HOLT

LITERATURE AND LANGUAGE ARTS

Warriner's Handbook

Second Course

TEACHER'S EDITION

Grammar • Usage • Mechanics • Sentences

 Mastering the CALIFORNIA STANDARDS in English-Language Conventions

Instructional Framework by

John E. Warriner

HOLT, RINEHART AND WINSTON

AUTHOR **JOHN E. WARRINER** taught for thirty-two years in junior and senior high schools and in college. He was a high school English teacher when he developed the original organizational structure for his classic *English Grammar and Composition* series. The approach pioneered by Mr. Warriner was distinctive, and the editorial staff of Holt, Rinehart and Winston have worked diligently to retain the unique qualities of his pedagogy in *Warriner's Handbook*. John Warriner also co-authored the *English Workshop* series and edited *Short Stories: Characters in Conflict.*

Requests for permission to make copies of any part of the work should be mailed to the following address: Permissions Department, Holt, Rinehart and Winston, 10801 N. MoPac Expressway, Building 3, Austin, Texas 78759.Acknowledgments and other credits appear on pages 551 and 552, which are extensions of the copyright page.

ISBN 978-0-03-09928-5

ISBN 0-03-099228-1

1 2 3 4 5 6 048 11 10 09 08

CONTENTS IN BRIEF

The Parts of a Sentence

CHAPTER 1

Standards Focus

Sentence Structure 1.1 Use correct and varied sentence types.

Sentence Structure 1.3 Use coordination to indicate clearly the relationship between ideas.

Grammar 1.4 Edit written manuscripts to ensure that correct grammar is used.

Parts of Speech Overview
Noun, Pronoun, Adjective

CHAPTER

2

🐻 Standards Focus

Grammar 1.4 Edit written manuscripts to ensure that correct grammar is used.

Punctuation and Capitalization 1.5 Use correct capitalization.

Parts of Speech Overview

CHAPTER

3

Verb, Adverb, Preposition, Conjunction, Interjection **50**

Standards Focus

Sentence Structure 1.3 Use coordination.

Grammar 1.4 Edit written manuscripts to ensure that correct grammar is used.

Punctuation and Capitalization 1.5 Use correct punctuation.

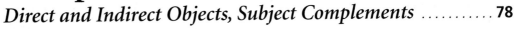

Complements

 CHAPTER

Direct and Indirect Objects, Subject Complements **78**

![bear icon] **Standards Focus**

Sentence Structure 1.1 Use correct and varied sentence types and sentence openings.

Grammar 1.4 Edit written manuscripts to ensure that correct grammar is used.

The Phrase

 CHAPTER

Prepositional, Verbal, and Appositive Phrases **94**

![bear icon] **Standards Focus**

Sentence Structure 1.1 Use correct and varied sentence openings.

Sentence Structure 1.3 Use apposition.

Grammar 1.4 Edit written manuscripts to ensure that correct grammar is used.

The Clause

 Standards Focus

Sentence Structure 1.1 Use correct and varied sentence types.

Sentence Structure 1.3 Use subordination.

Grammar 1.4 Edit written manuscripts to ensure that correct grammar is used.

Sentence Structure

CHAPTER

7

Standards Focus

Sentence Structure 1.1 Use correct and varied sentence types and sentence openings.

Sentence Structure 1.3 Use coordination.

Grammar 1.4 Edit written manuscripts to ensure that correct grammar is used.

Punctuation and Capitalization 1.5 Use correct punctuation and capitalization.

Agreement

CHAPTER 8

Subject and Verb, Pronoun and Antecedent **154**

Standards Focus

Grammar 1.4 Edit written manuscripts to ensure that correct grammar is used.

Using Verbs Correctly

CHAPTER 9

Principal Parts, Regular and Irregular Verbs,
Tense, Voice **184**

Standards Focus

Grammar 1.4 Edit written manuscripts to ensure that correct grammar is used.

Using Pronouns Correctly

Standards Focus

Grammar 1.4 Edit written manuscripts to ensure that correct grammar is used.

Jump Start reprinted by permission of
United Feature Syndicate, Inc.

Using Modifiers Correctly

CHAPTER

11

Comparison and Placement **236**

Standards Focus

Grammar 1.4 Edit written manuscripts to ensure that correct grammar is used.

A Glossary of Usage

CHAPTER 12

Standards Focus

Grammar 1.4 Edit written manuscripts to ensure that correct grammar is used.

Spelling 1.6 Use correct spelling conventions.

Capital Letters

CHAPTER 13

Standards Focus

Grammar 1.4 Edit written manuscripts to ensure that correct grammar is used.

Punctuation and Capitalization 1.5 Use correct capitalization.

Punctuation

Standards Focus

Sentence Structure 1.3 Use apposition.

Grammar 1.4 Edit written manuscripts to ensure that correct grammar is used.

Punctuation and Capitalization 1.5 Use correct punctuation.

Punctuation

Underlining (Italics), Quotation Marks, Apostrophes,
Hyphens, Parentheses, Brackets, Dashes 340

CHAPTER

15

Standards Focus

Grammar 1.4 Edit written manuscripts to ensure that correct grammar is used.

Punctuation and Capitalization 1.5 Use correct punctuation and capitalization.

Spelling

CHAPTER 16

Improving Your Spelling **368**

Standards Focus

Grammar 1.4 Edit written manuscripts to ensure that correct grammar is used.

Spelling 1.6 Use correct spelling conventions.

Correcting Common Errors

Key Language Skills Review **398**

Standards Focus

Language Convention 1.0 Students write and speak with a command of standard English conventions appropriate to this grade level.

PART 2 **Sentences**...**434**

Writing Effective Sentences 436

 **Standards Focus**

Sentence Structure 1.1 Use correct and varied sentence types and sentence openings to present a lively and effective personal style.

Sentence Structure 1.2 Identify and use parallelism, including similar grammatical forms, in all written discourse to present items in a series and items juxtaposed for emphasis.

Sentence Structure 1.3 Use subordination, coordination, apposition, and other devices to indicate clearly the relationship between ideas.

DIAGNOSTIC PREVIEW...**436**
    A. Identifying Sentences, Sentence Fragments, and Run-ons
    B. Combining Sentences
    C. Revising Stringy and Wordy Sentences
    D. Revising a Paragraph to Improve Sentence Style

WRITING CLEAR SENTENCES **438**
    Sentence Fragments **438**
    Run-on Sentences **441**

COMBINING SENTENCES...................................**444**
    Combining by Inserting Words **445**
    Combining by Inserting Phrases **446**
    Combining by Using Connecting Words **448**
    Combining by Using a Subordinate Clause **451**

IMPROVING SENTENCE STYLE **454**
    Revising Stringy Sentences **454**
    Revising Wordy Sentences................................**457**
    Using Parallel Structure **459**

BEYOND SENTENCE STYLE **461**
    Varying Sentence Beginnings **461**
    Varying Sentence Structure **463**
    Using Transitions **465**

Sentence Diagramming 472

Standards Focus

Language Convention 1.0 Students write and speak with a command of standard English conventions appropriate to this grade level.

Why should I study grammar, usage, and mechanics?

Many people would say that you should study grammar to learn to root out errors in your speech and writing. Certainly, *Warriner's Handbook* can help you learn to avoid making errors and to correct the errors you do make. More important, though, studying grammar, usage, and mechanics gives you the skills you need to take sentences and passages apart and to put them together, to learn which parts go together and which don't. Instead of writing sentences and passages that you hope sound good, you can craft your sentences to create just the meaning and style you want.

Knowing grammar, usage, and mechanics gives you the tools to understand and discuss your own language, to communicate clearly the things you want to communicate, and to develop your own communication style. Further, mastery of language skills can help you succeed in your other classes, in future classes, on standardized tests, and in the larger world, including, eventually, the workplace.

How do I use *Warriner's Handbook*?

Warriner's Handbook is part of the Holt Literature and Language Arts program. The skills taught in *Warriner's Handbook* are important to your success in the reading, writing, speaking, and listening components of this program.

Not only can you use this book as a complete grammar, usage, and mechanics textbook, but you can also use it as a reference guide when you work on any piece of writing. Whether you are writing a personal letter, a report for your social studies class, or some other piece of writing, you can use *Warriner's Handbook* to answer your questions about grammar, usage, capitalization, punctuation, and spelling.

How is *Warriner's Handbook* organized?

Warriner's Handbook is divided into three main parts:

PART 1 The **Grammar, Usage, and Mechanics** chapters provide instruction on and practice using the building blocks of language—words, phrases, clauses, capitalization, punctuation, and spelling. Use these chapters to discover how to take sentences apart and put them together. The last chapter, **Correcting Common Errors,** provides additional practice on key language skills as well as standardized test practice in grammar, usage, and mechanics.

PART 2 The **Sentences** chapters include Writing Effective Sentences and Sentence Diagramming. **Writing Effective Sentences** provides instruction on and practice with writing correct, clear, and interesting sentences. **Sentence Diagramming** teaches you to analyze and diagram sentences so you can see how the parts of a sentence relate to each other.

PART 3 The **Resources** section includes **History of English,** a concise history of the English language; **Test Smarts,** a handy guide to taking standardized tests in grammar, usage, and mechanics; and **Grammar at a Glance,** a glossary of grammatical terms.

How are the chapters organized?

Each chapter begins with a Diagnostic Preview, a short test that covers the whole chapter and alerts you to skills that need improvement, and ends with a Chapter Review, another short test that tells you how well you have mastered that chapter. In between, you'll see rules, which are basic statements of grammar, usage, and mechanics principles. The rules are illustrated with examples and followed by exercises and reviews that help you practice what you have learned.

What are some other features of this textbook?

- **Oral Practice**—spoken practice and reinforcement of rules and concepts
- **Writing Applications**—activities that let you apply grammar, usage, and mechanics concepts in your writing
- **Tips & Tricks**—easy-to-use hints about grammar, usage, and mechanics

- **Meeting the Challenge**—questions or short activities that ask you to approach a concept from a new angle
- **Style Tips**—information about formal and informal uses of language
- **Help**—pointers to help you understand either key rules and concepts or exercise directions

Warriner's Handbook on the Internet

As you move through *Warriner's Handbook*, you will find the best online resources at **go.hrw.com**.

What are the California standards?

The California State Board of Education has adopted a set of standards for achievement in Written and Oral English Language Conventions. You will be expected to master these standards during the school year. Each chapter of *Warriner's Handbook* begins with a box listing the California standards that you will cover in that chapter.

1.0 Written and Oral English Language Conventions

Students write and speak with a command of standard English conventions appropriate to this grade level.

Sentence Structure

1.1 Use correct and varied sentence types and sentence openings to present a lively and effective personal style.

1.2 Identify and use parallelism, including similar grammatical forms, in all written discourse to present items in a series and items juxtaposed for emphasis.

1.3 Use subordination, coordination, apposition, and other devices to indicate clearly the relationship between ideas.

Grammar

1.4 Edit written manuscripts to ensure that correct grammar is used.

Punctuation and Capitalization

1.5 Use correct punctuation and capitalization.

Spelling

1.6 Use correct spelling conventions.

Teaching Strands

This teaching-strand chart shows you some ways to connect grammar instruction and writing instruction.

Warriner's Handbook is designed to be a flexible teaching tool that accommodates many teaching philosophies and styles. For example, some teachers will prefer to use the handbook as a reference source, having students refer to it only as the need for explicit grammar instruction arises. Others will use the handbook as a teaching text, having their classes work through the instruction, examples, and exercises in a more methodical fashion. Your personal teaching style and the needs of your students will determine the best way for you to teach this material.

GO TO: go.hrw.com
KEYWORD: HLLA

All resources for this handbook are available for preview on the *Teacher One Stop DVD-ROM.* All worksheets and tests may be printed from the DVD-ROM.

Writing Assignments	Rationale
NARRATION	Writers of personal narratives use first person to tell their stories. To explain their ideas, writers usually choose chronological order, which can be indicated by adverbs, adverb phrases, and adverb clauses, but they must watch for stringy sentences as they describe the action. Dialogue, colorful modifiers, and sentence variety will enliven the narratives.
RESPONSE TO LITERATURE	In a book evaluation, carefully chosen words can capture the work's essence. A reviewer will cite titles, details, and direct quotations from the book, all of which must be properly capitalized and punctuated. Using adjective clauses helps the writer avoid short, choppy sentences.
TECHNICAL DOCUMENTS	Explaining a complex process requires precise thinking and writing. Signal words, properly set off, indicate an inference drawn or a chronological step. Accurate and consistent verb tenses maintain order. Correctly punctuated phrases may define unique terms or new vocabulary.
RESEARCH	Writers initially pose questions to guide their research. In developing and phrasing answers to these questions, writers must be careful to use correctly punctuated subordinate clauses and correct subject-verb and pronoun-antecedent agreement. Citing references for supporting data requires correct capitalization and punctuation.
PERSUASION	To interest and persuade readers, writers of persuasive essays use strong verbs, correct forms of adjectives and adverbs, and varied sentence beginnings and structures as well as precise language that is appropriate to the audience. Support involves a skillful blend of reasons, evidence, and emotional appeals.

Links to Grammar	Links to Usage	Links to Mechanics
→ first-person pronouns (Ch. 2)	→ pronoun case (Ch. 10)	→ capitalization of *I* (Ch. 13)
→ adverbs (Ch. 3); phrases (Ch. 5); clauses (Ch. 6)	→ placement of phrases and clauses (Ch. 11)	→ punctuation of compound and complex sentences (Ch. 14)
→ sentence structures (Ch. 7); kinds of sentences (Ch. 1)	→ subject-verb agreement (Ch. 8)	→ end punctuation (Ch. 14); capitalization and punctuation of dialogue (Ch. 13 & Ch. 15)
→ adjectives, nouns (Ch. 2)	→ adjective forms (Ch. 11)	→ spelling suffixes (Ch. 16)
→ pronouns (Ch. 2); complements (Ch. 4); adjective clauses, relative pronouns (Ch. 6)	→ pronoun case using *who* and *whom* (Ch. 10); *who, which, that* (Ch. 12); placement of adjective clauses (Ch. 11)	→ punctuating essential and nonessential clauses (Ch. 14)
→ kinds of sentences (Ch. 1); sentence structure (Ch. 7)		→ capitalizing and punctuating titles and quotations (Ch. 13 & Ch. 15)
→ adverbs (Ch. 3)	→ adverb forms (Ch. 11)	→ punctuating introductory words and phrases (Ch. 14)
→ verbs (Ch. 3)	→ verb tense (Ch. 9)	
→ verbal and appositive phrases (Ch. 5)	→ placement of phrases (Ch. 11)	→ punctuating parenthetical material (Ch. 15)
→ interrogatory sentences (Ch. 1); relative clauses (Ch. 6)	→ *who, whom* (Ch. 10)	→ end punctuation and commas (Ch. 14)
→ pronouns (Ch. 2); subjects and predicates (Ch. 1); complements (Ch. 4)	→ subject-verb and pronoun-antecedent agreement (Ch. 8)	→ capitalizing and punctuating titles in citations (Ch. 13–15)
→ action verbs (Ch. 3)	→ consistency of tense (Ch. 9)	
→ adjectives, adverbs (Ch. 2 & Ch. 3); verbal phrases (Ch. 5); clauses (Ch. 6); sentence structure (Ch. 7)	→ correct use of modifiers, placement of modifiers (Ch. 11)	→ punctuation of compound-complex sentences, semicolons between independent clauses, colons before lists and examples (Ch. 14)

By Amy Benjamin

Dispelling the Myths about Grammar Instruction

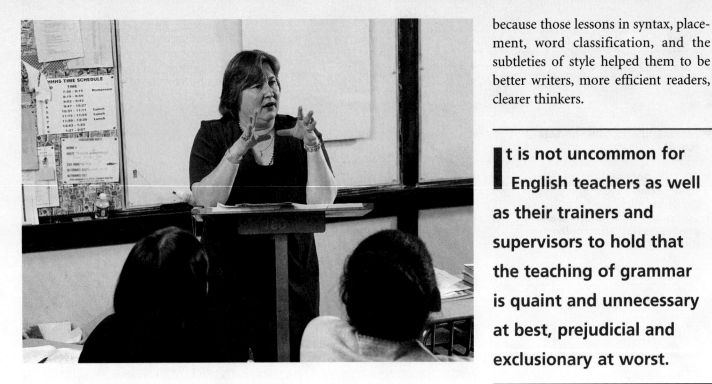

because those lessons in syntax, placement, word classification, and the subtleties of style helped them to be better writers, more efficient readers, clearer thinkers.

It is not uncommon for English teachers as well as their trainers and supervisors to hold that the teaching of grammar is quaint and unnecessary at best, prejudicial and exclusionary at worst.

I know an excellent English teacher whose students, many years after graduation, remember her for her grammar lessons. Unfortunately, instead of being proud of this, she is chagrined. . . . "*Grammar*!? Of all things in my class to remember! Why *grammar*? Why can't they remember me for all the wonderful literature I taught them? for what I taught them about composition? expression? creativity? Why just *grammar*? I don't even teach *grammar* anymore. I teach the *writing* process."

Perhaps these students remembered their grammar lessons because of the usefulness of those lessons or because of the satisfaction that they derived from learning challenging material. Perhaps they remembered

How lamentable it is that teaching writing through a process approach has become an orthodoxy in which the grammatical strand of English language arts is pitted against the literary strand, as if the two are not intertwined. Who set up this false dichotomy? The notion that grammar instruction is antithetical to the writing process is specious. My purpose in this essay is to debunk some of the myths about grammar instruction and to refurbish its tarnished reputation.

It is not uncommon for English teachers as well as their trainers and supervisors to hold that the teaching of grammar is quaint and unnecessary at best, prejudicial and exclusionary at worst. The problem begins with muddy terminology. Some people conflate the terms *grammar, usage,* and *mechanics,* as well as the terms *correct/incorrect* and *standard/ nonstandard.* Before I turn my fire extinguisher on the grammar myths, let me clarify my terms: By *grammar,* I refer to the rules which govern how words function in a sentence to make meaning. That *man bites dog* means something different from *dog bites man* is a function of grammar. By *usage,* I refer to the social conventions that determine what is considered standard. By *standard,* I do not mean *correct.* I mean that style of the English language which most educated people accept in formal circumstances. By *mechanics,* I refer to physical manifestations of language such as spelling, punctuation, capitalization and other conventions. In the case of *mechanics,* the terms *correct* and *incorrect* are more appropriate than they are when we are talking about matters of usage, but even spelling is not without gray areas.

Reasonable people can disagree over matters of content and methodology in teaching. However, I think everyone would agree that to understand a complicated system we need to know the names of its parts, their forms and functions, how the parts relate to the whole, and where these parts belong if the system is to operate at maximum efficiency. That said, here's what some people say about grammar instruction, and why I disagree with them.

Myth #1:

The explicit teaching of grammar does not improve writing ability, so time spent on grammar is time not spent on more worthy pursuits in the English classroom.

Think about it. Suppose my car is making a funny noise. Suppose I have no better understanding of what is going on under the hood than that. I take it to my mechanic, trusting his knowledge, integrity, and skill. He'll figure out what's wrong with my car and fix the problem. I'll pay the bill, and if all is not well, I'll get either another mechanic or another car. That is how many car owners (myself included) operate. We don't have the time or the inclination to learn the taxonomy, nomenclature, and anatomy of our cars.

When we don't speak explicitly to students about grammar, syntax, diction, and coherence, we have to resort to the "funny noise" method: We have to say "This part just doesn't sound right here," or "You're not saying this clearly." We may be able to help writers fix the sentence, but we haven't given them the generality that will allow them to apply what they've learned to similar circumstances.

On the other hand, I can know the names of all the tools in my toolbox, what each is for, and how they relate to one another; but if I don't use them to facilitate an actual job in progress, then my knowledge does not fulfill its intended purpose. For many of us, the grammar lessons that we learned in school were about "picking out." We'd "pick out" all kinds of structures: the parts of speech, subjects and predicates, simple subjects, helping verbs. Later, we'd hunt down adverbial clauses, subject complements, infinitives. We'd underline and double underline. We'd diagram. The trouble with our instruction was not that it was misguided, but that it was unfinished. Having learned to spot prepositional phrases, we may not have learned why doing so could improve our discourse.

How can we *use* our ability to identify grammatical structures such as prepositional phrases in our own reading and writing? We may have learned that the object of a preposition must be in the objective case, and that the object of a preposition is never the subject of the sentence. This knowledge helps us solve some usage problems, but that is not its main value. Knowing how to discern the subject and verb can help us read dense prose. When reading dense prose, the reader needs strategies. One such strategy is to reduce the sentence to its subject and verb. That done, the reader sees prepositional phrases for what they are: details. Beyond that, knowing about prepositions helps writers add sentence variety, as they learn not to begin sentence after sentence with the subject. Beginning a sentence with a prepositional phrase can set the stage for the action, but we have to be judicious: Sometimes, that prepositional phrase can be distracting or redundant. As modifiers, prepositional phrases can be movable, and their placement affects meaning, rhythm, and emphasis. Prepositional phrases, "time and place words," add detail and dimension. The novice writer who has difficulty fleshing out a topic can do well to consciously add more prepositional phrases. It is knowing what prepositional phrases can and can't do for you that makes being able to identify them worthwhile. Selecting standard pronoun case, creating purposeful variety in sentence structure, adding detail and dimension, and eliminating redundancy are some good reasons for being able to recognize prepositional phrases.

It is knowing what prepositional phrases can and can't do for you that makes being able to identify them worthwhile.

Recognition of a grammatical structure is only the beginning. If we think of grammar instruction as building an awareness of language choices available to the careful writer, then we view such instruction in two phases: recognition and application. Too often, the application phase does not happen. When it does not, the recognition phase seems to lack practicality. Thus does grammar instruction fall out of favor.

Myth #2:

Grammar instruction applies only to the editing phase of the writing process.

When people operate under this myth, they are confusing grammar with usage and mechanics. Usage and mechanics may be seen as "touch-ups," part of the finishing-off of a written piece. As such, they are not essential to the real intellectual work of the process, although no one should minimize their importance. Usage and mechanics can determine the first and last impressions that the reader gets of the writer's work. The point is that we should not limit our understanding of grammar to the surface features of usage and mechanics.

Along with diction and rhetoric, grammar (unlike usage and mechanics) is *organic* to the crafting of sentences and text. Writers with an awareness of grammar can make informed choices about how word order affects meaning. Picture a

carpenter. He doesn't just blindly reach into his toolbox, pull out a screwdriver, try to make it do the work of a wrench, and figure he'll just sand down the rough spots later. We can make our students better writers if we teach them to use grammatical knowledge consciously as they match their syntax to their intentions.

We understand the power of graphic organizers in both reading and writing for many learners. We teach students to map their ideas as a prewriting strategy. We teach them to make Venn diagrams to show similarities and differences, and flowcharts to express sequence. Sentence structures are patterns. We can think in terms of certain grammatical templates, containers, that work well for certain types of ideas. Parallel structure and compound sentences or simple sentences with compound constituents are good containers for *like* elements bearing equal importance. Complex sentences are good containers to use when we need to show the backgrounding and foregrounding of elements that do not bear equal importance. Sentence structure selections occur in the drafting and revision stages of the writing process, as the writer searches for the clearest, most efficient way to express thoughts.

Many writers have an intuitive sense of what kinds of containers work best with what kinds of ideas. When we bring this underlying awareness of grammar to the conscious level, we help students manage inchoate ideas in the same way that a graphic organizer, such as a Venn diagram, might. Indeed, there is much to be said for using one of the many versions of graphic organizers *along with* sentence structure templates. The writer can then look at a branch diagram or a cluster, decide how the ideas are related, and then consider an array of syntactical containers to suit them.

What I've described is a way of understanding the role of grammar in the writing process that is deeper than what is commonly thought, i.e., that grammatical thinking enters the picture only as the cleanup man. In fact, we already make intuitive grammatical choices as we compose our thoughts. Those intuitive choices may or may not be the best ones for the purpose. By building awareness of sentence and textual structure, we can increase our chances that our message is clear, efficient, and graceful.

Myth #3:
Grammar is boring.

There are many ways to make our classrooms boring. We can "cover material" in a perfunctory way, "going over" the exercises done for homework or as seatwork. We can convey to students that their language is "wrong" and ours is "right." We can be language prudes, fainting and blanching at every double negative or misplaced modifier that dares to show its face in our presence. We can insist that the answer key is always the authority and that grammar is a "no

discussion" subject. We can isolate the study of grammar, treat it as something we "have to get through" before moving on to literature. We can fail to make any connection between grammar and journalism, grammar and advertising, grammar and novels, grammar and drama, grammar and music, grammar and poetry. These are ways to make grammar boring.

I've heard teachers claim that grammar instruction interferes with creativity.

I've heard teachers claim that grammar instruction interferes with creativity. "Grammar is boring," they say. "And writing should be fun and interesting." This is a misguided notion, because creativity thrives within structure. The sonneteer works within a strictly prescribed structure, choosing that structure because it is the best container for particular ideas. The sonnet form is not constraining but liberating: The format frees the writer from decisions about rhythm and rhyme scheme. Because of the structure, half the work is done. I can't think of any creative pursuit—music, fine arts, dance, photography, drama, writing—that does not demand mastery of technique. I can't think of any creative pursuit in which there is no terminology, no anatomy, no structure, no tradition, no rules. Why would learning any kind of writing, much less creative writing, be

detached from the fundamentals? Knowledge of structure is not a hindrance, but a guide that enables, rather than impedes, creativity.

Sometimes, grammar instruction is thought of as "drill and kill." This pejorative implies that the instruction will consist of lower level thinking skills, mindless repetition, and lack of application to authentic language. We picture fill-in-the-blank workbook-type questions in which there is one right answer. The book that you have in your hands is an extremely useful, in fact indispensable, tool for the teaching of language. However, any grammar text is most effective when used *along with*, not in place of, literature and student writing. It might seem that students would naturally make the crossover from what they learn in grammar exercises to their own language use, but such is not necessarily the case. As teachers, we have to make that crossover happen very deliberately, pointing out structures that students have learned and how those structures are used to make meaning in authentic contexts. Thus does grammar instruction transcend the practice exercises that illustrate targeted concepts.

Everybody loves language; children and teenagers love it especially, because they are in the process of defining their own culture by laying claim to words and expressions all their own. When we invite students to analyze their own neologisms, grammatical idiosyncrasies, and dialectical styles, we enliven grammar lessons immeasurably. As English teachers, we embrace all forms of the English language even while we recognize that mastery of standard English is essential for success in certain precincts of society.

Another way to make grammar instruction interesting is to let students discover how language changes right before our eyes. Movies and novels set in various pockets of the English-speaking world are museums of linguistic anthropology. Compare the idioms of *To Kill A Mockingbird* to those of *The Color Purple*. Analyze the language of a movie set in New Orleans and compare it to the language of a movie set in Los Angeles.

There are many ways to make our classrooms interesting. Our love of the subject is contagious. Grammar is exciting and rewarding to learn not because we get the answers right, but because we've applied logic and found patterns, and because there may be more than one answer, depending on the circumstances, audience, and purpose. Contrary to myth, a good grammar lesson can invite a lively discussion about ambiguities in meaning and the best way to express thought in a particular context. It can even ignite a discussion about social power structures, prejudices, and immigration. This is not boring stuff.

Myth #4:
Grammar applies only to English classes.

For lack of a better term, we refer to subjects other than English as "content areas." Aside from the obvious expectation that we use standard English in school, how can students apply grammar to their content area classes?

Every teacher wants students to be better readers. A law student told me recently that she was glad that she knew something about grammar, because she needed it to read complex materials in her courses. She found that by mentally pulling out the subject and verb, she could follow the lines of technical text.

Needless to say, grammatical knowledge of the English language is essential for learning another language. Just as grammar has fallen out of favor in many English classes, it has suffered a similar blow in the pedagogy of learning other languages as well, where grammar instruction has been supplanted by "conversation." The predictable consequence has been much confusion and frustration for both teachers, who feel that their hands are tied, and students, many of whom are bewildered by the gymnastics of the French verb when they don't even know how English verbs behave.

What about science, math, social studies, the arts? All teachers love words. The biology teacher is fussy about the difference between *osmosis* and *diffusion*. Getting students to make fine distinctions is an important part of teaching students to think like scientists. Teachers want to give away the words of their subject areas the way grandmothers want to give away food. We want to invite our students into the professional conversation of our subject areas.

Teachers want to give away the words of their subject areas the way grandmothers want to give away food.

As English teachers, we love words about words, language about language. To us, there is a vast difference between an action verb and a linking verb, a predicate nominative and a direct object, a transitive verb and an intransitive verb. In teaching students to talk the talk, we turn them into licensed operators, not just amateurs. A licensed operator can make the machinery run more efficiently, can anticipate potential problems, and can fix what is wrong. An amateur *hopes* that the sentence "sounds good."

Grammar should be the permeable membrane that allows knowledge learned in English class to transform into skill in the content area classes. Active voice may be preferable in English classes where the subject is often *people doing things* (S-V-O). In composing a lab report, however, passive voice may be the better choice. *The difference in pressure was recorded* might sound more scientific than *I recorded the difference in pressure*. In the language of lab reports, the fact that the technician did the action is irrelevant. A radiologist writes her report in the passive voice: *No abnormalities were found*, rather than *I found no abnormalities*. In English class, we show students the difference in tone between active and passive voice.

It is important to learn to think in action verbs in all subject areas. A student who is writing about the Reformation needs to focus on who did what: *Martin Luther <u>translated</u> the Bible into the German vernacular. His translation <u>enabled</u> more people to read the Bible.* The action verbs tell the story. They give students a starting point when writing and a focus when reading. All subject areas use this concept; it is we English teachers who actually teach it in our grammar lessons.

The social studies teacher and the science teacher may not know it, but the benefits of grammar instruction are carried through the student's entire day.

Myth #5:

Grammar instruction is ethnocentric and prejudicial.

As English teachers, we need to avoid giving the impression that we are the designated Keepers of the Language. We can teach the etiquette of standard English without denying a student the right to his or her own dialect.

An educated person has that social thermostat that linguists call code-switching. The metaphor of table manners is apt: What we are expected to do at an outdoor barbecue differs from what we're expected to do at Thanksgiving dinner. Those of us who can't tell the difference, who can't code-switch, are socially awkward. This is not to say that standard English is better than any particular dialect. Standard English is not more expressive, more poetic, or even more accurate. It is simply the expected currency of mainstream society in formal situations. We don't have to use it all of the time, but if we *can't* use it when it is expected, then we are at a cultural disadvantage that our education should remedy.

We are constantly making impressions that indicate our understanding of our social context. Those who are successful in their chosen fields,

indeed, those for whom a chosen field is an option in the first place, know how to control the impression that others have of them. People judge our status and education levels not only through language, but also through dress, manners, and gesture.

Once we acknowledge that standard English is just another form of English that is appropriate for certain situations but not for all, then we are free to enjoy the dialects of English that we find in authentic literature, regional speech, song lyrics, and casual conversation. We can look at new coinages, popular metaphors, slang, and jargon with the interest of a linguist rather than the arrogance of a pedant.

We can teach the etiquette of Standard English without denying a student the right to his or her own dialect.

That language is a changing social contract is evidenced by grammar books of yore. Even in one generation, the *who/whom* distinction has attenuated, as has the use of the past perfect tense of verbs. Certain usages, such as the nominative case after a linking verb, sound stuffy. We have yet to solve the problem that exists because we lack a generic singular pronoun: *He,* once preferred, is thought to be sexist; *one* sounds stilted and British; *they* is a grammatical mismatch. That leaves *he or she*, which can seem awfully conspicuous. It's interesting to have students compare the style guides of various publications on sensitive points such as this.

Myth #6:

As native speakers, we don't have to learn grammar.

It is true that we already know grammar intuitively. Native speakers learn, quite naturally, how to put words together to make meaning. What we don't learn naturally is the metalanguage, that is, the language of language. Absent that, we can't explain what we mean about what we are trying to say, and others are at a loss to help us.

Terminology is powerful.

Recently, I worked with a group of elementary school teachers who were looking for teaching strategies that would improve their students' writing skills. When I suggested that they develop a scope and sequence in grammar skills, they were skeptical. "They already know how to use adjectives, nouns, and verbs," one teacher said. "Why do they have to know the *names* of these things?" "That just isn't the way we teach anymore," said another with a wave of her hand. "We don't want to interfere with the children's creativity. Teaching them grammar would interrupt their flow." A fourth-grade teacher added, "But that isn't on the state test, and we really don't have time for anything that doesn't get the scores up." Here's what I would answer:

Terminology is powerful. We can't improve our sentences until we understand the crucial role played by verbs. We certainly can't understand that role until we know how to identify verbs in context and that verbs come in various flavors: finite verbs, infinitives, participles, gerunds.

Further, creativity and "flow" are enhanced, not impeded, by knowledge of language structure and what certain kinds of phrases and sentences can and can't do. When the reader has to stumble over and re-read awkward, redundant, convoluted, or misplaced structures within sentences, does it matter how creative the writer was? Doesn't the logic of grammar *improve* the flow of prose?

To answer the last objection, the statewide tests may or may not have explicit questions regarding grammar. Some do; some don't, and the nature of those tests can and will change. What will not change is that a writer who knows where commas belong makes the job easier on the reader, as does the writer who understands subordination, agreement, and overall

Essays on Teaching Grammar

sentence management. If we acknowledge that the whole purpose of writing is to communicate, and that communication is accomplished by writing clearly, then we can see the application of grammar to writing. Of course, if grammar instruction never makes the leap from identification of a structure to its effective application, then these teachers are right to reject it as largely irrelevant.

What Knowing Grammar Can Do for Writers

Finally, here is a list of what you can do when you know a few things about grammar:

- If you know how to use parallel structure, you can make your message smoother, clearer, easier on the reader, more logical, and more memorable.

- If you know when to use active voice and when to use passive voice, you can control the directness or indirectness of your message. You control the power and impact of your words. You can also avoid the trouble that comes from being too direct or accusatory.

- If you know how to use verb tense consistently, you can guide your reader through the tangle of time in your narrative.

- If you know how to vary the grammatical constructs in your sentence

structure, you can make your flow of sentences more musical, more nuanced, less choppy.

- If you know the difference between a phrase, a clause, and a sentence, you can guide your reader by using well-placed punctuation.

Like poetry, grammar is about the beauty of expressing exactly what we mean by placing the words just right.

Understanding how grammar works puts the writer on the right path. When writers begin a definition by saying "Osmosis is *when . . .*" they are failing to apply the concept that a subject complement, not an adverbial clause, must follow a linking verb. The "*is when . . .*" definition is going to fall on its face because the key term has not been handled properly in the sentence. Definitions call for classification. First, we must place the term in its proper realm: "Osmosis is a . . . process? means? phenomenon?" The writer must stop and think about what *kind* of thing osmosis is. Such categorical thinking is absolutely essential to the scientist, but it does not happen with the ungrammatical ". . . *is when*" structure. This example demonstrates the relation-

ship between grammar and the logical progression of ideas.

Knowing grammar is useful, but even if it weren't, learning it would still be worthwhile because it is interesting. Like chess, grammar is about how power and proximity govern relationships and possibilities. Like engineering, grammar is about structure, balance, efficiency and strength. Like mathematics, grammar is about patterns and forms. Like geology, grammar is at once eternal and dynamic. Like poetry, grammar is about the beauty of expressing exactly what we mean by placing the words just right. ∎

Amy Benjamin is an English teacher at Hendrick Hudson High School in Montrose, New York. In addition, she is a consultant to teachers, administrators, staff developers, and people in the business world. Amy specializes in showing people how to use clear, concise language. She has written several books about teaching literacy skills in all subject areas, as well as two plays (Romeo and Juliet Will Not Be Performed Tonight *and* Romeo and Juliet: Still Not Dead) *and a young adult novel* (Russell Kim: My Real Name). *Amy lives in Fishkill, New York, with her husband Howard and son Mitch.*

By Brock Haussamen

Grammar: Why Teach It?

Why should students learn—and teachers teach—grammar? Simply memorizing the parts of speech doesn't, by itself, make students better writers. Worrying about errors can quickly dampen student enthusiasm for a writing project. Over the past three decades, grammar's reputation has suffered. Is grammar useful? Why teach it?

I believe the central reason for teaching and learning grammar is that it gives all of us a language for talking about language, and certainly the ability to talk about language is a fundamental educational goal. It is difficult to discuss sentences without knowing basic grammar in the same way that it is difficult to talk about a sport or a science or politics without knowing the names of its elements and how they are organized. Knowing basic grammar is what enables students to discuss the sentences in a book they are reading or in a paper they are writing, and to discuss their native language or a second language.

Think of grammar as having two faces. One is its public face, which can be quite formal. The other face is private and more friendly.

The Two Faces of Grammar

To teach grammar effectively, we need to show students how to put it to use. The language of grammar—the names for the parts of speech and other sentence components that appear in the grammar section of this textbook—has two distinct kinds of uses. Think of grammar as having two faces. One is its public face, which can be quite formal. The other face is private and more friendly.

Public Grammar

The public face of grammar consists of all the rules we teach students to follow in their writing and all the errors we tell them to avoid making. In this textbook it is the material in the sections on usage and mechanics. I call usage and mechanics "public grammar" because they identify the conventions of the standard American dialect in which our society carries on its formal writing and speaking. There are many good reasons to teach these conventions. Such a standard dialect helps people from different places and different backgrounds to communicate clearly. The conventions of public grammar help sustain the uniformity of our writing system, on which our society depends utterly. Finally, they reflect the language of economic power. In general, people who can write and speak according to the standard conventions have a better chance at participating in the influential core of our society. People who do not master those conventions will likely face obstacles at every turn.

It is important for us to remember and to remind our students that public grammar is different from, not inherently better than, the language students normally use. The do's and don'ts of public grammar create an illusion that they are rigorously logical, like the rules of mathematics, and that they are permanent. Neither of these claims is true. The do's and don'ts are sometimes illogical, and they change. Just a few decades ago, grammar textbooks like this one would have insisted on the distinction between *will* and *shall*; today that distinction is all but gone. A few decades into the future, a book such as this will probably simplify and may even omit the distinction between *who* and *whom*, which is already fading in informal English.

The "right" clothes, like the "right" grammar, depend on what is appropriate or expected in a given situation.

Try explaining to your students that their grammar is like the clothes they wear. The "right" clothes, like the "right" grammar, depend on what is appropriate or expected in a given situation. Around their friends, students talk and dress in particular ways. At formal occasions or in the workplace, they will be required to dress, to talk, and to write in other ways. This approach will less likely demean those students who do not routinely hear and use standard English. It also gives grammatical correctness a practical value and encourages your students to see language differences as an example of social diversity and opportunity.

Private Grammar

The other face of grammar is much more personal. By "private grammar," I mean the language structure that all of us already carry around in our heads and put to use when we communicate or think. In contrast to the study of public grammar, which has evolved over centuries, the description of our inherent language ability has grown from the work of linguists over the last several decades. Such grammar is private in the sense that it operates inside our heads, so quickly we are not even conscious of it. You won't find questions about private grammar on standardized tests; it is what students possess in order to read the tests in the first place.

If using public grammar can be compared to wearing socially acceptable formal clothes, private grammar can be compared to doing what comes naturally, to physical skills such as walking or running or throwing. Ask students to take a statement and turn it into a question in their native language. They can do it easily. They can fit new slang words into sentences fluidly. They know quickly when the language they hear or read sounds confusing or clear, choppy or smooth. They do all this with their private grammar.

Private grammar can be compared to doing what comes naturally, to physical skills such as walking or running or throwing.

If they can do all this already, how will studying grammar help them do more? The answer is that any skill that already comes somewhat naturally, like throwing a ball or making music, will improve if we learn about it and practice it. Students will be using the language of grammar to some degree when they revise and combine sentences in the section on "Writing Effective Sentences" in this textbook. They will do so to a greater degree whenever you show them how to improve the style of their writing by finding active verbs or expanding sentences with participles or prepositional phrases.

Putting Grammar to Use

As you can see from these descriptions of public and private faces, the language of basic grammar has many uses. Nonetheless, it is a difficult language for students to grow com-fortable with; its vocabulary looks large and forbidding; many of the terms combine with each other in ways that seem strange to students ("adjective clause"); and because it is a language about language, it strains the verbal skills of many of its students, both children and adults. So, like any language it must be practiced often and put to use in a variety of contexts. Here are some general suggestions.

Use Private Grammar to Teach Public Grammar

As language users, we all have an intuitive sense that sentences are made up of sections. Give students a sentence and ask them to divide it into chunks and to group the words that go together. This approach can remain basic or can become more refined as students divide and cluster clauses and phrases.

This sort of activity easily leads to sentence diagramming. If you are not familiar with diagramming, see Chapter 19. I teach students not the whole of it but just the basic components; even elementary diagrams help many students see the subject-predicate core of a sentence more clearly. If you choose to teach diagramming more thoroughly, students will be able to analyze difficult sentences that they encounter in reading and will build their comprehension. Many students enjoy constructing the diagrams; the activity taps students' visual and spatial skills in addition to their verbal ones.

Another way to draw on students' private grammatical ability is to provide them with practical shortcuts for getting at the essential points of grammar. Grammarians over the years have assembled a number of these simple methods, and your students will love you for telling them about these methods. One good book on the subject is Rei Noguchi's *Grammar and the Teaching of Writing: Limits and Possibilities* (NCTE). Students find the shortcuts practical, and they also appreciate the positive reinforcement of their grammatical instincts.

Use Grammar for Reading

Although grammar is most closely associated with writing, students can put grammar to use when they read.

Knowing grammatical terminology gives students the tools they need to discuss a difficult sentence in a story or a poem. Ask students to pick out the main verb and then the simple subject; finding these can help them figure out the rest of the sentence. Poets bend sentences around a good deal, but most poetry consists of recognizable sentences and sentence parts. Often you can help students move beyond their perplexity about a poem by reminding them to look for the sentences and their basic parts.

In discussing with students what they enjoy or don't enjoy about a writer's style, look for the grammatical characteristics of the writer's sentences. What parts of speech stand out in the sentences? Some writers specialize in strong, active verbs, with few forms of the verb *be*. In other writers' texts, *is* and *are* abound, but the nouns stand out. In still others', the adjectives and adverbs catch the reader's attention.

Another approach is to ask students how long a writer's sentences are, on average. What characteristic sentence lengths do students notice among types of writers, or the writers of different periods? This approach can lead to a discussion of the different structures that make up a writer's sentences. Some writers like to add modifiers, phrases, and clauses; other writers keep sentences short to

highlight the main nouns and verbs. Some start a sentence with long introductory word groups; others go right to the subject.

Bring grammar into the reading of advertisements, political language, and the World Wide Web. Advertisements provide good examples of sentence fragments, imperative verbs, and words that look like nouns but act like adjectives ("a Labor Day sofa sale"). Political speeches and slogans make interesting use of *we* and other personal pronouns. E-mail seems to encourage sentences that are variously clipped, casual, funny, skillful, and careless. Ask students to bring in examples for discussion.

Use Grammar for Revision

When students write, help them use grammar not just in the final editing stage, when they hunt out their violations of public grammar, but in the revising stage as well, when they can experiment with private grammar to develop their style as writers.

This textbook shows students how to combine sentences by inserting words or using conjunctions. Students can use some of the same methods to build a single sentence. They can build their sentences by adding participles (especially *–ing* participles that function half

as an active verb, half as an adjective) and also by adding appositives. "A spider, **a repulsive, hairy creature, no bigger than a tarantula,** crawled into the room. . . . **Hands trembling, sweat dripping from his face,** he flung the magazine left and right, **trying to kill the spiders,** but there were too many." That example of an eighth-grader's work is from Harry Noden's *Image Grammar: Using Grammatical Structures to Teach Writing,* an excellent source for these and other techniques. Students can also add phrases, especially prepositional phrases, and clauses to a sentence, expanding the information about their main point, giving more details in order to paint a picture, building, and penetrating further into their topic. (The sentence that you just read is one example; you can find more—and better ones—in the work of most accomplished writers.) Students may think at first that they are merely making sentences longer, but they will quickly find that they are also saying more.

Conclusion

The suggestions in this essay are only a sample of the good ideas for using the language of grammar to help students become better readers and writers. The books I have mentioned will lead you to other ideas. And your colleagues in language arts can provide you with many other suggestions for using grammar in the classroom. If you think of grammar as a language for talking about language and you keep in mind the differences

Weaver, Constance. *Teaching Grammar in Context.* Portsmouth: Boynton/Cook, 1996.

William, Joseph M. Style: *The Lessons in Clarity and Grace.* 6th ed. New York: Longman, 2000. ∎

Brock Haussamen has taught at Raritan Valley Community College in New Jersey since 1968. He is the author of Revising the Rules: Traditional Grammar and Modern Linguistics *(Kendall/Hunt) and also of a book on the history of the local New Jersey railroads. He began serving as president of the Assembly for the Teaching of English Grammar in 2000. His hobby and passion recently is playing ragtime piano.*

between public and private grammar, you can make grammar a valuable part of your students' language education.

For Further Reading

Assembly for the Teaching of English Grammar. www.ateg.org.

Berk, Lynn M. *English Syntax: From Word to Discourse.* New York: Oxford UP, 1999.

Haussamen, Brock. *Revising the Rules: Traditional Grammar and Modern Linguistics.* 2nd ed. Dubuque: Kendall/Hunt, 2000.

Kolln, Martha. *Rhetorical Grammar: Grammatical Choices, Rhetorical Effect.* 3rd ed. Boston: Allyn and Bacon, 1998.

Kolln, Martha, and Robert Funk (contributor). *Understanding English Grammar.* 5th ed. Needham: Allyn and Bacon, 1998.

Noden, Harry R. *Image Grammar: Using Grammatical Structures to Teach Writing.* Portsmouth: Heinemann/Boynton Cook, 1999.

Noguchi, Rei. *Grammar and the Teaching of Writing: Limits and Possibilities.* Urbana: NCTE, 1991.

By Rei R. Noguchi

Getting Down to Basics:
Using What Students Already Know

Like sentences, subjects and verbs are among the most basic elements of grammar and writing instruction.

Too often we struggle in teaching basic grammar to our students. Yet what really are the basics and how should we teach them? The most basic—the rock-bottom minimum—are sentence, verb, and subject. Surprisingly, we can teach these three basic elements by taking advantage of the unconscious linguistic knowledge that students already possess, their private grammar, so to speak. By tapping this unconscious knowledge, we can help students identify more easily the three basic elements, and, more important, help them better understand subsequent instruction in grammar, usage, and mechanics.

Why are the sentence, verb, and subject the very basics of grammar instruction? Take the notion of sentence. The sentence constitutes the most important unit in written texts, particularly in writing for school. A shaky grasp of what counts as a written sentence inevitably and unintentionally leads to distracting sentence fragments, fused sentences, and comma splices. Clearly, to master formal written English, students need to differentiate between a genuine sentence and an inappropriate nonsentence. Like sentences, subjects and verbs are among the most basic elements of grammar and writing instruction. Besides helping to define a sentence, subjects and verbs constitute elements on which a great deal of grammar and writing instruction builds. Without a reliable way of identifying subject and verb, students can almost certainly expect rough going.

How can we teach the concepts of subject, verb, and sentence so that students can identify them easily? I would suggest that, rather than relying solely on semantic definitions, we take fuller advantage of what we often ignore or downplay in our teaching of grammar, namely, the tremendous unconscious knowledge that all fluent or near-fluent speakers of English bring to the classroom every day. Put more bluntly, our students know a great deal more about grammar than many of us think. This grammar is not school grammar but their "private grammar," the system of rules unconsciously learned and unconsciously used by all fluent speakers of English in everyday conversation. We cannot teach this personal underlying grammar for the simple reason that our students already know it. All we can do is bring this knowledge to the surface and exploit it to the fullest.

Identifying the Sentence

Exploiting the unconscious linguistic knowledge of students is the key to teaching the very basics of grammar. For students unaccustomed or resistant to working with abstract definitions, identifying sentences and fragments may prove difficult. To identify fragments, students must, at minimum, understand that a fragment is an "incomplete sentence"; to apply this definition, however, students must understand what a sentence is. To understand what a sentence is, students must understand such terms as subject, predicate, and independent clause. Each of these terms may require further definitions yet.

Exploiting the unconscious linguistic knowledge of students is the key to teaching the very basics of grammar.

To avoid the chain of seemingly endless definitions to identify sentences and fragments, teachers can take advantage of their students' unconscious knowledge of what constitutes a complete sentence. Teachers can, for example, use the following frame to help students tap what they already know.

Sentence Frame:
They liked the idea that

_____.

Many word groups will fit in the frame, but whatever they are, they will all be genuine declarative sentences. Students can try out fragments you provide, such as *Thinking of joining the team* or *Because he joined the team,* as well as any suspicious word groups they themselves may write. If students discover a fragment, they can add or delete words to make it fit into the frame and thereby change the fragment into a genuine sentence. There is no need to define a sentence formally at this stage. If students can perform the simple test given here, they already unconsciously know what a sentence is, and with that knowledge they can easily identify fragments, which are just parts of sentences. With a bit of guidance and exploration, students will discover that fused sentences and comma splices won't fit in the empty slot either.

Identifying Verbs

If we tap the private grammar of our students, we can also help them identify specific and important parts of the sentence. Below are two frames that will help students identify words that can serve as main verbs.

Main-Verb Frame 1:
They might _____ (it) now.

Main-Verb Frame 2:
They aren't _____-ing (it) now.

Any word that fits in the empty slots above will be the base form (infinitive) of the main verb, the form listed in the dictionary (e.g., *eat, collect, finish, sleep*). There is no need here to define *main verb.* If the word fits in the empty slot, it's a word that English speakers and writers can and do use as a main verb in sentences.

Because verbs don't always occur in the base form in actual sentences, students need other strategies to identify verbs, especially in the sentences they compose. Here again, we can take advantage of the unconscious linguistic knowledge of students, this time their uncanny ability to produce negative sentences and yes-no questions, to assist students in identifying helping verbs.

If we examine the following sentences, we see that a helping verb is a word that immediately precedes the negative element (*–n't* or *not*) in negated sentences or the word that gets fronted in yes-no questions.

EXAMPLES

1. Jim should go to the football game.
   [*Transform this into a negative sentence or a question.*]

   Jim **should**n't go to the football game.

   Should Jim go to the football game?

2. Jim went to the football game.

   Jim **did**n't go to the football game.

   Did Jim go to the football game?

If we have students transform declarative sentences into either negative sentences or yes-no questions, we can help them identify helping verbs. Again, there is no need to define *helping verb* formally. Though students may have never heard of the term *helping verb* (or *auxiliary verb*) before, they already unconsciously know what it is if they can produce a corresponding negative sentence or a corresponding yes-no question from a declarative sentence. Making such transformations requires complex linguistic knowledge. Yet, remarkably, we don't have to teach students how to do this. If students are fluent or near-fluent in spoken English, they already know it, as amply demonstrated in their daily speech. What we need to do, however, is to

take advantage of this knowledge in teaching the basics of grammar.

Main Verb *Be*

The main verb *be* (as in *They were friends*) is especially tricky because, unlike other main verbs, it moves to the front in yes-no questions (*Were they friends?*). It also takes the negative element in negative sentences (*They weren't friends*). The main verb *be* can thus masquerade as the helping verb *be* (compare *They were friends* to *They were running*). To make matters worse, the main verb *be* appears frequently in student writing. Indeed, when we complain that our students write with too many *be* verbs, we really mean the main verb *be*, not the helping verb *be*. This gives all the more reason for students to be able to identify the

main verb *be*. Teaching students to use the main-verb frames and the helping-verb transformations can reduce confusion over the function of *be* in a sentence. Further, having students memorize the main-verb forms of *be* can reduce the confusion even more.

Identifying Subjects

Once students have identified the verb of a sentence, they can easily identify the subject. To identify the latter, they can insert the verb in the question frame below and then answer the question.

Simple-Subject Frame:
Who or what _____?

In most cases, the answer to the question will be the subject of the sentence.

non-native, bring to the language arts classroom every day.

Further References

DeBeaugrande, Robert. "Forward to the Basics: Getting Down to Grammar." *College Composition and Communication* 35 (1984): 358–67.

Noguchi, Rei R. *Grammar and the Teaching of Writing: Limits and Possibilities*. Urbana, IL: National Council of Teachers of English. 1991. ∎

Rei R. Noguchi, Professor of English and Linguistics at California State University, Northridge, has taught courses in linguistics to practicing and prospective language arts teachers for over seventeen years. He is the author of Grammar and the Teaching of Writing: Limits and Possibilities *(NCTE). When not teaching or writing, he enjoys reading, bicycling, and following various kinds of sports, particularly baseball.*

Applying Knowledge of Subjects and Verbs

Being able to identify subjects and verbs brings considerable payoffs. It will help students understand *clause*, which, in turn, will help them understand *independent* (or *main*) *clause* and *subordinate* (or *dependent*) *clause*. Understanding these terms will help them better understand the notion of *sentence*, which, in turn, will help them better understand and correct any unintentional fragment or run-on sentence. (Think also of all the punctuation rules that directly or indirectly refer to these structures.) Being able to identify subjects and verbs will certainly help students identify errors in subject-verb agreement, errors in verb-tense consistency, and even the overuse of main verb *be*. This skill can also help students identify verbs in the passive voice and can help students choose the correct case of personal pronouns. In short, knowing how to identify subjects and verbs leads to an understanding of a host of other concepts.

Conclusion

For many language arts teachers, teaching grammar is both a labor of love and a love of labor. Many of us like the notion of grammar as a system, the wholes and parts fitting into place. Yet too often we struggle with difficult concepts and often with indifferent students. We can make the labor of teaching grammar less—and, hopefully, the love of grammar more for both teacher and student—if we take advantage of the prodigious private linguistic knowledge that all fluent speakers of English, native and

By Billy T. Boyar, Ph.D.

Raising Expectations:
The Importance of Teaching Grammar to ESL Students

In the sixth grade, my class was taught sentence diagramming. Trying to superimpose our simple schoolbook diagrams on the infinity of language felt mysterious. Studying grammar in such a systematic way was like mapping the stars: We named unidentified words and charted their relationships. Words and phrases depended on other words like moons held to planets by gravity, and verbs sparkled like stars. I was not surprised, years later, to learn that the word *grammar* is etymologically related to *glamour* and *gramarye*,

> **S**tudying grammar in such a systematic way was like mapping the stars: We named unidentified words and charted their relationships.

suggesting magic. To me, the study of grammar has always been interesting and provocative in its own right. There are, however, important practical reasons for studying grammar and even more important practical reasons for ESL students to study it.

In the past, some people have disparaged the formal, systematic teaching of grammar to the ESL student. When people emphasize the importance of the natural way of learning language, beginning with hearing and mimicking, I agree with them. When they stress the necessity of creating a relaxed noncritical environment in which the ESL student feels free to practice speaking his or her new language, I agree with them. I agree that the study of literature and written composition is crucial. I even agree that grammar, if taught to young children or to ESL beginners of any age, should be fun and games, or should not be taught at all. However, when people advocate such approaches to the exclusion of a formal program of grammar for ESL students who are at least on an intermediate level and at least in the sixth grade, their argument is extreme, and I disagree with them.

Why is the study of grammar, usage, and mechanics important for appropriately mature and advanced ESL students?

Avoiding False Analogies

A study of English grammar, usage, and mechanics helps ESL students to avoid developing English language habits based on false analogies with the rules for their primary language. A comparative study of different languages shows that the basic patterns of grammar, conventions such as punctuation and capitalization, and the special uses of words can be vastly different. For example, a Spanish sentence doesn't necessarily need a subject (the subject can be implied by the verb); Spanish uses the present tense where English would sometimes use the past tense; question marks and exclamation points are placed both at the beginning and at the end of sentences; and a double negative is considered standard usage. English is even further from the grammatical expectations of Chinese and other non-Western ESL students.

In the past, some people have disparaged the formal, systematic teaching of grammar to the ESL student.

In my composition class, a Mexican American student submitted an essay that contained this sentence: "The Christmas party resulted well." The cognates *to result* (English) and *resultar* (Spanish) have confusingly similar meanings, yet their usage is distinctly different. Here, *resultar* could be translated *to turn out*. My student meant that the party turned out well, but she was basing her English usage on a false analogy with Spanish usage.

Not only does the ESL student tend to base English grammar rules on such false analogies, but also he or she often hears nonstandard usage repeated by friends and family. Being continually reinforced, the false analogy becomes an ingrained habit. Without the formal, systematic study of English grammar, usage, and mechanics, the ESL student may always have difficulty with standard English.

Promoting Academic Success

Teaching grammar to ESL students will help them succeed academically, especially if they plan to attend college. I have taught ESL and English at both high school and college. In composition classes, which also often contain ESL students, I frequently need to explain a point of grammar in order to help students understand why I am asking them to revise their papers. I want them to understand the principle so that they can avoid committing the same error over and over in future essays. For example, I ask them not to separate the subject and verb with only one comma (as in *Sara, who lives nearby is on my soccer team.*). This comment inevitably requires a further explanation: "Here you have inserted a nonessential clause between the subject and verb."

"But Mister," asks one ESL student, "what do you mean . . . *nonessential?*"

"A nonessential clause is a clause that can be removed. . . ."

"But what's a clause?"

"A clause contains a subject and a verb—it can be independent or subordinate. There are three kinds of subordinate . . ."

"What do you mean *subordinate*?"

"I mean that they have a subject and verb but that they cannot stand . . ."

"So what's a subject?"

"A subject is the noun or pronoun doing the . . ."

"Noun?"

The problem is that trying to teach a little bit of grammar is like trying to paint a little bit of a wall: It doesn't work.

I encounter situations like this all the time—and of course, ESL students aren't the only ones who don't know formal English grammar. The problem is that trying to teach a little bit of grammar is like trying to paint a little bit of a wall: It doesn't work. In a college composition class, instructors typically explain points of grammar, usage, and mechanics as they are related to essays submitted by students. However, it would not be appropriate to stop the composition class in order to devote the rest of the course to the basics of grammar. The result is that the ESL student who knows no formal English grammar is poorly served because he or she cannot take full advantage of the instructor's explanations.

Like many a native English speaker's, the ESL student's grammar and usage may never be perfect. Rather than perfection, the goal is a workable compromise. If students can communicate effectively in English, does it matter that they speak with an accent? The lives of ESL students will not be destroyed, for example, if they do not master the subjunctive mood. As teachers, we must demand excellence, but at the same time, we should carefully consider what exactly we want students to master.

Supporting Career Success

Studying grammar will help ESL students succeed professionally. Recently, a city employee asked me to tutor him in English. He had started out as a garbage collector, but after a few years his bosses recognized his ability and promoted him, then promoted him again. He suddenly found himself having to write memos and job descriptions. Now, in order to keep the job, he was required to improve his English grammar, usage, and mechanics.

The reality is that proficiency in standard English is a badge required for acceptance in many careers and professions in the United States. Teachers, lawyers, doctors, and so forth may not be given the respect and trust they deserve if their use of language departs too far from the standard. Beyond this country, English has become the foremost international language. The dialect of the neighborhood, rightly cherished, will not succeed very well in commerce on the World Wide Web. The formal, systematic study of grammar, usage, and mechanics helps the ESL student separate neighborhood dialect from public language, in order to develop that public language in a clear and conscious way. Being truly bilingual, of

countless others, a refined bilingualism can open doors to wider possibilities.

Increasing Language Ownership

ESL students will benefit from the formal study of English because a better understanding of language patterns, a confidence in punctuation, and a command of the special uses of words will help them internalize English as a language of their own. Language ownership is an important topic. Language is a huge part of personal identity. It is a major reference point in our understanding of who we are. However, it should be emphasized that we can own more than one language; we can have two or more languages and dialects as expressions of our identity. It is helpful, healing, and sane for ESL students whose home is the United States to adopt English and care for it as their own. The problem is that immigrants have not always been welcomed with open arms, which is ironic in a land of immigrants. Our ESL students may therefore feel somewhat alien and sense that the English language is the language of others. One category of ESL students speaks English most of the time. They speak English in school; they speak it in their after-school jobs; and they even speak it most of the time at home: with brothers and sisters nearly all of the time, with parents some of the time, but with grandparents not at all. Even though these students speak English

The reality is that proficiency in standard English is a badge required for acceptance in many careers and professions in the United States.

course, is more than merely owning a badge. Coupling a career or professional training with authentic bilingualism will broaden opportunities in ways that are numerous and unforeseen: as a police officer, nurse, doctor, lawyer, salesperson, diplomat, translator, flight attendant, psychotherapist, teacher, construction supervisor, municipal work supervisor, governor, or president. In any of these careers and professions and most of the time, they paradoxically still consider English their second language. In addition, since they use their "primary" (home) language less and less, it does not grow.

The knowledge of grammar, usage, and mechanics is one tool in many, but we should not underestimate its importance.

These ESL students can be left in a world of little language indeed. A systematic study of grammar, usage, and mechanics in a friendly environment will tend to cut through the cycle of alienation. In the same way that we may feel better about our own cars when we learn how they work and can repair them ourselves, ESL students can learn how English works and can feel the pride of ownership.

Conclusion

Finally, ESL students are in the advantageous position of having a head start on bilingualism. If they continue to grow in their first language and if we give them the tools that they need for their second language, they will become truly bilingual. They need many tools in their language tool kits: the training to hear English phonemes, so that they can be good listeners; the skill of pronunciation, so that they can speak clearly; the knowledge of literature, so that they can contemplate the values of English-language cultures and the cultures of the rest of the world; and the art of writing compositions, so that they can express their own truths. The knowledge of grammar, usage, and mechanics is one tool in many, but we should not underestimate its importance. For ESL students, grammatical knowledge is a *sine qua non* of becoming bilingual on a professional level. On this level of bilingualism, the advantages are many, but it seems we and our students sometimes set our sights too low. Perhaps we have been guilty of not expecting our ESL students to accomplish as much as other students. They can aspire to the same—or better—careers and professions and can partake richly of the larger culture. Beyond these avenues, however, from the point of view of those of us who love language, ESL students will be able to look at language from a higher vantage point. From this aerial view, perhaps some will even rediscover the old meaning of grammar: magic. ■

Billy Boyar has taught composition, literature, and ESL in high schools and community colleges for twenty years. Billy lives in Austin, Texas, where he teaches at Austin Community College. He has worked with juvenile offenders, volunteered with Hospice, and mediated as an ombudsman in nursing homes. In his free time, he enjoys studying Spanish and reading philosophy and finds his garden rewarding and a great way to unwind. He believes that a formal, systematic study of grammar is an important part of an ESL program.

Warriner's Handbook

▶ Your **California Roadmap** to Grammar, Usage, and Mechanics Mastery

Now more than ever before, there is a demand for students at all grade levels to develop competence in the language arts and facility with the English language. Students need to be able to access information with ease, to appreciate the literary arts, and perhaps most importantly, to apply their language skills at levels demanded in the twenty-first century.

GIVING MIDDLE SCHOOL STUDENTS ACCESS TO LANGUAGE SKILLS

Students in each classroom—including English language learners, special education students, students with learning difficulties, and advanced learners—are at varying levels of preparation and have different strengths and needs. Giving these students the tools they need to succeed is no easy task. That's where *Warriner's Handbook* comes in.

Designed specifically for middle school teachers and students in California, *Warriner's Handbook* is an integral part of a comprehensive, balanced language arts program called *Holt Literature and Language Arts*. This program leads the charge in providing a carefully researched method for not only helping your students meet and master the California standards in the language arts, but also helping them to embrace the power of the English language in all its forms.

The motivating force behind the organization and instructional delivery of *Warriner's Handbook* is the desire to offer teachers and students a method to focus on the written and oral English language conventions required by the standards—to provide a compelling and effective way to teach and learn grammar, usage, and mechanics skills. Based on John Warriner's time-tested model for instruction, *Warriner's Handbook* can also stand alone as a powerful tool for giving students access to the language skills they need most.

Covering All Your Students Need to Know About **Grammar, Usage, and Mechanics**

THREE MAIN PARTS COVER THE BASICS

PART I: GRAMMAR, USAGE, AND MECHANICS chapters help students use and practice using the building blocks of language— words, phrases, clauses, capitalization, punctuation, and spelling. The last chapter, **Correcting Common Errors,** gives students more practice building key language skills and taking tests in standardized formats.

PART II: The **SENTENCES** section is divided into two main areas of instruction: The **Writing Effective Sentences** chapter focuses on building grammatically correct, clear, and interesting sentences; the **Sentence Diagramming** chapter teaches students how the parts of a sentence relate to each other.

PART III: The **RESOURCES** chapters include **History of English,** a concise history of the English language; **Test Smarts,** a guide to taking standardized tests in grammar, usage, and mechanics; and **Grammar at a Glance,** a glossary of grammatical terms.

PART **1** Grammar, Usage, and Mechanics

PART **2** Sentences

PART **3** Resources

Instructional Delivery
That Keeps Students on Track

Each chapter in **Warriner's Handbook** is carefully sequenced so that students are introduced to and taught new rules and skills at the right time. Each chapter includes entry-level diagnosis, direct instruction of the rules followed immediately by exercises, ongoing assessment, and application of new knowledge through writing. This direct and practical instructional approach allows you to keep track of your students' pace, progress, and degree in mastering each California standard.

DIAGNOSTIC PREVIEW
Short tests that cover the whole chapter let you pretest for the most essential knowledge and skills.

RULE, EXAMPLE, EXERCISE
The introduction of a new rule is followed immediately by examples and exercises.

2

1.0 Written and Oral English Language Conventions
Students write and speak with a command of standard English conventions appropriate to this grade level.
1.4 Edit written manuscripts to ensure that correct grammar is used.
1.5 Use correct capitalization.

Numerals in brackets refer to rules tested by the items in the Diagnostic Preview.

1. [2p]
2. [2p]
3. [2h, o, a, b]
4. [2h, l, a, g]
5. [2h, m, l]
6. [2h, j, a]
7. [2h, i, p]
8. [2h, i, a]
9. [2h, o, a]
10. [2a, d]

Parts of Speech Overview
Noun, Pronoun, Adjective

Diagnostic Preview

A. Identifying Nouns, Pronouns, and A...

Tell whether each italicized word or word group i... sentences is used as a *noun*, a *pronoun*, or an *adjec...*

EXAMPLE 1. *Each* student is required to take a for... language.
   1. *Each*—adjective; *language*—noun

1. *That* drummer is the *best* performer.
2. That *German shepherd* puppy is a sweet-natur... rascal.
3. *Everybody* says that *high school* will be more w... fun, too.
4. *This* is the greatest year the junior varsity volle... ever had.
5. *Who* can tell me whose bicycle *this* is?
6. Jenna prepared a special breakfast for her par... this *morning*.
7. This is their fault because *they* ignored all the...
8. *We* received word that they aren't in *danger*.
9. *Each* of these clubs decorated a float for the Ci... *parade*.
10. The runner *Carl Lewis* won several Olympic *medals*.

Common Nouns and Proper Nouns

2c. A *common noun* names any one of a group of persons, places, things, or ideas.

A common noun generally does not begin with a capital letter.

2d. A *proper noun* names a particular person, place, thing, or idea.

A proper noun begins with a capital letter.

Common Nouns	Proper Nouns
poem	"The Raven," *I Am Joaquín*
country	Spain, Ivory Coast
athlete	Joe Montana, Zina Garrison
ship	*Mayflower, U.S.S. Constitut...*
newspaper	*The New York Times, USA T...*
river	Rio de la Plata, Ohio River
street	Market Street, University A...
day	Friday, Independence Day
city	Los Angeles, New Delhi, Ho...
organization	National Forensic League, G... of America

Exercise 3 Identifying Nouns

Identify the nouns in each of the following sentences, and label them *common* or *proper*.

EXAMPLE 1. My family likes to visit California when we are vacationing.
   1. *family*—common; *California*—proper

1. My whole family visited San Francisco during our vacation last year.
2. The city is famous for its hilly landscape.
3. Some of the steepest streets in the world can be found in the downtown area.
4. The city is also well-known for its system of streetcars.
5. San Francisco and Oakland, which is across the bay, have a number of teams that play professional sports.

Review A Writing the Past and Past Participle Forms
of Irregular Verbs

Write the correct past or past participle form of the italicized
verb given before each of the following s...

EXAMPLE   **1.** *tell*   Has Alameda ___ y...
                        Indian Tipi: Its Histor...

          1. told

1. *write*   Reginald and Gladys Laubin ...
                 others about American India...
2. *build*   The Laubins ___ their own ...
3. *stand*   Tepees of various sizes once ...
                 Great Plains.   **3.** stood
4. *see*   I have ___ pictures of camp...
                 decorated tepees.   **4.** seen
5. *make*   For many years, American In...
                 out of cloth rather than buffa...
6. *come*   The word *tepee*, or *tipi*, has ...
                 the Sioux language.   **6.** com...

Review B Writing the Past and Past Participle Forms
of Irregular Verbs

Write the correct past or past participle form of the italicized
verb given before each of the following sentences.

EXAMPLE   **1.** *write*   I ___ a report on Jim Thorpe.
          1. wrote

1. *blow*   Yesterday the wind ___ the leaves into our yard.
2. *break*   My pen pal from Australia has never ___ his
                 promise to write once a week.
3. *bring*   I ___ the wrong book to class.
4. *burst*   The children almost ___ with excitement.
5. *choose* The director ___ James Earl Jones for the role.
6. *come*   My aunt and her friend ___ to dinner last night.
7. *do*   I have always ___ my homework right after supper.
8. *drink*   The guests ___ fruit punch and lemonade.
9. *fall*   One of Julian's Russian nesting dolls has ___ off
                 the shelf.
10. *freeze* Has the pond ___ yet?
11. *go*   We have never ___ to see the Parthenon in
                 Nashville.
12. *know*   Had I ___, I would have called you sooner.
13. *ring*   Suddenly the fire alarm ___.
14. *run*   Joan Samuelson certainly ___ a good race.
15. *see*   I ___ you in line at the movies.
16. *shrink* The apples we dried in the sun have ___.
17. *speak* After we had ...
                 to play domi...
18. *swim*   We ___ out...

REVIEW EXERCISES

Short reviews after practice exercises
offer cumulative assessment so that you
can plan future instruction to help all
students meet or master the standards.

Chapter Review

A. Using Irregular Verbs

Write the correct past or past participle form of the italicized
irregular verb provided before each sentence.

1. *break*   The thunder ___ the silence.
2. *ring*   Who ___ the fire alarm so quickly?
3. *shrink*   This shirt must have ___ in the dryer.
4. *throw*   You've ___ the ball out of bounds!
5. *lead*   Julio ___ the parade last year, so now it's my turn.
6. *rise*   The sun ___ over the pyramids of Giza in Egypt.
7. *swim*   We have ___ only three laps.
8. *choose*   Vera was ___ as captain of the volleyball team.
9. *go*   I have ___ to visit the Grand Canyon twice.
10. *sit*   The tiny tree frog ___ motionless.
11. *write*   Joan has ___ a story about aliens from the
                  Andromeda galaxy.
12. *do*   During class, Jorge ___ the first five problems of his
                  homework assignment.
13. *steal*   Three runners ___ bases during the first inning.
14. *break*   This summer's heat wave has ___ all records.
15. *drink*   Have you ___ all of the tomato juice?
16. *sink*   The log had slowly ___ into the quicksand.
17. *lie*   The old postcards have ___ in the box for years.
18. *drive*   Have you ever ___ across the state of Texas?
19. *begin*   Our local PBS station ___ its fund-raising drive.
20. *set*   Have you ___ the paper plates and napkins on the
                  picnic table?

CHAPTER REVIEWS

These tests offer
additional practice
and opportunities
for ongoing
assessments.

Writing Application
Using Verbs in a Story

Verb Forms and Tenses   A local writers' club is sponsoring a
contest for the best "cliffhanger" opening of an adventure story.
Write an exciting paragraph to enter in the contest. Your paragraph should leave readers wondering "What happens next?" In
your paragraph, use at least five verbs from the lists of Common
Irregular Verbs in this chapter.

Prewriting   First, you will need to imagine a suspenseful situation to describe. Jot down several ideas for your story opening.
Then, choose the one you like best. With that situation in mind,
scan the lists of irregular verbs. Note at least ten verbs you can
use. Include some lively action verbs like *burst*, *swing*, and *throw*.

Writing   As you write your rough draft, think of your readers.
Choose words that create a suspenseful, believable scene.
Remember that you have only one paragraph to catch your
readers' interest.

Revising   Ask a friend to read your paragraph. Does your
friend find it interesting? Can he or she picture the scene clearly?
If not, you may want to add, delete, or revise some details.

Publishing   Check your spelling, usage, punctuation, and
grammar. Check to make sure the forms of verbs are correct and
the tenses are consistent. You may want to exchange your
cliffhanger with a partner, and complete each other's stories.
With your teacher's permission, you can then read the completed
stories aloud to the class.

WRITING APPLICATIONS

These end-of-chapter
activities guide
students in applying
new grammar, usage,
and mechanics skills
in their writing.

1.0 Written and Oral English Language Conventions

1.2 Understand sen-
tence construction (e.g.,
parallel structure, sub-
ordination, proper
placement of modifiers)
and proper English
usage (e.g., consistency
of verb tenses).

1.3 Demonstrate an
understanding of
proper English usage
and control of gram-
mar, paragraph and
sentence structure, dic-
tion, and syntax.

Instruction Based on
California Standards

CALIFORNIA STANDARDS

At the beginning of each chapter, students are alerted to the
California standards that will be covered. They understand
immediately what they are expected to learn.

Instruction Based on
Warriner's Model

An English teacher for thirty years, John Warriner developed the original instructional approach used throughout the grammar, usage, and mechanics chapters in **Warriner's Handbook** *Student Edition*. His logical model of instruction is based on a three-step process: Teach students the rule, show examples of the rule in action, and provide immediate practice to reinforce the skill or concept. This model has been the authoritative standard for teaching grammar, usage, and mechanics skills for over fifty years.

RULE
Clearly stated rules are always presented in red.

EXERCISE
Exercises give immediate practice for rules.

EXAMPLES
A variety of student-friendly examples illustrate the language skill or concept being taught.

┌─HELP─┐

Most regular verbs that end in e drop the e before adding *–ing*. Some regular verbs double the final consonant before adding *–ing* or *–ed*.

EXAMPLES
shake—shak**ing**
hug—hu**gged**

Reference Note
For more about **spelling rules,** see Chapter 16. For information on **standard and nonstandard English,** see page 245.

Regular Verbs

9b. A *regular verb* forms its past and past participle by adding *–d* or *–ed* to the base form.

Base Form	Present Participle	Past	Past Participle
clean	[is] cleaning	cleaned	[have] cleaned
hope	[is] hoping	hoped	[have] hoped
inspect	[is] inspecting	inspected	[have] inspected
slip	[is] slipping	slipped	[have] slipped

One common error in forming the past or the past participle of a regular verb is to leave off the *–d* or *–ed* ending.

NONSTANDARD   Our street use to be quieter.
STANDARD   Our street **used** to be quieter.

Another common error is to add unnecessary letters.

NONSTANDARD   The swimmer almost drownded in the riptide.
STANDARD   The swimmer almost **drowned** in the riptide.

NONSTANDARD   The kitten attackted that paper bag.
STANDARD   The kitten **attacked** that paper bag.

Using Regular Verbs

owing sentences aloud, stressing the

meet at the

d to buy the

called me about

used to live in

could go to the

WOOF
WOOFS
WOOFING
WOOFED

© 1992 by Sidney Harris.

USAGE

---

6. The chairs have been *moved* into the hall for the dance.
7. That salesclerk has *helped* my mother before.
8. Eli may not have *looked* under the table for the cat.

Exercise 1 **Writing the Forms of Regular Verbs**

Write the correct present participle, past, or past participle form of the italicized verb given before each of the following sentences.

EXAMPLES   **1.** *learn*   Many people today are ____ folk dances from a variety of countries.

1. *learning*

2. *hope*   Dad and I had ____ to take lessons in folk dancing this summer.

2. *hoped*

1. *practice*   These Spanish folk dancers must have ____ for a long time.

2. *perform*   Notice that they are ____ in their colorful native costumes.

3. *wish*   Have you ever ____ that you knew how to do any folk dances?

4. *use*   Virginia reels ____ to be popular dances in the United States.

5. *promise*   Mrs. Stamos, who is from Greece, ____ to teach her daughter the Greek chain dance.

6. *lean*   The young Jamaican dancer ____ backward before he went under the pole during the limbo dance competition.

7. *start*   The group from Estonia is ____ a dance about a spinning wheel.

8. *request*   Someone in the audience has ____ an Irish square dance called "Sweets of May."

9. *dance*   During the Mexican hat dance, the woman ____ around the brim of the sombrero.

10. *fill*   The Jewish wedding dance ____ the room with both music and movement.

Features That Help Students Along the Way

Oral Practice 5 Using Forms of *Rise* and *Raise* Correctly

Read the following sentences aloud, stressing the italicized verbs.

1. Mount Everest *rises* over 29,000 feet.
2. He *raises* the flag at sunrise.
3. The TV reporter *raised* her voice to be heard.
4. She *rose* from her seat and looked out the window.
5. The constellation Orion had not yet *risen* in the southern sky.
6. They had *raised* the piñata high in the tree.
7. I hope the bread is *rising*.
8. He will be *raising* the bucket from the well.

ORAL PRACTICE
Spoken practice and reinforcement of rules and concepts

TIPS & TRICKS

Sometimes a fragment is really a part of a nearby sentence. You can correct the fragment by attaching it to the sentence that comes before or after it.

SENTENCE WITH FRAGMENT
Mark is practicing his hook shot. Because he wants to try out for the basketb

SENTENCE
Mark is
hook sh
wants
the bas

When you
ment to a
to check y
for correc
capitaliza

TIPS & TRICKS
Easy-to-use hints that help students master language skills

MEETING THE CHALLENGE

Write a poem, correctly using each of the six troublesome verbs, *sit, set, rise, raise, lie,* and *lay.* Be sure to check your poem for correct usage of the troublesome verbs.

MEETING THE CHALLENGE
Questions and short activities that ask students to approach a concept from a new angle

STYLE TIP

The verb *lie* can also mean "to tell an untruth." Used in this way, *lie* still does not take an object.

EXAMPLE
Don't **lie** to her, Beth.

The past and past participle forms of this meaning of *lie* are *lied* and [*have*] *lied.*

STYLE TIPS
Information that guides students in making sound decisions about style and usages.

HELP
Some of the subjects and verbs in Review B are compound.

HELP
Pointers that help students understand key rules or exercise directions

Unique Strategies Make
Planning Lessons Easy

The **Warriner's Handbook** *Teacher's Edition* helps you organize your lessons into manageable segments—preteaching, direct teaching, and reteaching, for example—so that students build skills in a systematic, accessible way. Suggestions for differentiating instruction are integrated with lessons to help you support students with special learning needs, including advanced learners, students with learning difficulties, and English-language learners. Features that direct you to program resources for each chapter and lesson are also there to help you along the way.

 STANDARDS FOCUS

Grade-Level Standards
(Boldface indicates concepts that are taught and tested in this chapter.)

- Language Conventions 1.0: Students write and speak with a command of standard Engli conventions appropriate to grade level.
- Grammar 1.2: Identify and p erly use indefinite pronoun and present perfect, past pe fect, and future perfect verl tenses; ensure that verbs ag with compound subjects.
- Capitalization 1.4: Use corre capitalization.

Prerequisite/Review Standards
- Grammar 1.2: Identify and correctly use verbs that are often misused (e.g., *lie/lay, rise/raise, sit/set*), modifiers, and pronouns.
- Capitalization 1.4: Use correct capitalization.

Standards Coming Up in the Next Grade Level
- Grammar 1.3: Identify all parts of speech and types and structure of sentences.
- Capitalization 1.6: Use correct capitalization.

STANDARDS FOCUS

Each chapter opens with a clearly presented summary of standards that will be taught and tested in the chapter, including **Grade-Level Standards, Prerequisite/Review Standards**, and **Standards Coming up in the Next Grade Level**.

PRETEACHING

Lesson Starter

Prior Knowledge. Ask students to supply words that describe the similarities and differences between an orange and a baseball. Students might begin by saying that both objects are round. You mi[gh]
Venn diagram
ask students t[o]

PRETEACHING

Located at the beginning of each chapter, these strategies help you identify prerequisite skills and build on the prior knowledge of your students.

DIRECT TEACHING

Modeling and Demonstration

Identifying Nouns. Model how to identify nouns by using the example *self-esteem*. First, ask whether the word names a person, place, thing, or idea. [idea] *Self-esteem* names an idea; therefore, *self-esteem* is a noun. Now, have a voluntee[r] another example from this c[ ] demonstrate how to identify

DIRECT TEACHING

Direct teaching strategies to help you present content include modeling and demonstrating new concepts.

RETEACHING

Pronouns

Activity. Ask students to write five descriptive sentences about a celebrity without ever mentioning the celebrity's name. Have two or three volunteers read their sentences, and let classmates try to guess the celebrity. Then, lead students to see that a common word in many of the sentences is *he* or *she*. Point out that pronouns like *he* and *she* are used in place of a noun, common or proper.

RETEACHING

Reteaching strategies offer techniques to help you present material from a fresh perspective.

EXTENSION

Critical Thinking
Metacognition. Point out to students that there are probably too many pronouns to memorize all of them by type. Ask students what their strategies are for remembering the different types of pronouns. Have students describe and rate the effectiveness of their strategies. Students having trouble with pronouns should develop new strategies. Have students meet in groups to share and compare their ideas.

DIFFERENTIATING INSTRUCTION

Advanced Learners
Have students read and discuss John Gardner's "Dragon, Dragon" or another folk tale that uses common nouns rather than proper names for its characters. Ask students to consider why the author uses common nouns rather than proper ones for the characters in the story. [*Students may say that there are so many characters in the story that it is easier for the reader to remember them with descriptive common nouns than with proper ones. Common nouns may also make the characters seem more universal.*]

CHAPTER RESOURCES

Internet
- go.hrw.com (keyword: HLLA)

Planning
- *Teacher One Stop DVD-ROM*
- *On Course: Mapping Instruction*

Practice & Review
- *Language & Sentence Skills Practice,* pp. 25–37; 38–40
- *Developmental Language & Sentence Skills,* pp. 7–16

Application & Enrichment
- *Language and Sentence Skills Practice,* pp. 43; 24, 41–42

EXTENSION
Activities and strategies ask students to apply grammar, usage, and mechanics concepts to the other language arts.

DIFFERENTIATING INSTRUCTION
These activities and suggestions help you reinforce language skills with learners having difficulty, English-language learners, advanced learners, and special education students.

CHAPTER RESOURCES
This handy feature lists all materials that support each chapter lesson.

Teaching Suggestions That Help Students Make Connections

Because language arts skills are so interconnected, the *Teacher's Edition* provides a variety of extension and application strategies that help students make connections between the grammar, usage, and mechanics skills you're teaching them and the writing, science, and social studies skills they need to succeed in other classes. In addition, the *Teacher's Edition* gives you suggestions for integrating an invaluable element of your students' learning experience—their families and communities.

MINI-LESSON · Mechanics

Punctuating Adjectives in a Series. Often two or more adjectives are used before a noun to make its meaning more specific. Remind students of the rules regarding comma usage with series of adjectives.

MINI-LESSON
These practical lessons help students link various grammar, usage, and mechanics skills to one another.

Learning for Life

Writing a Personal Profile. For various reasons, adults are sometimes asked to write personal profiles, which require careful attention to verb tense. Ask your students to write profiles of themselves, including only material they are comfort-

LEARNING FOR LIFE
These real-world suggestions help students relate grammar, usage, and mechanics skills to their own lives and to workplace skills they'll need in the future.

CONTENT-AREA CONNECTIONS

Social Studies
Places and Names. To give students practice in naming proper nouns, have students complete a team race on a social studies topic that they are studying. Divide the class into groups of four. Give each group a social studies category, and have the groups write as many proper nouns as they can in five minutes. All group members are responsible for generating answers. (Possible categories include states and their capitals, continents, oceans, rivers, countries, presidents, and

FAMILY/COMMUNITY ACTIVITY

Introductions. Most students have had or will have opportunities to introduce people to each other. In doing so, students will use complements. Provide the following examples:

1. Hi! I'm <u>Ms. King</u>. I teach <u>language arts</u> at Carson Middle School.
2. Maria, this is <u>Tom Jones</u>. Tom is <u>new</u> to our school. Tom, this is <u>Maria Gomez</u>. Maria is my best <u>friend</u>.

CONTENT-AREA CONNECTIONS
These extension activities reinforce the notion that language arts skills are relevant to other disciplines like science and social studies.

FAMILY/COMMUNITY ACTIVITY
These activities offer a real-world forum for students' language arts skills.

Additional **Practice** and **Strategies** to Help Students Succeed

LANGUAGE & SENTENCE SKILLS PRACTICE

These worksheets provide practice, reinforcement, and extension for topics covered in *Warriner's Handbook*. Traditional worksheets offer additional practice for every rule taught in the *Student Edition*. **Language in Context** worksheets let students apply and extend their study of grammar, usage, and mechanics to other areas in the language arts and to content in other disciplines. These worksheets include **Choices** worksheets, **Proofreading Application** worksheets, **Literary Model** worksheets, and **Writing Application** worksheets.

UNIVERSAL ACCESS: DEVELOPMENTAL LANGUAGE & SENTENCE SKILLS

These remedial worksheets provide instruction, practice, and reinforcement to supplement lessons in *Warriner's Handbook* and in *Language & Sentence Skills Practice*. Targeted to those students who have not yet mastered specific concepts taught in *Warriner's Handbook*, special features of this workbook include **Tips** that help students grasp abstract concepts with mnemonic devices, identification tests, and recognition strategies; **Points of Instruction** that explain how the rule applies to the examples provided; and **Guided Practice** that helps students with the first items of each exercise by asking guiding questions.

ENGLISH-LANGUAGE CONVENTIONS PROGRESS-MONITORING TESTS

This booklet contains chapter tests in standardized test format for the grammar, usage, mechanics, and sentences chapters in *Warriner's Handbook.* Presented in multiple-choice format, each test offers a sound means of assessing your students' grasp of key English language conventions and, at the same time, offers students opportunities to practice their test-taking skills. The answer key provides useful references to specific rules that tie the answers to relevant instruction in *Warriner's Handbook* and helps you pinpoint which skills and concepts students have mastered and which need further attention.

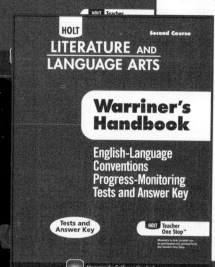

FORMAL ASSESSMENT: DIAGNOSTIC, PROGRESS-MONITORING, AND SUMMATIVE TESTING

These assessments test students' knowledge of English-language conventions and writing strategies in a multiple-choice format. In addition, these tests provide an opportunity for students to respond to on-demand writing prompts. The diagnostic test given at the beginning of the year uses multiple tasks in writing to assess mastery of the standards required in the forthcoming year as well as the previous year's standards. The progress-monitoring tests as well as the summative tests include questions related to sentence structure, grammar, punctuation, spelling, and capitalization.

READING AND WRITING TRANSPARENCIES

This binder contains transparencies that help students practice vocabulary, proofreading, reading, and sentence-combining skills. Reinforcing grammar, usage, and mechanics skills covered in *Warriner's Handbook,* the proofreading warm-up transparencies offer quick, five- to ten-minute proofreading activities. Sentence-combining transparencies include activities that direct students to combine sentences by inserting a word or phrase, to combine sentences in order to create a particular meaning, and to combine three sentences in different ways.

SPELLING LESSONS AND ACTIVITIES

This component focuses on both sound-pattern and word-analysis strategies. The worksheets provide both instruction and practice in spelling strategies such as determining word parts from other languages, learning related words, and understanding prefixes and suffixes. Review tests are included for each unit, as well as creative games and activities for reviewing the words.

FAMILY INVOLVEMENT ACTIVITIES: A GUIDE TO STANDARDS MASTERY

This booklet contains a number of letters that invite parents and guardians to participate in what students are learning. Each of these letters gives suggestions on how parents can integrate grammar, usage, or mechanics instruction into students' lives at home, and prompts them to consider relationships between the skills required by the California guidelines and everyday applications of those skills.

HOLT Teacher One Stop™

with Test Generator and State-Specific Resources

DVD-ROM for Macintosh® and Windows®

DVD-ROM Technology
Reinforces Learning— and Helps You Teach

HOLT **Teacher One Stop™**

with Test Generator and State-Specific Resources

DVD-ROM for Macintosh® and Windows®

TEACHER ONE STOP DVD-ROM with EXAMVIEW TEST GENERATOR
(for Macintosh® and Windows®)

Planning and managing lessons has never been easier than with the *Teacher One Stop DVD-ROM with Examview Test Generator.* This convenient, all-in-one planning tool includes all the teaching resources for *Warriner's Handbook,* as well as valuable planning and assessment tools. The *Teacher One Stop* includes

- an easy-to-use test generator that lets you find test items quickly
- previews of all teaching resources, including assessments and worksheets directly linked to the *Student Edition*
- printable program resources
- a direct launch to the **go.hrw.com** Internet site

Teaching resources are presented in easy-to-understand, point-and-click formats. To preview a transparency or to print out tests and worksheets for your students, simply make your selection and click your mouse.

Extend Grammar, Usage, and Mechanics Learning to the **Internet**!

GO.HRW.COM

Internet references in the *Student Edition* part openers direct students to **go.hrw.com**, a Web site that links students to resources related to concepts, rules, and assignments in **Warriner's Handbook.**

HOW IT WORKS

When students see the **go.hrw.com** logo and a keyword in the textbook, they can go to the **go.hrw.com** site, enter the keyword, and link instantly to resources that support the grammatical concept or rule they are studying.

INTERACTIVE EXERCISES IN GRAMMAR, USAGE, AND MECHANICS

Among the resources available to students on the **go.hrw.com** site are interactive exercises in grammar, usage, and mechanics. Students can practice skills with short assignments and then complete chapter tests and other assessments—scored immediately—so that students have immediate feedback on their progress.

California Standards Correlation Chart

This chart outlines the chapters of *Warriner's Handbook*, the California standards those chapters cover, and the resources available in the *Holt Literature and Language Arts* program to help you teach those standards. The chart lists materials appropriate for use with on-level students, advanced students, learners having difficulty, special education students, and English-language learners. Many of these resources are available on the *Teacher One Stop™*, on other DVD-ROMs, or at go.hrw.com.

Warriner's Handbook Chapter	California Written and Oral English-Language Standards	Differentiating Instruction	
		Advanced Learners	**On-Level Learners**
1 The Parts of a Sentence	**1.0** Students write and speak with a command of standard English conventions appropriate to this grade level. **1.1** Use correct and varied sentence types. **1.3** Use coordination to indicate clearly the relationship between ideas. **1.4** Edit written manuscripts to ensure that correct grammar is used.	• Teacher's Edition, pp. 8, 10 • Language & Sentence Skills Practice, pp. 22–24	• Teacher's Edition, pp. 2–23 • Language & Sentence Skills Practice, pp. 1–24
2 Parts of Speech Overview: Noun, Pronoun, Adjective	**1.0** Students write and speak with a command of standard English conventions appropriate to this grade level. **1.4** Edit written manuscripts to ensure that correct grammar is used. **1.5** Use correct capitalization.	• Teacher's Edition, pp. 29, 37 • Language & Sentence Skills Practice, pp. 43–45	• Teacher's Edition, pp. 24–49 • Language & Sentence Skills Practice, pp. 25–45
3 Parts of Speech Overview: Verb, Adverb, Preposition, Conjunction, Interjection	**1.0** Students write and speak with a command of standard English conventions appropriate to this grade level. **1.3** Use coordination. **1.4** Edit written manuscripts to ensure that correct grammar is used. **1.5** Use correct punctuation.	• Teacher's Edition, p. 53 • Language & Sentence Skills Practice, pp. 67–69	• Teacher's Edition, pp. 50–77 • Language & Sentence Skills Practice, pp. 46–69

Differentiating Instruction		Assessment	Additional Resources
Learners Having Difficulty	**English-Language Learners & Special Education Students**		
• Teacher's Edition, p. 20 • Developmental Language & Sentence Skills, pp. 1–8	• Teacher's Edition, (ELL) pp. 8, 13, 19 • Universal Access: Differentiating Instruction • Universal Access: Supporting Instruction in Five Languages	• Formal Assessment • Progress-Monitoring Tests, pp. 1–2, 48 • Test Generator (Teacher One Stop DVD-ROM)	• Reading and Writing Transparencies • Spelling Lessons & Activities • go.hrw.com (keyword: HLLA) • WordSharp: An Interactive Vocabulary Tutor
• Teacher's Edition, pp. 33, 35, 40 • Developmental Language & Sentence Skills, pp. 9–18	• Teacher's Edition, (ELL) pp. 28, 39 • Universal Access: Differentiating Instruction • Universal Access: Supporting Instruction in Five Languages	• Formal Assessment • Progress-Monitoring Tests, pp. 3–4, 48 • Test Generator (Teacher One Stop DVD-ROM)	• Reading and Writing Transparencies • Spelling Lessons & Activities • go.hrw.com (keyword: HLLA) • WordSharp: An Interactive Vocabulary Tutor
• Teacher's Edition, p. 73 • Developmental Language & Sentence Skills, pp. 19–28	• Teacher's Edition, (ELL) pp. 52, 53, 67; (SE) p. 51 • Universal Access: Differentiating Instruction • Universal Access: Supporting Instruction in Five Languages	• Formal Assessment • Progress-Monitoring Tests, pp. 5–6, 48 • Test Generator (Teacher One Stop DVD-ROM)	• Reading and Writing Transparencies • Spelling Lessons & Activities • go.hrw.com (keyword: HLLA) • WordSharp: An Interactive Vocabulary Tutor

(continued on next page)

Warriner's Handbook Chapter	California Written and Oral English-Language Standards	Differentiating Instruction	
		Advanced Learners	On-Level Learners
4 Complements	**1.0** Students write and speak with a command of standard English conventions appropriate to this grade level. **1.1** Use correct and varied sentence types and sentence openings. **1.4** Edit written manuscripts to ensure that correct grammar is used.	• Teacher's Edition, p. 88 • Language & Sentence Skills Practice, pp. 84–86	• Teacher's Edition, pp. 78–93 • Language & Sentence Skills Practice, pp. 70–86
5 The Phrase	**1.0** Students write and speak with a command of standard English conventions appropriate to this grade level. **1.1** Use correct and varied sentence openings. **1.3** Use apposition. **1.4** Edit written manuscripts to ensure that correct grammar is used.	• Teacher's Edition, p. 107 • Language & Sentence Skills Practice, pp. 115–117	• Teacher's Edition, pp. 94–117 • Language & Sentence Skills Practice, pp. 87–117
6 The Clause	**1.0** Students write and speak with a command of standard English conventions appropriate to this grade level. **1.1** Use correct and varied sentence types. **1.3** Use subordination. **1.4** Edit written manuscripts to ensure that correct grammar is used.	• Teacher's Edition, p. 129 • Language & Sentence Skills Practice, pp. 135–137	• Teacher's Edition, pp. 118–137 • Language & Sentence Skills Practice, pp. 118–137

Differentiating Instruction		Assessment	Additional Resources
Learners Having Difficulty	**English-Language Learners & Special Education Students**		
• Teacher's Edition, pp. 80, 83, 84 • Developmental Language & Sentence Skills, pp. 29–36	• Teacher's Edition, (ELL) p. 87; (SE) p. 83 • Universal Access: Differentiating Instruction • Universal Access: Supporting Instruction in Five Languages	• Formal Assessment • Progress-Monitoring Tests, pp. 7–8, 48 • Test Generator (Teacher One Stop DVD-ROM)	• Reading and Writing Transparencies • Spelling Lessons & Activities • go.hrw.com (keyword: HLLA) • WordSharp: An Interactive Vocabulary Tutor
• Teacher's Edition, pp. 97, 102, 103, 110 • Developmental Language & Sentence Skills, pp. 37–46	• Teacher's Edition, (ELL) pp. 97, 98, 102, 103, 109, 110; (SE) p. 113 • Universal Access: Differentiating Instruction • Universal Access: Supporting Instruction in Five Languages	• Formal Assessment • Progress-Monitoring Tests, pp. 9–10, 48 • Test Generator (Teacher One Stop DVD-ROM)	• Reading and Writing Transparencies • Family Involvement Activities: A Guide to Standards Mastery • Family Involvement Activities: In Five Languages • Spelling Lessons & Activities • go.hrw.com (keyword: HLLA) • WordSharp: An Interactive Vocabulary Tutor
• Teacher's Edition, pp. 131, 132 • Developmental Language & Sentence Skills, pp. 47–50	• Teacher's Edition, (ELL) pp. 125, 128 • Universal Access: Differentiating Instruction • Universal Access: Supporting Instruction in Five Languages	• Formal Assessment • Progress-Monitoring Tests, pp. 11–12, 48 • Test Generator (Teacher One Stop DVD-ROM)	• Reading and Writing Transparencies • Spelling Lessons & Activities • go.hrw.com (keyword: HLLA) • WordSharp: An Interactive Vocabulary Tutor

(continued on next page)

Warriner's Handbook Chapter	California Written and Oral English-Language Standards	Differentiating Instruction	
		Advanced Learners	On-Level Learners
7 Sentence Structure	**1.0** Students write and speak with a command of standard English conventions appropriate to this grade level. **1.1** Use correct and varied sentence types and sentence openings. **1.3** Use coordination. **1.4** Edit written manuscripts to ensure that correct grammar is used. **1.5** Use correct punctuation and capitalization.	• Teacher's Edition, p. 146 • Language & Sentence Skills Practice, pp. 149–151	• Teacher's Edition, pp. 138–153 • Language & Sentence Skills Practice, pp. 138–151
8 Agreement	**1.0** Students write and speak with a command of standard English conventions appropriate to this grade level. **1.4** Edit written manuscripts to ensure that correct grammar is used.	• Teacher's Edition, p. 168 • Language & Sentence Skills Practice, pp. 175–178	• Teacher's Edition, pp. 154–183 • Language & Sentence Skills Practice, pp. 152–178
9 Using Verbs Correctly	**1.0** Students write and speak with a command of standard English conventions appropriate to this grade level. **1.4** Edit written manuscripts to ensure that correct grammar is used.	• Teacher's Edition, pp. 192, 206 • Language & Sentence Skills Practice, pp. 198–201	• Teacher's Edition, pp. 184–213 • Language & Sentence Skills Practice, pp. 179–201

Differentiating Instruction		Assessment	Additional Resources
Learners Having Difficulty	**English-Language Learners & Special Education Students**		
• Teacher's Edition, pp. 144, 148, 149 • Developmental Language & Sentence Skills, pp. 51–54	• Teacher's Edition, (ELL) p. 140; (SE) p. 144 • Universal Access: Differentiating Instruction • Universal Access: Supporting Instruction in Five Languages	• Formal Assessment • Progress-Monitoring Tests, pp. 13–14, 48 • Test Generator (Teacher One Stop DVD-ROM)	• Reading and Writing Transparencies • Family Involvement Activities: A Guide to Standards Mastery • Family Involvement Activities: In Five Languages • Spelling Lessons & Activities • go.hrw.com (keyword: HLLA) • WordSharp: An Interactive Vocabulary Tutor
• Teacher's Edition, pp. 160, 174 • Developmental Language & Sentence Skills, pp. 55–64	• Teacher's Edition, (ELL) pp. 158, 162, 167, 174, 175 • Universal Access: Differentiating Instruction • Universal Access: Supporting Instruction in Five Languages	• Formal Assessment • Progress-Monitoring Tests, pp. 15–16, 48 • Test Generator (Teacher One Stop DVD-ROM)	• Reading and Writing Transparencies • Family Involvement Activities: A Guide to Standards Mastery • Family Involvement Activities: In Five Languages • Spelling Lessons & Activities • go.hrw.com (keyword: HLLA) • WordSharp: An Interactive Vocabulary Tutor
• Teacher's Edition, pp. 191, 202 • Developmental Language & Sentence Skills, pp. 65–70	• Teacher's Edition, (ELL) pp. 190, 195, 197, 200 • Universal Access: Differentiating Instruction • Universal Access: Supporting Instruction in Five Languages	• Formal Assessment • Progress-Monitoring Tests, pp. 17–18, 48 • Test Generator (Teacher One Stop DVD-ROM)	• Reading and Writing Transparencies • Family Involvement Activities: A Guide to Standards Mastery • Family Involvement Activities: In Five Languages • Spelling Lessons & Activities • go.hrw.com (keyword: HLLA) • WordSharp: An Interactive Vocabulary Tutor

(continued on next page)

Warriner's Handbook Chapter	California Written and Oral English-Language Standards	Differentiating Instruction	
		Advanced Learners	**On-Level Learners**
10 Using Pronouns Correctly	**1.0** Students write and speak with a command of standard English conventions appropriate to this grade level. **1.4** Edit written manuscripts to ensure that correct grammar is used.	• Teacher's Edition, p. 222 • Language & Sentence Skills Practice, pp. 217–220	• Teacher's Edition, pp. 214–235 • Language & Sentence Skills Practice, pp. 202–220
11 Using Modifiers Correctly	**1.0** Students write and speak with a command of standard English conventions appropriate to this grade level. **1.4** Edit written manuscripts to ensure that correct grammar is used.	• Teacher's Edition, p. 250 • Language & Sentence Skills Practice, pp. 240–243	• Teacher's Edition, pp. 236–261 • Language & Sentence Skills Practice, pp. 221–243
12 A Glossary of Usage	**1.0** Students write and speak with a command of standard English conventions appropriate to this grade level. **1.4** Edit written manuscripts to ensure that correct grammar is used. **1.6** Use correct spelling conventions.	• Teacher's Edition, p. 266 • Language & Sentence Skills Practice, pp. 253–266	• Teacher's Edition, pp. 262–283 • Language & Sentence Skills Practice, pp. 244–256
13 Capital Letters	**1.0** Students write and speak with a command of standard English conventions appropriate to this grade level. **1.4** Edit written manuscripts to ensure that correct grammar is used. **1.5** Use correct capitalization.	• Teacher's Edition, pp. 292, 293 • Language & Sentence Skills Practice, pp. 275–278	• Teacher's Edition, pp. 284–309 • Language & Sentence Skills Practice, pp. 257–278

Differentiating Instruction		Assessment	Additional Resources
Learners Having Difficulty	**English-Language Learners & Special Education Students**		
• Teacher's Edition, p. 229 • Developmental Language & Sentence Skills, pp. 71–76	• Teacher's Edition, (ELL) pp. 217, 221, 223, 227; (SE) p. 227 • Universal Access: Differentiating Instruction • Universal Access: Supporting Instruction in Five Languages	• Formal Assessment • Progress-Monitoring Tests, pp. 19–20, 48 • Test Generator (Teacher One Stop DVD-ROM)	• Reading and Writing Transparencies • Spelling Lessons & Activities • go.hrw.com (keyword: HLLA) • WordSharp: An Interactive Vocabulary Tutor
• Teacher's Edition, pp. 243, 252, 256 • Developmental Language & Sentence Skills, pp. 77–86	• Teacher's Edition, (ELL) pp. 239, 242, 249; (SE) pp. 244, 253 • Universal Access: Differentiating Instruction • Universal Access: Supporting Instruction in Five Languages	• Formal Assessment • Progress-Monitoring Tests, pp. 21–22, 48 • Test Generator (Teacher One Stop DVD-ROM)	• Reading and Writing Transparencies • Family Involvement Activities: A Guide to Standards Mastery • Family Involvement Activities: In Five Languages • Spelling Lessons & Activities • go.hrw.com (keyword: HLLA) • WordSharp: An Interactive Vocabulary Tutor
• Teacher's Edition, pp. 270, 271, 278 • Developmental Language & Sentence Skills, pp. 87–92	• Teacher's Edition, (ELL) pp. 267, 275, 276 • Universal Access: Differentiating Instruction • Universal Access: Supporting Instruction in Five Languages	• Formal Assessment • Progress-Monitoring Tests, pp. 23–24, 48 • Test Generator (Teacher One Stop DVD-ROM)	• Reading and Writing Transparencies • Family Involvement Activities: A Guide to Standards Mastery • Family Involvement Activities: In Five Languages • Spelling Lessons & Activities • go.hrw.com (keyword: HLLA) • WordSharp: An Interactive Vocabulary Tutor
• Teacher's Edition, pp. 292, 302, 304 • Developmental Language & Sentence Skills, pp. 93–106	• Teacher's Edition, (ELL) pp. 287, 289, 294, 301, 305, 306; (SE) pp. 288, 304 • Universal Access: Differentiating Instruction • Universal Access: Supporting Instruction in Five Languages	• Formal Assessment • Progress-Monitoring Tests, pp. 25–26, 48 • Test Generator (Teacher One Stop DVD-ROM)	• Reading and Writing Transparencies • Family Involvement Activities: A Guide to Standards Mastery • Family Involvement Activities: In Five Languages • Spelling Lessons & Activities • go.hrw.com (keyword: HLLA) • WordSharp: An Interactive Vocabulary Tutor

(continued on next page)

Correlation Chart **T67**

Warriner's Handbook Chapter	California Written and Oral English-Language Standards	Differentiating Instruction	
		Advanced Learners	On-Level Learners
14 Punctuation: End Marks, Commas, Semicolons, and Colons	1.0 Students write and speak with a command of standard English conventions appropriate to this grade level. 1.3 Use apposition. 1.4 Edit written manuscripts to ensure that correct grammar is used. 1.5 Use correct punctuation.	• Teacher's Edition, p. 318 • Language & Sentence Skills Practice, pp. 299–302	• Teacher's Edition, pp. 310–339 • Language & Sentence Skills Practice, pp. 279–302
15 Punctuation: Underlining (Italics), Quotation Marks, Apostrophes, Hyphens, Parentheses, Brackets, Dashes	1.0 Students write and speak with a command of standard English conventions appropriate to this grade level. 1.4 Edit written manuscripts to ensure that correct grammar is used. 1.5 Use correct punctuation and capitalization.	• Teacher's Edition, p. 342 • Language & Sentence Skills Practice, pp. 324–327	• Teacher's Edition, pp. 340–367 • Language & Sentence Skills Practice, pp. 303–327
16 Spelling	1.0 Students write and speak with a command of standard English conventions appropriate to this grade level. 1.4 Edit written manuscripts to ensure that correct grammar is used. 1.6 Use correct spelling conventions.	• Teacher's Edition, pp. 381, 382, 383 • Language & Sentence Skills Practice, pp. 354–357	• Teacher's Edition, pp. 368–397 • Language & Sentence Skills Practice, pp. 328–357

Differentiating Instruction		Assessment	Additional Resources
Learners Having Difficulty	**English-Language Learners & Special Education Students**		
• Teacher's Edition, pp. 313, 316, 317, 320, 321, 323 • Developmental Language & Sentence Skills, pp. 107–112	• Teacher's Edition, (ELL) pp. 315, 319; (SE) p. 325 • Universal Access: Differentiating Instruction • Universal Access: Supporting Instruction in Five Languages	• Formal Assessment • Progress-Monitoring Tests, pp. 27–28, 48 • Test Generator (Teacher One Stop DVD-ROM)	• Reading and Writing Transparencies • Family Involvement Activities: A Guide to Standards Mastery • Family Involvement Activities: In Five Languages • Spelling Lessons & Activities • go.hrw.com (keyword: HLLA) • WordSharp: An Interactive Vocabulary Tutor
• Teacher's Edition, p. 346 • Developmental Language & Sentence Skills, pp. 113–122	• Teacher's Edition, (ELL) pp. 345, 346, 351, 352, 355, 358 • Universal Access: Differentiating Instruction • Universal Access: Supporting Instruction in Five Languages	• Formal Assessment • Progress-Monitoring Tests, pp. 29–30, 48 • Test Generator (Teacher One Stop DVD-ROM)	• Reading and Writing Transparencies • Spelling Lessons & Activities • go.hrw.com (keyword: HLLA) • WordSharp: An Interactive Vocabulary Tutor
• Teacher's Edition, pp. 371, 372, 373, 374, 377, 381, 384 • Developmental Language & Sentence Skills, pp. 123–134	• Teacher's Edition, (ELL) pp. 373, 375, 376, 381; (SE) p. 383 • Universal Access: Differentiating Instruction • Universal Access: Supporting Instruction in Five Languages	• Formal Assessment • Progress-Monitoring Tests, pp. 31–32, 48 • Test Generator (Teacher One Stop DVD-ROM)	• Reading and Writing Transparencies • Family Involvement Activities: A Guide to Standards Mastery • Family Involvement Activities: In Five Languages • Spelling Lessons & Activities • go.hrw.com (keyword: HLLA) • WordSharp: An Interactive Vocabulary Tutor

(continued on next page)

Warriner's Handbook Chapter	California Written and Oral English-Language Standards	Differentiating Instruction	
		Advanced Learners	On-Level Learners
17 Correcting Common Errors	**1.0** Students write and speak with a command of standard English conventions appropriate to this grade level.	• Teacher's Edition • Language & Sentence Skills Practice, pp. 392–396	• Teacher's Edition, pp. 398–433 • Language & Sentence Skills Practice, pp. 358–396
18 Writing Effective Sentences	**1.0** Students write and speak with a command of standard English conventions appropriate to this grade level. **1.1** Use correct and varied sentence types and sentence openings to present a lively and effective personal style. **1.2** Identify and use parallelism, including similar grammatical forms, in all written discourse to present items in a series and items juxtaposed for emphasis. **1.3** Use subordination, coordination, apposition, and other devices to indicate clearly the relationship between ideas.	• Teacher's Edition, p. 445	• Teacher's Edition, pp. 436–471 • Language & Sentence Skills Practice, pp. 397–428
19 Sentence Diagramming	**1.0** Students write and speak with a command of standard English conventions appropriate to this grade level.	• Teacher's Edition, pp. 472–491	• Teacher's Edition, pp. 472–491

Differentiating Instruction		Assessment	Additional Resources
Learners Having Difficulty	**English-Language Learners & Special Education Students**		
• Developmental Language & Sentence Skills, pp. 135–136	• Universal Access: Differentiating Instruction • Universal Access: Supporting Instruction in Five Languages	• Formal Assessment • Progress-Monitoring Tests, pp. 33–34, 48 • Test Generator (Teacher One Stop DVD-ROM)	• Reading and Writing Transparencies • Spelling Lessons & Activities • go.hrw.com (keyword: HLLA) • WordSharp: An Interactive Vocabulary Tutor
• Teacher's Edition, p. 445 • Developmental Language & Sentence Skills, pp. 137–154	• Teacher's Edition, (ELL) pp. 449, 451, 452, 465 • Universal Access: Differentiating Instruction • Universal Access: Supporting Instruction in Five Languages	• Formal Assessment • Progress-Monitoring Tests, pp. 35–39, 48 • Test Generator (Teacher One Stop DVD-ROM)	• Reading and Writing Transparencies • Family Involvement Activities: A Guide to Standards Mastery • Family Involvement Activities: In Five Languages • Spelling Lessons & Activities • go.hrw.com (keyword: HLLA) • WordSharp: An Interactive Vocabulary Tutor
• Teacher's Edition, pp. 472–491	• Teacher's Edition, (ELL) pp. 472–491 • Universal Access: Differentiating Instruction • Universal Access: Supporting Instruction in Five Languages	• Test Generator (Teacher One Stop DVD-ROM)	• Reading and Writing Transparencies • go.hrw.com (keyword: HLLA)

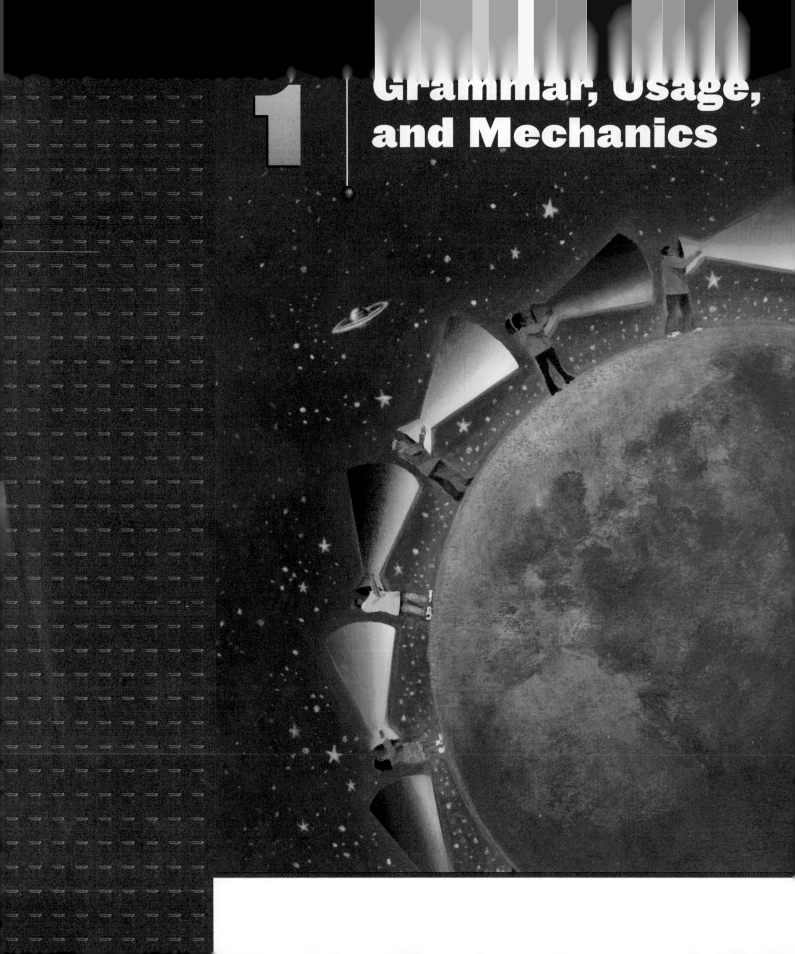

1 Grammar, Usage, and Mechanics

Grammar

Usage

Mechanics

GO TO: go.hrw.com
KEYWORD: HLLA

STANDARDS FOCUS

Grade-Level Standards

(Boldface indicates concepts that are taught and tested in this chapter.)

- Language Convention 1.0: **Students write and speak with a command of standard English conventions appropriate to this grade level.**

- Sentence Structure 1.1: **Use correct and varied sentence types** and sentence openings to present a lively and effective personal style.

- Sentence Structure 1.3: **Use** subordination, **coordination,** apposition, and other devices **to indicate clearly the relationship between ideas.**

- Grammar 1.4: **Edit written manuscripts to ensure that correct grammar is used.**

Prerequisite/Review Standard

- Grammar 1.3: Identify all parts of speech and types and structure of sentences.

Standard Coming Up in the Next Grade Level

- Grammar and Mechanics of Writing 1.2: Understand sentence construction (e.g., parallel structure, subordination, proper placement of modifiers) and proper English usage (e.g., consistency of verb tenses).

▼

INTRODUCING THE CHAPTER

- This chapter explains the difference between complete sen-

(continued)

1.0 Written and Oral English Language Conventions

Students write and speak with a command of standard English conventions appropriate to this grade level.

1.1 Use correct and varied sentence types.

1.3 Use coordination to indicate clearly the relationship between ideas.

1.4 Edit written manuscripts to ensure that correct grammar is used.

Numerals in brackets refer to rules tested by the items in the Diagnostic Preview.

1. sent. [1a]
2. frag.—are popular [1a]
3. frag.—I just bought [1a]
4. frag.—These stamps are interesting [1a]
5. sent. [1a]

The Parts of a Sentence

Subject and Predicate, Kinds of Sentences

Diagnostic Preview

A. Identifying Sentences and Sentence Fragments

Identify each group of words as a *sentence* or a *sentence fragment.* If the word group is a sentence fragment, correct it by adding the words necessary to make a complete sentence.

EXAMPLES
1. Do you like the U.S. Postal Service's special postage stamps?
1. *sentence*

2. When my parents buy stamps.
2. *sentence fragment—When my parents buy stamps, they ask for new commemorative ones.*

1. Commemorative stamps are issued to give recognition to someone or something special.
2. Stamps with pictures of animals or famous people
3. A block of four different, colorful stamps that commemorate Earth Day.
4. Because all four of the winning designs for the Earth Day 1995 stamps were created by young people.
5. I like "Love" stamps and holiday stamps.

CHAPTER RESOURCES

Internet
- go.hrw.com (keyword: HLLA)

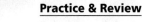

go. hrw .com

Planning
- *Teacher One Stop DVD-ROM* 💿
- *On Course: Mapping Instruction*

Practice & Review
- *Language & Sentence Skills Practice,* pp. 2–17; 18–21
- *Developmental Language & Sentence Skills,* pp. 1–8

Application & Enrichment
- *Language & Sentence Skills Practice,* pp. 24; 1, 22–23

B. Identifying Subjects and Predicates

Classify each italicized group of words as the *complete subject* or the *complete predicate* of the sentence. Then, identify the *simple subject* or the *verb* in each italicized word group.

EXAMPLES
1. *Anyone searching for the highest mountains* must look on land and in the sea.
   1. complete subject; simple subject—Anyone

2. Not all mountains *are easy to see*.
   2. complete predicate; verb—are

6. *Much of the earth's surface* is mountainous.
7. *Can* you *name the world's highest mountain*?
8. *Mount Everest in the Himalayas* claims that title.
9. In fact, *seven of the world's highest mountains* are in the Himalayan mountain range.
10. Mount Everest *towers to a height of 29,028 feet above sea level*.
11. *The Alps in Europe, the Rockies in North America, and the Andes in South America* are other high mountain ranges.
12. High mountains *also have been discovered under the ocean*.
13. Down the middle of the Atlantic Ocean floor runs *the earth's longest continuous mountain range*.
14. The peaks of some undersea mountains *rise above the surface of the water and form islands*.
15. *The islands of Hawaii* are actually the peaks of submerged mountains in the Pacific Ocean.

6. comp. sub. [1b,c]
7. comp. pred. [1d,e]
8. comp. sub. [1b,c]
9. comp. sub. [1b,c]
10. comp. pred. [1d,e]
11. comp. sub. [1b,c]
12. comp. pred. [1d,e]
13. comp. sub. [1b,c]
14. comp. pred. [1d,e]
15. comp. sub. [1b,c]

C. Classifying Sentences

Classify each of the following sentences as *declarative*, *interrogative*, *imperative*, or *exclamatory*. Then, write the last word of each sentence and provide appropriate end punctuation.

EXAMPLE
1. Write your name and the date on your paper
   1. imperative—paper.

16. Juana plans to study architecture after she graduates.
17. Isn't this the right answer to the question?
18. How confused we are!
19. Bring me the map of Paraguay, please.
20. I can't right now, Andy, because I am carrying two boxes.

16. dec. [1h]
17. int. [1j]
18. exc. [1k]
19. imp. [1i]
20. dec. [1h]

GRAMMAR

tences and sentence fragments and then covers subjects and predicates—complete and simple—and compound subjects and verbs. The last part of the chapter deals with classifying sentences by purpose.

■ The chapter closes with a **Chapter Review** including a **Writing Application** feature that asks students to write a paragraph using complete sentences.

■ For help in integrating this chapter with writing assignments in *Holt Literature and Language Arts,* use the **Teaching Strands** chart on pp. T24–T25.

ASSESSING

Entry-Level Assessment
Diagnostic Preview. Use the **Diagnostic Preview** to gauge students' familiarity with sentence completeness, subjects and predicates, and classifying sentences by purpose. In addition, you may wish to evaluate sentences in students' writing samples to determine areas where students need practice.

PRETEACHING

Lesson Starter
Background Information. An unabridged dictionary gives the etymology of the word *predicate* as "from Latin, meaning *to proclaim*." Ask students to describe how the predicate in the sentence "Marco's brother delivers pizzas" proclaims the sentence's meaning. [*Without the complete predicate,* delivers pizzas, *there would be no statement.*]

Differentiating Instruction
■ UA: Differentiating Instruction
■ UA: Supporting Instruction in Five Languages
Assessment
■ Formal Assessment
■ Progress-Monitoring Tests, pp. 1–2, 48

■ Test Generator (Teacher One Stop DVD-ROM) 🎧
Other Language Resources
■ Spelling Lessons & Activities
■ WordSharp: An Interactive Vocabulary Tutor
■ Reading and Writing Transparencies

The Sentence

Rule 1a *(pp. 4–7)*

OBJECTIVES

- To identify sentences and sentence fragments
- To identify sentences and revise sentence fragments to form complete and interesting sentences

APPLICATION

Revising Sentence Fragments

Ask pairs of students to find a song that contains sentence fragments in the lyrics. Remind students that lyrics must be suitable for classroom discussion. Then, have students rewrite the fragments to form complete sentences. You might ask volunteers to sing their revised songs for the class, rearranging the melodies in order to make them fit the new lyrics. Then, ask students about their opinions of the resulting songs. For example, why do you think the lyricist used fragments instead of complete sentences?

Reference Note

For more about the **understood subject,** see page 19.

Reference Note

For more information about **correcting sentence fragments,** see page 438.

COMPUTER TIP

Some style-checking software programs can identify sentence fragments. Such programs are useful, but they are not perfect. The best way to eliminate fragments from your writing is still to check each sentence yourself. Make sure that each of your sentences has a subject and a verb and that it expresses a complete thought.

The Sentence

In casual conversation, people often leave out parts of sentences. In your writing at school, however, it is almost always best to use complete sentences. They help make your meaning clear to the reader.

1a. A *sentence* is a word group that contains a subject and a verb and that expresses a complete thought.

A sentence begins with a capital letter and ends with a period, a question mark, or an exclamation point.

EXAMPLES   **S**ean was chosen captain of his soccer team**.**

Have you ever seen a Broadway musical**?**

What a thrilling adventure we had**!**

Stop**!** [The understood subject is *you*.]

A ***sentence fragment*** is a word group that looks like a sentence but does not contain both a subject and a verb or does not express a complete thought.

SENTENCE FRAGMENT	Was a well-known ragtime pianist. [This group of words has a verb (*Was*), but the subject is missing. *Who* was a well-known ragtime pianist?]
SENTENCE	**Scott Joplin** was a well-known ragtime pianist.
SENTENCE FRAGMENT	A butterfly with bright blue wings and long antennae. [This group of words has a subject (*butterfly*), but the verb is missing. *What* did the butterfly do?]
SENTENCE	A butterfly with bright blue wings and long antennae **landed.**
SENTENCE FRAGMENT	Even though she had worked a long time. [This group of words has a subject (*she*) and a verb (*had worked*), but it does not express a complete thought. *What happened* even though she had worked a long time?]
SENTENCE	**Louise Nevelson had not completed the sculpture** even though she had worked on it a long time.

4   Chapter 1   The Parts of a Sentence

RESOURCES

The Sentence

Practice

- *Language & Sentence Skills Practice*, pp. 2–4, 18
- *Developmental Language & Sentence Skills*, pp. 1–2

Exercise 1 **Identifying Sentences and Sentence Fragments**

Tell whether each of the following groups of words is a *sentence* or a *sentence fragment*.

EXAMPLES
1. Can you name the famous American woman in the picture below?
   1. *sentence*

2. A woman who made history.
   2. *sentence fragment*

1. One of the best-known women in American history is Sacagawea. **1.** sent.
2. A member of the Lemhi band of the Shoshone. **2.** frag.
3. She is famous for her role as interpreter for the Lewis and Clark expedition. **3.** sent.
4. Which was seeking the Northwest Passage. **4.** frag.
5. In 1800, the Lemhis had encountered a war party of the Hidatsa. **5.** sent.
6. Who captured some of the Lemhis, including Sacagawea. **6.** frag.
7. Later, with Charbonneau, her French Canadian husband, and their two-month-old son. **7.** frag.
8. Sacagawea joined the Lewis and Clark expedition in what is now North Dakota. **8.** sent.
9. Her knowledge of many languages enabled the explorers to communicate with various peoples. **9.** sent.
10. Sacagawea also searched for plants that were safe to eat. **10.** sent.
11. And once saved valuable instruments during a storm. **11.** frag.
12. As they traveled farther. **12.** frag.
13. The explorers came across the Lemhis. **13.** sent.
14. From whom Sacagawea had been separated years before. **14.** frag.

The Granger Collection, New York.

The Sentence **5**

PRACTICE

Guided and Independent
You may wish to use items 1–10 in **Exercise 1** as guided practice. Then, have students complete items 11–20 as independent practice.

HOMEWORK

DIRECT TEACHING

Modeling and Demonstration
Identifying Sentences. Model how to identify a complete sentence by using the example: *Can you name the famous American woman in the picture below?* Remind students that a sentence must contain both a subject and a verb and express a complete thought. Then, have students identify the subject. [*you*] Next, have them identify the verb. [*Can name*] Ask whether the sentence expresses a complete thought. [*yes*] Point out that the example meets the three requirements of a complete sentence. Now, have a volunteer use another example from this chapter to demonstrate how to identify a complete sentence.

DIRECT TEACHING

Correcting Misconceptions
Imperatives. Because imperative sentences do not have stated subjects, students may misidentify imperatives as sentence fragments. On the chalkboard, write an imperative sentence, such as "Please step forward." Then, ask students who is expected to perform the action of the verb *step*. [*you*] Have them explain how to tell whether a sentence is imperative. Then, remind students that even though its subject is understood rather than stated, an imperative sentence is considered a complete sentence.

15. The Lemhis helped the explorers. **15.** sent.
16. By giving them guidance. **16.** frag.
17. After they returned from the expedition. **17.** frag.
18. Clark encouraged Sacagawea and Charbonneau to settle in St. Louis. **18.** sent.
19. However, the couple moved back to Sacagawea's native land. **19.** sent.
20. Where this famous woman died in 1812. **20.** frag.

Oral Practice **Identifying Sentences and Revising Sentence Fragments**

POSSIBLE ANSWERS
Revisions will vary but should all be complete sentences.
1. Sentence fragment—After he caught the baseball with both hands, he hurled it to second base.
2. Sentence fragment—Do you enjoy doing the multiplication tables?
3. Sentence fragment—Inside the castle we found a long, narrow passage with a hidden door at each end.
4. Sentence fragment—After waiting for six hours, I finally gave up and went home.
5. Sentence
6. Sentence
7. Sentence fragment—Instead of calling the doctor this morning about her sore throat, Mom got up and went to work.
8. Sentence
9. Sentence fragment—The bats were roosting on beams beneath the tall ceiling of the church.
10. Sentence

Oral Practice **Identifying Sentences and Revising Sentence Fragments**

Read each of the following word groups aloud, and tell whether the word group is a sentence or a sentence fragment. If the word group is a sentence fragment, add words to make it a complete sentence.

EXAMPLES
1. Classes in mountain climbing will begin soon.
1. sentence

2. Living alone in the mountains.
2. sentence fragment—Living alone in the mountains, the couple make their own furniture and clothes.

1. After he caught the baseball with both hands.
2. Doing the multiplication tables?
3. A long, narrow passage with a hidden door at each end.
4. After waiting for six hours.
5. The gymnasium is open.
6. Last night there were about six television commercials every half-hour.
7. Instead of calling the doctor this morning about her sore throat.
8. Are you careful about turning off unnecessary lights?
9. Beneath the tall ceiling of the church.
10. In the back of the storeroom stands a stack of boxes.

Exercise 2 **Writing Interesting Sentences**

Revise each sentence fragment by adding words to make an interesting sentence. Answers will vary.

EXAMPLE
1. At the last minute.
1. At the last minute, his parachute opened.

1. On the last day of summer , we went swimming
2. Found only in the country. This type of flower is
3. A graceful ballerina danced across the stage
4. Burning out of control! The fire is
5. The old building by the lake? Who bought
6. The duck-billed platypus looks funny
7. Three days after Thanksgiving , we still had leftover turkey
8. Until I finish my work. I can't read my book
9. Singing loudly in the woods. The birds were
10. In the final quarter of the game. Jeremy played his best

The Subject and the Predicate

Sentences consist of two basic parts: *subjects* and *predicates*.

The Subject

1b. A *subject* tells *whom* or *what* the sentence is about.

EXAMPLES   **Aunt Louise** found a beautiful antique lamp at the garage sale.

The kitten with the white paws is called Boots.

Where are **your mittens**, Kris?

How surprised **we** were!

To find the subject, ask *who* or *what* is doing something or *about whom* or *what* something is being said.

EXAMPLES   Laughing and running down the street were **two small boys.** [Who were laughing and running down the street? Two small boys were.]

A sealed envelope rested near the edge of the desk. [What rested near the edge of the desk? A sealed envelope rested there.]

Are **Dalmatians** very good watchdogs? [About what is something being said? Something is being said about Dalmatians.]

Can **horses and cattle** swim? [What can swim? Horses and cattle can swim.]

MEETING THE CHALLENGE

To find the subject in a question, turn the question into a statement. Then, ask *who* or *what* is doing something or *about whom* or *what* something is being said.

Turn each of the following questions into a statement. Then, identify the subject of each statement.

1. Did they win the race?

2. Would you like to ride with us?

3. Will she and her cousin get back in time?

ANSWERS
1. They did win the race.—They
2. You would like to ride with us.—You
3. She and her cousin will get back in time.—She and her cousin

The Subject and the Predicate
Rules 1b–e (pp. 7–14)

OBJECTIVES

- **To identify complete subjects and simple subjects in sentences**
- **To identify complete predicates and simple predicates (verbs) in sentences**
- **To write sentences by adding complete subjects or complete predicates**

The Subject and the Predicate   **7**

DIFFERENTIATING INSTRUCTION

English-Language Learners

General Strategies. Because word order in some languages is more flexible than it is in English, you may want to work through several examples of common subject placement in English sentences.

Advanced Learners

Challenge students to find examples of sentences in which the subject-verb order is inverted. Suggest that students explore various media—newspapers, magazines, novels, and books of poetry. Remind students that reversing the order of the subject and the verb is a good way to add variety to their sentences. Have students create a bulletin board display with their examples, which they may want to group under headings such as "Beginning with *Here* or *There*," "Questions," and so forth.

RETEACHING

Subjects and Predicates

You may want to introduce diagramming to help students see the relationship between subjects and predicates in sentences. Refer students to **Chapter 19: Sentence Diagramming,** p. 472.

Reference Note

For more information about **compound nouns,** see page 26.

Reference Note

For more information about **prepositional phrases,** see page 96.

TIPS & TRICKS

Sometimes crossing out the prepositional phrases in a sentence can help you find the subject.

EXAMPLE
The girl ~~in the red boots~~ is Marlene.

The **complete subject** consists of all the words that tell *whom* or *what* the sentence is about. The simple subject is part of the complete subject.

1c. The **simple subject** is the main word or word group that tells *whom* or *what* the sentence is about.

EXAMPLES   The dangerous **trip** over the mountains took four days. [The complete subject is *The dangerous trip over the mountains.*]

Someone in this room is about to get a big surprise! [The complete subject is *Someone in this room.*]

In the last forty years, **he** has missed seeing only one home game. [The complete subject is *he.*]

Pacing back and forth in the cage was a hungry **tiger.** [The complete subject is *a hungry tiger.*]

Joey arrived late for the dance. [The complete subject is *Joey.*]

As you can see in the following examples, the simple subject may consist of more than one word.

EXAMPLES   **Stamp collecting** is my father's favorite hobby.

Containing over eighty million items, the **Library of Congress** is the nation's largest single library.

Madeleine Johnson was appointed secretary.

Accepting the award was **Leo Kolar.**

The simple subjects in the four preceding examples are all compound nouns.

The subject of a sentence is never in a prepositional phrase.

EXAMPLES   **Several** of the players hit home runs. [Who hit home runs? *Several* hit home runs. *Players* is part of the prepositional phrase *of the players.*]

At the end of our street is a **bus stop.** [What is? *Bus stop* is. *End* and *street* are parts of the prepositional phrases *At the end* and *of our street.*]

NOTE   In this book, the term *subject* generally refers to the simple subject unless otherwise noted.

MINI-LESSON   Grammar

Compound Nouns as Simple Subjects.
Tell students that simple subjects may have more than one word. Write the following words on the chalkboard.

give-and-take   sister-in-law
water-skiing   roller coaster
high school   first aid

Have each student write a sentence using one of the words in the list as the simple subject. [Water-skiing requires balance and

Exercise 3 Identifying Complete Subjects and Simple Subjects

Identify the *complete subject* and the *simple subject* in each of the following sentences.

EXAMPLE   **1.** My favorite teams compete in the Caribbean Baseball Leagues.

         1.   *complete subject—My favorite teams; simple subject—teams*

1. People throughout Latin America enjoy going out to a ballgame.
2. The all-American sport of baseball has been very popular there for a long time.
3. In fact, fans in countries such as Cuba, Panama, and Venezuela go wild over the game.
4. As a result, the Caribbean Baseball Leagues were formed more than fifty years ago.
5. Each year the teams in Latin America play toward a season championship.
6. That championship is known as the Caribbean World Series.
7. A total of more than one hundred players compete in the series.
8. Many talented Latin American players are recruited by professional United States teams each year.
9. The list of these players includes such baseball greats as José Canseco, Ramón Martinez, and Fernando Valenzuela.
10. In addition, a number of U.S. players train in the Latin American winter leagues.

The Predicate

1d. The **predicate** of a sentence tells something about the subject.

The **complete predicate** consists of a verb and all the words that describe the verb and complete its meaning.

EXAMPLES   Marco's brother **delivers pizzas.**

          Under a large bush sat the tiny rabbit.

          Does this copier **staple and fold documents**?

          How talented you **are**!

The Subject and the Predicate   **9**

Reference Note

For more about **verb phrases,** see page 52.

Sometimes the complete predicate appears at the beginning of a sentence. In the following examples, vertical lines separate the complete subjects from the complete predicates.

EXAMPLES   comp. pred. | comp. subj.
On the tiny branch perched | a chickadee.

comp. pred. | comp. subj.
Covering the side of the hill were | wildflowers.

Part of the predicate may appear on one side of the subject and the rest on the other side.

EXAMPLES   pred. | comp. subj. | pred.
Before winter | many birds | **fly south.**

pred. | comp. subj. | pred.
Yesterday | the movie star | **signed autographs.**

1e. The *simple predicate,* or *verb,* is the main word or word group that tells something about the subject.

A simple predicate may be a one-word verb, or it may be a *verb phrase* (a main verb and one or more helping verbs).

EXAMPLES   comp. subj. | comp. pred.
These books | **are** available in the media center.

comp. subj. | comp. pred.
Our English class | **is reading** the novel *Frankenstein.*

comp. subj. | comp. pred.
The musicians | **have been rehearsing** since noon.

NOTE   In this book, the term *verb* generally refers to the simple predicate.

The words *not* (*–n't*) and *never,* which are frequently used with verbs, are not part of a verb phrase. Both of these words are adverbs.

EXAMPLES   She **did** not **believe** me.

They **have**n't **left** yet.

The two cousins **had** never **met.**

I **will** never **eat** there again!

10   Chapter 1   The Parts of a Sentence

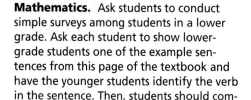

Exercise 4 — Identifying Complete Predicates and Verbs

Identify the underlined complete predicate and the underlined verb in each of the following sentences.

EXAMPLE   **1.** A ton and a half of groceries may seem like a big order for a family of five.

　　　　　1. complete predicate—*may seem like a big order for a family of five; verb—may seem*

HELP

Keep in mind that parts of the complete predicate may come before and after the complete subject.

1. Such a big order is possible in the village of Pang.
2. This small village is near the Arctic Circle.
3. Once a year the people of Pang receive their groceries.
4. A supply ship can visit Pang only during a short time each summer.
5. In spring, families order their year's supply of groceries by mail.
6. A few months later the huge order is delivered to Pang.
7. The people store the groceries in their homes.
8. Frozen food is kept outdoors.
9. Too costly for most residents is the airfreight charge for a grocery shipment to Pang.
10. Villagers also must hunt and fish for much of their food.

Exercise 5 — Identifying Simple Predicates

Identify the underlined simple predicate in each of the following sentences.

EXAMPLE   **1.** Samuel Pepys was an English government worker.

　　　　　1. *was*

HELP

Remember that a simple predicate can be a one-word verb or a verb phrase.

1. Between 1660 and 1669, Samuel Pepys kept a diary.
2. He wrote the diary in a secret shorthand.
3. This secret shorthand was finally decoded after many years of hard work.
4. In 1825, *The Diary of Samuel Pepys* was published.
5. The diary presents a personal look at life in England during the seventeenth century.
6. In many entries Pepys told about his family and friends.
7. Some of these accounts are quite humorous.
8. In other entries Pepys described very serious events.
9. For example, in entries during 1666, Pepys gave a detailed account of the Great Fire of London.
10. What other events might be described in the diary?

EXTENSION

Critical Thinking

Metacognition. After students have completed **Review A**, have them analyze the process they use to identify subjects and verbs. Ask them to work in pairs to answer the following questions.

1. Do you read sentences through before starting to look for the subjects and verbs?

2. Do you go back and look at the rules and examples as you try to find the subjects and verbs?

3. Do you use any special shortcuts to find the subjects and verbs?

4. What is the most difficult part of finding subjects and verbs?

5. How do you check your work to make sure it is correct?

PRACTICE

Guided and Independent

You may wish to use **Review B** as guided practice. Then, have students complete **Review C** as independent practice. **HOMEWORK**

Review A **Identifying Subjects and Verbs**

Identify the <u>subject</u> and the <u>verb</u> in each of the following sentences.

EXAMPLE **1.** In Greek mythology, Medusa was a horrible monster.

1. *subject—Medusa; verb—was*

1. On Medusa's head <u>grew</u> <u>snakes</u> instead of hair.
2. According to Greek myth, a <u>glance</u> at Medusa <u>would turn</u> a mortal into stone.
3. However, one proud <u>mortal</u>, Perseus, <u>went</u> in search of Medusa.

4. Fortunately, <u>he</u> <u>received</u> help from the goddess Athena and the god Hermes.
5. From Athena, <u>Perseus</u> <u>accepted</u> a shiny shield.
6. With Hermes as his guide, <u>Perseus</u> soon <u>found</u> Medusa.
7. <u>He</u> <u>knew</u> about Medusa's power.
8. Therefore, <u>he</u> <u>did</u> not <u>look</u> directly at her.
9. Instead, <u>he</u> <u>watched</u> her reflection in the shiny shield.
10. The <u>picture</u> on the left <u>shows</u> Perseus's victory over the evil Medusa.

Review B **Identifying Complete Subjects and Complete Predicates**

Copy the following sentences. Separate the complete subject from the complete predicate with a vertical line.

EXAMPLE **1.** Legends and folk tales have been repeated and enjoyed throughout the Americas.

1. *Legends and folk tales | have been repeated and enjoyed throughout the Americas.*

1. The Chorotega people|lived in Nicoya, Costa Rica, hundreds of years ago.

2. One Chorotega folk tale|tells the story of the Chorotegan treasure and praises Princess Nosara for protecting it from the Chirenos.
3. Chireno warriors|landed, according to the story, on the Nicoya Peninsula and attacked the Chorotegas.
4. The Chorotegas|were surprised but reacted quickly.
5. Princess Nosara|grabbed the treasure and ran to her friend's house for help.
6. Nosara and he|took a bow and some arrows and fled into the woods.
7. The couple|ran from the enemy all night and at last reached a river.
8. The brave girl|dashed into the mountains alone, hid the treasure, and returned to the river.
9. Chireno warriors|attacked shortly after her return, however, and killed the princess and her friend.
10. The murderous warriors|searched for the treasure but never found it.

Review C **Identifying Complete Subjects and Complete Predicates**

Copy each of the following sentences. Underline the complete subject once and the complete predicate twice.

EXAMPLE   1. The word *acrostic* comes from the Greek word for "line of verse."

            1. The word *acrostic* comes from the Greek word for "line of verse."

1. Are you familiar with acrostics?
2. Counting the letters of your name starts the fun.
3. Ruled paper with enough lines for the letters is needed.
4. One letter of your name goes on each line of the paper.
5. Sometimes the names of people and places are used.
6. The letters are the starting points for lines of poetry or prose.
7. Ink or pencil may be used to do the writing.
8. Complete sentences on each line are not necessary.
9. Have you noticed what the first letters of the eight preceding sentences spell?
10. Acrostics and other writing help you express yourself.

─HELP─

Remember that the subject may come between parts of the predicate.

DIFFERENTIATING INSTRUCTION

English-Language Learners

Vietnamese. For the most part, Vietnamese uses S+V+O word order as English does, so students will expect verbs to follow subjects. However, Vietnamese does not use *it* as the subject in weather, time, and distance expressions such as "It's raining" or "It's 11:00" or in expressions such as "It's easy to . . ." or "It's necessary to. . . ." Remind students that *it* can be used as a subject in English sentences without referring to an antecedent, and have students practice the form by responding to questions or activities requiring *it* to be in the answers.

What time is it?
***It's** 10:00.*

How far is it?
***It's** two miles.*

Tell us the time now.
***It's** 2:30.*

What's the weather today?
***It's** sunny and warm.*

GRAMMAR

Review D — Writing Sentences

POSSIBLE ANSWERS

1. The tent collapsed in the storm, and all of our gear got soaked.
2. The rabbits hop around the yard.
3. Had neighbors gone to their aid?
4. The hours passed slowly as we waited out the storm.
5. The Hawaiian shirt was inappropriate for the occasion.
6. For the party, eight piñatas will be fastened to tree branches.
7. The horses ran all the way back to the barn.
8. Every Sunday, more than a hundred cars compete in the flat-track race.
9. Africa contains nearly every kind of scenery.
10. Is Japan the first stop on your trip to East Asia?

Review E — Writing Sentences

POSSIBLE ANSWERS

1. A <u>two-year-old</u> <u>should</u> not <u>be left</u> alone.
2. The vacant <u>lot</u> down the street <u>serves</u> as our baseball field.
3. The graceful <u>couple</u> <u>danced</u> across the floor.
4. The <u>puppy</u> <u>looked</u> mysteriously at us.
5. Their best <u>player</u> <u>won</u> the trophy.
6. The famous <u>movie star</u> <u>winked</u> at me.
7. <u>Mom</u> <u>is going</u> to the game.
8. <u>One</u> of the Jackson twins <u>visited</u> Charla.
9. My <u>books</u> <u>could have been left</u> on the bus.
10. The neighborhood watch <u>group</u> <u>had</u> a social gathering last Tuesday.

—HELP—

Remember to capitalize the first word of each sentence and to use appropriate end marks. Even though two sentences are given for the example, you need to write only one for each item.

—HELP—

Remember to capitalize the first word of each sentence and to use appropriate end marks.

Review D — Writing Sentences

Add words to each of the following subjects and verbs to make detailed, complete sentences.

EXAMPLE   1. kite flew
  1. *The kite that we made from balsa wood and paper flew very high.*

  or

  A large green-and-purple kite just flew into our backyard.

1. tent collapsed
2. rabbits hop
3. had neighbors gone
4. hours passed
5. shirt was
6. piñatas will be fastened
7. horses ran
8. cars compete
9. Africa contains
10. is Japan

Review E — Writing Sentences

Some of the following word groups are complete subjects, and some are complete predicates. Write each word group, adding the part needed to make a sentence. Then, underline the subject once and the verb twice.

EXAMPLE   1. had been marching for five hours
  1. *The <u>members</u> of the band <u>had been marching</u> for five hours.*

1. should not be left alone
2. the vacant lot down the street
3. danced across the floor
4. looked mysteriously at us
5. their best player
6. the famous movie star
7. is going to the game
8. one of the Jackson twins
9. could have been left on the bus
10. the neighborhood watch group

The Compound Subject

1f. A *compound subject* consists of two or more connected subjects that have the same verb.

The most common connecting words are *and* and *or*.

EXAMPLES **Keshia** and **Todd** worked a jigsaw puzzle.

Either **Carmen** or **Ernesto** will videotape the ceremony tomorrow.

Among the guest speakers were an **astronaut,** an **engineer,** and a **journalist.**

> **Exercise 6** **Identifying Compound Subjects and Their Verbs**

Identify the *compound subject* and the *verb* in each of the following sentences.

EXAMPLE   1. Festivals and celebrations are happy times throughout the world.

      1. compound subject—*Festivals, celebrations;* verb—*are*

1. Children and nature are honored with their own festivals in Japan.
2. Among Japanese nature festivals are the Cherry Blossom Festival and the Chrysanthemum Festival.
3. Fierce dragons and even huge ships fly in the sky during Singapore's Kite Festival.
4. Elaborate masks and costumes are an important part of the Carnival Lamayote in Haiti.
5. Flowers or other small gifts are presented to teachers during Teacher's Day in the Czech Republic.
6. Brave knights and their ladies return each year to the medieval festival at Ribeauvillé, France.
7. During Sweden's Midsommar (midsummer) Festival, maypoles and buildings bloom with fresh flowers.
8. Wrestling and pole climbing attract crowds to the Tatar Festival of the Plow in Russia.
9. Games, dances, and feasts highlight the Green Corn Dance of the Seminole Indians in the Florida Everglades.
10. In Munich, Germany, floats and bandwagons add color to the Oktoberfest Parade.

The Subject and the Predicate   **15**

Modeling and Demonstration

Identifying Compound Verbs.
Model how to identify a compound verb by using the example *Some plants sprout, bloom, and wither quickly.* First, ask students to identify the verb or verbs in the sentence. Remind students that a connecting word like *and, or,* or *but* is used between compound verbs. [*And* connects three verbs: *sprout, bloom, wither.*] Then, ask students whether the verbs all have the same subject. [*yes*] Now, have a volunteer use another example from this chapter to demonstrate how to identify a compound verb.

Relating to Writing

Display various action pictures, such as a carnival or a sporting event, and have each student use compound subjects and compound verbs to write an informative paragraph about one of the pictures. Then, encourage students to share their paragraphs with the rest of the class.

Dialogue

Give students practice using compound subjects and compound verbs by assigning each student to write ten sentences of dialogue between two historical figures. Allow students to brainstorm a list of possible figures and ideas for conversations. You may need to review the punctuation rules for direct quotations in **Chapter 15: Punctuation,** p. 340.

STYLE	TIP

You can use compound subjects and verbs to combine sentences and reduce wordiness in your writing.

WORDY
Anne Brontë wrote under a male pen name. Charlotte Brontë wrote under a male pen name. Emily Brontë wrote under a male pen name.

REVISED
Anne, Charlotte, and Emily Brontë wrote under male pen names.

The Compound Verb

1g. A *compound verb* consists of two or more verbs that have the same subject.

A connecting word—usually *and, or,* or *but*—is used between the verbs.

EXAMPLES The dog **barked** and **growled** at the stranger.

The man **was convicted** but later **was found** innocent of the crime.

Some plants **sprout, bloom,** and **wither** quickly.

You **can leave** now or **wait** for the others.

Notice in the last sentence that the helping verb *can* is not repeated before *wait.* In compound verbs, the helping verb may or may not be repeated before the second verb if the helper is the same for both verbs.

Exercise 7 Identifying Subjects and Compound Verbs

Identify the *subject* and the *compound verb* in each of the following sentences.

EXAMPLE 1. The hikers loaded their backpacks and studied the map of the mountain trails.

1. subject—hikers; compound verb—loaded, studied

1. Linda wrote her essay and practiced the piano last night.
2. Miami is the largest city in southern Florida and has been a popular resort area since the 1920s.
3. According to Greek mythology, Arachne angered Athena and was turned into a spider.
4. Martina Arroyo has sung in major American opera halls and has made appearances abroad.
5. This year the Wildcats won seven games and lost five.
6. During special sales, shoppers arrive early at the mall and search for bargains.
7. Maria Montessori studied medicine in Italy and developed new methods for teaching children.
8. Jim Rice autographed baseballs and made a short speech.
9. General Lee won many battles but lost the war.
10. In the summer many students go to music camps or take music lessons.

FAMILY/COMMUNITY ACTIVITY   *Continued on pp. 17–18*

Letters to the Editor. Effective written communication relies on complete sentences; interesting communication takes advantage of varied sentence construction. To show students a practical example of communicating effectively, bring to class examples of letters to the editor. Try to include a variety of sources: school, neighborhood, city, and national newspapers as well as various magazines.

Have students work in small "discovery" groups to compile a list of guidelines for

Both the subject and the verb of a sentence may be compound. In such a sentence, each subject goes with each verb.

EXAMPLE

       S   **S** **V**   **V**

The **guide** and the **hikers sat** inside and **waited** for the storm to pass. [The guide sat and waited, and the hikers sat and waited.]

NOTE There are times when a sentence may contain more than one subject or verb without containing a compound subject or a compound verb.

      S   **V**   **S** **V**

EXAMPLES **Noah entered** the race, and **he won.** [compound sentence]

        S   **V**   **S** **V**

When **you go** to the store, **you can get** more milk. [complex sentence]

        S   **V**   **S** **V**

The **puppies ran** to the fence, and **they barked** at

                 S **V**

the mail carrier **who was** outside. [compound-complex sentence]

Reference Note

For more about **compound, complex,** and **compound-complex sentences,** see Chapter 7.

Exercise 8 **Identifying Compound Subjects and Compound Verbs**

Identify the <u>subjects</u> and the <u>verbs</u> in each of the following sentences.

EXAMPLE **1.** Aaron Neville and his brothers, pictured here, have often performed at the New Orleans Jazz and Heritage Festival.

     1. subjects—Aaron Neville, brothers; verb—have performed

1. <u>Aaron</u>, <u>Art</u>, <u>Charles</u>, and <u>Cyril</u> <u><u>are</u></u> the Neville Brothers.

2. The four <u>brothers</u> <u>play</u> different instruments and <u>have</u> their own individual styles.

The Subject and the Predicate **17**

---

such letters. As each group shares its guidelines with the rest of the class, make a list on the chalkboard. The list might look something like this:

- has a strong, clear opinion statement
- has relevant supporting information
- is organized logically
- has emotional appeal
- has a strong ending, perhaps with a call to action

    Then, ask students to work individually

TEACHING (TIP)

Exercise 8 You may want to remind students that some verbs are combined with other words to form idiomatic expressions often referred to as phrasal verbs. For example, *grew up* in the sixth sentence is considered a phrasal verb. If students have questions, encourage them to consult a dictionary.

3. They formed their act and performed together in 1977.
4. Before then, the brothers performed and toured separately.
5. New Orleans is their hometown and has greatly influenced their music.
6. They grew up hearing music at home and found it everywhere.
7. New Orleans gospel sounds and jazz rhythms fill many of the brothers' songs.
8. The four brothers have strong opinions and often sing about social issues.
9. *Yellow Moon* and *Brother's Keeper* are two of their most popular albums.
10. The children and grandchildren of the Neville Brothers have now joined in this family's musical tradition.

—HELP—

Some sentences in Review F contain compound subjects, compound verbs, or both.

Review F Identifying Subjects and Verbs

Identify the subjects and verbs in each of the following sentences. If a sentence has an understood subject, write *(you)*.

EXAMPLES
1. Valerie and Tranh have been best friends since third grade.
1. *subjects—Valerie, Tranh; verb—have been*

2. Pass the potatoes, please.
2. *subject—(you); verb—pass*

1. The train to Baltimore must have left the station at exactly 12:03 P.M.
2. To my surprise, out of my backpack spilled the golf balls.
3. Is Emily or her sister taking a computer animation class this summer?
4. On the hiking trail we spotted two brown bear cubs.
5. For Vietnamese noodles, James and I always go to Kim Phung Restaurant.
6. Have you met Marisa and her younger brother?
7. Please gather the birthday cards and hand them to me. 7. (you)
8. In the garage were stacked old boxes, hundreds of magazines, and rusty cans of paint.
9. Rows of wheat and corn sprouted and grew in the rich soil.
10. Last night Hector and the varsity team played well but lost the game anyway.

FAMILY/COMMUNITY ACTIVITY *Continued from p. 17*

to write letters to the editor. Encourage them to focus on issues about which they feel strongly and to target specific publications that would be receptive to their issues.

Remind students to check that sentences are complete, and encourage them to use variety in the position of the subject and verb and to use appropriate compound forms.

Classifying Sentences by Purpose

A sentence may be classified, depending on its purpose, as *declarative, imperative, interrogative,* or *exclamatory.*

1h. A *declarative sentence* makes a statement and ends with a period.

EXAMPLES   Miriam Colón founded the Puerto Rican Traveling Theatre.

Curiosity is the beginning of knowledge.

Lani wondered why the sky looks blue.

1i. An *imperative sentence* gives a command or makes a request. Most imperative sentences end with a period. A strong command ends with an exclamation point.

EXAMPLES   John, please close the door. [request]

Do your homework each night. [mild command]

Stop her! [strong command]

The subject of an imperative sentence is always *you.* Often the *you* is not stated. In such cases, *you* is called the **understood subject.**

EXAMPLES   [You] Do your homework each night.

[You] Stop her!

John, [you] please close the door. [*John* is a noun of direct address identifying the person spoken to in the sentence. The understood subject is still *you.*]

1j. An *interrogative sentence* asks a question and ends with a question mark.

EXAMPLES   What do you know about glaciers?

Was the game exciting?

How do diamonds form?

1k. An *exclamatory sentence* shows excitement or strong feeling and ends with an exclamation point.

EXAMPLES   What a sight the sunset is!

How thoughtful Tim was to rake the leaves!

I'm so happy that Sarah won the VCR!

Reference Note

A sentence may also be classified according to its structure. For information about **classifying sentences by structure,** see Chapter 7.

Reference Note

For information about **punctuating nouns of direct address,** see page 324.

STYLE TIP

Many people overuse exclamation points. In your own writing, save exclamation points for sentences that really do express strong emotion. When overused, this punctuation mark loses its impact.

Classifying Sentences by Purpose   **19**

GRAMMAR

Classifying Sentences by Purpose
Rules 1h–k *(pp. 19–20)*

OBJECTIVE

- To classify sentences according to purpose and to add appropriate end marks

DIRECT TEACHING

Modeling and Demonstration

Imperative Sentences. Model how to identify imperative sentences by using the following examples: *John, please close the door* and *Stop her!* First, point out that an imperative sentence gives a command or makes a request. Then, ask students whether *John, please close the door* is a request or command. [*request*] Explain that most imperative sentences, especially requests, end with a period. Then, ask whether *Stop her!* is a request or a command. [*command*] Point out that strong commands such as this one end with an exclamation point. Then, have a volunteer use another example from this chapter to demonstrate how to identify imperative sentences.

DIFFERENTIATING INSTRUCTION

English-Language Learners

General Strategies. To simplify the writing of different kinds of sentences, give students a base declarative sentence from which to form the other three types of sentences. For example, use the base sentence "The game was fun."
[*interrogative—Was the game fun? exclamatory—What a fun game that was! imperative—Tell me whether the game was fun.*]

DIFFERENTIATING INSTRUCTION

Learners Having Difficulty

Because voice inflection can indicate a sentence's purpose, you may want to read the sentences in **Exercise 9** aloud.

APPLICATION

Classifying Sentences

Have students bring in the comics from the Sunday newspaper, or keep a collection of your own for this and future assignments. Ask each student to search the comic strips and to find and label examples of the four kinds of sentences. You may want to display the examples on a bulletin board.

Review G Writing a Variety of Sentences

POSSIBLE ANSWERS

1. Toni Morrison and Zora Neale Hurston are excellent writers.
2. Open the window and enjoy the fresh air.
3. My grandmother paints beautiful landscapes.
4. Have you or your friends ever seen the intriguing paintings of Frida Kahlo?
5. Does the museum open at noon and offer guided tours?
6. What a fabulous exhibit we saw!
7. Look at the pastels in this watercolor.
8. The storm began as expected and ended quickly.
9. How wildly it rained and thundered!
10. Karla and her brother ran for cover and found shelter in a bus station.

dec. = declarative
int. = interrogative
imp. = imperative
exc. = exclamatory

1. dec.
2. dec.
3. int.
4. exc.
5. dec. [or exc.]
6. dec.
7. exc. [or dec.]
8. int.
9. dec.
10. exc.

Exercise 9 Classifying Sentences

Write the final word of each sentence, and add appropriate punctuation. Then, classify each sentence according to its purpose.

EXAMPLE   1. Do you know what the word *Hopi* means
          1. *means?—interrogative*

1. It means "good, peaceful," I believe.
2. The Hopi live primarily in northeastern Arizona.
3. Have you been to Arizona?
4. Wow, the Grand Canyon is awesome!
5. You must go see it. [or !]
6. Meteor Crater is interesting, too.
7. The fall of that meteor would have been something to see! [or .]
8. Have you seen western movies with red cliffs in them?
9. They may have been filmed near Sedona, Arizona.
10. How exciting it is to visit new places!

Review G Writing a Variety of Sentences

Write your own sentences according to the following guidelines. Use different subjects and verbs for each sentence.

EXAMPLE   1. Write an interrogative sentence with a single subject and a single verb.
          1. *Is Danielle bringing dessert?*

1. Write a declarative sentence with a compound subject.
2. Write an imperative sentence with a compound verb.
3. Write a declarative sentence with a single subject and a single verb.
4. Write an interrogative sentence with a compound subject.
5. Write an interrogative sentence with a compound verb.
6. Write an exclamatory sentence with a single subject and a single verb.
7. Write an imperative sentence with a single verb.
8. Write a declarative sentence with a compound verb.
9. Write an exclamatory sentence with a compound verb.
10. Write a declarative sentence with a compound subject and a compound verb.

1. sent. [1a]
2. frag. [1a]
3. sent. [1a]
4. sent. [1a]
5. sent. [1a]
6. frag. [1a]
7. frag. [1a, j]
8. sent. [1a]
9. frag. [1a]
10. sent. [1a]

Chapter Review

A. Identifying Sentences and Sentence Fragments

Identify each group of words as a *sentence* or a *sentence fragment*. If the word group is a sentence fragment, correct it by adding words to make a complete sentence. Answers will vary.

1. Where can the lion live with the lamb?
2. Just as Miguel entered the Korean restaurant‸   2. , he saw Terry
3. My stepbrother helped me with this.
4. With their songs, whales can communicate throughout the oceans.
5. My sister in college is studying all night.
6. ‸Excited by the news that Grandfather was to come soon.   6. Gina was
7. ‸Where the horses are stabled?   7. Do you know
8. Deep in the forest, a broken-down cabin sheltered us.
9. ‸Jesse Owens, who won four gold medals in the 1936 Olympics.
10. The many-colored lights delighted the viewers.   9. I read about

B. Identifying Subjects and Predicates

Identify each italicized group of words as the *complete subject* or the *complete predicate* of the sentence. Then, identify the <u>simple subject</u> or the <u>verb</u> in each word group.

11. pred. [1d,e]
12. sub. [1b,c]
13. sub. [1b,c]
14. pred. [1d,e]
15. sub. [1b,c]
16. sub. [1b,c]
17. pred. [1d,e]
18. sub. [1b,c]

11. Mr. Adams *gave me his old croquet set.*
12. Why did *that large, new <u>boat</u>* sink on such a clear day?
13. *<u>Trees</u> and <u>bushes</u> all over the neighborhood* had been torn out by the storm.
14. Walking to school, Bill *was <u>splashed</u> by a passing car.*
15. *My old <u>bicycle</u> with the drop-style handlebars* is rusting away in the garage now.
16. *The <u>creek</u> behind my house* rises during the summer rains.
17. Sandy's little sister *bravely <u>dived</u> off the high board at the community pool.*
18. *<u>Fridays</u> and other test <u>days</u>* always seem long to me.

Chapter Review   **21**

ASSESSING

Monitoring Progress
Chapter Review. To assess student progress, you may want to compare the types of items missed on the **Diagnostic Preview** to those missed on the **Chapter Review.** If students have not made significant progress, you could refer them to **Chapter 17: Correcting Common Errors, Exercises 1–5,** for additional practice.

GRAMMAR

RESOURCES

The Parts of a Sentence
Review
- *Language & Sentence Skills Practice,* pp. 18–21

Assessment
- *Formal Assessment*
- *Progress-Monitoring Tests,* pp. 1–2, 48
- *Test Generator (Teacher One Stop DVD-ROM)*

19. pred. [1d,e]
20. pred. [1d,e]

19. My cousins and I *played basketball* and *walked* over to the mall yesterday.

20. *Does* Max *want* another serving of spaghetti?

C. Classifying Sentences

Identify each of the following sentences as *declarative*, *interrogative*, *imperative*, or *exclamatory*. Then, write the last word of each sentence and give the correct end punctuation.

21. dec. [1h]
22. exc. [1k]
23. int. [1j]
24. imp. [1i]
25. dec. [*or* exc.]
    [1h,k]
26. dec. [1h]
27. dec. [1h]
28. int. [1j]
29. dec. [1h]
30. exc. [1k]

21. The sea horse is a very unusual kind of fish.

22. What a beautiful butterfly that is!

23. Can you believe that most polar bears don't hibernate?

24. Daniel, find out how many miles per hour a rabbit can hop.

25. Some jack rabbits can hop forty miles per hour. [*or* !]

26. That is not as fast as a cheetah can run, though.

27. The cheetah is the fastest land animal on earth.

28. How fast can a cheetah run?

29. A cheetah can run at a top speed of fifty to seventy miles per hour.

30. Wow, they could break the speed limit in some places!

D. Identifying Subjects and Verbs

Identify the subject and the verb in each of the following sentences. If a sentence contains a *compound subject* or a *compound verb*, write both words that make up the compound.

31. [1c,e]
32. [1c,e]
33. [1c,g]
34. [1c,e]
35. [1f,e]
36. [1c,e]
37. [1c,e]
38. [1c,e]
39. [1f,e]
40. [1c,e]

31. Charles de Gaulle was a famous French general and statesman.

32. Lille, de Gaulle's birthplace, is a city in northern France.

33. Young de Gaulle served and fought in the French Army before and during World War I.

34. As a soldier, he was loyal and courageous.

35. In World War II, he and the Free French Forces led French resistance against the occupying Germans.

36. After World War II, de Gaulle hoped to retire from public life.

37. However, he returned to politics in 1958.

38. The French people twice elected him president.

39. A political crisis and low public support led to his resignation in 1969.

40. Controversial at home and abroad, de Gaulle died in 1970.

Writing Application
Using Subjects and Predicates in a Paragraph

Writing Complete Sentences   Your best friend is on vacation, and you are pet-sitting. Write a paragraph about your experiences taking care of your friend's pet.

Prewriting   You can write about a pet you know or one that is unfamiliar to you. Jot down notes about the pet you choose. Then, think about what you might do or what might happen while you are taking care of the pet.

Writing   As you write your first draft, think about how to organize your notes and your thoughts. Tell about your experiences in a logical order, and use complete sentences. Your tone can be humorous or serious.

Revising   Read through your paragraph to be sure that each sentence has a subject and a predicate. Does your paragraph tell about your experience in an interesting way? Add, delete, or rearrange details to make your paragraph more entertaining or informative.

Publishing   Read over your paragraph once more, correcting errors in punctuation, spelling, and capitalization. Ask a classmate to read the paragraph, and use the completed paragraph as a basis of a class discussion. With your teacher's permission you may also want to post it on your class bulletin board or Web page, if available.

APPLICATION

Writing Application

Prewriting Tip. You may want to provide pictures of various pets for students who do not have pets. Allow students to use the pictures and their imaginations to complete the writing assignment. You may want to pair students who do not have pets with pet owners for a brainstorming session about pet behavior.

Analysis. As students revise their paragraphs, have them check to see that they have arranged the events in a logical order. The most obvious choice is chronological order, but dramatic effect or humor may be achieved by stating the outcome at the beginning and then filling in the preceding events. Students should be able to explain the logic of their sequence of events.

Scoring Rubric. While you will want to pay particular attention to students' use of complete sentences, you will also want to evaluate students' overall writing performance. You may want to give a split score to indicate development and clarity of the composition as well as grammar skills.

Grade-Level Standards

(Boldface indicates concepts that are taught and tested in this chapter.)

- Language Convention 1.0: **Students write and speak with a command of standard English conventions appropriate to this grade level.**

- Grammar 1.4: **Edit written manuscripts to ensure that correct grammar is used.**

- Punctuation and Capitalization 1.5: **Use correct** punctuation and **capitalization.**

Prerequisite/Review Standards

- Grammar 1.3: Identify all parts of speech and types and structure of sentences.

- Capitalization 1.6: Use correct capitalization.

Standard Coming Up in the Next Grade Level

- Grammar and Mechanics of Writing 1.3: Demonstrate an understanding of proper English usage and control of grammar, paragraph and sentence structure, diction, and syntax.

▼

INTRODUCING THE CHAPTER

- This chapter covers three of the eight parts of speech: nouns, pronouns, and adjectives. You may want students to review adjectives when they study modifiers, **Chapter 11,** and pronouns when they study pronoun-antecedent agreement, **Chapter 8.**

(continued)

1.0 Written and Oral English Language Conventions
Students write and speak with a command of standard English conventions appropriate to this grade level.
1.4 Edit written manuscripts to ensure that correct grammar is used.
1.5 Use correct capitalization.

Numerals in brackets refer to rules tested by the items in the Diagnostic Preview.

1. [2p]
2. [2p]
3. [2h, o, a, b]
4. [2h, l, a, g]
5. [2h, m, l]
6. [2h, j, a]
7. [2h, i, p]
8. [2h, i, a]
9. [2h, o, a]
10. [2a, d]

Parts of Speech Overview
Noun, Pronoun, Adjective

Diagnostic Preview

A. Identifying Nouns, Pronouns, and Adjectives

Tell whether each italicized word or word group in the following sentences is used as a *noun*, a [*pronoun*], or an *adjective*.

EXAMPLE   1. *Each* student is required to take a foreign language.

1. *Each—adjective; language—noun*

1. *That* drummer is the *best* performer.
2. That *German shepherd* puppy is a sweet-natured and *lively* rascal.
3. [*Everybody*]says that *high school* will be more work but more fun, too.
4. [*This*]is the greatest year the junior varsity volleyball *team* has ever had.
5. [*Who*]can tell me whose bicycle [*this*] is?
6. Jenna prepared a special breakfast for her parents and [*herself*] this *morning*.
7. This is their fault because [*they*]ignored all the *danger* signals.
8. [*We*]received word that they aren't in *danger*.
9. [*Each*]of these clubs decorated a float for the Cinco de Mayo *parade*.
10. The runner *Carl Lewis* won several Olympic *medals*.

B. Identifying Nouns, Pronouns, and Adjectives

Tell whether each italicized word or word group in the following paragraph is used as a *noun*, a *pronoun*, or an *adjective*.

EXAMPLES   The [1] *president* travels in a [2] *reserved* jet known as Air Force One.
1. *president—noun*
2. *reserved—adjective*

[11] *American* presidents have used many different types of transportation. President Thomas Jefferson's way of getting to his first inauguration was [12] *simple*. [13] *He* walked there and then walked home after taking the [14] *oath* of office. President Zachary Taylor proudly rode the [15] *same* horse throughout the [16] *Mexican War* and later during his term of office. James Monroe had the [17] *honor* of being the first president to ride aboard a steamship. In 1899, William McKinley became the [18] *first* president to ride in an automobile. President Theodore Roosevelt, [19] *who* is remembered for his love of adventure, rode in a submarine in 1905. Probably [20] *nobody* was surprised when the president himself took over the controls.

11. [2p]
12. [2p]
13. [2h, i]
14. [2a, c]
15. [2p]
16. [2a, b, d]
17. [2a, f]
18. [2p]
19. [2h, n]
20. [2h, o]

The Noun

2a. A ***noun*** is a word or word group that is used to name a person, a place, a thing, or an idea.

Persons	Alice Walker, Dr. Lacy, women, team
Places	forest, town, Canada, Grand Rapids
Things	jewelry, rain, pets, *Skylab*, Eiffel Tower
Ideas	fairness, care, loyalty, idealism, beauty

Exercise 1 Identifying Nouns

Identify all the nouns in each of the following sentences.

EXAMPLE   1. Many American Indian leaders have been known for their courage and wisdom.
1. *leaders, courage, wisdom*

- The chapter closes with a **Chapter Review** including a **Writing Application** that asks students to write a movie review, using at least ten each of nouns, pronouns, and adjectives.
- For help in integrating this chapter with writing assignments in *Holt Literature and Language Arts,* use the **Teaching Strands** chart on pp. T24–T25.

ASSESSING

Entry-Level Assessment
Diagnostic Preview. The **Diagnostic Preview** consists of twenty sentences in which students are asked to identify nouns, pronouns, and adjectives. The results of the preview will help you determine the needs of individual students and the areas that require teaching or review.

The Noun
Rules 2a–g *(pp. 25–31)*

OBJECTIVES

- To identify nouns in sentences
- To identify compound nouns in sentences
- To identify common, proper, concrete, abstract, and collective nouns in sentences

---

Differentiating Instruction
- *UA: Differentiating Instruction*
- *UA: Supporting Instruction in Five Languages*

Assessment
- *Formal Assessment*
- *Progress-Monitoring Tests,* pp. 3–4, 48

- *Test Generator (Teacher One Stop DVD-ROM)* 🎧

Other Language Resources
- *Spelling Lessons & Activities*
- *WordSharp: An Interactive Vocabulary Tutor*
- *Reading and Writing Transparencies*

Lesson Starter

Prior Knowledge. Write the word *modify* on the chalkboard, and ask students to explain its meaning. [*to change or reshape something*] Then, write the word *house* on the chalkboard, and ask students to suggest words to change, or modify, the meaning of *house.* When students have generated a list of words such as *old, brick, clean,* and *white,* point out that they have used adjectives to modify the meaning of *house.* Remind students that adjectives are *modifiers* because they change the meaning of a noun or pronoun.

TEACHING TIP

Exercise 1 In sentences 2 and 8, some students may correctly identify *speaking* and *leading* as nouns. Take the opportunity to explain to students that here, *speaking* and *leading* are verbals—verb forms used as another part of speech. Specifically, the two words are gerunds, verb forms used as nouns. For more on verbals, see **Chapter 5: The Phrase.**

DIRECT TEACHING

Modeling and Demonstration

The Noun. Model how to identify a noun by using the example *loyalty.* Ask whether the word names a person, place, thing, or idea. [*idea*] *Loyalty* names an idea; therefore, *loyalty* is a noun. Now, have a volunteer use another example from this chapter to demonstrate how to identify a noun.

1. Chief Joseph of the Nez Perce was a wise leader.
2. He was an educated man; he wrote that his people believed in justice and honor.
3. In this photograph, Satanta, a Kiowa chief, wears a medal with the profile of President James Buchanan on it.
4. Satanta wore the medal during a famous council for peace at Medicine Lodge Creek in Kansas.
5. In a moving speech, Satanta described the love that his people had for the Great Plains and the buffalo.
6. *The Autobiography of Black Hawk* is an interesting book by the chief who fought for land in the Mississippi Valley.
7. Sitting Bull and his warriors soundly defeated General George Custer and his troops at the Battle of the Little Bighorn.
8. In his later years, Sitting Bull toured with Buffalo Bill and his Wild West Show.
9. Red Cloud of the Oglala Sioux and Dull Knife of the Cheyennes were other powerful leaders.
10. Chief Washakie received praise for his leadership of the Shoshones, and he was also a noted singer and craftsman.

Compound Nouns

2b. A *compound noun* is made up of two or more words used together as a single noun.

The parts of a compound noun may be written as one word, as separate words, or as a hyphenated word.

RESOURCES

The Noun
Practice
- *Language & Sentence Skills Practice,* pp. 26–30
- *Developmental Language & Sentence Skills,* pp. 9–10

One Word	basketball, filmmaker, drugstore, doghouse, grasshopper, grandson, Passover, Greenland, Iceland
Separate Words	fire drill, chain reaction, *The Call of the Wild*, Thomas A. Edison, House of Representatives, North Americans
Hyphenated Word	self-control, cross-references, fund-raiser, eighteen-year-olds, mother-in-law, out-of-doors, president-elect

NOTE When you are not sure how to write a compound noun, look it up in a dictionary.

Exercise 2 **Identifying Compound Nouns**

Identify the compound noun in each of the following sentences.

EXAMPLE 1. Did you know that the most famous alphabet used by people with visual impairments was invented by a fifteen-year-old?

1. *fifteen-year-old*

1. Louis Braille was born in 1809 in France.
2. His father was a saddlemaker who often let Louis play with pieces of leather.
3. In 1812, when the three-year-old tried to punch a hole in a piece of leather, the tool slipped and injured his left eye.
4. Infection from the wound spread to both eyes, and Louis completely lost his eyesight.
5. Louis left for Paris in 1819 to attend the National Institute for the Blind.
6. By 1824, Louis made real his daydream to develop an alphabet for the blind.
7. His first version used both dots and dashes, but that system had drawbacks.
8. As a young teacher at the National Institute for Blind Children, Braille perfected an alphabet of raised dots.
9. Now a machine called a braillewriter is used.
10. Braille died in 1852, and although his alphabet is widely appreciated and used now, it never was during his lifetime.

PRACTICE

Compound Nouns
You may want to give your students more practice in identifying the three forms of compound nouns. Have each student look through a dictionary to find five compound nouns that are written as separate words, five that are hyphenated, and five that are closed compounds. Then, have volunteers read compound nouns from their lists, and have the rest of the class try to write the nouns correctly.

DIFFERENTIATING INSTRUCTION

English-Language Learners

General Strategies. The writing systems of many languages do not use capital letters. Because capital letters are one way to distinguish proper nouns from common nouns, speakers of these languages might have difficulty with this convention. Write nouns one at a time on the chalkboard, and ask English-language learners to identify them as proper or common nouns. Have students give reasons for their choices.

Reference Note

For information on **capitalizing proper nouns,** see page 288.

Common Nouns and Proper Nouns

2c. A *common noun* names any one of a group of persons, places, things, or ideas.

A common noun generally does not begin with a capital letter.

2d. A *proper noun* names a particular person, place, thing, or idea.

A proper noun begins with a capital letter.

Common Nouns	Proper Nouns
poem	"The Raven," *I Am Joaquín*
country	Spain, Ivory Coast
athlete	Lance Armstrong, Venus Williams
ship	*Mayflower*, U.S.S. *Constitution*
newspaper	*The New York Times, USA Today*
river	Rio de la Plata, Ohio River
street	Market Street, University Avenue
day	Friday, Independence Day
city	Los Angeles, New Delhi, Houston
organization	National Forensic League, Girl Scouts of America

Exercise 3 **Identifying Nouns**

Identify the nouns in each of the following sentences, and label them *common* or *proper*.

EXAMPLE   **1.** My family likes to visit California when we are vacationing.

　　　　　1. family—common; California—proper

1. My whole family visited San Francisco during our vacation last year.
2. The city is famous for its hilly landscape.
3. Some of the steepest streets in the world can be found in the downtown area.
4. The city is also well-known for its system of streetcars.
5. San Francisco and Oakland, which is across the bay, have a number of teams that play professional sports.

6. The campuses of many colleges and universities can also be found in the region.
7. Sacramento, which is the capital of California, is closer to San Francisco than Los Angeles is.
8. My family rented a car so that we could drive around and see more of the area.
9. My favorite moment of the trip came when we drove across the Golden Gate Bridge.
10. Below the bridge, I could see boats on the water.

Concrete Nouns and Abstract Nouns

2e. A *concrete noun* names a person, place, or thing that can be perceived by one or more of the senses (sight, hearing, taste, touch, and smell).

2f. An *abstract noun* names an idea, a feeling, a quality, or a characteristic.

Concrete Nouns	hummingbird, telephone, teacher, popcorn, ocean, Golden Gate Bridge, Jesse Jackson
Abstract Nouns	knowledge, patriotism, love, humor, self-confidence, beauty, competition, Zen Buddhism

Collective Nouns

2g. A *collective noun* is a word that names a group.

People	Animals	Things
audience	brood	batch
chorus	flock	bundle
committee	herd	cluster
crew	litter	collection
faculty	pack	fleet
family	pride	set

MEETING THE CHALLENGE

Nouns that stand for specific objects are usually clearly concrete. Nouns that stand for characteristics are usually clearly abstract. However, sometimes it isn't easy to decide whether a noun is concrete or abstract. For instance, consider how you would classify the noun *knitting*. What about *hour*?

Make a list of five nouns that you think are hard to classify. Then, for each one, write down whether you think it is more concrete or more abstract. Write a short explanation saying why you think each noun is hard to classify.

ANSWER
Lists will vary but should include five nouns.

┌ **HELP** ─
Nouns that are not collective have to be made plural to name a group. The singular form of a collective noun names a group.

The Noun **29**

MINI-LESSON **Usage** *Continued on p. 30*

Choosing Verbs to Agree with Collective Nouns. A collective noun that is singular in form names a group of persons, animals, or things. Therefore, when a collective noun is the subject of a sentence, determining whether the verb should be singular or plural can be tricky for many students. Explain that when a collective noun subject refers to the group as a unit, it takes a singular verb. However, if a collective noun subject refers to the individual members or parts

DIFFERENTIATING INSTRUCTION

Advanced Learners

Have pairs of students create proper names that describe professions or jobs. Ask each pair to think of five different jobs and then create names that are puns related to these jobs. Remind students to write the names as proper nouns.

You may want to write the following examples on the chalkboard and read them aloud to help students get started.

1. dentist—Dr. U. R. Gumms
2. florist—Ima Flower
3. lawyer—Sue N. Court
4. actor—B. A. Hamm
5. astronomer—Professor C. D. Star

Once students have compiled their lists, have each pair write their list on the chalkboard.

DIRECT TEACHING

Correcting Misconceptions

Collective Nouns. Some students may incorrectly identify plurals as collective nouns. Although plural words such as *teeth, mice,* and *ships* name groups, they are not collective nouns; the singular forms (*tooth, mouse,* and *ship*) name just one item. Tell students that singular collective nouns, however, name a group. [*a litter of kittens*] Plural collective nouns name more than one grouping. [*three litters of kittens*] Have students practice distinguishing between ordinary plural nouns and collective nouns.

Review A Identifying and Classifying Nouns

ANSWERS

1. day—common, abstract;
   crowds—common, concrete, collective;
   Lincoln Memorial—proper, concrete;
   Washington, D.C.—proper, concrete.

2. memorial—common, concrete;
   setting—common, concrete;
   monuments—common, concrete;
   Capitol—proper, concrete.

3. Lincoln Memorial—proper, concrete;
   Jefferson Memorial—proper, concrete;
   Tidal Basin—proper, concrete.

4. memorial—common, concrete;
   Washington Monument—proper, concrete;
   pools—common, concrete.

5. Lincoln Memorial—proper, concrete;
   architect—common, concrete;
   time—common, abstract;
   Henry Bacon—proper, concrete.

6. memorial—common, concrete;
   temple—common, concrete;
   columns—common, concrete;
   state—common, concrete;
   union—common, concrete [*or* abstract];
   time—common, abstract;
   death—common, abstract;
   Lincoln—proper, concrete.

7. photograph—common, concrete;
   inside—common, concrete;
   Lincoln Memorial—proper, concrete;
   hall—common, concrete.

8. statue—common, concrete;
   Lincoln—proper, concrete;
   sculptor—common, concrete;
   Daniel Chester French—proper, concrete;
   blocks—common, concrete;
   marble—common, concrete.

Review A Identifying and Classifying Nouns

Identify the nouns in each of the following sentences. Classify each noun as *common* or *proper* and as *concrete* or *abstract*. Also tell whether a noun is *collective*.

EXAMPLE   **1.** I went with a group of students to see the monument that commemorates Abraham Lincoln.

     1. *group—common, concrete, collective; students—common, concrete; monument—common, concrete; Abraham Lincoln—proper, concrete*

1. Each day huge crowds visit the Lincoln Memorial, which is in Washington, D.C.
2. The memorial is in a beautiful setting not far from two other presidential monuments and the Capitol.
3. The Lincoln Memorial is separated from the Jefferson Memorial by the Tidal Basin.
4. Between the memorial and the Washington Monument are two long, shallow pools.
5. The Lincoln Memorial was designed by a noted architect of the time, Henry Bacon.
6. The memorial is styled to look like a Greek temple and has thirty-six columns, one for each state in the union at the time of the death of Lincoln.
7. As you can see in the photograph, the inside of the Lincoln Memorial is a large marble hall.
8. The gigantic statue of Lincoln, designed by the sculptor Daniel Chester French, was carved from blocks of white marble.

MINI-LESSON   **Usage**   *Continued from p. 29*

of the group, then it takes a plural verb.
Write the following sentences on the chalkboard, and have students choose the correct verb form.

1. The fifth-grade class (does, do) a science experiment every Thursday. [*does*]

2. The basketball team (washes, wash) their own uniforms. [*wash*]

For more about subject-verb agreement, refer students to **Chapter 8: Agreement,** p. 154.

9. The statue of Lincoln depicts him sitting in a large armchair as if in deep meditation.
10. In the lower lobby of the memorial, a set of murals by Jules Guerin shows allegories of Emancipation and Reunion.

The Pronoun

2h. A *pronoun* is a word used in place of one or more nouns or pronouns.

EXAMPLES   When Kelly saw the signal, Kelly pointed the signal out to Enrique.
When Kelly saw the signal, **she** pointed **it** out to Enrique.

Lee and Pat went fishing. Lee caught three bass, and Pat caught three bass.
Lee and Pat went fishing. **Each** caught three bass.

The word that a pronoun stands for is called its *antecedent.*

 antecedent   pronoun
EXAMPLES   Elena read the **book** and returned **it** to the library.

 antecedent   pronoun
The **models** bought **themselves** new dresses.

 antecedent   pronoun   pronoun
Catherine told **her** father **she** would be late.

Sometimes the antecedent is not stated.

 pronoun
EXAMPLES   **Who** invented the telephone?

 pronoun
No one could solve the riddle.

 pronoun   pronoun   pronoun
I thought **you** said that **everybody** would help.

Exercise 4   **Identifying Pronouns**

Identify the <u>pronoun or pronouns</u> in each of the following sentences. After each pronoun, write the <u>antecedent</u> to which the pronoun refers. If a pronoun does not refer to a specific antecedent, write [*unidentified.*]

Reference Note
For more about **pronouns,** see Chapter 10: Using Pronouns Correctly.

Reference Note
For more about choosing **pronouns that agree with their antecedents,** see page 173.

┌ H E L P ─
In Exercise 4, the antecedent may appear before or after the pronoun, or even in a previous sentence.

The Pronoun   **31**

RESOURCES

The Pronoun

Practice
■ *Language & Sentence Skills Practice,* pp. 31–35
■ *Developmental Language & Sentence Skills,* pp. 11–16

Review A   **Identifying and Classifying Nouns**

ANSWERS continued

9. statue—common, concrete; Lincoln—proper, concrete; armchair—common, concrete; meditation—common, abstract.
10. lobby—common, concrete; memorial—common, concrete; set—common, collective, abstract; murals—common, concrete; Jules Guerin—proper, concrete; allegories—common, abstract [*or* concrete]; Emancipation—proper, abstract; Reunion—proper, abstract.

The Pronoun
Rules 2h–o *(pp. 31–38)*

OBJECTIVES

■ **To identify pronouns and their antecedents in sentences**

■ **To identify and classify forms of pronouns as personal, reflexive, or intensive**

■ **To identify demonstrative, interrogative, and relative pronouns correctly in sentences**

■ **To insert indefinite pronouns into sentences**

RETEACHING

Antecedents
Have students look up the prefix *ante–* in a dictionary. Point out that this prefix comes from Latin and that it means "before." Tell students that in English sentences, antecedents of pronouns usually, but not always, come before the pronouns.

The Pronoun   **31**

1. When the luggage cart fell on its side, the bags and their contents scattered everywhere.

1. *its—cart; their—bags*

1. The passengers scrambled to find their luggage and even got down on hands and knees to pick up their belongings.
2. In no time, the travelers found themselves quibbling.
3. One person shouted, "The brown bag belongs to me!"
4. "It has my name on it," somebody replied.   **4.** It–bag/it–bag
5. "Are you sure the blue socks are yours?" asked another traveler.
6. "I have a pair just like them."   **6.** I–traveler/them–socks
7. A young couple asked, "Who owns a pink and yellow shirt?"
8. "This isn't our shirt."   **8.** this–shirt/our–couple
9. "Those are the birthday presents I bought for a friend of mine!" yelled an angry man in a blue suit.
10. As a crowd of people gathered, some just laughed, but several offered to help.

Personal Pronouns

2i. A ***personal pronoun*** refers to the one speaking (*first person*), the one spoken to (*second person*), or the one spoken about (*third person*).

Personal Pronouns	
First Person	I, me, my, mine, we, us, our, ours
Second Person	you, your, yours
Third Person	he, him, his, she, her, hers, it, its, they, them, their, theirs

EXAMPLES   Last spring, **I** visited **my** relatives. [first person]

Did **you** say that this pen is **yours**? [second person]

The coach gathered the players around **her** and gave **them** a pep talk. [third person]

Reference Note
For more about **possessive forms of pronouns,** see page 225.

NOTE   In this book, the words *my, your, his, her, its,* and *their* are called pronouns. Some authorities prefer to call these words adjectives. Follow your teacher's instructions regarding possessive forms.

DIRECT TEACHING

Modeling and Demonstration

Identifying Antecedents. Model how to identify the antecedent of a pronoun by using the example *When the luggage cart fell on its side, the bags and their contents scattered everywhere.* First, ask students to identify each pronoun. [*its, their*] Then, ask what fell on its side. [*The cart fell on its side.*] *Cart* is the antecedent of *its.* Next, ask which contents scattered everywhere. [*The contents of the bags scattered.*] *Bags* is the antecedent of *their.* Now, have a volunteer use another example from this chapter to demonstrate how to identify the antecedent of a pronoun.

TEACHING TIP

Exercise 4   If you teach students to classify possessive forms as adjectives, exclude the following answers: both instances of *their* in sentence 1 and *our* in sentence 8. (See Note on this page.)

EXTENSION

Relating to Literature

If your literature textbook contains "The Ransom of Red Chief" by O. Henry, have students read the first few paragraphs and identify some of the first-person pronouns. [*I, me, myself, we,* and so on] Then, have students discuss the effects of the author's use of the first person and of the first-person pronouns in particular. [*Since the narrator is one of the main characters, the use of the first person and first-person pronouns contributes to character development and creates a conversational tone.*]

Reflexive and Intensive Pronouns

2j. A *reflexive pronoun* refers to the subject and functions as a complement or an object of a preposition.

2k. An *intensive pronoun* emphasizes a noun or another pronoun.

Notice that reflexive and intensive pronouns have the same form.

Reflexive and Intensive Pronouns	
First Person	myself, ourselves
Second Person	yourself, yourselves
Third Person	himself, herself, itself, themselves

REFLEXIVE   The rescuers did not consider **themselves** heroes. [direct object]

Juan wrote **himself** a note. [indirect object]

She is **herself** again. [predicate nominative]

I don't feel like **myself.** [object of the preposition]

INTENSIVE   Amelia designed the costumes **herself.**

I **myself** sold more than fifty tickets.

Exercise 5   **Identifying Pronouns and Antecedents**

Identify the pronoun or pronouns in each of the following sentences as *personal, reflexive,* or *intensive*. After each pronoun, write the antecedent to which the pronoun refers. If a pronoun does not refer to a specific antecedent, write *unidentified*.

EXAMPLE   **1.** Italian explorer Marco Polo traveled to China, where he and Emperor Kublai Khan became friends.

     1. he—personal—Marco Polo

1. The British explorer Sir Richard Burton himself wrote many books about his adventures in Africa.
2. We watched the movie about Robert O'Hara Burke's trip across Australia in the 1800s.
3. Queen Isabella of Spain herself gave approval for the famous voyages of Christopher Columbus.

Reference Note

For more about **complements,** see Chapter 4. For more about the **objects of prepositions,** see page 66.

TIPS & **TRICKS**

If you are not sure whether a pronoun is reflexive or intensive, try omitting the pronoun. If the basic meaning of the sentence stays the same, the pronoun is intensive. If the meaning changes, the pronoun is reflexive.

EXAMPLES

Rachel painted the fence herself.

Rachel painted the fence. [Without *herself,* the meaning stays the same. The pronoun is intensive.]

They treated themselves to a picnic.

They treated to a picnic. [Without *themselves,* the sentence doesn't make sense. The pronoun is reflexive.]

HELP

In Exercise 5, the antecedent may appear before or after the pronoun, or even in a previous sentence.

DIFFERENTIATING INSTRUCTION

Learners Having Difficulty
Distinguishing between the different kinds of pronouns might be a challenge for some students. You can help solve this problem by creating wall charts that contain visual organizers. Draw a chart on poster board, including the following headings: Personal, Reflexive and Intensive, Demonstrative, Interrogative, Relative, and Indefinite. Then, ask students to decide which pronouns belong in each cell. Keep the chart on display so students can refer to it as they work through the chapter.

Exercise 5   **Identifying Pronouns and Antecedents**

ANSWERS

1. himself—intensive—Sir Richard Burton
   his—personal—Sir Richard Burton
2. We—personal—unidentified
3. herself—intensive—Queen Isabella

Exercise 5 Identifying
Pronouns and Antecedents

ANSWERS continued

4. himself—reflexive—Matthew
   Henson

5. He—personal—Matthew Henson
   his—personal—Matthew Henson

6. I—personal—unidentified
   myself—intensive—I

7. themselves—reflexive—Lewis,
   Clark
   their—personal—Lewis, Clark

8. them—personal—Lewis, Clark

9. you—personal—unidentified
   himself—reflexive—Francisco
   Coronado

10. Our—personal—unidentified
    us—personal—unidentified

TEACHING TIP

Exercise 5 After discussing the
Note on p. 32, you probably established whether you want students to
label possessive forms as pronouns or
as adjectives. If you have instructed
students to label possessives as adjectives, *his* in sentences 1 and 5, *their* in
sentence 7, and *Our* in sentence 10
may be identified as adjectives.

---

4. Matthew Henson prided himself on being part of the first
   expedition to reach the North Pole.
5. He wrote *A Negro Explorer at the North Pole,* a book about his
   expeditions with Commander Robert E. Peary.
6. I myself just read about the Dutch explorer Abel Tasman's
   voyages on the South Seas.
7. Lewis and Clark surely considered themselves lucky to have
   Sacagawea, a Shoshone woman, as their guide.
8. President Thomas Jefferson sent them to explore the land
   west of the Mississippi River.
9. Do you think the Spanish explorer Francisco Coronado really
   pictured himself finding the Seven Cities of Gold?
10. Our teacher told us about Samuel de Champlain's founding
    of the colony of Quebec.

Demonstrative Pronouns

2l. A *demonstrative pronoun* points out a person, a place,
a thing, or an idea.

Demonstrative Pronouns			
this	that	these	those

EXAMPLES   **This** is the most valuable baseball card I have, but
that is also valuable.

These are the names of **those** who volunteered.

NOTE   When the words *this, that, these,* and *those* are used to
modify a noun or a pronoun, they are considered adjectives, not
pronouns.

EXAMPLE   **This** card is my favorite.

Interrogative Pronouns

2m. An *interrogative pronoun* introduces a question.

Interrogative Pronouns				
what	which	who	whom	whose

Reference Note
For more about **demon-
strative adjectives,** see
page 40.

MINI-LESSON **Grammar**

Interrogative Pronouns. *Which, who,
whom,* and *whose* are used as both interrogative and relative pronouns. Remind students that an interrogative pronoun always
introduces a direct or indirect question.

Reinforce recognizing interrogative
pronouns by asking students to classify the
pronouns in the following sentences as
interrogative or relative.

EXAMPLES **What** is the largest planet in our solar system?

Who scored the most points in the game?

NOTE When the words *what, which,* and *whose* are used to modify a noun or a pronoun, they are considered adjectives, not pronouns.

EXAMPLE **Which** player scored the most points?

Relative Pronouns

2n. A *relative pronoun* introduces an adjective clause.

Reference Note

For information on **relative pronouns** and **subordinate clauses,** see Chapter 6.

Common Relative Pronouns				
that	which	who	whom	whose

EXAMPLES The Bactrian camel, **which** has two humps, is native to central Asia.

Ray Charles was a performer **who** had many hit recordings.

Exercise 6 **Identifying Demonstrative, Interrogative, and Relative Pronouns**

Identify the demonstrative, interrogative, and relative pronouns in each of the following sentences.

EXAMPLE **1.** Which of you has heard of *The Mustangs of Las Colinas,* a sculpture that is located in Irving, Texas?

1. *Which—interrogative; that—relative*

1. The nine mustangs that make up the work appear to gallop across Williams Square in the Las Colinas Urban Center.
2. The Mustang Sculpture Exhibit, which is housed in a building near the statue, provides more information.
3. The horses, whose images are cast in bronze, form the world's largest equestrian (horse) sculpture.
4. That is an amazing sight!
5. What is the name of the sculptor who created the mustangs?
6. Robert Glen, who was born in Kenya, is the artist whom you mean.

DIFFERENTIATING INSTRUCTION

Learners Having Difficulty
Some students may have difficulty learning the names of the different kinds of pronouns. One way to assist them is to have them develop and use a set of flashcards.

Assign students to groups of four, and ask each group member to write on an index card a sentence using one of the types of pronouns studied thus far. Have students highlight the pronoun. Then, have them write on the back of the card the name of the type of pronoun. Ask students to check the cards within their group to make sure the cards are correct.

Collect the cards from all the groups, and shuffle them thoroughly. Then, distribute equal numbers of cards to each group, and let group members practice identifying the type of pronoun in each sentence.

Exercise 6

DISTRIBUTED REVIEW
Use **Exercise 6** to review classifying sentences by purpose. Have students identify sentences 3, 4, and 5 by type. [3. *declarative,* 4. *exclamatory,* 5 *interrogative*]

---

1. Who wrote *Romeo and Juliet*? [*interrog.*]
2. Of the scenes in the play, which did Henry like best? [*interrog.*]
3. Our class wondered whom the story affected most. [*relative*]

7. This is a picture of the sculpture, (which) is made up of bronze horses (that) are larger than life-size.
8. Looking at the sculpture, you can imagine the amount of time (that) Glen has spent studying wildlife.
9. Who told me mustangs are descended from horses brought to the Americas by the Spanish?
10. Horses like these roamed wild over Texas and other western states in the 1800s.

Indefinite Pronouns

2o. An *indefinite pronoun* refers to a person, a place, a thing, or an idea that may or may not be specifically named.

Reference Note

For more about the **agreement of indefinite pronouns and their antecedents,** see page 174.

Common Indefinite Pronouns				
all	both	everything	neither	other
another	each	few	nobody	several
any	each other	many	none	some
anybody	either	more	no one	somebody
anyone	everybody	most	nothing	someone
anything	everyone	much	one	something

EXAMPLES   **Everyone** completed the test before the bell rang.

            Neither of the actors knew what costume the **other** was planning to wear.

Many words that can be used as indefinite pronouns can also be used as adjectives.

ADJECTIVE   Look in **both** cabinets. [*Both* is an adjective modifying *cabinets*.]

PRONOUN   **Both** contain winter clothing. [*Both* is an indefinite pronoun.]

ADJECTIVE   **Each** player took **one** cap. [*Each* is an adjective modifying *player*; *one* is an adjective modifying *cap*.]

PRONOUN   **Each** of the players took **one** of the caps. [*Each* and *one* are indefinite pronouns.]

Exercise 7   **Using Indefinite Pronouns**

Write an indefinite pronoun for the blank in each of the following sentences. Use a different pronoun for each blank.
Answers may vary.

EXAMPLE   1. We hope _____ in the Science Club knows about the meeting.

            1. *everyone*

1. _____ of the members are working on their science fair projects.   **1. Many**
2. _____ of these reports on pollution levels in Smith's Pond are by Aba and Benito.   **2. Both**
3. They need _____ of the science students to help collect and test water.   **3. most**
4. Kwan, Lucy, and William have taken _____ of the pictures through a telescope.   **4. some**
5. They have developed and printed _____ of their pictures themselves.   **5. all**
6. Zane has found that bacteria will grow in _____ of the mouthwash.   **6. some**
7. _____ Zane decides to do is unusual.   **7. Everything**
8. Shannon has offered to draw _____ of the illustrations for posters.   **8. several**
9. We hope that _____ misses the fair.   **9. no one**
10. Last year _____ went well.   **10. all**

WE HAD DREAMS OF GREATNESS.

WE WERE GOING TO WIN THE KENTUCKY DERBY.

WE WERE GOING TO TAKE THE TRIPLE CROWN.

WE WERE GOING TO HAVE A FANTASTIC YEAR.

YOU BLEW IT!

WHAT HAPPENED TO 'WE' ALL OF A SUDDEN?

BERRY'S WORLD reprinted by permission of Newspaper Enterprise Association, Inc.

DIFFERENTIATING INSTRUCTION

Advanced Learners
The introduction of indefinite pronouns is a good time to discuss issues of gender agreement. Traditionally, masculine pronouns (*he, him, his*) were always used with singular indefinite pronouns when the gender of the antecedent was unknown. *Everyone turned in* his *test before the bell rang.* Ask the class to discuss why some people might find this practice annoying or even offensive. Ask them to suggest alternatives to using the masculine pronouns [*using* his or her *instead of* his; *revising the sentence so that the antecedent is plural and plural pronouns* (they, them, their) *are used*].

The Pronoun   **37**

TEACHING TIP

Review B   As mentioned in the **Note** on p. 32, possessive forms are sometimes called adjectives. Such possessive pronouns appear three times in **Review B**: *his* in sentence 1, *whose* in sentence 6, and *their* in sentence 9.

EXTENSION

Critical Thinking

Metacognition. Ask students to write brief answers to the following questions after they have completed **Review B**.

1. How did you decide which word was a pronoun?

2. What helped you the most in deciding how to label each pronoun?

The Adjective

Rule 2p *(pp. 38–43)*

OBJECTIVES

- To add specific and vivid adjectives to sentences
- To identify adjectives and proper adjectives and the words they modify

---

Review B   **Identifying Kinds of Pronouns**

Identify each pronoun in the following sentences as *personal*, *reflexive*, *intensive*, *demonstrative*, *interrogative*, *relative*, or *indefinite*.

EXAMPLE   **1.** Can you name some of the many famous Hispanic entertainers who have their stars on Hollywood's Walk of Fame?

   1. you—personal; some—indefinite; who—relative; their—personal

1. Who is the actor that played Zorro?   **1.** int./dem.

2. He is Antonio Banderas, and he received his star on the Walk of Fame in 2005.   **2.** per./per./per.

3. Emilio Estefan won the honor himself in the same year for his years of writing and performing great music.   **3.** ref./per.

4. I think you will agree that to win the honor is exciting.   4. per./per./dem.

5. Everybody has heard of some of the entertainers honored with bronze stars on Hollywood 5. ind./ind. Boulevard.

6. A musician whose name you might recognize appeared on the old *I Love Lucy* TV show, which is still shown.   **6.** rel./per./per./rel.

7. Of course, that was Desi Arnaz, who was a Cuban bandleader.   **7.** dem./rel.

8. Can you name some Hispanic singers who have stars on the Walk of Fame?   **8.** per./rel.

9. All of the following singers have their stars there: Julio Iglesias, Tony Orlando, Ritchie Valens, and José Feliciano.   **9.** ind./per.

10. The actors José Ferrer, Cesar Romero, and Ricardo Montalbán—all of them have stars.   **10.** ind./per.

The Adjective

2p. An *adjective* is a word used to modify a noun or a pronoun.

To *modify* a word means to describe the word or to make its meaning more definite. An adjective modifies a word by telling *what kind, which one, how much,* or *how many.*

RESOURCES

The Adjective

Practice

- *Language & Sentence Skills Practice,* pp. 36–38
- *Developmental Language & Sentence Skills,* pp. 17–18

What Kind?	Which One?	How Much? or How Many?
stone house	**another** one	**seven** rings
rushing river	**next** customer	**more** money
Irish linen	**first** day	**some** water
eager clerk	**those** people	**several** others
tired dog	**that** dress	**many** books
secret message	**these** mangoes	**larger** share

Exercise 8 Using Appropriate Adjectives

For each of the following sentences, replace each italicized question with an appropriate adjective.

EXAMPLE   1. They sold *how many?* tickets for the *which one?* show.
1. They sold *fifty tickets for the first show.*

1. Even though we had already run *how many?* laps around the track, we still had to run *how many?* more.
2. *Which one?* weekend, *how many?* hikers went on a *what kind?* trip to the *what kind?* park.
3. We rode in a *what kind?* van that carried *how many?* people and drove *how many?* miles to the game.
4. There was *how much?* time left when I started to answer the *which one?* question on the test.
5. During the *what kind?* afternoon we washed more than *how many?* cars and earned *how many?* dollars.
6. The recipe calls for *what kind?* flour and *how many?* eggs.
7. The *what kind?* paint livened up the *what kind?* room.
8. There were *how many?* rabbits hopping around in our *what kind?* yard this morning.
9. *How many?* musicians in the band are in *which one?* grade.
10. *Which one?* books on *which one?* table have *what kind?* stories for the *what kind?* children.

Articles

The most frequently used adjectives are *a, an,* and *the.* These adjectives are called **articles.** The adjectives *a* and *an* are called **indefinite articles** because they refer to any member of a general

---

STYLE TIP

You can make your writing more lively and interesting by using specific adjectives. Avoid overused adjectives such as *good, nice,* and *big.* Instead, use specific, vivid adjectives to make your descriptions come alive.

DULL
    The small man was accompanied by two big dogs.

VIVID
    The short, slim man was accompanied by two massive dogs.

COMPUTER TIP

Some word-processing programs have thesauruses. You can use an electronic thesaurus to help you find specific, descriptive adjectives to use in your writing. To make sure an adjective has the connotation you intend, look up the word in a dictionary.

Exercise 8 Using Appropriate Adjectives

ANSWERS
Adjectives will vary. As reinforcement for the kinds of questions that adjectives answer, you may want to have students underline the adjectives they add to the sentences.

DIFFERENTIATING INSTRUCTION

English-Language Learners
General Strategies. In English, adjectives usually precede the noun they modify [*fast car*]. In some languages, such as French, Spanish, and Vietnamese, adjectives usually follow the noun [*car fast*]. If students who speak these languages try to identify adjectives in English by their position, they might think *fast* is the noun and *car* is the adjective. You may wish to stress the adjective-noun order in English by writing adjective-noun pairs on the chalkboard and by having students identify the parts of speech and the order.

Hmong. Because Hmong speakers are accustomed to a complex system of more than one hundred noun classifiers, each of which can be used only with nouns of the same class, shape, group, or form, English-language learners may be uncomfortable with the relative simplicity of English article usage. Remind Hmong students that English relies on its indefinite articles, *a* and *an*, and its definite article, *the,* as its primary noun "classifiers."

The Adjective   **39**

DIFFERENTIATING INSTRUCTION

Learners Having Difficulty

Some students might have problems deciding when to use the article *a* and when to use the article *an*. Remind students that *a* precedes a word beginning with a consonant sound and *an* precedes a word beginning with a vowel sound.

Write the following words on the chalkboard. Have students read the words aloud with you and stress the beginning sounds. Then, ask for volunteers to tell when to use the article *a* and when to use the article *an*.

orange	family
newspaper	airplane
watermelon	egg
umbrella	jar
icicle	heir
one-day sale	unicorn

[*Answers:* orange, umbrella, icicle, airplane, egg, *and* heir *are preceded by* an; *the others by* a.]

DIRECT TEACHING

Modeling and Demonstration

The Adjective. Model how to identify adjectives by using the example *The blouse, once bright, now looks faded.* First, ask students to identify any nouns in the sentence. [*blouse*] Then, ask what word or words describe *blouse* by telling what kind or which one. [*The, bright,* and *faded* identify which blouse.] Point out that *the, bright,* and *faded* are adjectives modifying *blouse.* Now, have a volunteer use another example from this chapter to demonstrate how to identify an adjective.

---

group. *A* is used before a word beginning with a consonant sound. *An* is used before a word beginning with a vowel sound.

EXAMPLES How is **a** gerbil different from **a** hamster?

Uncle Bill wears **a** uniform to work. [The article *a* is used because *uniform* begins with a consonant sound.]

An accident stalled traffic for **an** hour. [The article *an* is used before *hour* because *hour* begins with a vowel sound.]

Reference Note

For more on using **adjectives,** see Chapter 11.

The adjective *the* is called the ***definite article*** because it refers to someone or something in particular.

EXAMPLES **The** astronaut appeared calm aboard **the** shuttle.

The key would not open **the** lock.

Demonstrative Adjectives

This, that, these, and *those* can be used both as adjectives and as pronouns. When they modify nouns or pronouns, they are called ***demonstrative adjectives.*** When they take the place of nouns or pronouns, they are called ***demonstrative pronouns.***

ADJECTIVE Did Jessica win **this** trophy or **that** one?
PRONOUN Did Jessica win **this** or **that**?

ADJECTIVE **These** flags are much more colorful than **those** banners are.
PRONOUN **These** are much more colorful than **those** are.

Reference Note

For more about **demonstrative pronouns,** see page 34.

Adjectives in Sentences

An adjective may come before or after the word it modifies.

EXAMPLES **Each** one of us brought **used** books for the auction.

The blouse, once **bright**, now looks **faded**.

These rare coins are extremely **valuable**.

NOTE An adjective that follows a linking verb and modifies the subject of the sentence is called a ***predicate adjective.***

Reference Note

For more about **predicate adjectives,** see page 87.

Exercise 9 Identifying Adjectives and the Words They Modify

Identify the adjectives and the words they modify in each of the following sentences. Do not include the articles *a, an,* and *the.*

EXAMPLE　1. Many people considered the old man unlucky.
　　　　　1. *Many—people; old—man; unlucky—man*

1. For eighty-four days, Santiago, an elderly Cuban fisherman, had not caught a single fish.
2. Despite his bad luck, he remained hopeful.
3. On the eighty-fifth day, he caught a ten-pound albacore.
4. Soon after this catch, he hooked a huge marlin.
5. For nearly two days, the courageous fisherman struggled with the mighty fish and finally harpooned it.
6. Exhausted but happy, Santiago sailed toward shore.
7. Within an hour, however, his bad luck returned.
8. What happened to the weary fisherman and his big catch?
9. Does the story have a happy ending?
10. You can find the answers in the classic novel *The Old Man and the Sea.*

Oral Practice　Revising Sentences

Read each of the following sentences aloud. Then, re-read each sentence aloud, adding specific, vivid adjectives to modify the nouns.

EXAMPLE　1. The children took a nap.
　　　　　1. *The five grumpy children took a long nap.*

1. Did Carolyn give a cat to her aunt?
2. Cesar donated books and jeans for the sale.
3. We watched the parade pass under our window.
4. The outfielder caught the baseball and made a throw to the catcher.
5. A dancer leaped across the stage.
6. Quickly, the hikers took shelter in the cabin.
7. The actor played the role of a detective.
8. Trapped, neither of the explorers could find a way out of the cave.
9. A lawyer questioned the witness.
10. Later, the knight fought the dragon and saved the village.

Exercise 9　If you have instructed students to label possessive pronouns as adjectives, include *his* as an adjective in sentences 2, 7, and 8.

Oral Practice　Revising Sentences

POSSIBLE ANSWERS
Adjectives will vary. Encourage students to avoid choosing overused adjectives such as *good, nice,* and *big.*

1. Did young Carolyn give a Siamese cat to her favorite aunt?
2. Generous Cesar donated used books and holey jeans for the yard sale.
3. We watched the lengthy parade pass under our third-floor window.
4. The agile outfielder caught the fly baseball and made a quick throw to the alert catcher.
5. A graceful dancer leaped across the wide stage.
6. Quickly, the two hikers took temporary shelter in the log cabin.
7. The first actor played the exciting role of a tough detective.
8. Trapped, neither of the inexperienced explorers could find a reasonable way out of the deep cave.
9. A sharp lawyer questioned the hostile witness.
10. Later, the brave knight fought the green dragon and saved the tiny village.

Reference Note

For more information about **capitalizing proper adjectives,** see page 298.

EXTENSION

Relating to Literature

Explain to students that specific adjectives can be used to describe sensory details—how something looks, smells, sounds, feels, and tastes. To show students the effective use of adjectives, have them read Arthur Gordon's "The Sea Devil" if the selection is available in your literature textbook. First, ask students to identify the adjectives that Gordon uses to describe the sights and sounds of his setting in the first two paragraphs [*tiny, cheerful, neat, orderly, dark, countless, dead, silent, green,* and *breathless*]. Then, have students finish reading the story, picking out effective uses of adjectives as they read and listing specific details about the sea devil's appearance and about its movements.

┌─HELP─

Some sentences in Exercise 10 contain more than one proper adjective.

Proper Adjectives

A *proper adjective* is formed from a proper noun and begins with a capital letter.

Proper Nouns	Proper Adjectives
Canada	**Canadian** citizen
China	**Chinese** calendar
Islam	**Islamic** law
Carter	**Carter** administration
New Jersey	**New Jersey** coast

Some proper nouns do not change spelling when they are used as adjectives.

PROPER NOUN   Seattle
PROPER ADJECTIVE   **Seattle** skyline

Exercise 10 Identifying Proper Adjectives

Identify the proper adjectives and the words they modify in the following sentences.

EXAMPLE   **1.** In recent years many American tourists have visited the Great Wall of China.

      1. American—tourists

1. Early Spanish explorers built forts along the Florida coast.
2. The professor of African literature gave a lecture on the novels of Camara Laye, a writer who was born in Guinea.
3. Which Arthurian legend have you chosen for your report?
4. The program about the Egyptian ruins was narrated by a British scientist and a French anthropologist.
5. Aeolus was the god of the winds in ancient Greek mythology.
6. The society of Victorian England was the subject of many British novels in the late 1800s.
7. During the press conference last night, the president commented on the American economy.
8. A friend who is Japanese gave me a kimono from Tokyo.
9. We saw a display of Appalachian crafts in the public library.
10. Marian McPartland, a jazz pianist from New York City, played several Scott Joplin songs.

Review C Identifying Adjectives

Identify the adjectives in each of the following sentences. Do not include the articles *a*, *an*, and *the*.

EXAMPLE 1. Have you heard of the Heidi Festival, a popular event in the small town of New Glarus, Wisconsin?

  1. *popular, small*

1. For geography class, I wrote a short paper about New Glarus.
2. It was founded by adventurous Swiss settlers in 1845, and people call it Little Switzerland.
3. As you can see in these photographs, colorful reminders of that Swiss heritage are everywhere.
4. The special emblems of the cantons, or states, of Switzerland are on street signs and buildings.
5. Many of the women make beautiful lace, and there is even an embroidery factory.
6. Dairying is big business, too, and the townsfolk make delicious cheeses.
7. In a historical village, visitors can see reconstructed buildings, such as a schoolhouse, a blacksmith shop, a church, and the cheese factory in this photograph.
8. In this village, pioneer tools and belongings are on display.
9. New Glarus also has a museum in a mountain lodge, or *chalet*.
10. Someday, I hope to see a summer festival, such as the Heidi Festival.

—HELP—

If an adjective is capitalized as part of a name, as in *New York* and *White House*, consider it part of the proper noun and not a separate adjective.

Determining Parts of Speech

The way that a word is used in a sentence determines what part of speech the word is. Some words may be used as nouns or as adjectives.

Determining Parts of Speech **43**

Determining Parts of Speech
(pp. 43–46)

OBJECTIVES

■ To identify nouns, pronouns, and adjectives in sentences

■ To write sentences using nouns, pronouns, and adjectives

Modeling and Demonstration

Noun or Adjective? Model how to determine whether a word is a noun or an adjective by using the example *These library books are overdue* and focusing upon the word *library*. First, have students identify any nouns (persons, places, things, or ideas) in the sentence. [*books*] Students may say that the word *library* is a noun (place). Point out that here, *library* answers the question *What books are overdue?* [These *library* books are overdue.] *Library* functions as an adjective modifying the noun *books*. Now, have a volunteer use another example from this chapter to demonstrate how to determine whether a word is a noun or an adjective.

Guided and Independent

You may wish to use items 1–10 in **Exercise 11** as guided practice. Then, have students complete items 11–20 as independent practice.

NOUN	How often do you watch **television**?
ADJECTIVE	What is your favorite **television** program?
NOUN	Return these books to the **library.**
ADJECTIVE	These **library** books are overdue.
NOUN	Would you like to have a cookout this **Labor Day**?
ADJECTIVE	Our annual **Labor Day** cookout is always a wonderful event.

Some words may be used as pronouns or adjectives.

PRONOUN	**That** is not a dragonfly; it's a damsel fly.
ADJECTIVE	**That** insect is not a dragonfly; it's a damsel fly.
PRONOUN	**Some** have gone to their dressing rooms.
ADJECTIVE	**Some** actors have gone to their dressing rooms.
PRONOUN	**Whose** are these?
ADJECTIVE	**Whose** gloves are these?

Exercise 11 Identifying Nouns, Pronouns, and Adjectives

Tell whether the italicized word in each of the following sentences is used as a *noun*, a *pronoun*, or an *adjective*.

EXAMPLE
1. The robin carried *some* twigs to its nest.
   1. adjective

1. This new *computer* program makes printers work twice as fast.
2. The program runs on this *computer*.
3. The *football* hit the ground and bounced right into his arms.
4. Are you going to the *football* game?
5. The book is much better than the *movie*.
6. The *movie* star rode at the front of the parade.
7. We'll start painting *that* section next.
8. *That* must be an interesting job.
9. *One* of the trees still has all its leaves.
10. The raccoon carried *one* baby at a time back to the nest.
11. The next race is scheduled for *Tuesday* night.
12. According to some surveys, *Tuesday* is the best day to get work done.

Learning for Life

Giving Accurate Directions. People often give others directions for getting to a specific place. Ask each student to write a set of directions for getting from the classroom to some other location in the school, such as the library or the cafeteria. Ask

them to use specific nouns, pronouns, and adjectives to describe the landmarks a person will encounter in following the directions.

After students complete their directions, have groups of four test the accuracy of their directions. Have each student read his

13. *Which* stars make up Orion's belt?
14. *Which* of the otters caught the first fish?
15. *All* mammals are vertebrates.
16. Matt has already memorized *all* of his lines in the play.
17. The only *mystery* is how it ended up in a box in the back of the closet.
18. The next guest speaker is a famous *mystery* writer.
19. If you lose *any* of the pieces, we won't be able to complete the puzzle.
20. Amazing things can be found by turning over almost *any* rock.

Review D **Identifying Nouns, Pronouns, and Adjectives**

Tell whether each underlined italicized word in the following sentences is used as a *noun*, a *pronoun*, or an *adjective*.

EXAMPLE   1. Remember, don't let *anyone* tell you that the age of exploration is over.
           1. *pronoun*

1. Two brothers, Lawrence and Lorne Blair, went on an amazing *adventure* that began in 1973.
2. For ten years they traveled among the nearly fourteen thousand *islands* of Indonesia.
3. *Each* of them returned with remarkable tales about the lands, animals, and people they had seen.
4. Their *adventure* story began when some pirates guided them through the Spice Islands.
5. There, the brothers located *one* of the world's rarest and most beautiful animals—the greater bird of paradise.
6. Another *island* animal that the brothers encountered was the frightening Komodo dragon.
7. *Some* Komodo dragons are eleven feet long and weigh more than five hundred pounds.
8. *Each* day brought startling discoveries, such as flying frogs and flying snakes.
9. On *one* island, Borneo, they found a group of people thought to be extinct.
10. To *some*, the brothers' stay with the cannibals of West New Guinea is the strangest part of their trip.

EXTENSION

Critical Thinking

Metacognition. After students complete **Reviews D** and **E**, ask them to discuss the following questions with a partner or in small groups.

1. Which are easiest to identify—nouns, pronouns, or adjectives?

2. Did you refer to rules and examples in previous parts of the chapter in completing the review exercises?

3. Did you find using the rules helpful? Why or why not?

4. Did you find using the examples helpful? Why or why not?

5. What advice would you give other students in learning to identify nouns, pronouns, and adjectives?

PRACTICE

Guided and Independent

You may wish to use **Review D** as guided practice. Then, have students complete **Review E** as independent practice.   **HOMEWORK**

or her directions to the group, and let group members add, delete, or clarify aspects of the directions to make them easier to follow. Visually oriented students may want to draw a map either before or after writing the directions.

TEACHING **TIP**

Review E You may want to make **Review E** more manageable by telling students how many nouns, pronouns, and adjectives there are in each sentence. *His* in sentence 4 and *their* and *his* in sentence 10 may be identified as adjectives.

Review F **Writing Sentences with Nouns, Pronouns, and Adjectives**

POSSIBLE ANSWERS

1. Let's play a game.—noun
   We saw some beautiful birds and animals at the game preserve.—adjective

2. Some think he is a hero.—pronoun
   Some people work long hours.—adjective

3. I am an American.—noun
   We fly an American flag.—adjective

4. Turn to the right.—noun
   Make a right turn here.—adjective

5. That is her mother.—pronoun
   You can wear that coat.—adjective

6. Her favorite color is green.—noun
   She put on her green plaid skirt.—adjective

7. Give me more.—pronoun
   We need more rain.—adjective

8. Saturday will be the first day of our vacation.—noun
   What are the bookstore's Saturday hours?—adjective

9. What did you find?—pronoun
   What answer did you give?—adjective

10. How much water should I add to the soup?—noun
    The water level is rising steadily.—adjective

─HELP─

You may want to go through Review E three times: First, look for nouns, then for pronouns, and finally for adjectives.

Review E **Identifying Nouns, Pronouns, and Adjectives**

Identify each *noun*, *pronoun*, and *adjective* in the following sentences. Do not include the articles *a*, *an*, and *the*.

EXAMPLE   1. Charles Drew was an American doctor.
            1. *Charles Drew—noun; American—adjective; doctor—noun*

1. Charles Drew developed innovative techniques that are used in the separation and preservation of blood.
2. During World War II, Dr. Drew himself was the director of donation efforts for the American Red Cross.
3. He established blood-bank programs.
4. His research saved numerous lives during the war.
5. Dr. Drew set up centers in which blood could be stored.
6. The British government asked him to develop a storage system in England.
7. Shortly before the beginning of World War II, Dr. Drew became a professor of surgery at Howard University.
8. After the war, he was appointed chief surgeon at Freedman's Hospital.
9. This physician and researcher made important contributions to medical science.
10. Many people who have needed blood owe their lives to his methods.

Review F **Writing Sentences with Nouns, Pronouns, and Adjectives**

Write two sentences with each of the following words. Use each word as two different parts of speech—*noun* and *adjective* or *pronoun* and *adjective*. Write the part of speech of the word after each sentence.

EXAMPLE   1. this
            1. *This bicycle is mine.—adjective*
               This cannot be the right answer.—pronoun

1. game   5. that   9. what
2. some   6. green   10. water
3. American   7. more
4. right   8. Saturday

2

Numerals in brackets refer to rules tested by the items in the Chapter Review.

1. [2a, c]
2. [2p, a, c]
3. [2h, o, p]
4. [2p, a, c]
5. [2h, m, p]
6. [2a, c, h, i]
7. [2a, d]
8. [2a, b, d, p]
9. [2p, h, o]
10. [2h, l, p]
11. [2p, a, c]
12. [2h, o, p]
13. [2a, h, i]
14. [2a, b, d, p]
15. [2a, c, e]
16. [2h, o]
17. [2a, c, e, h, j]
18. [2p, a, c]
19. [2p, h, i]
20. [2h, i, p]

Chapter Review

A. Identifying Nouns, Pronouns, and Adjectives

Identify each italicized word or word group as a *noun,*[*pronoun,*] or *adjective.*

1. I don't feel happy when the dark *sky* threatens *rain.*
2. My little sister, *afraid* of *thunder* and lightning, hid under the bed.
3. Inger's mother gave [*each*] of us a glass of *cold* milk.
4. One by one, *each* husky ventured out into the *cold.*
5. [*Who*] went to the movie on *Saturday* night?
6. When the famous *performer* came to town, we went to [*his*] concert.
7. The house across the street has been up for *sale* since *Tuesday.*
8. *Michelangelo Buonarroti* painted many *large* murals in the Sistine Chapel.
9. *That* jacket doesn't belong to [*anyone.*]
10. [*That*] is an *Aleut* mask.
11. Give me *some* iced *lemonade,* please.
12. [*Somebody*] said that there would be no more *discount* movie tickets.
13. I got a *discount* on [*our*] tickets, though.
14. *Mr. Taylor* donated the *sports* equipment for the new middle school in our town.
15. In high school, Uncle Todd excelled in *track* and several other *sports.*
16. [*Everyone*] liked one painting or the [*other.*]
17. Juana went to the *mall* by [*herself.*]
18. Hobbies take up so *much* time that they often become *work.*
19. My aunt's very busy *work* schedule often takes [*her*] out of town for several days at a time.
20. This parakeet screeches if [*it*] doesn't get *enough* food.

Chapter Review **47**

GRAMMAR

B. Identifying Pronouns

Identify the <u>pronoun or pronouns</u> in each of the following sentences as *personal, reflexive, intensive, demonstrative, interrogative, relative,* or *indefinite.*

21. per./per. [2i]
22. ref. [2j]
23. its. [2k]
24. per. [2i]
25. int./per. [2m, i]
26. ref. [2j]
27. per./per./ind. [2i, o]
28. its. [2k]
29. rel./per. [2n, i]
30. its. [2k]
31. per. [2i]
32. ref. [2j]
33. dem./rel./per. [2l, n, i]
34. ind. [2o]
35. ind./per. [2o, i]
36. rel. [2n]
37. int./per. [2m, i]
38. ind. [2o]
39. ind. [2o]
40. per./ref. [2i, j]

21. <u>Our</u> teacher and Ms. de la Garza said <u>they</u> would be at the meeting.
22. The members of the cast checked <u>themselves</u> in the dressing-room mirrors.
23. Mr. O'Shaughnessy <u>himself</u> said the quiz might be postponed.
24. The late Senator Duddington was a giving, generous, and warm human being, wasn't <u>he</u>?
25. <u>Which</u> of the science classes is <u>she</u> taking next year?
26. The chimpanzee taught <u>itself</u> to use a remote control.
27. A friend of <u>mine</u> said <u>you</u> had won <u>several</u> of the events at the 4-H competition.
28. Did Sally paint the apartment <u>herself</u>?
29. The zebras took the same path <u>that</u> <u>they</u> had always taken across the veldt.
30. Darryl answered the phone <u>himself</u>.
31. Is Queen Elizabeth I remembered because <u>she</u> was a great leader of England?
32. Kimiko wrote <u>herself</u> a note.
33. <u>These</u> are the books <u>that</u> <u>I</u> mentioned earlier.
34. The choice was hard, as <u>both</u> were excellent students.
35. Almost <u>everything</u> <u>my</u> grandfather did was motivated by concern for the family.
36. The council member <u>whom</u> the reporter wants to interview is out of town today.
37. <u>Who</u> may <u>I</u> say is calling?
38. <u>Somebody</u> has given Benno the Dalmatian a bath.
39. According to Sanjay, <u>either</u> of the two movies is worth seeing.
40. <u>We</u> found <u>ourselves</u> in an awkward situation.

Writing Application
Writing a Movie Review

Using Nouns, Pronouns, and Adjectives   Write a paragraph about a movie you have recently seen and enjoyed. Be sure to use at least ten each of nouns, pronouns, and adjectives.

Prewriting   You could write about a movie you have seen that is very popular or one that is less well-known but that you enjoyed. Write down some thoughts about the movie—what you especially liked, what you think worked, and what you think didn't work. Read some short newspaper movie reviews for an idea of the kind of style you might use.

Writing   Think about how to organize your notes and your ideas. Write down your impressions of the movie in a logical order, starting with your overall opinion, then going into a little more detail about the story, and concluding with a short summary.

Revising   Does your paragraph give your opinion of the movie in an interesting way? Add, delete, or rearrange details to make your paragraph more entertaining or informative. Read through your paragraph to make sure that you have used at least ten each of nouns, pronouns, and adjectives.

Publishing   Check for errors in grammar, punctuation, and spelling. Then, ask a classmate to read the paragraph, and post the completed paragraph on the class bulletin board or Web page, if available.

3

STANDARDS FOCUS

Grade-Level Standards
(Boldface indicates concepts that are taught and tested in this chapter.)

■ Language Convention 1.0: **Students write and speak with a command of standard English conventions appropriate to this grade level.**

■ Sentence Structure 1.3: **Use** subordination, **coordination,** apposition, and other devices to indicate clearly the relationship between ideas.

■ Grammar 1.4: **Edit written manuscripts to ensure that correct grammar is used.**

■ Punctuation and Capitalization 1.5: **Use correct punctuation and capitalization.**

Prerequisite/Review Standard

■ Grammar 1.3: Identify all parts of speech and types and structure of sentences.

Standard Coming Up in the Next Grade Level

■ Grammar and Mechanics of Writing 1.3: Demonstrate an understanding of proper English usage and control of grammar, paragraph and sentence structure, diction, and syntax.

▼

INTRODUCING THE CHAPTER

■ This chapter focuses on identifying and using verbs, adverbs, prepositions, conjunctions, and interjections. Students might find this chapter useful when they are

(continued)

3

1.0 Written and Oral English Language Conventions
Students write and speak with a command of standard English conventions appropriate to this grade level.
1.3 Use coordination.
1.4 Edit written manuscripts to ensure that correct grammar is used.
1.5 Use correct punctuation.

┌─HELP─

Keep in mind that correlative conjunctions can be made up of more than one word.

Numerals in brackets refer to rules tested by the items in the Diagnostic Preview.

1. a.v./prep. [3a, c]
2. prep./a.v. [3c, a]
3. l.v./conj. [3a, d]
4. adv./a.v. [3b, a]
5. prep./adv. [3c, b]

Parts of Speech Overview
Verb, Adverb, Preposition, Conjunction, Interjection

Diagnostic Preview

A. Identifying Different Parts of Speech

Identify each italicized word or word group in the following sentences as a *verb,* an *adverb,* a *preposition,* or a *conjunction.* For each verb, indicate whether it is an *action verb* or a *linking verb.*

EXAMPLE   **1.** You probably know that Christopher Columbus was a famous explorer, *but* do you know anything *of* his personal life?

   1. but—conjunction; of—preposition

1. I *have discovered* some interesting facts *about* Christopher Columbus.

2. He was born *into* a hard-working Italian family and *learned* how to sail as a boy.

3. He *became,* in fact, *not only* a master sailor *but also* a map maker.

4. Although he had *barely* any formal education, he *studied* both Portuguese and Spanish.

5. The writings *of* ancient scholars about astronomy and geography *especially* interested him.

CHAPTER RESOURCES

Internet

■ go.hrw.com (keyword: HLLA)

go. hrw .com

Planning

■ *Teacher One Stop DVD-ROM* 🅢

■ *On Course: Mapping Instruction*

Practice & Review

■ *Language & Sentence Skills Practice,* pp. 47–63; 64–66

■ *Developmental Language & Sentence Skills,* pp. 19–28

Application & Enrichment

■ *Language & Sentence Skills Practice,* pp. 69, 46, 67–68

6. Columbus *apparently* also *had* keen powers of observation.
7. These *served* him *well* on his expeditions.
8. On his voyages to find a sea route *to* the East Indies, Columbus *was* a determined, optimistic leader.
9. He let *neither* doubters *nor* hardships interfere *with* his plans.
10. Many people mistakenly think that Columbus was poor when he died in 1506, *but* he was actually *quite* wealthy.

B. Identifying Different Parts of Speech

Identify each italicized <u>word or word group</u> in the following sentences as a *verb*, an *adverb*, a *preposition*, a *conjunction*, or an *interjection*.

EXAMPLE   1. I *am reading* a book *about* baseball cards.
            1. am reading—verb; about—preposition

11. We *watched* as the skywriter *carefully* spelled out the words "Marry me, Alice."
12. *Both* the dog *and* the cat *are* dirty and need baths.
13. *Whoops*! I dropped my ring *under* the counter.
14. *Today* we studied the contributions that ancient North Africans made *to* mathematics.
15. Clever replies *never* occur to me until it is *too* late.
16. Sandy *does* not *have* enough granola *for* breakfast.
17. The girl *tried* climbing the rock face again *in spite of* her previous difficulty.
18. *Well*, I really want to see *either* Key West *or* the Everglades when we go to Florida next summer.
19. How *did* the other team *win* *so* easily?
20. The beans with rice *tasted* good, *for* we were hungry after a long day of yardwork.

The Verb

3a. A **verb** is a word used to express action or a state of being.

In this book, verbs are classified in three ways—(1) as *helping* or *main verbs*, (2) as *action* or *linking verbs*, and (3) as *transitive* or *intransitive verbs*.

6. adv./a.v. [3b, a]
7. a.v./adv. [3a, b]
8. prep./l.v. [3c, a]
9. conj./prep. [3d, c]
10. conj./adv. [3d, b]

┌─HELP─
Keep in mind that verbs, correlative conjunctions, and some prepositions can be made up of more than one word.

11. v./adv. [3a, b]
12. conj./v. [3d, a]
13. int./prep. [3e, c]
14. adv./prep. [3b, c]
15. adv./adv. [3b]
16. v./prep. [3a, c]
17. v./prep. [3a, c]
18. int./conj. [3e, d]
19. v./adv. [3a, b]
20. v./conj. [3a, d]

evaluating and revising writing assignments or studying style in composition and in literature.
■ The chapter closes with a **Chapter Review** including a **Writing Application** feature that asks students to write a summary of an incident from a book, movie, or television show.
■ For help in integrating this chapter with writing assignments in *Holt Literature and Language Arts,* use the **Teaching Strands** chart on pp. T24–T25.

ASSESSING

Entry-Level Assessment
Diagnostic Preview. The **Diagnostic Preview** asks students to identify verbs, adverbs, prepositions, conjunctions, and interjections and to classify the verbs as action or linking verbs. You can use this preview to assess your students' knowledge of these parts of speech and to group students to meet individual needs.

DIFFERENTIATING INSTRUCTION

Special Education Students
Because this chapter includes many terms, you may want to repeat important ideas frequently and to begin each lesson with a summary of material covered the previous day. This repetition should help students improve recall.

Differentiating Instruction
■ *UA: Differentiating Instruction*
■ *UA: Supporting Instruction in Five Languages*
Assessment
■ *Formal Assessment*
■ *Progress-Monitoring Tests,* pp. 5–6, 48

■ *Test Generator (Teacher One Stop DVD-ROM)* 🎧
Other Language Resources
■ *Spelling Lessons & Activities*
■ *WordSharp: An Interactive Vocabulary Tutor*
■ *Reading and Writing Transparencies*

The Verb

Rule 3a *(pp. 51–61)*

OBJECTIVES

- To identify verb phrases in sentences

- To identify action verbs in sentences

- To use linking verbs in sentences and to identify the words linked

- To identify subjects, verbs, and words linked to subjects

- To identify helping and main verbs and action and linking verbs

- To identify transitive and intransitive verbs in sentences

- To use transitive and intransitive verbs in sentences and to underline the objects of transitive verbs

DIFFERENTIATING INSTRUCTION

English-Language Learners

Hmong. In Hmong, the verb *be* is implied by, rather than used with, predicate adjectives; therefore, Hmong speakers may see the verb as redundant when it's used with a predicate adjective. Students may sometimes omit the verb entirely, writing "I happy," "She tall," or "He busy" rather than "I am happy," "She is tall," or "He is busy." Remind English-language learners that verbs are necessary in complete sentences in English, and offer practice with the use of *be*, stressing the verb forms in posed questions and answers: *Are you happy? I am happy. Is she tall? She is tall. Is he busy? He is busy.*

CALVIN & HOBBES copyright 1993 Watterson. Reprinted with permission of Universal Press Syndicate. All rights reserved.

Helping Verbs and Main Verbs

A *helping verb* helps the *main verb* express action or a state of being. Together, a main verb and at least one helping verb (also called an *auxiliary verb*) make up a *verb phrase.*

The following sentences contain verb phrases.

EXAMPLES Seiji Ozawa **will conduct** many outstanding orchestras. [The main verb is *conduct.*]

He **has been praised** for his fine conducting. [The main verb is *praised.*]

His recordings **should be heard** by anyone interested in classical music. [The main verb is *heard.*]

He **will be leading** the orchestra tonight. [The main verb is *leading.*]

Commonly Used Helping Verbs			
Forms of *Be*	am	been	was
	are	being	were
	be	is	
Forms of *Do*	do	does	did
Forms of *Have*	had	has	have
Other Helping Verbs	can	might	should
	could	must	will
	may	shall	would

NOTE Some helping verbs may also be used as main verbs.

EXAMPLES Did he **do** his homework?

She will **be** here soon.

We do not **have** enough time, but we **have** a plan.

Sometimes a verb phrase is interrupted by another part of speech. In most cases, the interrupter is an adverb. In a question, however, the subject often interrupts a verb phrase.

RESOURCES

The Verb

Practice

- *Language & Sentence Skills Practice*, pp. 47–53
- *Developmental Language & Sentence Skills*, pp. 19–22

EXAMPLES   The newspaper **has** finally **arrived.**

Because of the fog, we **did** not [or didn't] **have** a clear view of the mountains.

Will the boy in the blue jacket **write** his report on Lucy Stone, the suffragist?

Notice in the second example that the word *not* is not included in the verb phrase. *Not* (as well as its contraction, *–n't*) is an adverb and is never part of a verb phrase.

Reference Note

For information about **contractions** such as *–n't,* see page 167.

Exercise 1 Identifying Verb Phrases

Identify the verb phrases in the following sentences. Then, underline each helping verb.

EXAMPLE   1. Many people are earning a living at unusual jobs.

 1. *are earning*

1. Even today people can find positions as shepherds, inventors, and candlestick makers.
2. It might seem strange, but these people have decided that ordinary jobs have become too boring for them.
3. Some people have been working as messengers.
4. You may have seen them when they were wearing clown makeup or costumes such as gorilla suits.
5. Other people have been finding work as mimes.
6. They can be seen performing at circuses, fairs, and festivals.
7. Chimney sweeps still do clean chimney flues for people.
8. Some chimney sweeps may even wear the traditional, old-time clothes of the trade.
9. With a little imagination, anyone can find an unusual job.
10. What unusual jobs can you name?

┌HELP─

Some sentences in Exercise 1 contain more than one verb phrase.

Action Verbs

An ***action verb*** is a verb that expresses either physical or mental activity.

Physical Activity	laugh, paint, leap, sneeze, play

EXAMPLES   Langston Hughes **wrote** volumes of poetry.

A distinguished cinematographer, James Wong Howe, **arrived.**

| COMPUTER TIP

Some word-processing programs come with built-in thesauruses. You can use a computer thesaurus to help you find fresh, lively action verbs to make your writing more interesting. Always make sure the verb you select has the precise meaning you wish to express.

The Verb   **53**

MINI-LESSON **Usage**   *Continued on pp. 54–55*

Tenses of Verbs. Point out that one way that helping verbs can "help" the main verb is by indicating verb tense. For example, the helping verb *will* is used to form the future tense, as in "Jena will leave soon." Similarly, *have* (or *has*) helps form the present perfect tense ("I have waited too long") or combines with *will* to form the future perfect tense ("I will have waited too long to cover the plants, if we

---

Lesson Starter

Motivating. To introduce action verbs, write the following sentences on the chalkboard.

1. The sailor swabbed the deck.

2. The trainer groomed the racehorse.

3. The student closed the door.

Ask volunteers to pantomime the sentences and then to underline the word in each sentence that indicates how to act out the sentence. [*swabbed, groomed, closed*] Point out that the words in a sentence that tell an actor what to do are the action verbs.

DIFFERENTIATING INSTRUCTION

English-Language Learners

Cantonese. Because Cantonese does not use helping verbs for questions or negatives, the use of *do* as a helping verb may be puzzling for Cantonese speakers. Students may use regular verb forms but omit the helping verb: *How much money you have?* Since the helping verb is unstressed in English sentences, students may have difficulty perceiving its use. Emphasize the use of *do* and other helping verbs when speaking to students to focus their attention on helping verbs.
Do you have a pen? Yes, I do.
Can you swim? No, I can't.

Advanced Learners

Explain to students that action verbs that express mental activity are often followed by noun clauses consisting of the word *that* and a subject and a verb, as in "I worry that I'll be late." This type of noun clause is used as the direct object of the verb. The word *that* is often deleted, as in "I worry I'll be late." Have students work in pairs to brainstorm other examples of this pattern.

EXTENSION

Verbs in Figurative Language

You could integrate the study of linking verbs with that of similes and metaphors. Explain to students that a simile compares two unrelated things by using *like* or *as,* often with a form of the verb *be,* while a metaphor makes a direct comparison without using *like* or *as.* Point out that a simile may also be used with an action verb, as in "Leslie snores as loud as a bull." Read the following two sentences aloud, and have students identify each as a *simile* or a *metaphor.*

1. Her eyes are like candles in the dark. [*simile*]

2. Her eyes are candles in the dark. [*metaphor*]

Ask students to create metaphors and similes using the nouns *heart, city,* and *wind.* Have them underline the verbs they use and identify them as action or linking verbs.

SAMPLE ANSWERS

1. My heart <u>pounds</u> like the ocean's steady tide. [*action verb, simile*]

2. The city <u>is</u> a ravenous wolf. [*linking verb, metaphor*]

3. The wind <u>seems</u> as soft as a kiss. [*linking verb, simile*]

Mental Activity	understand, wish, trust, realize, dream

EXAMPLES The scientist **studied** the ant colony.

Mario **knew** the answer to every question on the test.

Exercise 2 **Identifying Action Verbs**

Identify the <u>action verb or verbs</u> in each of the following sentences.

EXAMPLE **1.** Joseph Bruchac writes and publishes poems and stories.

1. writes, publishes

1. Bruchac, of Slovak and Abenaki heritage, <u>tells</u> personal histories also.
2. He and his wife Carol <u>own</u> and <u>run</u> Greenfield Review Press.
3. The press <u>publishes</u> the work of American Indian writers.
4. Bruchac himself <u>wrote</u> more than fifty books for adults and children.
5. One of his books, *Lasting Echoes,* <u>tells</u> the history of American Indians.
6. Bruchac <u>subtitled</u> the book *An Oral History of Native American People.*
7. *Lasting Echoes* <u>describes</u> the importance of the land to the American Indian.
8. Bruchac <u>shares</u> the stories he <u>wishes</u> he <u>had heard</u> as a child.
9. American Indians <u>narrate</u> their own experiences and ideas.
10. Bruchac <u>believes</u> their stories <u>should be told</u> and <u>remembered</u>.

Linking Verbs

A **linking verb** connects the subject to a word or word group that identifies or describes the subject. The noun, pronoun, or adjective that is connected to the subject by a linking verb completes the meaning of the verb.

MINI-LESSON **Usage** *Continued from p. 53*

have a freeze while I am away"). *Had* helps form the past perfect tense ("The governor had spoken earlier").

Write the following sentences on the chalkboard, omitting the underlining.

For each sentence, have a volunteer underline the entire verb phrase once and the helping verb(s) twice. Then, ask students to identify the verb tense of each sentence.

EXAMPLES Tranh **is** one of the finalists. [Tranh = one]

    Marie Curie **became** a famous scientist. [Marie Curie = scientist]

    Wild animals **remain** free on the great animal reserves in Africa. [free animals]

    The watermelon **looks** ripe. [ripe watermelon]

Commonly Used Linking Verbs

Forms of *Be*	am	be	being	was
	are	been	is	were
Other Verbs	appear	grow	seem	stay
	become	look	smell	taste
	feel	remain	sound	turn

NOTE The forms of the verb *be* are not always used as helping verbs or linking verbs. When followed by a word or word group that tells *when* or *where*, a form of *be* is a **state-of-being verb.**

EXAMPLE Your roller skates **are** in the attic.

Exercise 3 Using Linking Verbs

Supply a linking verb for each blank in the following sentences. Try to use a different verb in each blank. Then, identify the words that each verb links.

EXAMPLE **1.** Judith Jamison _____ calm during the première of the dance.

    1. Judith Jamison remained calm during the première of the dance.

    Judith Jamison—calm

1. The first day _____ long.
2. Your suggestion _____ good to me.
3. Our room _____ festive after we decorated it for the party.
4. The orange _____ a little too sweet.
5. In the novel the main character _____ a doctor, and he returns home to set up a clinic.
6. Before a storm the air _____ wet and heavy.
7. Did she _____ happy about living in Florida?

STYLE ✏ TIP

Overusing the linking verb *be* can make your writing dull and lifeless. When possible, replace a dull *be* verb with a verb that expresses action.

BE VERB
 Edgar Allan Poe **was** a writer of poems and frightening short stories.

ACTION VERB
 Edgar Allan Poe **wrote** poems and frightening short stories.

COMPUTER TIP

The overuse of *be* verbs is a problem that a computer can help you solve. Use the computer's search function to find and highlight each occurrence of *am, are, is, was, were, be, been,* and *being.* For each such use, decide whether the *be* verb is needed or whether it could be replaced with an action verb for greater variety.

DIRECT TEACHING

Modeling and Demonstration

Action Verbs and Linking Verbs. Model how to identify action verbs and linking verbs by using the examples *The scientist studied the ant colony* and *Marie Curie became a famous scientist.* First, have students identify the verbs. [*studied; became*] Next, ask whether each verb expresses an action or links the subject to another word in the sentence. [*studied—action; became—linking*] Tell students that *studied* is an action verb, while *became* is a linking verb. Now, have a volunteer use another example from this chapter to demonstrate how to identify an action verb or a linking verb.

Exercise 3

Using Linking Verbs

POSSIBLE ANSWERS
1. The first day seemed long.
 day—long
2. Your suggestion sounds good to me.
 suggestion—good
3. Our room looked festive after we decorated it for the party.
 room—festive
4. The orange tastes a little too sweet.
 orange—sweet
5. In the novel the main character is a doctor, and he returns home to set up a clinic.
 character—doctor
6. Before a storm, the air turns wet and heavy.
 air—wet, heavy
7. Did she appear happy about living in Florida?
 she—happy

---

1. Lewis <u>has</u> <u>written</u> a poem. [*present perfect*]

2. On Sunday, Brenda <u>will</u> <u>ride</u> her bike to the park. [*future*]

3. That morning I <u>had</u> <u>fed</u> the cats as usual. [*past perfect*]

4. Leon and Candace <u>will</u> probably <u>run</u> in the marathon. [*future*]

5. By next week we <u>will have</u> <u>read</u> both articles. [*future perfect*]

Exercise 3
Using Linking Verbs

**POSSIBLE ANSWERS
continued**

8. The diver seemed more confident with each dive she made.
diver—confident

9. They became quiet as the theater lights dimmed.
They—quiet

10. The lilacs in the garden smelled lovely.
lilacs—lovely

EXTENSION

Relating to Literature

If your literature textbook contains the poem "O Captain! My Captain!" by Walt Whitman, have students read the selection. Then, have them compare the effects created by the linking verbs with those created by the action verbs, such as *rise, hear,* and *trills.* [*The action verbs are more forceful and direct. Linking verbs place emphasis on the words connected with the subject rather than on any kind of action.*]

Exercise 4

DISTRIBUTED REVIEW
For a quick review of adjectives, have students find the adjectives in sentences 3, 8, and 9 [3. *important, Mexican;* 8. *spicy, hot;* 9. *many*].

┌─ **TIPS** & **TRICKS** ─┐

Try the following test to determine whether a verb is a linking verb or an action verb. Substitute a form of *be* for the verb. If the sentence still makes sense, the verb is probably a linking verb. If not, the verb is most likely an action verb.

EXAMPLES
Mona felt sleepy.
Mona was sleepy. [The sentence still makes sense. Here, *felt* is a linking verb.]

Mona felt the soft fabric.
Mona is the soft fabric. [This sentence does not make sense. Here, *felt* is an action verb.]

---

8. The diver ____ more confident with each dive she made.
9. They ____ quiet as the theater lights dimmed.
10. The lilacs in the garden ____ lovely.

Most linking verbs, not including the forms of *be* and *seem*, may also be used as action verbs. Whether a verb is used to link words or to express action depends on its meaning in a sentence.

LINKING   Those plums **appeared** ripe.
ACTION   Those plums **appeared** on our back porch.

LINKING   The soup **tasted** good.
ACTION   I **tasted** the soup.

LINKING   She **had grown** tired of playing.
ACTION   She **had grown** into the new coat.

Exercise 4   Verbs and Their Subjects

Identify the verb and its subject in each of the following sentences. If the verb is a linking verb, identify also the [word or words that the verb links to its subject].

EXAMPLES   1. People enjoy the International Championship Chili Cook-off in Terlingua, Texas.
   1. enjoy, People

   2. The event, first held in 1967, is extremely popular.
   2. is, event—popular

1. Chili cook-offs throughout the Southwest attract fans.
2. Real fans grow [hungry] at the mention of chili peppers and chili powder.
3. These are important [ingredients] in Mexican cooking.
4. Chili cooks start with their favorite chili powder.
5. Basic chili powder consists of ground, dried chilies and other spices.
6. The most common chili is [chili con carne].
7. This is a thick, spicy meat [stew], often with beans in it.
8. Chili varies from somewhat spicy to fiery hot.
9. You also find many recipes for chili without meat.
10. Regardless of the other ingredients in a batch of chili, the chili powder smells [wonderful] to chili fans.

Exercise 5 **Identifying Verbs**

Identify the verb or verbs in each of the following sentences. If the verb is a linking verb, identify also the words that the verb links.

EXAMPLES
1. Do you know Tomás Herrera?
1. *Do know*

2. He is a friend of mine who lives next door to me.
2. *is, He—friend; lives*

1. Tomás is a young musician.
2. He likes all kinds of music and practices many hours each week.
3. His parents are proud of his talent and discipline.
4. One afternoon Tomás became restless.
5. The notes sounded wrong, and none of his music seemed right to him.
6. He wrote some notes on several sheets of music paper.
7. After a little careful revision, he formed the notes into an original harmony.
8. That night he performed his song for some of his friends.
9. Cristina exclaimed, "Tomás, that was excellent!"
10. "Is that really your first original song?"

Review A **Identifying Helping and Main Verbs and Action and Linking Verbs**

Identify each verb or verb phrase in the following sentences as an *action verb* or a *linking verb*. For each verb phrase, underline the main verb twice and each helping verb once.

EXAMPLE
1. Who were the Vikings, and where did they live?
1. *were—linking verb; did live—action verb*

1. The Vikings were Norsemen who roamed the seas from A.D. 700 to 1100.
2. The term *Vikings* applies to all Scandinavian sailors of this period, whether they were Norwegians, Swedes, or Danes.
3. People in other countries considered the Vikings the terror of Europe.
4. Vikings worshiped such fierce gods as Thor and Odin.
5. Viking warriors were hopeful that they would die in battle.

┌HELP┐
Some sentences in Review A contain more than one verb.

1. l.v./a.v.

2. a.v./l.v.

3. a.v.

4. a.v.

5. l.v./a.v.

The Verb   **57**

TECHNOLOGY **TIP**

If students write using a computer word-processing program, they can use the thesaurus to replace dull verbs with lively action verbs. However, point out to students that they should use the thesaurus to remind them of words they already know and use in their speech and writing. Sometimes using a thesaurus to discover new words can be disastrous, since most thesauruses do not list the connotations of words or give subtle differences in meaning.

6. a.v./a.v./a.v.

7. a.v.

8. a.v./a.v.

9. a.v.

10. a.v./a.v.

6. They[believed] that if they[died] in battle, they[would go] to Valhalla.

7. In Valhalla, they[could] always[enjoy] battles and banquets.

8. Each day, the warriors in Valhalla[would go] out to the battle-field and[would receive] many wounds.

9. Then, in spite of their injuries, at the end of the day they [would] all[meet] back at the banquet hall.

10. Their wounds[would] promptly[heal], and they[could boast] about their great bravery in battle.

Review B **Identifying Helping and Main Verbs and Action and Linking Verbs**

Identify each[verb or verb phrase] in the following sentences as an *action verb* or a *linking verb*. For each verb phrase, underline the main verb twice and each helping verb once.

┌─HELP───
Some sentences in Review B contain more than one verb.

EXAMPLES **1.** Have you heard of Mary McLeod Bethune?

1. *Have heard—action verb*

2. She dedicated her life to young people.

2. *dedicated—action verb*

1. l.v.
2. a.v./a.v.
3. a.v./a.v.
4. l.v./a.v.
5. a.v.
6. a.v.

1. Mary McLeod Bethune[is] a major figure in American history.
2. Bethune[taught] school after she[had completed] her education in South Carolina.
3. In 1904, she[moved] to Florida and[opened] a school of her own.
4. This school eventually[became] Bethune-Cookman College, and Mary Bethune[served] as its president.
5. In 1930, Bethune[was invited] to a presidential conference on child health and protection.
6. Then, during Franklin Roosevelt's administration, she and others[founded] the National Youth Administration.
7. Her outstanding efforts [impressed] President Roosevelt, and he[established] an office for minority affairs.
8. This office[gave] money to serious students so that they[could continue] their education.
9. In 1945, Bethune[was] an observer at the conference that [organized] the United Nations.
10. Throughout her long life, Bethune[remained] interested in education, and her efforts[earned] her national recognition.

7. a.v./a.v.
8. a.v./a.v.
9. l.v./a.v.
10. l.v./a.v.

Transitive and Intransitive Verbs

A *transitive verb* is a verb that expresses an action directed toward a person, place, thing, or idea.

EXAMPLES   Joel **held** the baby. [The action of *held* is directed toward *baby*.]

Loretta **brought** flowers. [The action of *brought* is directed toward *flowers*.]

Did Grandpa **sharpen** the ax this morning? [The action of *Did sharpen* is directed toward *ax*.]

With transitive verbs, the action passes from the doer—the subject—to the receiver of the action. Words that receive the action of transitive verbs are called *objects.*

EXAMPLES   Our scout troop made a **quilt.** [*Quilt* is the object of the verb *made*.]

The voters elected **him.** [*Him* is the object of the verb *elected*.]

How quickly the dog chased the **cat!** [*Cat* is the object of the verb *chased*.]

Reference Note

For more about **objects** and their uses in sentences, see page 81.

An *intransitive verb* expresses action (or tells something about the subject) without the action passing to a receiver, or object.

EXAMPLES   **Did**n't Samuel Ramey **sing** beautifully in the opera *Don Giovanni*?

The Evans twins **played** quietly indoors the whole day.

How long **have** you **been painting,** Mary?

A verb may be transitive in one sentence and intransitive in another.

EXAMPLES   Janet **swam** ten laps. [transitive]
Janet **swam** well. [intransitive]

The teacher **read** a poem. [transitive]
The teacher **read** aloud. [intransitive]

NOTE Because linking verbs do not have objects, they are classified as intransitive verbs.

Exercise 6 Identifying Transitive Verbs and Intransitive Verbs

Identify each italicized verb as *transitive* or *intransitive*. Be prepared to identify the (object) of each transitive verb.

EXAMPLE   **1.** Whether you *know* it or not, many cowboys in the United States were African Americans.

       1. transitive

1. During the years after the Civil War, thousands of African American cowboys *rode* the cattle (trails) north from Texas.
2. They *worked* alongside Mexican, American Indian, and European American trail hands.
3. All the members of a cattle drive *slept* on the same hard, sometimes rocky ground.
4. They *ate* the same (food) and did the same hard jobs.
5. When the day was done, they *enjoyed* each other's (company) as they swapped stories.
6. Often they also *sang* around the campfire.
7. After long weeks on the trail, they finally *reached* their (destinations) with their herds.
8. Then they *celebrated* by having rodeos, parades, and shooting contests.
9. Nat Love, one of the most famous African American cowboys, *wrote* about his experiences on the range.
10. In his book, Love *recalls* (many) of the times that he and the other cowboys looked out for one another, regardless of skin color.

Exercise 7 Writing Sentences with Transitive Verbs and Intransitive Verbs

For each of the verbs on the following page, write two sentences. In the first sentence, use the verb as a *transitive* verb and underline its object. In the second, use the verb as an *intransitive* verb. You may use different tenses of the verb.

EXAMPLE   **1.** read

    1. For tomorrow, read the <u>chapter</u> that begins on page 441. (transitive)

    I think I'll read this evening instead of watching television. (intransitive)

Exercise 7 Writing Sentences with Transitive Verbs and Intransitive Verbs

ANSWERS

Sentences will vary. Here are some possibilities. The first sentence in each pair uses a transitive verb.

1. Juan won the <u>race</u>.
   He won easily.

2. Please move that <u>chair</u> now.
   When did they move here?

3. Tani plays a <u>clarinet</u>.
   He plays well.

4. Ana ran a <u>marathon</u> last month.
   Don't run in the halls.

5. I will freeze the <u>leftovers</u>.
   Our garden froze last night.

6. Judith built a <u>house</u> for her dog.
   Build upon your earlier training.

7. Rosa jumped the <u>hurdle</u>.
   The child jumped into the puddle.

8. Dad cooked <u>breakfast</u>.
   Does he cook well?

9. Don't paint the <u>trim</u> yet.
   We painted all day.

10. Help your <u>sister</u> with her homework.
    Can I help?

1. win 3. play 5. freeze 7. jump 9. paint
2. move 4. run 6. build 8. cook 10. help

The Adverb

3b. An *adverb* is a word that modifies a verb, an adjective, or another adverb.

Just as an adjective makes the meaning of a noun or pronoun more definite, an adverb makes the meaning of a verb, an adjective, or another adverb more definite. An adverb tells *where, when, how,* or *to what extent* (*how much or how long*).

Where?	When?
They said the forest fire started **here.**	Louis **promptly** rounded up suspects.
The couple was married **nearby.**	**Then** several suspects were questioned.

How?	To What Extent?
The accident occurred **suddenly.**	Ms. Kwan was **quite** proud of the girls' debate team.
The prime minister spoke **carefully.**	She has **scarcely** begun the math lesson.

Adverbs Modifying Verbs

Adverbs may come before or after the words they modify.

EXAMPLES **Slowly** the man crawled **down.** [The adverb *Slowly* tells *how* the man crawled, and the adverb *down* tells *where* he crawled.]

I **seldom** see you **nowadays.** [The adverb *seldom* tells *to what extent* I see you, and the adverb *nowadays* tells *when* I see you.]

Adverbs may come between the parts of verb phrases.

EXAMPLES Keisha has **already** completed her part of the project. [The adverb interrupts and modifies *has completed*.]

Many students did **not** understand the directions. [The adverb interrupts and modifies *did understand*.]

The Adverb **61**

RESOURCES

The Adverb

Practice

■ *Language & Sentence Skills Practice,* pp. 54–56

■ *Developmental Language & Sentence Skills,* pp. 23–24

Reference Note

For information on **adjectives,** see page 38.

MEETING THE CHALLENGE

Write a riddle for your classmates to solve. Choose a person, animal, or thing, and brainstorm a list of vivid verbs that tell what he, she, or it does. Then, brainstorm a list of adverbs that make your verbs more descriptive. Finally, use at least five of your verbs and at least five of your adverbs to create a "What am I?" riddle.

EXAMPLE
I **glide smoothly**
I **spin around**
I **zoom about joyfully**
I **slip suddenly** and **hurtle wildly** down the pavement
I **stop—luckily!**

What am I?

ANSWER
an in-line skater

ANSWER
Riddles will vary.

The Adverb

Rule 3b *(pp. 61–66)*

OBJECTIVES

■ To identify adverbs and the verbs, adjectives, and adverbs they modify

■ To choose adverbs to modify adjectives

DIRECT TEACHING

Modeling and Demonstration

Identifying Adverbs. Model how to identify an adverb by using the example *They said the forest fire started here.* First, write the sentence on the chalkboard, along with the questions *Where? When? How?* and *To what extent?* Next, ask students whether any words in the sentence answer any of those questions. [*here—Where?*] Tell students that *here* is an adverb modifying *started.* Now, have a volunteer use another example from this chapter to demonstrate how to identify an adverb.

RETEACHING

Adverbs

Activity. Copy the chart on this page onto chart paper, but leave out the adverb example sentences. Label each empty example space with a number from one to four, and have the class count off from one to four to create four groups. Ask students to write a brief sentence to go in the cell corresponding to their number. Collect all the number one sentences, and read each one aloud. Repeat this procedure for all four numbers, writing good examples of sentences in the corresponding cells. You can post the chart in the classroom for the duration of this section of the chapter.

EXTENSION

Relating to Literature

If your literature textbook contains Dr. Martin Luther King, Jr.'s speech "I Have a Dream," ask a volunteer to read the speech aloud. Tell students to pay close attention to the adverbs that show time and to analyze the effect created by the deliberate repetition of many of these adverbs. [The material excerpted may vary from textbook to textbook. The following sentences provide one possible answer. *Adverbs give the speech a historical framework as well as a sense of history in the making. Ago, later, and still link the past (1863) to the time the speech was presented (1963). Today and now ground the ideals of equality and justice to the time of the speech. Never and forever link these ideals to the future. The repetition of later, still, never, and today creates a sense of outrage that racial injustice continues and a sense of urgency that this injustice be corrected.*]

Reference Note

For information on two other kinds of adverbs, **relative adverbs** and **conjunctive adverbs,** see pages 125 and 332.

Adverbs are sometimes used to ask questions.

EXAMPLES   **Where** are you going?

How did you do on the test?

Exercise 8 **Identifying Adverbs That Modify Verbs**

Identify the <u>adverbs</u> and the <u>verbs they modify</u> in the following sentences.

EXAMPLE   1. How can I quickly learn to take better pictures?
            1. How—can learn; quickly—can learn

1. You can listen carefully to advice from experienced photographers, who usually like to share their knowledge.
2. Nobody always takes perfect pictures, but some tips can help you now.
3. To begin with, you should never move when you are taking pictures.
4. You should stand still and hold your camera firmly.
5. Some photographers suggest that you move your feet apart and put one foot forward to help maintain your balance.
6. Many beginners do not stand near the subject when they take pictures.
7. As a result, subjects frequently are lost in the background, and the photographers later wonder what happened to their careful compositions.
8. A good photographer automatically thinks about what will be in a picture and consequently avoids disappointment with the result.
9. Nowadays, many cameras have built-in light meters, but you should still check the lighting.
10. You may already have heard the advice to stand with your back to the sun when taking pictures, and that tip is often a good one.

Learning for Life

Using Adverbs in Persuasive Speeches. Taking an active role in effecting change can be an important and satisfying aspect of civic pride. Have students prepare short, persuasive speeches that focus on something they would like to change. Perhaps students feel that a school policy is unfair, or they might have alternative ways to deal with issues in the news. Have students jot down their thoughts and arrange them in a logical order.

Students should carefully choose their

Adverb or Adjective?

Many adverbs end in –*ly*. Many of these adverbs are formed by adding –*ly* to adjectives.

Adjective	+	–*ly*	=	Adverb
bright	+	–*ly*	=	brightly
loud	+	–*ly*	=	loudly

However, some words ending in –*ly* can be used as adjectives.

EXAMPLES   friendly   monthly   lonely
               likely   timely   only

Adverbs Modifying Adjectives

EXAMPLES   An **unusually** fast starter, Karen won the race. [The adverb *unusually* modifies the adjective *fast,* telling *how fast* the starter was.]

Our committee is **especially** busy at this time of year. [The adverb *especially* modifies the adjective *busy,* telling *to what extent* the committee is busy.]

Exercise 9 Identifying Adverbs That Modify Adjectives

Identify the adverbs and the adjectives they modify in the following sentences.

EXAMPLE   **1.** Because so many bicycles have been stolen, the principal hired a guard.

        1. so—many

1. The team is extremely proud of its record.
2. Frogs may look quite harmless, but some are poisonous.
3. The class was unusually quiet today.
4. The Mardi Gras celebration in New Orleans is very loud and remarkably colorful.
5. The coach said we were too careless during the play.
6. I waited nearly two hours to get tickets to that show.
7. When the kittens are with their mother, they look thoroughly contented.

TIPS & TRICKS

If you are not sure whether a word is an adjective or an adverb, ask yourself what the word modifies. If it modifies a noun or a pronoun, it is an adjective.

EXAMPLE
She gave us the **daily** report. [*Daily* modifies the noun *report* and so is used as an adjective.]

If a word modifies a verb, an adjective, or an adverb, then it's an adverb.

EXAMPLE
Alicia **recently** won the spelling bee. [The adverb *recently* modifies the verb *won.*]

HELP

A sentence in Exercise 9 contains more than one adverb that modifies an adjective.

EXTENSION

Relating to Writing

Ask students to select a piece of their own writing to evaluate. Have them locate and underline every adverb in the sample. Then, ask students to write a brief statement about how adverbs helped them communicate their ideas more clearly.

Next, ask students to find five sentences in their writing that do not contain adverbs. Have them rewrite the sentences, adding adverbs where appropriate.

Finally, lead a discussion about the ways in which adverbs can improve writing.

---

words in order to be convincing. Encourage them to use strong, specific adverbs to make their persuasive speeches more effective.

Have student pairs take turns giving their speeches. As one student presents his or her speech, the other should pay close attention to the use of adverbs and how they affect the persuasiveness of the speech.

ANSWERS

Adverbs will vary. Here are some possibilities.

1. surprisingly
2. terribly
3. extremely
4. incredibly
5. consistently
6. exceptionally
7. tremendously
8. quite
9. especially
10. breathtakingly

EXTENSION

Relating to Vocabulary

To help students expand their vocabulary, have the class play a game of opposites with adverbs. Assign students to groups of three or four. After calling out an adverb such as *gracefully, noisily, happily,* or *suddenly,* let each group think of an antonym and use it in a sentence. Then, let the class decide which group has the best response.

STYLE TIP

The adverb *very* is often overused. In your writing, try to replace *very* with more descriptive adverbs. You can also revise a sentence so that other words carry more of the descriptive meaning.

EXAMPLE
Vikram Seth's novel *A Suitable Boy* is very long.

REVISED
Vikram Seth's novel *A Suitable Boy* is **extremely** long.

or

Vikram Seth's novel *A Suitable Boy* is **1,349 pages** long and **weighs four pounds.**

8. Weekends are especially hectic for me when all of my teachers assign homework.
9. Those fajitas seem much spicier than these.
10. The exchange student from Norway is surprisingly fluent in English.

Oral Practice Choosing Adverbs to Modify Adjectives

Say each of the following adjectives aloud. Then, choose an adverb other than *very* to modify each adjective.

EXAMPLE **1.** strong
   1. *incredibly strong*

1. cheerful   4. messy   7. heavy   9. calm
2. sour   5. honest   8. long   10. graceful
3. wide   6. timid

Adverbs Modifying Other Adverbs

EXAMPLES Elena finished the problem **more** quickly than I did. [The adverb *more* modifies the adverb *quickly,* telling *how quickly* Elena finished the problem.]

Our guest left **quite** abruptly. [The adverb *quite* modifies the adverb *abruptly,* telling *to what extent* our guest left abruptly.]

Exercise 10 Identifying Adverbs That Modify Other Adverbs

Identify each adverb that modifies another adverb in the following sentences. Then, write the adverb that it modifies.

EXAMPLE **1.** Condors are quite definitely among the largest living birds.
   1. *quite—definitely*

1. The California condor and the Andean condor are almost entirely extinct.
2. So very few California condors exist today outside captivity.
3. Andean condors are slightly more numerous, and more of them can still be seen in the wild.

4. You can see from these photographs why some people think that condors are <u>most</u> <u>assuredly</u> the ugliest birds.
5. However, once in the air, condors soar <u>so</u> <u>gracefully</u> that they can look beautiful.
6. Condors fly <u>amazingly</u> <u>gracefully</u> considering that some weigh more than <u>fifteen</u> pounds.
7. The heads of the Andean and California condors differ <u>quite</u> <u>distinctly</u>.
8. The California condor in the photograph on the right has a head that is <u>very</u> <u>handsomely</u> shaped compared to that of the Andean condor.
9. The Andean condor's head has a large fleshy caruncle protruding <u>quite</u> <u>noticeably</u> above the beak.
10. The extinction of condors is happening <u>especially</u> <u>quickly</u>, so the time left to observe them may be sadly short.

Review C — Identifying Adverbs

Identify the adverbs in each of the following sentences. After each adverb, write the word that the adverb modifies.

EXAMPLE   1. Sherlock Holmes solved the case very quickly.
            1. *very—quickly; quickly—solved*

1. I have been a fan of mystery stories since I was quite young.
2. Some stories are incredibly exciting from start to finish.
3. Others build suspense very slowly.
4. If I like a story, I almost never put it down until I finish it.
5. In many cases, I can scarcely prevent myself from peeking at the last chapter to see the ending.
6. I never start reading a mystery story if I have homework because then it is more tempting to read than to study.
7. My favorite detectives are ones who cleverly match wits with equally clever villains.
8. I especially like detectives who carefully hunt for clues.

┌─HELP─
Some sentences in Review C have more than one adverb.

Review C — Identifying Adverbs

ANSWERS

1. quite—young
2. incredibly—exciting
3. very—slowly; slowly—build
4. almost—never; never—put; down—put
5. scarcely—can prevent
6. never—start; then—is; more—tempting
7. cleverly—match; equally—clever
8. especially—like; carefully—hunt

9. The clues that they uncover are almost always found in unexpected, spooky places.
10. It's amazing how detectives can use these clues to solve the most complicated cases.

The Preposition

3c. A **preposition** is a word that shows the relationship of a noun or pronoun, called the **object of the preposition**, to another word.

Notice how a change in the preposition changes the relationship between *package* and *tree* in each of the following examples.

EXAMPLES   The package **under** the tree is mine.
            The package **near** the tree is mine.
            The package **next to** the tree is mine.
            The package **in front of** the tree is mine.

NOTE   As a general rule, the object of the preposition follows the preposition.

EXAMPLE   Melissa is writing **about** her **stay in** the **hospital.** [*Stay* is the object of the preposition *about; hospital* is the object of the preposition *in.*]

Sometimes, however, the object of the preposition comes before the preposition.

EXAMPLE   **What** I'm most concerned **about** is your safety. [*What* is the object of the preposition *about.*]

Commonly Used Prepositions			
aboard	along	at	but (meaning *except*)
about	along with	before	
above	amid	below	by
according to	among	beneath	down
across	around	beside	during
after	aside from	besides	except
against	as of	between	for

Review C **Identifying Adverbs**

ANSWERS continued

9. almost—always; always—are found
10. how—can use; most—complicated

The Preposition

Rule 3c *(pp. 66–69)*

OBJECTIVES

■ To identify prepositions, including compound prepositions, in sentences

■ To identify prepositional phrases in sentences

■ To write sentences using words as adverbs, then as prepositions

DIRECT TEACHING

Modeling and Demonstration

Identifying Prepositions. Model how to identify prepositions by using the example *The package under the tree is mine.* First, ask what word shows the relationship between *package* and *tree.* [*under*] Note that the preposition *under* shows where the package is in relation to the tree. Then, read the example aloud, using different prepositions. Point out how the different prepositions change the relationship between the package and the tree. Now, have a volunteer use another example from this chapter to demonstrate how to identify a preposition. Have the volunteer supply different prepositions to change the relationship between the noun or pronoun and another word in the sentence.

| STYLE ✎ TIP |

In formal writing, many people consider it best to avoid ending a sentence with a preposition. However, this practice is becoming more accepted in casual speech and informal writing. You should follow your teacher's instructions on sentences ending with prepositions.

RESOURCES

The Preposition
Practice

■ *Language & Sentence Skills Practice,* pp. 57–59

■ *Developmental Language & Sentence Skills,* pp. 25–26

Commonly Used Prepositions			
from	near	over	until
in	next to	past	unto
in addition to	of	since	up
in front of	off	through	upon
inside	on	throughout	with
in spite of	on account of	to	within
instead of		toward	without
into	out	under	
like	out of	underneath	

NOTE Prepositions that consist of more than one word, such as *in front of*, are called **compound prepositions**.

Exercise 11 Identifying Prepositions

Identify each underlined preposition in the following sentences. Be sure to include all parts of any compound prepositions you find.

EXAMPLE   **1.** Throughout the centuries people have read about the legend of Romulus and Remus.

   1. Throughout, about, of

1. According to legend, Mars, the god of war in Roman mythology, was the father of the twin brothers Romulus and Remus.
2. When the twins were infants, an evil ruler had them placed in a basket and cast into the Tiber River.
3. Fortunately, they safely drifted to the bank of the river.
4. There they were rescued by a wolf.
5. Later they were found by a shepherd and his wife.
6. When the twins were adults, they tried building a city on the site where they had been rescued.
7. Instead of working together, however, the twins fought against each other.
8. During the quarrel Romulus killed Remus.
9. Then, the legend continues, Romulus founded the city of Rome in approximately 753 B.C.
10. Out of hundreds of legends about the founding of Rome, this one has remained among the best known.

DIFFERENTIATING INSTRUCTION

English-Language Learners

Spanish. In Spanish, the single preposition *en* is used to denote *in, on,* and *at.* Therefore, the following generalizations about English prepositions may be useful to Spanish speakers.

1. *In* is often used for cities, states, and countries. (We live *in* Denver, *in* Colorado, *in* the United States.)
2. *On* is often used for streets, avenues, and roads. (We live *on* Elm Street.)
3. *At* is often used for addresses that include the number. (We live *at* 112 Elm Street.)

You may want to create a fill-in-the-blank exercise about a family moving from one state or country to another and have students fill in the correct prepositions.

Cantonese. Unlike English, Cantonese does not have a large range of prepositions. Since English preposition use is often unpredictable and idiomatic, Cantonese speakers may find prepositions difficult to master. Help students learn the patterns of preposition usage by teaching the prepositions with words they generally follow, for example, *go to, come from, hope for.* Emphasize the prepositions when speaking to students.

*Did you go **to** the store?*
*Tell us where that came **from**.*
*I hope **for** good things.*

CONTENT-AREA CONNECTIONS

Social Studies. Ask students to read a portion of the Declaration of Independence and to write down the prepositional phrases they find in it. Then, ask them to work in groups to rewrite that same portion, simplifying the sentence structure by eliminating or combining prepositional phrases whenever possible. Remind students to preserve the meaning of the original text. Allow volunteers to share their efforts with the class.

Relating to Literature

If your literature textbook contains Abraham Lincoln's Gettysburg Address, have students read it and take a closer look at the prepositions *of, by,* and *for* in the final clause of the speech. Each of these prepositions uses the word *people* as its object, and all three prepositional phrases modify the word *government.* Discuss how the meaning of each phrase is different. [Of *shows possession. The people own the government.* By *shows a relationship in which the people empower the government.* For *shows a need fulfilled or service performed. The government serves the people.*]

Reference Note

For more information about **prepositional phrases,** see page 96.

Reference Note

For more about **infinitives,** see page 108.

The Prepositional Phrase

All together, the preposition, the object of the preposition, and any modifiers of the object are called a ***prepositional phrase.***

EXAMPLE   The tired tourists climbed **onto the crowded bus.** [The prepositional phrase consists of the preposition *onto,* its object *bus,* and two adjectives modifying the object—*the* and *crowded.*]

NOTE   Be careful not to confuse a prepositional phrase that begins with *to* (*to town, to her club*) with an infinitive that begins with *to* (*to run, to be seen*). Remember: A prepositional phrase has a noun or a pronoun as an object.

Exercise 12 Identifying Prepositional Phrases

Identify the prepositional phrase or phrases in each of the following sentences. Then, underline each preposition.

EXAMPLE   1. Walt Whitman wrote the very moving poem "O Captain! My Captain!" about President Abraham Lincoln.

    1. *about President Abraham Lincoln*

1. In Whitman's poem, the captain directs his ship toward a safe harbor.
2. The captain represents Abraham Lincoln, and the ship is the ship of state.
3. The captain has just sailed his ship through stormy weather.
4. This voyage across rough seas symbolizes the Civil War.
5. On the shore, people joyfully celebrate the ship's safe arrival.
6. One of the ship's crew addresses his captain, "O Captain! My Captain! rise up and hear the bells."
7. Sadly, everyone except the captain can hear the rejoicing.
8. The speaker in the poem says that the captain "has no pulse nor will."
9. The captain has died during the voyage, just as Lincoln died at the end of the Civil War.
10. According to many people, "O Captain! My Captain!" is one of Whitman's finest poems.

Adverb or Preposition?

Some words may be used as both prepositions and adverbs. To tell an adverb from a preposition, remember that a preposition always has a noun or pronoun as an object.

ADVERB   The plane circled **above.**
PREPOSITION   The plane circled **above** the field.

ADVERB   Please go **inside** soon.
PREPOSITION   Please go **inside** the house soon.

Exercise 13 **Writing Sentences with Adverbs and Prepositions**

Use each of the following words in two sentences, first as an adverb and then as a preposition. Underline the given word.

EXAMPLE   **1.** along
    1. *Do you have to bring your little brother* <u>along</u>*?*
       Wildflowers were blooming <u>along</u> *the riverbank.*

1. off   **3.** below   **5.** down   **7.** on   **9.** around
2. across **4.** outside   **6.** under   **8.** about **10.** near

The Conjunction

3d. A *conjunction* is a word used to join words or groups of words.

Coordinating conjunctions join words or groups of words that are used in the same way.

Coordinating Conjunctions						
and	but	for	nor	or	so	yet

EXAMPLES   Maria, Han, Theo, **or** Tyler [four nouns]

quickly **but** carefully [two adverbs]

away from town, through a forest, **and** across a river [three prepositional phrases]

Cocker spaniels make good pets, **but** they require a lot of grooming. [two clauses]

TIPS & TRICKS

You can remember the coordinating conjunctions as FANBOYS.
For
And
Nor
But
Or
Yet
So

Exercise 13 **Writing Sentences with Adverbs and Prepositions**

POSSIBLE ANSWERS

1. Take the hat <u>off</u>.
   He threw a rock <u>off</u> the bridge.

2. He crawled <u>across</u> easily.
   The car went <u>across</u> the bridge.

3. Let's go <u>below</u> to the galley.
   It's <u>below</u> zero outside.

4. What is hiding <u>outside</u>?
   It was just <u>outside</u> the door.

5. Put the basket <u>down</u>.
   The turtle crawled <u>down</u> the hill.

6. Should I jump over or crawl <u>under</u>?
   The cleansers are <u>under</u> the sink.

7. Move <u>on</u>, please.
   <u>On</u> the table was a large vase.

8. The papers are scattered <u>about</u>.
   Have you heard <u>about</u> the game?

9. The birds were flying <u>around</u>.
   Wear it <u>around</u> your waist.

10. The time is <u>near</u>.
    Do not sit <u>near</u> the heater.

The Conjunction
Rule 3d *(pp. 69–71)*

OBJECTIVE

■ **To identify coordinating and correlative conjunctions and the words they join**

RESOURCES

The Conjunction
Practice

■ *Language & Sentence Skills Practice,* pp. 60–61
■ *Developmental Language & Sentence Skills,* pp. 27–28

DIRECT TEACHING

Modeling and Demonstration

Identifying Conjunctions. Model how to identify coordinating conjunctions by using the examples *Maria, Han, Theo, or Tyler; away from town, through a forest, and across a river;* and *Cocker spaniels make good pets, but they require a lot of grooming.* [*or* joins four nouns; *and* joins three prepositional phrases; *but* joins two clauses]. First, explain to students that a *junction* is the place at which two roads join; a *conjunction* is a word that joins words, phrases, or clauses. Then, read the examples aloud, emphasizing the conjunctions. Now, have a volunteer demonstrate how to identify a conjunction by following the pattern of the examples and using the same conjunctions to join new words, phrases, and clauses. [*red or blue; over the hill, under the bridge, and into the water; Homemade pizza is delicious, but it takes time to prepare.*]

STYLE   TIP

The coordinating conjunction *so* is often overused. For variety, reword a sentence to avoid using *so*.

EXAMPLE
You are new, **so** you might get lost.

REVISED
Because you are new, you might get lost.

Reference Note

A third kind of conjunction—the **subordinating conjunction**—is discussed on page 128.

┌HELP─

In the example, the conjunction *and* joins the nouns *man* and *women*.

NOTE When *for* is used as a conjunction, it connects clauses. On all other occasions, *for* is used as a preposition.

CONJUNCTION   We wrote to the tourist bureau, **for** we wanted information on places to visit.

PREPOSITION   We waited patiently **for** a reply.

Correlative conjunctions are pairs of conjunctions that join words or word groups that are used in the same way.

Correlative Conjunctions		
both . . . and	either . . . or	neither . . . nor
whether . . . or	not only . . . but also	

EXAMPLES   **Both** horses **and** cattle were brought to North America by the Spanish. [The correlative conjunction joins two nouns.]

The student council will meet **not only** on Tuesday **but also** on Thursday. [The correlative conjunction joins two prepositional phrases.]

I don't know **whether** to walk **or** to ride my bike to the grocery store. [The correlative conjunction joins two infinitive phrases.]

Either help me set the table now, **or** wash the dishes later. [The correlative conjunction joins two clauses.]

Exercise 14 Identifying Coordinating and Correlative Conjunctions

Identify each of the conjunctions in the following sentences as *coordinating* or *correlative*. Be prepared to tell what words or word groups the conjunctions join.

EXAMPLE   1. The man and women in the picture on the next page are wearing African clothes.

1. *and—coordinating*

1. African clothing is fashionable today for both men and women in the United States.

2. People wear <u>not only</u> clothes of African design <u>but also</u> Western-style clothes made of African materials.

3. American women have worn modified African headdresses for years, <u>but</u> nowadays men are wearing African headgear, too.

4. Men <u>and</u> women sometimes wear *kufi* hats, which originated with Muslims.

5. <u>Both</u> women's dresses <u>and</u> women's coats are especially adaptable to African fashions.

6. Many women wear African jewelry <u>or</u> scarves.

7. Clothes made of such materials as *kente* cloth from Ghana, *ashioke* cloth from Nigeria, <u>and</u> *dogon* cloth from Mali have become quite popular.

8. These fabrics are decorated <u>either</u> with brightly colored printed designs <u>or</u> with stripes.

9. African-inspired clothes usually fit in <u>whether</u> you are at work <u>or</u> at play.

10. African styles are popular, <u>for</u> they show appreciation of ancient cultures.

The Interjection

3e. An *interjection* is a word used to express emotion.

An interjection has no grammatical relation to other words in the sentence. Usually an interjection is followed by an exclamation point. Sometimes an interjection is set off by a comma or commas.

EXAMPLES   **Oh!** You surprised me.

            Wow! Am I tired!

            Aha, you've discovered the secret.

            Could you, **well,** be quiet, please?

NOTE   Interjections are common in informal writing and speaking situations. However, interjections are rarely used in formal situations, except as part of written dialogue.

The Interjection   **71**

Exercise 15 Identifying Interjections

ANSWERS

Speakers: Jack of "Jack and the Beanstalk," (1, 3, 8); *Baby Bear from "Goldilocks and the Three Bears,"* (2, 9); *Little Red Riding Hood* (4, 6); *and the Wolf from "The Three Little Pigs"* (5, 7, 10)

Determining Parts of Speech

Rule 3f *(pp. 72–74)*

OBJECTIVES

- To identify the parts of speech of words in sentences

- To add interjections, conjunctions, prepositions, adverbs, and verbs to sentences

DIRECT TEACHING

Modeling and Demonstration

Adverb or Preposition? Model how to determine whether a word is an adverb or a preposition by using the examples *The raccoon climbed down* (sentence 1) and *The raccoon climbed down the hill* (sentence 2). First, ask students whether *down* modifies a word in sentence 1. [*Down* modifies the verb *climbed,* telling *where.*] *Down* modifies a verb; therefore, *down* is an adverb. Then, have students identify how *down* functions in sentence 2. [*Down* is a preposition in the prepositional phrase *down the hill.*] Now, have a volunteer use another example from the chapter to demonstrate how to determine whether a word is an adverb or a preposition.

The four fairy-tale characters are, in order of appearance, Jack from "Jack and the Beanstalk," Baby Bear from "Goldilocks and the Three Bears," Little Red Riding Hood, and the Wolf from "The Three Little Pigs."

Exercise 15 **Identifying Interjections**

Some fairy-tale characters are meeting to discuss their image. They are worried that the familiar fairy tales make them look stupid or silly. Identify the ten <u>interjections</u> used in the following dialogue. Then, try to guess who the four fairy-tale speakers are.

EXAMPLE **1.** "Hooray! We're finally getting a chance to tell our side of the stories!"

 1. *Hooray*

1. "<u>Beans</u>! It's not fair what they say. I knew I was taking a giant step that day."

2. "<u>Well</u>, it's not fair what they say about us, either. Don't you think Papa and Mama saw that little blond girl snooping around our house?"

3. "<u>Yeah</u>! Don't you think I intended to buy magic beans?"

4. "You guys don't have it as bad as I do. <u>Ugh</u>! How dumb do people think I am? Of course I'd know my own grandmother when I saw her."

5. "<u>Sure</u>! I think your cloak was over your eyes, but how about me? I didn't go near those three pigs."

6. "<u>What</u>! Next you'll probably tell me that I didn't see your brother at Grandmother's house."

7. "<u>Humph</u>! I don't know what you really saw. It's difficult to tell sometimes in the woods."

8. "<u>Aw</u>, let's not argue. We've got to put our best feet forward— all the way up the beanstalk if need be."

9. "<u>Yes</u>! I want to give people the real story about that kid who broke my bed."

10. "<u>Great</u>! I'm ready to squeal on those three little pigs!"

Determining Parts of Speech

3f. The way a word is used in a sentence determines what part of speech the word is.

The same word may be used as different parts of speech.

PRONOUN	**Each** was painted blue.
ADJECTIVE	**Each** ornament was painted blue.
ADVERB	The raccoon climbed **down.**
PREPOSITION	The raccoon climbed **down** the hill.

| NOUN | The crew has spotted **land.** |
| VERB | The crew can **land** here safely. |

| INTERJECTION | **Well,** he seems healthy. |
| ADJECTIVE | He seems **well.** |

Review D Identifying Parts of Speech

Identify the part of speech of the italicized word in each sentence. Be prepared to explain your answers.

EXAMPLES
   1. The *ship* entered the harbor slowly.
   1. noun

   2. Did they *ship* the package to Dee and Seth?
   2. verb

1. The English test was easy *for* him.
2. He didn't go to the movies, *for* he wanted to practice on the drums.
3. It was a steep *climb,* but we made it to the top of the hill.
4. Kimiko and I *climb* the stairs for exercise.
5. *Some* volunteered to sell tickets.
6. We donated *some* clothes to the rummage sale.
7. Looking for shells, the girl strolled *along* the shore.
8. When we went sailing, Raúl and Manuel came *along.*
9. I lost *my* book report!
10. *My!* This is not a good day!

Review E Identifying Parts of Speech

Identify the part of speech of each italicized word or word group in the following paragraphs.

EXAMPLES
Dancing **[1]** *may be* easy for **[2]** *some,* but I have **[3]** *always* had **[4]** *two* left **[5]** *feet.*

   1. verb   *3. adverb*   *5. noun*
   2. pronoun *4. adjective*

  [1] *Yesterday* after **[2]** *school,* one of my friends **[3]** *tried* to teach **[4]** *me* some new dance steps. **[5]** *Well,* I was **[6]** *so* embarrassed I could have hidden **[7]** *in* the **[8]** *closet.* My feet **[9]** *seem* to have **[10]** *minds* of **[11]** *their* own **[12]** *and* do **[13]** *not* do what I want them to.

Determining Parts of Speech   **73**

┌HELP──
You may want to review Chapter 2 before working on Review D.

1. preposition
2. conjunction

3. noun
4. verb
5. pronoun
6. adjective
7. preposition
8. adverb
9. pronoun
10. interjection

┌HELP──
You may want to review Chapter 2 before working on Review E.

1. adverb	8. noun
2. noun	9. verb
3. verb	10. noun
4. pronoun	11. pron.
5. interjection	12. conj.
6. adverb	13. adverb
7. preposition	

DIFFERENTIATING INSTRUCTION

Learners Having Difficulty
Encourage students to play with the parts of speech in much the same way they would piece together the parts of a puzzle. Using colored construction paper, make six sets of word cards, one set each for nouns, pronouns, adjectives, verbs, adverbs, and prepositions. Each set of cards will be a different color. Ask students to take three word cards from each set and to create three complete sentences by stringing the parts of speech together appropriately. Students are free to use any extra words, as necessary, but they must make use of all the parts of speech that they select.

PRACTICE

Guided and Independent
You may wish to use **Review D** as guided practice. Then, have students complete **Review E** as independent practice.

HOMEWORK

T E A C H I N G TIP

Reviews D and E (See Note on p. 32.) *My* in sentence 9 of Review D and *their* in item 11 of Review E may be identified as adjectives.

14. adverb
15. conjunction
16. pronoun
17. verb
18. interjection
19. adverb
20. pronoun
21. verb
22. adverb
23. verb
24. adverb
25. adjective

"You're **[14]** *too* tense when you dance, **[15]** *or* you're trying too hard. **[16]** *You* **[17]** *should relax* more," my friend told me.

[18] "*What!* **[19]** *How* can I relax?" I groaned. **[20]** "*No one* **[21]** *can relax* when his body goes **[22]** *left* and his feet go right!" At that point, I **[23]** *decided* to give up dancing, but I know I'll try **[24]** *again* **[25]** *another* day.

Review F **Using Different Parts of Speech**

Complete the following poem by adding words that are the parts of speech called for in the blank spaces.

EXAMPLES   Why **[1]** (___verb___) Robin all alone?
[2] (___adverb___) have all the others gone?

1. Why sits Robin all alone?
2. Where have all the others gone?

[1] (interjection), Robin thought her day was just fine.
She **[2]** (___verb___) to the concert, and there wasn't a line.

Then when she got in **[3]** (conjunction) sat herself down,
People were leaving **[4]** (preposition) rows all around.

You can see that Robin looks **[5]** (___adverb___) dejected;
She thinks that she **[6]** (___verb___) rejected.

If only she could have the chairs as her friends—
[7] (interjection)!—she'd have friends without end.

She sat **[8]** (___adverb___) and worried and pondered.
Was the problem with her **[9]** (conjunction) the others? she wondered.

Then she **[10]** (___verb___) at her ticket and saw she was late,
So she imagined the concert, and it was just great!

Responses will vary. Here are some possibilities.
1. Well   6. has been
2. went   7. Hooray
3. and   8. there
4. from   9. or
5. extremely   10. looked

GRAMMAR

Numerals in brackets refer to rules tested by the items in the Chapter Review.

1. conj. [3d]
2. int. [3e]
3. l.v. [3a]
4. adv. [3b]
5. prep. [3c]
6. a.v. [3a]
7. adv. [3b]
8. prep. [3c]
9. prep. [3c]
10. a.v. [3a]
11. conj. [3d]
12. adv. [3b]
13. int. [3e]
14. a.v. [3a]
15. a.v. [3a]
16. prep. [3c]
17. l.v. [3a]
18. adv. [3b]
19. conj. [3d]
20. l.v. [3a]

Chapter Review

A. Identifying Verbs, Adverbs, Prepositions, Conjunctions, and Interjections

Label the underlined word or word group in each of the following sentences as an *action verb*, a *linking verb*, an *adverb*, a *preposition*, a *conjunction*, or an *interjection*.

1. Rosie hit a home run *and* tied up the score.
2. *Wow*, that's the best meal I've eaten in a long time!
3. School *can be* fun sometimes.
4. Neither Carlos nor Jan wanted to go *very* far into the water.
5. That dog looks mean *in spite of* his wagging tail.
6. *Have* you ever *celebrated* Cinco de Mayo?
7. If Ken will *not* help us finish the project, then he cannot share in the rewards.
8. My older sister was a cheerleader *during* her senior year.
9. The road that runs *near* the railroad tracks is usually crowded.
10. Several of my friends *enjoy* the music of Quincy Jones.
11. No one could do much to help, *for* the damage had already been done.
12. *Where* have you been putting the corrected papers?
13. *Oh*, I didn't know he had already volunteered.
14. Jodie *was taking* in the wash for her mother.
15. Surely Ms. Kwan *does*n't *expect* us to finish our art projects by today.
16. May I have a glass of milk and a club sandwich *without* onions?
17. James *became* impatient, but he waited quietly.
18. My uncle *always* brings us interesting presents when he visits during Hanukkah.
19. The car swerved suddenly to avoid the dog, *yet* the driver remained in control.
20. The rose *smells* lovely.

GRAMMAR

Monitoring Progress
Chapter Review. To assess student progress, you may want to compare the types of items missed on the **Diagnostic Preview** to those missed on the **Chapter Review**. You may want to work out specific goals for mastering essential information with individual students who are still having difficulty.

RESOURCES

Parts of Speech Overview
Review
■ *Language & Sentence Skills Practice,* pp. 64–66

Assessment
■ *Formal Assessment*
■ *Progress-Monitoring Tests,* pp. 5–6, 48
■ *Test Generator (Teacher One Stop DVD-ROM)*

┌HELP──

Keep in mind
that correlative conjunc-
tions and some preposi-
tions have more than
one word.

21. v./prep. [3f, a, c]
22. v./conj. [3f, a, d]
23. adv./conj. [3f, b, d]
24. adv./adv. [3f, b]
25. prep./v. [3f, c, a]
26. adv./prep. [3f, b, c]
27. conj. [3f, d]
28. adv./prep. [3f, b, c]
29. v. [3f, a]
30. adv./v. [3f, b, a]

┌HELP──

You may want
to review Chapter 2 before
working on Part C.

31. pro. [3f, 2h]
32. adj. [3f, 2p]
33. conj. [3f, d]
34. prep. [3f, c]
35. noun [3f, 2a]
36. verb [3f, a]

B. Identifying Different Parts of Speech

Identify each <u>italicized word or word group</u> in the following sentences as a *verb*, an *adverb*, a *preposition*, or a *conjunction*.

21. I *read* an interesting article *about* the great Italian composer Giuseppe Verdi.

22. Born near Parma in 1813, the son of a grocer, he *studied* music locally *but* was rejected by the prestigious Milan Conservatory.

23. *Bravely*, he persevered, *and* when he was twenty-six, his first opera was accepted by the famous La Scala opera house.

24. *Shortly* afterward, personal tragedy hit him hard, and he *nearly* gave up.

25. The success *of* his next opera, <u>Nabucco</u>, *inspired* him to continue.

26. Verdi, an Italian patriot, *soon* became a symbol of Italy's struggle *for* unity.

27. He was admired *not only* for his operas, *but also* for his political career.

28. In fact, he was *eventually* elected a senator *in* the new parliament of united Italy.

29. At the same time, he *was becoming* famous for operatic masterpieces such as <u>La Traviata</u>, <u>Rigoletto</u>, and <u>Aida</u>.

30. Giuseppe Verdi was *so* admired by his fellow Italians that a period of national mourning *was declared* following his death in 1901.

C. Identifying Parts of Speech

Identify the part of speech of the <u>italicized word</u> in each sentence. Be prepared to explain your answers.

31. *Some* even made it to the top before noon.

32. They bought *some* tomatoes and peppers in the market.

33. The lion cubs waited their turn, *for* an adult lion was drinking at the water hole.

34. These large tires are made especially *for* that kind of mountain bicycle.

35. Every morning, Fran goes out for a *run*.

36. My doctor recommended that I *run* in moderation.

37. I wanted to nap, _so_ I went home early.

38. The dogs were _so_ excited that one of them knocked over the coat rack.

39. I enjoyed walking _along_ Ipanema Beach in Rio.

40. Come _along_; it's time to go!

Writing Application
Using Verbs in a Story

Action Verbs   Your little sister likes for you to tell her exciting stories, but you've run out of new ones. To get ideas for new stories, you think about events you've read about or seen. Write a summary of an exciting incident from a book, a movie, or a television show. Use action verbs that are fresh and lively.

Prewriting   Think about books that you've read recently or movies and television shows that you've seen. Choose an exciting incident from one of these works, and write what you remember about that incident.

Writing   As you write your first draft, think about how you're presenting the information. When telling a story, you should usually use chronological order. This method would be easiest for your young reader to follow. Try to use fresh, lively action verbs.

Revising   Imagine that you are a young child hearing the story for the first time. Look over your summary, and ask yourself if the verbs used in the story would help you picture what happened.

Publishing   Make sure that each verb you use is in the correct form and tense. Also, check to make sure that any pronouns, conjunctions, adverbs, and interjections are used correctly. Proofread your story for errors in usage, spelling, and punctuation. Then, with your teacher's permission, share your story with the class by reading it aloud or posting the completed story on a class bulletin board.

37. conj. [3f, d]
38. adv. [3f, b]
39. prep. [3f, c]
40. adv. [3f, b]

4 Complements
Direct and Indirect Objects, Subject Complements

Numerals in brackets refer to rules tested by the items in the Diagnostic Preview.

1. i.o. [4c]
2. d.o. [4b]
3. p.a. [4f]
4. p.n. [4e]
5. d.o. [4b]
6. p.n. [4e]
7. d.o. [4b]
8. p.a. [4f]
9. i.o. [4c]
10. d.o. [4b]
11. p.n. [4e]
12. p.a. [4f]
13. p.n. [4e]
14. p.n. [4e]
15. d.o. [4b]

Diagnostic Preview

Identifying Complements

Identify each italicized word in the following paragraphs as a *direct object*, an *indirect object*, a *predicate nominative*, or a *predicate adjective*.

EXAMPLES   I enjoy [1] *cooking*, but it can be hard [2] *work*.

1. cooking—direct object
2. work—predicate nominative

My dad has been giving [1] *me* cooking [2] *lessons* since last summer. At first, I was [3] *reluctant* to tell the guys because some of them think that cooking is a girl's [4] *job*. Dad told me to remind them that we guys eat [5] *meals* just as often as girls do. He also said that cooking is an excellent [6] *way* for us to do our share of the work around the house.

When I began, I could hardly boil [7] *water* without fouling up, but Dad remained [8] *patient* and showed [9] *me* the correct and easiest ways to do things. For example, did you know that water will boil faster if it has a little [10] *salt* in it or that cornstarch can be an excellent thickening [11] *agent* in everything from batter to gravy?

My first attempts tasted [12] *awful*, but gradually I've become a fairly good [13] *cook*. My best main dish is chicken [14] *stew*. Although stew doesn't require the highest [15] *grade* of chicken, a good baking hen will give [**16**] *it* a much better taste. I am always very [**17**] *careful* about choosing the vegetables, too. Maybe I am too [**18**] *picky,* but I use only the best [**19**] *ingredients.* I know, though, that when I serve my [**20**] *family* my stew, they say it is their favorite dish.

16. i.o. [4c]
17. p.a. [4f]
18. p.a. [4f]
19. d.o. [4b]
20. i.o. [4c]

Recognizing Complements

4a. A ***complement*** is a word or a word group that completes the meaning of a verb.

Every sentence has at least one subject and verb. Often a verb also needs a complement to make the sentence complete.

	S	V	
INCOMPLETE	Marlene	brought	[*what?*]

	S	V	C
COMPLETE	Marlene	brought	**sandwiches.**

	S	V	
INCOMPLETE	Carlos	thanked	[*whom?*]

	S	V	C
COMPLETE	Carlos	thanked	**her.**

	S	V	
INCOMPLETE	We	were	[*what?*]

	S	V	C
COMPLETE	We	were	**hungry.**

As you can see, a complement may be a noun, a pronoun, or an adjective.

EXAMPLES   My uncle sent **me** a **postcard.** [The pronoun *me* and the noun *postcard* complete the meaning of the verb by telling *what* was sent and *to whom* it was sent.]

The Ephron sisters are **writers.** [The noun *writers* completes the meaning of the verb *are* by identifying the sisters.]

This story is **exciting.** [The adjective *exciting* completes the meaning of the verb *is* by describing the story.]

Recognizing Complements   79

■ The chapter closes with a **Chapter Review** including a **Writing Application** feature that asks students to use direct objects and indirect objects in a personal letter.

■ For help in integrating this chapter with writing assignments in *Holt Literature and Language Arts,* use the **Teaching Strands** chart on pp. T24–T25.

ASSESSING

Entry-Level Assessment
Diagnostic Preview. You could use the **Diagnostic Preview** to determine the amount of study students need on complements. If students do well on the preview, have them move through the chapter quickly, perhaps working only the Review exercises.

Recognizing Complements
Rule 4a (*pp. 79–81*)

OBJECTIVES

■ **To identify subjects, verbs, and complements in sentences**

■ **To write sentences containing complements**

Assessment

■ *Formal Assessment*
■ *Progress-Monitoring Tests,* pp. 7–8, 48
■ *Test Generator*
  (Teacher One Stop DVD-ROM)

Other Language Resources

■ *Spelling Lessons & Activities*
■ *WordSharp: An Interactive Vocabulary Tutor*
■ *Reading and Writing Transparencies*

Lesson Starter

Motivating. Challenge students with the following puzzle: Can you change the word *complement* to the word *complete* in three moves? A move consists of either (1) removing a letter or (2) changing the position of a letter. Have students write the word *complement* on a piece of paper and try to solve the puzzle. [*Three moves are* 1. *remove the second* m, 2. *remove the* n, *and* 3. *move the* t *to between the two* e's.] Point out to students that a complement *completes* the meaning of a verb.

DIFFERENTIATING INSTRUCTION

Learners Having Difficulty

To provide students help in completing **Exercise 1,** list the following steps on the chalkboard, and suggest that students follow this sequence in analyzing each sentence in the exercise.

1. Delete the prepositional phrases (as a reminder that essential sentence parts cannot be within prepositional phrases).
2. Locate the verb.
3. Find the subject.
4. Find the word that completes the meaning of the verb.

Reference Note

For information on **adverbs,** see page 61. For information on **prepositional phrases,** see page 68.

TIPS & TRICKS

If you have trouble finding the complement in a sentence, try this trick. Cross out all the prepositional phrases first. Then, look for the subject, verb, and complement in the rest of the sentence.

EXAMPLE

Juanita wrote the letter ~~on a sheet of plain notebook paper.~~ [The subject is *Juanita.* The verb is *wrote. Sheet* and *paper* cannot be complements because they are both in prepositional phrases. The complement is *letter.*]

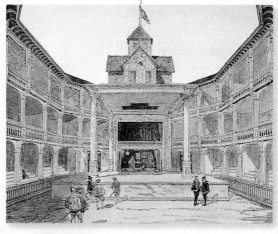

The Granger Collection, New York

An adverb is never a complement.

| ADVERB | The dog is **outside.** [*Outside* modifies the verb by telling where the dog is.] |
| COMPLEMENT | The dog is **friendly.** [The adjective *friendly* modifies the subject by telling what kind of dog.] |

A complement is never part of a prepositional phrase.

| OBJECT OF PREPOSITION | Ben is studying for his geography **test.** [*Test* is the object of the preposition *for.*] |
| COMPLEMENT | Ben is studying his geography **notes.** |

Exercise 1 Identifying Subjects, Verbs, and Complements

Identify the subject, verb, and complement in each of the following sentences.

EXAMPLE
1. William Shakespeare was one of the owners of the Globe Theatre.

1. *William Shakespeare—subject; was—verb; one—complement*

1. During Shakespeare's time, plays were a common form of entertainment in England.
2. A great many people watched plays at the most popular playhouse in London—the Globe Theatre.
3. Richard and Cuthbert Burbage built the Globe in 1599.
4. In this drawing, you can see many of the differences between the Globe and most modern theaters.
5. The Globe Theatre was a building with eight sides.
6. The building enclosed a spacious inner courtyard.
7. The stage was a raised platform at one end of the courtyard.
8. Some of the audience watched the play from seats around the courtyard.
9. Many playgoers, however, did not have seats during a performance.
10. These people filled the courtyard in front of the stage.

Recognizing Complements
Practice
- *Language & Sentence Skills Practice,* p. 71
- *Developmental Language & Sentence Skills,* pp. 29–30

Oral Practice Creating Sentences with Complements

Create ten different sentences aloud by adding a different complement, along with other necessary words, to each of the following subject-verb pairs.

	Subject	Verb
EXAMPLE	**1.** kittens	like

1. *The kittens like cream.*

	Subject	Verb
1.	men	asked
2.	days	are
3.	Pam	sent
4.	runner	seemed
5.	weather	will be
6.	girls	climbed
7.	letter	contained
8.	elephant	is
9.	neighbors	kept
10.	dog	wants

Objects of Verbs

Direct objects and *indirect objects* complete the meaning of transitive verbs.

Direct Objects

4b. A *direct object* is a noun, pronoun, or word group that tells who or what receives the action of the verb.

A direct object answers the question "Whom?" or "What?" after a transitive verb.

EXAMPLES   Our history class built a **model** of the Alamo. [The noun *model* receives the action of the verb *built* and tells *what* the class built.]

Has the freeze destroyed **some** of the crop? [The pronoun *some* receives the action of the verb *Has destroyed* and tells *what* the freeze has destroyed.]

Mr. Ito greets **whoever comes into the shop.** [The noun clause *whoever comes into the shop* receives the action of the verb *greets* and tells *whom* Mr. Ito greets.]

Reference Note

For more information about **transitive verbs,** see page 59.

┌HELP─

To find the direct object in a sentence, say the verb and then ask "What?" or "Whom?"

EXAMPLE
In his free time, Eduardo writes mystery stories. [Writes what? Stories.] *Stories* is the direct object.

Reference Note

For more about **noun clauses,** see page 130.

Objects of Verbs   **81**

RESOURCES

Objects of Verbs

Practice

■ *Language & Sentence Skills Practice,* pp. 72–75
■ *Developmental Language & Sentence Skills,* pp. 31–32

Oral Practice Creating Sentences with Complements

ANSWERS
Sentences will vary. You may want to have students identify each complement as a noun, a pronoun, or an adjective.

Objects of Verbs

Rules 4b, c *(pp. 81–85)*

OBJECTIVES

■ **To identify verbs and their direct objects in sentences**

■ **To identify direct objects and indirect objects in sentences**

RETEACHING

Direct Objects

Write the following sentences on the chalkboard.

1. Sylvia bought a new _____.

2. The baseball player hit the _____.

Have students fill in the blanks; then, tell them they have added direct objects. Next, ask students to locate the verb in each sentence. [*bought, hit*] Ask them what question the direct object answers. [*what*] Point out that the direct object answers the question *What?* or *Whom?* after a transitive verb.

APPLICATION

Direct Objects

Activity. Many figurative uses of language start out as fresh, colorful phrases but become clichés through overuse. The following clichés contain direct objects. Have students replace these tired expressions with original sentences that describe the same ideas and that contain direct objects.

1. The early bird gets the worm.

2. Keep your nose to the grindstone.

3. Make hay while the sun shines.

TEACHING TIP

Exercise 2 To prepare students for items 5, 7, and 10 in **Exercise 2,** you may want to guide students through the process of finding the verbs and complements in interrogative sentences. Remind students to turn a question into a statement before they attempt to analyze it.

Reference Note
For more about **linking verbs,** see page 54.

Reference Note
For more information about **prepositional phrases,** see page 68.

─HELP─
One sentence in Exercise 2 contains a compound direct object.

NOTE A direct object can never complete the meaning of a linking verb because a linking verb does not express action.

LINKING VERB   William Wordsworth **became** poet laureate of England in 1843. [The verb *became* does not express action. Therefore, it has no direct object.]

A direct object is never part of a prepositional phrase.

EXAMPLE   He walked for hours in the English countryside. [*Hours* is not a direct object of the verb *walked*. It is the object of the preposition *for*. *Countryside* is not a direct object either. It is the object of the preposition *in*. The sentence has no direct object.]

NOTE A direct object may be compound.

EXAMPLES   Mrs. Neiman planted **tulips** and **daffodils.**

The man wore a white **beard,** a red **suit,** and black **boots.**

Exercise 2 **Identifying Verbs and Direct Objects**

Identify the verb and its direct object in each of the following sentences.

EXAMPLE   1. Volunteers distributed food and water to the flood victims.

1. *distributed—food, water*

1. On the plains of the American West, the Cheyenne hunted buffalo for food and clothing.

2. We watched a performance of Lorraine Hansberry's *A Raisin in the Sun.*

3. During most of its history, the United States has welcomed refugees from other countries.

4. The leading man wore a hat with a large plume.

5. Are you recycling bottles and cans?

6. After the game, the coach answered questions from the sports reporters.

7. Did you see her performance on television?

8. The researchers followed the birds' migration from Mexico to Canada.

MINI-LESSON   Usage

Objective Case. Discuss pronoun case with students, and explain that pronouns used as direct or indirect objects are in the objective case. Write the following list of objective case pronouns on the chalkboard, and review them with students.

me	us
you	you
him, her, it	them

Then, read the following sentences aloud, asking students to fill in the blanks with

9. Mayor Fiorello La Guardia <u>governed</u> <u>New York City</u> during the Depression.
10. <u>Have</u> the movie theaters <u>announced</u> the special <u>discount</u> for teenagers yet?

Indirect Objects

4c. An *indirect object* is a noun, pronoun, or word group that sometimes appears in sentences containing direct objects.

An indirect object tells *to whom* or *to what* or *for whom* or *for what* the action of the verb is done.

EXAMPLES   Luke showed the **class** his collection of comic books. [The noun *class* tells *to whom* Luke showed his collection.]

  Sarita bought **us** a chess set. [The pronoun *us* tells *for whom* Sarita bought a chess set.]

  Dad gave **whatever needed fixing** his full attention. [The noun clause *whatever needed fixing* tells *to what* Dad gave his attention.]

NOTE Linking verbs do not have indirect objects.

LINKING VERB   Her mother **was** a collector of rare books. [The linking verb *was* does not express action, so it cannot have an indirect object.]

    An indirect object, like a direct object, is never in a prepositional phrase. A noun or pronoun that follows *to* or *for* is the object of the preposition, not an indirect object.

OBJECT OF PREPOSITION   He gave some flowers to his **sister.** [*Sister* is the object of the preposition *to.*]

INDIRECT OBJECT   He gave his **sister** some flowers.

NOTE Like a direct object, an indirect object may be compound.

EXAMPLES   Uncle Alphonso bought my **brother** and **me** an aquarium.

  Tanya sent **Kim, Raymond,** and **him** invitations.

TIPS & TRICKS

A sentence with an indirect object will always have a direct object, too. What are the direct objects in the examples following Rule 4c? collection, set, attention

Reference Note

For more about **noun clauses,** see page 130.

HELP

An indirect object usually comes between a verb and a direct object.

Objects of Verbs   **83**

DIFFERENTIATING INSTRUCTION

GRAMMAR

Learners Having Difficulty

Some students might find it helpful to have a visual representation of the kinds of questions answered by direct and indirect objects. Using a chart like the following one, ask students to supply the questions under each heading.

DIRECT OBJECT	INDIRECT OBJECT
[whom?	[to what?
what?]	to whom?
	for what?
	for whom?]

Special Education Students

Some students might more easily recognize direct and indirect objects by hearing them rather than seeing them. You may want to place students in small groups and have members take turns reading aloud the sentences in the examples and in the exercises.

DIRECT TEACHING

Modeling and Demonstration

Direct Objects and Indirect Objects. Model how to identify direct objects and indirect objects by using the example *He gave his sister some flowers.* First, have students identify the subject and verb. [*He—subject; gave—verb*] Next, ask whether the subject and verb express a complete thought by themselves. [*no*] Then, ask what he gave. [*flowers*] Explain that *flowers* is the direct object of the verb. Finally, ask to whom the flowers were given. [*sister*] *Sister* is the indirect object of the verb. Now, have a volunteer use another example from this chapter to demonstrate how to identify direct and indirect objects.

appropriate objective case pronouns. Have students tell whether the pronoun is used as a direct object or an indirect object.

1. Did Vanessa show _____ the cards? [*indirect object*]

2. Dad drove _____ to the game. [*direct object*]

3. Leroy lent Sara that book, but she has already returned _____. [*direct object*]

Objects of Verbs   **83**

DIRECT TEACHING

Correcting Misconceptions

Indirect Objects and Objects of Prepositions. Students may be confused by the difference between indirect objects and objects of prepositions. Write these two sentences on the chalkboard.

Bob gave him the message.
Bob gave the message to him.

Tell students that in the first sentence, *him* is an indirect object of the verb *gave*. Tell them that in the second sentence, *him* is part of the prepositional phrase *to him*. Remind students that if a noun or a pronoun is part of a prepositional phrase, that noun or pronoun cannot be an indirect object.

PRACTICE

Guided and Independent

You may wish to use **Exercise 3** as guided practice. Then, have students complete **Review A** as independent practice. **HOMEWORK**

DIFFERENTIATING INSTRUCTION

Learners Having Difficulty

Some students may find it motivating to work on the chalkboard to mark direct objects and indirect objects. Write the following sentences on the chalkboard, and ask students to draw arrows from the verbs to the direct objects and to circle the indirect objects.

1. She wrote (me) a letter.

2. He gave his (dog) a bone.

3. Tom brought (us) the newspaper.

4. Sue sang her (sister) a lullaby.

HELP—

Not every sentence in Exercise 3 has an indirect object.

HELP—

Not every sentence in Review A has an indirect object.

CLYDE BURK

Exercise 3 Identifying Direct Objects and Indirect Objects

Identify the <u>direct objects</u> and the <u>indirect objects</u> in the following sentences.

EXAMPLE   1. They gave us their solemn promise.
          1. *promise—direct object; us—indirect object*

1. They sent <u>me</u> on a wild-goose chase.
2. Gloria mailed the <u>company</u> a <u>check</u> yesterday.
3. The speaker showed the <u>audience</u> the <u>slides</u> of Zimbabwe.
4. Juan would not deliberately tell <u>you</u> and <u>me</u> a lie.
5. The coach praised the <u>students</u> for their school spirit.
6. I sent my <u>cousins</u> some embroidered <u>pillows</u> for their new apartment in New York.
7. The art teacher displayed the students' <u>paintings</u>.
8. Sue's parents shipped <u>her</u> the <u>books</u> and the <u>magazines</u>.
9. Carly, Mary Ellen, and Doreen taught <u>themselves</u> the <u>importance</u> of hard work.
10. In most foreign countries, United States citizens must carry their <u>passports</u> for identification.

Review A Identifying Direct Objects and Indirect Objects

Identify the <u>direct objects</u> and the <u>indirect objects</u> in each of the following sentences.

EXAMPLE   1. The spring rodeo gives our town an exciting weekend.
          1. *weekend—direct object; town—indirect object*

1. This year Mrs. Perez taught our <u>class</u> many interesting facts about rodeos.
2. She told <u>us</u> <u>stories</u> about the earliest rodeos, which were held more than a hundred years ago.
3. The word *rodeo* means "roundup" in Spanish.
4. Mrs. Perez also showed <u>us</u> <u>drawings</u> and <u>pictures</u> of some well-known rodeo performers.
5. The Choctaw roper Clyde Burk especially caught the <u>interest</u> of our class.
6. The Rodeo Cowboys Association awarded <u>Burk</u> four world <u>championships</u> during his career.
7. For years, Burk entertained <u>audiences</u> with his roping skill.

84   Chapter 4   Complements

8. He also trained <u>some</u> of the best rodeo horses available.
9. The picture on the previous page shows <u>Clyde Burk</u> on his horse Baldy.
10. Burk often gave <u>Baldy</u> <u>credit</u> for their success.

Subject Complements

4d. A *subject complement* is a word or word group that completes the meaning of a linking verb and that identifies or describes the subject.

EXAMPLES   Alice Eng is a dedicated **teacher.** [The noun *teacher* completes the meaning of the linking verb *is* and identifies the subject *Alice Eng.*]

The lemonade tastes **sour.** [*Sour* completes the meaning of the linking verb *tastes* and describes the subject *lemonade.*]

The new pliers were **what she wanted.** [The noun clause *what she wanted* completes the meaning of the linking verb *were* and identifies the subject *pliers.*]

There are two kinds of subject complements—the *predicate nominative* and the *predicate adjective.*

Predicate Nominatives

4e. A *predicate nominative* is a word or word group that is in the predicate and that identifies the subject or refers to it.

A predicate nominative may be a noun, a pronoun, or a word group that functions as a noun. A predicate nominative completes the meaning of a linking verb.

EXAMPLES   Mr. Richards became **mayor** of a small town in Ohio. [The noun *mayor* identifies the subject *Mr. Richards.*]

My aunt's niece is **she.** [The pronoun *she* identifies *niece.*]

Is the winner **whoever gets the most votes**? [The noun clause *whoever gets the most votes* identifies the subject *winner.*]

Reference Note
For more about **linking verbs,** see page 54.

Reference Note
For more about **noun clauses,** see page 130.

┌─────────────────────┐
│ TIPS & TRICKS │
└─────────────────────┘
To find the subject complement in an interrogative sentence, rearrange the sentence to make a statement.

EXAMPLE
Was the dog muddy?
The dog was **muddy.**

To find the subject complement in an imperative sentence, insert the understood subject *you.*

EXAMPLE
Stay still.
(You) stay **still.**

Subject Complements   85

Subject Complements
Rules 4d–f *(pp. 85–90)*

OBJECTIVES

■ To identify predicate nominatives in sentences

■ To identify predicate adjectives in sentences

DIRECT TEACHING

Modeling and Demonstration

Identifying Subject Complements. Model how to identify a subject complement by using the example *Hernando de Soto was a soldier and a diplomat.* First, ask students to identify the subject. [*Hernando de Soto*] Next, ask them to identify the complete predicate. [*was a soldier and a diplomat*] Then, ask whether there is a word or word group in the predicate that identifies or describes Hernando de Soto. [*soldier; diplomat*] Explain that both *soldier* and *diplomat* are subject complements. Now, have a volunteer use another example from this chapter to demonstrate how to identify subject complements.

┌──────────────────────────────┐
│ **RESOURCES** │

Subject Complements
Practice
■ *Language & Sentence Skills Practice,* pp. 76–83
■ *Developmental Language & Sentence Skills,* pp. 33–36
└──────────────────────────────┘

Correcting Misconceptions
Nominative Case Pronouns.
Students may not be aware that formal English requires that nominative case pronouns (**Chapter 10,** pp. 216–220) be used after linking verbs (for example, "This is *she*" rather than "This is *her*"). Ask pairs of students to practice using as many of these constructions as possible in dialogues. Encourage creativity and humor. Ask volunteers to perform their dialogues for the class.

Exercise 4

DISTRIBUTED REVIEW
Have students review prepositions by finding the prepositions and their objects in sentences 2, 4, and 5.
[*2. Through—germination; 4. for—people; 5. With—light, moisture*]

Predicate nominatives do not appear in prepositional phrases.

EXAMPLE   **Sophia is one of my closest friends.** [*One* is the predicate nominative. *Friends* is the object of the preposition *of,* not the predicate nominative.]

NOTE   Predicate nominatives may be compound.

EXAMPLE   Hernando de Soto was a **soldier** and a **diplomat.**

Exercise 4 Identifying Predicate Nominatives

Identify the <u>predicate nominatives</u> in each of the following sentences.

EXAMPLE   **1.** Botany, a branch of biology, is the study of plants.
            1. study

1. Horticulture is the <u>art</u> or <u>science</u> of growing flowers, fruits, vegetables, and other plants.
2. Through germination, a seed becomes a <u>plant</u>.
3. The developing plant is a <u>seedling</u>.
4. Growing plants is a <u>pleasure</u> for many people.
5. With light and moisture, seedlings will become healthy <u>plants</u>.
6. Nasturtiums are <u>flowers</u> that can be eaten.
7. Rain is a welcome <u>sight</u> for gardeners.
8. *Helio,* from the Greek language, is a <u>word</u> meaning "sun."
9. Some flowers that turn to the sun, like sunflowers, are <u>heliotropes</u>.
10. Some other flowers always remain shade <u>lovers</u>.

CONTENT-AREA CONNECTIONS

Social Studies
Complements. Give small groups copies of a historical document written in formal English, such as the *Federalist Papers.* Have each group analyze a specific passage from the document, underlining the verbs, circling the complements, and then classifying the complements as direct or indirect objects, predicate nominatives, or predicate adjectives. Let groups report on the number of each type of complement identified. Discuss the characteristics of the document's writing style with students.

Predicate Adjectives

4f. A *predicate adjective* is an adjective that is in the predicate and that describes the subject.

A predicate adjective completes the meaning of a linking verb.

EXAMPLES   A nuclear reactor is very **powerful.** [The adjective *powerful* completes the meaning of the linking verb *is* and describes the subject *reactor.*]

This chili tastes **spicy.** [The adjective *spicy* completes the meaning of the linking verb *tastes* and describes the subject *chili.*]

How **cheerful** the baby is! [The adjective *cheerful* completes the meaning of the verb *is* and describes the subject *baby.*]

NOTE   Predicate adjectives may be compound.

EXAMPLE   A computer can be **fun, helpful,** and sometimes **frustrating.**

Exercise 5   Identifying Predicate Adjectives

Identify the predicate adjective or adjectives in each of the following sentences.

EXAMPLE   1. San Francisco's Chinatown is large and colorful.
         1. *large, colorful*

1. The great stone dogs that guard the entrance to Chinatown look a bit frightening.
2. The streets there are crowded and full of bustling activity.
3. The special foods and beverages at the tearooms and restaurants smell wonderful.
4. To an outsider, the mixture of Chinese and English languages can sound both mysterious and intriguing.
5. The art at the Chinese Culture Center is impressive.
6. The Chinese Historical Society of America is fascinating.
7. Taking a walking tour of Chinatown is tiring.
8. Chinatown appears huge, and it is; it covers about sixteen square blocks.
9. To be in the midst of it feels exciting.
10. After a while, the surroundings become familiar.

STYLE TIP

Overusing the linking verb *be* can make writing dull and lifeless. As you review your writing, you may get the feeling that nothing is happening, that nobody is doing anything. That feeling is one sign that your writing may contain too many *be* verbs. Wherever possible, replace a dull *be* verb with a verb that expresses action.

BE VERB
   A secret hope **was** in his heart.

ACTION VERB
   A secret hope **surged** in his heart.

GRAMMAR

DIFFERENTIATING INSTRUCTION

English-Language Learners

Vietnamese. Vietnamese rarely uses the equivalent of the English verb *be.* Therefore, Vietnamese speakers sometimes drop forms of *be* in sentences having subject complements: *I very tired.* Because the verb *be* is often contracted in conversation, it is especially difficult to hear. Model correct forms of *be,* and provide practice for students.
Teacher: I'm hungry. Are you?
Student: Yes, I'm hungry, too.
Teacher: Is Emily hungry?
Student: Yes, she's hungry.

EXTENSION

Relating to Writing

Have students write an autobiographical paragraph using each type of complement—direct object, indirect object, predicate nominative, and predicate adjective. Students' paragraphs might include information about their families; their favorite music, sports, or books; and their goals. Remind students to include information they would not mind sharing in class.

TECHNOLOGY TIP

Give students practice identifying complements while familiarizing them with word-processing formatting options. When students revise their autobiographical paragraphs (see **Relating to Writing,** above), suggest that they double-space, add one-inch margins, and underline verbs. Students could then label verbs and complements by writing the following abbreviations in the spaces above the words: *AV* (action verb), *LV* (linking verb), *DO* (direct object), *IO* (indirect object), *PN* (predicate nominative), *PA* (predicate adjective).

DIFFERENTIATING INSTRUCTION

Advanced Learners

Have students form groups of three or four. Explain to students that they will take turns composing sentences with complements. The first person will create a sentence with a direct object, for example, *James ate a sandwich.* The second person will create a new sentence using that complement as a subject and introducing a new complement, this one a predicate adjective, for example, *The sandwich was delicious.* In the next sentence, because an adjective cannot be the subject of a sentence, the third member must use the complement to modify a new subject, for example, *The delicious juice is sweet.*

If a student creates a sentence such as "The sweet kitten scratched me," the object pronoun (*me*) becomes a subject (*I*), and the next sentence could be "I play soccer."

Allow time for each group to complete several rounds of the game.

MEETING THE CHALLENGE

A **mnemonic** is a visual cue, rhyme, or other device that people use to help themselves remember something. For instance, the rhyme "*i* before *e*, except after *c*" is a mnemonic.

Create a mnemonic device to help your classmates remember the different kinds of complements covered in this chapter.

ANSWER
Mnemonics will vary but should cover each kind of complement.

Some verbs, such as *look, grow,* and *feel,* may be used as either linking verbs or action verbs.

LINKING VERB	The gardener **grew** tired. [*Grew* is a linking verb; it links the predicate adjective *tired* to the subject *gardener.*]
ACTION VERB	The gardener **grew** carrots. [*Grew* is an action verb; it is followed by the direct object *carrots,* which tells what the gardener grew.]

Review B · Identifying Linking Verbs and Subject Complements

Identify the <u>linking verb</u> and the <u>subject complement</u> in each of the following sentences. Then, identify each complement as a *predicate nominative* or a *predicate adjective.*

EXAMPLE   1. The raincoat looked too short for me.

     1. *looked; short—predicate adjective*

1. The package from Aunt Janice <u>felt light</u>.   **1.** p.a.
2. I <u>am</u> the <u>one</u> who called you yesterday.   **2.** p.n.
3. Many public buildings in the East <u>are proof</u> of I. M. Pei's architectural skill.   **3.** p.n.
4. The downtown mall <u>appeared</u> especially <u>busy</u> today.   **4.** p.a.
5. Sally Ride <u>sounded excited</u> and <u>confident</u> during the television interview.   **5.** p.a.
6. The actress playing the lead <u>is she</u>.   **6.** p.n.
7. These questions <u>seem easier</u> to me than the ones on the last two tests.   **7.** p.a.
8. The singer's clothing <u>became a symbol</u> that her fans imitated.   **8.** p.n.
9. Some poems, such as "The Bells" and "The Raven," <u>are</u> delightfully <u>rhythmical</u>.   **9.** p.a.
10. While the mountain lion looked around for food, the fawn <u>remained</u> perfectly <u>still</u>.   **10.** p.a.

Review C · Identifying Subject Complements

Each of the following sentences has at least one subject complement. Identify each complement as a *predicate nominative* or a *predicate adjective.*

EXAMPLE   1. All the food at the Spanish Club dinner was terrific.

     1. *terrific—predicate adjective*

Learning for Life

Writing a Letter of Inquiry. Ask students to write a letter or an e-mail message asking for information about a subject that interests them. Remind students that to get the information they want, they must make their letter specific and clear. Encourage them to use direct objects, indirect objects, predicate nominatives, and predicate adjectives that are precise and that help make the request clear to the reader.

As a prewriting activity, you might have students make a list of topics about which

1. Of the Mexican foods brought to the dinner, the tacos and Juan's fajitas were the most popular <u>dishes</u>.
2. The *ensalada campesina,* or peasant salad of Chile, which contained chickpeas, was Rosalinda's <u>contribution</u>.
3. The Ecuadorean tamales not only looked <u>good</u> but also tasted <u>great</u>.
4. The baked fish fillets from Bolivia were <u>spicy</u> and quite <u>appetizing</u>.
5. Peru is <u>famous</u> for its soups, and the shrimp soup was a <u>winner</u>.
6. The noodles with mushroom sauce are a <u>specialty</u> of Paraguay.
7. The Spanish cauliflower with garlic and onions was a <u>treat</u> but seemed too <u>exotic</u> for some students.
8. However, the pan of *hallacas,* the national cornmeal dish of Venezuela, was soon <u>empty</u>.
9. *Arroz con coco,* or coconut rice, from Puerto Rico quickly became the most requested <u>dessert</u>.
10. After dinner, all of us certainly felt <u>full</u> and much more <u>knowledgeable</u> about foods from Spanish-speaking countries.

Review D **Identifying Complements**

For each of the following sentences, identify each italicized complement as a *direct object,* an *indirect object,* a *predicate nominative,* or a *predicate adjective.*

EXAMPLE   **1.** Because they want artistic *freedom,* many people from other countries become United States *citizens.*

　　　　　 1. freedom—direct object; citizens—predicate nominative

1. Gilberto Zaldivar's story is a good *example.*　**1.** p.n.
2. Zaldivar was an *accountant* and a community theater *producer* in Havana, Cuba, in 1961.　**2.** p.n./p.n.
3. He became *unhappy* and *frustrated* with the Cuban government's control over the arts.　**3.** p.a./p.a.
4. He left his *job* and his *homeland* and started a new *life* in New York City.　**4.** d.o./d.o./d.o.
5. The change brought *Zaldivar* many *opportunities.*　**5.** i.o./d.o.
6. It also gave *audiences* in the United States a new entertainment *experience.*　**6.** i.o./d.o.

Subject Complements　**89**

Review E Writing Sentences with Complements

POSSIBLE ANSWERS

1. Yesterday I sold the <u>car</u>.

2. All of the members of the team were fifteen-year-old <u>girls</u>.

3. Was the apple <u>ripe</u>?

4. Hand <u>me</u> the <u>papers</u> now.

5. José slid into third base.

6. Grandmother sent <u>Myra</u> and <u>Toni</u> a <u>gift</u>.

7. Ms. Griffin is a <u>teacher</u> and <u>coach</u>.

8. Feed the <u>dog</u> and the <u>parakeet</u>.

9. The peaches tasted <u>sweet</u> and <u>juicy</u>.

10. Joy placed the <u>photo</u>, the <u>candle</u>, and a small <u>mirror</u> on the shelf.

---

7. p.n.

7. Zaldivar was a *cofounder* of the Repertorio Español in 1968.

8. This company quickly established a *reputation* as the country's best Spanish-language theater troupe. **8.** d.o. **9.** p.a./p.a.

9. Their productions were *fresh* and *unfamiliar* to audiences.

10. Throughout the years, the company has performed numerous Spanish *classics* as well as new plays. **10.** d.o.

Review E Writing Sentences with Complements

Write sentences according to the following guidelines. Underline each direct object, indirect object, predicate nominative, or predicate adjective that you write.

EXAMPLE **1.** Write a sentence with a three-part compound predicate adjective.

    1. The fire is <u>warm</u>, <u>cheery</u>, and <u>fragrant</u>.

1. Write a sentence with a direct object.

2. Write a sentence with a predicate nominative.

3. Write a sentence with a predicate adjective.

4. Write a sentence with an indirect object and a direct object.

5. Write a sentence without a complement.

6. Write a sentence with a compound indirect object and a direct object.

7. Write a sentence with a compound predicate nominative.

8. Write a sentence with a compound direct object.

9. Write a sentence with a compound predicate adjective.

10. Write a sentence with a three-part compound direct object.

Chapter Review

Numerals in brackets refer to rules tested by the items in the Chapter Review.

1. [4a, c, b]
2. [4a, b]
3. [4a, b]
4. [4a, b]
5. [4a, c, b]
6. [4a, b]
7. [4a, b, c]
8. [4a, c, b]
9. [4a, b]
10. [4a, b, c]

A. Identifying Direct Objects and Indirect Objects

Identify the <u>direct objects</u> and the <u>indirect objects</u> in the following sentences.

1. The coach awarded <u>her</u> a varsity <u>letter</u>.

2. My pen pal from Guatemala visited <u>me</u> last summer.

3. Did you hear the <u>news</u>?

4. The car stalled, and we couldn't restart <u>it</u>.

5. Dad told <u>him</u> and <u>me</u> <u>stories</u> about growing up in Idaho.

6. I bought a <u>CD</u> of Italian folk songs for her birthday.

7. We called the <u>dogs</u> and gave <u>them</u> their <u>food</u>.

8. Timmy, could you give the <u>baby</u> his <u>bath</u>?

9. Our dog and cat need rabies <u>vaccinations</u>.

10. Anita proudly mounted the <u>dais</u>, and the principal gave <u>her</u> the gold <u>medal</u>.

11. [4a, d, e]
12. [4a, d, f]
13. [4a, d, f]
14. [4a, d, f]
15. [4a, d, e]
16. [4a, d, f]
17. [4a, d, e]
18. [4a, d, e]
19. [4a, d, f]
20. [4a, d, f]

B. Identifying Subject Complements

Each of the following sentences has at least one subject complement. Write each complement, and identify it as a *predicate nominative* or a *predicate adjective*.

11. Enid Blyton has always been <u>one</u> of the most popular children's authors.

12. All of the astronauts look <u>confident</u>.

13. The entrance to the cave looks a bit <u>narrow</u> to me.

14. That soil seems awfully <u>dry</u>.

15. Angela has become a very good <u>runner</u>.

16. The breeze from the sea feels <u>fresh</u> and <u>cool</u>.

17. James Joyce was a <u>novelist</u> and a short-story <u>writer</u>.

18. History is the <u>study</u> of the past.

19. The cast members seem <u>happy</u> and <u>excited</u> about the good reviews in today's newspapers.

20. You should be <u>careful</u>; that rope is <u>frayed</u>.

Chapter Review **91**

C. Identifying Complements

Identify each of the italicized words or word groups in the following sentences as a *direct object*, an *indirect object*, a *predicate nominative*, or a *predicate adjective*.

21. d.o. [4b]
22. p.a. [4f]
23. p.n. [4e]
24. p.a. [4f]
25. i.o. [4c]
26. p.a. [4f]
27. p.n. [4e]
28. d.o. [4b]
29. d.o. [4b]
30. i.o. [4c]
31. i.o. [4c]
32. p.a. [4f]
33. d.o. [4b]
34. p.a. [4f]
35. p.n. [4e]
36. d.o. [4b]
37. i.o. [4c]
38. p.n. [4e]
39. i.o. [4c]
40. p.n. [4e]

21. Pilar caught the *ball* and threw it to first base.

22. Your cousin seems *nice*.

23. I'm not the *one* who did that.

24. The sun grew *hotter* as the day went on.

25. Mrs. Sato gave *me* a passing grade.

26. Peter Sellers was *famous* for comedy.

27. Amy's two cousins are both truck *drivers*.

28. Have you bought your *tickets* yet?

29. Did James ride his new *bike* to school today?

30. The angry customer sent the *manager* a letter of complaint.

31. The nurse gave *Linda* a flu shot.

32. Josh often looks *tired* on Monday mornings.

33. With his calloused hands he cannot feel the *texture* of velvet.

34. My sister's room is always *neater* than mine.

35. Heather, who is new at our school, is the nicest *girl* I know.

36. The Algonquians used *toboggans* to haul goods over snow and ice.

37. Dave, throw *Eric* a screen pass.

38. When left to dry in the sun, certain kinds of plums become *prunes*.

39. Dr. Charles Drew gave *science* a better way to process and store blood.

40. Ms. Rosada will be our Spanish *teacher* this fall.

Writing Application
Using Objects in a Letter

Direct and Indirect Objects   Imagine that you have just returned from an interesting and enjoyable shopping trip. Write a letter to a friend telling about what happened on this trip. Use direct objects and indirect objects in your letter.

Prewriting   You may want to write about an actual shopping trip that you have made recently, perhaps to a shopping mall or a flea market. Otherwise, you can make up a shopping trip to another country or even another planet. Make a list of what you did, what you saw, and what you bought for whom.

Writing   As you write your first draft, think about describing your shopping trip in a way that will interest your friend. Use vivid action verbs and specific direct objects and indirect objects. Be sure to tell when and where your trip took place.

Revising   Read over your paragraph. Does it clearly tell why the shopping trip was so interesting and enjoyable? If not, you may want to add or change some details. Be sure that your paragraph follows a consistent and sensible order.

Publishing   Proofread your paragraph for errors in grammar, punctuation, and spelling. If you wrote about real places that are near your home, you can use a telephone book to check the spelling of names of stores, shopping malls, or shopping centers. With your teacher's permission, you may want to gather your class's letters together in a binder and create a Smart Shoppers' Guide.

GRAMMAR

5

The Phrase
Prepositional, Verbal, and Appositive Phrases

Diagnostic Preview

Identifying Prepositional, Verbal, and Appositive Phrases

Identify each italicized phrase in the following paragraphs as a *prepositional*, *participial*, *gerund*, *infinitive*, or *appositive phrase*. You need not separately identify a prepositional phrase that is part of a larger phrase.

EXAMPLES   After [1] *giving me my allowance,* my father said [2] *not to spend it all in one place.*

    1. giving me my allowance—gerund phrase
    2. not to spend it all in one place—infinitive phrase

    Gina, [1] *my best friend since elementary school,* and I decided [2] *to go to the mall after school yesterday.* At first Gina suggested [3] *taking the back way* so that we could jog, but I was wearing sandals [4] *instead of my track shoes,* so we just walked. Along the way we saw Cathy [5] *sitting on her front porch* and asked her if she wanted [6] *to join us.* She was earning a little spending money by [7] *baby-sitting her neighbor's children,* though, and couldn't leave.

    [8] *Walking up to the wide glass doors at the mall,* Gina and I looked in our purses. We both had some money and our student passes, so we stopped [9] *to get orange juice* while we checked

Numerals in brackets refer to rules tested by the items in the Diagnostic Preview.

   1. app. [5l]
   2. inf. [5j]
   3. ger. [5h]
   4. prep. [5b]
   5. part. [5f]
   6. inf. [5j]
   7. ger. [5h]
   8. part. [5f]
   9. inf. [5j]

what movies were playing. None [10] *of the four features* looked interesting to us. However, Deven Bowers, [11] *a friend from school and an usher at the theater,* said that there would be a sneak preview [12] *of a new adventure film* later, so we told him we'd be back then.

Since stores usually do not allow customers to bring food or drinks inside, Gina and I gulped down our orange juice before [13] *going into our favorite dress shop.* We looked [14] *through most of the sale racks,* but none of the dresses, [15] *all of them formal or evening gowns,* appealed to us. A salesclerk asked if we were shopping [16] *for something special.* After [17] *checking with Gina,* I told the clerk we were just looking, and we left.

We walked past a couple of shops—[18] *the health food store and a toy store*—and went into Music World. [19] *Seeing several CDs by my favorite group,* I picked out one. By the time we walked out of Music World, I'd spent all my money, so we never did get [20] *to go to the movie that day.*

What Is a Phrase?

5a. A *phrase* is a group of related words that is used as a single part of speech and that does not contain both a verb and its subject.

PREPOSITIONAL PHRASE	a message **from the other members of the debate team**
PARTICIPIAL PHRASE	monkeys **swinging through the dense jungle**
INFINITIVE PHRASE	asking **to go with them on their Antarctic expedition**
APPOSITIVE PHRASE	a painting by van Gogh, **the famous Dutch painter**

NOTE A group of words that has both a verb and its subject is called a *clause.*

EXAMPLES Leta is watching television. [*Leta* is the subject of the verb *is watching.*]

before the train arrived [*Train* is the subject of the verb *arrived.*]

10. prep. [5b]
11. app. [5l]
12. prep. [5b]
13. ger. [5h]
14. prep. [5b]
15. app. [5l]
16. prep. [5b]
17. ger. [5h]
18. app. [5l]
19. part. [5f]
20. inf. [5j]

Reference Note
For more about **clauses,** see Chapter 6.

What Is a Phrase? **95**

■ Grammar and Mechanics of Writing 1.2: Understand sentence construction (e.g., parallel structure, subordination, proper placement of modifiers) and proper English usage (e.g., consistency of verb tenses).

▼
INTRODUCING THE CHAPTER

■ The first section of this chapter defines phrases and may be used as a preview or review. The rest of the chapter is divided into three sections: prepositional phrases, verbal phrases, and appositive phrases. The section on verbal phrases discusses participial phrases, gerund phrases, and infinitive phrases.

■ The chapter closes with a **Chapter Review** including a **Writing Application** that asks students to write a short story, using a variety of adjective and adverb phrases.

■ For help in integrating this chapter with writing assignments in *Holt Literature and Language Arts,* use the **Teaching Strands** chart on pp. T24–T25.

ASSESSING

Entry-Level Assessment
Diagnostic Preview. Use the **Diagnostic Preview** to determine which types of phrases give students the greatest difficulty. Then, have students work on activities and exercises specifically targeted to a particular type of phrase.

Differentiating Instruction
■ *UA: Differentiating Instruction*
■ *UA: Supporting Instruction in Five Languages*
■ *Family Involvement Activities: In Five Languages*

Assessment
■ *Formal Assessment*

■ *Progress-Monitoring Tests,* pp. 9–10, 48
■ *Test Generator (Teacher One Stop DVD-ROM)* 💿

Other Language Resources
■ *Spelling Lessons & Activities*
■ *WordSharp: An Interactive Vocabulary Tutor*
■ *Reading and Writing Transparencies*

PRETEACHING

Lesson Starter
Prior Knowledge. Get students thinking about phrases by having them brainstorm common idioms that they may hear or say. (An idiom is an expression the meaning of which differs from the literal meaning of its elements taken together.) Record their suggestions on the chalkboard; some examples are *in hot water, raining cats and dogs,* and *reading between the lines.* Have students evaluate what is similar in the construction of the phrases. Lead students to recognize that a phrase is a group of related words that does not contain both a subject and a verb.

The Prepositional Phrase
Rules 5b–d *(pp. 96–101)*

OBJECTIVES

■ To identify prepositional phrases

■ To identify adjective and adverb phrases and the words they modify

DIRECT TEACHING

Modeling and Demonstration
Identifying Prepositional Phrases. Model how to identify a prepositional phrase by using the example *During the stormy night, the black horse ran off.* First, ask students to identify any prepositions. [*During*] Then, ask which word is the object of the preposition. [*night*] Ask if there are any modifiers. [*the; stormy*] Then, point out that the preposition, the object, and any modifiers of that object make up a prepositional phrase; therefore, *During the stormy night* is a prepositional phrase. Now, have a volunteer use another example from this chapter to demonstrate how to identify a prepositional phrase.

Reference Note
For a list of commonly used **prepositions,** see page 66.

S T Y L E   T I P

Sometimes you can combine two short, choppy sentences by taking a prepositional phrase from one sentence and inserting it into the other.

CHOPPY
That day Lettie received a package. It was from her grandmother.

REVISED
That day Lettie received a package **from her grandmother.**

Reference Note
For more information about **infinitives,** see page 108.

The Prepositional Phrase

5b. A *prepositional phrase* includes a preposition, a noun or pronoun called *the object of the preposition,* and any modifiers of that object.

EXAMPLES   The Seine River flows **through Paris.** [The noun *Paris* is the object of the preposition *through.*]

The car **in front of us** slid **into an icy snowbank.** [The pronoun *us* is the object of the compound preposition *in front of.* The noun *snowbank* is the object of the preposition *into.*]

CRANKSHAFT copyright 1996 Mediagraphics. Reprinted with permission of Universal Press Syndicate. All rights reserved.

Any modifier that comes between a preposition and its object is part of the prepositional phrase.

EXAMPLE   **During the stormy night,** the black horse ran off. [The adjectives *the* and *stormy* modify the object *night.*]

An object of the preposition may be compound.

EXAMPLE   The dish is filled **with raw carrots and celery.** [Both *carrots* and *celery* are objects of the preposition *with.*]

NOTE   Be careful not to confuse a prepositional phrase with an infinitive. A prepositional phrase always has an object that is a noun or a pronoun. An infinitive is a verb form that usually begins with *to.*

PREPOSITIONAL   When we went **to Florida,** we saw the old
PHRASE   Spanish fort in St. Augustine.

INFINITIVE   When we were in Florida, we went **to see** the old Spanish fort in St. Augustine.

RESOURCES

The Prepositional Phrase
Practice

■ *Language & Sentence Skills Practice,* pp. 88–93

■ *Developmental Language & Sentence Skills,* pp. 37–40

Exercise 1 **Identifying Prepositional Phrases**

Identify the prepositional phrase or phrases in each of the following sentences.

EXAMPLE   1. Do you recognize the man in this picture?

1. *in this picture*

1. Hubert "Geese" Ausbie was well known for both his sunny smile and his athletic skill during his career.
2. For twenty-five years, Ausbie played on one of the most popular teams in basketball's history.
3. He was a star with the Harlem Globetrotters.
4. The team, which was started in 1927, is famous for its humorous performances.
5. Ausbie discovered that ability must come before showmanship.
6. The combination of skill and humor is what appeals to Globetrotter fans throughout the world.
7. Ausbie, a native of Oklahoma, sharpened his skill on the basketball team at Philander Smith College in Little Rock, Arkansas.
8. In 1961, while he was still in college, he joined the Globetrotters.
9. When he retired from the Globetrotters, Ausbie formed a traveling museum of his many souvenirs.
10. His collection includes the autographs of two presidents and boxing gloves from Muhammad Ali.

The Adjective Phrase

5c. A prepositional phrase that modifies a noun or a pronoun is called an ***adjective phrase.***

An adjective phrase tells *what kind* or *which one.*

EXAMPLES   Wang Wei was a talented painter **of landscapes.** [The prepositional phrase *of landscapes* modifies the noun *painter,* telling what kind of painter.]

Mrs. O'Meara is the one **on the left.** [The prepositional phrase *on the left* modifies the pronoun *one,* telling which one Mrs. O'Meara is.]

The Prepositional Phrase   97

English-Language Learners
General Strategies. The use of prepositions varies from language to language. If you notice the incorrect use of prepositions in students' writing, you could help them understand the correct uses of both the preposition they used and the preposition they should have used, providing examples and a simple definition of each one.

Exercise 2

DISTRIBUTED REVIEW
Point out that sentences 8 and 9 contain direct objects. Ask students to find the direct objects in these two sentences. [8. *trouble;* 9. *problem*]

An adjective phrase usually follows the word it modifies. That word may be the object of another prepositional phrase.

EXAMPLES Sicily is an island **off the coast of Italy.** [The phrase *of Italy* modifies *coast,* which is the object of the preposition *off.*]

Rena took notes **on her experiment for science class.** [The phrase *for science class* modifies *experiment,* which is the object of the preposition *on.*]

More than one adjective phrase may modify the same word.

EXAMPLE The glass **of juice on the counter** is for Alise. [The phrases *of juice* and *on the counter* modify the noun *glass.*]

Exercise 2 Identifying Adjective Phrases

Most of the following sentences contain at least one adjective phrase. Identify each adjective phrase and the word it modifies. If a sentence contains no adjective phrase, write *none.*

EXAMPLE 1. Megan read a book on the origins of words.
1. *on the origins—book; of words—origins*

1. Mike's sister Tanya, a real terror with a whale of a temper, shouts "Beans!" whenever something goes wrong.
2. Some words for the expression of anger have Latin origins.
3. Many of us in English class wanted to discuss how people express their annoyance.
4. Imagine what would happen if everybody with a bad temper had a bad day simultaneously.
5. We agreed that the best thing to do is to avoid people with chips on their shoulders.
6. Perhaps, whenever they feel bad, those people should use printed signs to warn others.   6. none
7. Happenings of little importance can cause some people to get angry.
8. A misunderstanding over some innocent remark may cause trouble.
9. The offended person often creates the real problem in communication.
10. We decided that we had better maintain our own senses of good will and humor.

MINI-LESSON **Usage**

Pronouns as Objects of Prepositions.
Pronouns used as objects of prepositions must be in the objective case in formal, standard English.
    Write the following two sentences on the chalkboard.

Give it to (*I, me*).
Wait for Susie and (*I, me*).

Ask students which pronoun sounds more natural in the first sentence, *I* or *me* [*me*]. Then, ask them which pronoun sounds more natural in the second sentence.

The Adverb Phrase

5d. A prepositional phrase that modifies a verb, an adjective, or an adverb is called an *adverb phrase.*

An adverb phrase tells *how, when, where, why,* or *to what extent* (*how long, how much,* or *how far*).

EXAMPLES   The snow fell **throughout the day.** [The phrase modifies the verb *fell,* telling *when* the snow fell.]

Are you good **at soccer**? [The phrase modifies the adjective *good,* telling *how* you are good.]

Elaine speaks French well **for a beginner.** [The phrase modifies the adverb *well,* telling to *what extent* Elaine speaks French well.]

Mr. Ortiz has taught school **for sixteen years.** [The phrase modifies the verb phrase *has taught,* telling *how long* Mr. Ortiz has taught.]

An adverb phrase may come before or after the word it modifies.

EXAMPLES   The sportswriter interviewed the coach **before the game.**
Before the game, the sportswriter interviewed the coach. [In each sentence, the phrase modifies the verb *interviewed.*]

More than one adverb phrase may modify the same word.

EXAMPLES   **Over the weekend,** the family went **to two different museums.** [Both phrases modify the verb *went.*]

On April 24, 1990, the Hubble Space Telescope was launched **into space.** [Both phrases modify the verb phrase *was launched.*]

┌ TIPS & TRICKS ┐

If you are not sure whether a prepositional phrase is an adjective phrase or an adverb phrase, remember that an adjective phrase almost always follows the word it modifies. If you can move the phrase without changing the meaning of the sentence, the phrase is probably an adverb phrase.

Exercise 3   Identifying Adverb Phrases

Identify the <u>adverb phrase</u> in each of the following sentences. Then, give the <u>word or words it modifies</u>.

EXAMPLE   **1.** The new restaurant was built over a river.

   1. over a river—was built

1. The Bali Hai Restaurant <u>has opened</u> <u>across the road.</u>

If students select *I,* cover or erase *Susie and,* and ask the question again [*me*].

Point out that *me* is the correct choice in both cases because *me* can be the object of a preposition, but *I* cannot be. You can sug-gest that students mentally block out the first part of a compound object of a preposition, as you demonstrated, in order to choose the correct pronoun.

2. The food is <u>fantastic</u> <u>beyond belief</u>.
3. Almost everyone <u>has gone</u> <u>to the new place</u>.
4. <u>At the Bali Hai</u> you can <u>eat</u> exotic food.
5. <u>Off the river</u> <u>blows</u> a cool breeze.
6. Customers <u>enjoy</u> themselves <u>in the friendly atmosphere</u>.
7. People <u>appear</u> <u>happy</u> <u>with the service</u>.
8. <u>For three weeks</u> the Bali Hai <u>has been crowded</u>.
9. When we went there, we <u>were seated</u> <u>on the patio</u>.
10. None <u>of the items</u> <u>on the menu</u> are too <u>expensive</u> <u>for most people</u>.

Review A — Identifying Adjective Phrases and Adverb Phrases

ANSWERS

1. of us—adj. (Few); of the pioneers—adj. (determination)

2. from the French word *travailler*—adv. (comes)

3. before dawn—adv. (began)

4. On the trip west—adv. (rode); in wagons—adv. (rode); like these—adj. (wagons)

5. During the day—adv. (traveled); over the mountains—adv. (traveled); across plains and deserts—adv. (traveled)

6. At dusk—adv. (were unhitched); from the wagons—adv. (were unhitched); around campfires—adv. (were pitched)

┌HELP┐
In the example for Review A, the phrase *Through old journals* modifies the verb phrase *have learned* and *about the pioneers* modifies the pronoun *much*.

Review A — Identifying Adjective Phrases and Adverb Phrases

Identify each prepositional phrase in the following sentences. Then, tell whether each phrase is an *adjective phrase* or an *adverb phrase*. Be prepared to tell which word or expression each phrase modifies.

EXAMPLE   1. Through old journals, we have learned much about the pioneers.

1. *Through old journals—adverb phrase; about the pioneers—adjective phrase*

1. Few of us appreciate the determination of the pioneers who traveled west.
2. The word *travel* comes from the French word *travailler*, which means "to work," and the pioneers definitely worked hard.
3. A typical day's journey began before dawn.
4. On the trip west, people rode in wagons like these.
5. During the day the wagon train traveled slowly over the mountains and across plains and deserts.
6. At dusk, the horses were unhitched from the wagons, and tents were pitched around campfires.

Worthington Whittredge, *Encampment on the Plains*. Autry Museum of Western Heritage, Los Angeles.

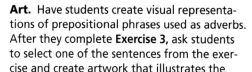

CONTENT-AREA CONNECTIONS

Art. Have students create visual representations of prepositional phrases used as adverbs. After they complete **Exercise 3**, ask students to select one of the sentences from the exercise and create artwork that illustrates the meaning of the phrase. Encourage creativity, and supply a variety of media for students to use, such as colored pencils, markers, or crayons.

7. The travelers often established a temporary camp in a valley for protection from the harsh winter weather.
8. Life in these camps was hard—food was often scarce, and many people never recovered from the hardships.
9. The pioneers who did survive by sheer determination usually continued their journey.
10. When the journey ended, these people worked hard to make homes for their families.

Verbals and Verbal Phrases

A *verbal* is a word that is formed from a verb but is used as a noun, an adjective, or an adverb. There are three kinds of verbals: the *participle*, the *gerund*, and the *infinitive*.

The Participle

5e. A *participle* is a verb form that can be used as an adjective.

(1) Present participles end in *–ing*.

EXAMPLES The **smiling** child waved. [*Smiling*, a form of the verb *smile*, modifies the noun *child*.]

The horses **trotting** past were not frightened by the crowd. [*Trotting*, a form of the verb *trot*, modifies the noun *horses*.]

(2) Most past participles end in *–d* or *–ed*. Some past participles are irregularly formed.

EXAMPLES The police officers searched the **abandoned** warehouse. [*Abandoned*, a form of the verb *abandon*, modifies the noun *warehouse*.]

This plate, **bought** at a flea market, is a valuable antique. [*Bought*, a form of the verb *buy*, modifies the noun *plate*.]

Chosen for her leadership abilities, Dawn was an effective team captain. [*Chosen*, a form of the verb *choose*, modifies the noun *Dawn*.]

Reference Note

For a list of **irregular past participles,** see page 190.

Verbals and Verbal Phrases **101**

RESOURCES

The Participle and the Participial Phrase

Practice

- *Language & Sentence Skills Practice,* pp. 94–97
- *Developmental Language & Sentence Skills,* pp. 41–42

Review A Identifying Adjective Phrases and Adverb Phrases

ANSWERS continued

7. in a valley—adv. (established); for protection—adv. (established); from the harsh winter weather—adj. (protection)
8. in these camps—adj. (Life); from the hardships—adv. (recovered)
9. by sheer determination—adv. (did survive)
10. for their families—adj. (homes)

The Participle and the Participial Phrase

Rules 5e, f *(pp. 101–105)*

OBJECTIVES

- To identify participles, participial phrases, and the words they modify

- To write sentences with participial phrases

- To combine sentences using participles and participial phrases

DIRECT TEACHING

Modeling and Demonstration

Identifying Participles. Model how to identify a participle by using the example *The smiling child waved.* First, ask students to identify the verb. [*waved*] Next, have students look for a verb form—a word that does not serve as the verb in the sentence but is a form of a verb. [*Smiling* is a form of the verb *smile*.] Then, ask whether *smiling* is used as an adjective. [Yes, *smiling* acts as an adjective modifying the noun *child*.] Now, have a volunteer use another example from this chapter to demonstrate how to identify a participle.

DIRECT TEACHING

Participles

Activity. Ask students to examine a piece of their own writing. Have them read the writing carefully and underline all the words that end in *–ing* and *–ed*. Have volunteers write sentences containing the underlined words on the chalkboard. After students have read the material about participles in the textbook, ask them to find any present and past participles in the examples on the board. As students analyze the examples, lead them to an understanding of what participles are and how they are used in sentences.

DIFFERENTIATING INSTRUCTION

Learners Having Difficulty

Because a participle used as an adjective and a participle used in a verb phrase can be easily confused, you may want to simplify **Exercise 4** by identifying for students the verbs in the sentences. You could do the same for **Exercise 5,** p. 103, or allow students to work together to identify the verbs before they try to locate the participles.

English-Language Learners

Spanish and Portuguese. Point out to students that the English suffix *–ing* corresponds to *–ando* and *–iendo* in Spanish (*hablando*) and *–ando, –endo,* and *–indo* in Portuguese. The English suffix *–(e)d* corresponds to *–ado* and *–ido* (*hablado*) in Spanish and Portuguese.

Reference Note

For information on **verb phrases,** see page 52.

┌ **HELP** ─

In the example for Exercise 4, both *whistling* and *chugging* are present participles.

1. past/past
2. pres.

3. past
4. past/past
5. pres.
6. past
7. pres.

8. pres./pres.
9. pres.
10. past

Reference Note

For more information about **complements,** see Chapter 4. For more about **modifiers,** see Chapter 11.

Do not confuse a participle used as an adjective with a participle used as part of a verb phrase.

ADJECTIVE	**Planning** their trip, the class learned how to read a road map.
VERB PHRASE	While they **were planning** their trip, the class learned how to read a road map.
ADJECTIVE	Most of the treasure **buried** by the pirates has never been found.
VERB PHRASE	Most of the treasure that **was buried** by the pirates has never been found.

Exercise 4 Identifying Participles

Identify the participles used as adjectives in the following sentences. Give the noun or pronoun each participle modifies. Be prepared to identify the participle as a *present participle* or a *past participle.*

EXAMPLE   1. We heard the train whistling and chugging in the distance.

   1. *whistling—train; chugging—train*

1. Records, cracked and warped, were in the old trunk in the attic.
2. Shouting loudly, Carmen warned the pedestrian to look out for the car.
3. Spoken in haste, the angry words could not be taken back.
4. The papers, aged and yellowed, were in the bottom drawer.
5. For centuries the ruins remained there, waiting for discovery.
6. Carefully decorated, the piñata glittered in the sunlight.
7. The charging bull thundered across the field of red and orange poppies.
8. Cheering and clapping, the spectators greeted their team.
9. The children, fidgeting noisily, waited eagerly for recess.
10. Recently released, the movie is not yet in local theaters.

The Participial Phrase

5f. A *participial phrase* consists of a participle and any modifiers or complements the participle has. The entire phrase is used as an adjective.

MINI-LESSON **Mechanics**

Punctuating Participial Phrases. Familiarize students with punctuation rules concerning participial phrases before assigning **Review B,** p. 104. First, write the following sentences on the chalkboard and underline the participial phrases.

1. Barking loudly, the dogs approached the front door.
2. The books stored in our attic were my great-grandmother's.
3. Uncle José, whistling a tune, just left for work.

A participle may be modified by an adverb or an adverb phrase and may also have a complement, usually a direct object.

EXAMPLES **Seeing itself in the mirror,** the duck seemed quite bewildered. [The participial phrase modifies the noun *duck.* The pronoun *itself* is the direct object of the present participle *Seeing.* The adverb phrase *in the mirror* modifies the present participle *Seeing.*]

After a while, we heard the duck **quacking noisily at its own image.** [The participial phrase modifies the noun *duck.* The adverb *noisily* and the adverb phrase *at its own image* modify the present participle *quacking.*]

Then, **disgusted with the other duck,** it pecked the mirror. [The participial phrase modifies the pronoun *it.* The adverb phrase *with the other duck* modifies the past participle *disgusted.*]

A participial phrase should be placed as close as possible to the word it modifies. Otherwise, the phrase may appear to modify another word and the sentence may not make sense.

MISPLACED Slithering through the grass, I saw a snake trimming the hedges this morning.

CORRECTED **Trimming the hedges this morning,** I saw a snake **slithering through the grass.**

Exercise 5 Identifying Participial Phrases

Identify the participial phrases in the following sentences. Give the word or words that each phrase modifies.

EXAMPLE
1. Myths are wonderful stories passed on from generation to generation.
1. *passed on from generation to generation—stories*

1. Noted for her beauty, Venus was sought by many gods as a wife.
2. Bathed in radiant light, Venus brought love and joy wherever she went.
3. Jupiter, knowing her charms, nevertheless married her to Vulcan, the ugliest of the gods.
4. Mars, known to the Greeks as Ares, was the god of war.
5. Terrified by Ares' power, many Greeks did not like to worship him.
6. They saw both land and people destroyed by him.

Reference Note

For more about **misplaced participial phrases,** see page 254.

STYLE TIP

Sometimes you can use a participial phrase to combine short, choppy sentences.

CHOPPY
The treasure was buried by the pirates. The treasure has never been found.

REVISED
The treasure **buried by the pirates** has never been found.

DIFFERENTIATING INSTRUCTION

English-Language Learners

Asian Languages. Because some Asian languages, such as Vietnamese, do not have participles, students might have difficulty identifying and using these verbals. To clarify the concept, list the verbs *jump, howl, march, polish, iron,* and *trust* on the chalkboard. Ask students to add *–ing* to the first three verbs, to add *–ed* to the last three verbs, and to follow these newly formed participles with nouns. [*Possibilities include* jumping frog, howling dog, marching army, polished floor, ironed shirt, *and* trusted friend.]

Learners Having Difficulty

To give students practice with participial phrases, divide the class into groups of three and seat each group in a small circle. Have each student write a participle on a sheet of paper and pass it to the group member on the right. Tell students to create participial phrases with the participles they receive and to pass the phrases to the right. Then, have students create sentences from the participial phrases they receive.

Each group should end up with three sentences containing participial phrases. Have a reporter from each group share the group's sentences.

Explain to students that a participial phrase at the beginning of a sentence is followed by a comma (first sentence). When the phrase is in the middle of the sentence and the information it presents is essential to the meaning of the sentence, no commas are needed (second sentence). However, if the phrase contains nonessential information, it is set off by commas (third sentence). You could reinforce these rules by discussing the use of commas in **Exercise 5.**

7. Observing his grim path, they said that Ares left blood, devastation, and grief behind him.
8. The Romans, having great respect for Mars, made him one of their three chief deities.
9. They imagined him dressed in shining armor.
10. Mars, supposedly the father of the founders of Rome, has a planet named after him.

Oral Practice Creating Sentences with Participial Phrases

ANSWERS
Sentences will vary. You could suggest that students vary the positions of the participial phrases within the sentences they create. Remind students, however, to place each phrase as close as possible to the word it modifies.

Oral Practice **Creating Sentences with Participial Phrases**

Read each of the following participial phrases aloud. Then, use the participial phrases in sentences you create, placing each phrase as close as possible to the noun or pronoun that it modifies.

EXAMPLE   1. standing in line
         1. *Standing in line, we waited twenty minutes for the store to open.*

1. waiting for the bus in the rain
2. broken in three places
3. planning the escape
4. jumping from stone to stone
5. hearing the whistle blow and feeling the train lurch
6. given to him by President Carter
7. saved over the years
8. looking down from the top of the Ferris wheel
9. hidden under the shrub
10. seeing the ocean for the first time

Review B **Using Participles and Participial Phrases to Combine Sentences**

You are the sports editor for the school newspaper. A new photographer just turned in several photographs from a district school track-and-field event. She also wrote captions to go under the photographs. The information is fine, but you want each caption to be a single sentence. Use participles and participial phrases to combine each set of sentences on the next page.

EXAMPLE   1. Tamara Jackson nears the finish line in the 100-meter dash. She looks happy because she's run her best.
         1. *Looking happy because she's run her best, Tamara Jackson nears the finish line in the 100-meter dash.*

1. In the 100-meter hurdles, Ruth Ann Garcia appears to be leading. She is known for her last-minute bursts of energy.
2. Discus thrower Zack Linquist shifts his weight to his left foot. He twists his body to the right and hurls the discus across the field.
3. Relay team member Krista Davidson reaches for the baton. She is prepared to run the last leg of the relay race.
4. In the pole vault, Dennis Nishimoto clears the crossbar. Every muscle in his body strains as he goes over the bar.
5. Julie McKay shows great promise in the broad jump. Most people favor her to win this year's event.

Review B Using Participles and Participial Phrases to Combine Sentences

POSSIBLE ANSWERS

1. Ruth Ann Garcia, known for her last-minute bursts of energy, appears to be leading in the 100-meter hurdles.
2. Shifting his weight to his left foot and twisting his body to the right, Zack Linquist hurls the discus across the field.
3. Prepared to run the last leg of the relay race, Krista Davidson reaches for the baton.
4. Every muscle in his body straining as he goes over, Dennis Nishimoto clears the crossbar in the pole vault.
5. Favored to win this year's event, Julie McKay shows great promise in the broad jump.

The Gerund and the Gerund Phrase
Rules 5g, h *(pp. 105–108)*

OBJECTIVES

- To identify gerunds and gerund phrases and indicate their functions within sentences
- To write sentences with gerund phrases

The Gerund

5g. A *gerund* is a verb form ending in *–ing* that is used as a noun.

SUBJECT	**Skiing** down that slope was fun.
PREDICATE NOMINATIVE	Dad's favorite pastime is **fishing** for trout and bass.
INDIRECT OBJECT	Give **sailing** a try.
DIRECT OBJECT	We enjoyed **hiking** in the Sangre de Cristo Mountains.
OBJECT OF PREPOSITION	Please sweep the front sidewalk after **mowing.**

Reference Note

For information on **subjects,** see page 7. For information on **predicate nominatives,** see page 85. For information on **indirect and direct objects,** see pages 83 and 81. For information on **objects of prepositions,** see page 66.

RESOURCES

The Gerund and the Gerund Phrase

Practice

- *Language & Sentence Skills Practice,* pp. 98–102

Modeling and Demonstration

Identifying Gerunds. Model how to identify a gerund by using the example *Typing the paper took an hour.* Have students look for words ending in *–ing.* [*Typing*] Ask them whether *Typing* acts as a noun. [Yes, *Typing* is the subject of the sentence.] Therefore, *Typing* is a gerund serving as the subject of the sentence. Now, have a volunteer use another example from this chapter to demonstrate how to identify a gerund.

Correcting Misconceptions

Gerund or Present Participle? Some students may confuse participles and gerunds. Use the example *Pausing, the deer was sniffing the wind before stepping into the meadow* to help students distinguish gerunds from present participles. Remind students that gerunds always act as nouns. Have students evaluate the *–ing* words in the sentence to determine which ones, if any, are nouns. *Pausing* is not a noun; it is a participle modifying *deer,* telling what the deer is doing. *Sniffing* is not a noun; it is part of the verb phrase *was sniffing.* The preposition *before* signals a need for an object of the preposition. *Stepping* is a noun that serves as the object of *before.* Therefore, *stepping* is a gerund.

HELP

If you are not sure whether an *–ing* word is a gerund or a participle, try this test. Substitute a pronoun for the *–ing* word. If the sentence still makes sense, the word is a gerund.

EXAMPLES

Running is good exercise.

It is good exercise.
[*It* makes sense in the sentence. *Running* is a gerund.]

We watched the dolphins playing with a ball.

We watched the dolphins it with a ball.
[*It* does not make sense here. *Playing* is a participle.]

While this test usually works, you may find that it does not work for every gerund.

Reference Note

For more information about **complements**, see Chapter 4. For more about **modifiers,** see Chapter 11.

Do not confuse a gerund with a present participle used as part of a verb phrase or as an adjective.

EXAMPLE   Pausing, the deer was sniffing the wind before **stepping** into the meadow. [*Pausing* is a participle modifying *deer,* and *sniffing* is part of the verb phrase *was sniffing.* *Stepping* is a gerund that serves as the object of the preposition *before.*]

Exercise 6   Identifying Gerunds

Find the gerunds in the following sentences. Identify each gerund as a *subject,* a *predicate nominative,* a *direct object,* or an *object of a preposition.* If a sentence does not contain a gerund, write *none.*

EXAMPLE   **1.** Typing the paper took an hour.
         1. Typing—subject

1. In the past, working took up most people's time six days a week.   **1.** s.
2. Dr. Martin Luther King, Jr.'s powerful speaking helped draw attention to the civil rights movement.   **2.** s.
3. My sister has always enjoyed riding horseback.   **3.** d.o.
4. Why won't that dog stop barking?   **4.** d.o.
5. I look forward to a rest after this tiring job is done.   **5.** none
6. Uncle Eli's specialty is barbecuing on the grill.   **6.** p.n.
7. Nobody could stand the child's unceasing whine.   **7.** none
8. The most exciting part of the ceremony will be the crowning of the new king.   **8.** p.n.
9. Studying usually pays off in higher scores.   **9.** s.
10. Considering the other choices, Melinda decided on walking.
        10. o.p.

The Gerund Phrase

5h. A *gerund phrase* consists of a gerund and any modifiers or complements the gerund has. The entire phrase is used as a noun.

Because a gerund is a verb form, it may be modified by an adverb or an adverb phrase and may have a complement, usually a direct object. Also, since a gerund functions as a noun, it may be modified by an adjective or an adjective phrase.

EXAMPLES   **Having a part-time job** may interfere with your
schoolwork. [The gerund phrase is the subject of the
sentence. The noun *job* is the direct object of the
gerund *Having*. The article *a* and the adjective
part-time modify *job*.]

The townspeople heard **the loud clanging of the fire
bell.** [The gerund phrase is the direct object of the verb
heard. The article *the*, the adjective *loud*, and the adjective phrase *of the fire bell* modify the gerund *clanging*.]

We crossed the stream by **stepping carefully from
stone to stone.** [The gerund phrase is the object of the
preposition *by*. The adverb *carefully* and the adverb
phrases *from stone* and *to stone* modify the gerund
stepping.]

NOTE When a noun or a pronoun comes immediately before a
gerund, use the possessive form of the noun or pronoun.

EXAMPLES   **Michael's** cooking is the best I've ever tasted.

The vultures didn't let anything disturb **their** feeding.

Exercise 7 **Identifying Gerund Phrases**

Find the gerund phrases in the following sentences. Identify each
phrase as a *subject*, a *predicate nominative*, a *direct object*, or an
object of a preposition.

EXAMPLE   1. The rain interrupted their building the bonfire.
          1. *their building the bonfire—direct object*

1. Angelo's pleading rarely influenced his mother's decisions.   1. s.
2. The eerie sound they heard was the howling of the wolves.   2. p.n.
3. We sat back and enjoyed the slow rocking of the boat.   3. d.o.
4. The blue jay's screeching at the cat woke us up at dawn.   4. s.
5. People supported Cesar Chavez and the United Farm   5. o.p.
   Workers by boycotting grapes.
6. Our greatest victory will be winning the state championship.   6. p.n.
7. The frantic darting of the fish indicated that a shark was nearby. 7. s.
8. She is considering running for class president.   8. d.o.
9. Ants try to protect their colonies from storms by piling up   9. o.p.
   sand against the wind.
10. In his later years, Chief Quanah Parker was known for   10. o.p.
    settling disputes fairly.

Verbals and Verbal Phrases   **107**

**DIFFERENTIATING
INSTRUCTION**

Advanced Students

Diagramming Gerunds. Some students may find it easier to understand the grammatical functions of
gerunds if they see gerunds in sentence diagrams. Diagram on the
chalkboard the example sentences
following **Rule 5g.** You may want to
refer students to **Chapter 19:
Sentence Diagramming.**

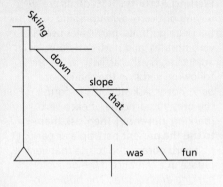

EXTENSION

Poetry
Gerunds can be useful poetic devices
because of their multiple uses as subjects, predicate nominatives, and
objects of verbs and prepositions.
Have students brainstorm ideas for
poems and then compose their own
poems using at least four gerunds.

Exercise 8 Writing Sentences with Gerund Phrases

ANSWERS

Sentences will vary. Check to see that students use the phrases correctly as gerund phrases.

RETEACHING

Participles and Gerunds

Writing Activity. If students are having difficulty distinguishing between gerunds, participles used in verb phrases, and participles used as adjectives, try this activity. Write the following verbs on the chalkboard: *bark, hover.* Ask students to form the present participle of each verb. [*barking, hovering*] Then, ask them to use the present participle as part of a verb phrase and to use that verb phrase in a sentence. [*The dog is barking at a squirrel; The humming-birds are hovering near the flower bed.*] Have students use the same participles as adjectives in similar sentences. [*The barking dog chased the squirrel; The hovering hummingbirds are beautiful.*] Finally, have students use the same verb forms as nouns (gerunds) in sentences. [*The barking of the dog warned the squirrel; Hovering allows hummingbirds to seize insects from flowers.*] Ask students to explain in their own words how to tell whether each –*ing* form functions as a gerund, a participle used in a verb phrase, or a participle used as an adjective.

The Infinitive and the Infinitive Phrase

Rules 5i, j *(pp. 108–112)*

OBJECTIVES

- To identify infinitives and infinitive phrases and indicate their part of speech

- To write sentences with infinitive phrases

Exercise 8 Writing Sentences with Gerund Phrases

Use each of the following gerund phrases in a sentence of your own. Underline the gerund phrase, and identify it as a *subject,* a *predicate nominative,* a *direct object,* an *indirect object,* or an *object of a preposition.*

EXAMPLE   **1.** hiking up the hill

         1. <u>Hiking up the hill</u> took us all morning.—subject

1. getting up in the morning
2. arguing among themselves
3. refusing to board the space shuttle
4. sharpening my pencil
5. listening to the tour guide
6. walking to the video store
7. jumping into the cold water
8. figuring out puzzles
9. repairing the tires on my bicycle
10. living near a castle

The Infinitive

5i. An **infinitive** is a verb form that can be used as a noun, an adjective, or an adverb. Most infinitives begin with *to.*

NOUNS	**To install** the ceiling fan took two hours. [*To install* is the subject of the sentence.]
	Winona's ambition is **to become** a doctor. [*To become* is a predicate nominative referring to the subject *ambition.*]
	Shina likes **to skate** but not **to ski.** [*To skate* and *to ski* are direct objects of the verb *likes.*]
ADJECTIVES	The best time **to visit** Florida is December through April. [*To visit* modifies *time.*]
	If you want information about computers, that is the magazine **to read.** [*To read* modifies *magazine.*]
ADVERBS	The gymnasts were ready **to practice** their routines. [*To practice* modifies the adjective *ready.*]
	The camel knelt at the pool **to drink.** [*To drink* modifies the verb *knelt.*]

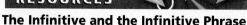

RESOURCES

The Infinitive and the Infinitive Phrase
Practice
- *Language & Sentence Skills Practice,* pp. 103–107, 112
- *Developmental Language & Sentence Skills,* pp. 43–44

NOTE Be careful not to confuse an infinitive with a prepositional phrase beginning with *to*. A prepositional phrase always has an object that is a noun or a pronoun. An infinitive is a verb form that usually begins with *to*.

| PREPOSITIONAL PHRASE | I handed the vase **to my mother.** |
| INFINITIVE | Is she ready **to swim?** |

Exercise 9 Identifying Infinitives

Identify the <u>infinitive</u> in each of the following sentences.

EXAMPLE **1.** The first time we met, June and I decided to be friends.

1. *to be*

1. After school, June and I like <u>to walk</u> home together.
2. Usually, we go to my house or her house <u>to listen</u> to CDs.
3. Sometimes I get up <u>to dance</u> to the music, but June never does.
4. I don't like <u>to sit</u> still when a good song is playing.
5. June finally told me that she had never learned how <u>to dance</u>.
6. "Do you want <u>to learn</u> some steps?" I asked.
7. "I want <u>to try</u>," she answered.
8. I decided <u>to start</u> with some simple steps.
9. For three weeks, we went to my house <u>to practice</u>.
10. Now, June is ready <u>to go</u> to the school dance after the game on Friday.

The Infinitive Phrase

5j. An *infinitive phrase* consists of an infinitive and any modifiers or complements the infinitive has. The entire phrase may be used as a noun, an adjective, or an adverb.

An infinitive may be modified by an adjective or an adverb; it may also have a complement.

EXAMPLES   The crowd grew quiet **to hear the speaker.** [The infinitive phrase is an adverb modifying the verb *grew*. The noun *speaker* is the direct object of the infinitive *to hear.*]

Verbals and Verbal Phrases   **109**

DIRECT TEACHING

Modeling and Demonstration

Identifying Infinitives. Model how to distinguish infinitives from prepositional phrases by using the example *Is she ready to swim?* First, have students look for the word *to*. Then, ask whether an object (a noun or pronoun) follows *to*. [No, *swim* follows *to* and is not a noun or a pronoun.] A prepositional phrase must have an object. Therefore, *to* does not serve as a preposition, and *to swim* is an infinitive. Now, have a volunteer use another example from this chapter to demonstrate how to identify an infinitive.

Exercise 9

DISTRIBUTED REVIEW
Have students identify the subject and verb in sentences 1, 2, 9, and 10. [1. *S—June, I; V—like;* 2. *S—we; V—go;* 9. *S—we; V—went;* 10. *S—June; V—is*]

DIFFERENTIATING INSTRUCTION

English-Language Learners
Romance Languages. Point out to students that in Spanish and Portuguese the infinitive ends in *–ar, –er,* or *–ir* (for example, *hablar, vender,* and *partir* in Spanish; *falar, vender,* and *partir* in Portuguese). In French the infinitive ends in *–er, –ir, –oir,* or *–re* (for example, *aimer, finir, recevoir, rompre*).

Learning for Life   *Continued on pp. 110–111*

Writing an Advertisement. Students sometimes confuse participles, gerunds, and infinitives with the main verbs of sentences and inadvertently write sentence fragments using these verbals. Sentence fragments, used purposely, can add style and power to some kinds of writing, but the key is to know how and when to use them.

Have students brainstorm examples of circumstances in which sentence fragments might be appropriate (for example, in dialogue, in lists, in newspaper ads). Ask

Peanuts and raisins are good snacks **to take on a camping trip.** [The infinitive phrase is an adjective modifying *snacks.* The adverb phrase *on a camping trip* modifies the infinitive *to take.*]

To lift those weights takes great strength. [The infinitive phrase is a noun used as the subject of the sentence. The noun *weights* is the direct object of the infinitive *To lift.*]

Exercise 10 Identifying Infinitive Phrases

Most of the following sentences contain infinitive phrases. Identify each <u>infinitive phrase</u>, and tell whether it is used as a *noun*, an *adjective*, or an *adverb*. If there is no infinitive phrase in a sentence, write *none*.

EXAMPLE 1. I told my aunt Elise that I wanted to take better care of my bicycle.

  1. *to take better care of my bicycle—noun*

1. adj. 1. Taking care of your bicycle is one way <u>to make it last.</u>
2. adv. 2. We used machine oil <u>to lubricate the chain.</u>
3. n.   3. I learned <u>to place a small drop of oil on each link.</u>
4. adv. 4. Then she showed me the valve that is needed <u>to fill the inner tube.</u>
5. none 5. Using Aunt Elise's hand pump, we added some air to the back tire.
6. adv. 6. We were careful <u>not to put in too much air.</u>
7. adv. 7. Next, we got out wrenches <u>to tighten some bolts.</u>
8. n.   8. My aunt said <u>not to pull the wrench too hard.</u>
9. none 9. Overtightening can cause as much damage to bolts as not tightening them enough.
10. adj. 10. When we finished, I thanked my aunt for taking the time <u>to give me tips about taking care of my bicycle.</u>

Exercise 11 Writing Sentences with Infinitive Phrases

Use each of the following infinitive phrases in a sentence of your own. Underline the infinitive phrase, and identify it as a *noun*, an *adjective*, or an *adverb*.

EXAMPLE 1. to leave school early on Tuesday

  1. *The principal gave me permission <u>to leave school early on Tuesday.</u>—adjective*

Learning for Life

Continued from p. 109

students to find examples of the various purposeful uses of fragments in publications and conversations.

Then, have students compose an advertisement using sentence fragments contain-ing infinitives, participles, and gerunds. Let students choose their own product and create the ad for whatever medium they wish (for example, TV, radio, newspaper, magazine, brochure).

1. to give the right answers
2. to go to another planet
3. to run toward the zebra
4. to read the entire book over the weekend
5. to spend the night at my cousin's house
6. to wait for the meteor shower
7. to finish the posters before Kwanzaa
8. to climb the mountain with my friends
9. to close all the windows in the house
10. to sing on stage

Review C **Identifying Verbals and Verbal Phrases**

Each of the following sentences contains at least one verbal or verbal phrase. Identify each underline{verbal or verbal phrase} as a *gerund*, a *gerund phrase*, a *participle*, a *participial phrase*, an *infinitive*, or an *infinitive phrase*.

EXAMPLE 1. Visiting Cahokia Mounds State Historic Site in Illinois is a wonderful experience.

1. *Visiting Cahokia Mounds State Historic Site in Illinois—gerund phrase*

1. Cahokia was a highly developed civilization in North America more than one thousand years ago.
2. Noting the importance of Cahokia, the United Nations Educational, Scientific, and Cultural Organization (UNESCO) set aside Cahokia Mounds as a World Heritage Site.
3. After studying the site, archaeologists were able to make a sketch of the ancient city.
4. The city was destroyed long ago, but the remaining traces of it show how huge it must have been.
5. This thriving community had a population of about 20,000 sometime between A.D. 700 and A.D. 1500.
6. You can see that the people chose to build their houses mostly inside the stockade wall.

1. part. phr.   2. part. phr.
3. ger. phr./   4. part.
   inf. phr.
5. part.   6. inf. phr.

Verbals and Verbal Phrases **111**

EXTENSION

Relating to Vocabulary Skills

Use this activity to introduce students to a variety of infinitives. Divide the class into groups of three, assign each group a specific letter, and give each group a dictionary and ten blank cards.

Tell each group to use the dictionary to find ten unusual verbs beginning with their assigned letter. Then, have the group members write sentences using each verb in an infinitive phrase, one sentence to a card. Have students write the meaning of the verb on the back of each card. (Example: The fire alarm forced us to *scud* outside.—"to move quickly") Then, pair the groups to have them define each other's infinitives.

Allow students to work with others to evaluate and revise their ads. Fragments that don't contribute to tone should be rewritten as complete sentences. You can allow students to publish their work by posting ads in the classroom.

GRAMMAR

7. inf. phr.

8. part.

9. ger. phr./part. phr.

10. inf.

7. It's still possible <u>to see</u> many of the earthen mounds.
8. The historic site includes about sixty-eight <u>preserved</u> mounds, which were probably used for ceremonial activities.
9. <u>Seeing the 100-foot-high Monks Mound</u> was <u>quite enlightening</u>.
10. The mound was built for the city's ruler as a place <u>to live</u>.

Appositives and Appositive Phrases

Appositives and Appositive Phrases

Rules 5k, l *(pp. 112–114)*

OBJECTIVE

- To identify appositives and appositive phrases and the words they identify

DIRECT TEACHING

Modeling and Demonstration

Identifying Appositives. Model how to identify appositives by using the example *The cosmonaut Yuri Gagarin was the first person in space.* First, have students identify the nouns and pronouns. [*cosmonaut; Yuri Gagarin; person; space*] Next, ask whether any of the nouns are directly next to each other. [*cosmonaut and Yuri Gagarin*] Then, ask whether *cosmonaut* and *Yuri Gagarin* refer to the same thing. [*yes*] Explain to students that *Yuri Gagarin* is the appositive of *cosmonaut.* Now, have a volunteer use another example in this chapter to demonstrate how to identify an appositive.

Reference Note

For more about the use of **commas with appositives,** see page 323.

Appositives and Appositive Phrases

5k. An *appositive* is a noun or a pronoun placed beside another noun or pronoun to identify or describe it.

EXAMPLES   The cosmonaut **Yuri Gagarin** was the first person in space. [The noun *Yuri Gagarin* identifies the noun *cosmonaut.*]

I chose one person, **her,** to organize the volunteers. [The pronoun *her* refers to the noun *person.*]

NOTE Commas are generally used with appositives that refer to proper nouns.

EXAMPLE   Rachel Carson, a **biologist** and **writer,** published the book ***Silent Spring*** in 1962. [The nouns *biologist* and *writer* describe the proper noun *Rachel Carson.* The noun *Silent Spring* identifies the common noun *book.*]

5l. An *appositive phrase* consists of an appositive and its modifiers.

EXAMPLES   Officer Webb, **one of the security guards,** caught the burglar. [The adjective phrase *of the security guards* modifies the appositive *one.*]

Leonardo da Vinci, **an Italian painter known for his artworks,** was also an architect, engineer, and scientist. [The article *an,* the adjective *Italian,* and the participial phrase *known for his artworks* modify the appositive *painter.*]

Appositives and appositive phrases that are not essential to the meaning of the sentence are set off by commas. If the appositive is essential to the meaning, it is generally not set off by commas.

RESOURCES

Appositives and Appositive Phrases
Practice

- *Language & Sentence Skills Practice,* pp. 108–111, 113–114
- *Developmental Language & Sentence Skills,* pp. 45–46

EXAMPLES My sister, **Lana,** has blond hair. [The writer has only one sister. The appositive is not essential to identify the sister. Because the information is nonessential, it is set off by commas.]

My sister **Lana** has blond hair. [The writer has more than one sister. The appositive is necessary to tell which sister is meant. Because this information is essential to the meaning of the sentence, it is not set off by commas.]

Exercise 12 Identifying Appositives and Appositive Phrases

Identify the appositives and appositive phrases in the following sentences. Then, give the word or words each appositive or appositive phrase identifies or describes.

EXAMPLE 1. My dog, the mutt with floppy ears, can do tricks.

1. *the mutt with floppy ears—dog*

1. Tacos, one of the most popular Mexican dishes, are served here.
2. My twin, Daniel, rode in a Mardi Gras parade.
3. Those two men, a truck driver and a sailor, helped my father push the car off the road.
4. I'll have a sandwich, tuna salad on rye bread, please.
5. Miguel has the same class, American history, this afternoon.
6. Barbara Jordan, one of my heroes, was a strong champion of both civil and human rights.
7. Shelley asked everyone where her friend Bianca had gone.
8. Somebody reported the hazard, a pile of trash containing broken bottles, to the police.
9. Be sure to bring the exact change, fifty cents.
10. They sang the song "I've Been Working on the Railroad" over and over all the way down the path.

Review D Identifying Verbals and Appositives

Find all the verbals and appositives in the following sentences. Identify each *participle, gerund, infinitive,* or *appositive.*

EXAMPLE 1. Skating on the sidewalk, my little brother Shawn tried to do some acrobatics.

1. *Skating—participle; Shawn—appositive; to do—infinitive*

Reference Note

For more on **essential and nonessential phrases,** see page 321.

STYLE TIP

You can use appositives and appositive phrases to combine short, choppy sentences.

CHOPPY
Santa Fe is a major tourist center. It is the capital of New Mexico.

REVISED
Santa Fe, **the capital of New Mexico,** is a major tourist center.

GRAMMAR

Review E Writing
Sentences with Prepositional,
Verbal, and Appositive Phrases

POSSIBLE ANSWERS

1. The celebration after the game was exciting.

2. I insisted that Vanessa borrow your sandals instead of your good shoes.

3. Iago is a character in the Shakespeare play we saw.

4. I actually enjoy going to school every day.

5. She compared living in the city to living in a small town.

6. Walking through the empty lot, Vi heard a kitten mewing.

7. Dressed in authentic costumes, our tribal council presented the award.

8. To drive a car for the first time will be a challenge.

9. Pasqual, the best athlete in our school, was awarded an academic scholarship.

10. Baking, my favorite pastime, makes my family happy, too.

MEETING THE CHALLENGE

Think about a specific location in or around your school. Then, write directions telling how to get to this location from your classroom. In your directions, use at least one example of each kind of phrase covered in this chapter. How well can someone else follow your directions?

ANSWERS
Directions will vary but should contain one of each kind of phrase.

1. Instead of <u>falling</u> on the soft ground, Shawn managed <u>to land</u> right on the sidewalk.   **1.** ger./inf.

2. The concrete, <u>broken</u> and <u>crumbling</u>, cut his legs.**2.** part./part.

3. We heard his <u>piercing</u> wail up at our house, and my mother and I rushed <u>to see</u> what had happened.   **3.** part./inf.

4. By the time we got to him, the cuts had already started <u>bleeding</u>, and he was struggling <u>to get</u> his skates off. **4.** ger./inf.

5. <u>Bending</u> down, Mom pulled off the skates and dabbed at the <u>seeping</u> red cuts and scrapes.   **5.** part./part.   **6.** app./ger.

6. Shawn, a brave little <u>boy</u> usually, could not keep from <u>crying</u>.

7. Mom carried Shawn to the house, and I followed with his skates, <u>scratched</u> and <u>scraped</u> almost as badly as he was. **7.** part./part. **8.** ger.

8. After <u>cleaning</u> Shawn's cuts, Mom took him to the clinic.

9. The doctor, a young <u>intern</u>, said that she would have <u>to close</u> one of the cuts with stitches.   **9.** app./inf.

10. When we got home, Mom said that she hoped Shawn had learned <u>to be</u> more careful; <u>knowing</u> Shawn, I'm sure he will be. **10.** inf./part.

Review E **Writing Sentences with Prepositional, Verbal, and Appositive Phrases**

Write ten sentences, using one of the following phrases in each sentence. Follow the directions in parentheses.

EXAMPLE   **1.** to write a descriptive paragraph (*use as an infinitive phrase that is the predicate nominative in the sentence*)

     1. *Our assignment for tomorrow is to write a descriptive paragraph.*

1. after the game (*use as an adjective phrase*)

2. instead of your good shoes (*use as an adverb phrase*)

3. in the Shakespeare play (*use as an adjective phrase*)

4. going to school every day (*use as a gerund phrase that is the direct object in the sentence*)

5. living in a small town (*use as a gerund phrase that is the object of a preposition*)

6. walking through the empty lot (*use as a participial phrase*)

7. dressed in authentic costumes (*use as a participial phrase*)

8. to drive a car for the first time (*use as an infinitive phrase that is the subject of the sentence*)

9. the best athlete in our school (*use as an appositive phrase*)

10. my favorite pastime (*use as an appositive phrase*)

5

Numerals in brackets refer to rules tested by the items in the Chapter Review.

1. ger. [5h]
2. part. [5f]
3. prep. [5b]
4. app. [5l]
5. inf. [5j]
6. part. [5f]
7. inf. [5j]
8. ger. [5h]
9. app. [5l]
10. prep. [5b]
11. prep. [5b]
12. ger. [5h]
13. inf. [5j]
14. app. [5l]
15. ger. [5h]
16. prep. [5b]
17. part. [5f]
18. app. [5l]

Chapter Review

A. Identifying Prepositional, Verbal, and Appositive Phrases

For each of the following sentences, identify the italicized phrase as a *prepositional phrase,* a *participial phrase,* a *gerund phrase,* an *infinitive phrase,* or an *appositive phrase.* Do not separately identify a prepositional phrase that is part of a larger phrase.

1. Ed likes *listening to music.*
2. The sea gulls *gliding through the air* looked like pieces of paper caught in the wind.
3. The school bus was on time *in spite of the traffic jam.*
4. Ms. Abdusalaam, *my science teacher,* got married last week.
5. There is no time left *to answer your questions.*
6. *Hoping for a new bicycle and a toy robot,* my brother couldn't sleep at all on Christmas Eve.
7. He tried *to do his best* in the race.
8. Nobody seems to be very interested in *going to the fireworks display.*
9. Have you seen my cat, *a long-haired Persian with yellow eyes*?
10. Chad said that he prefers the bike *with all-terrain tires and the wider, more comfortable seat.*
11. At the carnival, the band played songs *with a lively samba beat.*
12. Rachel talked her friends into *watching that Three Tenors video.*
13. In the United States, citizens have the right *to speak their minds.*
14. My aunt's car, *an old crate with a torn-up interior and a rattling engine,* used to belong to my grandfather.
15. The Dutch artist Jan Vermeer enjoyed *painting pictures of house interiors.*
16. Last Sunday, we all piled in the car and went *to the beach, the bowling alley, and the mall.*
17. The shark *chasing the school of fish* looked like a hammerhead.
18. Nobody wanted to read the book, *a thick hardback with a faded cover.*

GRAMMAR

ASSESSING

Monitoring Progress

Chapter Review. To assess student progress, you may want to compare the types of items missed on the **Diagnostic Preview** to those missed on the **Chapter Review.** You may want to work out specific goals with individual students who are still having difficulty mastering essential information.

RESOURCES

The Phrase

Review

- *Language & Sentence Skills Practice,* pp. 112–114

Assessment

- *Formal Assessment*
- *Progress-Monitoring Tests,* pp. 9–10, 48
- *Test Generator (Teacher One Stop DVD-ROM)*

19. part. [5f]
20. inf. [5j]

19. All of the invitations *sent to the club members* had the wrong date on them.

20. Mr. Patel and Mr. Kim recruited neighborhood children *to help decorate the storefronts for Independence Day.*

B. Identifying Gerunds and Gerund Phrases

Identify the <u>gerunds and gerund phrases</u> in the following sentences.

21. [5h]
22. [5g]
23. [5h]
24. [5h]
25. [5h]
26. [5h]
27. [5h]
28. [5g]
29. [5h]
30. [5h]

21. <u>Reaching an agreement between the parties</u> is the goal of every negotiator.

22. <u>Smoking</u> has become less common in the United States.

23. The incessant <u>raining</u> put a damper on our holiday.

24. <u>Relaxing at home on the weekend</u> can be beneficial to your peace of mind.

25. When she is abroad, Aunt Ida especially enjoys <u>meeting other travelers</u>.

26. After a long and tiring day, <u>swimming a lap or two</u> can relax your muscles.

27. Cousin Mark's summer job is <u>selling produce at the farmers' market</u>.

28. <u>Singing</u> is Nina's favorite pastime.

29. <u>Living across the street from school</u> is convenient.

30. The only sound they heard was <u>the barking of the seals</u>.

C. Identifying Verbals, Verbal Phrases, Appositives, and Appositive Phrases

The following sentences contain verbals and appositives. Identify each <u>verbal or verbal phrase</u> as a *participle*, a *participial phrase*, a *gerund*, a *gerund phrase*, an *infinitive*, or *an infinitive phrase*. Also identify each *appositive* or *appositive phrase*.

31. app. [5k]
32. part. phr. [5f]
33. inf. phr. [5j]
34. ger. phr. [5h]
35. inf. phr. [5j]

31. The architect <u>Bernini</u> designed the entrance of St. Peter's Basilica in Rome.

32. We saw the raccoon <u>escaping through the backdoor</u>.

33. <u>To finish what you have started</u> is an accomplishment.

34. <u>The honking of the car horn</u> awoke him from his nap.

35. Gerald M. Hopkins, Jr., is the candidate <u>to watch in the next election</u>.

36. <u>Waxed</u> floors can be dangerously slippery.
37. Babs and Tim listened to <u>the beautiful singing of the soprano.</u>
38. Aunt Anne got her degree in zoology, <u>the scientific study of animal life.</u>
39. They may have paid less attention than usual because they were so eager <u>to finish.</u>
40. <u>The dog's constant barking</u> annoyed the entire neighborhood.

36. part. [5e(2)]
37. ger. phr. [5h]
38. app. phr. [5l]
39. inf. [5i]
40. ger. phr. [5h]

Writing Application
Using Prepositional Phrases in a Story

Adjective and Adverb Phrases Your class is writing and illustrating a book of original stories. The book will be given to a second-grade class during National Library Week. For the book, write a short story about a search for sunken treasure. In your story, use a variety of adjective and adverb phrases.

Prewriting Begin by thinking about stories you have read or heard about sunken treasures. Then, write down some details from these real or fictional stories. Next, use your imagination to think of a setting and some characters for your own story. Choose a point of view (first person or third person), and start writing.

Writing As you write your first draft, try to make your story exciting and interesting for second-grade readers. Because you are telling a story, arrange the events in chronological order. Remember to include details in prepositional phrases whenever possible.

Revising Read the story aloud to a friend or a younger child. Notice what reactions you get from your listener. Have you included enough details to make the story seem real? You may need to cut some details or add some information. New information often can be added easily in prepositional phrases.

Publishing Proofread your story for any errors in grammar, usage, and punctuation. Publish your story, along with any illustrations for it, in a class book. Your class may want to read the stories aloud to younger students.

Grade-Level Standards
(Boldface indicates concepts that are taught and tested in this chapter.)

- Language Convention 1.0: **Students write and speak with a command of standard English conventions appropriate to this grade level.**

- Sentence Structure 1.1: **Use correct and varied sentence types** and sentence openings to present a lively and effective personal style.

- Sentence Structure 1.3: **Use subordination,** coordination, apposition, and other devices to indicate clearly the relationship between ideas.

- Grammar 1.4: **Edit written manuscripts to ensure that correct grammar is used.**

Prerequisite/Review Standard

- Grammar 1.3: Identify all parts of speech and types and structure of sentences.

Standards Coming Up in the Next Grade Level

- Grammar and Mechanics of Writing 1.1: Identify and correctly use clauses (e.g., main and subordinate), phrases (e.g., gerund, infinitive, and participial), and mechanics of punctuation (e.g., semicolons, colons, ellipses, hyphens).

- Grammar and Mechanics of Writing 1.2: Understand sentence construction (e.g., parallel structure, subordination, proper placement of modifiers) and

(continued)

Numerals in brackets refer to rules tested by the items in the Diagnostic Preview.

1. adv. [6c, e]
2. adj. [6c, d]
3. n. [6c, f]
4. adv. [6c, e]
5. [6b]
6. [6b]
7. adv. [6c, e]
8. [6b]
9. adj. [6c, d]
10. n. [6c, f]

The Clause
Independent Clauses and Subordinate Clauses

Diagnostic Preview

Identifying Independent and Subordinate Clauses

Identify each italicized clause in the following paragraphs as an *independent clause* or a *subordinate clause.* Then, tell whether each italicized subordinate clause is used as a *noun,* an *adjective,* or an *adverb.*

EXAMPLES   When my mother got a new job, **[1]** *we had to move to another town.*

1. independent clause

[2] *When my mother got a new job,* we had to move to another town.

2. subordinate clause—adverb

[1] *Because I didn't want to transfer to another school,* I didn't want to move. This is the fourth time [2] *that I have had to change schools,* and every time I've wished [3] *that I could just stay at my old school.* [4] *As soon as I make friends in a new place,* I have to move again and leave them behind. [5] *Then I am a stranger again at the new school.*

[6] *We lived in our last house for three years,* which is longer than in any other place [7] *since I was little.* [8] *Living there so long, I had a chance to meet several people* [9] *who became good friends of mine.* My best friends, Chris and Marty, said [10] *that they would write to me,* and I promised to write to them, too.

However, the friends [11] *that I've had before* had promised to write, but [12] *after a letter or two we lost touch.* [13] *Why this always happens* is a mystery to me.

I dreaded having to register at my new school [14] *after the school year had begun.* [15] *By then, everyone else would already have made friends,* and [16] *I would be an outsider,* as I knew from experience. There are always some students who bully and tease [17] *whoever is new at school* or anyone else [18] *who is different.* Back in elementary school I would get angry and upset [19] *when people picked on me.* Since then, I've learned how to fit in and make friends in spite of [20] *whatever anyone does to hassle me or make me feel uncomfortable.*

Everywhere [21] *that I've gone to school,* some students are friendly and offer to show me around. [22] *I used to be shy,* and I wouldn't take them up on their invitations. Since they didn't know [23] *whether I was shy or unfriendly,* they soon left me alone. Now, [24] *whenever someone is friendly to me at a new school or in a new neighborhood,* I fight my shyness and act friendly myself. It's still hard to get used to new places and new people, but [25] *it's much easier with a little help from new friends.*

11. adj [6c, d]
12. [6b]
13. n. [6c, f]
14. adv. [6c, e]
15. [6b]
16. [6b]
17. n. [6c, f]
18. adj. [6c, d]
19. adv. [6c, e]
20. n. [6c, f]
21. adj. [6c, d]
22. [6b]
23. n. [6c, f]
24. adv. [6c, e]
25. [6b]

What Is a Clause?

6a. A *clause* is a word group that contains a verb and its subject and that is used as a sentence or as part of a sentence.

Every clause has a subject and a verb. However, not every clause expresses a complete thought.

SENTENCE	Writers gathered at the home of Gertrude Stein when she lived in Paris.

           S   **V**

CLAUSE   Writers gathered at the home of Gertrude Stein
[complete thought]

           S   **V**

CLAUSE   when she lived in Paris [incomplete thought]

There are two kinds of clauses: the *independent clause* and the *subordinate clause.*

proper English usage (e.g., consistency of verb tenses).

■ Grammar and Mechanics of Writing 1.3: Demonstrate an understanding of proper English usage and control of grammar, paragraph and sentence structure, diction, and syntax.

▼

INTRODUCING THE CHAPTER

■ The first section of this chapter gives a brief introduction to clauses. The rest of the chapter discusses independent and subordinate clauses, focusing on the function of subordinate clauses as adjective clauses, adverb clauses, and noun clauses.

■ The chapter closes with a **Chapter Review** including a **Writing Application** feature that asks students to write a paragraph defining a term, using at least four adjective clauses in their definitions.

■ For help in integrating this chapter with writing assignments in *Holt Literature and Language Arts,* use the **Teaching Strands** chart on pp. T24–T25.

ASSESSING

Entry-Level Assessment

Diagnostic Preview. In evaluating students' writing, you may discover that some students do not use a variety of sentence structures. You could use the **Diagnostic Preview** to assess students' understanding of independent and subordinate clauses. Then, have students work individually or in small groups on activities and exercises designed to develop understanding in the areas in which they show weakness.

Differentiating Instruction
■ *UA: Differentiating Instruction*
■ *UA: Supporting Instruction in Five Languages*
Assessment
■ *Formal Assessment*
■ *Progress-Monitoring Tests,* pp. 11–12, 48

■ *Test Generator (Teacher One Stop DVD-ROM)* 🎵
Other Language Resources
■ *Spelling Lessons & Activities*
■ *WordSharp: An Interactive Vocabulary Tutor*
■ *Reading and Writing Transparencies*

GRAMMAR

The Independent Clause and the Subordinate Clause

Rules 6b, c *(pp. 120–123)*

OBJECTIVES

- To identify the subjects and verbs in independent clauses
- To identify word groups as independent or subordinate clauses
- To identify subordinate clauses and their subjects and verbs
- To write sentences with independent and subordinate clauses

---

PRETEACHING

Lesson Starter

Motivating. Help students recognize the difference between independent and subordinate clauses by reading clauses aloud, exaggerating the incompleteness of the subordinate clause. Here are some examples that you can read to the class.

1. While you were away . . .
2. When he answered correctly . . .
3. After we had breakfast . . .

Point out that all three clauses leave the hearer wanting more information, which an independent clause would provide.

┌HELP─

Before doing Exercise 1, you may want to review subjects and verbs in Chapter 1: The Parts of a Sentence.

The Independent Clause

6b. An *independent* (or *main*) *clause* expresses a complete thought and can stand by itself as a complete sentence.

EXAMPLES

        S   V
The sun set an hour ago. [This entire sentence is an independent clause.]

   S   V
Jean Merrill wrote *The Pushcart War,* **and**

   S   V
Ronni Solbert illustrated the book. [This sentence contains two independent clauses.]

           S   V
After I finish studying, **I will go to the movies.** [This sentence contains one subordinate clause and one independent clause.]

Exercise 1 **Identifying Subjects and Verbs in Independent Clauses**

Identify the <u>subject</u> and <u>verb</u> in each italicized independent clause in the following sentences.

EXAMPLE   **1.** Before she left for college, *my sister read the comics in the newspaper every day.*

        1. *sister—subject; read—verb*

1. *She told me* that Jump Start was her favorite.
2. Since she liked it so much, *I made a point of reading it, too.*
3. *The comic strip was created by this young man, Robb Armstrong,* who lives and works in Philadelphia.
4. *Jump Start features a police officer named Joe and his wife, Marcy,* who is a nurse.

RESOURCES

The Independent Clause and the Subordinate Clause

Practice

- *Language & Sentence Skills Practice,* pp. 119–122

5. If you aren't familiar with the strip, *you may not recognize Joe and Marcy standing behind their creator.*

6. Like many readers, *I like funny strips best.*

7. *Other people like more serious comics* that feature an ongoing drama.

8. *Ask your family and friends* what comics they like best.

9. *You can see* whether Jump Start is among their favorites.

10. During the holidays, *I plan to draw my own comic strip.*

8. understood *you*

The Subordinate Clause

6c. A *subordinate* (or *dependent*) *clause* does not express a complete thought and cannot stand by itself as a complete sentence.

A word such as *that, what,* or *since* often signals the beginning of a subordinate clause.

SUBORDINATE CLAUSES

$$\overset{S}{} \overset{V}{}$$
that I wanted

$$\overset{S}{} \overset{V}{}$$
what she saw

$$\overset{S}{} \overset{V}{}$$
since most plants die without light

The meaning of a subordinate clause is complete only when the clause is attached to an independent clause.

SENTENCES
The store did not have the video game **that I wanted.**

The witness told the police officers **what she saw.**

Since most plants die without light, we moved our houseplants closer to the window.

Sometimes the word that begins a subordinate clause is the subject of the clause.

EXAMPLES
$$\overset{S}{} \overset{V}{}$$
The animals **that are in the wildlife preserve** are protected from hunters.

$$\overset{S}{} \overset{V}{}$$
Can you tell me **who wrote "America the Beautiful"?**

STYLE TIP

A subordinate clause that is capitalized and punctuated as a sentence is a **sentence fragment**. Avoid using sentence fragments in formal writing.

Reference Note

For more about **sentence fragments**, see page 4.

DIRECT TEACHING

Modeling and Demonstration

The Clause. Model how to identify independent and subordinate clauses by using the example clauses *After I finish supper* and *I will go to the movies*. First, ask students to identify the subject of the first example. [*I*] Next, ask them to identify the verb. [*finish*] Then, ask whether the clause expresses a complete thought and can stand by itself. [*no*] Therefore, the clause is a subordinate clause. Next, repeat the procedure with the second clause. [*I—subject; will go—verb phrase; yes*] The second example can stand by itself; therefore, it is an independent clause. Tell students they can combine the two clauses to create the independent clause *After I finish supper, I will go to the movies*. Now, have a volunteer use another example from this chapter to demonstrate how to identify independent and subordinate clauses.

The Subordinate Clause **121**

Critical Thinking

Metacognition. After students complete the **Oral Practice** and **Exercise 2,** ask them to write brief answers to the following questions.

1. How did the way you read the items in the **Oral Practice** help you decide whether the items were independent or subordinate clauses?

2. How did you apply the rules and examples to identify subordinate clauses?

3. What process did you use to identify the verbs in subordinate clauses?

4. What process did you use to select the subjects in subordinate clauses?

Oral Practice Identifying Independent and Subordinate Clauses

Read the following word groups aloud, and identify each one as an *independent clause* or a *subordinate clause.*

EXAMPLE   **1.** as I answered the telephone

     1. subordinate clause

1. we memorized the lyrics   **1.** ind.
2. as they sat on the back porch   **2.** sub.
3. if no one is coming   **3.** sub.
4. my sister was born on Valentine's Day   **4.** ind.
5. which everyone enjoyed   **5.** sub.
6. the flood destroyed many crops   **6.** ind.
7. the singer wore a silk scarf   **7.** ind.
8. when the lights were flickering   **8.** sub.
9. since we talked to Maria   **9.** sub.
10. that the lion's cage was empty   **10.** sub.

Exercise 2 Identifying Subordinate Clauses and Their Subjects and Verbs

Identify the subordinate clause in each of the following sentences. Give the subject and the verb of each subordinate clause.

EXAMPLE   **1.** My report is about the plague that spread across Europe in the fourteenth century.

     1. that spread across Europe in the fourteenth century; subject—that; verb—spread

1. In 1347, trading ships arrived at the Mediterranean island of Sicily from Caffa, which was a port city on the Black Sea.
2. When the sailors went ashore, many of them carried a strange illness.
3. No medicine could save the stricken sailors, who died quickly and painfully.
4. Bubonic plague, which is the most common form of the illness, causes swelling in the legs, neck, and armpits.
5. The disease was spread by fleas, which traveled between cities in Europe on rats and other animals.
6. Millions of people became sick and died as the plague spread from Sicily across Europe.

7. On this map, you can trace how quickly the plague spread.

8. Many terrified survivors thought that the world was coming to an end.

9. No one is sure of the total number of people who died from the dreaded plague.

10. Since modern medicine offers new ways for controlling the plague, the spread of this disease is unlikely today.

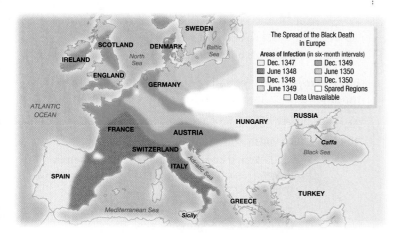

The Spread of the Black Death in Europe
Areas of Infection (in six-month intervals)
☐ Dec. 1347   ☐ Dec. 1349
■ June 1348   ☐ June 1350
■ Dec. 1348   ☐ Dec. 1350
☐ June 1349   ☐ Spared Regions
☐ Data Unavailable

Exercise 3 Writing Sentences with Independent Clauses and Subordinate Clauses

Write a sentence by adding an independent clause to each subordinate clause. Draw one line under the subject and two lines under the verb of each clause.

EXAMPLES   1. who came late

     1. *Anica is the volunteer who came late.*

     2. as the horn blared

     2. *As the horn blared, I was running out the door.*

1. when the ice melts
2. if my teacher approves
3. since you insist
4. when they act silly
5. who borrowed my notes
6. as she began to shout
7. when we danced on stage
8. who gave the report
9. since I sleep soundly
10. that I bought yesterday

The Subordinate Clause   **123**

Exercise 3 Writing Sentences with Independent Clauses and Subordinate Clauses

POSSIBLE ANSWERS

1. When the ice melts, we will wear boots.

2. If my teacher approves, I will make a diorama including dinosaurs for my science project.

3. Since you insist, I will stay for dinner.

4. When they act silly, Mom separates the twins.

5. The one who borrowed my notes has not returned them.

6. The band stopped playing as she began to shout.

7. I broke the heel on my shoe when we danced on stage.

8. I do not remember who gave the report.

9. The alarm will not wake me since I sleep soundly.

10. The shoes that I bought yesterday are in that box.

The Adjective Clause

GRAMMAR

Rule 6d (*pp. 124–127*)

OBJECTIVES

- To identify adjective clauses, the relative pronoun in each clause, and the word or words to which the relative pronoun refers

- To add adjective clauses to sentences

DIRECT TEACHING

Modeling and Demonstration

The Adjective Clause. Model how to identify an adjective clause by using the example *Leonardo da Vinci was the artist who painted the* Mona Lisa. First, have students identify the subordinate clause. [*who painted the* Mona Lisa] Ask students whether the clause begins with *who, which, that, whom,* or *whose.* [yes] Next, ask what question the clause answers. [*which one*] Then, tell students that because the clause answers the question *which one* and begins with the relative pronoun *who,* it is an adjective clause. Now, have a volunteer use another example from this chapter to demonstrate how to identify an adjective clause.

STYLE TIP

Adjective clauses can bring clarity and good description to your writing. Be careful, though, not to use too many adjective clauses. Overusing adjective clauses can make your writing wordy. You might want to replace some of them with adjectives or brief phrases.

WORDY
They live in the apartment building **that is made of brick** and **that is located next to the fire station.**

BETTER
They live in the **brick** apartment building **next to the fire station.**

Reference Note
For information on using **who** and **whom** correctly, see page 226.

The Adjective Clause

Like an adjective or an adjective phrase, an adjective clause may modify a noun or a pronoun.

ADJECTIVE	the **blonde** woman
ADJECTIVE PHRASE	the woman **with blonde hair**
ADJECTIVE CLAUSE	the woman **who has blonde hair**

ADJECTIVE	a **steel** bridge
ADJECTIVE PHRASE	a bridge **of steel**
ADJECTIVE CLAUSE	a bridge **that is made of steel**

6d. An *adjective clause* is a subordinate clause that modifies a noun or a pronoun.

An adjective clause usually follows the word or words it modifies and tells *which one* or *what kind.*

EXAMPLES Ms. Jackson showed slides **that she had taken in Egypt.** [The adjective clause modifies the noun *slides,* telling *which* slides.]

The brownie cap is a mushroom **that grows in lawns and other grassy areas.** [The adjective clause modifies the noun *mushroom,* telling *what kind* of mushroom.]

That one, **which is my favorite,** was bought in Kenya. [The adjective clause modifies the pronoun *one,* telling *which* one.]

Relative Pronouns

An adjective clause is usually introduced by a *relative pronoun.*

Common Relative Pronouns				
that	which	who	whom	whose

A *relative pronoun* relates an adjective clause to the word or words the clause modifies.

EXAMPLES Leonardo da Vinci was the artist **who painted the Mona Lisa.** [The relative pronoun *who* begins the adjective clause and relates it to the noun *artist.*]

RESOURCES

The Adjective Clause

Practice

- *Language & Sentence Skills Practice,* pp. 123–125
- *Developmental Language & Sentence Skills,* pp. 47–48

The magazine, **which arrived in the mail today,** is torn. [The relative pronoun *which* begins the adjective clause and relates it to the noun *magazine*.]

NOTE The relative pronoun *that* can be used to refer both to people and to things. The relative pronoun *which* is used to refer to things only.

Sometimes a relative pronoun is preceded by a preposition that is part of the adjective clause.

EXAMPLES   Have you read the book **on which the movie is based**?

The actor **to whom I am referring** is Sir Alec Guinness.

In addition to relating a subordinate clause to the rest of the sentence, a relative pronoun often has a grammatical function in the subordinate clause.

EXAMPLES   Is this tape the one **that is on sale**? [*That* relates the subordinate clause to the word *one* and also functions as the subject of the subordinate clause.]

The jeweler **to whom I took the broken bracelet** repaired it quickly. [*Whom* relates the subordinate clause to the word *jeweler* and functions as the object of the preposition *to*.]

To modify a place or a time, an adjective clause may be introduced by *when* or *where*. When used to introduce adjective clauses, these words are called **relative adverbs.**

EXAMPLES   This is the spot **where we caught most of the fish.**

Mrs. Itoh looks forward to Saturday afternoons, **when she works in her garden.**

In some cases, the relative pronoun or adverb can be omitted.

EXAMPLES   We haven't seen the silver jewelry **[that] she brought back from Mexico.**

Do you remember the time **[when or that] the dog caught the skunk**?

A boy **[whom or that] I know** is a nationally ranked tennis player.

Reference Note
For information on **when to set off adjective clauses with commas,** see page 321.

DIFFERENTIATING INSTRUCTION

English-Language Learners

Spanish. Spanish speakers may sometimes use the relative pronoun *that* even in cases where *who* or *which* would sound more natural in English. You may want to show them some sentences containing *that, who,* and *which* in adjective clauses, allowing them to investigate in which situations each relative pronoun is used. Allow them to practice inserting appropriate relative pronouns into sentences and to ask questions about what they do not understand.

Spanish. In Spanish it is considered awkward to end a clause with a verb. For example, in an English sentence such as "I like the book that Maria is reading," the Spanish speaker may want to invert the subject and the verb in the adjective clause: *Me gusta el libro que está leyendo Maria* ("I like the book that is reading Maria"). You may want to give students a list of sentences in which the adjective clause ends in a verb, and emphasize the subject-verb order. Also, suggest that students practice reading the sentences aloud.

The Subordinate Clause   **125**

MINI-LESSON **Grammar**   *Continued on p. 126*

Combining Sentences by Using Adjective Clauses. Two short sentences can often be combined into a longer and smoother sentence by converting one of the sentences into an adjective clause. Write the following sentences on the chalkboard, and ask stu-

dents to combine them by making one sentence an adjective clause. Ask students to point out the relative pronouns in the new sentences. Student responses may vary.

This is the apple tree.
This apple tree produces the best apples.

PRACTICE

PRACTICE

Guided and Independent

You may wish to use **Exercise 4** as guided practice and have students complete **Exercise 5** as independent practice.

HOMEWORK

RETEACHING

Relative Pronouns

The omission of the relative pronoun or relative adverb can be confusing to some students. To show that omitting such words often makes sentences more readable and more like spoken English, read the following two sentences aloud and ask which sounds better.

1. I like the haircut that you got yesterday.

2. I like the haircut you got yesterday.

[*Most students will prefer the second sentence.*]

Offer similar sentences to show students how to supply the missing relative pronouns or relative adverbs when analyzing these sentences. Then, ask students to write several sentences in which the relative pronouns or relative adverbs are omitted.

Exercise 4 Identifying Adjective Clauses

Identify the adjective clause in each of the following sentences. Give the relative pronoun and the word or word group to which the relative pronoun refers.

EXAMPLE **1.** Our friends have a canary that is named Neptune.

1. that is named Neptune; that—canary

1. Most proverbs are sayings that give advice.

2. Trivia questions have been organized into games that have become quite popular.

3. A black hole, which results after a star has collapsed, can trap energy and matter.

4. The school presented a special award to the student whose work had improved most.

5. Frances Perkins, who served as secretary of labor, was the first woman to hold a Cabinet position.

6. The problem that worries us right now is the pollution of underground sources of water.

7. We enjoyed the poems of Gwendolyn Brooks, who for years was poet laureate of Illinois.

8. In *Walden*, Henry David Thoreau shared ideas that have influenced many people.

9. Athena, who ranked as an important Greek deity, protected the city of Athens.

10. A friend is a person whom you can trust.

Exercise 5 Identifying Adjective Clauses

Identify the adjective clause in each of the following sentences. Give the relative pronoun or relative adverb and the word or word group to which the pronoun refers.

EXAMPLE **1.** Crispus Attucks was an African American patriot who was killed during the Boston Massacre.

1. who was killed during the Boston Massacre; who—patriot

1. Coco Chanel is the woman for whom the perfume Chanel No. 5 is named.

2. Here is the concert hall where we heard the great cello player Pablo Casals.

3. The cello is an instrument to which I could listen for hours.

MINI-LESSON **Grammar** *Continued from p.125*

[*This is the apple tree that produces the best apples.*]
My cousin lives in Miami.
My cousin came to visit us.
[*My cousin who lives in Miami came to visit us.*]

The cupboard doors are pale pink.
We painted them ourselves.
[*The cupboard doors, which we painted ourselves, are pale pink.*]

4. Ella Fitzgerald, (who) started singing in New York City, was famous throughout the world.
5. The English playwright Christopher Marlowe wrote of Helen of Troy, "Was this the face (that) launched a thousand ships?"
6. Anita was one of the sopranos (who) sang in the chorus.
7. In the play *My Fair Lady*, Eliza Doolittle, a poor flower seller, becomes a woman (whom) everyone admires.
8. The Kinderhook was the creek in (which) we found the shells.
9. Janet Flanner, (who) wrote dispatches from Paris, used the pen name Genêt.
10. The astronauts, to (whom) travel in the space shuttle is almost routine, must always keep in shape.

Exercise 6 Using Adjective Clauses

Add an adjective clause to each of the following sentences. Write the entire sentence. Circle the relative pronoun, underline the adjective clause once, and underline twice the word to which the pronoun refers.

EXAMPLE   **1.** The book is a detective story.
         1. *The book (that) I read is a detective story.*

1. A new book is here.
2. My cousin likes to draw.
3. The class will go on a field trip.
4. My family traveled to my favorite state.
5. A deer and fawn were in the park.
6. Kwame and Joachim built the bookcase.
7. After the game we are going to the mall.
8. Damita won the 10K run.
9. Before the art show, there will be an international meal.
10. The author will speak tomorrow at the assembly.

The Adverb Clause

Unlike an adverb or an adverb phrase, an adverb clause has a subject and a verb.

ADVERB	He will leave **soon.**
ADVERB PHRASE	He will leave **in a few minutes.**
ADVERB CLAUSE	He will leave **when he is ready.** [*He* is the subject of the adverb clause, and *is* is the verb.]

Exercise 6   Using Adjective Clauses

POSSIBLE ANSWERS

1. A new book (that) I ordered is here.
2. My cousin, (who) lives in Georgia, likes to draw.
3. The class will go on a field trip, (which) begins at 6:00 A.M.
4. My family traveled to my favorite state, (which) is Florida.
5. A deer and fawn, (which) were hard to see against the fall landscape, were in the park.
6. Kwame and Joachim, (who) are neighbors, built the bookcase.
7. After the game, (which) should end around 4:00 P.M., we are going to the mall.
8. Damita, (who) had never competed in a racing event before, won the 10K run.
9. Before the art show, there will be an international meal, (which) I am planning to attend.
10. The author, (whose) book we studied in social studies, will speak tomorrow at the assembly.

The Adverb Clause
Rule 6e *(pp. 127–130)*

OBJECTIVES

■ To identify adverb clauses and the subordinating conjunction, subject, and verb in each

■ To write sentences with adverb clauses and to identify the subordinating conjunction, the subject, and the verb in each adverb clause

GRAMMAR

Modeling and Demonstration

The Adverb Clause. Model how to identify an adverb clause by using the example *When winter sets in, many animals hibernate.* First, have students identify the subordinate clause. [*When winter sets in*] Next, ask what question the clause answers. [*When do many animals hibernate?*] Then, tell students that because the clause answers the question *when,* it is an adverb clause. Now, have a volunteer use another example from this chapter to demonstrate how to identify an adverb clause.

English-Language Learners

General Strategies. Most languages use structures similar to adverb clauses; however, the order of the subject and the verb is often inverted. You may want to have students use the **Common Subordinating Conjunctions** chart to practice saying and writing sentences with adverb clauses. Emphasize the subject-verb pattern that is most common in English by having students identify the subject and the verb of each clause they write.

Relating to Writing

Ask students to describe a situation by writing sentences containing adverb clauses. For example, ask them what experiences they have had that could be explained with the help of an adverb clause beginning with *Since.* You might illustrate by saying, "Since I got up this morning, I have been happy that today is Monday."

| STYLE | TIP |

In most cases, deciding where to place an adverb clause is a matter of style, not of correctness. Both sentences below are correct.

EXAMPLES

Though she was almost unknown during her lifetime, Emily Dickinson is now known as a major American poet.

Emily Dickinson is now known as a major American poet **though she was almost unknown during her lifetime.**

Reference Note

For more about using **commas** with **adverb clauses,** see page 321.

6e. An *adverb clause* is a subordinate clause that modifies a verb, an adjective, or an adverb.

An adverb clause tells *where, when, how, why, to what extent,* or *under what condition.*

EXAMPLES You may sit **wherever you wish.** [The adverb clause modifies the verb *may sit,* telling *where* you may sit.]

When winter sets in, many animals hibernate. [The adverb clause modifies the verb *hibernate,* telling *when* many animals hibernate.]

Jessica and Anaba look **as though they have some exciting news for us.** [The adverb clause modifies the verb *look,* telling *how* Jessica and Anaba look.]

Happy **because he had made an A,** Tony hurried home. [The adverb clause modifies the adjective *Happy,* telling *why* Tony was happy.]

Gabrielle can type faster **than I can.** [The adverb clause modifies the adverb *faster,* telling *to what extent* Gabrielle can type faster.]

If it does not rain tomorrow, we will go to Crater Lake. [The adverb clause modifies the verb *will go,* telling *under what condition* we will go to Crater Lake.]

Notice that when an adverb clause begins a sentence, it is followed by a comma.

Subordinating Conjunctions

An adverb clause is introduced by a *subordinating conjunction*—a word that shows the relationship between the adverb clause and the word or words that the clause modifies.

Common Subordinating Conjunctions			
after	as though	since	when
although	because	so that	whenever
as	before	than	where
as if	how	though	wherever
as long as	if	unless	whether
as soon as	in order that	until	while

NOTE The words *after*, *as*, *before*, *since*, and *until* are also commonly used as prepositions.

PREPOSITION   **After** lunch we'll finish making the model airplane.

SUBORDINATING   **After** you wash the dishes, I'll dry them and
CONJUNCTION   put them away.

Reference Note

For more information about **prepositions**, see page 66.

Exercise 7 **Identifying Adverb Clauses**

Identify the |adverb clause| in each of the following sentences. In each clause, circle the subordinating conjunction, and underline the subject once and the verb twice.

EXAMPLE   **1.** Although they lived in different regions of North America, American Indian children all across the continent enjoyed playing similar kinds of games.

   1. (Although) they lived in different regions of North America

1. These children once used many natural objects in games |(since) no toy stores existed there at the time.|

2. Many American Indian children played darts with large feathers (as) these Arapaho children are doing.|

3. |(If) you look closely at the tree,| you can see the children's target, a hole in the trunk.

4. These children are throwing goose feathers attached to bones, but players also used wild turkey feathers (whenever) they could find them.|

5. |(Although) they played many kinds of games,| American Indians in the Southwest especially liked kickball races.

6. The children made balls out of materials such as wood and tree roots (before) they started playing.|

The Subordinate Clause   **129**

DIRECT TEACHING

GRAMMAR

Correcting Misconceptions
Subordinating Conjunctions.
Students may incorrectly identify adverb clauses as prepositional phrases because some prepositions such as *after*, *as*, *before*, and *since* may be used as subordinating conjunctions. Remind students that a preposition is followed by a noun or pronoun (the object of the preposition), and a prepositional phrase does not contain a subject or a verb. [*after lunch*] An adverb clause, however, must contain a subject and a verb. In the example *after you wash the dishes, you* is the subject and *wash* is the verb.

Exercise 7

DISTRIBUTED REVIEW
Ask students to identify the verbals and verbal phrases listed below.

4. attached to bones [*participial phrase*]

6. playing [*gerund*]

8. to find [*infinitive*]

DIFFERENTIATING INSTRUCTION

Advanced Learners
Activity. To demonstrate how important it is to be clear and precise when writing instructions, ask each student to create and describe a game using a common object, such as a paper clip or a pen. Have students use adverb clauses in explaining how the games are played. When students have finished writing the descriptions, have them underline the adverb clauses. You may want to let students make and then play their games.

7. (After) snow had fallen, | Seneca children raced small, hand-made "snow boats."

8. Pine cones were used in many games | (because) they were so easy to find. |

9. (While) some children played catch with pine cones, | others had cone-throwing contests.

10. Games gave the children practice in skills they would need (when) they became adults. |

Exercise 8 **Writing Sentences with Adverb Clauses**

Add an adverb clause to each of the following sentences. Write the entire sentence. Circle the subordinating conjunction, and underline the subject of each adverb clause once and the verb twice.

EXAMPLE
    1. The movie finally ended.
     1. (After) we had spent three hours in the theater, the movie finally ended.

1. Most of the members of the Drama Club auditioned for the play.
2. Erica speaks three languages.
3. We prepared moussaka, a Greek dish with lamb and eggplant, for our Cooking Club's international supper.
4. The Goldmans have visited Acapulco several times.
5. Jill daydreams in class.
6. We students planted fifteen oak trees at our school on Arbor Day.
7. Timothy fixes computers.
8. Mr. Washington worked for a newspaper.
9. The eighth-graders in Mrs. Maranjian's class offered to decorate the gym.
10. The soccer field is closed.

The Noun Clause

6f. A *noun clause* is a subordinate clause that is used as a noun.

A noun clause may be used as a subject, as a complement (such as a predicate nominative, a direct object, or an indirect object), or as an object of a preposition.

Exercise 8 **Writing Sentences with Adverb Clauses**

POSSIBLE ANSWERS

1. (After) the drama coach promoted the production, most of the members of the Drama Club auditioned for the play.
2. (Because) she lived in several countries as a child, Erica speaks three languages.
3. (Although) we were afraid the recipe might be too difficult, we prepared moussaka, a Greek dish with lamb and eggplant, for our Cooking Club's international supper.
4. (Because) they like to practice their Spanish, the Goldmans have visited Acapulco several times.
5. (When) spring weather arrives, Jill daydreams in class.
6. (After) we raised the money, we students planted fifteen oak trees at our school on Arbor Day.
7. (Since) he trained at an electronics school, Timothy fixes computers.
8. Mr. Washington worked for a newspaper (when) he lived in the Middle East.
9. The eighth-graders in Mrs. Maranjian's class offered to decorate the gym (so that) they could hold a winter dance.
10. The soccer field is closed (because) the snow has not melted.

The Noun Clause

Rule 6f *(pp. 130–134)*

OBJECTIVE

- To identify noun clauses and their functions in sentences

┌HELP─

Knowing where clauses are placed in a sentence can help you decide whether a clause is an adjective clause or an adverb clause. Adjective clauses usually follow the noun or pronoun they modify. Adverb clauses often may be moved around in a sentence without changing the meaning of the sentence. Also, adverb clauses often begin or end a sentence.

EXAMPLES

Daniel, **whom I have known for many years,** is the pitcher for our team. [The adjective clause *whom I have known for many years* describes or modifies *Daniel.* Moving the clause elsewhere would either change the meaning of the sentence or make the sentence very awkward.]

Because Daniel is such a strong pitcher, our team has won many games. [The adverb clause *Because Daniel is such a strong pitcher* tells *why* the team has won many games. The clause would also make sense at the end of the sentence.]

RESOURCES

The Noun Clause

Practice

- *Language & Sentence Skills Practice,* pp. 129–134

SUBJECT	**That they were angry** was obvious to the others.
PREDICATE NOMINATIVE	Three dollars was **what Daniel offered for the trinket**.
DIRECT OBJECT	Anthony and Peter remembered **who he was.**
INDIRECT OBJECT	The hostess gives **whoever enters** a menu.
OBJECT OF A PREPOSITION	Eager to please the speaker, we listened to **whatever he said.**

Common Introductory Words for Noun Clauses

how	whatever	which	whom
that	when	who	whomever
what	whether	whoever	why

The word that introduces a noun clause often has a grammatical function within the clause.

EXAMPLES   Give a free pass to **whoever asks for one.** [The introductory word *whoever* is the subject of the verb *asks*.]

Lani would not show either of us **what he wrote.** [The introductory word *what* is the direct object of the verb *wrote*—he wrote what.]

Sometimes the word that introduces a noun clause is omitted but is understood.

EXAMPLE   She said **[that] the milk was sour.**

Exercise 9   Identifying Noun Clauses and Their Functions

Identify the <u>noun clause</u> in each of the following sentences. Then, tell whether the noun clause is used as a *subject*, a *predicate nominative*, a *direct object*, an *indirect object*, or an *object of a preposition*.

EXAMPLE   1. We couldn't find what was making the noise.
   1. *what was making the noise—direct object*

1. <u>Whatever you decide</u> will be fine with us.

Reference Note

For information about **subjects,** see page 7. For information about **complements,** see page 79. For information about **objects of prepositions,** see page 66.

TIPS & TRICKS

Notice that noun clauses and adjective clauses sometimes begin with the same words (*that, which, who, whom, whose*). To tell the difference between an adjective clause and a noun clause, you must decide how the clause functions in the sentence.

ADJECTIVE CLAUSE
Did you find any plates **that are chipped**? [*That are chipped* modifies the noun *plates*.]

NOUN CLAUSE
I can see **that this plate is chipped.** [*That this plate is chipped* tells what I can see and functions as a direct object.]

Reference Note

For information on using *who, whom, whoever,* and *whomever* correctly, see page 226.

1. s.

DIRECT TEACHING

Modeling and Demonstration

The Noun Clause. Model how to identify a noun clause by using the example *Anthony and Peter remembered who he was.* First, have students identify the subordinate clause. [*who he was*] Next, ask whether the clause acts as a noun. [*Yes, the clause is the direct object of the verb* remembered.] Now, have a volunteer use another example from this chapter to demonstrate how to identify a noun clause.

DIFFERENTIATING INSTRUCTION

Learners Having Difficulty

Noun Clauses. To help students understand that noun clauses function as nouns, point out that a simple noun or pronoun can be substituted for a noun clause. Usually, the word *it* can be substituted. As an example, write the following sentence on the chalkboard, cross out the noun clause, and replace it with *it:*

<u>That Josh won the match</u> surprised everyone.

<u>It</u> surprised everyone.

Encourage students to use this technique of substituting as they complete **Exercise 9.**

The Subordinate Clause   **131**

2. p.n. 2. No, these results are not <u>what we had planned</u>.

3. d.o. 3. Do you know <u>what happened to the rest of my sandwich?</u>

4. o.p. 4. Stuart is looking for <u>whoever owns that red bicycle</u>.

5. d.o. 5. Checking our supplies, we discovered <u>that we had forgotten the flour</u>.

6. p.n. 6. The story's worst flaw is <u>that it doesn't have a carefully developed plot</u>.

7. s. 7. <u>Whoever takes us to the beach</u> is my friend for life.

8. i.o. 8. The painter gave <u>whatever spots had dried on the wall</u> another coat of primer.

9. o.p. 9. At lunch, my friends and I talked about <u>what we should do as our service project</u>.

10. s. 10. <u>That Jennifer won the race</u> surprised no one at the track meet.

Review A Identifying Adjective, Adverb, and Noun Clauses

Identify each <u>subordinate clause</u> in the following sentences, and tell whether it is used as an *adjective*, an *adverb*, or a *noun*.

EXAMPLE 1. Is this the jacket that you bought?
      1. *that you bought—adjective*

┌HELP┐
Remember that the relative pronoun sometimes is omitted.

1. adj. 1. My aunt found the teapot <u>that my grandfather brought back from Thailand</u>.

2. adv. 2. James skied the advanced slope <u>as if he were an expert</u>.

3. n. 3. Did anyone ask her <u>what sort of present she would like for her birthday?</u>

4. adv. 4. Eduardo can play the drums better <u>than Alex can</u>.

5. adj. 5. Have you seen the painting <u>to which I am referring?</u>

6. n. 6. Their solution was <u>that we work on the extra-credit project as a team</u>.

7. n. 7. Linda told Ken <u>that Monica volunteered to help with the Special Olympics</u>.

8. n. 8. <u>Whoever wins the student council election</u> will have a great deal of responsibility.

9. adv. 9. <u>Because the tropical storm gained strength</u>, our flight to Belize was canceled.

10. adj. 10. I can't find the baseball and mitt <u>my cousin lent me</u>.

Learning for Life

Imitating Magazine Writers. The use of subordinate clauses makes writing more interesting. Select from respected magazines several paragraphs that contain long sentences with embedded subordinate clauses.

Allow students to work in groups, and give each group a different paragraph to analyze. Ask them to break down the sentences into a series of simple sentences and to write the simple sentences in paragraph form.

Review B **Identifying Subordinate Clauses**

Each of the following sentences contains a subordinate clause.
Identify each subordinate clause as an *adjective clause*, an *adverb
clause*, or a *noun clause*.

EXAMPLE　　**1.** The Museum of Appalachia, which is in Norris,
　　　　　　　Tennessee, is a re-created pioneer village.

　　　　　1. *which is in Norris, Tennessee—adjective clause*

1. If you've ever wanted to step into the past, you'll like this
museum. **1.** adv.

2. You can see many pioneer crafts and tools that are still used
at the museum. **2.** adj.　　　　　　　　　**3.** adj.

3. For example, the men on the right are splitting shingles with
tools that were used in their boyhood.

4. Two other men show how plowing
was done before the development
of modern equipment. **4.** n.

5. I think that the 250,000 pioneer tools
and other items on display will
amaze you. **5.** n.

6. What some visitors like to do is to
tour the village's log buildings and
then take a rest. **6.** n.　　　　　　**7.** adv.

7. While they're resting, they can often
listen to some mountain music.

The Subordinate Clause　　**133**

Next, ask the groups to swap the
student-written paragraphs with one
another. Then, ask each group to rewrite
the paragraphs as they think the original
authors wrote them.

After students have rewritten the paragraphs, let them compare their work to the
original paragraphs from the magazines.
Have students in groups discuss the effectiveness of both the originals and the students' work.

8. Listen to all the different instruments <u>that the musicians are playing</u>. **8.** adj.

9. At Homecoming, you might even meet the museum's founder, John Rice Irwin, <u>who grew up in the Appalachian Mountains</u>. **9.** adj.

10. <u>When I went to the museum's annual Homecoming</u>, I saw the fiddler pictured on the previous page perform. **10.** adv.

Review C **Writing Sentences with Independent and Subordinate Clauses**

Write your own sentences according to the following instructions. Underline the subordinate clauses.

EXAMPLE **1.** Write a sentence containing an independent clause and an adjective clause.

1. *I am going to the game with Gilbert, <u>who is my best friend</u>.*

1. Write a sentence containing an independent clause and no subordinate clause.
2. Write a sentence containing an independent clause and one subordinate clause.
3. Write a sentence containing an adjective clause that begins with a relative pronoun.
4. Write a sentence containing an adjective clause in which a preposition precedes the relative pronoun.
5. Write a sentence containing an introductory adverb clause.
6. Write a sentence containing an adverb clause and an adjective clause.
7. Write a sentence containing a noun clause used as a direct object.
8. Write a sentence containing a noun clause used as a subject.
9. Write a sentence containing a noun clause used as the object of a preposition.
10. Write a sentence containing a noun clause and either an adjective clause or an adverb clause.

Review C **Writing Sentences with Independent and Subordinate Clauses**

POSSIBLE ANSWERS

1. I like salads of all kinds.
2. <u>Although I eat many other kinds of food</u>, I like salads best.
3. I especially enjoy salads <u>that have several kinds of sprouts</u>.
4. My sister Tara is the person <u>with whom I most enjoy fixing salads</u>.
5. <u>When Tara and I visit the supermarket</u>, I go to the produce section first.
6. <u>When Tara can't find me</u>, she always knows the place <u>where I will be</u>.
7. Tara knows <u>what I like</u>.
8. <u>That I like salads with all the fixings</u> is very clear.
9. Sometimes she may get tired of hearing me talk about <u>what I'd most like to have for the next meal</u>.
10. <u>What I'd like tonight</u> is a mixed salad <u>that has Boston lettuce, red cabbage, and raisins</u>.

MEETING THE CHALLENGE

Think of a humorous or interesting incident that has happened to you. You may also choose to invent an incident. Then, write a brief account of that incident. In your account, use at least one example of each kind of clause covered in this chapter. Can your classmates identify the types of clauses you have used?

ANSWERS
Accounts will vary but should contain one of each kind of clause.

CONTENT-AREA CONNECTIONS

Mathematics. Hand out copies of an article or paragraph that demonstrates a well-developed writing style. Have students analyze the style of the piece by first underlining each subordinate clause and labeling it by type. Ask students to calculate the percentage of sentences in the piece that contain at least one subordinate clause. To find this figure, students should divide the number of sentences containing at least one subordinate clause by the total number of sentences. Then, have students determine what percentage of the subordinate clauses are adjective clauses, adverb clauses, and noun clauses. Explain that a variety of different types of clauses makes writing more interesting.

Numerals in brackets refer to rules tested by the items in the Chapter Review.

1.–10. [6a, c]

Chapter Review

A. Identifying Subordinate Clauses

Identify the subordinate clause in each of the following sentences.

1. The officer who gave us directions to the concert was helpful.
2. Since none of my family has been to Chicago, we decided to go there for vacation.
3. How the school team would do in the playoffs became the topic of the town.
4. Monica had written six thank-you notes when her pen ran out of ink.
5. The woman at the theater told us that the movie was sold out.
6. We decided to eat at whatever restaurant was the nearest one.
7. My brother's greatest fear was that he would miss the bus.
8. After she had purchased a book, she went to the park and started reading it.
9. Our neighbors returned the rake they borrowed last autumn.
10. When my father took the defective watch back to the store, the clerk asked to see a receipt.

B. Identifying Independent and Subordinate Clauses

Identify each italicized clause in the following sentences as an *independent clause* or a *subordinate clause*. Indicate whether each italicized subordinate clause is used as an *adjective*, an *adverb*, or a *noun*.

11. adv. [6c, e]
12. adj. [6c, d]
13. [6b]
14. n. [6c, f]
15. adv. [6c, e]
16. [6b]

11. *After it had been snowing for several hours,* we took our sleds out to Sentry Hill.
12. The ring *that I lost at the beach last summer* had belonged to my great-grandmother.
13. If he doesn't get here soon, *I'm leaving.*
14. Do you know *who she is?*
15. I have not seen Sean *since the football game ended.*
16. *In the morning they gathered their belongings and left* before the sun rose.

Chapter Review **135**

ASSESSING

Monitoring Progress

Chapter Review. To assess student progress, you may want to compare the types of items missed on the **Diagnostic Preview** to those missed on the **Chapter Review.** You may want to work out specific goals with individual students who are still having difficulty mastering essential information.

RESOURCES

The Clause

Review

■ *Language & Sentence Skills Practice,* pp. 132–134

Assessment

■ *Formal Assessment*
■ *Progress-Monitoring Tests,* pp. 11–12, 48
■ *Test Generator* *(Teacher One Stop DVD-ROM)*

17. n. [6c, f]
18. [6b]
19. adj. [6c, d]
20. n. [6c, f]
21. adv. [6c, e]
22. n. [6c, f]
23. adj. [6c, d]
24. [6b]
25. adj. [6c, d]
26. adv. [6c, e]
27. [6b]
28. adv. [6c, e]
29. adj. [6c, d]
30. n. [6c, f]

17. Nobody knew *that Derrick had worked out the solution*.
18. *The Hopi and the Zuni built their homes out of adobe*, which is a kind of sun-dried earth.
19. My dad says never to trust strangers *who seem overly friendly*.
20. *That he had been right* became obvious as the problem grew worse.
21. Julio knew the right answer *because he looked it up*.
22. Today's assignment is to write a three-paragraph composition on *how a bill becomes law*.
23. On our vacation we visited my dad's old neighborhood, *which is now an industrial park*.
24. *Mr. Johnson told us* that in the late 1800s at least one fourth of all the cowboys in the West were African Americans.
25. Did you get the package *that your mother sent?*
26. Tranh raked up the leaves *while his father stuffed them into plastic bags*.
27. *In Israel, the tour group visited several kibbutzim*, which are communal farms.
28. We will be over *as soon as Sandy finishes his lunch*.
29. That is the man *whose dog rescued my sister*.
30. Free samples were given to *whoever asked for them*.

C. Identifying Adjective, Adverb, and Noun Clauses

Identify each <u>subordinate clause</u> in the following sentences. Then, tell whether each is used as an *adjective*, an *adverb*, or a *noun*.

31. adv. [6a, c, e]
32. adj. [6a, c, d]
33. adj. [6a, c, d]
34. adj. [6a, c, d]
35. adj. [6a, c, d]

31. <u>When my family went to New York last summer</u>, we visited the Theodore Roosevelt museum.
32. The museum has been established on the site <u>where Theodore Roosevelt was born</u>.
33. It is located in the reconstructed house, <u>which is on East Twentieth Street</u>.
34. The museum contains books, letters, and documents <u>that tell about Roosevelt's public life</u>.
35. There are mounted heads of animals, a stuffed lion, and zebra skins from the days <u>when Roosevelt went big-game hunting in Africa</u>.

36. <u>That he had been a cowboy</u> is obvious from the branding irons and chaps.

37. <u>Before Roosevelt became president</u>, he gained fame in the Spanish-American War.

38. During that war he led the Rough Riders, <u>who made the famous charge up San Juan Hill</u>.

39. <u>Whoever rode with the Rough Riders</u> shared in Roosevelt's later fame.

40. The Roosevelt Memorial Association, <u>which established the museum</u>, charges a nominal admission fee to visitors.

36. n. [6a, c, f]
37. adv. [6a, c, e]
38. adj. [6a, c, d]
39. n. [6a, c, f]
40. adj. [6a, c, d]

Writing Application

Writing a Specific Definition

Using Adjective Clauses Sometimes, people misunderstand each other because they aren't thinking of the same meanings for words. Write a paragraph defining one of the people or things listed below or another term that you choose. Use at least four adjective clauses. Underline those clauses.

a clean room	a loyal friend	a fun weekend
a good teacher	an ideal pet	a good-looking outfit

Prewriting First, choose a term that interests you. Then, take a few minutes to write down whatever thoughts come to mind about that term. Write specific names and details.

Writing State your definition of the term—your main idea—in a topic sentence. As you write your supporting sentences, refer to your notes for specific names and details.

Revising Read over your paragraph. Would your reader understand your definition? Would he or she agree with it? Remember that all details in your paragraph should relate to your definition. If they do not, you may need to add, cut, or revise some information.

Publishing Proofread your paragraph for errors in grammar, spelling, and punctuation. You and your classmates may enjoy comparing different definitions of the same term. You could also gather the definitions together to create a class dictionary.

Sentence Structure
The Four Basic Sentence Structures

Diagnostic Preview

Identifying the Four Kinds of Sentence Structure

Identify each of the following sentences as *simple,* *compound,* *complex,* or *compound-complex.*

EXAMPLE   **1.** When my grandmother came to visit, she taught us how to make our own holiday ornaments.

　　　　1. complex

1. Last year my grandmother came to stay with us from the middle of December until my brother's birthday in January.
2. While we were getting out the holiday decorations, Mom and Grandma told us all about how people used to make their own decorations.
3. Mom said that she remembered making beautiful decorations and that it used to be great fun, so we decided to try making some of our own.
4. My dad, my brother, and I drove out to the nearby woods to gather pine cones.
5. We had forgotten to ask what size to get, and since Dad had never made decorations, he didn't know.
6. We decided to play it safe and get all different sizes, especially since doing so would be easy with pine cones everywhere.

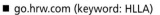

CHAPTER RESOURCES

Internet
- go.hrw.com (keyword: HLLA)

Planning
- *Teacher One Stop DVD-ROM*
- *On Course: Mapping Instruction*
- *Family Involvement Activities: A Guide to Standards Mastery*

Practice & Review
- *Language & Sentence Skills Practice,* pp. 139–145; 146–148
- *Developmental Language & Sentence Skills,* pp. 51–54

Application & Enrichment
- *Language & Sentence Skills Practice,* pp. 151; 138, 149–150

7. My brother picked up all the little hard ones, and my dad and I threw medium and big ones into the trunk of the car.

8. When Mom and Grandma saw how many we had, they laughed and said we had enough to decorate ten houses.

9. First, we sorted the cones; the little hard ones went into one pile, and the bigger ones went into another.

10. Dad and I painted the little ones silver, and Mom and Grandma painted stripes, dots, and all sorts of other designs on them.

11. Then we tied strings to the tops of the cones; later, when we put them up, they made great ornaments.

12. We painted the bigger pine cones all different colors and glued on cranberries and beads so that each cone looked like a miniature fir tree.

13. We saved some smaller ones for the dining room table, and we put most of the others all around the house.

14. My brother took some to school for a holiday party, too.

15. Besides the pine-cone decorations, we made some strings to decorate the mantel.

16. My mom got needles and a spool of heavy thread out of her sewing basket, and we strung the rest of the cranberries on six-foot lengths of the thread.

17. Mom and Grandma cut several more long pieces of thread, and we used them to make strings of popcorn like our strings of cranberries.

18. We left some of the popcorn strings white, painted the others different colors, and hung them around the living room and dining room.

19. Decorating was even more fun than usual, and I think that the whole house looked prettier, too, with all our homemade ornaments.

20. From now on, we're going to make all of our own holiday decorations every year.

7. cd. [7b]
8. cx. [7c]
9. cd. [7b]
10. cd. [7b]
11. cd.-cx. [7d]
12. cx. [7c]
13. cd. [7b]
14. s. [7a]
15. s. [7a]
16. cd. [7b]
17. cd. [7b]
18. s. [7a]
19. cd.-cx. [7d]
20. s. [7a]

What Is Sentence Structure?

The *structure* of a sentence refers to the kinds and the number of clauses it contains. The four kinds of sentences are *simple,* *compound, complex,* and *compound-complex.*

Reference Note

For information about **classifying sentences according to purpose,** see page 19.

understanding of proper English usage and control of grammar, paragraph and sentence structure, diction, and syntax.

INTRODUCING THE CHAPTER

- This chapter builds on the instruction covered in **Chapter 6: The Clause.** The four kinds of sentence structures are covered individually and collectively.

- The chapter closes with a **Chapter Review** including a **Writing Application** feature that asks students to write out the message they will leave on their answering machine, explaining that they have missed their ride home and are at a friend's house. Students should use a variety of sentence structures.

- For help in integrating this chapter with writing assignments in *Holt Literature and Language Arts,* see the **Teaching Strands** chart on pages T24–T25.

ASSESSING

Entry-Level Assessment

Diagnostic Preview. The results of the **Diagnostic Preview** will tell you which students can identify the four kinds of sentence structures in exercises but will not show you whether students can use the structures in their writing. In addition to the preview, you may wish to give a writing assignment preview or to use existing writing samples as an aid in evaluation.

GRAMMAR

Simple Sentences

Rule 7a (pp. 140–141)

OBJECTIVE

- To identify subjects and verbs in simple sentences

PRETEACHING

Lesson Starter

Prior Knowledge. Ask students to compose one sentence imitating the structure of each of the following sentences. Students should replace each noun with a noun, each verb with a verb, and so on to create sentences with the patterns given in brackets.

1. [*single subject and single verb*]
   Bob rode his bicycle all summer.
2. [*compound subject and single verb*]
   My dog and my cat play together.
3. [*single subject and compound verb*]
   Tarika picked a whole basket of raspberries and ate them all.
4. [*compound subject and compound verb*]
   Li and Tim came over and helped me with my math project.

DIFFERENTIATING INSTRUCTION

English-Language Learners

General Strategies. In many languages, the ordering of sentence elements is much less restricted than it is in English. Consequently, English-language learners may have problems identifying subjects and verbs in sentences. Start by having students identify subjects and verbs in simple sentences. Once students have mastered doing so, have them move on to compound sentences.

┌HELP─

A *clause* is a group of words that contains a verb and its subject and that is used as a sentence or as part of a sentence.

Reference Note

For more about **clauses,** see Chapter 6.

Reference Note

For more about **compound subjects** and **compound verbs,** see pages 15 and 16. For more about the types of **phrases,** see Chapter 5.

┌HELP─

Some sentences in the Oral Practice have compound subjects or compound verbs.

Simple Sentences

7a. A *simple sentence* contains one independent clause and no subordinate clauses.

EXAMPLES

        S   V
The hairstylist gave Latrice a new look.

        S   V
Ernesto has volunteered to organize the recycling campaign.

A simple sentence may contain a compound subject, a compound verb, and any number of phrases.

EXAMPLES

     S   S   V
Beth Heiden and **Sheila Young won** Olympic medals. [compound subject]

    S   V   V
Lawrence caught the ball but then **dropped** it. [compound verb]

       S   S   V
The **astronomer** and her **assistant studied** the

          V
meteor and **wrote** reports. [compound subject and compound verb]

  S   V
Both of the scientists on the expedition **stood** still, waiting for the jungle cat to move away. [three prepositional phrases, one participial phrase, and one infinitive phrase]

Oral Practice — **Identifying Subjects and Verbs in Simple Sentences**

Read each of the following simple sentences aloud. Then, identify the <u>subjects</u> and <u>verbs</u>.

EXAMPLE   1. Throughout history, people have invented and used a variety of weapons.

        1. people—subject; have invented, used—verbs

1. As protection from such weapons, <u>warriors</u> in battle <u>needed</u> special equipment.
2. Some <u>warriors</u> <u>used</u> shields of wood or animal hides.

RESOURCES

Simple Sentences

Practice

- *Language & Sentence Skills Practice,* p. 139
- *Developmental Language & Sentence Skills,* pp. 51–52

3. In ancient Assyria, <u>soldiers</u> <u>wore</u> leather armor with bronze reinforcements.
4. By 1800 B.C., the <u>Greeks</u> <u>had made</u> the first metal armor out of bronze.
5. Later, the <u>Romans</u> <u>manufactured</u> strong iron armor and <u>designed</u> special equipment, such as shinguards.
6. Before and during the Middle Ages, European <u>knights</u> and foot <u>soldiers</u> often <u>dressed</u> in shirts of chain mail.
7. <u>You</u> <u>can see</u> the tiny steel links of the chains in this picture.
8. In comparison with chain mail, <u>suits</u> of steel armor <u>gave</u> better protection and therefore <u>became</u> more popular.
9. <u>Helmets</u> and shoulder <u>pieces</u> like these <u>protected</u> a knight's head and neck.
10. Over his legs and feet, a <u>knight</u> <u>wore</u> greaves and sollerets into battle.

helmet

shoulder piece

greave (shinguard)

solleret (shoe)

DIRECT TEACHING

Modeling and Demonstration

Identifying Simple Sentences.
Model how to identify a simple sentence by using the example *The hairstylist gave Latrice a new look.* First, have students identify the subject. [*hairstylist*] Next, have them identify the verb. [*gave*] Then, explain to students that because there is one subject and one verb, the sentence is a simple sentence. Also, explain that a simple sentence may have a compound subject or a compound verb or both. Now, have a volunteer use another example from this chapter to demonstrate how to identify a simple sentence.

Oral Practice

DISTRIBUTED REVIEW
Ask students to find the direct objects in sentences 1 through 3. [1. *equipment,* 2. *shields,* 3. *armor*] For a more extensive review, have students find the direct objects in other sentences in the exercise. [*Every sentence except sentence 6 contains at least one direct object.*]

GRAMMAR

Compound Sentences

Rule 7b (pp. 142–144)

OBJECTIVES

- To identify subjects, verbs, and conjunctions in compound sentences
- To identify simple sentences and compound sentences

DIRECT TEACHING

Modeling and Demonstration

Identifying Compound Sentences. Model how to identify a compound sentence by using the example *Alberto led for half the distance, and then Jared took the lead.* First, ask students to identify the subject or subjects. [*Alberto; Jared*] Next, have them identify the verb or verbs. [*led; took*] Then, ask students whether the sentence has a comma and a coordinating conjunction. [*yes*] Next, ask students how many independent clauses the sentence has. [*two*] Then, ask students whether the sentence has any subordinate clauses. [*no*] Explain to students that because there are at least two independent clauses and no subordinate clauses, the sentence is a compound sentence. Now, have a volunteer use another example from this chapter to demonstrate how to identify a compound sentence.

DIRECT TEACHING

Correcting Misconceptions

Compound Sentences. If students are confusing compound sentences with simple sentences that have compound subjects and verbs, highlight the Note on p. 142. You may want to refer students to Chapter 1, pp. 15–18, for a review of compound subjects and compound verbs.

Reference Note

For more information on **independent clauses,** see page 120.

Reference Note

For more about using **semicolons** and **conjunctive adverbs** in **compound sentences,** see pages 331 and 332.

Compound Sentences

7b. A *compound sentence* contains two or more independent clauses and no subordinate clauses.

The independent clauses are usually joined by a comma and a coordinating conjunction: *and, but, for, nor, or, so,* or *yet.*

EXAMPLES
According to legend, **Betsy Ross made** our first S   V

flag, but **little evidence supports this claim.** [two S   V independent clauses joined by the conjunction *but*]

The whistle blew, the drums rolled, and **the** S V   S V

crowd cheered. [three independent clauses, the last two S V joined by the conjunction *and*]

NOTE Do not confuse a compound sentence with a simple sentence that contains a compound subject, a compound verb, or both.

SIMPLE SENTENCE
Alberto and **Jared increased** their speed and S   S   V
passed the other runners. [compound subject and V compound verb]

COMPOUND SENTENCE
Alberto led for half the distance, and then **Jared** S V   S
took the lead. [two independent clauses] V

    The independent clauses in a compound sentence may also be joined by a semicolon or by a semicolon, a conjunctive adverb, and a comma.

EXAMPLES
Many mathematical concepts originated in North S   V
Africa; the ancient Egyptians used these concepts in S   V building the pyramids.

RESOURCES

Compound Sentences

Practice

- *Language & Sentence Skills Practice,* pp. 140–141
- *Developmental Language & Sentence Skills,* pp. 51–52

S   V
Lynn called Marty with the good news**; however,**

S   V
he was not at home.

Exercise 1 **Identifying Subjects, Verbs, and Conjunctions in Compound Sentences**

Each of the following sentences is a compound sentence. Identify the subject and the verb in each of the independent clauses in each sentence. Then, give any punctuation marks, coordinating conjunctions, or conjunctive adverbs that join the independent clauses.

EXAMPLE   1. Many strange things happen backstage during a performance, but the audience usually does not know about them.

    1. *things—subject; happen—verb; audience—subject; does know—verb; comma + but*

1. The director of a theater-in-the-round visited our class, and we listened to his stories for almost an hour.
2. According to him, the workers in charge of properties are usually alert and careful; however, they still make mistakes sometimes.
3. For example, in one production of *Romeo and Juliet*, the character Juliet prepared to kill herself with a dagger, but no dagger was on the stage.
4. Audiences at theaters-in-the-round can also be a problem, for they sit very close to the stage.
5. Members of the audience often set things on stage tables, or they hang their coats on the actors' coat racks.
6. Sometimes these actions are overlooked by the stagehands, and the results can be very challenging for the actors.
7. For example, the main clue in one mystery play was a scarf on the stage floor, but the audience had gathered on the stage during intermission.
8. After the intermission, the detective in the play found two scarves instead of one, yet he could not show any surprise.
9. During another mystery drama, a spectator became too involved in the play; he leaped up on the stage and tackled the villain.
10. Directors cannot always predict the reactions of the audience, nor can they always control the audience.

MINI-LESSON **Mechanics** | *Continued on p. 144*

Using Semicolons. Remind students that a semicolon or a semicolon, a conjunctive adverb, and a comma may be used in place of a comma and conjunction to join two parts of a compound sentence. Assign students to write three sentences to demonstrate this point. You may want to offer topics such as Saturday's football game, a holiday, and the seasons. For example:

• Marilyn and her twin went to the football

GRAMMAR

RETEACHING

Compound Sentences

Activity. To demonstrate that compound sentences are made up of at least two independent clauses, have each student write a simple sentence on the same topic, such as pets. Have a volunteer write his or her sentence on the chalkboard. Then, ask another volunteer to turn that sentence into a compound sentence by adding his or hers to it. Students may find that some revising of the second sentence may be necessary. You could have several pairs of volunteers repeat the process. Point out that the two parts of a compound sentence should be logically related in some way.

PRACTICE

Guided and Independent
You may want to have students complete **Exercise 1** as guided practice and **Exercise 2** as independent practice.

HOMEWORK

Exercise 2

DISTRIBUTED REVIEW
Have students find the following kinds of phrases in the designated sentences.

5. an infinitive phrase [*to receive Academy Awards*]

6. two prepositional phrases [*as military men, for their performances*]

9. an appositive phrase [*a film about African American fighter pilots during WWII*]

DIFFERENTIATING INSTRUCTION

Special Education Students
Some students may not be able to distinguish among the four basic sentence structures. You may want to have a helper work with these students, focusing on identifying subjects and verbs of simple and compound sentences until students begin to understand that task.

Learners Having Difficulty
Have each student write a simple sentence on the same topic, using individual note cards or slips of paper. Next, have students make another set of cards with a comma and a coordinating conjunction on each card. Then, have pairs of students use the cards to build compound sentences. You may wish to remind students of semicolons by asking if they can think of another way to combine two independent clauses.

Exercise 2 **Identifying Simple Sentences and Compound Sentences**

Identify each <u>subject</u> and <u>verb</u> in the following sentences. Then, tell whether the sentence is a *simple sentence* or a *compound sentence*.

EXAMPLES 1. African American actors and actresses performed in many early Hollywood movies.

1. *actors, actresses—subjects; performed—verb; simple sentence*

2. Hattie McDaniel, for example, made many films, and she is best known for her role in *Gone with the Wind.*

2. *Hattie McDaniel—subject; made—verb; she—subject; is known—verb; compound sentence*

1. Over the years, African American <u>performers</u> <u>have earned</u> much acclaim and <u>won</u> a number of Academy Awards. **1.** s.

2. <u>Hattie McDaniel</u> <u>won</u> an Oscar for her role in *Gone with the Wind* in 1939. **2.** s.

3. <u>Sidney Poitier</u> <u>acted</u> in stage plays and <u>made</u> several movies early in his career. **3.** s.

4. <u>Poitier</u> <u>won</u> an Oscar in 1963 for *Lilies of the Field*, and <u>he</u> later <u>made</u> many other popular films. **4.** cd.

5. <u>McDaniel</u> and <u>Poitier</u> <u>were</u> the first African Americans to receive Academy Awards. **5.** s.

6. More recently, <u>Lou Gossett, Jr.</u>, and <u>Denzel Washington</u> <u>played</u> supporting roles as military men and <u>won</u> Academy Awards for their performances. **6.** s.

7. Another <u>winner</u>, Whoopi Goldberg, first <u>gained</u> fame as a stand-up comic; then <u>she</u> <u>made</u> several hit movies. **7.** cd.

8. <u>Critics</u> <u>praised</u> her performance in *The Color Purple*, and in 1991, <u>she</u> <u>won</u> an Academy Award for her role in *Ghost.* **8.** cd.

9. *The Tuskegee Airmen*, a film about African American fighter pilots during WWII, and *As Good As It Gets* <u>brought</u> Cuba Gooding, Jr., much attention. **9.** s.

10. In 1996, <u>Gooding</u> <u>was nominated</u> for an Oscar for a role as a professional football player, and <u>he</u> <u>won</u> the award for best supporting actor. **10.** cd.

144 **Chapter 7** Sentence Structure

MINI-LESSON **Mechanics** *Continued from p. 143*

game on Saturday, but their brother John went swimming.

- I enjoy the parades on Independence Day; my younger sister prefers the fireworks.

- I love the cool evenings of autumn; how-

ever, my brother prefers the cold and snow of winter.

Refer students to **Chapter 14: Punctuation: End Marks, Commas, Semicolons, Colons** for more information on punctuating compound sentences.

Complex Sentences

7c. A *complex sentence* contains one independent clause and at least one subordinate clause.

EXAMPLES

$\overset{\text{S}}{\text{When}}\ \overset{\text{V}}{\text{I watch}}$ Martha Graham's performances,

$\overset{\text{S}}{\text{I}}\ \overset{\text{V}}{\text{feel}}$ like studying dance.

| *Independent clause* | I feel like studying dance |
| *Subordinate clause* | When I watch Martha Graham's performances |

In *Gone with the Wind,* $\overset{\text{S}}{\text{when}}$ Scarlett $\overset{\text{V}}{\text{is faced}}$

with near-starvation, $\overset{\text{S}}{\text{she}}$ $\overset{\text{V}}{\text{vows}}$ that $\overset{\text{S}}{\text{she}}$ never

$\overset{\text{V}}{\text{will be}}$ hungry again.

Independent clause	In *Gone with the Wind,* she vows
Subordinate clause	when Scarlett is faced with near-starvation
Subordinate clause	that she never will be hungry again

Independent clauses can be interrupted by subordinate clauses.

EXAMPLE

$\overset{\text{S}}{\text{All of the stars}}$ that $\overset{\text{S}}{\text{we}}$ $\overset{\text{V}}{\text{can see}}$ without a telescope

$\overset{\text{V}}{\text{are}}$ part of the Milky Way galaxy.

| *Independent clause* | All of the stars are part of the Milky Way galaxy |
| *Subordinate clause* | that we can see without a telescope |

Notice in the examples above that a subordinate clause can appear at the beginning, in the middle, or at the end of a complex sentence.

Reference Note

For more information on **independent** and **subordinate clauses,** see pages 120 and 121.

GRAMMAR

Complex Sentences
Rule 7c *(pp. 145–146)*

OBJECTIVE

- To identify independent clauses and subordinate clauses in complex sentences

DIRECT TEACHING

Modeling and Demonstration

Identifying Complex Sentences.
Model how to identify a complex sentence by using the example *All of the stars that we can see without a telescope are part of the Milky Way galaxy.* First, ask students how many independent clauses the sentence has. [*one—All of the stars are part of the Milky Way.*] Then, ask students whether the sentence has any subordinate clauses. [*yes—that we can see without a telescope*] Explain to students that because there is one independent clause and at least one subordinate clause, the sentence is a complex sentence. Now, have a volunteer use another example from this chapter to demonstrate how to identify a complex sentence.

RESOURCES

Complex Sentences

Practice
- *Language & Sentence Skills Practice,* pp. 142–143
- *Developmental Language & Sentence Skills,* pp. 53–54

EXTENSION

Relating to Writing

Have students examine the sentence structures in a piece of their own writing and answer the following questions.

- Which sentence structures have been used?
- How does the use of different sentence structures contribute to the effectiveness of the piece?

Ask students to revise the piece, using a variety of sentence structures in the most effective way possible. Then, have students exchange writing samples and offer constructive feedback to each other on the use and variety of sentence structures in the sample.

DIFFERENTIATING INSTRUCTION

Advanced Learners

Divide the class into groups to practice creating sentences with different structures. Tell students that each group's task is to create a series of sentences all related to the same topic. The first student in each group begins by stating a simple sentence on the topic of his or her choice. The second student then provides a compound sentence on the same subject. The third student creates a simple sentence, and the fourth student adds a subordinate clause to make a complex sentence.

Have groups repeat the process three more times, exchanging tasks each time so that each student has a chance to choose a topic and to help create each kind of sentence structure.

—HELP—

In the first example in Exercise 3, the independent clause contains the subject *China* and the verb *is*. The subordinate clause contains the subject *which* and the verb *has*. In the second example, the independent clause contains the subject *brother* and the verb *bought*. The subordinate clause contains the subject *it* and the verb *was*.

Students should be prepared to identify these subjects and verbs:

1. show appeared/it became

2. most are sitting/parents have

3. Richard E. Byrd is/who traveled

4. studies continued/facts were discovered

5. group recorded/who donated/that made

6. ruler was/who wrote

7. we finish/we may go

8. students, teachers knew/group visited

9. crew was constructing/ performers continued/ which went

10. she had/Wilma Rudolph became

Exercise 3 Identifying Independent Clauses and Subordinate Clauses in Complex Sentences

Identify each of the clauses in the following sentences as *independent* or *subordinate*. Be prepared to give the subject and the verb of each clause. [Hint: A sentence may have more than one subordinate clause.]

EXAMPLES

1. China, which has a population of more than one billion people, is a largely agricultural country.

1. *China is a largely agricultural country—independent; which has a population of more than one billion people—subordinate*

2. Although it was nearly worthless, my brother bought one of those old coins for his collection.

2. *Although it was nearly worthless—subordinate; my brother bought one of those old coins for his collection—independent*

1. The detective show appeared on television for several weeks before it became popular with viewers.
2. Most of the albums that my parents have from the 1970s are sitting in the corner of the basement behind the broken refrigerator.
3. Richard E. Byrd is but one of the explorers who traveled to Antarctica.
4. As studies continued, many important facts about nutrition were discovered.
5. A group of popular singers, who donated their time, recorded a song that made people aware of a famine in Ethiopia.
6. The Hawaiian ruler who wrote the famous song *"Aloha Oe"* ("Farewell to Thee") was Queen Liliuokalani.
7. After we finish our report on the history of computers, we may go to the basketball game.
8. Although few students or teachers knew about it, a group of sociologists visited our school to study the relationship between classroom environment and students' grades.
9. While the stage crew was constructing the sets, the performers continued their rehearsal, which went on into the night.
10. Although she had polio as a child, Wilma Rudolph became a top American Olympic athlete.

CONTENT-AREA CONNECTIONS

Social Studies. Complex and compound-complex sentences show relationships that are sometimes difficult to express in simple sentences alone. To illustrate this point, ask students to rewrite the Preamble to the U.S. Constitution in simple sentences. You can allow students to work independently, in pairs, or in groups of three on this activity. Ask volunteers to read their rewrites to the class.

Compound-Complex Sentences

7d. A *compound-complex sentence* contains two or more independent clauses and at least one subordinate clause.

        S   V

EXAMPLES   Yolanda began painting only two years ago, but

        S   V

already she has been asked to show one of her

               S   V

paintings at the exhibit that is scheduled for May.

Independent clause	Yolanda began painting only two years ago
Independent clause	already she has been asked to show one of her paintings at the exhibit
Subordinate clause	that is scheduled for May

      S V S   V   S   V

When Bill left, he locked the door, but he forgot to turn off the lights.

Independent clause	he locked the door
Independent clause	he forgot to turn off the lights
Subordinate clause	When Bill left

    S   V   S   V

Emilia has several hobbies that she enjoys, but the

    S   S   V   V

one on which she spends the most time is woodcarving.

Independent clause	Emilia has several hobbies
Independent clause	the one is woodcarving
Subordinate clause	that she enjoys
Subordinate clause	on which she spends the most time

MEETING THE CHALLENGE

Simple sentences are best used to express single ideas. To describe more complicated ideas and to show how the ideas fit together, use compound, complex, and compound-complex sentences.

Using only simple sentences, write a paragraph describing what you would do if you had a million dollars. Then, revise the paragraph by combining the simple sentences into compound, complex, and compound-complex sentences. Which paragraph do you prefer?

ANSWER

Paragraphs will vary—the first paragraph should contain only simple sentences, and the revision should contain the other three sentence structures.

Compound-Complex Sentences

Rule 7d *(pp. 147–150)*

OBJECTIVE

- To identify independent and subordinate clauses in compound-complex sentences

DIRECT TEACHING

Modeling and Demonstration

Identifying Compound-Complex Sentences. Model how to identify a compound-complex sentence by using the example *When Bill left, he locked the door, but he forgot to turn off the lights.* First, ask students how many independent clauses the sentence has. [*two—He locked the door; He forgot to turn off the lights.*] Then, ask students whether the sentence has any subordinate clauses. [*yes—When Bill left*] Explain to students that because there are at least two independent clauses and at least one subordinate clause, the sentence is a compound-complex sentence. Now, have a volunteer use another example from this chapter to demonstrate how to identify a compound-complex sentence.

RESOURCES

Compound-Complex Sentences

Practice

- *Language & Sentence Skills Practice,* pp. 144–148
- *Developmental Language & Sentence Skills,* pp. 53–54

DIRECT TEACHING

Compound-Complex Sentences

Activity. To show how compound-complex sentences are formed, build a sentence for students as an example. Begin with a simple sentence, add a second independent clause, and then add a subordinate clause.

EXAMPLE

1. John went to a ski resort on Monday.

2. John went to a ski resort on Monday, and he enrolled in an expert skiers' class.

3. John went to a ski resort on Monday, and he enrolled in an expert skiers' class because he wanted to win the big race on Saturday.

Ask students to create compound-complex sentences by following your model.

DIFFERENTIATING INSTRUCTION

Learners Having Difficulty

Encourage students to visualize compound-complex sentences as a series of units. To help visualization, have students copy **Exercise 4** and highlight each type of clause in a different color as they work on the exercise.

HELP

The four kinds of sentence structures are created by using only two kinds of clauses—independent clauses and subordinate clauses. Every sentence has at least one independent clause.

EXAMPLES

Eric likes peas. [simple sentence with one independent clause]

Eric likes peas, but Liza prefers green beans. [compound sentence with two independent clauses]

Eric likes peas when they are cooked a short time. [complex sentence with one independent clause and one subordinate clause]

Eric likes peas, but Liza prefers green beans when they are steamed. [compound-complex sentence with two independent clauses and one subordinate clause]

Exercise 4 Identifying Clauses in Compound-Complex Sentences

Identify each of the clauses in the following sentences as *independent* or *subordinate*.

EXAMPLE

1. When they returned from their vacation, they collected their mail at the post office, and they went to the supermarket.

   1. *When they returned from their vacation—subordinate; they collected their mail at the post office—independent; they went to the supermarket—independent*

1. Before we conducted the experiment, we asked for permission to use the science lab, but the principal insisted on teacher supervision of our work.

2. Inside the old trunk in the attic, which is filled with boxes and toys, we found some dusty photo albums; and one of them contained pictures from the early 1900s.

3. We told them that their plan wouldn't work, but they wouldn't listen to us.

4. Every expedition that had attempted to explore that region had vanished without a trace, yet the young adventurer was determined to map the uncharted jungle because he couldn't resist the challenge.

5. The smoke, which steadily grew thicker and darker, billowed through the dry forest; the animals ran ahead of the fire as it spread quickly.

6. Our new neighbors, who moved in last month, have painted their house, and the children have put up a basketball hoop.

7. Because Traci, Sheila, and Tomas like to compete, they swim laps in the pool in the park, and they keep a chart of who wins each time.

8. We bought tortillas, cheese, tomatoes, and onions; and Ernesto made enchiladas, which everyone enjoyed.

9. Gabriel and Daniel earned the money that they wanted for new bikes, but then they put the money into their savings accounts instead.

10. I was glad that the school bus came early the day of the science fair; I needed extra time at school to set up my exhibit.

Learning for Life

Continued on pp. 149–150

Writing to a Public Official. Sentence structure is one way for a writer to set the tone of a piece of writing. The tone of a letter or other document can be as important as the ideas it contains.

Ask students to write a letter to a public

official expressing disagreement with a decision the official has made concerning curfew, noise laws, or another issue of interest. Once students have selected an issue to write about, ask them to consider the attitude they wish to communicate (for

Review A Identifying the Four Kinds of Sentence Structure

Identify each of the following sentences as *simple*, *compound*, *complex*, or *compound-complex*.

EXAMPLE 1. If she had not practiced, my cousin Sheila could not have become a good skater.
          1. *complex*

1. People who are learning a new sport begin by mastering basic skills. **1.** cx.
2. After people have practiced basic skills for a while, they can progress to more difficult moves. **2.** cx.
3. At this point a beginner may become discouraged, and the temptation to quit grows strong. **3.** cd.
4. One of the most common problems that beginners face is lack of coordination; another is muscular aches and pains. **4.** cd.-cx.
5. A beginner who is not careful can injure muscles, yet strenuous activity usually strengthens the muscle tissues. **5.** cd.-cx.
6. When enough oxygen reaches the warmed-up muscles, the danger of injury lessens, and the muscles grow in size. **6.** cd.-cx.
7. At the same time, coordination grows with confidence. **7.** s.
8. The hours of practice that a beginner puts in usually result in rewarding improvements. **8.** cx.
9. As a rule, learning something new takes time and work, or it will not seem worthwhile. **9.** cd.
10. In sports, as in most other activities, persistence and patience often pay off. **10.** s.

Review B Writing a Variety of Sentence Structures

Write your own original sentences according to the following instructions.

EXAMPLE 1. Write a compound sentence with two independent clauses joined by a comma and *and*.
          1. *My mother usually serves us spaghetti for supper once a week, and she makes the best spaghetti in the world.*

1. Write a simple sentence with a compound subject.
2. Write a simple sentence with a compound verb.
3. Write a compound sentence with two independent clauses joined by a comma and *but*.

Compound-Complex Sentences **149**

example, alarm, outrage, helpfulness). Ask them how they would express their ideas and feelings in a face-to-face encounter with the official, and encourage them to translate that expression into their writing. Encourage them to use different sentence structures to reflect their feelings but to avoid being disrespectful to their reader.

After students have finished writing, have them work in groups to evaluate their letters. To let the writer know whether the attitude he or she wants to

Review B — Writing a Variety of Sentence Structures

POSSIBLE ANSWERS continued

4. Alan can play tennis after school, or he can run track.

5. We bought the car last year; it is already causing us trouble.

6. The man who is wearing the red shirt is my uncle.

7. After we came home, I rode the horse that belongs to my neighbor.

8. As soon as the rabbit saw me, it hopped away.

9. The cicadas in the trees were so loud that they almost deafened me.

10. When we went to the baseball game, John was paged, and we had to leave early.

TECHNOLOGY TIP

Since each item in **Review B** requires a sentence with a different structure, have students demonstrate those differences in the appearance of their sentences. If students have access to a word-processing program, encourage them to use plain text for independent clauses, italics for subordinate clauses, and boldface for conjunctions.

4. Write a compound sentence with two independent clauses joined by a comma and *or*.

5. Write a compound sentence with two independent clauses joined by a semicolon.

6. Write a complex sentence with one subordinate clause.

7. Write a complex sentence with two subordinate clauses.

8. Write a complex sentence with a subordinate clause at the beginning of the sentence.

9. Write a complex sentence with a subordinate clause at the end of the sentence.

10. Write a compound-complex sentence.

I'M THE STORE SANTA CLAUS. ERNIE IS, IF YOU WILL EXCUSE THE EXPRESSION, A SUBORDINATE CLAUS.

FRANK & ERNEST reprinted by permission of Newspaper Enterprise Association, Inc.

Learning for Life

Continued from p. 149

communicate comes across to readers, each group member who reads a letter should attach a self-adhesive note stating the attitude conveyed.

As students revise their letters, have them evaluate how structure reflects attitudes. For example, using mostly short, simple sentences may communicate opposition more effectively than using longer compound and complex sentences.

7

Numerals in brackets refer to rules tested by the items in the Chapter Review.

1. cd. [7b]
2. cx. [7c]
3. s. [7a]
4. s. [7a]
5. cd.-cx. [7d]
6. cx. [7c]
7. s. [7a]
8. s. [7a]
9. cx. [7c]
10. cd.-cx. [7d]
11. cd. [7b]
12. cx. [7c]
13. cd.-cx. [7d]
14. cd. [7b]
15. s. [7a]
16. cd.-cx. [7d]
17. cd. [7b]
18. s. [7a]
19. cd.-cx. [7d]
20. cx. [7c]

Chapter Review

A. Identifying Sentence Structures

Identify each of the following sentences as *simple,* *compound,* *complex,* or *compound-complex.*

1. Christina left on time, but her bus was late.
2. When the rabbit saw us, it ran into the bushes.
3. In 1967, Thurgood Marshall became the first African American on the U.S. Supreme Court.
4. You can either buy a new bicycle or fix the old one.
5. Yoko said that this would be the shortest route, but I disagree.
6. How could we tell what had really happened?
7. That seems to me like the answer to the first problem.
8. Mercedes Rodriguez of Miami, Florida, entered and won the contest.
9. Do you know who wrote this note and left it on my desk?
10. I'm not sure what you mean, but I think that I agree.
11. Nobody is worried about that, for it will never happen.
12. Whatever you decide will be fine with me.
13. Is the movie that we want to see still playing in theaters, or is it available on video?
14. Rommel knew the plan, and he assigned each unit a part.
15. Amphibians and some insects can live both on the land and in water.
16. The detectives searched for the woman who had been wearing a blue beret, but there weren't any other clues.
17. The tornado cut across the edge of the housing development yesterday morning, and seven homes were damaged.
18. By July of 1847, the Mormons had reached the Great Salt Lake valley.
19. Before the game started, all the football players ran out onto the field, and everyone cheered.
20. My father helped the family whose car had broken down on the highway.

ASSESSING

Monitoring Progress
Chapter Review. To assess student progress, you may want to compare the types of items missed on the **Diagnostic Preview** with those missed on the **Chapter Review.** You may want to help students who are still having difficulty set specific goals for mastering essential information.

GRAMMAR

RESOURCES

Sentence Structure
Review
- *Language & Sentence Skills Practice,* pp. 146–148

Assessment
- *Formal Assessment*
- *Progress-Monitoring Tests,* pp. 13–14, 48
- *Test Generator* (Teacher One Stop DVD-ROM)

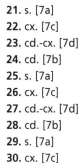

21. s. [7a]
22. cx. [7c]
23. cd.-cx. [7d]
24. cd. [7b]
25. s. [7a]
26. cx. [7c]
27. cd.-cx. [7d]
28. cd. [7b]
29. s. [7a]
30. cx. [7c]

21. My cousin sent me a present for my birthday.
22. When I jog, the dog next door often follows me.
23. Tara opened the door, but when she saw the snow, she decided to stay inside.
24. Delsin drew the picture, and I added the text.
25. Are those letters from New Jersey for me?
26. When birds fly during a rainstorm, the rain will probably last all day.
27. Eagerly, we unpacked the tent, and my uncle who had been in the army helped us set it up in the side yard.
28. The lake was filled with trout, and we caught enough fish for a delicious dinner.
29. Gordon Parks wrote *The Learning Tree* and directed the film version of the novel.
30. Alaska's flag was designed by a boy who was in the seventh grade.

B. Identifying Clauses in Compound, Complex, and Compound-Complex Sentences

Identify each clause in the sentences in the following paragraph as *independent* or *subordinate*.

31. [7c]
32. [7b]
33. [7c]
34. [7b]
35. [7b]
36. [7b]
37. [7c]

[31] Jan Vermeer (pronounced yahn vuhr-MEER) was a seventeenth-century Dutch painter who used the pointillist method of painting. [32] With this method, the painter uses small dots, or points, of unmixed color, and the result is almost like putting gauze in front of a camera lens. [33] In paintings such as *The Lacemaker,* this technique gives the light a soft, blurry quality that has become the best-known characteristic of Vermeer's work. [34] His paintings are now world-famous, but Vermeer never left his hometown of Delft in the Netherlands. [35] In fact, he did not work primarily as a painter at all; he spent most of his life as an art dealer and innkeeper. [36] Vermeer's paintings deal with many subjects, including landscapes, but they are primarily known for their scenes of house interiors. [37] They show young people who are talking, playing musical

instruments, reading letters, and laughing, all in a relaxed and peaceful atmosphere. [38] Many of his subjects are caught in moments of concentration, yet the overall feeling is calm. [39] Perhaps his own paintings are unique because he never left his hometown and therefore did not see much of other artists' work. [40] Vermeer's paintings are alive with color, and they shine with a pure, serene light that is rarely found in art or life.

38. [7b]

39. [7c]

40. [7d]

Writing Application

Using Sentence Variety in a Telephone Message

Sentence Structures   Imagine that you have missed your ride home after school, so you have gone to a friend's house. No one is at your home now, but you know you should call and leave a message on the answering machine. Write out the message that you will leave. Use a variety of sentence structures.

Prewriting   First, decide what will be in your message. You will want to tell where you are, why you are there, and why you missed your ride. You may also want to say when you will be home and whether arrangements should be made to pick you up. Make notes on all these details.

Writing   Use your notes to write your first draft. As you write, remember that your message must be short but clear and informative. Think about how you can combine ideas.

Revising   Read your message aloud, and listen to how it sounds. Are your explanations and plans complete? Do they sound logical? Check to be sure that you have used a variety of sentence structures.

Publishing   Read over your message again, checking for errors in grammar, spelling, and punctuation. You and your classmates may want to hold a contest to determine the best of several messages. Once the best message has been chosen, you may want to post it on a class bulletin board or Web page.

Reference Note

For more information about **punctuating compound sentences,** see pages 319 and 331. For more about **using commas with subordinate clauses,** see page 327.

8

STANDARDS FOCUS

Grade-Level Standards

(Boldface indicates concepts that are taught and tested in this chapter.)

- Language Convention 1.0: **Students write and speak with a command of standard English conventions appropriate to this grade level.**

- Grammar 1.4: **Edit written manuscripts to ensure that correct grammar is used.**

Prerequisite/Review Standard

- Grammar 1.2: Identify and use infinitives and participles and make clear references between pronouns and antecedents.

Standard Coming Up in the Next Grade Level

- Grammar and Mechanics of Writing 1.3: Demonstrate an understanding of proper English usage and control of grammar, paragraph and sentence structure, diction, and syntax.

▼

INTRODUCING THE CHAPTER

- This chapter discusses agreement of subjects and verbs and of pronouns and antecedents, including grammatical number and problems in agreement.

- The chapter closes with a **Chapter Review** including a **Writing Application** that asks students to write a brief report using at least five collective nouns.

(continued)

1.0 Written and Oral English Language Conventions

Students write and speak with a command of standard English conventions appropriate to this grade level.

1.4 Edit written manuscripts to ensure that correct grammar is used.

Numerals in brackets refer to rules tested by the items in the Diagnostic Preview.

1. has [8c, l, b(1)]
2. take [8g, b(2)]
3. doesn't [8d, k, b(1)]
4. C [8h, b(1)]
5. Don't [8k, j, b(2)]
6. are [8j, b(2)]
7. like [8f, b(2)]
8. C [8e, b(2)]
9. are [8p, b(2)]
10. is [8h, n, b(1)]

8 Agreement
Subject and Verb, Pronoun and Antecedent

Diagnostic Preview

A. Identifying Verbs That Agree with Their Subjects

In each of the following sentences, if the underlined italicized verb does not agree with its subject, write the correct form of the verb. If a sentence is already correct, write *C*.

EXAMPLES
   1. The people on the bus *have* all been seated.
   1. C

   2. The fish, bass and perch mostly, *has* started feeding.
   2. have

1. The swarm of bees *have* deserted its hive.
2. My spelling lessons and science homework sometimes *takes* me hours to finish.
3. Somebody who is on the council *don't* approve of the new rule.
4. Neither Danny Glover nor Morgan Freeman *stars* in tonight's movie.
5. *Doesn't* those children still take piano lessons?
6. There *is* probably a few children who don't like strawberries.
7. Most of the guests *likes* the inn's Irish soda bread.
8. Both of those varsity players *exercise* for an hour each day.
9. Evenings *is* the best time to visit her.
10. Physics or mathematics *are* the subject you should study.

CHAPTER RESOURCES

Internet

- go.hrw.com (keyword: HLLA)

Planning

- *Teacher One Stop DVD-ROM*
- *On Course: Mapping Instruction*
- *Family Involvement Activities: A Guide to Standards Mastery*

Practice & Review

- *Language & Sentence Skills Practice,* pp. 153–170; 171–174
- *Developmental Language & Sentence Skills,* pp. 55–64

Application & Enrichment

- *Language & Sentence Skills Practice,* pp. 175, 178; 152, 176–177

B. Identifying Pronouns That Agree with Their Antecedents

In each of the following sentences, if the underlined italicized pronoun does not agree with its antecedent, write the correct form of the pronoun. If a sentence is already correct, write *C*.

EXAMPLES

1. Either of the men could have offered *their* help.

1. *his*

2. Both of the flowers had opened *their* petals.

2. *C*

11. Why doesn't somebody raise *their* hand and ask Mr. Liu for directions?

12. One of the birds lost most of *their* tail feathers.

13. Joey sold *his* last ticket to Heather.

14. The old tennis court has weeds growing in *their* net.

15. The Smithsonian's National Museum of the American Indian had closed *their* doors for the day.

16. I don't understand how chameleons sitting on green shrubbery change *their* color.

17. Alex has studied gymnastics for many years, and he is now very good at *them*.

18. These girls can choose *her* own materials from the supply room.

19. The senior class has chosen *their* theme for homecoming.

20. Island of the Blue Dolphins is my sister's favorite book, and she has read *it* three times.

11. his or her [8t(1), q]
12. its [8t(1), q]
13. C [8q]
14. its [8q]
15. its [8y]
16. C [8q]
17. it [8w, q]
18. their [8q]
19. its [8u, q]
20. C [8x]

Number

Number is the form a word takes to indicate whether the word is singular or plural.

8a. When a word refers to one person, place, thing, or idea, it is *singular* in number. When a word refers to more than one person, place, thing, or idea, it is *plural* in number.

Singular	egg	person	fox	I	die	each
Plural	eggs	people	foxes	we	dice	all

Reference Note

For more about forming **plurals of nouns,** see page 376.

Number **155**

Differentiating Instruction
- UA: Differentiating Instruction
- UA: Supporting Instruction in Five Languages
- Family Involvement Activities: In Five Languages

Assessment
- Formal Assessment

- Progress-Monitoring Tests, pp. 15–16, 48
- Test Generator (Teacher One Stop DVD-ROM)

Other Language Resources
- Spelling Lessons & Activities
- WordSharp: An Interactive Vocabulary Tutor
- Reading and Writing Transparencies

USAGE

- For help in integrating this chapter with writing assignments in *Holt Literature and Language Arts,* see the **Teaching Strands** chart on pp. T24–T25.

ASSESSING

Entry-Level Assessment
Diagnostic Preview. The **Diagnostic Preview** can pinpoint specific strengths and weaknesses students might have with agreement. Encourage students to circle verbs and pronouns when proofreading and to check each one for correct agreement with its subject or antecedent.

PRETEACHING

Lesson Starter
Prior Knowledge. Tell students that they use subject-verb agreement every day. Write the following nonsense sentences on the chalkboard, and ask students to select the correct verbs.

1. The shink (*grimp, grimps*) the vork.
2. The shinks (*grimp, grimps*) the vork.

Even though the sentences are composed of nonsense words, most students will agree that *The shink* (singular) *grimps the vork* and that *The shinks* (plural) *grimp the vork.* Ask students to write similar nonsense sentences, and have partners select the correct verbs.

Number
Rule 8a *(pp. 155–156)*

OBJECTIVES

■ To read expressions aloud and classify the nouns and pronouns they contain as singular or plural

■ To classify nouns and pronouns by number

DIRECT TEACHING

Modeling and Demonstration

Number. Model how to classify nouns and pronouns as singular or plural using the examples *egg, person, fox, I,* and *each.* First, read the words aloud. Then, ask students how the plural of each word is formed. [*eggs, persons* or *people, foxes, we, all*] Explain that most nouns form the plural by adding *s,* but that some nouns, such as *fox,* form the plural by adding *es.* Other nouns, such as *person,* may change their base form in the plural. Point out that personal pronouns, such as *I,* and indefinite pronouns, such as *each,* also take irregular forms in the plural. Now, have a volunteer use another example from this chapter to demonstrate how to classify nouns and pronouns as singular or plural.

PRACTICE

Guided and Independent

Exercise 1 You may wish to use the first ten items of **Exercise 1** as guided practice and have students complete the exercise as independent practice. **HOMEWORK**

Reference Note

The plurals of some nouns do not end in *s* (for example, *feet, children, moose*). For more about **irregularly formed plurals,** see page 377.

TIPS & TRICKS

Generally, nouns ending in *s* are plural (*bands, thoughts, friends, lizards*), and verbs ending in *s* are singular (*jumps, hears, borrows, waits*). However, verbs used with the singular pronouns *I* and *you* do not end in *s.*

EXAMPLES

The **friends talk.**

The **friend talks.**

I talk.

You talk.

Oral Practice 1 **Classifying Nouns and Pronouns by Number**

Read the following expressions aloud. Tell whether each italicized noun or pronoun is *singular* or *plural.*

1. The *lion* yawns. 1. s.
2. The *cubs* play. 2. p.
3. *No one* stays. 3. s.
4. The *refugees* arrive. 4. p.
5. *She* wins. 5. s.
6. The *play* opens. 6. s.
7. *Everyone* goes. 7. s.
8. *All* applaud. 8. p.

Exercise 1 **Classifying Nouns and Pronouns by Number**

Classify each of the following words as *singular* or *plural.*

EXAMPLE   1. cat
          1. *singular*

1. rodeos 1. p.
2. book 2. s.
3. they 3. p.
4. I 4. s.
5. many 5. p.
6. igloo 6. s.
7. geese 7. p.
8. we 8. p.
9. friends 9. p.
10. it 10. s.
11. lake 11. s.
12. heroes 12. p.
13. oxen 13. p.
14. aunt 14. s.
15. roof 15. s.
16. year 16. s.
17. children 17. p.
18. those 18. p.
19. mice 19. p.
20. skate 20. s.
21. shoes 21. p.
22. bases 22. p.
23. him 23. s.
24. license 24. s.
25. guess 25. s.

Agreement of Subject and Verb

8b. A verb should agree in number with its subject.

(1) Singular subjects take singular verbs.

EXAMPLES   The **car comes** to a sudden stop. [The singular verb *comes* agrees with the singular subject *car.*]

On that route the **airplane flies** at a very low altitude. [The singular verb *flies* agrees with the singular subject *airplane.*]

RESOURCES

Number

Practice

■ *Language & Sentence Skills Practice,* p. 153

(2) Plural subjects take plural verbs.

EXAMPLES   Many **senators oppose** the new tax bill. [The plural verb *oppose* agrees with the plural subject *senators*.]

The **dolphins leap** playfully in the channel. [The plural verb *leap* agrees with the plural subject *dolphins*.]

In a verb phrase, the first helping verb agrees in number with the subject.

EXAMPLES   **He is building** a bird feeder. [The singular helping verb *is* agrees with the singular subject *He*.]

They are building a bird feeder. [The plural helping verb *are* agrees with the plural subject *They*.]

Does anyone know the answer? [The singular helping verb *Does* agrees with the singular subject *anyone*.]

Do any **students know** the answer? [The plural helping verb *Do* agrees with the plural subject *students*.]

Reference Note

For more about **helping verbs,** see page 52.

Exercise 2   **Identifying Verbs That Agree in Number with Their Subjects**

Choose the form of the <u>verb</u> in parentheses <u>that agrees with the given subject.</u>

EXAMPLES   **1.** it (*is, are*)
1. *is*

2. they (*does, do*)
2. *do*

1. this (*costs, cost*)
2. Chinese lanterns (*glows, glow*)
3. the swimmer (*dives, dive*)
4. we (*considers, consider*)
5. the men (*was, were*)
6. she (*asks, ask*)
7. these (*needs, need*)
8. those tacos (*tastes, taste*)
9. that music (*sounds, sound*)
10. lessons (*takes, take*)
11. several actors (*accepts, accept*)
12. children (*interferes, interfere*)
13. they (*says, say*)
14. counselor (*advises, advise*)
15. the woman (*leads, lead*)
16. you (*chooses, choose*)
17. mice (*approaches, approach*)
18. friends (*tries, try*)
19. the officer (*appreciates, appreciate*)
20. I (*swims, swim*)

COMPUTER TIP

Some word-processing programs can find problems in subject-verb agreement. You can use such programs to search for errors when you proofread your writing. However, such programs are not perfect. If you are not sure that an error found by the word processor is truly an error, check the relevant rule in this book.

Agreement of Subject and Verb

Rule 8b *(pp. 156–158)*

OBJECTIVE

■ To choose verbs that agree in number with their subjects

DIRECT TEACHING

Modeling and Demonstration

Agreement of Subject and Verb. Model how to determine that a subject and verb agree in number by using the example *He is building a bird feeder.* First, ask students to identify the subject. [*He*] Next, ask whether this subject is singular or plural. [*singular*] Then, ask which word or words make up the verb. [*is building*] Ask whether this verb phrase is singular or plural. [*singular*] Point out that singular subjects take singular verbs, and plural subjects take plural verbs. Also, point out that in a verb phrase, the first helping verb (in this case *is*) agrees with the subject in number. Now, have a volunteer use another example from this chapter to demonstrate how to determine that a subject and verb agree in number.

PRACTICE

Guided and Independent

Exercises   You may wish to use **Exercise 2** as guided practice. Then, have students complete **Exercise 3** as independent practice.

HOMEWORK

USAGE

Exercise 3

DISTRIBUTED REVIEW

Ask students to identify the sentence structure of sentences 1, 2, 4, and 8. [1. *simple*; 2. *complex*; 4. *compound-complex*; 8. *compound*]

DIFFERENTIATING INSTRUCTION

English-Language Learners

General Strategies. Some English-language learners may be confused by the meaning of the word *agreement*. They might expect that when the subject ends in *s*, the verb must also end in *s*. It may be helpful to emphasize that *agreement* means that a singular subject requires a singular verb, which usually ends in *s*.

Also, some speakers of languages other than English do not use plural forms in certain circumstances. If other words in a sentence clearly indicate plurality, students who speak such languages may consider the plural to be optional, as in *I have about a million baseball card*. You can help students by pointing out that the plural form is needed in this situation in English.

Spanish. In Spanish, *la gente*, "people," is a singular noun, so Spanish-speaking students might use sentences such as "The people is going to the game." Emphasize that *people* is plural in English, and provide practice in correct subject-verb agreement by using *people* as the subject of a number of sentences.

Problems in Agreement

Rule 8c *(pp. 158–159)*

OBJECTIVE

■ To identify subjects and verbs that agree in number when a phrase or clause follows the subject

USAGE

Exercise 3 **Identifying Verbs That Agree in Number with Their Subjects**

Choose the correct form of the verb in parentheses in each of the following sentences.

EXAMPLE　**1.** The sport of basketball (*enjoys, enjoy*) great popularity worldwide.

　　　　　1. enjoys

1. Successful basketball leagues (*exist, exists*) in many countries, but the National Basketball Association remains the world's major league.
2. Around the world, children (*dreams, dream*) of one day playing in the NBA.
3. NBA teams (*selects, select*) some of the best international players, along with college players, in the yearly NBA draft.
4. The NBA (*appeals, appeal*) to a global audience through these talented foreign-born players.
5. One such player (*is, are*) Emanuel Ginobili of Argentina.
6. Ginobili (*plays, play*) for the San Antonio Spurs as well as the Argentine national team.
7. In Argentina, fans (*follows, follow*) the career of their beloved "Manu."
8. (*Do, Does*) many people know that Ginobili is the only player in history to win a Euroleague championship, an NBA championship, and an Olympic gold medal?
9. With such accomplishments, he (*has, have*) proven to be a winner wherever he plays.
10. Other international stars (*includes, include*) Yao Ming of China, Pau Gasol of Spain, and Nenê of Brazil.

Problems in Agreement
Phrases and Clauses Between Subjects and Verbs

8c. The number of a subject is not changed by a phrase or clause following the subject.

EXAMPLES　The **lights** on the Christmas tree **create** a festive atmosphere. [The prepositional phrase *on the Christmas tree* does not affect the number of the subject *lights*.]

RESOURCES

Problems in Agreement
Practice
■ *Language & Sentence Skills Practice,* p. 155

The **distance** between the two posts **is** eight feet. [The prepositional phrase *between the two posts* does not affect the number of the subject *distance*.]

Karen's **brother**, who has always enjoyed bicycle repair and maintenance, **works** at the bike shop on weekends. [The adjective clause *who has always enjoyed bicycle repair and maintenance* does not affect the number of the subject *brother*.]

NOTE If the subject is the indefinite pronoun *all, any, more, most, none,* or *some,* its number may be determined by the object of a prepositional phrase that follows it.

EXAMPLES **All** of the vegetables **were** peeled. [*All* refers to the plural word *vegetables*.]

All of the salad **was** eaten. [*All* refers to the singular word *salad*.]

Exercise 4 **Identifying Subjects and Verbs That Agree in Number**

Identify the <u>subject</u> in each sentence. Then, choose the form of the <u>verb</u> in parentheses <u>that agrees with the subject</u>.

EXAMPLE 1. The houses on my block (*has, have*) two stories.
    1. *houses—subject; have*

1. The <u>launch</u> of a space shuttle (<u>*attracts*</u>, *attract*) the interest of people throughout the world.
2. Our <u>thermos</u>, which is in the picnic basket, (<u>*is*</u>, *are*) filled with apple juice.
3. That <u>collection</u> of poems (*is, are*) *Where the Sidewalk Ends.*
4. <u>People</u> in some countries (*observes*, <u>*observe*</u>) Friendship Day at the beginning of August.
5. The <u>children</u> of the world (*needs*, <u>*need*</u>) food and medicine.
6. That <u>house</u> on the hill (*is, are*) where my grandfather was born.
7. <u>Koalas</u> that live in the wild (*eats*, <u>*eat*</u>) mainly eucalyptus leaves and shoots.
8. The <u>principal</u> of each high school (<u>*awards*</u>, *award*) certificates to honor students.
9. <u>Stories</u> about Hank Aaron always (*makes*, <u>*make*</u>) me want to play baseball.
10. The <u>cucumbers</u> in my garden (*grows*, <u>*grow*</u>) very quickly.

| TIPS & TRICKS |

The subject of a sentence is never in a prepositional phrase.

EXAMPLE
The **files** in this drawer **are** neat and organized. [The subject is *files. Drawer* is part of the prepositional phrase *in this drawer*.]

As well as, along with, together with, and *in addition to* are compound prepositions. Phrases beginning with compound prepositions do not affect the number of the subject or verb.

EXAMPLE
The **conductor,** as well as the musicians, **wears** formal wear at every performance. [The prepositional phrase *as well as the musicians* does not affect the number of the subject *conductor*.]

Reference Note
For a list of **common prepositions,** see page 66.

Problems in Agreement **159**

DIRECT TEACHING

Modeling and Demonstration

Problems in Agreement. Model how to determine whether a subject and verb agree in number when a phrase or clause follows the subject by using the example from **Exercise 4,** *The houses on my block have two stories.* First, ask students to identify the subject and verb in the example. [*houses; have*] Point out to students that *on my block* is a prepositional phrase; therefore, the object of the preposition, *block,* cannot be the subject of the sentence. Now, ask whether *houses* is singular or plural. [*plural*] Then, ask what the verb's number is. [*plural*] Tell students that the intervening phrase *on my block* does not change the subject's number. Now, have a volunteer use another example from this chapter to demonstrate how to identify subject-verb agreement.

DIRECT TEACHING

Irregular Plurals

Remind students that some words can be the same in both their singular and plural forms. For example, some animal names like *deer* and *fish* are both singular and plural. Ask students to suggest other animal names that can be the same in both singular and plural forms. [*Possibilities include* sheep, shrimp, moose, reindeer, squid, trout.]

MINI-LESSON **Usage**

Intervening Prepositional Phrases. Review prepositions and prepositional phrases, pp. 66–69. Then, ask each student to write two sentences using prepositional phrases between each subject and verb. Write a few of the sentences on the chalk-board, highlighting correct subject-verb agreement. Omit intervening phrases in incorrect sentences, and ask students to correct the verb forms. Remind them that verbs agree with the subjects of sentences, not the objects of prepositions.

Indefinite Pronouns
Rules 8d–f (pp. 160–163)
OBJECTIVE

■ To identify indefinite pronouns used as subjects and to choose the verbs that agree with them

DIRECT TEACHING

Modeling and Demonstration

Indefinite Pronouns. Model how to identify subject-verb agreement with an indefinite pronoun as a subject by using the example *One of the books belongs to Sabrena.* First, ask students to identify the subject and the verb. [*One; belongs*] Next, ask whether the subject is singular or plural. [*singular*] Then, ask what the verb's number is. [*singular*] Tell students that the phrase *of the books* does not change the subject's number. Explain that the indefinite pronoun *one*, like the other pronouns listed in **Rule 8d**, is singular. Now, have a volunteer use another example from this chapter to demonstrate how to identify subject-verb agreement.

DIFFERENTIATING INSTRUCTION

Learners Having Difficulty

Have groups of three students make charts or other visual representations for **Rules 8d–f.** Each student can take one of the three rules, creating the text for the parts of the visual that apply to that rule. The chart or visual should include a list of the indefinite pronouns to which each rule applies, an indication of the number of the pronouns, and example sentences demonstrating each rule. Display the visuals in the classroom while students study this chapter.

TIPS & TRICKS

The words *body, one,* and *thing* are singular. The indefinite pronouns that contain these words are singular as well.

EXAMPLES

Was any**body** there?

Some**one is** inside.

Every**thing has** been done.

HELP

Some indefinite pronouns, such as *both, each,* and *some,* can also be used as adjectives. When an indefinite adjective comes before the subject of a sentence, the verb agrees with the subject as it normally would.

EXAMPLES

Children love playing in the park.

Both children love playing in the park.

The **child loves** playing in the park.

Each child loves playing in the park.

Reference Note

For more about **indefinite pronouns,** see page 36.

Indefinite Pronouns

You may recall that personal pronouns refer to specific people, places, things, or ideas. Some pronouns do not refer to a definite person, place, thing, or idea and are therefore called *indefinite pronouns.*

8d. The following indefinite pronouns are singular: *anybody, anyone, anything, each, either, everybody, everyone, everything, neither, nobody, nothing, no one, one, somebody, someone,* and *something.*

EXAMPLES   **Everyone was invited** to the celebration.

Either of the answers **is** correct.

One of the tapes **belongs** to Sabrena.

Someone in the stands **has been waving** at us.

Pronouns like *each* and *one* are frequently followed by prepositional phrases. Remember that, for these pronouns, the verb agrees with the subject of the sentence, not with a word in a prepositional phrase.

8e. The following indefinite pronouns are plural: *both, few, many,* and *several.*

EXAMPLES   **Both** of the apples **are** good.

Few know about the surprise.

Many of the students **walk** to school.

Several of the club's members **have** not **paid** their dues.

8f. The indefinite pronouns *all, any, more, most, none,* and *some* **may be singular or plural, depending on their meaning in a sentence.**

Often, the object in a prepositional phrase that follows these pronouns indicates whether the pronoun is singular or plural. Usually, if the object of the preposition is singular, the pronoun is singular. If the object is plural, the pronoun usually is plural.

EXAMPLES   **All** of the room **has** been painted. [*All* refers to the singular object *room.*]

All of the rooms **have** been painted. [*All* refers to the plural object *rooms.*]

RESOURCES

Indefinite Pronouns
Practice

■ *Language & Sentence Skills Practice,* pp. 156–157
■ *Developmental Language & Sentence Skills,* pp. 59–60

Some of the equipment **has been stored** in the garage. [*Some* refers to the singular object *equipment*.]

Some of the supplies **have been stored** in the garage. [*Some* refers to the plural object *supplies*.]

NOTE The pronouns listed in Rule 8f are not always followed by prepositional phrases.

EXAMPLES **All have** left.

Some was eaten.

In such cases, you should look at the context—the other words and sentences surrounding the pronoun—to see if the pronoun refers to a singular or a plural word.

Exercise 5 **Identifying Subjects and Verbs That Agree in Number**

Identify the subject in each of the following sentences. Then, choose the form of the verb in parentheses that agrees with the subject.

EXAMPLE 1. Each of the marchers (*was, were*) carrying a sign protesting apartheid.

     1. Each—subject; was

1. All of my friends (*has, have*) had the chickenpox.
2. Everyone at the party (*likes, like*) the hummus dip.
3. Both of Fred's older brothers (*celebrates, celebrate*) their birthdays in July.
4. Some of the story (*is, are*) funny.
5. None of those rosebushes in my mother's garden ever (*blooms, bloom*) in February.
6. Several of those colors (*do, does*) not appeal to me.
7. Many of Mrs. Taniguchi's students (*speaks, speak*) fluent Japanese.
8. Nobody in these beginning painting classes (*has, have*) displayed work in the annual art show.
9. Most of the food here (*tastes, taste*) delicious.
10. One of Georgia O'Keeffe's paintings (*shows, show*) a ram's skull.

| COMPUTER TIP

Using indefinite pronouns correctly can be tricky. To help yourself, you may want to create an indefinite pronoun guide. First, summarize the information in Rules 8d–8f and 8t. Then, choose several examples to illustrate the rules. If you use a computer, you can create a "Help" file in which to store this information.

Call up your "Help" file whenever you run into difficulty with indefinite pronouns in your writing. If you do not use a computer, keep a writing notebook.

RETEACHING

Indefinite Pronouns

To help students remember that singular indefinite pronouns require singular verbs, encourage students to read compound indefinite pronouns as though they were two separate words with the word *single* between the two parts. For example, encourage students to think of *everybody* as *every single body* to help them recognize that *body* is singular and thus requires a singular verb.

EXTENSION

Critical Thinking

Inclusive Language. In the past, singular masculine pronouns were used to refer to singular indefinite pronouns whose gender was mixed or unknown, as in *Everyone bought his ticket to the game.* Ask students to discuss why this practice is offensive to some people. [*Responses will vary. Some students might point out that using masculine pronouns ignores the existence of females or, at least, assumes that masculine forms are capable of standing for all human beings.*]

Review A Proofreading Sentences for Subject-Verb Agreement

┌HELP──

Some sentences in Review A have more than one verb.

Many of the following sentences contain ~~errors in subject-verb agreement~~. If a verb does not agree with its subject, write the correct form of the verb. If a sentence contains no errors, write *C*.

EXAMPLES
1. One of the best-known prehistoric monuments in the world stand in a field in Britain.
   1. *stands*
2. Today everybody calls the monument Stonehenge, and thousands of people visits it each year.
   2. *visit*

1. want
2. challenge
3. C
4. is
5. believe
6. remain
7. C
8. say

1. All of the visitors to Stonehenge ~~wants~~ to know why the structure was built.
2. The huge rocks at Stonehenge ~~challenges~~ tourists and scientists alike to uncover their mysteries.
3. Most people easily recognize the monument as it looks in the photograph below.
4. However, nobody ~~are~~ sure how Stonehenge looked long ago.
5. Some of the archaeologists studying the site ~~believes~~ that Stonehenge once looked very different.
6. Few of the stones ~~remains~~ in their original places.
7. Many visitors to Stonehenge assume that ancient Druids built the monument.
8. Most scientists, though, ~~says~~ it was built many years before the Druids—perhaps four thousand years ago.

9. After seeing Stonehenge, few doubt that the stones~~weighs~~ as much as fifty tons.

9. weigh

10. Of course, nearly everyone~~seem~~ to have a theory about how these stones were set in place and what they were used for, but no one knows for sure.

10. seems

Compound Subjects

8g. Subjects joined by *and* usually take a plural verb.

Most compound subjects joined by *and* name more than one person or thing and take plural verbs.

EXAMPLES **Antonia Brico** and **Sarah Caldwell are** famous conductors. [Two persons are conductors.]

Last year a **library,** a **gazebo,** and a **museum were built** in our town. [Three things were built.]

A compound subject that names only one person or thing takes a singular verb.

EXAMPLES The **secretary** and **treasurer** of the science club **is** Leona. [One person is both the secretary and the treasurer.]

Chicken and dumplings is a favorite Southern dish. [*Chicken and dumplings* is one dish.]

Reference Note

For more about **compound subjects,** see page 15.

Exercise 6 **Choosing Verbs That Agree in Number with Compound Subjects**

Identify the compound subject in each of the following sentences as *singular* or *plural*. Then, choose the form of the verb that agrees with the compound subject.

EXAMPLE **1.** Cleo and Pam (*is, are*) here.
  1. plural—are

1. March and April (*is, are*) windy months.
2. The mechanic and shop owner (*is, are*) preparing his estimate.
3. The Bulldogs and the Pirates (*plays, play*) in the finals today.
4. Red beans and rice (*is, are*) my favorite Cajun dish.

1. pl.
2. s.
3. pl.
4. s.

Compound Subjects
Rules 8g–i *(pp. 163–166)*

OBJECTIVES

■ To identify compound subjects in sentences as singular or plural and to choose the verbs that agree in number with their subjects

■ To choose verbs that agree in number with compound subjects in sentences

USAGE

DIRECT TEACHING

Modeling and Demonstration

Compound Subjects. Model how to identify verbs that agree with their compound subjects by using the example *Last year a library, a gazebo, and a museum were built in our town.* First, ask students to identify the subject of the sentence. [*library, gazebo, museum*] Next, ask whether this subject is singular or plural. [*plural*] Then, ask what number the verb phrase *were built* is. [*plural*] Explain that compound subjects joined by *and* usually take a plural verb. Now, have a volunteer use another example from this chapter to demonstrate how to identify verbs and compound subjects that agree in number.

TEACHING **TIP**

Exercise 6 You may wish to have your students do **Exercise 6** orally. If students make errors, you can give guided practice in how to choose the correct verb.

Review B Choosing Verbs That Agree in Number with Their Subjects

Choose the form of the verb in parentheses that agrees with its subject in each of the following sentences.

EXAMPLE   **1.** *Pan dulce* and other baked goods (*sells, sell*) well at the Mexican American bakery shown below.

    1. sell

1. The wonderful smells at the bakery (*invites, invite*) hungry customers.
2. Children and their parents always (*enjoy, enjoys*) choosing and tasting the baked treats.
3. Display cases and large bowls (*holds, hold*) the fresh breads and pastries.
4. Rolls with powdered toppings and braided breads (*goes, go*) quickly.
5. Either an empanada or some giant biscuits (*are, is*) likely to be someone's breakfast.

6. Pumpkin or sweet potato (*is, are*) often used to fill the empanadas.
7. Most children (*likes, like*) volcano-shaped pastries known as *volcanes*.
8. Some raisin bars or a *buñuelo* (*makes, make*) a special after-school treat.
9. Bakeries like this one (*prepares, prepare*) mainly traditional Mexican American breads.
10. Holidays and special occasions (*calls, call*) for extra-fancy baked goods.

Other Problems in Agreement

8j. When the subject follows the verb, find the subject and make sure the verb agrees with it.

The subject usually follows the verb in sentences beginning with *here* or *there* and in questions.

EXAMPLES   Here **is** my **seat**.
                    Here **are** our **seats**.

Other Problems in Agreement
Rules 8j–p *(pp. 166–173)*

OBJECTIVES

- To choose the verb forms that agree in number with their subjects
- To read aloud sentences using *don't* and *doesn't*
- To use *don't* and *doesn't* correctly in sentences

RESOURCES

Other Problems in Agreement
Practice

- *Language & Sentence Skills Practice*, pp. 159–163, 171

There **is** an exciting **ride** at the fair.

There **are** exciting **rides** at the fair.

Where **is** the **bread**?

Where **are** the **loaves** of bread?

Does he know them?

Do they know him?

Exercise 9 **Choosing Verbs That Agree in Number with Their Subjects**

For each of the following sentences, choose the word or word group in parentheses that correctly completes the sentence.

EXAMPLE   1. (*Here's, Here are*) the jazz CDs I borrowed.

1. *Here are*

1. According to this map, (*there's, there are*) seven countries in Central America.
2. Where (*is, are*) the rough draft you were proofreading for me?
3. (*Has, Have*) they returned from the cafeteria yet?
4. There (*has, have*) been fewer rainy days this month than last month.
5. (*Here's, Here are*) the team's new uniforms.
6. (*There's, There are*) no reason we can't finish these math problems on time.
7. When (*is, are*) the next lunar eclipse?
8. (*Does, Do*) your parents know about the new schedule?
9. Janelle, (*here's, here are*) a question only you can answer.
10. When (*does, do*) you expect to hear from your cousin in Singapore again?

8k. The contractions *don't* and *doesn't* should agree with their subjects.

The word *don't* is a contraction for *do not*. Use *don't* with all plural subjects and with the pronouns *I* and *you*.

EXAMPLES   These **gloves don't** fit.

I don't want to be late.

Don't you feel well?

TIPS & TRICKS

When the subject of a sentence follows part or all of the verb, the word order is said to be *inverted*. To find the subject of a sentence with inverted order, restate the sentence in normal word order.

INVERTED   Here **is Eileen.**
NORMAL   **Eileen is** here.

INVERTED   **Are they** on time?
NORMAL   **They are** on time.

INVERTED   Into the woods **ran** the **deer.**
NORMAL   The **deer ran** into the woods.

HELP

The contractions *here's, there's,* and *where's* contain the verb *is* and should be used with only singular subjects.

NONSTANDARD
Here's your keys.

STANDARD
Here **are** your **keys.**

STANDARD
Here**'s** your **key.**

Reference Note

For more information about **contractions,** see page 354.

DIFFERENTIATING INSTRUCTION

English-Language Learners

General Strategies. An oral drill can help clear up confusion about the use of *don't* and *doesn't*. Read aloud a few sentences that have the same pattern, exaggerating the italicized words.

1. I used to live in Texas, but *I don't* anymore.
2. Luke used to play video games, but *he doesn't* anymore.
3. Our teams used to win all the tournaments, but *they don't* anymore.

Shake your head to emphasize negation when you say *don't* and *doesn't*. When students understand the pattern, let them volunteer their own sentences.

USAGE

USAGE

STYLE TIP

Some people consider contractions informal. Therefore, it is generally best not to use them in formal writing and speech.

The word *doesn't* is a contraction of *does not.* Use *doesn't* with all singular subjects except the pronouns *I* and *you.*

EXAMPLES   The **music box doesn't** play.

Doesn't she like cold weather?

It doesn't matter.

Oral Practice 2 Using *Doesn't* and *Don't* with Singular Subjects

Read the following sentences aloud, emphasizing the italicized words.

1. *Don't Oktoberfest* and the *Fall Carnival* start Saturday?
2. *We don't* call meetings often.
3. *One doesn't* interrupt a speaker.
4. *They don't* play their stereo loudly.
5. *Doesn't* the television *set* work?
6. *It doesn't* look like a serious wound.
7. *She doesn't* play basketball.
8. *Fido doesn't* like his new dog food.

Exercise 10 Using *Doesn't* and *Don't* Correctly

Complete each sentence by inserting the correct contraction, *doesn't* or *don't.*

EXAMPLE   1. _____ they go to our school?
             1. *Don't*

1. Doesn't
2. doesn't
3. don't
4. don't
5. doesn't
6. Don't
7. don't
8. doesn't
9. Doesn't
10. doesn't

1. _____ anyone in the class know any interesting facts about Susan B. Anthony?
2. Bill Bradley _____ play professional basketball anymore.
3. They _____ have enough people to form a softball team.
4. You _____ need to change your schedule.
5. It _____ hurt very much.
6. _____ the Japanese celebrate spring with a special festival?
7. Those snow peas _____ look crisp.
8. Hector _____ win every track meet; sometimes he places second.
9. _____ anybody know the time?
10. He _____ know the shortest route from Dallas to Peoria.

CONTENT-AREA CONNECTIONS

Health

Writing About Nutrition. Ask students to bring to class the packaging from a food product such as pasta, cereal, soup, or a frozen entree. Have students work in groups of three or four to interpret the "Nutrition Facts" box on one of the packages.

Then, ask each group to write four or five sentences about the nutritional value of the product. The sentences should give specific

8l. A collective noun may be either singular or plural, depending on its meaning in a sentence.

The singular form of a *collective noun* names a group of persons, animals, or things.

Common Collective Nouns			
army	club	fleet	public
assembly	committee	flock	swarm
audience	crowd	group	team
class	family	herd	troop

Reference Note
For more about **collective nouns**, see page 29.

A collective noun is

- singular when it refers to the group as a unit
- plural when it refers to the individual parts or members of the group

EXAMPLES Tomorrow the science **class is taking** a field trip to the planetarium. [The class as a unit is taking a field trip.]

The science **class are working** on their astronomy projects. [The members of the class are working on various projects.]

The **family has moved** to Little Rock, Arkansas. [The family as a unit has moved.]

The **family have been** unable to agree on where to spend their next vacation. [The members of the family have different opinions.]

Review C **Proofreading Sentences for Subject-Verb Agreement**

Most of the following sentences contain ~~errors in subject-verb agreement~~. If a sentence contains an error in agreement, write the correct form of the verb. If a sentence is already correct, write *C*.

EXAMPLE **1.** There is a man and a woman here to see you.
    1. are

1. Leilani and Yoshi ~~doesn't~~ know how to swim.
2. Here are the vegetables for the stir-fry.
3. The Seminoles of Florida ~~sews~~ beautifully designed quilts and jackets.

1. don't
2. C
3. sew

Problems in Agreement **169**

USAGE

information about calories, fat content, vitamins and minerals, and so on. Finally, have students check the subject-verb agreement in their sentences, underlining each subject once and each verb twice. If time permits, have students share their sentences orally with the class.

4. (Here) are
5. costs
6. celebrates
7. were
8. flies
9. C
10. (Where) are

4. ~~Here's~~ the sweaters I knitted for you.
5. Each of these ten-speed bicycles ~~cost~~ more than two hundred dollars.
6. The soccer team always ~~celebrate~~ each victory with a cookout at Coach Rodriguez's house.
7. The jury ~~was~~ arguing among themselves.
8. The flock of geese ~~fly~~ over the lake at dawn.
9. Doesn't that Thai dish with chopped peanuts taste good?
10. ~~Where's~~ the bus schedules for downtown routes?

Review D **Proofreading Sentences for Subject-Verb Agreement**

Some of the following sentences contain ~~errors in subject-verb agreement.~~ If a sentence contains an error in agreement, write the correct form of the verb. If a sentence is already correct, write *C*.

EXAMPLE   1. Don't this neon sign light up the night with color?
           1. Doesn't

1. The public ~~have~~ been fascinated with neon lights since they were introduced in the 1920s.   **1.** has [*or* C]
2. ~~There's~~ neon lights in large and small cities all over the world.   **2.** (There) are
3. Times Square in New York City and Tokyo's Ginza district ~~is~~ two places famous for their neon lights.   **3.** are
4. Some of today's neon signs are very large and creative.   **4.** C
5. Many signs like the one shown here ~~is~~ used in advertising.   **5.** are
6. Nowadays you sometimes see neon decorations and sculptures.   **6.** C
7. Our science class ~~are~~ learning how neon lights work.   **7.** is
8. Neon lights ~~is~~ made from hollow glass tubes filled with neon gas.   **8.** are

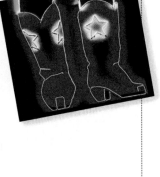

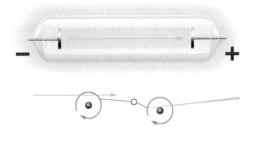

TEACHING TIP

Review D   In sentence 1, *public* could be either singular or plural. Referring to a unit, the word is singular; referring to individuals, it is plural.

DIRECT TEACHING

Correcting Misconceptions

Collective Nouns. Students may confuse collective nouns with plural nouns and so have problems with subject-verb agreement. Write the following nouns on a chalkboard or on a transparency: *mice, children, teeth, fleet, family, audience.* Tell students that the first three words are plural nouns, while the last three words are collective nouns. Remind students that in singular form, collective nouns can refer to members of a unit or the unit as a single whole, whereas plural nouns always refer to more than one.

Learning for Life

Preparing a Speech. Ask students to brainstorm topics about which they are knowledgeable, such as hobbies, career interests, or sports. Then, have each student choose a topic and prepare a three-minute speech on that topic. Each student should make an outline and a set of note cards for his or her chosen subject. Remind students to focus on organization and to include pertinent information. Let students practice their speeches, and then have pairs evaluate each other's speeches, listening closely

9. An electric current shot through the tube makes the gas glow.

10. The diagrams on the previous page ~~shows~~ the action of a neon light.
∧

8m. An expression of an amount (a measurement, a percentage, or a fraction, for example) may be singular or plural, depending on how it is used.

An expression of an amount is

- singular when the amount is thought of as a unit
- plural when the amount is thought of as separate units

SINGULAR   **Three years seems** like a long time.

PLURAL   **Two years** in particular **were** difficult for the family.

A fraction or a percentage is singular when it refers to a singular word and plural when it refers to a plural word.

SINGULAR   **Two thirds** of the city council **was** at the meeting.
             Eighty percent of the student body **is** present.

PLURAL   **Two thirds** of the council members **were** present.
             Eighty percent of the students **are** present.

Expressions of measurement (such as length, weight, and area) are usually singular.

EXAMPLES   **Ten feet** of yarn **is needed** for this art project.

           Two gallons of that paint **covers** approximately two hundred square feet.

8n. Some nouns that are plural in form take singular verbs.

The following nouns take singular verbs.

civics	genetics	mathematics	physics
economics	gymnastics	molasses	summons
electronics	linguistics	news	

EXAMPLES   **Economics is** my sister's favorite subject.

           The evening **news begins** at 6:00.

MEETING THE CHALLENGE

Create a recipe listing ingredient amounts and directions. You may wish to create a recipe for your favorite dish or for an abstract idea, like happiness or success. Write the recipe directions in complete sentences; at least five sentences should express ingredient amounts. Be sure to include both singular and plural expressions of amounts and to check for correct subject-verb agreement.

Meeting the Challenge

ANSWER

Recipes will vary but should include at least five amounts and both singular and plural expressions of amounts.

USAGE

for any agreement problems. Have listeners give feedback, using the following questions.

1. Is the speech well organized and easy to follow?

2. Does the speaker stick to the important information?

3. Are there any problems with agreement?

However, some nouns that are plural in form and that name singular objects take plural verbs.

binoculars	pants	shears
eyeglasses	pliers	shorts
Olympics	scissors	slacks

EXAMPLES   Your **binoculars have** complicated controls.

The **slacks are** torn in two different spots.

The **pliers belong** in the toolbox.

8o. Even when plural in form, the title of a creative work (such as a book, song, movie, or painting) or the name of a country, city, or organization generally takes a singular verb.

EXAMPLES   *Blue Lines* **is** an early Georgia O'Keeffe painting. [one painting]

The Souls of Black Folk **has** often **been cited** as a classic of African American literature. [one book]

"**Greensleeves**" **is** an old English folk song. [one song]

The **Netherlands has** thousands of canals. [one country]

Cedar Rapids is a manufacturing center in the Midwest. [one city]

Friends of the Earth was founded in 1969. [one organization]

8p. A verb agrees with its subject but not necessarily with a predicate nominative.

                        S   V   PN

EXAMPLES   The best **time** to visit **is** weekday **mornings.** [The verb *is* agrees with the singular subject *time,* not the plural predicate nominative *mornings.*]

                        S   V   PN

Weekday **mornings are** the best **time** to visit. [The verb *are* agrees with the plural subject *mornings,* not the singular predicate nominative *time.*]

STYLE ✏ **TIP**

If a construction like one shown under Rule 8p sounds awkward to you, revise the sentence so that it does not contain a predicate nominative.

AWKWARD
The main attraction is the marching bands.

REVISED
The audience considers the marching bands the main attraction.

USAGE

Review E — Choosing Verbs That Agree in Number with Their Subjects

Choose the <u>form of the verb</u> in parentheses <u>that agrees with the subject</u> in each of the following sentences.

EXAMPLE   **1.** There (*is, are*) many new students this year.
     1. *are*

1. The audience (*loves, love*) the mime performance.   1. [*or* love]
2. The story "Flowers for Algernon" (*makes, make*) me appreciate what I have.
3. Eight dollars (*is, are*) too much for that baseball card.
4. Andy's gift to Janelle (*was, were*) two roses.
5. Here (*is, are*) the letters I have been expecting.
6. The public (*differs, differ*) in their opinions on the referendum.
7. Physics (*was, were*) my sister's favorite subject.
8. The softball team usually (*practices, practice*) every Saturday morning.
9. His legacy to us (*was, were*) words of wisdom.
10. Where (*is, are*) the limericks you wrote?

Agreement of Pronoun and Antecedent

A pronoun usually refers to a noun or another pronoun called its *antecedent.* Whenever you use a pronoun, make sure that it agrees with its antecedent.

8q. **A pronoun should agree in both number and gender with its antecedent.**

Some singular personal pronouns have forms that indicate gender. Masculine pronouns (*he, him, his*) refer to males. Feminine pronouns (*she, her, hers*) refer to females. Neuter pronouns (*it, its*) refer to things (neither male nor female) and sometimes to animals.

EXAMPLES   **Bryan** lost **his** book.

Dawn lent **her** book to Bryan.

The **book** had Dawn's name written inside **its** cover.

> **Reference Note**
> For more information about **antecedents,** see page 31.

Agreement of Pronoun and Antecedent
Rules 8q–y (pp. 173–180)
OBJECTIVES

- To proofread and revise sentences for correct pronoun-antecedent agreement
- To complete sentences by identifying antecedents and writing pronouns that agree with them
- To identify antecedents for pronouns in sentences and to choose the forms of the pronouns that agree in number with the antecedents

DIRECT TEACHING

Modeling and Demonstration

Agreement of Pronoun and Antecedent. Model how to determine whether a pronoun's gender and number agree with the noun or pronoun to which it refers, using the example *Bryan lost his book.* First, ask students to identify any pronouns in the example. [*his*] Next, ask whether this pronoun refers to a noun. [*yes; Bryan*] Then, ask what the gender and number of this noun is. [*masculine, singular*] Ask whether the pronoun has the same gender and number as the noun to which it refers. [*yes*] Point out that pronouns and antecedents should agree in number and gender. Now, have a volunteer use another example from this chapter to demonstrate how to identify correct pronoun-antecedent agreement.

USAGE

DIFFERENTIATING INSTRUCTION

Learners Having Difficulty

To help students see the relationship of pronouns to antecedents, write on the chalkboard some of the examples under **Rule 8q.** Then, draw an arrow from each pronoun to its antecedent. Have volunteers contribute sentences and draw appropriate arrows.

English-Language Learners

Hmong. Some speakers of Hmong may find pronoun-antecedent agreement, especially in the possessive case, troublesome. Explain that English possessive pronouns fulfill the same function as do combinations of classifiers and pronouns in Hmong. Remind students that pronouns must correctly identify their antecedents and agree with them in gender and number. Have students review the feminine, masculine, and neuter pronouns, along with their cases.

STYLE TIP

Even when used correctly, the construction *his or her* sounds awkward to many people. To avoid using *his or her*, try to revise the sentence, using a plural pronoun and antecedent.

AWKWARD
Everyone in the club paid his or her dues.

Each of the mechanics uses his or her own tools.

REVISED
All of the club members paid **their** dues.

The **mechanics** use **their** own tools.

Sentences with singular antecedents joined by *or* or *nor* can sound awkward if the antecedents are of two different genders. Revise awkward sentences to avoid the problem.

AWKWARD
Ben or Maya will present his or her oral report.

REVISED
Ben will present **his** oral report, or **Maya** will present **hers.**

The antecedent of a personal pronoun can be another kind of pronoun, such as *each, neither,* or *one.* Often, the object of a prepositional phrase that follows the antecedent indicates the gender of the pronoun.

EXAMPLES **Each** of the men put on **his** hat. [*Men,* the object of the preposition *of,* indicates that the pronoun *Each* refers to males.]

Neither of those women got what **she** ordered. [*Women,* the object of the preposition *of,* indicates that the pronoun *Neither* refers to females.]

Some singular antecedents may be either masculine or feminine. When referring to such antecedents, use both the masculine and the feminine forms.

EXAMPLES Did **someone** in this line lose **his or her** ticket?

Everybody in the class wanted to know **his or her** grade.

8r. Use a singular pronoun to refer to two or more singular antecedents joined by *or* or *nor.*

EXAMPLES **Julio or Van** will bring **his** football.

Neither the **mother nor** the **daughter** had forgotten **her** running shoes.

8s. Use a plural pronoun to refer to two or more antecedents joined by *and.*

EXAMPLES My **mother and father** send **their** regards.

My **dog and cat** never share **their** food.

8t. Some indefinite pronouns are plural, some are singular, and some may be either.

(1) Use a singular pronoun to refer to *anybody, anyone, anything, each, either, everybody, everyone, everything, neither, nobody, no one, nothing, one, somebody, someone,* and *something.*

EXAMPLES **Anyone** who has finished **his or her** sketch should show it to the teacher.

Each of the birds built **its** own nest.

(2) The following indefinite pronouns are plural: *both, few, many,* and *several.*

EXAMPLES   **Several** of the ice sculptures are melting. How can we save **them**?

           Were **both** of the concerts canceled, or were **they** just rescheduled?

(3) The indefinite pronouns *all, any, more, most, none,* and *some* **may be singular or plural, depending on their meaning in a sentence.**

These pronouns are singular when they refer to a singular word and plural when they refer to a plural word.

EXAMPLES   **Some** of the test is hard, isn't **it**? [*Some* refers to the singular noun *test.*]

           Some of the questions are easy. I'll do **them** first. [*Some* refers to the plural noun *questions.*]

           All of the casserole looks burned, doesn't **it**?
           All of the potatoes look burned, don't **they**?

           Was **any** of the music original, or had you heard **it** all before?
           Were **any** of the songs original, or were **they** covers of old hits?

Exercise 11   **Proofreading for Pronoun-Antecedent Agreement**

Many of the following sentences contain ~~errors~~ in pronoun-antecedent agreement. If a sentence contains an error in agreement, write the underlined antecedent and the ∧correct form of the pronoun. If a sentence is already correct, write *C.*

EXAMPLE   **1.** Everyone in my English class will give their oral report on Friday.

           1. Everyone—his or her

1. Either Don or Buddy will be the first to give ~~their~~ report on literary devices.   **1.** his
2. Several others volunteered to give theirs first.   **2.** C
3. Everybody else in class wanted to put off giving ~~their~~ report as long as possible.   **3.** his or her

USAGE

Critical Thinking

Analysis. You might ask students to consider how pronoun-antecedent agreement compares to subject-verb agreement. They might consider what factors make a pronoun agree with its antecedent. [*for all personal pronouns: person and number; for third-person singular pronouns: gender*] Then, ask what factors are considered in making a subject agree with its verb. [*person and number*]

Reference Note

For information on the correct usage and spelling of the pronouns *its,* *their,* and *your,* see pages 272, 276, and 278.

4. Last year my friend Sandy and I figured out that waiting to give our reports was worse than actually giving them. **4.** C
5. I am surprised that more <u>people</u> did not volunteer to give <u>his or her</u> reports first. **5.** their
6. <u>Someone</u> else will be third to give <u>their</u> report; then I will give mine. **6.** his or her
7. <u>Some</u> of the students will show slides or play music with <u>his or her</u> reports. **7.** their
8. Our teacher, Mrs. Goldenburg, says that <u>anyone</u> who is nervous about giving <u>their</u> report should try rehearsing it in front of a mirror. **8.** his or her
9. Most of us think that giving a <u>report</u> later will leave more time to work on <u>them</u>. **9.** it
10. While <u>they</u> may put off giving <u>his or her</u> reports till later, I would rather do mine as soon as possible. **10.** their

Exercise 12 Identifying Antecedents and Writing Pronouns That Agree with Them

Complete the following sentences with pronouns that agree with their antecedents. Identify each <u>antecedent</u>.

EXAMPLE **1.** Ann Marie and Margaret wore _____ cheerleader uniforms.

   1. *their—Ann Marie and Margaret*

1. their
2. its
3. his or her
4. their
5. their
6. his
7. he or she
8. its
9. their
10. their

1. The <u>trees</u> lost several of _____ branches in the storm.
2. <u>Each</u> of the early Spanish missions in North America took pride in _____ church bell.
3. Anthony, do you know whether <u>anyone</u> else has turned in _____ paper yet?
4. <u>Many</u> in the mob raised _____ voices in protest.
5. The <u>creek</u> and the <u>pond</u> lost much of _____ water during the drought.
6. <u>One</u> of my uncles always wears _____ cowboy hat to work.
7. <u>No one</u> should be made to feel that _____ is worth less than someone else.
8. <u>One</u> of the dogs had gotten out of _____ collar.
9. A <u>few</u> of our neighbors have decided to fence _____ backyards.
10. <u>Lucinda</u> and <u>Val</u> looked forward to _____ chance to play basketball during the district playoffs.

Review F **Proofreading for Pronoun-Antecedent Agreement**

Many of the following sentences contain ~~errors in pronoun-antecedent agreement~~. If a sentence contains an error in agreement, write the <u>antecedent</u> and the correct form of the pronoun. If a sentence is already correct, write *C*.

EXAMPLE   1. Each of the president's Cabinet officers gave their advice about what to do.

    1. *Each—his or her*

1. <u>All</u> of the nation's presidents have had ~~his~~ own Cabinets, or groups of advisors.
2. Shortly after taking office, presidents appoint the members of their Cabinets.
3. <u>Everyone</u> appointed to the Cabinet is an expert in ~~their~~ field.
4. <u>George Washington</u> and <u>John Adams</u> met regularly with ~~his~~ advisors.
5. <u>Neither</u> had more than five people in ~~their~~ Cabinet.
6. The Cabinet received its name from James Madison, the fourth president.
7. Congress and the president have used their power over the years to create new government agencies.
8. In 1979, <u>Shirley M. Hufstedler</u> took ~~their~~ place on the Cabinet as the first secretary of education.
9. Neither <u>President Reagan</u> nor <u>President George H. W. Bush</u> created a new post in ~~their~~ Cabinet.
10. The <u>room</u> where the Cabinet meets now has more than fifteen chairs around ~~their~~ large table.

1. their
2. C
3. his or her
4. their
5. his
6. C
7. C
8. her

9. his
10. its

8u. Either a singular or a plural pronoun may be used to refer to a collective noun, depending on the meaning of the sentence.

EXAMPLES   The first **group** will give **its** presentation next Friday. [The group as a unit will give the presentation.]

    The **group** shared **their** ideas for topics. [The members of the group had various ideas.]

    The **committee** has given **its** full approval. [The committee as a unit has given approval.]

    After a brief debate, the **committee** recorded **their** final votes. [The committee members recorded their individual votes.]

Reference Note

For a list of **collective nouns,** see page 29.

Agreement of Pronoun and Antecedent   **177**

Critical Thinking

Metacognition. As a concluding activity and review, ask students to list examples of their own subject-verb or pronoun-antecedent agreement errors.

SAMPLE CHART

INCORRECT	CORRECT
There's two buildings.	There are two buildings.
Each of the boys wore their uniform.	Each of the boys wore his uniform.

Then, ask them to formulate a plan for eliminating errors. [*For example: When a sentence starts with* there, *the subject will usually follow the verb. Find the subject, and check for subject-verb agreement.*]

8v. An expression of an amount may take a singular or plural pronoun, depending on how the expression is used.

EXAMPLES **Ten dollars** is all I need. I think I can earn **it** over the weekend. [The amount is thought of as a unit.]

Where are the **two dollars** that were on the counter? Have **they** been taken? [The amount is thought of as individual pieces or parts.]

8w. Some nouns that are plural in form take singular pronouns.

The following nouns take singular pronouns.

civics	gymnastics	news
economics	linguistics	physics
electronics	mathematics	summons
genetics	molasses	

EXAMPLES Stacy enjoys **physics** even though **it** is a difficult subject.

I spilled the **molasses** and had to clean **it** up.

However, some nouns that are plural in form and that name singular objects take plural pronouns.

binoculars	pants	shears
eyeglasses	pliers	shorts
Olympics	scissors	slacks

EXAMPLES Jason removed his **eyeglasses** and placed **them** on the table.

Please hand me the **scissors** when you are finished with **them**.

8x. Use a singular pronoun to refer to the title of a creative work (such as a book, song, movie, or painting).

EXAMPLES After reading **"Neighbors,"** I recommended **it** to Juanita. [one story]

Terms of Endearment is my mom's favorite movie, and she has seen **it** six times. [one movie]

Reference Note

For information on using **italics** and **quotation marks with titles,** see pages 342 and 349.

8y. Use a singular pronoun to refer to the name of a country, city, or organization.

EXAMPLES   The **Philippines** is located in the southwest Pacific Ocean; **it** consists of thousands of islands. [one country]

The **Knights of Pythias** expects **its** members to maintain high moral standards. [one organization]

Exercise 13 Choosing Pronouns That Agree in Number with Their Antecedents

In each of the following sentences, identify the antecedent for the pronouns in parentheses. Then, choose the form of the pronoun that agrees with the antecedent.

EXAMPLE   **1.** I looked for my binoculars until I remembered that I had lent (*it, them*) to my sister.

   1. binoculars—them

1. The chess club decided that (*it, they*) would each bring two cans of food for the food drive.
2. *Cats* is one of Joan's favorite musicals, and she is very excited that (*it, they*) will be performed in town soon.
3. Lourdes is a famous town in France; (*it, they*) may attract as many as two million visitors each year.
4. Next, I carefully measured out three cups of water and poured (*it, them*) into the mixing bowl.
5. Once Janette started paying close attention to the news, she found (*it, them*) fascinating.
6. The flock of ducks flapping (*its, their*) wings gracefully overhead made very little noise.
7. When he got paid for mowing lawns, Jason's little brother put the four dollars in separate places so that he wouldn't spend (*it, them*) all at once.
8. The Bear Backers is what our high school booster club calls (*itself, themselves*).
9. When you are finished, be sure to put the scissors back where you found (*it, them*).
10. Have you visited the Netherlands? I heard (*it, they*) is a beautiful country.

Answers to items 1, 4, 7, and 8 may vary.

Review G **Proofreading Sentences for Subject-Verb and Pronoun-Antecedent Agreement**

Most of the following sentences contain errors in pronoun-antecedent agreement or subject-verb agreement. Identify each ~~error in agreement~~, and give the correct pronoun or verb. If a sentence is already correct, write∧C.

EXAMPLE   1. Ray Bradbury, shown below, is a favorite writer of many young people because he makes science fun for him or her.
           1. *him or her—them*

1. One reason for his stories' popularity∧~~are~~ that they are usually about people, not things. **1.** is
2. There∧~~is~~ some science fiction writers who care more about the gadgets they can imagine than the characters who use them. **2.** are
3. Bradbury tries to show that a person is more important than the technology that affects∧~~them~~. **3.** him or her
4. If you have not read his most famous book, *The Martian Chronicles,* you should read∧~~them~~ right away. **4.** it
5. In one of his short stories, children on Venus∧~~sees~~ the sun only once every seven years. **5.** see

6. One girl, who grew up on Earth, remembers what the heat of the sun is like. **6.** C
7. Some of the other children make fun of her, and they lock her in a closet. **7.** C
8. When the rain stops and the sun comes out, each of the other children∧~~have~~ fun outside. **8.** has
9. After the rain starts again, all of the children feel bad about what∧~~he or she~~ did to their classmate. **9.** they
10. Even though the story is set in the future and on another planet, human emotions, as opposed to technology,∧~~is~~ the focus of the story. **10.** are

8

Numerals in brackets refer to rules tested by the items in the Chapter Review.

1. are [8j, b(2)]
2. doesn't [8k, b(1)]
3. has [8d, b(1)]
4. C [8d, b(1)]
5. were [8g, b(2)]
6. has [8h, b(1)]
7. C [8f, b(2)]
8. Doesn't [8k, j, b(1)]
9. has [8d, b(1)]
10. gives [8o, b(1)]

Chapter Review

A. Identifying Verbs That Agree with Their Subjects

For each of the following sentences, if the italicized verb does not agree with its subject, rewrite the sentence, using the correct form of the verb. If the sentence is already correct, write *C*.

1. When *is* Bill's parents coming to pick us up?
2. Mr. Epstein said that it *don't* look like rain today.
3. Neither of the bar mitzvahs *have* been scheduled yet.
4. Everyone who wears eyeglasses *is* having vision tests today.
5. My baseball bat and my catcher's mitt *was* in my room.
6. Neither Esteban nor Tina *have* tried out for the play yet.
7. All of our guests *have* been to Fort Worth's Japanese garden.
8. *Don't* the team captain plan to put her into the game soon?
9. One of the men *have* decided that he will get his car washed.
10. The Bill of Rights *give* citizens of the United States the right to worship where they please.

B. Identifying Pronouns That Agree with Their Antecedents

For each of the following sentences, if the italicized pronoun does not agree with its antecedent, rewrite the sentence, using the correct form of the pronoun.

11. his [8t(1), q]
12. her [*or* its] [8t(1), q]
13. their [8t(3), q]
14. his or her [8t(1), q]
15. their [8t(2), q]
16. her [8r, q]
17. its [8q]
18. himself [8t(1), q]
19. them [8q]
20. his or her [8t(1), q]

11. Each of the boys brought *their* permission slip.
12. One of the does was accompanied by *their* fawn.
13. Have all of the winners taken *his or her* science projects home?
14. Everyone going to the concert should bring *their* own food.
15. Many of the buildings had yellow ribbons on *its* windows.
16. Neither Stephanie nor Marilyn had brought *their* book bag.
17. Every dog had a numbered tag hanging from *their* collar.
18. Someone in the Boy Scout troop camped near poison ivy and has gotten it all over *themselves.*
19. Only a few workers had brought tools with *him or her.*
20. One of the contest winners had *their* picture taken.

Chapter Review **181**

ASSESSING

Monitoring Progress

Chapter Review. To assess student progress, you may want to compare the types of items missed on the **Diagnostic Preview** with those missed on the **Chapter Review.** If students have not made significant progress, you may want to refer them to **Chapter 17: Correcting Common Errors, Exercises 6–9,** for additional practice.

USAGE

RESOURCES

Agreement
Review
■ *Language & Sentence Skills Practice,* pp. 171–174

Assessment
■ *Formal Assessment*
■ *Progress-Monitoring Tests,* pp. 15–16, 48
■ *Test Generator* (Teacher One Stop DVD-ROM)

C. Proofreading a Paragraph for Subject-Verb Agreement

Some of the following sentences contain errors in subject-verb agreement. If a sentence contains an ~~error in agreement~~, write the ∧correct form of the verb. If a sentence is already correct, write *C*.

21. have [8c, b(2)]
22. have [8g, b(2)]
23. exist [8b(2)]
24. is [8c, b(1)]
25. is [8b(1)]
26. C [8c, b(2)]
27. enjoy [8c, b(2)]
28. is [8d, b(1)]
29. C [8b(1)]
30. is [8c, b(1)]

[**21**] People in Switzerland ~~has~~ four national languages. [**22**] German is spoken by most Swiss, but French and Italian, as well as the old Latin dialect Romansh, ~~has~~ equal status. [**23**] Not many speakers of Romansh ~~exists~~, but the Romansh language, which is also called Grishun, has semiofficial national status. [**24**] Romansh, along with German, ~~are~~ spoken in the mountains of eastern Switzerland. [**25**] In the Western cities of Geneva and Lausanne, French ~~are~~ the language of most inhabitants. [**26**] To the north, the people in Bern, the capital, and in the famous banking centers of Basel and Zürich speak German. [**27**] Visitors in search of an Italian lifestyle ~~enjoys~~ the Italian-speaking city of Lugano, in the south. [**28**] One of Switzerland's larger cities ~~are~~ actually divided between two languages. [**29**] Truly bilingual, the city is called Biel on the German-speaking side and Bienne on the French-speaking side. [**30**] Communication between the two sides ~~are~~ no problem, because everybody in Biel/Bienne grows up speaking both languages!

D. Proofreading Sentences for Pronoun-Antecedent Agreement

Many of the following sentences contain errors in pronoun-antecedent agreement. If a sentence contains an ~~error in agreement~~, write the <u>antecedent</u> and the ∧correct form of the pronoun. If a sentence is already correct, write *C*.

31. her [8r, q]
32. their [8s]
33. its [8q]
34. its [8u]
35. C [8t(1), q]

31. If you see either <u>Maggie</u> or <u>Melanie</u>, will you please tell ~~them~~∧ I won't be able to stay after school?

32. <u>Tom</u> and <u>Mike</u> meet every Friday with ∧~~his~~ teammates to discuss strategy.

33. The museum's portrait <u>gallery</u> now has more than ten portraits on ∧~~their~~ walls.

34. Each <u>club</u> has ∧~~their~~ own service project.

35. One of the women in the acting class designs her own costumes.

36. <u>Linda</u> or <u>Rosa</u> will donate ~~their~~ time to the project.
_∧

37. <u>One</u> of the parrots escaped from ~~their~~ cage.
_∧

38. Did either <u>George</u> or <u>Patrick</u> forget to bring ~~their~~ birth
_∧
certificate?

39. <u>People</u> who film an animal in its natural habitat face many
problems.

40. <u>All</u> of the students shouted ~~his or her~~ approval.
_∧

36. her [8r, q]
37. its [*or* C] [8t(1), q]
38. his [8r, q]
39. C [8q]
40. their [8t(3), q]

Writing Application

Using Correct Agreement in a Report

Agreement with Collective Nouns   You are on the committee in charge of organizing your school's participation in the local Thanksgiving Day Parade. Write about the committee's plans in a brief report, which you will read at the next student council meeting. Use at least five collective nouns in your report.

Prewriting   Write down the names of some clubs or organizations that might be in the parade. Think about collective nouns to use in your report.

Writing   Use your notes to help you write your first draft. Begin with a main idea statement that tells other student council members what progress your committee has made. Then, tell about some of the groups that have asked to be in the parade and what those groups are planning to do.

Revising   As you read your report, ask yourself these questions: Is it clear what kind of participation is planned? Have I included important details? Do the committee's plans sound logical? Revise any parts of the report that are unclear.

Publishing   Proofread your report for any errors in grammar, spelling, and punctuation. Make sure that you have used five collective nouns and that the verbs and pronouns you use agree with them. Your class may wish to have each student present his or her report. Then, vote on which parade proposal is most entertaining.

Reference Note
You may want to refer to the list of **collective nouns** on page 29.

USAGE

1.0 Written and Oral English Language Conventions
Students write and speak with a command of standard English conventions appropriate to this grade level.
1.4 Edit written manuscripts to ensure that correct grammar is used.

Terms and numerals in brackets refer to concepts and rules tested by the items in the Diagnostic Preview.

1. bought [9a, c, d]
2. teaching [9a, c, d]
3. eaten [9a, c, d]
4. running [9a, c, d]
5. broke [9a, c, d]
6. rung [9a, c, d]
7. frozen [9a, c, d]
8. sang [9a, c, d]
9. begun [9a, c, d]
10. brought [9a, c, d]

Using Verbs Correctly
Principal Parts, Regular and Irregular Verbs, Tense, Voice

Diagnostic Preview

A. Using Correct Forms of Irregular Verbs

Give the <u>correct form</u> (past, past participle, or present participle) of the verb in parentheses in each of the following sentences.

EXAMPLES **1.** The deer (*run*) right in front of our path.
  1. ran

  2. Her dog has (*run*) away from home.
  2. run

1. Eileen (*buy*) several boxes decorated with Amish designs.
2. Joan had been (*teach*) preschool for three years.
3. I shouldn't have (*eat*) that last handful of sunflower seeds.
4. The water was (*run*) over the rocks.
5. When the medicine finally began to work, his fever (*break*).
6. That phone has (*ring*) every five minutes since I got home.
7. If that had happened to me, I would have (*freeze*) with fear.
8. Through the murky depths, the whales (*sing*) to one another.
9. We knew that it would start to rain soon because the crickets had (*begin*) chirping.
10. The waiter (*bring*) us couscous, a popular North African dish.

4

B. Choosing the Forms of *Lie* and *Lay*, *Sit* and *Set*, and *Rise* and *Raise*

Choose the correct verb in parentheses in each of the following sentences.

EXAMPLES **1.** My cat (*lies, lays*) around the house all day.
    1. lies

    2. Did any contestants (*rise, raise*) their hands?
    2. raise

11. The drawbridge had (*risen, raised*) before we sailed out into the bay.
12. (*Sit, Set*) that down in the chair, will you?
13. The treasure had (*lay, lain*) at the bottom of the sea for more than four hundred years.
14. Nashota read a folk tale about Coyote, the trickster, as we (*sat, set*) on the porch.
15. To avoid stepping on a snake, look on the other side of any logs (*lying, laying*) in the path.

11. [*rise, raise;* 9c, d]
12. [*sit, set;* 9c, d]
13. [*lie, lay;* 9c, d]
14. [*sit, set;* 9c, d]
15. [*lie, lay;* 9c, d]

C. Making Tenses of Verbs Consistent

For each of the following sentences, write the italicized verb in the correct tense.

EXAMPLES **1.** My father looked at his watch and *decides* that it was time to leave.
    1. decided

    2. Alejandra *calls* three times, but no one answered the phone.
    2. called

16. Before Marjorie's sister gave us a ride in her car, she *asks* us to lend her some money for gas.
17. He says he is sorry, but he *didn't* mean it.
18. In that forest, the pine trees grow close together and *had* straight trunks.
19. When the show ended, we *get* up to leave, but the crowd had already blocked the aisles.
20. Several mechanics worked on my aunt's car before one of them finally *finds* the problem.

16. asked [9e, d]
17. doesn't [9e, d, c]
18. have [9e, d, c]
19. got [9e, d, c]
20. found [9e, d, c]

■ The chapter closes with a **Chapter Review** including a **Writing Application** that asks students to include at least ten irregular verbs in a narrative poem.
■ For help in integrating this chapter with writing assignments in *Holt Literature and Language Arts,* see the **Teaching Strands** chart on pp. T24–T25.

USAGE

ASSESSING

Entry-Level Assessment
Diagnostic Preview. Use the **Diagnostic Preview** to pinpoint students' strengths and weaknesses in using verbs correctly. Evaluate students' responses to determine which rules need review. Even though students may show mastery on the preview, they may make tense, consistency, or voice errors in their writing.

PRETEACHING

Lesson Starter
Prior Knowledge. Write the following verbs on the chalkboard: *begun, eaten, gone, lain, swum,* and *sung,* and ask students to write a sentence with each verb. Then, let student pairs compare sentences. Students may discover that the verb forms need helping verbs. (Some students may find uses for the verbs as participial modifiers.)

Differentiating Instruction
■ *UA: Differentiating Instruction*
■ *UA: Supporting Instruction in Five Languages*
■ *Family Involvement Activities: In Five Languages*

Assessment
■ *Formal Assessment*

■ *Progress-Monitoring Tests,* pp. 17–18, 48
■ *Test Generator (Teacher One Stop DVD-ROM)* 🌀

Other Language Resources
■ *Spelling Lessons & Activities*
■ *WordSharp: An Interactive Vocabulary Tutor*
■ *Reading and Writing Transparencies*

USAGE

The Principal Parts of a Verb

Rules 9a–c *(pp. 186–196)*

OBJECTIVES

- To pronounce and use the past and past participle forms of regular verbs

- To pronounce and use the past and past participle forms of irregular verbs

- To proofread sentences for correct verb forms

DIRECT TEACHING

Modeling and Demonstration

The Principal Parts of a Verb.
Model how to use principal parts of regular and irregular verbs with the examples *work* and *sing*. First, ask students whether *work* takes *–d* or *–ed* to form the past tense. [*–ed*] Next, ask what the principal parts of *work* are. [*work, (is) working, worked, (have) worked*] Then, ask whether *work* is a regular or irregular verb. [*regular*] Now, ask students whether *sing* takes *–d* or *–ed* to form the past tense. [*neither*] Ask what the principal parts of *sing* are. [*sing, (is) singing, sang, (have) sung*] Ask whether *sing* is a regular or irregular verb. [*irregular*] Show students how the past participle of *sing* is used by saying aloud *We have sung all over the state.* Now, have a volunteer use another example from this chapter to demonstrate how to use principal parts of regular and irregular verbs.

D. Identifying Active and Passive Voice

Tell whether the verb in each of the following sentences is in *active voice* or *passive voice*.

EXAMPLES
  1. This colorful woven sash was imported from Guatemala.
    1. passive voice

  2. On vacation last year, we traveled by train to Prague and Budapest.
    2. active voice

21. passive [9f]
22. active [9f]
23. passive [9f]
24. passive [9f]
25. active [9f]

21. We were told about the contest by our favorite teacher.
22. Water rushed through the ravine and into the pool below.
23. The gate to the factory was left open all weekend.
24. A crystal glass was set too close to the edge of the coffee table.
25. The energetic puppy is chasing its tail again.

The Principal Parts of a Verb

The four basic forms of a verb are called the *principal parts* of the verb.

9a. The four principal parts of a verb are the *base form,* the *present participle,* the *past,* and the *past participle.*

The words *is* and *have* are included in the following chart because helping verbs are used with the present participle and past participle to form some tenses.

Base Form	Present Participle	Past	Past Participle
work	[is] working	worked	[have] worked
sing	[is] singing	sang	[have] sung

EXAMPLES
  I **sing** in the school a cappella chorus.

  We **are singing** at the music festival tonight.

  Mahalia Jackson **sang** spirituals at Carnegie Hall.

  We **have sung** all over the state.

RESOURCES

The Principal Parts of a Verb
Practice

- *Language & Sentence Skills Practice,* pp. 180–186, 194
- *Developmental Language & Sentence Skills,* pp. 65–66

Regular Verbs

9b. A *regular verb* forms its past and past participle by adding *–d* or *–ed* to the base form.

Base Form	Present Participle	Past	Past Participle
use	[is] using	used	[have] used
suppose	[is] supposing	supposed	[have] supposed
attack	[is] attacking	attacked	[have] attacked
drown	[is] drowning	drowned	[have] drowned

Avoid the following common errors when forming the past or past participle of regular verbs.

1. leaving off the *–d* or *–ed* ending

NONSTANDARD	She use to work in the library.
STANDARD	She **used** to work in the library.

NONSTANDARD	Who was suppose to bring the decorations?
STANDARD	Who was **supposed** to bring the decorations?

2. adding unnecessary letters

NONSTANDARD	A swarm of bees attackted us in the orange grove.
STANDARD	A swarm of bees **attacked** us in the orange grove.

NONSTANDARD	Several people nearly drownded in the flood.
STANDARD	Several people nearly **drowned** in the flood.

Oral Practice 1 **Using the Past and Past Participle Forms of Regular Verbs**

Read each of the following sentences aloud, stressing the italicized verbs.

1. She *has crossed* this street many times on the way to school.
2. The raccoon *visited* our camp every morning last summer.

—HELP—

Most regular verbs that end in e drop the e before adding *–ing*. Some regular verbs double the final consonant before adding *–ing* or *–ed*.

Reference Note

For more information on correctly **adding suffixes**, see page 373.

Reference Note

For a discussion of **standard and non-standard English**, see page 265.

STYLE TIP

A few regular verbs have alternative past forms ending in *t*. For example, the past form of burn is *burned* or *burnt*. Both forms are correct.

TEACHING TIP

Spelling. Remind students of the following spelling guidelines for adding *–d* or *–ed* to a verb to form the past or past participle.

1. For verbs ending in *y* preceded by a consonant, change the *y* to *i* before adding *–ed*.

cry + ed = cried

marry + ed = married

2. For verbs ending in *y* preceded by a vowel, keep the *y* when adding *–ed*.

pray + ed = prayed

destroy + ed = destroyed

(exceptions: laid, paid, said)

3. Double the final consonant before adding *–ed* if the verb (1) has only one syllable or has the accent on the last syllable and (2) ends in a single consonant preceded by a single vowel.

skip + ed = skipped

prefer + ed = preferred

Before students turn in **Exercise 1,** ask them to check the spellings of the answers.

---

3. Ryan and Annie *repaired* the engine in less than an hour.
4. Scientists *have discovered* that birds use the sun as a compass.
5. Some people say that Stone Age surgeons in Peru *operated* on the human brain.
6. Alexandra and Anthony *have baked* Bavarian pretzels for the party.
7. The actors *jumped* across the stage to catch the falling door.
8. Sylvia *has used* her computer every day this week.

Exercise 1 · Using Past and Past Participle Forms of Regular Verbs

Give the correct past or past participle form of the verb in parentheses in each of the following sentences.

EXAMPLE   1. My aunt has (*live*) in New York State for many years.
    1. *lived*

1. enjoyed

2. asked

3. raised

4. knitted [*or* knit]

5. wished

6. opened

7. applied

8. fascinated

9. called

10. started

1. As a child, she (*enjoy*) living on one of the Shetland Islands, off the coast of Scotland.
2. Several months before her sixth birthday, she (*ask*) for a Shetland pony and got one.
3. Back then, her family (*raise*) sheep and had a Shetland sheep-dog, a dog like a small collie.
4. Last year for my birthday, my aunt (*knit*) me a fine, soft sweater out of Shetland wool.
5. Recently she (*wish*) that she could go back to Scotland to visit her old home.
6. A new art museum that features the work of Mexican artists has (*open*) downtown.
7. Since reading about it, Dolores and Dario have (*apply*) for jobs there.
8. For a long time the works of Diego Rivera and José Clemente Orozco have (*fascinate*) them.
9. On Monday, the gallery manager (*call*) them.
10. They (*start*) work yesterday and will work at the museum for the rest of the summer.

Irregular Verbs

9c. An ***irregular verb*** forms its past and past participle in some other way than by adding *–d* or *–ed* to the base form.

An irregular verb forms its past and past participle in one of the following ways:

- changing vowels
- changing consonants
- changing vowels *and* consonants
- making no changes

Base Form	Past	Past Participle
ring	rang	[have] rung
make	made	[have] made
bring	brought	[have] brought
burst	burst	[have] burst

NOTE Since most English verbs are regular, people sometimes try to make irregular verbs follow the regular pattern. However, such words as *throwed, knowed, shrinked,* or *choosed* are considered nonstandard.

Avoid the following common errors when forming the past or past participle of an irregular verb.

1. using the past form with a helping verb

NONSTANDARD	Carlos has went to the shopping mall.
STANDARD	Carlos **went** to the shopping mall.
	or
STANDARD	Carlos **has gone** to the shopping mall.

2. using the past participle form without a helping verb

NONSTANDARD	I seen all of her movies.
STANDARD	I **have seen** all of her movies.

3. adding –*d* or –*ed* to the base form

NONSTANDARD	The right fielder throwed the ball to the shortstop.
STANDARD	The right fielder **threw** the ball to the shortstop.

─HELP─

When you are not sure whether a verb is regular or irregular, check a dictionary. Entries for irregular verbs generally list the principal parts.

USAGE

DIFFERENTIATING INSTRUCTION

English-Language Learners

General Strategies. As is true in many languages, most of the verbs that are irregular in English are also the most common. It is especially important, therefore, that students learn these verbs well. You may want to pair English-language learners with native speakers of English, first for help in defining unknown words and learning correct pronunciations (especially of the past and past participle, whose pronunciations are often quite different from the base form), and again later for informal quizzing and reteaching of the definitions and pronunciations.

Spanish. Remind Spanish speakers that the English present participle suffix *–ing* is equivalent to the Spanish *–ando* and *–iendo* (e.g., *hablando,* "speaking," from *hablar,* "to speak," and *comiendo,* "eating," from *comer,* "to eat") and that the English past participle suffix *–(e)d* is equivalent to the Spanish *–ado* and *–ido* (e.g., *marcado,* "marked," from *marcar,* "to mark," and *adquirido,* "acquired," from *adquirir,* "to acquire"). In English and in Spanish, the past participle can also function as an adjective.

| STYLE | TIP |

Using the standard forms of verbs is important in almost all of the writing that you do for school. Your readers expect standard usage in essays and reports.

On the other hand, readers expect the dialogue in plays and short stories to sound natural. For dialogue to sound natural, it must reflect the speech patterns of real people, and real people speak in all sorts of non-standard ways.

NONSTANDARD (DIALOGUE)
"I seen it, but I don't no way believe it!" exclaimed Jimmy.

STANDARD
Jimmy said he could not believe what he had seen.

You may want to discuss the use of nonstandard verb forms with your teacher. Together you can decide when and where such forms can be used appropriately in your writing.

Common Irregular Verbs

Base Form	Present Participle	Past	Past Participle
become	[is] becoming	became	[have] become
begin	[is] beginning	began	[have] begun
bite	[is] biting	bit	[have] bitten *or* bit
blow	[is] blowing	blew	[have] blown
break	[is] breaking	broke	[have] broken
bring	[is] bringing	brought	[have] brought
build	[is] building	built	[have] built
burst	[is] bursting	burst	[have] burst
buy	[is] buying	bought	[have] bought
catch	[is] catching	caught	[have] caught
choose	[is] choosing	chose	[have] chosen
come	[is] coming	came	[have] come
cost	[is] costing	cost	[have] cost
cut	[is] cutting	cut	[have] cut
do	[is] doing	did	[have] done
draw	[is] drawing	drew	[have] drawn
drink	[is] drinking	drank	[have] drunk
drive	[is] driving	drove	[have] driven
eat	[is] eating	ate	[have] eaten
fall	[is] falling	fell	[have] fallen
feel	[is] feeling	felt	[have] felt
fight	[is] fighting	fought	[have] fought
find	[is] finding	found	[have] found
fly	[is] flying	flew	[have] flown
forgive	[is] forgiving	forgave	[have] forgiven
freeze	[is] freezing	froze	[have] frozen
get	[is] getting	got	[have] got *or* gotten
give	[is] giving	gave	[have] given
go	[is] going	went	[have] gone
grow	[is] growing	grew	[have] grown

MINI-LESSON **Usage**

Practice with Irregular Verbs. Some irregular verbs cause students more difficulty than others. Help students by assessing which verbs are the most difficult and then providing additional practice.

Scan the list of irregular verbs on pp. 190–192, and select the ones you've noticed cause students difficulty. Common problem verbs include *begin, bring, catch, do, drink, eat, fly, go, grow, know, lay, lead, lie, ring, see, shake, sing, sink, swim, swing,* and *take.* Assess students' knowledge of

Common Irregular Verbs			
Base Form	Present Participle	Past	Past Participle
have	[is] having	had	[have] had
hear	[is] hearing	heard	[have] heard
hide	[is] hiding	hid	[have] hidden *or* hid
hit	[is] hitting	hit	[have] hit
hold	[is] holding	held	[have] held
hurt	[is] hurting	hurt	[have] hurt
keep	[is] keeping	kept	[have] kept
know	[is] knowing	knew	[have] known
lay	[is] laying	laid	[have] laid
lead	[is] leading	led	[have] led
leave	[is] leaving	left	[have] left
lend	[is] lending	lent	[have] lent
let	[is] letting	let	[have] let
lie	[is] lying	lay	[have] lain
light	[is] lighting	lighted *or* lit	[have] lighted *or* lit
lose	[is] losing	lost	[have] lost
make	[is] making	made	[have] made
meet	[is] meeting	met	[have] met
pay	[is] paying	paid	[have] paid
put	[is] putting	put	[have] put
read	[is] reading	read	[have] read
ride	[is] riding	rode	[have] ridden
ring	[is] ringing	rang	[have] rung
rise	[is] rising	rose	[have] risen
run	[is] running	ran	[have] run
say	[is] saying	said	[have] said
see	[is] seeing	saw	[have] seen
seek	[is] seeking	sought	[have] sought
sell	[is] selling	sold	[have] sold

(continued)

DIFFERENTIATING INSTRUCTION

Learners Having Difficulty

Problem Verbs. As students work through the exercises in this chapter, have them list irregular verbs that cause them problems. They could make charts like the following one with the base, past, and past participle forms of these verbs and keep the charts in their notebooks for reference when they are completing writing assignments.

BASE FORM	PAST FORM	PAST PARTICIPLE FORM
catch	caught	caught
see	saw	seen
go	went	gone

the past tense and past participle forms of these verbs by calling out the base form and having students write the other two forms.

After you have discovered which verbs are the most difficult, have students use all three forms of each verb in a sentence. If some students have trouble with many of the irregular verbs, spread the activity over several days or weeks, concentrating on two or three verbs at a time.

(continued)

Common Irregular Verbs

Base Form	Present Participle	Past	Past Participle
send	[is] sending	sent	[have] sent
set	[is] setting	set	[have] set
shake	[is] shaking	shook	[have] shaken
sing	[is] singing	sang	[have] sung
sink	[is] sinking	sank *or* sunk	[have] sunk
sit	[is] sitting	sat	[have] sat
speak	[is] speaking	spoke	[have] spoken
spend	[is] spending	spent	[have] spent
spin	[is] spinning	spun	[have] spun
spread	[is] spreading	spread	[have] spread
stand	[is] standing	stood	[have] stood
steal	[is] stealing	stole	[have] stolen
swim	[is] swimming	swam	[have] swum
swing	[is] swinging	swung	[have] swung
take	[is] taking	took	[have] taken
teach	[is] teaching	taught	[have] taught
tear	[is] tearing	tore	[have] torn
tell	[is] telling	told	[have] told
think	[is] thinking	thought	[have] thought
throw	[is] throwing	threw	[have] thrown
wear	[is] wearing	wore	[have] worn
win	[is] winning	won	[have] won

The verb *be* is probably the most common irregular verb.

The Principal Parts of *Be*

Base Form	Present Participle	Past	Past Participle
be	[is] being	was, were	[have] been

RETEACHING

Oral Learning

Reciting the principal parts of verbs to a rhythmic beat can help students learn the forms. Divide the class into groups of three or four students; assign each group ten irregular verbs, and have the groups prepare rhythmic oral presentations that include the base, past, and past participle forms of the verbs. The presentations can be poems, songs, stories, or recitations, and students can use movement to keep the beat or to act out their verbs.

DIFFERENTIATING INSTRUCTION

Advanced Learners

Denotations and Connotations. Discussions about denotations and connotations of words often center on adjectives, but verbs can have connotations as well. Give students the following pairs of verbs, which are similar in denotation, and ask them to discuss how the two verbs differ in connotation.

1. cover—hide
2. remain—endure
3. work—toil
4. compliment—flatter

Oral Practice 2 Using the Past and Past Participle
Forms of Irregular Verbs

Read each of the following sentences aloud, stressing the
italicized verb.

1. Charles *has written* many essays.
2. Leigh *did* everything the instructions said.
3. She *knew* the best route to take.
4. Maria Tallchief *chose* a career as a dancer.
5. He *ate* chicken salad on whole-wheat bread for lunch.
6. The monkey *had stolen* the food from its brother.
7. Felipe and Tonya *sang* a duet in the talent show.
8. The shy turtle *came* closer to me to reach the lettuce I
   was holding.

Exercise 2 Using the Past and Past Participle Forms
of Irregular Verbs

Give the correct past or past participle form of the verb in
parentheses in each of the following sentences.

EXAMPLE **1.** Nobody knew why he (*do*) that.
         1. did

1. Did you say that the telephone (*ring*) while I was in the
   shower?
2. The outfielder (*throw*) the ball to home plate.
3. Diana Nyad (*swim*) sixty miles—from the Bahamas all the
   way to Florida.
4. Uncle Olaf has (*ride*) his new snowmobile up to Gunther's
   ski lodge.
5. The librarian has (*choose*) a book by Jose Aruego.
6. I'm afraid that the bean seedlings and the herbs in the garden
   have (*freeze*).
7. After she finished the race, she (*drink*) two glasses of water.
8. He (*tell*) me that *waffle* and *coleslaw* are words that came
   from Dutch.
9. We had (*drive*) all night to attend my stepsister's college
   graduation ceremony.
10. Marianne (*sit*) quietly throughout the discussion.

1. rang

2. threw

3. swam

4. ridden

5. chosen

6. frozen

7. drank

8. told

9. driven

10. sat

Exercise 2

DISTRIBUTED REVIEW
Have students find the subordinate
clauses in sentences 6 and 7. [6. *that
the bean seedlings and the herbs in
the garden have frozen;* 7. *After she
finished the race*]

PRACTICE

Guided and Independent

Exercises You may want to have
students complete **Exercise 2** as
guided practice and **Exercise 3** as
independent practice.

HOMEWORK

The Principal Parts of a Verb **193**

Exercise 3 Using the Past and Past Participle Forms of Irregular Verbs

Give the correct past or past participle form of the irregular verb in parentheses in each of the following sentences.

EXAMPLE   **1.** Have you (*read*) about the Underground Railroad?
              1. read

1. wrote
2. drew
3. had
4. went
5. left
6. rode
7. run
8. got
9. came
10. said

1. Mr. Tucker, our new history teacher, (*write*) the words *Underground Railroad* on the chalkboard.
2. Then he (*draw*) black lines on a map to show us where the Underground Railroad ran.
3. What strange tracks this railroad must have (*have*)!
4. The lines even (*go*) into the Atlantic Ocean.
5. As you may imagine, this map (*leave*) the class very confused.
6. Then Mr. Tucker explained that no one actually (*ride*) on an underground railroad.
7. The railroad was really a secret network to help slaves who had (*run*) away.
8. Between 1830 and 1860, thousands of slaves (*get*) their freedom by traveling along the routes marked on this map.
9. The name *Underground Railroad* (*come*) from the use of railroad terms as code words.
10. Mr. Tucker (*say*) that hiding places were called "stations" and that people who helped slaves were called "conductors."

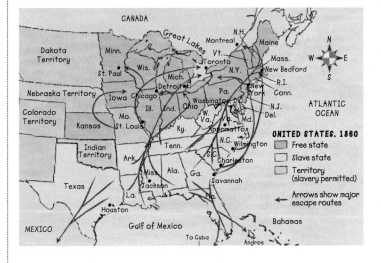

Review A Proofreading Sentences for Correct Regular and Irregular Verb Forms

Many of the following sentences contain incorrect verb forms. If a sentence has an incorrect verb form, write the correct form. If a sentence is already correct, write *C*.

EXAMPLE   1. I had spoke to my parents last week about this restaurant.

1. *had spoken*

1. My big brother Mark drived us there in Mom's car.
2. When we arrived at the restaurant, I runned ahead of everyone else and told the hostess we needed five seats.
3. We sitted down, and the waiter brought our menus.
4. Have you ever drunk water with lemon slices in the glasses?
5. Dad chose the ravioli.
6. My little sister Emilia taked two helpings of salad.
7. The waiter bringed out our dinners on a huge tray.
8. Mark given me a taste of his eggplant parmigiana.
9. Emilia stealed a bite of my lasagna.
10. Dad telled the waiter that the food was delicious.

1. drove
2. ran

3. sat
4. C
5. C
6. took
7. brought
8. gave
9. stole
10. told

Review B Proofreading Sentences for Correct Verb Forms

Some of the following sentences contain incorrect verb forms. If a sentence has an incorrect verb form, write the correct form. If a sentence is already correct, write *C*.

EXAMPLE   1. I thinked I had a copy of *A Journey to the Center of the Earth.*

1. *thought*

1. During the 1800s, Jules Verne wrote many scientific adventure tales. 1. C
2. Back then, readers founded his stories amazing. 2. found
3. Some people believe that he seen into the future. 3. saw
4. For example, in some of his novels he telled about 4. told space exploration and boats that traveled underwater.
5. These books fascinated readers in the days before space travel and submarines! 5. C
6. Verne lead a quiet life but had incredible adventures in his imagination. 6. led

The Principal Parts of a Verb   **195**

USAGE

Verb Tense

Rules 9d–f *(pp. 196–201)*

OBJECTIVES

- To proofread a paragraph to make the verb tense consistent
- To identify the use of active and passive voice in sentences

---

DIRECT TEACHING

Modeling and Demonstration

Verb Tense. Model how to proofread for correct use of verb tense by using the example *The scouts had hiked five miles before they stopped for lunch.* First, ask students what tense the verb *stopped* is. [*past*] Then, ask when this action occurred. [*in the past*] Next, ask what tense the verb phrase *had hiked* is. [*past perfect*] Ask when this action occurred. [*before the scouts stopped*] Explain how this sentence displays correct use of verb tense, because *had hiked* and *stopped* correctly use different tenses to describe events that occurred at different times in the past. Now, have a volunteer use another example from this chapter to demonstrate how to proofread for correct use of verb tense.

Meeting the Challenge

ANSWERS

Dialogues will vary but should include five of the six tenses; the tenses should be labeled.

---

9. or have been made

10. or People gave

MEETING THE CHALLENGE

Write a dialogue in which two people discuss a past event and how it will affect the future. In your dialogue, use at least five of the six verb tenses. Identify the verb tense or tenses in each sentence.

---

7. He ~~writed~~ some wonderful stories. **7.** wrote

8. Some inventors of modern rockets have said that they read Verne's stories. **8.** C

9. Some of his books, such as *Twenty Thousand Leagues Under the Sea,* ~~been~~ made into great movies. **9.** were

10. People have ~~gave~~ Verne the title "Father of Modern Science Fiction." **10.** given

Verb Tense

9d. The *tense* of a verb indicates the time of the action or of the state of being expressed by the verb.

The six tenses are *present, past, future, present perfect, past perfect,* and *future perfect*. These tenses are formed from the principal parts of verbs.

Each of the six tenses has its own uses. The time line below shows how the six tenses are related to one another.

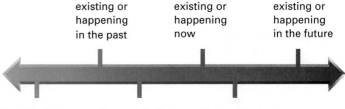

Past	Present	Future
existing or happening in the past	existing or happening now	existing or happening in the future

Past Perfect	Present Perfect	Future Perfect
existing or happening before a specific time in the past	existing or happening sometime before now; may be continuing now	existing or happening before a specific time in the future

EXAMPLES Melissa **has saved** [present perfect] her money, and now she **has** [present] enough for a guitar.

The scouts **had hiked** [past perfect] five miles before they **stopped** [past] for lunch.

The executive **will have seen** [future perfect] the report by next week and **will make** [future] a decision.

RESOURCES

Verb Tense

Practice

- *Language & Sentence Skills Practice,* pp. 187–188, 195
- *Developmental Language & Sentence Skills,* pp. 67–68

Listing the different forms of a verb in the six tenses is called *conjugating* a verb.

Conjugation of the Verb *Write*	
Singular	**Plural**
Present Tense	
I write	we write
you write	you write
he, she, *or* it writes	they write
Past Tense	
I wrote	we wrote
you wrote	you wrote
he, she, *or* it wrote	they wrote
Future Tense	
I will (shall) write	we will (shall) write
you will (shall) write	you will (shall) write
he, she, *or* it will (shall) write	they will (shall) write
Present Perfect Tense	
I have written	we have written
you have written	you have written
he, she, *or* it has written	they have written
Past Perfect Tense	
I had written	we had written
you had written	you had written
he, she, *or* it had written	they had written
Future Perfect Tense	
I will (shall) have written	we will (shall) have written
you will (shall) have written	you will (shall) have written
he, she, *or* it will (shall) have written	they will (shall) have written

STYLE TIP

In the past, careful speakers and writers of English used *shall* and *will* in different ways. Now, however, *shall* can be used almost interchangeably with *will*.

USAGE

DIRECT TEACHING

Correcting Misconceptions

Progressive Forms. Students may misidentify the progressive forms of certain verbs as passive-voice forms. Write the following sentences on the chalkboard or on a transparency.

Anne will be writing an essay.
An essay will be written by Anne.

Tell students that in the first sentence, *will be writing* is in the future progressive form, and that in the second sentence, *will be written* is in the passive voice. Remind students that although both the passive voice and the progressive form use forms of the verb *be* as helping verbs, the progressive forms always end with an *–ing* present participle, whereas passive-voice forms end with a past participle.

STYLE · · · · · · · · · · TIP

The emphatic form is also used in questions and negative statements. These uses do not place any special emphasis on the verb.

QUESTION
Why **do** bears hibernate?

NEGATIVE STATEMENT
If the car **does**n't [does not] start, check the battery.

Each of the six tenses has an additional form called the ***progressive form,*** which expresses continuing action or state of being. It consists of the appropriate tense of the verb *be* plus the present participle of a verb. The progressive is not a separate tense but rather another form of each of the six tenses.

Present Progressive	am, are, is writing
Past Progressive	was, were writing
Future Progressive	will (shall) be writing
Present Perfect Progressive	has been, have been writing
Past Perfect Progressive	had been writing
Future Perfect Progressive	will (shall) have been writing

Only the present and the past tenses have another form, called the ***emphatic form,*** which is used to show emphasis. In the present tense, the emphatic form consists of the helping verb *do* or *does* and the base form of a verb. In the past tense, the emphatic form consists of the verb *did* and the base form of a verb.

Present Emphatic	do, does write
Past Emphatic	did write

Consistency of Tense

9e. Do not change needlessly from one tense to another.

When describing events that occur at the same time, use verbs in the same tense.

INCONSISTENT	When we were comfortable, we begin our homework. [*Were* is past tense, and *begin* is present tense.]
CONSISTENT	When we **are** comfortable, we **begin** our homework. [Both *are* and *begin* are present tense.]
CONSISTENT	When we **were** comfortable, we **began** our homework. [Both *were* and *began* are past tense.]
INCONSISTENT	Suddenly the great door opened, and an uninvited guest comes into the dining hall. [*Opened* is past tense, and *comes* is present tense.]
CONSISTENT	Suddenly the great door **opens,** and an uninvited guest **comes** into the dining hall. [Both *opens* and *comes* are present tense.]

Learning for Life *Continued on pp. 199–200*

Writing a Personal Profile. For various reasons, adults are sometimes asked to write personal profiles, which require careful attention to verb tense. Ask your students to write profiles of themselves, including only material they are comfort-able sharing. Content could include basic information about where they were born and have lived, special interests they have, unusual experiences they have found memorable, and anything else about their backgrounds that would help readers get a

CONSISTENT   Suddenly the great door **opened,** and an uninvited guest **came** into the dining hall. [Both *opened* and *came* are past tense.]

When describing events that occur at different times, use verbs in different tenses to show the order of events.

EXAMPLES   Lisa **plays** basketball now, but last year she **was** on the volleyball team. [Lisa's basketball playing is occurring in the present, so *plays* is correct. Her volleyball playing occurred at a time in the past, so the past tense, *was,* is correct.]

Susana **won** the regional spelling bee; next week she **will compete** in the state tournament. [Susana won the spelling contest sometime in the past, so the past tense, *won,* is correct. The state spelling tournament will occur in the future, so *will compete* is correct.]

Exercise 4 Proofreading a Paragraph to Make the Verb Tense Consistent

Read the following paragraph, and decide whether to rewrite it in the present or past tense. Then, change verb forms to correct any unnecessary changes in tense.

EXAMPLE   **[1]** At my grandparents' house, I wake up before anyone else and quietly grabbed the fishing pole and head for the pond.

1. *At my grandparents' house, I wake up before anyone else and quietly grab the fishing pole and head for the pond.*

or

At my grandparents' house, I woke up before anyone else and quietly grabbed the fishing pole and headed for the pond.

[1] Across the water, I saw the ripples. [2] "I hope the fish are cooperative," I say to myself. [3] I threw my lure near where I see the ripples and reeled in the line. [4] The fish are not biting. [5] I saw more ripples and throw the line in the water again. [6] "I have a strike!" I shout to the trees around me. [7] As I reeled in the line, a beautiful trout jumps out of the water and spit out the hook. [8] Gloomily, I walk back to the house. [9] Grandpa was sitting at the kitchen table with a bowl of hot oatmeal for me. [10] I say, "Oh well, maybe tomorrow we'll have fresh trout for breakfast."

Verb Tense   **199**

USAGE

Exercise 4 Proofreading a Paragraph to Make the Verb Tense Consistent

ANSWERS
Students can choose either present or past tense, but tenses must be consistent throughout the paragraph. Verbs in direct quotations should not be changed. In the following answers, the present tense is given first and the past tense is in parentheses.

1. see (saw)
2. say (said)
3. throw, see, reel (threw, saw, reeled)
4. are biting (were biting)
5. see, throw (saw, threw)
6. shout (shouted)
7. reel, jumps, spits (reeled, jumped, spit)
8. walk (walked)
9. is sitting (was sitting)
10. say (said)

picture of who they are. The profiles should also include information about students' plans for the future or goals they hope to accomplish in years to come.
    As students generate ideas for their pro-files, encourage them to use web diagrams to show the relationships among the experiences they wish to share with others.
    Direct students to use strong action verbs to communicate precisely what they want

DIFFERENTIATING INSTRUCTION

English-Language Learners

Hmong. Hmong relies primarily upon the active voice, so the distinction in English between the active and passive voice may pose both translation difficulties and writing challenges for some Hmong speakers. Remind students of the purpose of the passive voice—to stress the object of a verb's action—and offer translation assistance when necessary.

EXTENSION

Relating to Writing

Have students select a piece of their own writing to analyze for active and passive voice. Have them look at each sentence to determine which voice they have used. For each sentence in the passive voice, students should ask themselves whether there is a good reason to use passive voice. If not, they should revise the sentence by using the active voice. Now, have each student exchange selections with another student for evaluation. Students should review both the original and the revised version of their partner's writing and provide feedback by answering these questions.

1. Which version keeps your attention better? Why do you think it does?

2. Which version sounds stronger and more direct?

3. How many passive-voice sentences remain in the revised version? Does each passive-voice sentence use the passive voice for a good reason?

| S T Y L E | T I P |

Overusing the passive voice makes your writing sound weak and awkward. In general, use the active voice to help make your writing direct and forceful.

WEAK
Shingles were torn from the roof by the high winds.

FORCEFUL
The high winds **tore** shingles from the roof.

Reference Note

For more about **helping verbs,** see page 52.

Active Voice and Passive Voice

9f. A verb in the *active voice* expresses an action done by its subject. A verb in the *passive voice* expresses an action done to its subject.

Compare the following sentences:

| ACTIVE VOICE | The school librarian **has formed** a book club. |
| PASSIVE VOICE | A book club **has been formed** by the school librarian. |

| ACTIVE VOICE | The architect **completed** the floor plans. |
| PASSIVE VOICE | The floor plans **were completed** by the architect. |

| ACTIVE VOICE | The illustrator **had used** watercolors. |
| PASSIVE VOICE | Watercolors **had been used** by the illustrator. |

| ACTIVE VOICE | Someone **mowed** the lawn yesterday. |
| PASSIVE VOICE | The lawn **was mowed** by someone yesterday. |

Notice that the object of the active sentence becomes the subject of the passive sentence. The subject of the active sentence is now expressed in a prepositional phrase. This prepositional phrase can be omitted.

| PASSIVE VOICE | The lawn **was mowed** yesterday. |

In a passive sentence, the verb phrase always includes a form of *be* and the past participle of the main verb. Other helping verbs may also be included.

| ACTIVE VOICE | Mrs. Edwin **fixed** the computer. |
| PASSIVE VOICE | The computer **was fixed** by Mrs. Edwin. |

| ACTIVE VOICE | Lucinda **had planted** those marigolds. |
| PASSIVE VOICE | Those marigolds **had been planted** by Lucinda. |

The passive voice emphasizes the person or thing receiving the action. The passive voice is useful when you do not know who performed the action or when you do not want to reveal the performer of the action.

Learning for Life   *Continued from p. 199*

to say. Remind them of the importance of consistency in the use of tenses, and point out that each section of their profile (such as the section on the future) may require tenses that are different from other sections.

Allow students to work in small groups to evaluate and revise their profiles. Encourage them to pay close attention to verb tenses, and remind them that their profiles should reflect who they are.

EXAMPLES These flowers **were left** on the doorstep sometime this
afternoon. [The performer is unknown.]

"A large donation **was given** anonymously," said
Mrs. Neal. [The speaker does not want to reveal the
performer of the action.]

Exercise 5 Identifying Active and Passive Voice

Tell whether each verb in the following sentences is in *active voice*
or *passive voice*.

EXAMPLE **1.** Jared's birthday dinner was paid for by his uncle.

        1. passive voice

1. Trees were being blown over by the wind.
2. The streetlights made long, scary shadows on the sidewalk.
3. The cave was explored by the science class.
4. The Gettysburg Address was written by Abraham Lincoln.
5. Marion considered the book an inspiration.
6. The grapes had been eaten by the time Sandy arrived.
7. Kenny's fans cheered him on to victory.
8. The snow drifted over the fence and across the road.
9. The swelling on Kehl's arm was caused by a bee sting.
10. Bob and Judy were setting out birdseed for the cardinals
    and chickadees.

1. passive
2. active
3. passive
4. passive
5. active
6. passive
7. active
8. active
9. passive
10. active

Special Problems with Verbs

Sit and *Set*

The verb *sit* means "to rest in an upright, seated position" or
"to be in a place." *Sit* seldom takes an object. The verb *set* means
"to put (something) in a place." *Set* usually takes an object.
Notice that *set* has the same form for the base form, past, and
past participle.

Reference Note

For information on
objects of verbs, see
page 81.

Base Form	Present Participle	Past	Past Participle
sit	[is] sitting	sat	[have] sat
set	[is] setting	set	[have] set

Exercise 5

DISTRIBUTED REVIEW
To review parts of speech, have students find the following items in the
designated sentences.

1. an adverb in sentence 1 [*over*]

2. two closed compound nouns in
   sentence 2 [*streetlights, sidewalk*]

3. two proper nouns in sentence 4
   [*Gettysburg Address, Abraham
   Lincoln*]

4. two prepositions in sentence 8
   [*over, across*]

USAGE

Special Problems
with Verbs
(pp. 201–210)

OBJECTIVES

■ **To pronounce and choose the
correct forms of *sit* and *set* and
to identify direct objects**

■ **To pronounce and choose the
correct forms of *lie* and *lay* and
to identify direct objects**

■ **To pronounce and choose the
correct forms of *rise* and *raise* and
to identify direct objects**

DIRECT TEACHING

Modeling and Demonstration

Special Problems with Verbs. Model how to use the verbs *sit* and *set* correctly by using the examples *Let's sit under the tree* and *Let's set our backpacks under the tree.* First, ask students whether a word in the first sentence receives the action of the verb. [no] The verb *sit* does not usually take a direct object; therefore, *sit* is correct here. Next, ask whether a word in the second sentence receives the action of the verb. [yes; backpacks] *Set* does usually take a direct object; therefore, *set* is correct in the second sentence. Now, have a volunteer use other examples from this chapter to demonstrate the correct use of the problem verbs *lie*, *lay*, *rise*, and *raise*.

DIFFERENTIATING INSTRUCTION

Learners Having Difficulty

Collages. Have students make collages of pictures that illustrate the verbs *sit/set, lie/lay,* and *rise/raise.* Students could look in magazines for pictures of people performing the actions of the verbs, arrange their pictures on poster board, and write under each picture a sentence using the appropriate verb.

┌─**HELP**─

You may know that the word *set* has more meanings than the one given on page 201. Check in a dictionary to see if the meaning you intend requires an object.

EXAMPLE
The sun **sets** in the West. [Here, *set* does not take an object.]

EXAMPLES
Let's **sit** under the tree. [no object]
Let's **set** our backpacks under the tree. [Let's set what? *Backpacks* is the object.]

The tourists **sat** on the bench. [no object]
The tourists **set** their suitcases on the bench. [The tourists set what? *Suitcases* is the object.]

We **had** just **sat** down when the telephone rang. [no object]
We **had** just **set** our books down when the telephone rang. [We had set what? *Books* is the object.]

Oral Practice 3 ▸ Using the Forms of *Sit* and *Set*

Read the following sentences aloud, stressing each italicized verb.

1. *Sit* down here, please.
2. The dog is *sitting* on the porch.
3. Our teacher *set* a deadline for our term projects.
4. Some mornings I *sit* on the steps and watch the sun rise.
5. I have always *sat* in the front row.
6. Please *set* the carton down inside the doorway.
7. Where have I *set* my book on judo?
8. After I had *set* the mop in the closet, I *sat* down to rest.

Exercise 6 ▸ Choosing the Forms of *Sit* and *Set*

Choose the correct verb in parentheses in each of the following sentences. If the verb you choose is a form of *set*, identify its object.

EXAMPLE 1. Please (*sit, set*) the serving platter on the table.
　　　　　　 1. set; object—platter

1. Has he (*sat, set*) anything down here?
2. The kitten cautiously (*sat, set*) down beside the Great Dane.
3. Jenny (*sat, set*) her notebook down on the kitchen counter.
4. I had been (*sitting, setting*) there all day.
5. (*Sit, Set*) the fine crystal in the china cabinet.
6. The referee is (*sitting, setting*) the ball on the fifty-yard line.
7. Aaron will (*sit, set*) the table for our Passover celebration.
8. Let's (*sit, set*) that aside until later.

9. Alex had to (*sit, set*) and catch his breath after joining in the Greek chain dance.
10. They had (*sat, set*) there for fifteen minutes without saying a word to each other.

Lie and Lay

The verb *lie* means "to rest," "to recline," or "to be in a place." *Lie* does not take an object. The verb *lay* means "to put (something) in a place." *Lay* usually takes an object.

Base Form	Present Participle	Past	Past Participle
lie	[is] lying	lay	[have] lain
lay	[is] laying	laid	[have] laid

EXAMPLES   The napkins **are lying** next to the plates. [no object]
The servers **are laying** extra napkins beside every plate for the barbecue. [The servers are laying what? *Napkins* is the object.]

The soldiers **lay** very still while the enemy passed. [no object]
The soldiers **laid** a trap for the enemy. [The soldiers laid what? *Trap* is the object.]

Rip Van Winkle **had lain** asleep for twenty years. [no object]
Rip Van Winkle **had laid** his knapsack on the ground. [Rip Van Winkle had laid what? *Knapsack* is the object.]

Oral Practice 4 Using the Forms of *Lie* and *Lay*

Read the following sentences aloud, stressing each italicized verb.

1. Don't *lie* in the sun until you put on some sunscreen.
2. You should not *lay* your papers on the couch.
3. The lion had been *lying* in wait for an hour.
4. The senator *laid* her notes aside after her speech.
5. I have *lain* awake, listening to Spanish flamenco music on the radio.

┌─HELP─
The verb *lie* can also mean "to tell an untruth." Used in this way, *lie* still does not take an object.

EXAMPLE
   Don't **lie** to her, Beth.

The past and past participle forms of this meaning of *lie* are *lied* and *[have] lied.*

USAGE

6. She has *laid* her books on the desk.
7. At bedtime, Toshiro *lies* down on a futon.
8. The exhausted swimmer *lay* helpless on the sand.

Exercise 7 Using the Forms of *Lie* and *Lay*

Complete each of the following sentences by supplying the correct form of *lie* or *lay*. If the verb you use is a form of *lay*, identify its object.

EXAMPLE   **1.** Leo _____ the disk next to the computer.
    1. laid; object—disk

1. After the race, Michael Andretti _____ his helmet on the car.
2. My dad was _____ down when I asked him for my allowance.
3. We _____ down the picnic blanket.
4. Have you ever _____ on a water bed?
5. Rammel had _____ his keys beside his wallet.
6. These days, my cat often _____ on the front porch.
7. Amy is _____ the coats on the bed in the guest room.
8. Yesterday that alligator _____ in the sun all day.
9. Lim Sing's great-grandfather _____ the glasses on the table.
10. The newspaper had _____ in the yard until the sun faded it.

Answers (left margin):
1. laid
2. lying
3. laid
4. lain
5. laid
6. lies
7. laying
8. lay
9. laid
10. lain

Exercise 8 Using Forms of *Lie* and *Lay* and *Sit* and *Set*

Give the correct form of *lie* or *lay* or *sit* or *set* for each of the following sentences.

EXAMPLE   **1.** Does anybody _____ in bed late on the farm?
    1. lie

1. The family _____ down to breakfast every day at 6:00 A.M.   **1. sits (or sat)**
2. One morning as they _____ around the table, they heard a terrible racket.   **2. sat**
3. Lily, one of the cats, had _____ out on a hunting expedition.   **3. set**
4. By mistake, she jumped on a snake that _____ asleep under a holly bush.   **4. lay**
5. The harmless, black snake struck at Lily, who yowled and then _____ back, growling.   **5. sat (or lay)**
6. The hens, who were _____ eggs, began to squawk and flap their wings.   **6. laying**
7. Lily seemed dazed, so the family brought her into the house and _____ her on a pillow.   **7. laid**

USAGE (side tab)

PRACTICE

Guided and Independent

Exercises You may wish to use **Exercise 7** as guided practice and have students complete **Exercise 8** as independent practice.

HOMEWORK

8. They _____ a pan of water near her, and then Lily rolled off the pillow into the pan. **8.** set (*or* laid)

9. She was frightened and would not _____ still to be dried. **9.** sit

10. Long after the family _____ down to sleep, they could hear Lily pacing through the rooms. **10.** lay

Rise and *Raise*

The verb *rise* means "to go up" or "to get up." *Rise* does not take an object. The verb *raise* means "to lift up" or "to cause (something) to rise." *Raise* usually takes an object.

Base Form	Present Participle	Past	Past Participle
rise	[is] rising	rose	[have] risen
raise	[is] raising	raised	[have] raised

EXAMPLES   My neighbors **rise** very early in the morning. [no object]

Every morning they **raise** their shades to let the sunlight in. [They raise what? *Shades* is the object.]

Sparks **rose** from the flames of the campfire. [no object]

The breeze **raised** sparks high into the air. [The breeze raised what? *Sparks* is the object.]

The senators **have risen** from their seats to show respect for the chief justice. [no object]

The senators **have raised** a number of issues. [The senators have raised what? *Number* is the object.]

┌HELP─

You may know that the verb *raise* has more meanings than the one given here.

EXAMPLE
   The Nelsons **raise** geese.
   [*Raise* does not mean "lift up" here, but it still takes an object.]

Oral Practice 5   **Using the Forms of *Rise* and *Raise***

Read each of the following sentences aloud, stressing the italicized verb.

1. The reporters *rise* when the president enters the room.

2. Students *raise* their hands to be recognized.

3. They have *raised* the curtain for the first act of the play.

4. Alex Haley *rose* to fame with his book *Roots*.

5. The sun was *rising* over the mountains.

6. The old Asian elephant slowly *rose* to its feet.
7. Who had *risen* first?
8. Two of the builders *raised* the cement block and set it in place.

Exercise 9 **Choosing the Forms of *Rise* and *Raise***

Choose the correct verb in parentheses in each of the following sentences. If the verb you choose is a form of *raise*, identify its object.

EXAMPLE   **1.** Please (*raise, rise*) your hand when you want to speak.
   1. raise; object—hand

1. The steam was (*rising, raising*) from the pot of soup.
2. That discovery (*rises, raises*) an interesting question about the Algonquian people of Canada.
3. The child's fever (*rose, raised*) during the night.
4. The sun (*rises, raises*) later each morning.
5. The student body's interest in this subject has (*risen, raised*) to new heights.
6. We must (*rise, raise*) the flag before school begins.
7. The children (*rise, raise*) the blinds to get a better look at the unusual visitor.
8. The kite has (*risen, raised*) above the power lines.
9. My father will (*rise, raise*) my allowance if I pull the weeds.
10. The art dealer (*rose, raised*) the price of the painting by Frida Kahlo.

Exercise 10 **Using the Forms of *Rise* and *Raise***

Complete each of the following sentences by supplying the correct past or past participle form of *rise* or *raise*.

EXAMPLE   **1.** Have you ever _____ before dawn?
   1. risen

1. We girls _____ early to start our hike to Lookout Mountain.   **1.** rose
2. From our position at the foot of the mountain, it looked as though the peak _____ straight up to the sky.   **2.** rose
3. However, we had not _____ at daybreak just to look at the high peak.   **3.** risen
4. We _____ our supply packs to our backs and started the long climb up the mountain.   **4.** raised

5. With every step we took, it seemed that the peak ____ that much higher. **5.** rose
6. Finally, after several hours, we reached the summit and ____ a special flag that we had brought for the occasion. **6.** raised
7. When our friends at the foot of the mountain saw that we had ____ the flag, they knew that all of us had reached the top safely. **7.** raised
8. They ____ their arms and shouted. **8.** raised
9. Our friends' shouts ____ from the valley below. **9.** rose
10. Then we felt glad that we had ____ early enough to climb to the top of Lookout Mountain. **10.** risen

Review C **Choosing the Forms of** *Sit* **and** *Set,* *Lie* **and** *Lay,* **and** *Rise* **and** *Raise*

Choose the <u>correct verb</u> in parentheses in each of the following sentences. Be prepared to explain your choices.

EXAMPLE **1.** The audience (*sat, set*) near the stage.

　　　　　1. sat

1. To study solar energy, our class (*sit, set*) a solar panel outside the window of our classroom.
2. Since I have grown taller, I have (*rose, raised*) the seat on my bicycle.
3. Didn't Mr. DeLemos (*lay, laid*) the foundation for the new Vietnamese Community Center building?
4. (*Sit, Set*) the groceries on the table while I start dinner.
5. The water level of the stream has not (*risen, raised*) since last summer.
6. Will you (*lie, lay*) the grass mats on the sand so that we can lie on them?
7. We (*sat, set*) under a beach umbrella so that we would not get sunburned.
8. When the sun rises, I often (*sit, set*) aside my covers and get up early to exercise before school.
9. He (*lay, laid*) his collection of Isaac Bashevis Singer stories on the table.
10. The crane operator (*rose, raised*) the steel beam and carefully set it in place.

┌HELP┐
The meaning of the verb in the example is "to be in a seated position." Therefore, *sat* is the correct answer.

Special Problems with Verbs　**207**

Review D Proofreading for Correct Verb Forms

Most of the following sentences contain an incorrect form of the verb *sit, set, lie, lay, rise,* or *raise.* If a sentence has an incorrect verb form, write the correct form. If a sentence is already correct, write *C.*

EXAMPLES
   1. We rose early for our journey to Havasu Canyon.
    1. C

   2. I laid awake for hours thinking about the trip.
    2. lay

                 1. set

1. I sat our bags in the car, and we headed for Havasu Canyon.

2. The canyon, which lies in northern Arizona, is home of the Havasupai Indian Reservation. **2.** C

3. At the canyon rim, a Havasupai guide helped me onto a horse and rose the stirrups so that I could reach them. **3.** raised

4. After we rode horses eight miles to the canyon floor, I set for a while because I was tired. **4.** sat

5. However, I knew I must sit a good example for my younger brother and not complain. **5.** set

6. As you can see, the trail we took is fairly narrow and lays along the side of a steep, rocky wall. **6.** lies

7. The sun raised high and hot as we rode through this beautiful canyon. **7.** rose

8. After we reached the village of Supai, I lay down to rest. **8.** C

9. Still, I quickly raised my hand to join the next tour to Havasu Falls. **9.** C

10. When we arrived, I was ready to lay under the spray of the waterfall shown below. **10.** lie

Choosing Correct Verb Forms

Each of the following sentences has at least one pair of verbs in parentheses. Choose the correct verb from each pair.

EXAMPLE   1. Josh (*catched, caught*) seven fish this morning.
             1. *caught*

1. Aretha Franklin has (*sang, sung*) professionally for more than forty years.
2. Have you (*began, begun*) your Scottish bagpipe lessons yet?
3. Cindy Nicholas was the first woman who (*swam, swum*) the English Channel both ways.
4. When the baby sitter (*rose, raised*) her voice, the children (*knew, knowed*) it was time to behave.
5. After we had (*saw, seen*) all of the exhibits at the county fair, we (*ate, eat*) a light snack and then (*went, gone*) home.
6. The egg (*burst, bursted*) in the microwave oven.
7. He (*lay, laid*) his lunch money on his desk.
8. The loud noise (*breaked, broke*) my concentration.
9. We (*sat, set*) through the movie three times because it was so funny.
10. We had (*rode, ridden*) halfway across the desert when I began to wish that I had (*brought, brung*) more water.

Identifying Correct Irregular Verb Forms

Each of the following sentences has a pair of verbs in parentheses. Choose the correct verb from each pair.

EXAMPLE   1. Have you ever (*saw, seen*) an animal using a tool?
             1. *seen*

1. I had (*thought, thinked*) that only humans use tools.
2. However, scientists have (*spended, spent*) many hours watching wild animals make and use tools.
3. Chimpanzees have been (*seen, saw*) using twigs to catch insects.
4. They (*taken, took*) sticks and poked them into termite holes, and termites climbed onto the sticks.
5. In that way, they (*caught, catched*) termites.
6. I have been (*telled, told*) that some finches use twigs to dig insects out of cracks in tree bark.

PRACTICE

Guided and Independent

Reviews You may wish to use Review E as guided practice. Then, have students complete Review F as independent practice.

HOMEWORK

USAGE

7. Sea otters have (*broke, broken*) open shellfish by banging them against rocks.
8. You may have (*knew, known*) that song thrushes also use that trick to get snails out of their shells.
9. Some animals have (*builded, built*) things, using their gluelike body fluids to hold objects together.
10. For example, scientists and others have watched as tailor ants (*spread, spreaded*) their sticky film on leaves to hold them together.

Review G **Proofreading Sentences for Correct Use of Past and Past Participles of Common Irregular Verbs**

Some of the following sentences contain incorrect forms of common irregular verbs. If a sentence has an incorrect verb form, write the correct form. If a sentence is already correct, write *C*.

EXAMPLE 1. The city of Guadalajara, Mexico, beginned in 1530.
 1. *began*

1. grown
1. Guadalajara now has grew into the second-largest city in Mexico, with a population of over three and a half million people.

2. chosen
2. Many people from the United States have choosed to retire in Guadalajara.

3. built
3. The city was builded in the Valley of Atemajac, where it attracted many settlers.

4. C
4. The area surrounding the city is part of Mexico's central plateau, where horse and cattle ranches have thrived.

5. found
5. People from many different places have finded Guadalajara's architecture charming.

6. lent
6. The city is filled with art and flowers and history; it also has lended itself to modern technology.

7. thought
7. Until recently no one thinked of Guadalajara as another "Silicon Valley," but it is becoming an electronics center.

8. C
8. Fortunately, the city has taken care to preserve and protect the historic downtown district and its six distinct plazas.

9. stolen
9. The jacaranda trees and bougainvillea that bloom everywhere have stealed many people's hearts.

10. sung
10. The mariachi singers rightly have singed the praises of the city through the years.

Chapter Review

Numerals in brackets refer to rules tested by the items in the Chapter Review.

1. lying [9a, c, d]
2. risen [9a, c, d]
3. set [9a, c, d]
4. writing [9a, c, d]
5. broken [9a, c, d]
6. burst [9a, c, d]
7. raised [9a, b, d]
8. saw [9a, c, d]
9. risen [9a, c, d]
10. rung [9a, c, d]
11. named [9a, b, d]
12. laid [9a, c, d]
13. frozen [9a, c, d]
14. chose [9a, c, d]
15. running [9a, c, d]
16. decided [9a, b, d]
17. took [9a, c, d]
18. bringing [9a, c, d]
19. bought [9a, c, d]
20. swam [9a, c, d]

A. Using the Present Participle, Past, and Past Participle Forms of Verbs

Give the correct form (present participle, past, or past participle) of the verb in parentheses in each of the following sentences.

1. The cat is (*lie*) down in front of the warm fire.
2. Since the storm began, the water has (*rise*) four feet.
3. Yolanda (*set*) the dictionary on the little table.
4. I have been (*write*) you a letter.
5. Two runners on our track team have (*break*) the school record for the mile run.
6. When the manager unlocked the door, a mob of shoppers (*burst*) into the store to take advantage of the sale.
7. Every morning last semester, the same cadet (*raise*) the flag.
8. The witness said that she (*see*) the blue truck run the red light.
9. Look in the oven to see if the muffins have (*rise*) yet.
10. Everyone should be in class after the bell has (*ring*).
11. Sitting Bull (*name*) his son Crowfoot.
12. Jeanette carefully (*lay*) her coat across the back of the chair.
13. By late December the pond has usually (*freeze*) solid.
14. Several of us (*choose*) to visit the Amish community in Pennsylvania.
15. Dana will be (*run*) five laps around the track.
16. Jan was late, so she (*decide*) to run the rest of the way.
17. The man at the gate (*take*) our tickets and said that we were just in time.
18. When he comes back from Philadelphia, Father is (*bring*) me a scale model of the Liberty Bell.
19. After Sarah told me about the book of Yiddish folk tales, I (*buy*) a copy.
20. In 1926, Gertrude Ederle, the first woman to swim across the English Channel, (*swim*) from France to England in 14 hours and 39 minutes.

Monitoring Progress
Chapter Review. To assess student progress, you may want to compare the types of items missed on the **Diagnostic Preview** with those missed on the **Chapter Review.** If students have not made significant progress, you may want to refer them for additional practice to **Chapter 17: Correcting Common Errors, Exercises 10–12.**

USAGE

RESOURCES

Using Verbs Correctly
Review
■ *Language & Sentence Skills Practice*, pp. 194–197

Assessment
■ *Formal Assessment*
■ *Progress-Monitoring Tests*, pp. 17–18, 48
■ *Test Generator*
(*Teacher One Stop DVD-ROM*)

B. Proofreading a Paragraph for Correct Verb Forms

Most of the following sentences contain ~~incorrect~~ verb forms. If a sentence has an incorrect verb form, write the correct form. If a sentence is already correct, write *C*.

21. spent [9c, d]
22. began [9c, d]
23. won [9c, d]
24. found [9c, d]
25. chose [9c, d]
26. brought [9c, d]
27. C [9b, d]
28. cared [9b, d]
29. raise [9b, d]
30. C [9c, d]

[21] Born in India, Ravi Arimilli ~~spended~~ most of his childhood years in Louisiana. [22] As a youngster, he ~~begun~~ playing tennis. [23] After starting college, he ~~winned~~ a spot on the Louisiana State University tennis team. [24] Arimilli ~~founded~~ that tennis was too limiting, so he studied electrical engineering instead. [25] After college, he ~~choosed~~ to work at IBM's office in Austin, Texas, because it put him in the middle of exciting computer projects. [26] Arimilli has ~~brung~~ talent and imagination to his job at IBM. [27] By 1998, he and his team had received eighteen patents for inventions, and Arimilli had been elected to the prestigious IBM Academy. [28] Arimilli has never ~~care~~ about those things too much, though. [29] Having what he calls an "I love me" wall in his office, covered with awards, would not ~~rise~~ his self-esteem. [30] Ravi Arimilli has always been more interested in making computer history than in just making a name for himself.

C. Identifying Active and Passive Voice

Tell whether each verb in the following sentences is in *active voice* or *passive voice*.

31. active [9f]
32. passive [9f]
33. active [9f]
34. active [9f]
35. passive [9f]
36. passive [9f]
37. passive [9f]
38. active [9f]
39. passive [9f]
40. active [9f]

31. Priscilla drew a quick sketch of the view from the terrace.
32. The ball was thrown too far to the left.
33. Mr. Bernstein gave each student a thesaurus.
34. Last night, we all worked on Dad's car.
35. Pedro or Carlie was given a raise last month.
36. The wart hogs were chased away by hyenas.
37. Houses are being painted all along the street.
38. The Empress Josephine requested a watch set in a bracelet.
39. Mom was amazed by the message.
40. Three of us asked the governor for his autograph.

USAGE

Writing Application
Using Verb Forms in a Poem

Verb Tense   You have decided to enter a local poetry contest. The theme of the contest is "Modern Adventures." Write a short narrative poem (a poem that tells a story) about a modern adventure. In your poem, use at least ten verbs from the list of Common Irregular Verbs on pages 190–192.

Prewriting   First, you will need to pick an adventure story to tell. You could tell a true story or an imaginary one. After you select a story, jot down some specific details that you want to include in your poem.

Writing   As you write your rough draft, try to express the excitement of the adventure. You may want to divide your poem into stanzas. Each stanza could tell a different event of your story.

Revising   Ask a friend to read your poem. Is the adventure story easy to follow? Is it interesting? If not, you may want to add, delete, or revise some details. If your poem is a ballad or other traditional type of poem, be sure that the rhythm and rhyme follow that poetic form. Does your poem contain enough sensory details? Make sure that you have not changed needlessly from one tense to another.

Publishing   Use your textbook to check the spelling of the irregular verbs in your poem. Be sure that you have used ten irregular verbs from the list. Read over your poem again, checking for errors in capitalization, spelling, and punctuation. With your teacher's permission, post the poem on the class bulletin board or Web page, if one is available.

Writing Application

Prewriting Tip. Have students brainstorm specific topics they think would be appropriate for their poems. Remind students that their work will be more engaging if they write about adventures that interest them. Possible topics include things they have done themselves, events they have heard about, or adventures they have imagined.

Scoring Rubric. While you will want to pay particular attention to students' use of verb forms, you will also want to evaluate overall writing performance. You may want to give a split score to indicate development and clarity of the composition as well as usage skills.

USAGE

Chapter Review   **213**

10

1.0 Written and Oral English Language Conventions
Students write and speak with a command of standard English conventions appropriate to this grade level.
1.4 Edit written manuscripts to ensure that correct grammar is used.

Using Pronouns Correctly
Case Forms of Pronouns; Special Pronoun Problems

Diagnostic Preview

A. Proofreading for Correct Forms of Pronouns

Each of the following sentences contains at least one pronoun that has been used incorrectly. Identify each ~~incorrect pronoun~~, and then give the ‸correct form.

EXAMPLE   1. The teacher told Derek and I a funny story.
              1. *I—me*

Numerals in brackets refer to rules tested by the items in the Diagnostic Preview.

1. whom [10g, e]
2. he [10b]
3. me [10c]
4. We [10h, a]
5. us [10h, d]
6. whom [10g, c]
7. him/me [10e]
8. him [10c]
9. him [10e]
10. they [10b]

1. To ~~who~~ did you and Marie send flowers?
2. The winners of the science fair were Felicia and ~~him~~‸.
3. That TV announcer's voice always irritates my father and ‸I.
4. ~~Us~~‸ teammates have to stick together, right?
5. Aunt Ida bought ‸we boys some roasted peanuts.
6. Is he the person ~~who~~‸ we met at Dan's party?
7. We split the vegetarian pizza between ‸he and ‸I.
8. The little boy asked Neil and ‸he for help.
9. May Kim and I sit next to Terrence and ‸he?
10. The best drummers in the high school band are ~~themselves~~‸.

CHAPTER RESOURCES

Internet
- go.hrw.com (keyword: HLLA)

go. hrw .com

Planning
- *Teacher One Stop DVD-ROM*
- *On Course: Mapping Instruction*

Practice & Review
- *Language & Sentence Skills Practice,* pp. 203–212; 213–216
- *Developmental Language & Sentence Skills,* pp. 71–76

Application & Enrichment
- *Language & Sentence Skills Practice,* pp. 217, 220; 202, 218–219

B. Identifying Correct Forms of Personal Pronouns

Choose the correct pronoun from the pair in parentheses in each of the following sentences.

EXAMPLE   **1.** Mrs. Lang gave (*we, us*) third-period students a list of good books for summer reading.

           1. *us*

11. Beth and (*I, me*) plan to read as many books as we can.

12. We asked (*she, her*) for some more information about the books she recommended.

13. (*She, Her*) said that *The Man Who Was Poe* is by Avi.

14. The author of *Nothing but the Truth* is also (*he, him*).

15. We probably will like Avi's books because (*they, them*) often combine fiction and history.

16. Both of (*we, us*) want to read *Where the Lilies Bloom* by Vera and Bill Cleaver, too.

17. Together, the two of (*they, them*) have written more than fifteen books for young readers.

18. The first book (*I, me*) will read is *The Cay* by Theodore Taylor.

19. Beth said that *A Gathering of Days* by Joan W. Blos will be the first book for (*she, her*).

20. Mrs. Lang told Beth and (*I, me*) that our summer reading project is a good idea.

11. [10a]
12. [10c]
13. [10a]
14. [10b]
15. [10a]
16. [10e]
17. [10e]
18. [10a]
19. [10e]
20. [10d]

C. Revising Sentences for Clear Pronoun Reference

Revise each of the following sentences, correcting each unclear pronoun reference.

EXAMPLE   **1.** When Marie met Becca, she had a cold.

           1. *Marie had a cold when she met Becca.*

┌─ HELP ─

Sentences in Part C of the Diagnostic Preview may have more than one possible answer.

21. Our game was rained out, and the meteorologist says to expect more of it this week.

22. Both the Hattons and the Prices own Persian cats, but that white one is theirs.

23. I was surprised to see Jo return from the library without borrowing a single one.

24. The soldiers saluted the queen and her family as they passed.

25. Home from the fishing trip, Paul lifted an ice chest full of them out of the truck.

21. [10j]
22. [10i]
23. [10j]
24. [10i]
25. [10j]

standard usage of *who* and *whom*, pronouns with appositives, and clear pronoun reference.

- The chapter closes with a **Chapter Review** including a **Writing Application** that asks students to write a letter, using pronouns correctly.

- For help in integrating this chapter with writing assignments in *Holt Literature and Language Arts,* see the **Teaching Strands** chart on pp. T24–T25.

ASSESSING

Entry-Level Assessment

Diagnostic Preview. The results of the **Diagnostic Preview** will tell you which students have difficulty with the nominative and objective cases and with troublesome pronoun usage.

Diagnostic Preview C

POSSIBLE ANSWERS

21. Our game was rained out, and the meteorologist says to expect more rain this week.

22. Both the Hattons and the Prices own Persian cats, but that white one is the Hattons'.

23. I was surprised to see Jo return from the library without borrowing a single book.

24. As the soldiers passed, they saluted the queen and her family.

25. Home from the fishing trip, Paul lifted an ice chest full of fish out of the truck.

Differentiating Instruction

- *UA: Differentiating Instruction*
- *UA: Supporting Instruction in Five Languages*

Assessment

- *Formal Assessment*
- *Progress-Monitoring Tests,* pp. 19–20, 48

- *Test Generator (Teacher One Stop DVD-ROM)* 🎧

Other Language Resources

- *Spelling Lessons & Activities*
- *WordSharp: An Interactive Vocabulary Tutor*
- *Reading and Writing Transparencies*

Case

(pp. 216–217)

OBJECTIVE

- To identify personal pronouns and their cases

PRETEACHING

Lesson Starter

Prior Knowledge. Have students insert first- or third-person pronouns into the sentence *Give it to _____*. If the pronoun fits this sentence and sounds "right," it's in the objective case—*Give it to us*. If it doesn't seem to fit, the pronoun is not in the objective case and so is in either the nominative or possessive case. Encourage students to create similar sentences to determine whether pronouns are in the nominative case or the possessive case. [*_____ ate the apple* and *This is _____ book*.]

DIRECT TEACHING

Modeling and Demonstration

Case. Model how to identify personal pronouns and their cases by using the example *I remembered to bring my homework with me*. First, ask students which words are pronouns. [*I, my, me*] Next, ask how the pronoun *I* is used in the sentence. [*as the subject*] Then, ask how *my* is used. [*to show possession*] Ask students how *me* is used. [*as the object of the preposition* with] Explain that the pronoun *I* is in the nominative case, *my* is in the possessive case, and *me* is in the objective case. Point out that a pronoun takes different forms depending on how it is used in a sentence. Now, have a volunteer use another example from this chapter to demonstrate how to identify pronouns and their cases.

Reference Note

For more information about **possessive forms of nouns,** see page 351.

HELP

As discussed in Chapter 2, a pronoun is a word used in place of one or more nouns or pronouns.

EXAMPLE
Kelly lent the book to David.
She lent **it** to **him.**

The word that a pronoun stands for is called its **antecedent**.

EXAMPLE
David read the **book** and returned **it.** [*Book* is the antecedent of the pronoun *it*.]

Be sure to review pronouns before you move on to topics such as case. If you need help, turn back to Chapter 2.

Case

Case is the form that a noun or a pronoun takes to show its relationship to other words in a sentence. In English, there are three cases: *nominative, objective,* and *possessive.*

The form of a noun is the same for both the nominative case and the objective case. For example, a noun used as a subject (nominative case) will have the same form when used as an indirect object (objective case).

NOMINATIVE CASE   The **singer** received a standing ovation. [subject]

OBJECTIVE CASE   The audience gave the **singer** a standing ovation. [indirect object]

A noun changes its form in the possessive case, usually by adding an apostrophe and an *s.*

POSSESSIVE CASE   Many of the **singer's** fans waited outside the theater.

Unlike nouns, most personal pronouns have different forms for all three cases. In the following example, the pronouns in boldface type all refer to the same person. They have three different forms because of their different uses.

EXAMPLE   **I** [nominative] remembered to bring **my** [possessive] homework with **me** [objective].

Personal Pronouns		
Nominative Case	**Objective Case**	**Possessive Case**
Singular		
I	me	my, mine
you	you	your, yours
he, she, it	him, her, it	his, her, hers, its
Plural		
we	us	our, ours
you	you	your, yours
they	them	their, theirs

RESOURCES

Case
Practice

- *Language & Sentence Skills Practice,* p. 203
- *Developmental Language & Sentence Skills,* pp. 71–72

Case   217

NOTE Some teachers prefer to call possessive pronouns such as *my, your,* and *our* adjectives. Follow your teacher's directions when labeling possessive forms.

Exercise 1 **Identifying Personal Pronouns and Their Cases**

Each of the following sentences contains at least one personal pronoun. Identify each <u>pronoun</u> and give its case.

EXAMPLE   **1.** Uncle Theo gave us this book about rock stars of the 1950s and 1960s.

    1. us—objective

1. Why don't we sit down and look through the book with Claire and <u>him</u>?   **1.** nom./obj.
2. We want to see what pictures <u>our</u> book has of the great American rock singers.   **2.** nom./poss.
3. I also look forward to reading more about <u>them</u>!   **3.** nom./obj.
4. The contributions <u>they</u> made to rock-and-roll affected popular music all over the world.   **4.** nom.
5. The stars in the pictures on this page look so different from the performers <u>we</u> have today.   **5.** nom.
6. That's Chuck Berry doing <u>his</u> famous "duckwalk."   **6.** poss.
7. These three women were known as the Supremes, and <u>they</u> had twelve number-one songs.   **7.** nom.
8. The woman in the middle may look familiar; <u>she</u> is Diana Ross.   **8.** nom.
9. Fans also liked the male vocal group the Four Tops and other groups like <u>them</u>.   **9.** obj.
10. Of course, <u>we</u> can't forget Little Richard, known for <u>his</u> wild piano playing.   **10.** nom./poss.

DIFFERENTIATING INSTRUCTION

English-Language Learners

Hmong. The objective and nominative uses of Hmong pronouns depend on their placement within the sentence rather than on the forms of the pronouns themselves, while the possessive case relies upon the use of a possessive classifier. Remind Hmong speakers that English pronouns change form in order to indicate their functions within a sentence. Offer additional review and practice using pronouns in their different cases.

Cantonese. Cantonese uses fewer pronouns than English and drops them when they are understood. *The nurse put a thermometer in (my) mouth.* Also, in Cantonese there is no difference between the nominative and objective forms. Have students practice correct forms of English pronouns by relating personal information, such as likes and dislikes, in speech or writing. Promote communication activities in which students converse with classmates about their families and interests.

TEACHING **TIP**

Exercise 1 Depending upon your instruction to students, *our* in sentence 2 and *his* in sentence 6 and in sentence 10 may be classified as adjectives. See the Note on p. 32 regarding labeling of possessive forms of pronouns.

DISTRIBUTED REVIEW
Ask students to find the antecedent of each personal pronoun in sentences 4, 6, and 8 of **Exercise 1**. [4. *singers,* 6. *Chuck Berry,* 8. *woman*]

The Nominative Case

Rules 10a, b *(pp. 218–220)*

OBJECTIVES

- To read aloud sentences that have pronouns as subjects
- To choose personal pronouns used as subjects
- To identify personal pronouns used as predicate nominatives

USAGE

EXTENSION

Relating to Literature

Poetry. Have each student find in his or her literature book a poem in which the poet has used first-person pronouns. Possible selections include "Mother to Son" by Langston Hughes and "Sugar Poem" by Aurora Levins Morales. Ask students to rewrite the poems by substituting third-person pronouns for the first-person forms. Have volunteers read the old versions and the new versions aloud. Discuss how the implications and force of a poem's message change when feelings and impressions are presented as a report about someone rather than as direct expressions from the heart and mind of the speaker.

Reference Note

For more about **finding the subject of a verb,** see page 7.

TIPS & TRICKS

To help you choose the correct pronoun in a compound subject, try each form of the pronoun separately.

EXAMPLE
Candida and (*me, I*) like to dance. [*Me like to dance* or *I like to dance?*]

ANSWER
Candida and **I** like to dance.

The Nominative Case

Nominative case pronouns—*I, you, he, she, it, we,* and *they*—are used as subjects of verbs and as predicate nominatives.

10a. The subject of a verb should be in the nominative case.

EXAMPLES | **I** like classical music. [*I* is the subject of *like*.]

Did **he** and **she** sell tickets? [*He* and *she* are the subjects of *Did sell*.]

They called while **we** were away. [*They* is the subject of *called. We* is the subject of *were*.]

Oral Practice 1 Using Pronouns as Subjects

Read the following sentences aloud, stressing the italicized pronouns.

1. *He* and *she* collect autographs.
2. My grandmother and *I* are painting the boat.
3. Both *they* and *we* were frightened.
4. Did Alicia or *she* answer the phone?
5. *We* are giving a fashion show.
6. *You* and *I* will stay behind.
7. Were *he* and *she* on the Old Spanish Trail?
8. My parents and *they* are good friends.

Exercise 2 Choosing Personal Pronouns Used as Subjects

Choose appropriate personal pronouns for the blanks in the following sentences. Use a variety of pronouns, but do not use *you* or *it*.   Answers may vary.

EXAMPLE | **1.** ____ and ____ will have a debate.
    1. We, they

1. I
2. we
3. he
4. She
5. he/she

1. Yesterday she and ____ went shopping.
2. Our cousins and ____ are ready for the race.
3. Neither ____ nor J. B. saw the zydeco band perform in concert last night.
4. ____ and Lim Sing have copies of the book.
5. When are ____ and ____ coming?

RESOURCES

The Nominative Case

Practice

- *Language & Sentence Skills Practice,* p. 204
- *Developmental Language & Sentence Skills,* pp. 71–72

6. Everyone remembers when ＿＿ won the big game.
7. Someone said that ＿＿ and ＿＿ are finalists.
8. Did you or ＿＿ ride in the hot-air balloon?
9. Both ＿＿ and ＿＿ enjoyed the stories about African American cowboys in the Old West.
10. Has ＿＿ or Eduardo seen that movie?

10b. A *predicate nominative* should be in the nominative case.

A *predicate nominative* is a noun or a pronoun that is in the predicate and that identifies or refers to the subject of the verb. A personal pronoun used as a predicate nominative follows a linking verb, usually a form of the verb *be* (*am, is, are, was, were, be,* or *been*).

EXAMPLES   The last one to leave was **he**. [*He* follows the linking verb *was* and identifies the subject *one.*]

Do you think the culprits may have been **they**? [*They* follows the linking verb *may have been* and identifies the subject *culprits.*]

Exercise 3 **Identifying Personal Pronouns Used as Predicate Nominatives**

Identify the correct personal pronoun in parentheses in each of the following sentences.

EXAMPLE   **1.** It was (*I, me*) at the door.
            1. *I*

1. We hoped it was (*her, she*).
2. That stranger thinks I am (*she, her*).
3. Luckily, it was not (*them, they*) in the accident.
4. If the singer had been (*her, she*), I would have gone to the concert.
5. Everyone believed it was (*we, us*).
6. It might have been (*him, he*), but I'm not sure.
7. Our opponents could have been (*them, they*).
8. I thought it was (*they, them*) from whom you bought the woven Navajo blanket.
9. It could have been (*she, her*) that he called.
10. Was the person who brought flowers Claudia or (*she, her*)?

---

6. we
7. she/I
8. he
9. she/he
10. he

TIPS & TRICKS

To help you choose the correct form of a pronoun used as a predicate nominative, remember that the pronoun could just as well be used as the subject in the sentence.

EXAMPLE
The group leaders will be **he** and **I**. [predicate nominatives]

He and **I** will be the group leaders. [subjects]

Reference Note

For more about **predicate nominatives,** see page 85.

STYLE **TIP**

Grammatically incorrect expressions such as *It's me, That's her,* and *It was them* are often used in informal situations. In formal speaking and writing, however, such expressions should be avoided.

Case   **219**

USAGE

DIRECT TEACHING

Modeling and Demonstration

The Nominative Case. Model how to identify personal pronouns used as subjects and predicate nominatives by using the example *He thinks the culprits may have been they.* First, ask students which word or words in the sentence are pronouns. [*He, they*] Then, ask how the pronoun *He* is used in the sentence. [as the subject of the verb thinks] Ask what case *He* is. [nominative] Next, ask how the pronoun *they* is used here. [they identifies culprits] Explain that since *they* follows the linking verb *may have been* and identifies that verb's subject, *culprits, they* is a predicate nominative and so is in the nominative case. Now, have a volunteer use another example from this chapter to demonstrate how to identify subjects and predicate nominatives.

DIRECT TEACHING

Correcting Misconceptions

Pronouns as Predicate Nominatives. Students may not know that it is correct to use nominative-case pronouns as predicate nominatives and may think that objective-case pronouns sound less awkward. Assure students that sentences such as "It is I" are correct, and encourage them to practice saying such sentences aloud to help make them more familiar. Remind students that they can rewrite sentences to make them sound more natural by swapping the subject and the predicate nominative. For example, in **Exercise 3,** sentence 7 would read *They could have been our opponents.*

Each of the following sentences contains a pair of personal pronouns in parentheses. Choose the <u>correct pronoun</u> from each pair.

EXAMPLE **1.** (*We, Us*) think of Leonardo da Vinci mostly as an artist.

    1. We

1. (*Me, I*) think you probably have seen some paintings by this Italian Renaissance master.

2. (*Him, He*) painted two works that are particularly famous.

3. The *Mona Lisa* and *The Last Supper* are (*they, them*).

4. In science class (*we, us*) were surprised by what our teacher said about Leonardo da Vinci.

5. (*Her, She*) said that he was also a brilliant inventor.

6. My friend Jill and (*me, I*) were amazed to hear that Leonardo designed a flying machine that looked like a helicopter.

7. Look at the propellers on the flying machine that (*he, him*) drew in 1488.

8. (*Me, I*) was also impressed by his drawing of a spring-driven car.

9. The designer of the diving bell and the battle tank was (*him, he*), too.

10. Scientists have studied Leonardo's work, and (*them, they*) have made models of many of his drawings.

CONTENT-AREA CONNECTIONS

Science

Pronouns. Have students research one of Leonardo da Vinci's inventions mentioned in **Review A.** Ask students to write four or five sentences about the invention. The sentences should include at least two personal pronouns used as subjects and two used as predicate nominatives. Have students label the pronouns as *subjects* or *predicate nominatives.*

The Objective Case

Objective case pronouns—*me, you, him, her, it, us,* and *them*—are used as direct objects, indirect objects, and objects of prepositions.

10c. A *direct object* should be in the objective case.

A *direct object* is a noun, pronoun, or word group that tells *who* or *what* receives the action of the verb.

EXAMPLES   Evan surprised **them.** [*Them* tells *whom* Evan surprised.]

        Uncle Ramón took **me** to the rodeo. [*Me* tells *whom* Uncle Ramón took.]

        The ranger guided **us** to the camp. [*Us* tells *whom* the ranger guided.]

        Did the class elect **you** and **me** to be the student council representatives? [*You* and *me* tell *whom* the class elected.]

Exercise 4 **Choosing Pronouns Used as Direct Objects**

Choose appropriate pronouns for the blanks in the following sentences. Use a variety of pronouns, but do not use *you* or *it.*

EXAMPLE   **1.** The teacher helped ____ with the assignment.
        1. us   Answers may vary.

1. The feisty little dog chased Adam and ____ for almost three blocks. **1.** me
2. They asked Ms. Shore and ____ for permission. **2.** her
3. Rita said that she can usually find Alberto, Tina, and ____ at your house. **3.** him
4. Did you know Jarvis and ____? **4.** her
5. The tour guide directed ____ to New York City's Little Italy neighborhood. **5.** us
6. Aunt Aggie took ____ and ____ to the zoo. **6.** her/me
7. Rochelle told my sister and ____ about last weekend's outdoor concert. **7.** me
8. Should we call Mark and ____ and tell them the good news about the play? **8.** him
9. Do you remember ____ and ____? **9.** her/me
10. All five judges have chosen ____ and ____ as the winners of the essay contest. **10.** him/her

Reference Note

For more about **direct objects,** see page 81.

TIPS & TRICKS

To help you choose the correct pronoun in a compound direct object, try each form of the pronoun separately in the sentence.

EXAMPLE
We met Tara and (*she, her*) at the video arcade. [*We met she* or *We met her*?]

ANSWER
We met Tara and **her** at the video arcade.

USAGE

The Objective Case and the Possessive Case
Rules 10c–f *(pp. 221–225)*

OBJECTIVES

- To use pronouns as direct objects, indirect objects, and objects of prepositions

- To read aloud sentences that use pronouns as direct objects, indirect objects, and objects of prepositions

DIFFERENTIATING INSTRUCTION

English-Language Learners

Spanish. Case usage differs in Spanish and English; therefore, Spanish-speaking students may need extra practice with English cases. Use students' names to create sentences such as *Roberto will ask Candace to take notes for Jorge.* Then, let volunteers substitute pronouns: _____ *will ask* _____ *to take notes for* _____. [*He will ask her to take notes for me.*]

Spanish also uses four different forms for third-person objective-case pronouns: one for direct objects, one for indirect objects, one for objects of prepositions, and another for reflexives. Tell students that in English, the objective-case pronouns are the same for all kinds of objects. Provide simple cloze activities for practice.

1. Mother called ____ to dinner. [*him, her, them*]

2. Mother gave ____ a book. [*him, her, them*]

3. Mother gave the book to ____. [*him, her, them*]

RESOURCES

The Objective Case and the Possessive Case
Practice

- *Language & Sentence Skills Practice,* pp. 205–208, 214
- *Developmental Language & Sentence Skills,* pp. 73–74

DIRECT TEACHING

Modeling and Demonstration

The Objective Case and the Possessive Case. Model how a pronoun takes the objective case when it is a direct object and the possessive case when it shows ownership by using the example *The teacher thanked me for finding her book.* First, ask which word or words in the sentence are pronouns. [*me, her*] Then, ask how the pronoun *me* is used in the sentence. [*as the direct object of the verb* thanked] Ask what case this pronoun is in. [*objective case*] Next, ask how the pronoun *her* is used here. [*to show possession*] Then, ask what case *her* is in. [*possessive case*] Now, have a volunteer use another example from this chapter to demonstrate the use of pronouns in the objective and possessive cases.

DIFFERENTIATING INSTRUCTION

Advanced Learners

Objective-Case Pronouns. Remind students that they use pronouns constantly, whether or not they identify them as such. Divide the class into teams. Provide a variety of magazines and newspapers, and set up a hunt for objective-case pronouns. Students could use highlighters to mark examples of pronouns. The team that records the most examples of objective-case pronouns in a given time period is the winner. Remind students that *you* and *it* may be in the objective case, depending on usage. Offer double credit if a team identifies which rule (**10c, d,** or **e**) each example illustrates.

TIPS & TRICKS

To help you choose the correct pronoun in a compound indirect object, try each form of the pronoun separately in the sentence.

EXAMPLE
Our neighbor gave Kristen and (*I, me*) a job for the summer. [*Our neighbor gave I a job* or *Our neighbor gave me a job*?]

ANSWER
Our neighbor gave Kristen and **me** a job for the summer.

Reference Note

For more about **indirect objects,** see page 83.

STYLE TIP

Just as there are good manners in behavior, there are also good manners in language. In English it is considered polite to put first-person pronouns (*I, me, mine, we, us, ours*) last in compound constructions.

EXAMPLE
Mr. Griffith lent **Juan and me** [not *me and Juan*] some magazines.

10d. An *indirect object* should be in the objective case.

Indirect objects often appear in sentences containing direct objects. An indirect object tells *to whom or what* or *for whom or what* the action of the verb is done. An indirect object usually comes between an action verb and its direct object.

EXAMPLES   Coach Mendez gave **them** a pep talk. [*Them* tells *to whom* Coach Mendez gave a pep talk.]

His mother built **him** a bookcase. [*Him* tells *for whom* his mother built a bookcase.]

The science teacher gave **us** posters of the solar system. [*Us* tells *to whom* the teacher gave posters.]

NOTE   Indirect objects do not follow prepositions. If a preposition such as *to* or *for* precedes an object, the object is an object of the preposition.

Oral Practice 2 **Using Pronouns as Direct Objects and Indirect Objects**

Read the following sentences aloud, stressing the italicized pronouns.

1. The sudden rain drenched Ahmad and *me.*
2. Li showed Raúl and *her* the new kite.
3. The stray dog followed *her* and *him* all the way to school.
4. Did you expect *us* or *them*?
5. The doctor gave *her* and *me* flu shots.
6. Carol helped Sarah and *him* with their chores.
7. Have you seen the Romanos or *them*?
8. After supper Mrs. Karras gave *us* some raspberries for dessert.

Exercise 5 **Using Personal Pronouns as Indirect Objects**

For each of the following sentences, fill in the blank with a correct personal pronoun.

EXAMPLE   **1.** My sister likes humorous poetry, so I lent _____ a copy of *Parents Keep Out: Elderly Poems for Youngerly Readers* by Ogden Nash.

1. **her**   Answers may vary.

 Usage

Using Pronouns in Sentences. Point out that the pronouns *you* and *it* can each be used in more than one case. The case is determined by the way the pronoun is used in the sentence, but the form of the pronoun stays the same.

Write on the chalkboard the pronouns *you* and *it* as well as the cases in which they can be used, and have students compose original sentences for each use.

1. She's happy because the book has given ____ many reasons to laugh.   **1.** her
2. When our family is all together, my sister reads ____ Ogden Nash poems.   **2.** us
3. Our uncle asked to borrow the book, but instead Sabrina bought ____ a copy of *You Can't Get There from Here.*   **3.** him
4. My uncle seeks me out and says, "Let me read ____ this poem. It's a really funny one!"   **4.** you
5. The family was curious about Ogden Nash's life, so I gave ____ some biographical information about him.   **5.** them
6. My literature book tells ____ his life span, which was 1902–1971.   **6.** us
7. He left ____ great humorous writings in movies, plays, and poems.   **7.** us
8. Sabrina asked ____ questions about Nash's childhood.   **8.** me
9. I provided ____ the information that he was born in Rye, New York, and grew up in cities along the East Coast.   **9.** her
10. Nash's creative works still bring ____ much enjoyment.   **10.** us

10e. An ***object of a preposition*** should be in the objective case.

A noun or a pronoun that follows a preposition is called the ***object of a preposition.*** Together, the preposition, its object, and any modifiers of that object make a ***prepositional phrase.***

EXAMPLES
to **Lee**	in an **hour**	like red **clay**
without **me**	near **her**	except **them**
for **him**	by **us**	next to **us**

A pronoun used as the object of a preposition should be in the objective case.

EXAMPLES   When did you mail the package to **them**? [*Them* is the object of the preposition *to.*]

Are you still planning to go to the movies with **us**? [*Us* is the object of the preposition *with.*]

The reward money was divided equally between **him** and **her**. [*Him* and *her* are the objects of the preposition *between.*]

Reference Note
For a list of **prepositions,** see page 66. For more about **prepositional phrases,** see page 96.

┌─────────────────────┐
│ TIPS & TRICKS │
└─────────────────────┘
To determine the correct pronoun form when the object of a preposition is compound, use each pronoun separately in the prepositional phrase.

EXAMPLE
Grandma sent a package to (*she, her*) and (*I, me*). [*To she* or *to her*? *To I* or *to me*?]

Grandma sent a package to **her** and **me**.

DIFFERENTIATING INSTRUCTION

English-Language Learners
General Strategies. To help English-language learners with **Exercise 5,** give them the option of making pronoun charts, such as the one on p. 216, to refer to as they work.

Exercise 5

DISTRIBUTED REVIEW
As a quick review of phrases and clauses, ask students to find the following items in the designated sentences.

2. an adverb clause [*When our family is all together*]

3. an infinitive phrase [*to borrow the book*]

5. a prepositional phrase [*about Ogden Nash's life* or *about him*]

6. an adjective clause [*which was 1902–1971*]

USAGE

1. you (nominative, objective)
[*You already have one.
Didn't Melissa hand you the grapes?*]

2. it (nominative, objective)
[*The day was long, but it was fun.
Hit it out of the park!*]

PRACTICE

Guided and Independent

Exercise 6 You may wish to use items 1–10 in **Exercise 6** as guided practice. Then, have students complete items 11–20 as independent practice. **HOMEWORK**

Oral Practice 3 Using Pronouns as Objects of Prepositions

Read the following sentences aloud, stressing the italicized words.

1. The safari continued *without her* and *me*.
2. Everyone *except us* saw the Navajo rugs.
3. We stood *beside* their families and *them* during the ceremony.
4. Do you have any suggestions *for* Jalen or *me*?
5. The firefighters talked *to* Lucy and *him*.
6. Please give this *to* either your father or *her*.
7. With the help *of* Juan and *her*, we built a fire and set up camp.
8. There was a contest *between us* and *them*.

Exercise 6 Choosing Pronouns Used as Objects of Prepositions

Choose appropriate pronouns for the blanks in the following sentences. Use a variety of pronouns, but do not use *you* or *it*.

EXAMPLE　　**1.** We could not find all of ＿＿＿.
　　　　　　1. them　Answers may vary.

1. me	1. The teacher read to André and ＿＿＿ a saying by Confucius about friendship.
2. him	2. I made an appointment for ＿＿＿ and you.
3. her	3. There are some seats behind Lusita and ＿＿＿.
4. me	4. No one except Patrice and ＿＿＿ was studying.
5. him	5. I couldn't have done it without you and ＿＿＿.
6. her	6. Why didn't you speak to Christie and ＿＿＿?
7. them	7. Our team has played basketball against the Jets and ＿＿＿.
8. her	8. I was near you and ＿＿＿ during the parade.
9. me	9. Just between you and ＿＿＿, I think our chances are good.
10. him	10. Did you go with ＿＿＿ to the Herb Harvest Fall Festival at the Ozark Folk Center?
11. her	11. The referee called fouls on ＿＿＿ and me.
12. him	12. Maggie is off fishing with ＿＿＿.
13. her	13. Without you and ＿＿＿ in the group, meetings have been dull.
14. us	14. They assigned the same lab equipment to them and ＿＿＿.
15. her	15. The duke sneered haughtily at ＿＿＿ and me.
16. him	16. The player tried to dodge between Sheridan and ＿＿＿.
17. her	17. Uncle Vic will get the details from Sofia and ＿＿＿ later.
18. them	18. I will talk about the next formation with ＿＿＿.

19. The letter you wrote to _____ and me was very funny.
20. The curious duck circled around Jade and _____.

19. him
20. me

The Possessive Case

10f. The personal pronouns in the possessive case—*my, mine, your, yours, his, her, hers, its, our, ours, their, theirs*— are used to show ownership or possession.

(1) The possessive pronouns *mine, yours, his, hers, its, ours,* and *theirs* are used as parts of a sentence in the same ways in which pronouns in the nominative and the objective cases are used.

SUBJECT	Your car and **mine** need tuneups.
PREDICATE NOMINATIVE	This jacket is **hers.**
DIRECT OBJECT	We painted **ours** yesterday.
INDIRECT OBJECT	Alice gave **theirs** her complete attention.
OBJECT OF A PREPOSITION	Next to **yours,** my bonsai crabapple tree looks puny.

(2) The possessive pronouns *my, your, his, her, its, our,* and *their* are used before nouns to show ownership or possession.

EXAMPLES   **My** CD player is on the desk.

Do you know **their** phone number?

NOTE   Some authorities prefer to call these words possessive adjectives. Follow your teacher's instructions regarding these possessive forms.

Special Pronoun Problems

Who and *Whom*

Nominative Case	who	whoever
Objective Case	whom	whomever

Special Pronoun Problems   **225**

RESOURCES

Special Pronoun Problems
Practice
■ *Language & Sentence Skills Practice,* pp. 209–213, 215–216
■ *Developmental Language & Sentence Skills,* pp. 75–76

10
g–j

USAGE

Special Pronoun Problems
Rules 10g–j *(pp. 225–232)*

OBJECTIVES

■ To read aloud sentences that contain *who* and *whom*

■ To identify correct forms of pronouns

■ To revise sentences for clear pronoun reference

DIRECT TEACHING

Modeling and Demonstration

Special Pronoun Problems. Model how to identify correct forms of *who* and *whom* by using the example *I like the baseball player (who, whom) hit the home run.* Ask students to identify the subordinate clause. [*(who, whom) hit the home run*] Then, ask them to identify the subject and verb of the subordinate clause. [*who* or *whom*—subject; *hit*— verb] Explain that since *who* or *whom* is the subject of the clause, then the pronoun should be in the nominative case, *who.* Now, have a volunteer use another example from the chapter to demonstrate how to choose correct forms of *who* and *whom.*

Special Pronoun Problems   **225**

RETEACHING

Who, Whom

Activity. Some students might find the steps for choosing between *who* and *whom* easier to comprehend and remember if they see them organized visually in a flowchart. Draw the following chart on the chalkboard, and ask students to copy it. Have students fill in each step as they read about it on this page.

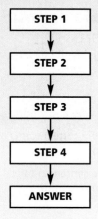

STEP 1

↓

STEP 2

↓

STEP 3

↓

STEP 4

↓

ANSWER

Meeting the Challenge

ANSWERS

Riddle poems will vary but should include three pronoun appositives and two uses of *who* or *whom.*

Reference Note

For information about **subordinate clauses,** see page 121.

STYLE TIP

In informal English, the use of *whom* is becoming less common. In fact, when you are speaking informally, you may begin a question with *who* regardless of the grammar of the sentence. In formal English, however, you should distinguish between *who* and *whom.*

MEETING THE CHALLENGE

Write a riddle poem. First, think of a person, place, thing, or idea you want to describe. Then, describe your topic without actually naming the item. Include at least two uses of *who* or *whom* and three pronoun appositives in your poem. Check for correct pronoun usage, and then trade poems with a classmate to see if you can guess each other's riddle.

10g. The use of *who* or *whom* in a subordinate clause depends on how the pronoun functions in the clause.

When you are choosing between *who* and *whom* in a subordinate clause, follow these steps.

STEP 1   Find the subordinate clause.

STEP 2   Decide how the pronoun is used in the clause—as a subject, predicate nominative, object of the verb, or object of a preposition.

STEP 3   Determine the case of the pronoun according to the rules of standard English.

STEP 4   Select the correct form of the pronoun.

EXAMPLE   Do you know (*who, whom*) they are?

STEP 1   The subordinate clause is (*who, whom*) they are.

STEP 2   The subject is *they,* the verb is *are,* and the pronoun is the predicate nominative: they are (*who, whom*).

STEP 3   A pronoun used as a predicate nominative should be in the nominative case.

STEP 4   The nominative form is *who.*

ANSWER   Do you know **who** they are?

EXAMPLE   Mayor Neiman, (*who, whom*) I have met, is intelligent.

STEP 1   The subordinate clause is (*who, whom*) I have met.

STEP 2   The subject is *I,* and the verb is *have met.* The pronoun is the direct object of the verb: I have met (*who, whom*).

STEP 3   A pronoun used as a direct object should be in the objective case.

STEP 4   The objective form is *whom.*

ANSWER   Mayor Neiman, **whom** I have met, is intelligent.

Oral Practice 4   Using *Who* and *Whom* Correctly

Read the following sentences aloud, stressing the italicized pronouns.

1. Our team needs a pitcher *who* can throw curve balls.
2. For *whom* do the gauchos in Argentina work?
3. They work for ranch owners *who* often live far away.
4. Dr. Martin Luther King, Jr., is a man *whom* we honor.
5. He told me *who* the author is.
6. The boy, *who* was new in town, was lost.

7. Is he the new student to *whom* this locker belongs?

8. *Whom* did they suggest for the job?

Appositives

10h. A pronoun used as an appositive is in the same case as the word to which it refers.

An *appositive* is a noun or pronoun placed next to another noun or pronoun to identify or describe it.

EXAMPLES   The runners—**he, she,** and **I**—warmed up on the track. [The pronouns are in the nominative case because they are used as appositives of the subject, *runners.*]

Every student except two, **him** and **her,** joined the archae-ological dig. [The pronouns are in the objective case because they are used as appositives of *two,* the object of the preposition *except.*]

The drama coach introduced the actors, Laura and **me.** [The pronoun is in the objective case because it is used as an appositive of the direct object, *actors.*]

Sometimes a pronoun is followed directly by an appositive. To help you choose which pronoun to use before an appositive, omit the appositive and try each form of the pronoun separately.

EXAMPLE   (*We, Us*) cheerleaders practice after school. [*Cheerleaders* is the appositive identifying the pronoun.]

We practice after school.

Us practice after school.

ANSWER   **We** cheerleaders practice after school.

EXAMPLE   The coach threw a party for (*we, us*) players. [*Players* is the appositive identifying the pronoun.]

The coach threw a party for *we.*

The coach threw a party for *us.*

ANSWER   The coach threw a party for **us** players.

Reflexive Pronouns

Reflexive pronouns such as *himself* and *themselves* can be used as objects. Do not use the nonstandard forms *hisself* and *theirselfs* or *theirselves* in place of *himself* and *themselves.*

NONSTANDARD   The mayor voted for hisself in May's election.

Reference Note
For more information about **appositives**, see page 112.

THE FAR SIDE®   By GARY LARSON

"So, then … Would that be 'us the people' or 'we the people'?"

Reference Note
For more about **reflexive pronouns,** see page 33.

Special Pronoun Problems   **227**

DIFFERENTIATING INSTRUCTION

English-Language Learners

Spanish. The Spanish equivalent of *who—que, quien,* and *quién—*does not change form when used as an object, so Spanish-speaking students do not have a first-language context for this concept. You may want to have students practice reading aloud sentences in which *who* and *whom* are used correctly. You could also have students work in pairs to create original sentences using *who* and *whom.* After you check for correct usage, suggest that students read the sentences aloud for reinforcement.

Special Education Students

Oral practices can be useful in teaching students to develop an ear for recognizing standard and non-standard usage. You might want to make recordings of the oral practices for use with special-needs students. Have a helper work with the students, playing the recordings and pointing out the different usages as students listen.

USAGE

Learning for Life

Continued on pp. 228–229

Writing a Permissions Request.
Virtually all published material is copyrighted, and before anyone can use it, he or she must obtain permission from the copyright owner.

Ask students to select a published photo

and to write a letter or an e-mail message to the copyright owner telling which image they wish to use, explaining how they plan to use it and for how long, and requesting permission to use the image.

Make sure students know how to

PRACTICE

Guided and Independent

You may wish to use **Exercise 7** as guided practice. Then, have students complete **Review B** as independent practice. **HOMEWORK**

COMPUTER TIP

A computer may be able to help you find pronoun problems in your writing. For example, if you sometimes use *who* and *whom* incorrectly, you can use the search feature to highlight all the uses of *who* and *whom*. Then, examine how each of these pronouns is used. If you have used an incorrect form, replace it with the correct form.

USAGE

Exercise 7 Identifying Correct Forms of Pronouns

Choose the correct pronoun in parentheses in each of the following sentences.

EXAMPLE
1. Mrs. Johnson said she was proud of (*we, us*) band members.

1. *us*

1. (*Who, Whom*) selected the new team captain?
2. They asked (*themselves, theirselves*) how the money from the fund-raiser should be spent.
3. The head nurse gave several volunteers—the Mullaneys, Ari, and (*she, her*)—a tour of the new hospital wing.
4. Did you know that (*we, us*) girls are going to the symphony tomorrow night?
5. From (*who, whom*) did you order the food?
6. Two runners, Jill and (*she, her*), finished in record time.
7. We are not sure (*who, whom*) the next president of the honor club will be.
8. (*We, Us*) members of the band hope to cut a demo tape soon.
9. (*Who, Whom*) shall we invite?
10. Robert took two helpings for (*hisself, himself*).

Review B Identifying Correct Forms of Pronouns

Identify the correct pronoun in parentheses in each of the following sentences. Then, tell whether the pronoun is used as a *subject*, a *predicate nominative*, a *direct object*, an *indirect object*, or an *object of a preposition*.

EXAMPLE
1. Say hello to (*she, her*) and Anna.

1. *her—object of a preposition*

1. d.o.
2. o.p.
3. p.n.

1. Tulips surround (*we, us*) during May in Holland, Michigan.
2. The audience clapped for Rudy and (*he, him*).
3. The best singer in the choir is (*she, her*).

Learning for Life **Continued from p. 227**

determine who owns the copyright. Copyright information can usually be found either in photo credits of a book or magazine, which appear with the acknowledgments, or within the individual photo captions themselves. If no copyright is

shown in the acknowledgments or captions, students can assume the publisher owns the copyright.

Encourage students to make their business letters or e-mail messages direct, concise, and clear. Allow students to work

4. The officer gave (*we, us*) girls a ride home.

5. I wrote a story about Grandpa and (*he, him*) last week.

6. Daniel and (*me, I*) read a book about Pelé, the soccer player.

7. Last year's winner was (*he, him*).

8. To (*who, whom*) did you send invitations?

9. Please tell me (*who, whom*) the girl in the yellow dress is.

10. (*We, Us*) sisters could help Dad with the dishes.

4. i.o.
5. o.p.
6. sub.
7. p.n.
8. o.p.
9. p.n.
10. sub.

Review C **Identifying Personal Pronouns and Their Uses**

Each of the following sentences contains at least one personal pronoun. Identify each personal pronoun, and tell whether it is used as a *subject*, a *predicate nominative*, a *direct object*, an *indirect object*, or an *object of a preposition*.

EXAMPLE   **1.** I enjoy watching Edward James Olmos in movies and television shows because he always plays such interesting characters.

   1. I—subject; he—subject

1. The cowboy in this picture from the movie *The Ballad of Gregorio Cortez* is he.   **1.** p.n.

2. In the movie he plays an innocent man hunted by Texas Rangers.   **2.** sub.

3. The film will give you a good idea of Olmos's acting talents.   **3.** i.o.

4. After I saw him in this movie, I wanted to know more about him.   **4.** sub./d.o./sub./o.p.   **5.** i.o.

5. A librarian gave me a book of modern biographies.

6. I read that Olmos's father came from Mexico but that the actor was born in Los Angeles.   **6.** sub.

7. Growing up, Olmos faced the problems of poverty and gang violence, but he overcame them.   **7.** sub./d.o.

8. Before becoming a successful actor, he played baseball, sang in a band, and moved furniture.   **8.** sub.

9. In 1978, Olmos's role in the play *Zoot Suit* gave him the big break he needed in show business.   **9.** i.o./sub.

10. Later, the movie *Stand and Deliver,* in which he played math teacher Jaime Escalante, earned him widespread praise.
   10. sub./i.o.

in groups of three or four to evaluate and revise their letters. In addition to evaluating writing for clarity and for the correct use of pronouns, students should make sure it contains all of the information specified in the assignment.

Students should produce their letters or e-mail messages using word-processing or e-mail software, if possible, and they should use the program's spelling and grammar-checking features before they proofread their writing in hard copy.

Choose the correct pronoun in parentheses in each of the following sentences. Then, tell whether each is used as a *subject*, a *predicate nominative*, a *direct object*, an *indirect object*, an *object of a preposition*, or an *appositive*.

EXAMPLE   **1.** Ms. Lee gave the debaters, (*they, them*) and us, name tags.

        1. them—appositive

1. app.
2. sub.
3. o.p.
4. i.o.
5. p.n.
6. d.o.
7. d.o.
8. p.n.
9. sub.
10. app.

1. The two winners, Sean and (*she, her*), received scholarships.

2. Will Marc and (*she, her*) run the concession stand this season?

3. Ms. Lozano asked them to carry the equipment for you and (*I, me*).

4. Did they buy (*theirselves, themselves*) new shoes?

5. The lighting crew for the production was Manuel and (*I, me*).

6. They treat (*whoever, whomever*) they hire very well.

7. They met Jenna and (*he, him*) at the airport.

8. I think that the people who were costumed as pirates are (*they, them*).

9. (*Us, We*) sophomores raised the most money for charity.

10. Coach Escobar congratulated the two starting forwards, Angela and (*I, me*).

Clear Reference

10i. Avoid an *ambiguous reference,* which occurs when any one of two or more words could be a pronoun's antecedent.

AMBIGUOUS   Melissa proofread Stacy's essay while she was at lunch.
                   [Was Melissa at lunch or was Stacy?]

     CLEAR   While Melissa was at lunch, she proofread Stacy's essay.

     CLEAR   Melissa proofread Stacy's essay while Stacy was at lunch.

10j. Avoid a *weak reference,* which occurs when a pronoun refers to an antecedent that has been suggested but not expressed.

To correct a weak pronoun reference, either replace the pronoun with an appropriate noun or give the pronoun a clear antecedent.

WEAK   We sat quietly bird-watching all afternoon, but we never saw any. [The antecedent of *any* is not expressed.]

CLEAR   We sat quietly bird-watching all afternoon, but we never saw any **birds.**

CLEAR   We sat quietly all afternoon watching for **birds,** but we never saw any.

Exercise 8 Revising Sentences for Clear Pronoun Reference

Revise the following sentences, correcting each ambiguous or weak pronoun reference.

EXAMPLE   **1.** Will Matthew and William be riding to the tennis tournament with his parents?

          1. Will Matthew and William be riding to the tennis tournament with Matthew's parents?

1. The oak tree and the maple tree in the backyard were both turning colors, but it had already started losing leaves.
2. Tanya spent almost an hour in the video store but never found one to rent.
3. Adela often fixes breakfast for Mrs. Snyder before she goes to school.
4. This batch of rolls turned out better than the last batch because it was baked at a higher temperature.
5. The volcanic eruption was sudden and violent, throwing it near the outskirts of the village.
6. As soon as Annie and Laura landed in San Diego, she called me.
7. Brad appears in plays and in movies, but he enjoys performing in them more.
8. Antonio is a watercolor painter; some of them have received awards.
9. Dolores drives Sara home from school whenever she doesn't have to work.
10. Sandra is a captivating and energetic speaker, and that was one of her best.

┌HELP─

Sentences in Exercise 8 may have more than one correct answer.

Review E Revising Sentences for Clear Pronoun Reference

POSSIBLE ANSWERS

1. After reviewing the vegetarian cookbook, I selected some dishes to make.
2. Dylan went to a different school before he began eighth grade with Michael.
3. While Emily was at karate practice, Mari Elena telephoned her.
4. The crowd roared in the final inning when Sammy hit the ball out of the ballpark!
5. If I could find the Irish setter, I would give it its flea medicine.
6. Whenever I come home from college, Mom and Dad prepare my favorite meals for dinner.
7. The Spanish Club will volunteer at the food bank to help sort the donations.
8. Gloria's writing has improved tremendously ever since she started working with Jennifer.
9. The toddler struck the cup along the edge of the bowl, spilling the bowl's contents onto the floor.
10. The Labrador retriever curled up by the sleeping kitten in the dog's basket.

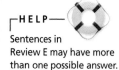

┌─HELP─
Sentences in Review E may have more than one possible answer.

Review E Revising Sentences for Clear Pronoun Reference

Revise the following sentences, correcting each ambiguous or weak pronoun reference.

EXAMPLE   **1.** Diane e-mailed Melissa while she was traveling in the Czech Republic.

        1. While Diane was traveling in the Czech Republic, she e-mailed Melissa.

1. After reviewing the vegetarian cookbook, I selected some to make.
2. Before Dylan began eighth grade with Michael, he went to a different school.
3. Mari Elena telephoned Emily while she was at karate practice.
4. The crowd roared in the final inning when Sammy hit it out of the ballpark!
5. I would give the Irish setter its flea medicine if I could find it.
6. Whenever I come home from college, Mom and Dad prepare my favorite ones for dinner.
7. The Spanish Club will volunteer at the food bank to help sort them.
8. Ever since Gloria started working with Jennifer, her writing has improved tremendously.
9. The toddler struck the cup along the edge of the bowl, spilling its contents onto the floor.
10. The Labrador retriever curled up by the sleeping kitten in its basket.

1. [10e]
2. [10g, c]
3. [10b]
4. [10c]
5. [10a]
6. [10b]
7. [10h, c]
8. [10e]
9. [10d]
10. [10d]
11. [10b]
12. [10d]
13. [10c]
14. [10g, a]
15. [10h, a]
16. C [10d]
17. whom [10g, e]
18. me [10d]
19. I [10a]

Chapter Review

A. Identifying Correct Forms of Pronouns

For each of the following sentences, identify the correct pronoun in parentheses.

1. Just between you and (*I*, *me*), I think he's wrong.
2. I don't know (*who*, *whom*) I'll invite to the dance.
3. The winners in the contest were Amelia and (*I*, *me*).
4. The wasp flew in the window and stung (*he*, *him*) on the arm.
5. Edward and (*she*, *her*) will give reports this morning.
6. The two scouts who have earned the most merit badges are Angelo and (*he*, *him*).
7. Several people in my neighborhood helped (*we*, *us*) boys clear the empty lot and measure out a baseball diamond.
8. May I sit next to Tori and (*he*, *him*)?
9. The tour guide showed Kimberly and (*she*, *her*) some Japanese *raku* pottery.
10. My aunt once gave (*me*, *I*) two dolls made from corn husks.
11. Did you know that it was (*I*, *me*) who called?
12. Our friends asked (*we*, *us*) if we could baby-sit.
13. Invite (*she*, *her*) and Joe to participate in the tournament.
14. Do you know (*who*, *whom*) received the award?
15. The jazz soloists—Lee and (*I*, *me*)—finally got to play.

B. Proofreading Sentences for Correct Forms of Personal Pronouns

Most of the following sentences contain a pronoun that has been used incorrectly. Write each ~~incorrect pronoun~~, and then write its correct form. If a sentence is already correct, write *C*.

16. The police officer told Pedro and him to move their bikes.
17. She was the counselor ~~who~~ I talked to last Friday.
18. He seemed eager to tell Sue and I how bad the movie was.
19. Danny and ~~me~~ like to make fajitas for the whole family.

ASSESSING

Monitoring Progress

Chapter Review. To assess student progress, you may want to compare the types of items missed on the **Diagnostic Preview** with those missed on the **Chapter Review.** If students have not made significant progress, you may want to refer them to **Chapter 17: Correcting Common Errors, Exercises 13–15,** for additional practice.

USAGE

RESOURCES

Using Pronouns Correctly

Review

■ *Language & Sentence Skills Practice,* pp. 213–216

Assessment

■ *Formal Assessment*
■ *Progress-Monitoring Tests,* pp. 19–20, 48
■ *Test Generator (Teacher One Stop DVD-ROM)* 🔘

20. We [10h, a]
21. C [10e]
22. us [10h, c]
23. me [10d]
24. he [10b]
25. me [10d]

20. Us students are enjoying the field trip to Rancho La Cima.
21. They gave the award to Maria and me.
22. The antics of the sea otters entertained we onlookers.
23. After the ceremony, Dad told Tim and I how proud he was.
24. The authors of the script were Amanda and him.
25. Ms. Pan told Nora and I the fable of the fox and the grapes.

C. Identifying Personal Pronouns and Their Uses

Each of the following sentences contains at least one personal pronoun. Identify each personal pronoun, and tell whether it is used as a *subject*, a *predicate nominative*, a *direct object*, an *indirect object*, or an *object of a preposition*.

26. p.n. [10b]
27. i.o. [10d]
28. sub. [10a]
29. o.p. [10e]
30. p.n. [10b]
31. sub. [10a]
32. d.o. [10c]
33. p.n. [10b]
34. i.o.[10d]
35. o.p. [10e]

26. Of the three applicants, the most promising is she.
27. With a sigh, the teacher handed him the letter.
28. She felt much better after taking vitamins and resting.
29. The albatross flew slowly over them.
30. Hello? Yes, this is he.
31. We are the best soccer players in the district.
32. When Winston Churchill was prime minister of Britain, the Canadian photographer Yousuf Karsh photographed him.
33. Half-hearted supporters are they.
34. The waiter gave us a complimentary serving of quesadillas.
35. The poster fell on her.

─HELP─

Sentences in Part D of the Chapter Review may have more than one possible answer.

36. [10i]
37. [10j]
38. [10j]
39. [10i]
40. [10i]

D. Revising Sentences for Clear Pronoun Reference

Revise each of the following sentences, correcting each unclear pronoun reference.

36. Seth will help Craig pick up trash on the beach so that he can complete the volunteer requirement.
37. Dai now has a potter's wheel but so far has not made any.
38. We weeded the garden and gave them some water.
39. Joshua offered Brent some hockey tickets before he left on vacation.
40. Brittney explained to Susan the duties of her new job.

Chapter Review D
POSSIBLE ANSWERS

36. So that Seth can complete the volunteer requirement, he will help Craig pick up trash on the beach.
37. Dai now has a potter's wheel but so far has not made any pottery.
38. We weeded the garden and gave the vegetables some water.
39. Before Joshua left on vacation, he offered Brent some hockey tickets.
40. Brittney explained to Susan the duties of Susan's new job.

Writing Application
Using Pronouns in a Letter

Nominative and Objective Case   A national magazine has asked its readers to send in letters telling about the people they respect the most. You decide to send in a letter. Write a letter to the magazine, telling about the person you most respect. You want your writing to appeal to many people, so be sure the pronouns you use are correct according to the rules of standard English.

Prewriting   Begin by thinking about a person you respect. The person could be someone you know, such as a family member, a teacher, or a friend; or it could be someone you have heard or read about (perhaps an author or a scientist). Choose one person as the topic of your letter. Then, make some notes about why you respect that person.

Writing   As you write your first draft, include only the most convincing details from your list. Think about how you want to group these details and how they will fit in your letter. Throughout your letter, use personal pronouns so that you do not keep repeating names.

Revising   As you read over your letter, imagine that you are a magazine editor. Ask yourself these questions:

- Is it clear why you respect the person?
- Have you supported all opinions with facts?

Mark any places where more information would be helpful. Delete any unnecessary information.

Publishing   Proofread your letter for any errors in grammar, usage, and mechanics. Check to be sure that all pronouns are in the correct case. You and your classmates could display your letters on a class bulletin board or Web page, if available. You might also want to send a copy of your letter to the person you described.

Grade-Level Standards

(Boldface indicates concepts that are taught and tested in this chapter.)

■ Language Convention 1.0: **Students write and speak with a command of standard English conventions appropriate to this grade level.**

■ **Grammar 1.4: Edit written manuscripts to ensure that correct grammar is used.**

Prerequisite/Review Standards

■ Sentence Structure 1.1: Place modifiers properly and use the active voice.

■ Grammar 1.2: Identify and use infinitives and participles and make clear references between pronouns and antecedents.

Standards Coming Up in the Next Grade Level

■ Grammar and Mechanics of Writing 1.1: Identify and correctly use clauses (e.g., main and subordinate), phrases (e.g., gerund, infinitive, and participial), and mechanics of punctuation (e.g., semicolons, colons, ellipses, hyphens).

■ Grammar and Mechanics of Writing 1.2: Understand sentence construction (e.g., parallel structure, subordination, proper placement of modifiers) and proper English usage (e.g., consistency of verb tenses).

1.0 Written and Oral English Language Conventions

Students write and speak with a command of standard English conventions appropriate to this grade level.

1.4 Edit written manuscripts to ensure that correct grammar is used.

┌─HELP─
Although some of the sentences in the Diagnostic Preview can be correctly revised in more than one way, you need to give only one revision for each sentence.

Numerals in brackets refer to rules tested by the items in the Diagnostic Preview.

1. most [11b(3), d]
2. C [11b]
3. other [11e]
4. better [11c]
5. anymore [11g]
6. better [11d, c]
7. else [11e]

11

Using Modifiers Correctly
Comparison and Placement

Diagnostic Preview

A. Using the Correct Forms of Modifiers

Most of the following sentences contain an error in the use of modifiers. Identify each error; then, revise the sentence, using the correct form of the modifier. If a sentence is already correct, write *C.*   Answers may vary.

EXAMPLE   **1.** I didn't want to live nowhere else.

   1. *didn't . . . nowhere—I didn't want to live anywhere else.*

1. The wonderfullest place in the whole world is my grandmother's house.

2. We lived there until we got a lovely apartment of our own.

3. Since her house is bigger than any house in the neighborhood, we all had plenty of room.

4. Grandma was glad to have us stay, because my dad can fix things so that they're gooder than new.

5. He plastered and painted the walls in one bedroom so that I wouldn't have to share a room no more with my sister.

6. I don't know which was best—having so much space of my own or having privacy from my sister.

7. My grandmother can sew better than anybody can.

---

8. She taught my sister and me how to make the ∧beautifull~~est~~ clothes.

9. She has three sewing machines, and I like her oldest one ∧~~better.~~

10. We started with the ~~more~~ simpler kinds of stitches.

11. After we could do those, Grandma showed us fancier stitches and sewing tricks.

12. For instance, she taught us to wrap thread behind buttons we sew on, so that they will be ~~more~~ easier to button.

13. We learned how to make skirts, blouses, and all sorts of other things, and now there is~~n't~~ hardly anything we can't make.

14. I was sad when we left Grandma's house, but I like our new apartment ~~more~~ better than I thought I would.

15. Luckily, we moved to a place near my grandmother's, and after school I can go over there or go home—whichever I want to do∧~~most.~~

B. Correcting Misplaced and Dangling Modifiers

The following sentences each contain a misplaced or a dangling modifier. Revise each sentence so that it is clear and correct.

EXAMPLE
  1. The cook will win a new oven that makes the best bread.

  1. *The cook that makes the best bread will win a new oven.*

16. Our math teacher told us∧that she had been a nurse∧~~yesterday.~~

17. ∧We read a story written by Jade Snow Wong∧~~in class.~~

18. ~~Destroyed by fire,~~ the man looked at the charred house∧.

19. After∧~~missing~~ the school bus, my mother gave me a ride.

20. ∧The fox escaped from the hounds pursuing it∧~~with a crafty maneuver into the hollow tree.~~

21. ∧~~Walking~~ through the park, the squirrels chattered and scurried along the path.

22. ∧~~Tearing~~ away his umbrella, Mr. Pérez became completely drenched.

23. The squid ~~fascinated the students~~ preserved in formaldehyde∧.

24. ∧~~Keeping~~ track of the race with binoculars, the blue car with a yellow roof pulled into the lead.

25. ∧Piling up in snowdrifts, our house was warm and toasty.

8. most [11b(3), d]
9. best [11d, c]
10. [11f]
11. C [11d, b(2)]
12. [11f]
13. [11g]
14. [11f]
15. more [11d, c]

Answers may vary.
16. yesterday [11h]
17. In class [11h]
18. that was destroyed by fire [11h]
19. I missed [11h]
20. With a crafty maneuver into the hollow tree, [11h]
21. As I walked [11h]
22. When the wind tore [11h]
23. fascinated the students [11h]
24. As we kept [11h]
25. While the snow was [11h]

▼
INTRODUCING THE CHAPTER

■ This chapter covers the correct use of adjectives and adverbs, including the distinction between *good* and *well;* the use of comparatives and superlatives; and the avoidance of double negatives. The last section addresses correct placement of modifying words, phrases, and clauses in sentences.

■ The chapter closes with a **Chapter Review**, which includes a **Writing Application** that asks students to write a letter, placing modifying phrases and clauses correctly.

■ For help in integrating this chapter with writing assignments in *Holt Literature and Language Arts,* see the **Teaching Strands** chart on pp. T24–T25.

ASSESSING

Entry-Level Assessment

Diagnostic Preview. Use the **Diagnostic Preview** to determine students' strengths and weaknesses. An assessment of students' responses should help you group students to meet individual needs or to make special assignments.

Differentiating Instruction

■ *UA: Differentiating Instruction*
■ *UA: Supporting Instruction in Five Languages*
■ *Family Involvement Activities: In Five Languages*

Assessment

■ *Formal Assessment*

■ *Progress-Monitoring Tests,* pp. 21–22, 48
■ *Test Generator (Teacher One Stop DVD-ROM)* 🎵

Other Language Resources

■ *Spelling Lessons & Activities*
■ *WordSharp: An Interactive Vocabulary Tutor*
■ *Reading and Writing Transparencies*

USAGE

Reference Note

For more information on **adjectives,** see page 38. For more on **adverbs,** see page 61.

What Is a Modifier?

A *modifier* is a word or word group that makes the meaning of another word or word group more specific. Two parts of speech are used as modifiers: adjectives and adverbs. *Adjectives* modify nouns and pronouns. *Adverbs* modify verbs, adjectives, and other adverbs.

ADJECTIVE	Ramona makes **beautiful** weavings.
ADVERB	Ramona weaves **beautifully.**

Adjective or Adverb?

Many adverbs end in *–ly*, but not all of them do. A few common adjectives also end in *–ly*. Therefore, you cannot tell whether a word is an adjective or an adverb simply by looking for the *–ly* ending.

ADJECTIVES	**lovely** dress	**likely** outcome
	silly story	**daily** exercise

To decide whether a word is an adjective or adverb, determine how the word is used in the sentence.

Adjectives	Adverbs
Greyhounds are **fast** dogs.	Greyhounds run **fast.**
Matt is my **second** cousin.	Matt came in **second.**
They took a **late** flight.	Their flight arrived **late.**

11a. If a word in the predicate modifies the subject of the verb, use the adjective form. If it modifies the verb, use the adverb form.

ADJECTIVE	His movements were **awkward.** [*Awkward* modifies the noun *movements.*]
ADVERB	He moved **awkwardly.** [*Awkwardly* modifies the verb *moved.*]
ADJECTIVE	The train moving down the tracks was **speedy.** [*Speedy* modifies the noun *train.*]
ADVERB	The train moved **speedily** down the tracks. [*Speedily* modifies the verb *moved.*]

238 Chapter 11   Using Modifiers Correctly

In many cases, linking verbs are followed by a predicate adjective.

Common Linking Verbs		
appear	grow	smell
be (am, is, are, etc.)	look	sound
become	remain	stay
feel	seem	taste

Reference Note

For more about **linking verbs,** see page 54.

EXAMPLES   That performance was **powerful.** [The predicate adjective *powerful* follows the linking verb *was* and describes the subject *performance.*]

The ground looks **muddy.** [The predicate adjective *muddy* follows the linking verb *looks* and describes the subject *ground.*]

NOTE Some verbs can be used as either linking verbs or action verbs. As action verbs they may be modified by adverbs.

ADJECTIVE   When we asked whether to turn right or left, Greg looked **blank.** [*Blank* modifies the noun *Greg.*]

ADVERB   Greg looked **blankly** at the sign. [*Blankly* modifies the action verb *looked.*]

Exercise 1 **Identifying Adjectives and Adverbs**

Identify the italicized word in each of the following sentences as either an adjective or an adverb.

EXAMPLE   **1.** They had been *best* friends since second grade.

    1. best—adjective

1. Does Mike's flight leave *early*?
2. Carolina was the *last* player on the field.
3. I can *hardly* hear the lead actor's monologue.
4. If we walk *fast*, we can make it to the gate on time.
5. The woven tapestry of *vivid* colors was lovely.
6. Have you met Kelly and her *younger* brother?
7. The *daily* news program begins in half an hour.
8. In the garage were stacked old boxes and *rusty* cans of paint.
9. Adrian and his sister boarded the airplane *last*.
10. Please hand me the small box on the *third* shelf.

1. adv.
2. adj.
3. adv.
4. adv.
5. adj.
6. adj.
7. adj.
8. adj.
9. adv.
10. adj.

What Is a Modifier?   **239**

DIRECT TEACHING

Modeling and Demonstration

What Is a Modifier? Model how to identify adjectives and adverbs by using the examples *His movements were awkward* and *He moved awkwardly.* First, ask students which word *awkward* describes in the first sentence. [*movements*] Then, ask what part of speech *movements* is. [*noun*] Explain that adjectives describe nouns; therefore, *awkward* is an adjective. Next, ask which word *awkwardly* describes in the second sentence. [*moved*] Then, ask what part of speech *moved* is. [*verb*] Since adverbs describe verbs, *awkwardly* is an adverb. Now, have a volunteer use another example from this chapter to demonstrate how to identify adjectives and adverbs.

DIFFERENTIATING INSTRUCTION

English-Language Learners

Hmong. As with speakers of many other languages, some Hmong English-language learners might place adjectives after the nouns they modify. For example, a Hmong speaker might write "a jacket red" rather than "a red jacket." Remind your Hmong speakers that in English, single-word adjectives usually precede the words they modify.

Exercise 1

DISTRIBUTED REVIEW
Have students identify the tense of the verbs in the following sentences:

3. [*present*]
6. [*present perfect*]
7. [*present*]
9. [*past*]

Reference Note

For more about *good* and *well,* see page 269.

DIRECT TEACHING

Correcting Misconceptions

Linking Verbs. Students may have difficulty distinguishing between adverbs and predicate adjectives because they mistakenly believe that a modifier after a linking verb modifies that verb. Make sure students understand that a linking verb is followed by an adjective rather than an adverb because the adjective modifies the subject of the verb, not the verb itself. Linking verbs that are forms of the verb *be* are relatively easy to identify, but some others may not be. Point out to students that a verb is a linking verb if the word *seem* can be substituted for it without significantly changing the meaning of the sentence. For example, one could change *This milk tastes sour* to *This milk seems sour. Tastes* is therefore used as a linking verb in this sentence.

Good and *Well*

Good is an adjective. It should be used to modify a noun or a pronoun. Use *well* to modify a verb.

EXAMPLES   Monica's voice sounded very **good** to me. [*Good* modifies the noun *voice.*]

                Monica sang the national anthem very **well.** [*Well* modifies the verb *sang.*]

Good should not be used to modify a verb.

NONSTANDARD   Paula does good in all her school subjects.

STANDARD   Paula does **well** in all her school subjects. [*Well* modifies the verb *does.*]

NONSTANDARD   The mariachi band can play good.

STANDARD   The mariachi band can play **well.** [*Well* modifies the verb *can play.*]

Well may be used either as an adjective or as an adverb. As an adjective, *well* has two meanings: "in good health" or "satisfactory."

EXAMPLES   Rammel is **well** today. [Meaning "in good health," *well* modifies the noun *Rammel.*]

                All is **well.** [Meaning "satisfactory," *well* modifies the pronoun *All.*]

NOTE   *Feel good* and *feel well* mean different things. *Feel good* means "to feel happy or pleased." *Feel well* means "to feel healthy."

EXAMPLES   I felt **good** [*happy*] when I got an A.

                He did not feel **well** [*healthy*] after lunch.

Oral Practice Using *Well* Correctly

Read the following sentences aloud, stressing the modifier *well.*

1. Everyone did *well* on the test.
2. We work *well* together.
3. Do you sing as *well* as your sister does?
4. I can't water-ski very *well.*
5. How *well* can you write?
6. All went *well* for the Korean gymnastics team.

7. Our class pictures turned out *well*.

8. The freshman goalie can block as *well* as the senior.

Exercise 2 **Using *Good* and *Well* Correctly**

Use *good* or *well* to complete each of the following sentences correctly.

EXAMPLE **1.** We danced _____ at the recital.
        1. well

1. Melba did not run as _____ during the second race.

2. The casserole looked _____ to us.

3. How _____ does she play the part?

4. Everyone could hear the huge Swiss alphorn very _____ when the man played it.

5. He certainly appears _____ in spite of his illness.

6. I gave them directions as _____ as I could.

7. The children behaved very _____.

8. Bagels with cream cheese always taste _____ to him.

9. The debate did not go as _____ as we had hoped.

10. How _____ the pool looks on such a hot day!

1. well
2. good
3. well
4. well
5. well
6. well
7. well
8. good
9. well
10. good

Comparison of Modifiers

The two kinds of modifiers—adjectives and adverbs—may be used to compare things. In making comparisons, adjectives and adverbs take different forms. The specific form that is used depends upon how many syllables the modifier has and how many things are being compared.

ADJECTIVES   This building is **tall.** [no comparison]

                 This building is **taller** than that one. [one compared with another]

                 This building is the **tallest** one in the world. [one compared with many others]

ADVERBS   I ski **frequently.** [no comparison]

                 I ski **more frequently** than she does. [one compared with another]

                 Of the three of us, I ski **most frequently.** [one compared with two others]

Comparison of Modifiers   **241**

RESOURCES

Comparison of Modifiers

Practice

■ *Language & Sentence Skills Practice,* pp. 225–230, 237

■ *Developmental Language & Sentence Skills,* pp. 79–82

---

11 b–f

USAGE

Comparison of Modifiers
Rules 11b–f (*pp. 241–248*)

OBJECTIVES

■ **To form the degrees of comparison of modifiers correctly**

■ **To use comparative and superlative forms of adjectives correctly in sentences**

■ **To proofread sentences for correct use of comparative and superlative forms**

■ **To use comparisons correctly in sentences**

DIRECT TEACHING

Modeling and Demonstration

Comparison of Modifiers. Model how to identify degrees of comparison by using the examples *This building is tall, This building is taller than that one,* and *This building is the tallest one in the world.* First, ask students which words in the first sentence are adjectives. [*This, tall*] Then, ask whether a comparison is made. [*no*] Since no comparison is made, the adjective *tall* is in the positive degree. (*This* is a demonstrative adjective.) Next, ask whether a comparison is made in the second sentence. [*yes*] Ask how many things are compared. [*two; This building, that one*] Since only two things are compared, the adjective *taller* is in the comparative degree. Finally, ask students what is compared in the third sentence. [*This building, many others in the world*] Three or more things are compared, so *tallest* is in the superlative degree. Now, have a volunteer use other examples from this chapter to demonstrate how to identify degrees of comparison.

Comparison of Modifiers   **241**

USAGE

DIFFERENTIATING INSTRUCTION

English-Language Learners

General Strategies. Frequently hearing the correct comparative forms of adjectives and adverbs will provide the aural reinforcement needed for students to learn those forms. You may want to have students take turns saying sentences aloud using the modifiers in the charts on this page and p. 243.

Spanish. Spanish speakers may need extra practice adding *–er* and *–est* because suffixes are not used to form comparatives and most superlatives in Spanish. For example, the English words *fast, faster,* and *fastest* are translated in Spanish as *rápido,* "fast"; *más rápido,* "more fast"; and *el más rápido,* "the most fast."

Vietnamese. Comparatives are expressed differently in Vietnamese. The comparison in Vietnamese follows the pattern noun+adjective+ *more than*+noun being compared, as in *Mr. Nguyen old more than Mr. Tran.* Students may use such constructions in English and may prefer the *more*+adjective form to the adjective+*–er* forms. Have students practice making comparisons in formal and informal class situations.

11b. The three degrees of comparison are the positive, the comparative, and the superlative.

Positive	Comparative	Superlative
sharp	sharper	sharpest
quickly	more quickly	most quickly
bad	worse	worst

Regular Comparison

(1) Most one-syllable modifiers form the comparative degree by adding *–er* and the superlative degree by adding *–est.*

Positive	Comparative	Superlative
meek	meeker	meekest
cold	colder	coldest
dry	drier	driest

(2) Two-syllable modifiers form the comparative degree by adding *–er* or using *more* and form the superlative degree by adding *–est* or using *most.*

Positive	Comparative	Superlative
simple	simpler	simplest
easy	easier	easiest
often	more often	most often

(3) Modifiers that have three or more syllables form the comparative degree by using *more* and the superlative degree by using *most.*

Positive	Comparative	Superlative
delicate	more delicate	most delicate
creative	more creative	most creative
carefully	more carefully	most carefully

| STYLE ✏ TIP |

Most two-syllable modifiers can correctly form the comparative and superlative degrees using either the suffixes *–er* and *–est* or the words *more* and *most.* If adding *–er* or *–est* sounds awkward, use *more* or *most.*

AWKWARD
  specialer

BETTER
  more special

(4) To show a decrease in the qualities they express, modifiers form the comparative degree by using *less* and the superlative degree by using *least*.

Positive	Comparative	Superlative
safe	less safe	least safe
expensive	less expensive	least expensive
often	less often	least often
gracefully	less gracefully	least gracefully
heartily	less heartily	least heartily

Exercise 3 Forming the Degrees of Comparison of Modifiers

Give the forms for the comparative and superlative degrees of the following modifiers.

EXAMPLE   **1.** rich
      1. richer, less rich; richest, least rich

1. sure	**4.** thankful	**7.** heavy	**10.** loyal
2. cautiously	**5.** possible	**8.** confident	
3. early	**6.** clean	**9.** seriously	

Irregular Comparison

11c. The comparative and superlative degrees of some modifiers are not formed by the usual methods.

Positive	Comparative	Superlative
good	better	best
bad	worse	worst
well	better	best
many	more	most
much	more	most
little	less	least
far	farther	farthest
	or further	*or* furthest

The word *little* also has regular comparative and superlative forms: *littler, littlest*. These forms are used to describe physical size (the **littlest** bunny). The forms *less* and *least* are used to describe an amount (**less** time).

Comparison of Modifiers   **243**

DIRECT TEACHING

Comparative and Superlative Forms

Tell students that most dictionaries list comparative and superlative forms only if there is a spelling change from one form to the other or if the forms are irregular.

DIFFERENTIATING INSTRUCTION

Special Education Students

Ask students to work in groups of three to demonstrate physically the positive, comparative, and superlative degrees of modifiers. Ask each group to select three adjectives or adverbs and practice how they would demonstrate the three degrees. Allow volunteers to perform for the class.

If some students seem particularly adept at this activity, allow them to form a group to perform improvisations for the class. Let class members suggest modifiers for the group to demonstrate without benefit of rehearsal.

PRACTICE

Guided and Independent

Review A You may wish to have students complete items 1–10 in **Review A** as guided practice and items 11–20 as independent practice.

HOMEWORK

Exercise 4 **Using Comparative and Superlative Forms of Adjectives**

Using the chart about skyscrapers that is provided below, give the correct form of an adjective for each of the following sentences.

EXAMPLE **1.** The Empire State Building is _____ than the John Hancock Center.

  1. *taller*   Answers may vary.

1. newest
2. most
3. newer
4. oldest
5. more
6. fewest
7. fewer

1. One Liberty Place, built in 1987, is the _____ of all the buildings listed.

2. The Sears Tower has the _____ stories of all the buildings listed in the chart below.

3. The Amoco Building, now known as the Aon Center, is four years _____ than the John Hancock Center.

4. The Chrysler Building is the _____ of all the buildings.

5. The Sears Tower has ten _____ stories than the John Hancock Center.

6. The Pittsburgh Plate Glass skyscraper has the _____ number of stories of all the buildings listed.

7. Pittsburgh has _____ skyscrapers on the list than Chicago has.

Sears Tower   Empire State Building   John Hancock Center   Amoco Building

SKYSCRAPERS IN THE UNITED STATES

Building	Height	Year Completed
Sears Tower, Chicago, IL	110 stories (1,454 feet)	1974
Empire State Building, New York City, NY	102 stories (1,250 feet)	1931
John Hancock Center, Chicago, IL	100 stories (1,127 feet)	1969
Amoco Building, Chicago, IL	83 stories (1,136 feet)	1973
Chrysler Building, New York City, NY	77 stories (1,046 feet)	1930
One Liberty Place, Philadelphia, PA	61 stories (945 feet)	1987
Pittsburgh Plate Glass, Pittsburgh, PA	40 stories (635 feet)	1984

8. Chicago's Sears Tower, at 1,454 feet, is the ____ building listed on the chart.

9. It would be fun to compare some of the ____ well-known buildings, too.

10. Although the Pittsburgh Plate Glass tower has the ____ stories of all the skyscrapers listed on the previous page, Pittsburgh residents think it is the most beautiful.

8. tallest

9. less

10. fewest

Review A Forming the Comparative and Superlative Degrees of Modifiers

Give the comparative and superlative forms of the following modifiers.

EXAMPLES   **1.** wasteful
             1. *more wasteful, less wasteful; most wasteful, least wasteful*

            2. *young*
             2. *younger, less young; youngest, least young*

1. sheepish	6. quick	11. furious	16. hot
2. simply	7. weary	12. enthusiastic	17. good
3. much	8. easily	13. suddenly	18. well
4. surely	9. many	14. frequently	19. bad
5. gracious	10. tasty	15. generous	20. old

Use of Comparative and Superlative Forms

11d. Use the comparative degree when comparing two things. Use the superlative degree when comparing more than two.

COMPARATIVE   The second problem is **harder** than the first.
               Luisa can perform the gymnastic routine **more gracefully** than I.
               Of the two CD players, this one costs **less**.

SUPERLATIVE   Crater Lake is the **deepest** lake in the United States.
               This is the **most valuable** coin in my collection.
               Of the three dogs, that one barks the **least**.

Review A Forming the Comparative and Superlative Degrees of Modifiers

ANSWERS

1. more (less) sheepish; most (least) sheepish
2. more (less) simply; most (least) simply
3. more (less); most (least)
4. more (less) surely; most (least) surely
5. more (less) gracious; most (least) gracious
6. quicker (less quick); quickest (least quick)
7. wearier *or* more weary (less weary); weariest *or* most weary (least weary)
8. more (less) easily; most (least) easily
9. more (fewer); most (fewest)
10. tastier *or* more tasty (less tasty); tastiest *or* most tasty (least tasty)
11. more (less) furious; most (least) furious
12. more (less) enthusiastic; most (least) enthusiastic
13. more (less) suddenly; most (least) suddenly
14. more (less) frequently; most (least) frequently
15. more (less) generous; most (least) generous
16. hotter (less hot); hottest (least hot)
17. better (worse); best (worst)
18. better (worse); best (worst)
19. worse (better); worst (best)
20. older (less old); oldest (least old)

USAGE

PRACTICE

Comparison of Modifiers

To give students practice using comparisons, ask them to choose two movies to compare and contrast. Suggest categories of evaluation for students to use, such as plot, character, special effects, and soundtrack. Encourage students to include as many comparative and superlative forms as possible. They could conclude their reviews with a star rating for each movie, from one star for poor to five stars for excellent.

EXTENSION

Relating to Writing

Divide the class into groups of four. Give each student a slip of paper with three modifiers written on it. Students are to work with their group to create a story that includes each of the modifiers—a total of twelve for each group. Encourage students to use the comparative and superlative forms when appropriate. Example story ideas include a space launch to Mars, an athletic contest between rival schools, or the arrival of surprise guests at a family reunion. The groups could read or dramatize their stories.

1. harder
2. more excited
3. best
4. most (or liveliest)
5. C

6. most

7. best

8. most

9. C (or lovelier)

10. C

Avoid the common mistake of using the superlative degree to compare two things.

NONSTANDARD   Of the two plans, this is the best one.
STANDARD   Of the two plans, this is the **better** one.

NONSTANDARD   Felicia is the youngest of the two girls.
STANDARD   Felicia is the **younger** of the two girls.

Review B Proofreading for Correct Use of Comparative and Superlative Forms

Some of the following sentences contain incorrect comparative and superlative forms. For each incorrect form, give the correct form. If a sentence is already correct, write *C*.

EXAMPLE   1. Julie and I spend the most time preparing for Cinco de Mayo than any other girls on our block.
   1. *the most—more*

1. Julie works even more hard than I do to prepare for the holiday.
2. I get exciteder about the parade and festivals, though.
3. I think Cinco de Mayo is the better holiday of the year.
4. At least it's the more lively one in our neighborhood.
5. Cinco de Mayo celebrates Mexico's most important victory over Napoleon III of France.
6. Of all the speakers each year, the mayor always gives the more stirring speech about the history of the day.
7. For me, the better part of the holiday is singing and dancing in the parade.
8. I get to wear the beautifulest dresses you've ever seen.
9. They're even more lovely than the ones worn by the girls in this picture.
10. Although these white dresses are certainly pretty, they are less colorful than mine.

11e. Include the word *other* or *else* when comparing one member of a group with the rest of the group.

NONSTANDARD   Jupiter is larger than any planet in the solar system. [Jupiter is one of the planets in the solar system and cannot be larger than itself.]

STANDARD   Jupiter is larger than any **other** planet in the solar system.

NONSTANDARD   Roland can type faster than anyone in his computer class. [Roland is one of the students in his computer class and cannot type faster than himself.]

STANDARD   Roland can type faster than anyone **else** in his computer class.

Exercise 5   **Using Comparisons Correctly in Sentences**

Write *other* or *else* to complete the meaning of each of the following sentences.

EXAMPLE   **1.** No one ＿＿ knows how much I love music.

            1. else

1. Several of my relatives think there are no ＿＿ careers from which to choose. **1.** other
2. I'd rather be a performer, playing the guitar or some ＿＿ musical instrument. **2.** other
3. A friend of mine plays the tenor saxophone better than anyone ＿＿ I've heard. **3.** else
4. Stringed instruments appeal to me more than ＿＿ kinds of instruments, such as brass. **4.** other
5. There are lutes, dulcimers, violins, cellos, sitars, harps, and many ＿＿ ancient strings. **5.** other
6. Everyone ＿＿ in my family expects me to become a music teacher. **6.** else
7. What ＿＿ could be as much fun as teaching music? **7.** else
8. The sound of acoustic music appeals to me more than anything ＿＿. **8.** else
9. Voice, strings, drums, and ＿＿ ancient ways of making music interest me. **9.** other
10. While I take guitar lessons, I will research the history of guitars and ＿＿ stringed instruments. **10.** other

Relating to Literature
Poetry. Initiate a brief discussion of the importance of word choice in poetry. Explain that because of poetry's condensed form and because poets use words to create images, word choice is particularly important. If your literature textbook contains "The Secret Heart" by Robert P. Tristram Coffin, have students read it. Ask them why they think the poet uses the superlative form *stillest* in the third line. [*Students might say that the superlative form indicates that this hour of the night differs from any other hour, thus making it special. The use of* stillest *also sets the mood of quiet and peace.*]

11f. Avoid using double comparisons.

A **double comparison** is the use of both *–er* and *more* (or *less*) or both *–est* and *most* (or *least*) to form a degree of comparison. For each degree, comparisons should be formed in only one of these two ways, not both.

| NONSTANDARD | The Asian elephant is more smaller than the African elephant. |
| STANDARD | The Asian elephant is **smaller** than the African elephant. |

| NONSTANDARD | Ribbon Falls, in Yosemite National Park, is the most beautifulest waterfall I have ever seen. |
| STANDARD | Ribbon Falls, in Yosemite National Park, is the **most beautiful** waterfall I have ever seen. |

Review C Revising for Correct Comparative and Superlative Forms

Most of the following sentences contain incorrect forms of comparison. Revise each incorrect sentence, using the correct form. If a sentence is already correct, write *C*.

EXAMPLES 1. It's the most homeliest dog in the world.
    1. *It's the homeliest dog in the world.*

    2. Which of these three is the more expensive?
    2. *Which of these three is the most expensive?*

1. other
2. The ~~most~~ largest ancient cliff dwellings in Arizona are in Navajo National Monument.
3. That modern sculpture is the ~~most~~ strangest I've ever seen.
4. more
5. (*or more sunny*)
6. Your cough sounds worse~~r~~ today.
7. C
8. other
9. Karl likes German sauerkraut ~~more~~ better than Korean kimchi.
10. C

1. The pitcher is worse at bat than any͜member of the team.
4. After watching the two kittens for a few minutes, Rudy chose to adopt the͜~~most~~ playful one.
5. This morning was ~~more~~ sunnier than this afternoon.
7. The music on this album is better for dancing than the music on that one.
8. New York City has a larger population than any͜city in the United States.
10. She was the most talented singer in the show.

The Double Negative

11g. Avoid using double negatives.

A *double negative* is the use of two negative words to express one negative idea.

Common Negative Words			
barely	never	none	nothing
hardly	no	no one	nowhere
neither	nobody	not (*or* –n't)	scarcely

Many negative words are used as modifiers.

NONSTANDARD	We don't have no extra chairs.
STANDARD	We have **no** extra chairs.
STANDARD	We do**n't** have **any** extra chairs.

NONSTANDARD	He couldn't hardly talk.
STANDARD	He **could hardly** talk.

Exercise 6 — Proofreading to Correct Double Negatives

Revise each of the following sentences to correct the double negative.   Answers will vary.

EXAMPLE	**1.**	We don't hardly have time to relax.
	1.	*We hardly have time to relax.*

1. Alejandro hasn't never been to Tennessee.
2. Because of the strong wind and heavy rain, we couldn't scarcely find our way home.
3. He never had no problem with public speaking.   **3.** any
4. The athletes don't hardly have a break between events.
5. The authorities don't allow no passenger cars on Michigan's popular Mackinac Island.   **5.** any
6. By the time I had made spring rolls for everyone else, I didn't have nothing left for myself.   **6.** anything
7. I never listen to no one who gossips.   **7.** anyone
8. Your answer doesn't make no difference to me.   **8.** any
9. The copier doesn't have no ink.   **9.** any
10. Don't never use both *not* and *scarcely* together.

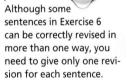

─HELP─

Although some sentences in Exercise 6 can be correctly revised in more than one way, you need to give only one revision for each sentence.

The Double Negative
Rule 11g *(pp. 249–251)*

OBJECTIVE

- To revise sentences to eliminate double negatives

DIRECT TEACHING

Modeling and Demonstration

Double Negatives. Model how to avoid double negatives by using the incorrect example *We don't have no extra chairs.* First, ask students which words in the sentence are negatives. [*don't, no*] Explain that only one negative is needed to express a negative idea. Ask how the sentence would read with one of the negatives eliminated. [*We don't have any extra chairs* or *We have no extra chairs.*] Point out that either negative can be eliminated to correct a double negative. Now, have a volunteer use another example to demonstrate how to identify and correct a double negative.

DIFFERENTIATING INSTRUCTION

English-Language Learners

Spanish. Students whose native language is Spanish may have difficulty avoiding double negatives. In Spanish, double and triple negatives are sometimes used in the same sentence. Acknowledge the correctness of this usage in Spanish, but stress that double negatives should be avoided in English.

USAGE

RESOURCES

The Double Negative

Practice

- *Language & Sentence Skills Practice*, p. 231

Guided and Independent

Reviews You may wish to use Review D as guided practice. Then, have students complete Review E as independent practice.

HOMEWORK

DIFFERENTIATING INSTRUCTION

Advanced Learners

Point out to students that some people maintain that double negatives are fundamentally illogical and should be avoided for that reason. Ask students to write a brief explanation of how double negatives can be considered illogical, and have volunteers share their explanations with the class. [*The traditional argument says that two negatives equal a positive, because in mathematics the product of the multiplication of two negative numbers is always positive. In effect, the negatives cancel one another out.*]

┌HELP─

Although some sentences in Reviews D and E can be correctly revised in more than one way, you need to give only one revision for each sentence.

Review D **Using Modifiers Correctly**

Most of the following sentences contain errors in the use of modifiers. Revise each incorrect sentence to correct the error. If a sentence is already correct, write *C*.   Answers may vary.

EXAMPLE   **1.** We don't never stay after school.

   1. *We never stay after school.*

1. Which did you like ~~best~~—the book or the movie?   **1.** better
2. Gina has more ideas for the festival than anyone.   **2.** else
3. The Suez Canal is ~~more~~ longer than the Panama Canal.
4. I can't hardly reason with her.
5. Jean and Dominic work ~~good~~ as a team.   **5.** well
6. Ben's bruise looks worse today than it did yesterday.   **6.** C
7. They haven't said ~~nothing~~ to us about it.   **7.** anything
8. Of the two singers, Mariah Carey has the ~~best~~ voice.   **8.** better
9. Which has better sound, your stereo or mine?   **9.** C
10. The cast performed extremely ~~good~~.   **10.** well

Review E **Proofreading for Correct Use of Modifiers**

Most of the following sentences contain errors in the use of modifiers. If a sentence contains an error, give the correct form of the modifier. If a sentence is already correct, write *C*. Answers may vary.

EXAMPLE   **1.** Of the three programs, the one on Japanese plays was the more interesting.

   1. *more—most*

1. Before the program, I didn't ~~hardly~~ know anything about Japanese theater.
2. I learned that Japanese theater is much ~~more old~~ than theater in many other countries.   **2.** older
3. *Noh* and *kabuki* are the two ~~most~~ best-known kinds of Japanese drama.
4. Dating from the Middle Ages, *noh* is different from any form of Japanese theater.   **4.** other

250 Chapter 11   Using Modifiers Correctly

5. *Noh* plays, which are narrated in an ancient language, are performed more slowly than *kabuki* plays.   5. C

6. *Noh* plays are seen less oftener than the more modern and dramatic *kabuki* plays.

7. In the West, we don't have ~~no~~ theater like Japan's *bugaku* for the Imperial Court.   7. any

8. I was more interested in Japan's puppet theater, the *bunraku*, than anyone in my class.   8. else

9. Puppet theater performers have a ~~more~~ harder job than other theater performers.

10. I didn't ~~never~~ know that it takes three people to operate one *bunraku* puppet.

Placement of Modifiers

Notice how the meaning of the following sentence changes when the position of the phrase *from Canada* changes.

EXAMPLE   The professor **from Canada** gave a televised lecture on famous writers. [The phrase modifies *professor*.]

The professor gave a televised lecture on famous writers **from Canada.** [The phrase modifies *writers*.]

The professor gave a televised lecture **from Canada** on famous writers. [The phrase modifies *gave*.]

11h. Place modifying words, phrases, and clauses as near as possible to the words they modify.

A modifier that seems to modify the wrong word in a sentence is called a ***misplaced modifier.***

MISPLACED   My aunt has almost seen all of the documentaries directed by Camille Billops.

CORRECT   My aunt has seen **almost** all of the documentaries directed by Camille Billops.

A modifier that does not clearly modify another word or word group in a sentence is called a ***dangling modifier.***

DANGLING   While vacationing in Mexico, snorkeling in the bay was the most fun.

CORRECT   **While vacationing in Mexico,** we had the most fun snorkeling in the bay.

MEETING THE CHALLENGE

A dangling modifier often occurs when a sentence is in the passive voice. Rewriting sentences in the active voice not only eliminates many dangling modifiers but also makes your writing more interesting and lively.

The following sentence contains a dangling modifier. Rewrite the sentence in the active voice to remove the dangling modifier.

1. Having emptied the drawers, the desk was found to be easier to carry.

ANSWER
Student responses will vary. Here is one possibility.

1. Having emptied the drawers, we found the desk easier to carry.

Placement of Modifiers   **251**

USAGE

Placement of Modifiers

Rule 11h *(pp. 251–258)*

OBJECTIVES

■ To revise sentences to correct misplaced and dangling modifiers

■ To correct misplaced prepositional phrases in sentences

■ To correct misplaced and dangling participial phrases in sentences

■ To correct sentences with misplaced adjective clauses

DIRECT TEACHING

Modeling and Demonstration

Placement of Modifiers. Model how a modifier should be placed as close as possible to the word or words it modifies, using the example *The professor from Canada gave a televised lecture on famous writers.* First, ask students which word the prepositional phrase *from Canada* modifies. [*professor*] Explain that *from Canada* immediately follows the noun *professor* because a modifier describes the word or words that are closest to it. Point out that if this prepositional phrase followed the noun *writers,* the meaning of the sentence would be different. Now, have a volunteer use another example from the chapter to demonstrate how a modifier should be placed as close as possible to the word it modifies.

USAGE

─HELP─

Although some sentences in Exercise 7 can be correctly revised in more than one way, you need to give only one revision for each sentence.

5. you must wash

7. cold water

9. From Canine Assistants

10. My sister was / and her

Reference Note

For more information about **prepositions**, see page 66. For more about **prepositional phrases**, see pages 68 and 96.

Exercise 7 **Correcting Misplaced Modifiers and Dangling Modifiers**

Revise each of the following sentences to correct the italicized misplaced or dangling modifier.

Answers may vary. Optional commas are underscored.

EXAMPLE 1. *Surprised,* the finish line was only fifty yards away!

1. *I was surprised that the finish line was only fifty yards away!*

1. Both Dr. Albert Sabin and Dr. Jonas Salk succeeded in *almost* developing polio vaccines at the same time.   **1.** almost

2. Kristi Yamaguchi won a gold medal ~~in the 1992 Olympics~~ *for figure skating.*   **2.** In the 1992 Olympics,

3. *Looking out the airplane window,* the volcano seemed ready to erupt.   **3.** I saw a / that

4. *As a new student,* the teacher introduced me to my classmates.   **4.** When I was

5. *Before eating supper,* your hands ~~must be washed.~~

6. Bessie Coleman dreamed of starting a flying school for African Americans *who was the first U.S. woman to earn an international pilot's license.*   **6.** , who was . . . license,

7. *Hot and tired,* ~~cold water was what~~ the team needed.

8. Did you look for the black-and-white photographs taken by Grandfather *in that old shoe box?*   **8.** in that old shoe box

9. My uncle got a service dog ~~from Canine Assistants~~ *that could open cabinets, pull a wheelchair, and go for help.*

10. *Thrilled,* ~~my sister's~~ face lit up with excitement.

Prepositional Phrases

A *prepositional phrase* consists of a preposition, a noun or pronoun called the *object of the preposition,* and any modifiers of that object.

A prepositional phrase used as an adjective should generally be placed directly after the word it modifies.

MISPLACED   This book describes Nat Turner's struggle for freedom by Judith Berry Griffin.

CORRECT   This book **by Judith Berry Griffin** describes Nat Turner's struggle for freedom.

A prepositional phrase used as an adverb should be placed near the word it modifies.

MISPLACED   Spanish explorers discovered gold along the river that runs near my house during the 1500s. [Did the river run near my house during the 1500s?]

CORRECT   **During the 1500s,** Spanish explorers discovered gold along the river that runs near my house.

CORRECT   Spanish explorers discovered gold **during the 1500s** along the river that runs near my house.

Avoid placing a prepositional phrase in a position where it can modify either of two words. Place the phrase so that it clearly modifies the word you intend it to modify.

MISPLACED   Emily said before sunset it might get colder. [Does the phrase modify *said* or *might get*?]

CORRECT   Emily said it might get colder **before sunset.** [The phrase modifies *might get.*]

CORRECT   **Before sunset** Emily said it might get colder. [The phrase modifies *said.*]

Exercise 8 **Correcting Misplaced Prepositional Phrases**

Find the underlined misplaced prepositional phrases in the following sentences. Then, revise each sentence, placing the phrase near the word it modifies. Answers may vary.

EXAMPLE   1. I read that a satellite was launched in the news today.
          1. *I read in the news today that a satellite was launched.*

1. The nature photographer told us about filming a herd of water buffalo in class today.
2. The quick steps of the Texas clog-dancing teams amazed us on the wooden stage.
3. The robotic mannequins drew a huge crowd in the futuristic window display.
4. Many people watched the Fourth of July fireworks in their cars.
5. We saw several capuchin monkeys on vacation in Costa Rica.
6. My aunt promised me on Saturday she will take me to the symphony.
7. There is one gymnast who can tumble as well as vault on our gymnastics team.

TIPS & TRICKS

To find misplaced prepositional phrases in a piece of your own writing, try this method: Look at each sentence, and circle each prepositional phrase. Then, draw an arrow from the circled phrase to the word it modifies.

Is the phrase near the word it modifies? If the phrase is used as an adjective, does it come right after the word it modifies? If not, move the misplaced phrase to the correct spot in your sentence.

HELP

Although some sentences in Exercise 8 can be correctly revised in more than one way, you need to give only one revision for each sentence.

USAGE

DIFFERENTIATING INSTRUCTION

Special Education Students
You may wish to have a helper make enlarged copies of **Exercise 8** so that students can cut the sentences apart and rearrange the parts to eliminate misplaced prepositional phrases.

Placement of Modifiers   **253**

CONTENT-AREA CONNECTIONS

Science
Writing Directions. To demonstrate the misunderstandings that misplaced modifiers can cause, have students work with a set of directions from a laboratory manual. Ask them to work in pairs to rewrite directions for an experiment, deliberately using misplaced modifiers to obscure the meaning of the directions. Have all students work on the same experiment. To illustrate how many different meanings a set of directions can have if modifiers are misplaced, ask one member from each pair to share the pair's work.

8. That man bought the rare painting of Pocahontas <u>with the briefcase</u>.

9. The model posed gracefully in front of the statue <u>in the designer gown</u>.

10. We saw the trapeze artist swinging dangerously through our field binoculars.

Participial Phrases

A *participial phrase* consists of a verb form—either a present participle or a past participle—and any modifiers or complements the participle has. A participial phrase modifies a noun or a pronoun.

Like a prepositional phrase, a participial phrase should be placed as close as possible to the word it modifies.

MISPLACED	Bandits chased the stagecoach yelling wildly. [Was the stagecoach yelling wildly?]
CORRECT	**Yelling wildly,** bandits chased the stagecoach.

MISPLACED	The vase was lying on the floor broken into several pieces. [Was the floor broken into pieces?]
CORRECT	The vase, **broken into several pieces,** was lying on the floor.

To correct a dangling participial phrase, supply a word that the phrase can modify, or change the phrase to a clause.

DANGLING	Jogging down the sidewalk, my ankle was sprained. [Was my ankle jogging down the sidewalk?]
CORRECT	Jogging down the sidewalk, **I** sprained my ankle.
CORRECT	I sprained my ankle **while I was** jogging down the sidewalk.

DANGLING	Dressed in warm clothing, the cold was no problem. [Was the cold dressed in warm clothing?]
CORRECT	Dressed in warm clothing, **we** had no problem with the cold.
CORRECT	**Since we were** dressed in warm clothing, the cold was no problem.

Reference Note

For more information on **participial phrases,** see page 102. For guidelines on using **commas with participial phrases,** see page 321.

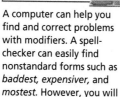

COMPUTER TIP

A computer can help you find and correct problems with modifiers. A spell-checker can easily find nonstandard forms such as *baddest, expensiver,* and *mostest.* However, you will need to examine the placement of phrase and clause modifiers yourself.

---

254 **Chapter 11** Using Modifiers Correctly

MINI-LESSON | **Mechanics**

Using Commas Correctly. Tell students that commas set off nonessential phrases and clauses, not essential ones. Write these examples on the chalkboard.

Elizabeth, **excited about the beautiful**

autumn day, went hiking. [*nonessential participial phrase*]

The fans **waiting at the side door** entered first. [*essential participial phrase*]

USAGE

Correcting Misplaced Modifiers

To help students correct misplaced modifying phrases or clauses, have them use the following procedure.

1. Find the simple subject and the simple predicate of the main clause.

2. Identify any direct or indirect objects or subject complements in the main clause.

3. Bracket all modifying phrases and clauses and determine what word or words they modify in the sentence.

Students can then revise the sentences by placing the modifiers near the words they modify.

Correcting Misplaced and Dangling Participial Phrases

Revise each incorrect sentence to eliminate the misplaced or dangling modifier. You may need to add, delete, or rearrange words. If a sentence is already correct, write *C.* Answers may vary.

EXAMPLE
1. Dressed in our clown costumes, the police officer waved and smiled.

   1. *Seeing us dressed in our clown costumes, the police officer waved and smiled.*

   or

   Dressed in our clown costumes, we saw the police officer wave and smile.

1. Standing on the dock, the boat didn't look safe to the sailors.
2. Pat found a secret passage exploring the old house.
3. Having brought in plenty of firewood, the cabin soon warmed up, and we fell asleep.
4. Wanting to see more of Mexico City, our vacation grew from one to two weeks.
5. Questioned by reporters, the governor's view on the matter became clear.
6. Suffering from a leg cramp, Al's chance of winning was slight.
7. Reading a book, my cat crawled into my lap.
8. The old suit hanging in the closet would make the perfect costume for the play.
9. Balancing precariously on the high wire, the tricks that the tightrope walker performed were amazing.
10. Exhausted after hiking in the Florida Everglades, a tall, cool glass of water was a welcome sight.

─HELP─
Although some of the sentences in Exercise 9 can be correctly revised in more than one way, you need to give only one answer for each sentence.

1. the sailors thought
2. Exploring the old house,
3. After we
4. Because we wanted
5. governor made his
6. Because he was
7. As I was
8. C
9. tricks
10. we welcomed the sight of

Adjective Clauses

An *adjective clause* is a subordinate clause that modifies a noun or a pronoun. Most adjective clauses begin with a relative pronoun—*that, which, who, whom,* or *whose.*

Like an adjective phrase, an adjective clause should be placed directly after the word it modifies.

MISPLACED The book was about insects that we read. [Did we read the insects?]

CORRECT The book **that we read** was about insects.

Reference Note

For more information on **adjective clauses,** see page 124. For more about **using commas with adjective clauses,** see page 321.

USAGE

My oldest brother, **who is in college,** is studying chemistry. [*nonessential adjective clause*]

The car **that Mom bought** is in excellent condition. [*essential adjective clause*]

Remind students that a nonessential phrase or clause adds information that isn't needed to understand the meaning of the sentence. For more information, refer students to **Chapter 14: Punctuation.**

DIFFERENTIATING INSTRUCTION

Learners Having Difficulty

To help students manipulate adjective clauses within sentences, create sentence strips with some of the sentences in **Exercise 10.** Have each student cut a sentence strip apart to remove the misplaced adjective clause. Then, have the student rearrange the pieces of the sentence to place the clause close to the word it modifies.

Exercise 10 Correcting Misplaced Adjective Clauses

POSSIBLE ANSWERS

1. The boy that won the contest is from my school.

2. In our heavy boots we tiptoed over the ice, which had begun to crack.

3. The jade sculpture that my cousin broke was by a famous Chinese artist.

4. On nice days we sometimes play soccer in one of the parks that are near the school.

5. Did the telethon that was on for more than thirty-six hours achieve its goal?

6. Nisei Week, which is celebrated by Japanese Americans in Los Angeles, is in August.

7. The friendly man, whose name I can't remember, said hello to my mother.

8. The sweater that has a V-shaped neck belongs to my best friend.

9. My married sister who lives in Ohio has the flu.

10. That documentary, which will be broadcast in the fall, was filmed in several countries.

MISPLACED	A little boy walked up to Jenny who was lost. [Who was lost, the little boy or Jenny?]
CORRECT	A little boy **who was lost** walked up to Jenny.
MISPLACED	His parents traded an old television for a new CD player, which they no longer wanted. [Did his parents no longer want a new CD player?]
CORRECT	His parents traded an old television, **which they no longer wanted,** for a new CD player.

┌HELP─

Although some of the sentences in Exercise 10 can be correctly revised in more than one way, you need to give only one answer for each sentence.

Exercise 10 Correcting Misplaced Adjective Clauses

Find the misplaced adjective clauses in the following sentences. Then, revise each sentence, placing the clause near the word it modifies.

EXAMPLE
1. I retyped the first draft on clean paper, which I had corrected.

1. *I retyped the first draft, which I had corrected, on clean paper.*

or

After I corrected the first draft, I retyped it on clean paper.

1. The boy is from my school that won the contest.
2. We tiptoed over the ice in our heavy boots, which had begun to crack.
3. The jade sculpture was by a famous Chinese artist that my cousin broke.
4. We sometimes play soccer in one of the parks on nice days that are near the school.
5. Did the telethon achieve its goal that was on for more than thirty-six hours?
6. Nisei Week is in August, which is celebrated by Japanese Americans in Los Angeles.
7. The friendly man said hello to my mother, whose name I can't remember.
8. The sweater belongs to my best friend that has a V-shaped neck.
9. My married sister has the flu who lives in Ohio.
10. That documentary was filmed in several countries, which will be broadcast in the fall.

Learning for Life

Continued on pp. 257–258

Writing a Newspaper Ad. Ask each student to prepare a newspaper ad for a product he or she wishes to sell. Tell students it is important to use strong, clear modifiers to create a vivid impression of the product's value. Specify that the ad should

be 8 1/2 x 11 inches in size and may contain graphics, but the text of the ad should be the primary means of communicating the product's worth.

Allow students to work in small groups to brainstorm lists of products. Encourage

Most sentences in the following paragraph contain misplaced or dangling modifiers. They may be words, prepositional phrases, participial phrases, or adjective clauses. Revise each sentence that contains a misplaced or dangling modifier. If a sentence is already correct, write *C*.

EXAMPLE
1. Living in cold and treeless areas, snow houses are built by some Native Arctic people.
1. *Living in cold and treeless areas, some Native Arctic people build snow houses.*

[1] You've probably seen pictures of houses on television built of snow. [2] Knowing that these houses are called igloos, other facts about them may be new to you. [3] At one time, the word *igloo*, which means "shelter," applied to all types of houses.[4] However, *igloo* has come to mean houses now built of snow. [5] For igloos, large blocks of snow are stacked together, which are used only during the winter. [6] Adapting to their environment long ago, snow houses provided protection against the bitter cold. [7] Looking at the drawing below, the three steps in the building of an igloo are shown. [8] First, blocks are carefully cut by the builders of snow. [9] Arranged in a circle about ten feet across, the builders slant the blocks inward. [10] The finished igloo that you see is dome shaped and has a hole at the top.

┌HELP┐

Although some of the sentences in Review F can be correctly revised in more than one way, you need to give only one answer for each sentence.

Placement of Modifiers **257**

Review F Proofreading for Misplaced Modifiers and Dangling Modifiers

POSSIBLE ANSWERS

1. You've probably seen on television pictures of houses built of snow.

2. Although you know that these houses are called igloos, other facts about them may be new to you.

3. C

4. However, *igloo* has now come to mean houses built of snow.

5. For igloos, which are used only during the winter, large blocks of snow are stacked together.

6. Adapting to their environment long ago, the native people built snow houses for protection against the bitter cold.

7. The drawing below shows the three steps in the building of an igloo.

8. First, blocks of snow are carefully cut by the builders.

9. The builders arrange the blocks in a circle about ten feet across and slant them inward.

10. C

USAGE

---

them to select products that have well-known competitors so the use of the comparative and superlative forms of modifiers is natural. You might want to display newspaper and magazine advertisements to serve as models. Encourage students to

notice the way modifiers are used in the model ads.

Remind students that although many ads make use of catchy titles or sentence fragments to attract attention, misplaced modifiers can distract and confuse readers.

TEACHING TIP

TEACHING TIP

Review G Explain to students that moving a misplaced modifier closer to the word it modifies may not be the best revision tactic. Instead, a sentence may need to be reworded for clarity. Write the following revisions of sentence 1 on the chalkboard to show students that the second revision is clearer.

1. During last night's charity concert, the singing group was protected by guards from being swarmed.

2. During last night's charity concert, guards protected the singing group from being swarmed.

Review G **Using Modifiers Correctly**

In each of the following sentences, a modifier is used incorrectly. The mistake may result from (1) a misuse of *good* or *well*, (2) an incorrect comparison, (3) the use of a double negative, or (4) a misplaced or dangling modifier. Revise each sentence so that it is clear and correct. Answers may vary.

EXAMPLE   1. That was the more entertaining concert I have ever seen.

　　　　　1. *That was the most entertaining concert I have ever seen.*

1. During last night's charity concert, the singing group was protected from being swarmed by guards.   1. guards protected

2. The group played before an extremely enthusiastic crowd performing most of their old hits as well as several new tunes.   2. , which performed most . . . tunes,

3. Years ago the singers wore strange costumes and makeup so that fans couldn't hardly tell what their faces looked like.

4. Bored, these gimmicks no longer appealed to the group's fans after a while.   4. bored

5. The band finally chose the most simply tailored look of the two looks they had considered.   5. more

6. Enthusiastic about the group's new look, a change in its performance style was barely noticed by the fans.   6. the fans barely noticed

7. Most fans couldn't never tell how nervous the singers were the first time they appeared in public after changing their style.

8. "That was the most scariest performance of my career," one singer remarked.

9. Cheering heartily, the singers' fears were relieved.   9. Because of the hearty

10. Both the concert and the picnic did exceptionally good at raising funds.   10. well

Learning for Life   **Continued from p. 257**

If students use word-processing or desktop publishing software to create their ads, have them print out their drafts, including any graphics they intend to use. Ask students to work in groups of four to evaluate each draft, focusing on the clear use of modifiers.

Numerals in brackets refer to rules tested by the items in the Chapter Review.

1. [11f]
2. better [11c, d]
3. [11g]
4. taller [11d, b(1)]
5. [11c, f]
6. any [11g]
7. most [11d, c]
8. more [11b(3), d]
9. [11f, c]
10. (or more easy) [11f]

Chapter Review

A. Using the Correct Forms of Modifiers

The following sentences contain errors in the use of modifiers. Rewrite each sentence to correct the errors.
Answers may vary.

1. Of all the characters in the movie, I think the gardener is the ~~most~~ funniest.
2. Alan thinks that this soup tastes ~~more~~ good than the others.
3. I couldn~~'t~~ hardly believe that she said that.
4. Yolanda is the ~~tallest~~ of the twins.
5. The house on Drury Avenue is the one we like the best~~est~~.
6. The book doesn't cost much, but I don't have ~~no~~ money.
7. They offer so many combinations that I don't know which one I like ~~more~~.
8. The movie made me ~~curiouser~~ about the Muslim period in Spanish history.
9. There's nothing I like ~~more~~ better to eat for supper than barbecued chicken.
10. Why doesn't the teacher ask questions that are ~~more~~ easier?

B. Correcting Misplaced and Dangling Modifiers

Each of the following sentences contains a misplaced or dangling modifier in italics. Rewrite each sentence so that it is clear and correct. Answers may vary.

11. we could not find [11h]
12. in our school [11h]
13. soundly sleeping [11h]
14. that I wanted to read [11h]
15. in a magazine, [11h]
16. We were alarmed when [11h]
17. the hikers thought [11h]

11. *Searching for hours,* the missing retainer ~~could not be found.~~
12. The library has several books about dinosaurs ~~in our school.~~
13. *Sleeping soundly,* Harry woke his father when supper was ready.
14. The book is not in the library ~~that I wanted to read.~~
15. Aunt Lucia found a coupon for free recipes ~~in a magazine.~~
16. *Alarmed,* a sudden gust of wind swept through the camp and battered our tent.
17. *Camping in the wilderness of the Big Thicket,* the night seemed long and eerie.

Chapter Review   **259**

ASSESSING

Monitoring Progress
Chapter Review. To assess student progress, you may want to compare the types of items missed on the **Diagnostic Preview** with those missed on the **Chapter Review.** If students have not made significant progress, you may want to refer them to **Chapter 17: Correcting Common Errors, Exercises 16–21,** for additional practice.

USAGE

RESOURCES

Using Modifiers Correctly
Review
■ *Language & Sentence Skills Practice,* pp. 236–239

Assessment
■ *Formal Assessment*
■ *Progress-Monitoring Tests,* pp. 21–22, 48
■ *Test Generator* *(Teacher One Stop DVD-ROM)*

18. they ate [11h]
19. As we watched them [11h]
20. we saw/catch [11h]

18. *After eating all their food,* we put the cats outside.
19. *Floating across the sky,* we could see shapes in the clouds.
20. *Sitting in the bleachers,* the outfielder caught the ball right in front of us.

C. Using Comparisons Correctly in Sentences

Write the following sentences, and complete the meaning of each sentence by using *other* or *else*.

21. else [11e]
22. other [11e]
23. other [11e]
24. else [11e]
25. else [11e]
26. else [11e]
27. other [11e]
28. other [11e]
29. else [11e]
30. other [11e]

21. Sharon sings better than anyone.
22. Rather than watch TV, I think I'll read *Adventures of Huckleberry Finn* or some book.
23. New York City has more inhabitants than any U.S. city.
24. Everyone in my class thinks my Spanish is better than I do.
25. The sun is brighter than anything in our solar system.
26. Riding a bike down a breezy lane in early summer is more fun than anything.
27. Marcy likes New Orleans better than any city in the United States.
28. Sharon would rather play kettledrums than any percussion instrument in the orchestra.
29. No one knows how much I miss Mexico.
30. The tulips Marcia and I planted last fall bloomed sooner than any flowers in our garden.

D. Proofreading a Paragraph for Correct Use of Modifiers and Comparative and Superlative Forms

Some of the sentences in the following paragraph contain incorrect uses and forms of modifiers. Write each sentence, giving the correct form or forms where needed. If a sentence is already correct, write *C*.

31. [11g]
32. most [11b(3), d]
33. C [11b(3), d]
34. he was raised in [11h]
35. hardest [11b(1), d]

[31] Before I saw this article on African American actors, I didn't hardly read anything about Sidney Poitier. [32] In his time, he was one of the popularest male leads in Hollywood. [33] His background is one of the most interesting things about him. [34] Born to poor tomato growers, south Florida and the Bahamas were where he was raised. [35] Poitier worked at some of the most hard jobs you can imagine before making his Broadway debut in

1946. [36] In 1963, his performance in the film *Lilies of the Field* won him an Academy Award as ~~better~~ actor. [37] In many ways, 1967 has been his ~~successfullest~~ year so far. [38] *In the Heat of the Night; To Sir, With Love;* and *Guess Who's Coming to Dinner* all came out that year, and they were some of the world's ~~favoritest~~ movies. [39] Still a Bahamian citizen, Poitier was appointed ambassador to Japan in 1997 by the Bahamian government. [40] The life of Sidney Poitier is certainly different from that of any movie star.

36. best [11c, d]
37. most [11b(3), d]
38. most [11b(3), d]
39. C [11h]
40. other [11e]

Writing Application
Using Modifiers in a Letter

Placement of Modifiers You have just received a letter from a favorite aunt who is a professional athlete. She wants to hear about your sports activities and any sports events you've been to or seen on TV. Write a letter to your aunt, telling her about your activities. Place modifying phrases and clauses correctly.

Prewriting You'll first need to choose a sports activity or event to write about. You may write about your own experiences in a school or community sport, or you may use your imagination. Before you begin writing, make notes about the activity or event you find most interesting.

Writing As you write your first draft, try to include specific details that will interest your aunt. Be sure to use the proper form for a personal letter.

Revising Read your finished letter. Is it interesting and lively? If not, revise it by adding more adjectives, adverbs, and action verbs to improve your descriptions.

Publishing Underline the prepositional phrases, participial phrases, and adjective clauses. Check to see that they are correctly placed near the words they modify. Check your letter for errors in spelling and punctuation. You and your classmates may want to post the letter on a class bulletin board or Web page.

Writing Application
Prewriting Tip. In the writing activity, students are asked to use modifiers in letters about their sports activities. You may want to let students who have little interest in sports write about any extracurricular activities in which they are involved.

Scoring Rubric. While you will want to pay particular attention to students' use of modifiers, you will also want to evaluate overall writing performance. You may want to give a split score to indicate development and clarity of the composition as well as usage skills.

USAGE

CHAPTER

12

A Glossary of Usage

Common Usage Problems

STANDARDS FOCUS

Grade-Level Standards

(Boldface indicates concepts that are taught and tested in this chapter.)

■ Language Convention 1.0: **Students write and speak with a command of standard English conventions appropriate to this grade level.**

■ Grammar 1.4: **Edit written manuscripts to ensure that correct grammar is used.**

■ Spelling 1.6: **Use correct spelling conventions.**

Prerequisite/Review Standard

■ Grammar 1.4: Demonstrate the mechanics of writing (e.g., quotation marks, commas at end of dependent clauses) and appropriate English usage (e.g., pronoun reference).

Standard Coming Up in the Next Grade Level

■ Grammar and Mechanics of Writing 1.3: Demonstrate an understanding of proper English usage and control of grammar, paragraph and sentence structure, diction, and syntax.

▼

INTRODUCING THE CHAPTER

■ Some of the common usage problems treated in this chapter involve correctly distinguishing between words that sound similar but have different meanings, such as *affect/effect*, *than/then*, *their/there/they're*, and *your/you're*. Other rules and

(continued)

Terms in brackets refer to concepts tested by the items in the Diagnostic Preview.

1. broke [*bust, busted*]
2. all ready[*all ready, already*]
3. isn't [*ain't*]

Diagnostic Preview

Identifying and Correcting Errors in Usage

One sentence in each of the following sets contains an error in formal, standard usage. Choose the letter of the sentence that contains an error. Then, revise the sentence, using formal, standard English. Revisions may vary.

EXAMPLE **1.** **a.** The chicken tastes bad.
  b. Where is the book about pandas at?
  c. There was agreement among the five dancers.

  1. *b.* *Where is the book about pandas?*

1. **a.** Bring your notes when you come over.
  b. The glass dish ~~busted~~. broke
  c. He could have danced.

2. **a.** Jennifer drew an apple.
  b. The cold affects that kind of plant.
  c. We are ~~already~~ all ready to go.

3. **a.** Manuel says that he ~~ain't~~ isn't going.
  b. She went everywhere.
  c. We have fewer chairs than we need.

CHAPTER RESOURCES

Internet

■ go.hrw.com (keyword: HLLA)

Planning

■ *Teacher One Stop DVD-ROM*

■ *On Course: Mapping Instruction*

■ *Family Involvement Activities: A Guide to Standards Mastery*

Practice & Review

■ *Language & Sentence Skills Practice,* pp. 245–249; 250–252

■ *Developmental Language & Sentence Skills,* pp. 87–92

Application & Enrichment

■ *Language & Sentence Skills Practice,* pp. 253, 256; 244, 254–255

4. a. They danced ~~good~~ at the party.
  b. If I had sung, you would have laughed.
  c. You ought to help.

5. a. It's cold.
  b. Samuel made ~~alot~~ of friends.
  c. Its knob is broken.

6. a. Teach me a song from the musical.
  b. That story is rather interesting.
  c. ~~Who's~~ dog is that?

7. a. Mr. Barnes is here for the meeting.
  b. I know why he left.
  c. Those ~~kind~~ of bikes are expensive.

8. a. These taste like oranges.
  b. Sing as she does.
  c. ~~Whose~~ in charge here?

9. a. Please come inside the house.
  b. I am ~~real~~ happy.
  c. The reason she laughed was that your dog looked funny.

10. a. ~~Take~~ me the book when you come over.
  b. Your forehand has improved somewhat.
  c. He sings better than I do.

11. a. Your coat is beautiful.
  b. You're a fast runner.
  c. I cannot leave ~~without~~ I wash the dishes first.

12. a. She is the student who plays the violin.
  b. We have only a short way to go.
  c. We read that a new store is opening in that ~~there~~ mall.

13. a. I ~~use~~ to read mysteries.
  b. Set that crate down over here.
  c. This hat is old.

14. a. I gave you ~~them~~ books.
  b. They bought themselves new shirts.
  c. There is the cat.

15. a. Sit down anywhere that looks comfortable.
  b. They're smiling.
  c. Where is the team ~~at~~?

4. well [*good, well*]
5. a lot [*a lot*]
6. Whose [*who's, whose*]
7. kinds [*kind, sort, type*]
8. Who's [*who's, whose*]
9. very [*real*]
10. Bring [*bring, take*]
11. unless [*without, unless*]
12. [*this here, that there*]
13. used [*use to, used to, suppose to, supposed to*]
14. those [*them*]
15. [*at*]

examples illustrate differences between standard and nonstandard usage that do not affect meaning but that can affect the impression one makes. The chapter also explains some expressions that are acceptable in informal English but that should be avoided in formal communication.

■ The chapter closes with a **Chapter Review** for checking students' mastery of common usage. In the **Writing Application,** students are asked to employ formal English usage in writing and presenting a speech.

■ For help in integrating this chapter with writing assignments in *Holt Literature and Language Arts,* see the **Teaching Strands** chart on pages T24–T25.

USAGE

ASSESSING

Entry-Level Assessment
Diagnostic Preview. If you notice that some students are having problems with usage in their compositions, the **Diagnostic Preview** will provide information about each student's ability to recognize common usage problems and to use standard, formal English. After reviewing students' performances on the **Diagnostic Preview,** you may decide to have them work on specific expressions or clusters of problems with which they have difficulty.

Differentiating Instruction
■ *UA: Differentiating Instruction*
■ *UA: Supporting Instruction in Five Languages*
■ *Family Involvement Activities: In Five Languages*

Assessment
■ *Formal Assessment*

■ *Progress-Monitoring Tests, pp. 23–24, 48*
■ *Test Generator (Teacher One Stop DVD-ROM)* 🎧

Other Language Resources
■ *Spelling Lessons & Activities*
■ *WordSharp: An Interactive Vocabulary Tutor*
■ *Reading and Writing Transparencies*

16. an [*a, an*]
17. effects [*affect, effect*]
18. nowhere [*anyways, anywheres, every-wheres, nowheres, somewheres*]
19. somewhat [*some, somewhat*]
20. can [*hardly, scarcely*]
21. to [*try and*]
22. fewer [*fewer, less*]
23. as [*like, as*]
24. have [*could of*]
25. Let [*leave, let*]

16. a. Gail did not feel well.
    b. Have a orange.
    c. You invited everyone except Cai.

17. a. I ate an apple with breakfast this morning.
    b. Sunscreen lessens the affects of the sun's rays.
    c. We already read the book in class.

18. a. Your answers are all right.
    b. They went nowheres.
    c. He looks as if he has lost something.

19. a. Nancy's ankle hurts some.
    b. The funds were divided among the three cities.
    c. The pipe burst.

20. a. I cannot hardly dance.
    b. Warm days make me feel good.
    c. It's pretty.

21. a. He must be somewhere.
    b. I can scarcely ride this bike.
    c. I try and like him because he is kind.

22. a. We have less shelves than we need.
    b. Those kinds of shirts are warm.
    c. This morning I could have slept longer.

23. a. Latoya doesn't put her books on the floor.
    b. Learn how to play this game.
    c. Do like he does.

24. a. They are inside the house.
    b. I could of eaten the entire sandwich.
    c. He placed the chair next to the table himself.

25. a. Leave my cats sleep.
    b. Do you need those books?
    c. Did you accept the apology?

About the Glossary

This chapter provides a compact glossary of common problems in English usage. A **glossary** is an alphabetical list of special terms or expressions with definitions, explanations, and examples. You'll notice that some examples in this glossary are labeled *nonstandard, standard, formal,* or *informal.*

The label **nonstandard** identifies usage that is suitable only in the most casual speaking situations and in writing that attempts to re-create casual speech. **Standard** English is language that is grammatically correct and appropriate in formal and informal situations. **Formal** identifies usage that is appropriate in serious speaking and writing situations (such as in speeches and in compositions for school). The label **informal** indicates standard usage common in conversation and in everyday writing such as personal letters. In doing the exercises in this chapter, be sure to use only standard English.

Formal	Informal
angry	steamed
unpleasant	yucky
agreeable	cool
very impressive	totally awesome
accelerate	step on it

a, an   Use *a* before words beginning with a consonant sound. Use *an* before words beginning with a vowel sound.

EXAMPLES   He did not consider himself **a** hero.

Market Avenue is **a** one-way street. [*One-way* begins with a consonant sound.]

An oryx is a large antelope.

We waited in line for **an** hour. [*Hour* begins with a vowel sound.]

accept, except   *Accept* is a verb that means "to receive." *Except* may be either a verb or a preposition. As a verb, *except* means "to leave out" or "to exclude"; as a preposition, *except* means "other than" or "excluding."

EXAMPLES   I **accept** your apology.

Children were **excepted** from the admission fee.

Mark has told all his friends **except** Trenell.

┌HELP─
The word *diction* is often used to refer to word choice. Your choice of words affects the tone and clarity of what you say and write. When you know which usages are formal, informal, standard, and nonstandard, you can choose diction that is appropriate to any audience.

Reference Note
For a list of **words often confused,** see page 380. Use the index at the end of the book to find discussions of other usage problems.

Reference Note
For more about **verbs,** see page 184. For more about **prepositions,** see page 66.

A, An–Bad, Badly
(pp. 265–267)

OBJECTIVE

■ **To identify correct usage**

DIRECT TEACHING

Modeling and Demonstration

A, An. Model how to correctly use *a* and *an* with the example *Market Avenue is a one-way street.* First, ask students whether *one-way* begins with a vowel or a consonant sound. [*consonant sound*] Next, ask whether *a* is used correctly. [*yes*] Then, ask whether *a* could be replaced with *an* here. [*no*] *A* is used before words beginning with a consonant sound, and *an* is used before words beginning with a vowel sound. Point out that the sound that begins a word, and not the actual letter, is what determines whether *a* or *an* should be used. Now, have a volunteer use another example from this chapter to demonstrate how to use *a* and *an* correctly.

RESOURCES

A, An–Bad, Badly
Practice
■ *Language & Sentence Skills Practice,* p. 245
■ *Developmental Language & Sentence Skills,* pp. 87–88

RETEACHING

Correct Usage

Mnemonics. Encourage students to develop personal memory devices to help them remember usage rules for sets of words that sound similar or the same. A memory device for *affect/effect,* for example, might be "If you *alter* something you *affect* it. If you *enact* something, you put it into *effect.*" Assign each pair of students a set of words, and ask them to come up with memory aids of this type.

DIFFERENTIATING INSTRUCTION

Advanced Learners

To inspire students to use alternatives for the overused *a lot,* bring in a copy of *An Exaltation of Larks* by James Lipton. This illustrated book lists traditional names for groups of animals, such as a "pride of lions." Lipton then coins a series of modern group names such as a "slouch of models" and a "wince of dentists." Have students work in small groups to come up with collective terms for numerous items or groupings in their world—books, teachers, homework, music videos, and so on.

Reference Note

For more about **nouns,** see page 25.

Reference Note

For more information about **adjectives,** see page 38. For more about **adverbs,** see page 61.

| S T Y L E | T I P |

Many writers overuse *a lot.* Whenever you run across *a lot* as you revise your own writing, try to replace it with a more exact word or phrase.

EXAMPLE

The Spaniards explored a lot of North America and South America.

The Spaniards explored **vast areas** [or **thousands of square miles**] of North America and South America.

affect, effect   *Affect* is a verb meaning "to influence." *Effect* used as a verb means "to bring about." Used as a noun, *effect* means "the result of some action."

EXAMPLES   The bad punt did not **affect** the outcome of the game.

The government's reforms **effected** great changes.

Read more about the **effects** of pollution.

ain't   Avoid using this word in speaking and writing; it is nonstandard English.

all ready, already   *All ready* means "completely prepared." *Already* means "previously."

EXAMPLES   The mechanic checked the engine parts to make sure they were **all ready** for assembly.

We have **already** served the refreshments.

all right   Used as an adjective, *all right* means "unhurt" or "satisfactory." Used as an adverb, *all right* means "well enough." *All right* should be written as two words.

EXAMPLES   Linda fell off the horse, but she is **all right.** [adjective]

Your work is **all right.** [adjective]

You did **all right** at the track meet. [adverb]

a lot   *A lot* should always be written as two words.

EXAMPLE   Her family donated **a lot** of money to the Red Cross.

among   See **between, among.**

anyways, anywheres, everywheres, nowheres, somewheres   Use these words without a final *s.*

EXAMPLE   I did not go **anywhere** [not *anywheres*] yesterday.

as   See **like, as.**

as if   See **like, as if, as though.**

at   Do not use *at* after *where.*

NONSTANDARD   Where is your saxophone at?
STANDARD   Where is your saxophone?

266   Chapter 12   A Glossary of Usage

CONTENT-AREA CONNECTIONS

Art

Illustrating Usage. Tell students that they will be creating an illustrated book to teach the words featured in this chapter. Suggest that students work with the words that gave them difficulty in the **Diagnostic Preview.**

Once students have seen the results of their previews, pair each student with another student who needs practice with the same words. Then, have students brainstorm visual ways to teach the words they need to practice. Students might create cartoon

bad, badly   *Bad* is an adjective. *Badly* is an adverb.

EXAMPLES   The fish smells **bad.** [*Bad* modifies the noun *fish*.]

The parrot recited the poem **badly.** [*Badly* modifies the verb *recited*.]

Exercise 1   **Identifying Correct Usage**

Choose the <u>correct word or word group</u> from the pair given in parentheses in each of the following sentences.

EXAMPLE   1. Korea has been in the news (*alot, a lot*) in recent years.

1. *a lot*

1. South Korea occupies the lower half of (*a, an*) peninsula between China and Japan.
2. According to an old Korean saying, you are never out of sight of mountains (*anywheres, anywhere*) in Korea.
3. The 1988 Olympic games in Seoul had a truly dramatic (*affect, effect*) on Korea's world image.
4. I looked on a map of Asia to find out where Korea's Lotte World (*is, is at*).
5. This cultural and athletic showcase is (*a, an*) attraction to visitors in Seoul.
6. Many Koreans come to the United States to join family members who (*all ready, already*) live here.
7. In Korea some girls practice on their neighborhood swings so that they won't perform (*bad, badly*) in swinging contests during *Tano*, a spring festival.
8. Most boys hope they do (*allright, all right*) in *Tano* wrestling matches.
9. In 1446, King Sejong the Great required the Korean people to use a new alphabet, which scholars and government officials readily (*accepted, excepted*).
10. Even if you (*ain't, aren't*) interested in dancing, you'd probably enjoy watching the lively Korean folk dancers shown here.

STYLE   TIP

In informal usage the expression "feel badly" has become acceptable, even though it is ungrammatical English.

INFORMAL
Marcia felt badly about her low grade.

FORMAL
Marcia felt **bad** about her low grade.

DIFFERENTIATING INSTRUCTION

English-Language Learners

Cantonese. Cantonese does not have the equivalent of the English articles *a, an,* or *the.* Students may omit articles (*I like book*), add articles unnecessarily (*She goes to the school every morning*), or confuse the two main types of articles (*Please lend me the pen and the piece of paper*). Articles are unstressed in English and difficult to hear for those whose language does not use articles. When introducing nouns, use the article with the noun. (*This is a noun, and this is an adjective.*) Also, have students practice the definite article *the* by using it to point to specific items.

Teacher: Which book do you want?
Student: The one with the red cover.

USAGE

---

drawings, three-dimensional clay figures, or even a tableau or computer graphics presentation to illustrate the concepts. Be sure that each important set of words is covered, but allow more than one pair of students to work on a specific set of words, if necessary.

Assign a photographer to make copies of any display that cannot be pasted directly into a book. Assign a volunteer to compile word entries, along with their illustrations, alphabetically into a book to be kept in the classroom for easy reference.

Because–Hardly, Scarcely

(pp. 268–271)

OBJECTIVE

- To identify correct usage

DIRECT TEACHING

Modeling and Demonstration

Between, Among. Model how to identify correct usage of *between* and *among* by using the example *In homeroom, Carlos sits between Bob and me.* First, ask what part of speech *between* is. [*preposition*] Next, ask what the object or objects of the preposition are. [*Bob, me*] Then ask if *between* is used correctly in this sentence. [*yes*] Explain that *between* should be used when referring to two things at a time, and *among* should be used when referring to a group of three or more. Now, have a volunteer use another example from the chapter to demonstrate how to identify correct usage of *between* and *among*.

---

because See **reason . . . because.**

between, among Use *between* when referring to two things at a time, even when they are part of a group containing more than two.

EXAMPLES   In homeroom, Carlos sits **between** Bob and me.

Some players practice **between** innings. [Although a game has more than two innings, the practice occurs only between any two of them.]

Use *among* when referring to a group rather than to separate individuals.

EXAMPLES   We saved ten dollars **among** the three of us. [As a group the three saved ten dollars.]

There was disagreement **among** the fans about the coach's decision. [The fans are thought of as a group.]

bring, take *Bring* means "to come carrying something." *Take* means "to go carrying something." Think of *bring* as related to *come* and of *take* as related to *go*.

EXAMPLES   **Bring** your skateboard when you come to my house this weekend.

Please **take** these letters with you to the post office when you go.

bust, busted Avoid using these words as verbs. Use a form of *burst* or *break* or *catch* or *arrest*.

EXAMPLES   The bubbles **burst** [not *busted*] when they touched the ceiling.

The officer **arrested** [not *busted*] the thief.

Reference Note

For more about **helping verbs,** see page 52.

could of Do not write *of* with the helping verb *could*. Write *could have*. Also avoid *ought to of, should of, would of, might of,* and *must of*.

EXAMPLE   Reva **could have** [not *could of*] played the piano.

Of is also unnecessary with *had*.

EXAMPLE   If I **had** [not *had of*] seen her, I would have said hello.

268   **Chapter 12**   A Glossary of Usage

RESOURCES

Because–Hardly, Scarcely

Practice

- *Language & Sentence Skills Practice,* p. 246
- *Developmental Language & Sentence Skills,* pp. 88–89

doesn't, don't   *Doesn't* is the contraction of *does not. Don't* is the contraction of *do not.* Use *doesn't,* not *don't,* with *he, she, it, this, that,* and singular nouns.

EXAMPLES   He **doesn't** [not *don't*] know how to swim.

The price **doesn't** [not *don't*] include tax.

effect   See **affect, effect.**

everywheres   See **anyways,** etc.

except   See **accept, except.**

fewer, less   *Fewer* is used with plural words. *Less* is used with singular words. *Fewer* tells "how many"; *less* tells "how much."

EXAMPLES   Do **fewer** plants grow in the tundra than in the desert?

Do desert plants require **less** water?

good, well   *Good* is an adjective. Do not use *good* as an adverb. Instead, use *well.*

NONSTANDARD   Nancy sang good at the audition.

STANDARD   Nancy sang **well** at the audition.

Although *well* is usually an adverb, *well* may also be used as an adjective to mean "healthy."

EXAMPLE   He didn't look **well** after eating the entire quiche all by himself.

NOTE   *Feel good* and *feel well* mean different things. *Feel good* means "to feel happy or pleased." *Feel well* means "to feel healthy."

EXAMPLES   I felt **good** [happy] when I got an A on my report.

Chris stayed home because he did not feel **well** [healthy] yesterday.

had of   See **could of.**

had ought, hadn't ought   The verb *ought* should not be used with *had.*

NONSTANDARD   Eric had ought to help us; he hadn't ought to have missed our meeting yesterday.

| TIPS & TRICKS |

Use *fewer* with things that can be counted. Use *less* with things that cannot be counted.

EXAMPLE
Yolanda has (*fewer, less*) pets than Kristi does.

ASK
Can you count pets? [yes]

ANSWER
Yolanda has **fewer** pets than Kristi does.

Reference Note

For more about the **differences between good and well,** see page 240.

DIRECT TEACHING

Correcting Misconceptions

***Fewer* and *Less*.** Students sometimes confuse the standard usage of *fewer* and *less*. Give them this simple rule that they can use to revise their writing: *Fewer* is used with things you can count; *less* is used with things you can't count. Have each student compose four sentences using *fewer* or *less* to modify nouns, applying the rule to the sentences.

APPLICATION

Activity

***Good, Well*.** Have students work in pairs for three minutes to generate two lists for the *good, well* entry: one list of things that might make someone feel good and a second list of things that might make someone feel well. Have each pair of students work with another pair to review the lists. Then, have students cross off items that appear on both pairs' lists and any item that is incorrectly classified. Students can then score one point for each item that remains and see which pair has the most points.

DIFFERENTIATING INSTRUCTION

Learners Having Difficulty

Some students may be better able to identify correct usage by listening to examples read aloud. Assign each student one of the following glossary entries, and ask him or her to write examples to demonstrate the usage rules.

bring, take	good, well
doesn't, don't	hardly, scarcely
fewer, less	

Once students have completed their sentences, have them read their examples out loud, emphasizing the key words. Students should listen carefully, using the examples to help reinforce their learning. If the examples are incorrect, have the students fix the errors orally with help from you or from classmates.

EXTENSION

Critical Thinking

Metacognition. After students complete **Exercise 2** and **Review A,** ask them to write brief answers to the following questions:

1. How did you approach the two different kinds of exercises?

2. Why was it easier to spot some usage errors than others?

3. Are there particular usage errors you need to work on? How do you plan to correct them?

STANDARD   Eric **ought to** help us; he **oughtn't to have** missed our meeting yesterday.

or

Eric **should** help us; he **shouldn't have** missed our meeting yesterday.

hardly, scarcely   The words *hardly* and *scarcely* convey negative meanings. They should not be used with another negative word to express a single negative idea.

EXAMPLES   I **can** [not *can't*] **hardly** read your handwriting.

We **had** [not *hadn't*] **scarcely** enough food.

Reference Note

For more about **double negatives,** see page 249.

Exercise 2 Identifying Correct Usage

Choose the <u>correct word or word group</u> from the pair given in parentheses in each sentence.

EXAMPLE   1. When you come to my house, (*bring, take*) that interesting book about U.S. presidents.

     1. bring

1. Theodore Roosevelt must have felt (*good, well*) about having the teddy bear named for him.
2. The letter *S* in Harry S. Truman's name (*don't, doesn't*) stand for anything.
3. William Henry Harrison served as president (*fewer, less*) days than any other president.
4. Herbert Hoover (*could of, could have*) kept his presidential salary, but he gave it to charity.
5. A president who (*doesn't, don't*) throw the first ball of the baseball season breaks a tradition started in 1910.
6. Theodore Roosevelt and his cousin Franklin Roosevelt were presidents of the United States; (*between, among*) them, they served a total of twenty years in office.
7. Abraham Lincoln's ability to write (*well, good*) helped him succeed in politics.
8. Woodrow Wilson believed that countries (*had ought, ought*) to work together in the League of Nations.
9. I (*can hardly, can't hardly*) imagine a president training horses, but Ulysses S. Grant did.
10. When Zachary Taylor went to the White House in 1849, he (*brought, took*) his old war horse with him.

Review A **Correcting Errors in Usage**

Each of the following sentences contains at least one error in
usage. Identify ~~each error~~, and write the correct word or words.

EXAMPLE   **1.** Between the various American Indian peoples, there
were alot of stories about mythological figures.

    1. Between—Among; alot—a lot

                              1. affected/badly

1. The Creek people believed that goblins, giants, and
dwarfs ~~effected~~ their lives ~~bad~~.   **2.** an/everywhere

2. The Micmacs believed that ~~a~~ enormous being named
Glooskap created humans and animals ~~everywheres~~.

3. This picture shows how humans ~~busted~~ into life because
of Glooskap's magic.   **3.** burst

4. The other animals don't appear to think that Glooskap's
new creations are ~~allright~~.   **4.** all right

5. The Tehuelche people of South America tell the story
of Elal, a hero who brought fire to where the people
were ~~at~~.

6. When the Mayas heard the thunderous approach of
their god Chac, they knew he was ~~taking~~ rain to their
dry fields.   **6.** bringing

7. The Pawnee people, who lived on the plains, ~~couldn't~~
hardly help noticing where the stars were.   **7.** could

8. They told stories about Morning Star, who fought really
~~good~~ and defeated star monsters.   **8.** well   **9.** accepted

9. One sad Tewa story is about Deer Hunter, who ~~had~~ ought to
have ~~excepted~~ the death of his wife, White Corn Maiden.

10. Her death ~~busted~~ poor Deer Hunter's heart, causing him to
disobey the laws of his people.   **10.** broke

Michael McCurdy, wood engraving.

he, she, it, they   Do not use an unnecessary pronoun after
a noun. This error is called the ***double subject.***

NONSTANDARD   Annika Sorenstam she is my favorite golfer.

STANDARD   Annika Sorenstam is my favorite golfer.

hisself   *Hisself* is nonstandard English. Use *himself.*

EXAMPLE   Ira bought **himself** [not *hisself*] a new silk tie.

how come   In informal situations, *how come* is often used
instead of *why*. In formal situations, *why* should be used.

A Glossary of Usage   **271**

RESOURCES

He, She, It, They–Like, As If, As Though
Practice
■ *Language & Sentence Skills Practice,* p. 247
■ *Developmental Language & Sentence Skills,* pp. 89–90

**DIFFERENTIATING
INSTRUCTION**

Learners Having Difficulty
Have students write two sample sentences to demonstrate the correct
form of any usage error they missed
in **Review A.** If many students do
poorly on the review, you might create a new practice exercise by using
the students' sentences.

***He, She, It, They–
Like, As If, As
Though***
(pp. 271–274)

O B J E C T I V E S

■ **To identify correct usage**

■ **To proofread for standard
English usage**

DIRECT TEACHING

**Modeling and
Demonstration**

He, She, It, They. Model how to
identify and correct double-subject
errors by using the incorrect example
Anna she is my favorite golfer. First,
ask students what the pronoun *she*
refers to in this sentence. [*Anna*]
Next, ask what the subject of the
sentence is. [*Anna*] Then, ask what
function *she* has in the sentence.
[She *is also a subject.*] Point out
that a pronoun (in this case *she*)
should not be used along with its
antecedent in a double subject. Ask
students how the sentence can be
written. [*Anna is my favorite golfer*
or *She is my favorite golfer.*] Now,
have a volunteer use another example from this chapter to demonstrate
how to identify and correct double-
subject errors.

APPLICATION

Activity

Its, It's. You can help reinforce the correct use of *its* and *it's* by playing a game with the whole class. Make ten flashcards, five with *its* on them and five with *it's*. Shuffle the cards and draw them randomly. Hold up a card, and ask a student volunteer to compose a sentence, correctly using the word on the card. If the student uses the word incorrectly, ask another volunteer to use the word correctly in a sentence. Continue this activity until you think the concept is sufficiently reinforced.

EXTENSION

Relating to Writing

Activity. Ask students to work in pairs to write short scripts involving a teacher who is trying to help a student overcome usage problems in the student's speech. Remind students that the teacher must be tactful and kind as he or she corrects the student's usage errors.

| TIPS & TRICKS |

When you are proofreading your own writing, find each use of *its* and *it's* and try substituting *it is* or *it has*. If the sentence sounds right with the substitution, the contraction *it's* is probably correct. If not, the possessive form *its* is probably correct.

EXAMPLE

Tourists flock to the island because it's so beautiful. [Does "Tourists flock to the island because *it is* so beautiful" make sense? Yes. *It's* is correct.]

Reference Note

For more about **possessive pronouns,** see page 225. For more about **contractions,** see page 354.

Reference Note

For more about **clauses,** see Chapter 6.

| INFORMAL | How come Nori's not here yet? |
| FORMAL | **Why** is Nori not here yet? |

its, it's   *Its* is a personal pronoun in the possessive form. *It's* is a contraction of *it is* or *it has*.

EXAMPLES   **Its** handle is broken. [possessive pronoun]

It's a hot day. [contraction of *it is*]

It's been a good trip. [contraction of *it has*]

kind, sort, type   The words *this, that, these,* and *those* should agree in number with the words *kind, sort,* and *type.*

EXAMPLES   Whitney likes **this kind** of music.

Those kinds of math problems are easy.

kind of, sort of   In informal situations, *kind of* and *sort of* are often used to mean "somewhat" or "rather." In formal English, *somewhat* or *rather* is preferred.

| INFORMAL | He seemed kind of embarrassed. |
| FORMAL | He seemed **somewhat** embarrassed. |

learn, teach   *Learn* means "to acquire knowledge." *Teach* means "to instruct" or "to show how."

EXAMPLES   I am **learning** how to type.

My father is **teaching** me how to type.

leave, let   *Leave* means "to go away" or "to depart from." *Let* means "to allow" or "to permit."

NONSTANDARD	Leave her go to the concert.
STANDARD	**Let** her go to the concert.
STANDARD	Let's **leave** on time for the concert.

less   See **fewer, less.**

lie, lay   See page 203.

like, as   In informal situations, the preposition *like* is often used instead of the conjunction *as* to introduce a clause. In formal situations, *as* is preferred.

EXAMPLE   I looked up several words in my dictionary, **as** [not *like*] our teacher had suggested.

272   **Chapter 12**   A Glossary of Usage

MINI-LESSON   Usage

Apostrophes. The use of *it's* instead of *its* as a possessive pronoun may stem from students' confusion of possessive nouns, which take an apostrophe (*the dog's bone*), with possessive personal pronouns, which do not (*its bone*). To emphasize that *its* is a possessive pronoun, write the following word groups on the chalkboard, and have students change them by using possessive pronouns.

- the eagle's eyes [*its eyes*]
- Bob's shoes [*his shoes*]

like, as if, as though   Informally, the preposition *like* is used for the compound subordinating conjunction *as if* or *as though*. In formal situations, *as if* or *as though* is preferred.

EXAMPLES   They behaved **as if** [not *like*] they hadn't heard him.

You looked **as though** [not *like*] you knew the answer.

Exercise 3   **Identifying Correct Usage**

For each of the following sentences, choose from the pair in parentheses the word or word group that is correct according to the rules of formal, standard English.

EXAMPLE   **1.** I'd like to know (*how come, why*) folk tales about animals that play tricks have always been popular.
       1. why

1. People all over the world enjoy stories about a creature that outsmarts (*it's, its*) enemies.
2. (*These kind, These kinds*) of stories are often referred to as trickster tales.
3. In the tales of American Indians of the Southwest, the trickster (*Coyote, Coyote he*) causes disorder and confusion.
4. In one story, Coyote (*kind of, somewhat*) playfully scatters stars across the sky.
5. In South American tales, the trickster known as Fox talks (*like, as though*) he is clever, but he really isn't.
6. Fox doesn't even understand (*how come, why*) a vulture beats him in a tree-sitting contest.
7. Our teacher (*learned, taught*) us about Brer Rabbit, a famous trickster in African American folklore.
8. Brer Rabbit gets (*himself, hisself*) into trouble by trying to trick Brer Fox.
9. In a tale from India, a monkey and a (*crocodile, crocodile they*) play tricks on each other.
10. Just (*as, like*) Aesop's tortoise defeats the hare, Toad wins a race against Donkey in a Jamaican tale.

Oral Practice   **Proofreading for Standard Usage**

Read aloud the sentences on the following page. Then, read aloud each sentence again, changing any ~~nonstandard or informal English~~ to formal, standard English.

- Karina's grades [*her grades*]
- the flowers we bought [*our flowers*]
- Billy's and Maria's project [*their project*]
- the trolley car's colors [*its colors*]

For more about possessive pronouns, direct students to **Chapter 10: Using Pronouns Correctly;** for more about apostrophes, direct them to **Chapter 15: Punctuation.**

EXTENSION

Relating to Writing

Activity. Pair students and write the following words on the chalkboard.

accept, except	good, well
affect, effect	its, it's
between, among	than, then
bring, take	

Have students take turns writing sentences using the words from the pairs given. If the first student uses *affect,* the second student should use *effect,* and so on. Students do not need to use every word pair; you may wish to specify the number of sentences each student should write. Challenge students to create a story by keeping the sentences on the same topic. You might wish to assign one student in each pair to proofread the story and the other to illustrate it.

EXAMPLE   **1.** Mr. Arlen had ought to be careful when he operates a crane like the one shown here.

   1. *Mr. Arlen ought to be careful when he operates a crane like the one shown here.*

Revisions may vary.

1. Mr. Arlen hisself owns and operates the crane.   **1.** himself

2. He learned Tony how to operate the crane.   **2.** taught

3. Those kind of machines are quite complicated but fun, Mr. Arlen says.   **3.** kinds

4. Tony he is young and learns new things very quickly.

5. He says these type of boom needs plenty of room in which to do its work.   **5.** this type of

6. The reason how come he looks high, low, and around is that the boom and the cab can move in a full circle.   **6.** why

7. Pulleys for the boom lines make the boom kind of like an arm that lifts and lowers things.   **7.** somewhat

8. As Mr. Arlen says, leave the crane do the heavy lifting.   **8.** let

9. Crane operators they can't be too careful.

10. Just like you would expect, cranes can easily unload heavy ship cargoes.   **10.** as

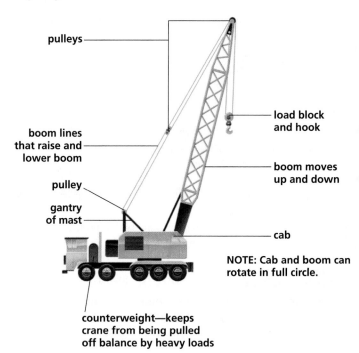

pulleys

load block and hook

boom lines that raise and lower boom

boom moves up and down

pulley

gantry of mast

cab

NOTE: Cab and boom can rotate in full circle.

counterweight—keeps crane from being pulled off balance by heavy loads

might of, must of See **could of.**

nowheres See **anyways,** etc.

of Do not use *of* after other prepositions such as *inside, off,* and *outside.*

EXAMPLES He quickly walked **off** [not *off of*] the stage.

She waited **outside** [not *outside of*] the school.

What is **inside** [not *inside of*] this cabinet?

ought to of See **could of.**

real In informal situations, *real* is often used as an adverb meaning "very" or "extremely." In formal situations, *very* or *extremely* is preferred.

INFORMAL My mother is expecting a real important telephone call.

FORMAL My mother is expecting a **very** important telephone call.

reason . . . because In informal situations, *reason . . . because* is often used instead of *reason . . . that.* However, in formal situations, you should use *reason . . . that.*

INFORMAL The reason I did well on the test was because I had studied hard.

FORMAL The **reason** I did well on the test was **that** I had studied hard.

rise, raise See page 205.

scarcely, hardly See **hardly, scarcely.**

should of See **could of.**

sit, set See page 201.

some, somewhat Do not use *some* for the adverb *somewhat.*

NONSTANDARD My fever has gone down some.

STANDARD My fever has gone down **somewhat.**

somewheres See **anyways,** etc.

sort See **kind, sort, type.**

sort of See **kind of, sort of.**

take See **bring, take.**

┌─HELP─
You can also revise your sentence to avoid using *reason.*

EXAMPLE
I did well on the test **because** I had studied hard.

A Glossary of Usage 275

Might of, Must of–Try and
(pp. 275–277)
OBJECTIVE

■ To identify correct usage

USAGE

DIRECT TEACHING

Modeling and Demonstration

Of. Model how to identify and correct errors in using *of* with the incorrect example *She waited outside of the school.* First, ask students to identify any prepositions in the sentence. [*outside, of*] Next, ask what the preposition *outside* describes. [*where she waited*] Then, ask whether the preposition *of* is necessary to the meaning of the sentence. [*no*] Explain that *of* should not be used with prepositions such as *inside, off,* and *outside* because *of* does not add meaning to a sentence when used with these prepositions. Now, have a volunteer use another example from the chapter to demonstrate how to identify and correct errors in using *of.*

DIFFERENTIATING INSTRUCTION

English-Language Learners
General Strategies. Some of the usage guidelines in this chapter depend on context, and others do not. For example, choosing among *their, there,* and *they're* depends on knowing other words in the sentence. However, the use of *themselves* rather than *theirselves* is always correct, regardless of context. You may wish to help students make reference lists of words and expressions that are preferred regardless of context.

RESOURCES

Might of, Must of–Try and
Practice
■ *Language & Sentence Skills Practice,* p. 248
■ *Developmental Language & Sentence Skills,* pp. 91–92

English-Language Learners

Vietnamese. Vietnamese students may confuse similar sounding words in English, such as *sit* and *set*, because Vietnamese lacks the vowel sounds found in *sit, had, fire,* and *hour.* Vietnamese-speaking students may substitute a close sound, but confusion may result with similar sounding words.

Also, Vietnamese uses a limited number of consonant sounds at the ends of words, which may cause problems with students' grammar and ability to comprehend English. Vietnamese students need opportunities to practice spoken English in an encouraging environment where correct pronunciation is modeled. They should work in groups with native English speakers whenever possible.

EXTENSION

Relating to Speaking

Activity. Assign one or two glossary entries to each student, and have students prepare minipresentations about their entries. Ask them to explain the usage rules in their own words and to create examples to demonstrate them. Students may also wish to include original memory devices. Students should give their minipresentations in front of the class, keeping the presentations under two minutes in length and focusing on effective speaking skills such as eye contact, voice control, and emphasis.

---

teach   See **learn, teach.**

than, then   *Than* is a subordinating conjunction; *then* is an adverb telling *when.*

EXAMPLES   Great Danes are larger **than** Dobermans are.

I finished my reading. **Then** I wrote some letters.

that   See **who, which, that.**

that there   See **this here, that there.**

their, there, they're   *Their* is the possessive form of *they. There* is used to mean "at that place" or to begin a sentence. *They're* is a contraction of *they are.*

EXAMPLES   **Their** team won the game. [*Their* tells whose team.]

We are planning to go **there** during spring vacation. [*There* tells at what place.]

There were twenty people at the party. [*There* is used to begin the sentence but does not add to the meaning of the sentence.]

They're the best players on the team. [*They're* is a contraction of *they are.*]

theirself, theirselves   *Theirself* and *theirselves* are nonstandard English. Use *themselves.*

EXAMPLE   They cooked **themselves** [not *theirself* or *theirselves*] a special dinner.

them   *Them* should not be used as an adjective. Use *those.*

EXAMPLE   Please put **those** [not *them*] cans in the recycling bin.

this here, that there   The words *here* and *there* are not necessary after *this* and *that.*

EXAMPLE   Do you like **this** [not *this here*] shirt or **that** [not *that there*] one?

this kind, sort, type   See **kind,** etc.

try and   In informal situations, *try and* is often used instead of *try to.* In formal situations, *try to* should be used.

INFORMAL   Try and be on time for the party.

FORMAL   **Try to** be on time for the party.

COMPUTER TIP

A word-processing program can help you find and correct usage errors in your own writing. For instance, if you tend to confuse the words *their, there,* and *they're,* you can use the search feature to find those words in your writing. Then, check each one to make sure you have used the correct spelling.

Exercise 4 **Identifying Correct Usage**

For each of the following sentences, choose from the pair in parentheses the <u>word or word group that is correct</u> according to the rules of formal, standard English.

EXAMPLE   1. Athletes find the physical and mental challenges of their sports (*real, very*) exciting.

    1. *very*

1. Yosemite Park Ranger Mark Wellman discovered new strengths (*inside of, inside*) himself when he climbed El Capitan, a rock formation in Yosemite National Park.
2. Wellman, paralyzed from the waist down, was anxious to (*try and, try to*) climb the 3,595-foot rock.
3. In this picture, Wellman strains (*somewhat, some*) as he climbs the granite peak.
4. The reason Wellman was strong enough for the climb is (*because, that*) he had trained for a year.
5. Like Wellman, many other people are able to swim, hike, cycle, and canoe in spite of (*there, their*) disabilities.
6. (*Them, Those*) newer, lighter, easier-to-use wheelchairs have helped many people enjoy a wider variety of sports activities.
7. Nowadays, national and state parks offer more services for physically challenged people (*than, then*) they used to offer.
8. (*This here, This*) magazine article lists dozens of sports organizations for athletes who have disabilities.
9. You (*might of, might have*) heard of the National Wheelchair Basketball Association, which sponsors teams and organizes tournaments.
10. Other athletes pride (*themselves, theirselves*) on being able to play wheelchair tennis.

use to, used to, suppose to, supposed to   Do not leave off the *d* when you write *used to* or *supposed to*.

EXAMPLES   We **used to** [not *use to*] live in Phoenix, Arizona.

I was **supposed to** [not *suppose to*] be home by dinner.

way, ways   Use *way*, not *ways*, in referring to a distance.

EXAMPLE   They still had a long **way** [not *ways*] to go.

A Glossary of Usage   **277**

RESOURCES

Use to, Used to, Suppose to, Supposed to–Your, You're
Practice
- *Language & Sentence Skills Practice*, pp. 249–252
- *Developmental Language & Sentence Skills*, p. 92

Use to, Used to, Suppose to, Supposed to–Your, You're
(pp. 277–280)

OBJECTIVE

■ **To identify correct usage**

DIRECT TEACHING

Modeling and Demonstration

Use to, Used to, Suppose to, Supposed to. Model how to identify and correct common errors in verb forms by using the incorrect example *I was suppose to be home by dinner.* First, ask students what word or word group makes up the verb in this sentence. [*was suppose*] Next, ask whether this verb phrase is in the correct form. [*no*] Ask what the correct form is. [*was supposed*] Point out that the *d* should not be left off the verb *supposed* in *supposed to,* just as the *d* should not be left off the verb *used* in *used to.* Now, have a volunteer use another example from the chapter to demonstrate how to identify and correct common errors in verb forms.

Reference Note

For more about **relative pronouns,** see page 35.

MEETING THE CHALLENGE

Write a review of a story or book you have recently read. Your analysis should include the correct use of at least five entries in the Glossary of Usage as well as the title of the work and its author. Proofread your review, checking for correct grammar, spelling, and punctuation.

well   See **good, well.**

when, where   Do not use *when* or *where* incorrectly to begin a definition.

NONSTANDARD	An infomercial is where a TV program is actually a long advertisement.
STANDARD	An infomercial is a TV program **that is** actually a long advertisement.

where   Do not use *where* for *that.*

EXAMPLE   I read **that** [not *where*] Sue won the tournament.

who, which, that   The relative pronoun *who* refers to people only; *which* refers to things only; *that* refers to either people or things.

EXAMPLES   Kim is the only one **who** got the right answer. [person]

My bike, **which** has ten speeds, is for sale. [thing]

He is the one person **that** can help you. [person]

This is the ring **that** I want to buy. [thing]

who's, whose   *Who's* is the contraction of *who is* or *who has. Whose* is used as the possessive form of *who* or as an interrogative pronoun.

EXAMPLES   I wonder **who's** keeping score.

Who's been using my computer?

Do you know **whose** baseball glove this is?

Whose is this?

without, unless   Do not use the preposition *without* in place of the subordinating conjunction *unless.*

EXAMPLE   My mother said that I can't go to the game **unless** [not *without*] I finish my homework first.

would of   See **could of.**

your, you're   *Your* is the possessive form of *you. You're* is the contraction of *you are.*

EXAMPLES   **Your** dinner is on the table.

You're one of my closest friends.

FAMILY/COMMUNITY ACTIVITY   *Continued on pp. 279–280*

Writing Thank-you Notes.   Students often have occasion to write thank-you notes and letters for gifts, favors, and other acts of kindness. While the tone should be informal and friendly, thank-you notes and letters should be free of usage errors.

Ask each student to write a thank-you letter to a family member, friend, or acquaintance. If students can't think of any recent real-life occasions for thank-you letters, ask them to think about such occasions from the past or about fictional occasions.

Choose the correct word or word group from the pair given in parentheses in each sentence.

EXAMPLE   **1.** Roseanne (*use, used*) to know the names of all thirty-three state birds.

      1. used

1. I read (*where, that*) some states have the same state birds.
2. The mockingbird, (*which, who*) mimics other birds, is the state bird of Texas, Mississippi, Arkansas, Tennessee, and Florida.
3. "Mimicking" is (*when a person or an animal imitates another, imitating another person or an animal*).
4. (*Your, You're*) probably familiar with New Mexico's state bird, the roadrunner, from cartoons.
5. My grandfather, (*who's, whose*) a fisherman, often hears the loud calls of Minnesota's state bird, the common loon.
6. The bluebird, the state bird of Missouri and New York, (*use, used*) to come around our house.
7. The bird on a baseball player's cap can represent both a state and a team quite (*good, well*).
8. (*Without, Unless*) I'm mistaken, you can guess what state claims the Baltimore oriole.
9. It travels a long (*way, ways*) between its summer and winter homes.
10. Would you (*of, have*) guessed that the cardinal is the official bird of the most states?

Review B Correcting Errors in Usage

Most of the following sentences contain an error in the use of formal, standard English. If a sentence contains an error, identify the error and write the correct form. If a sentence is already correct, write *C*.   Answers may vary.

EXAMPLE   **1.** It was the pirate Jean Laffite which established an early settlement on Texas's Galveston Island.

      1. which—who (or *that*)

1. Since ancient times, pirates ~~they~~ have terrorized sailors on all the world's seas.
2. Bands of pirates ~~use~~ to build fortified hide-outs from which they attacked ships.   **2.** used

DISTRIBUTED REVIEW
Ask students to identify the case of the following pronouns:

1. *I* in sentence 1 [*nominative*]

2. *our* in sentence 6 [*possessive*]

3. *its* in sentence 9 [*possessive*]

USAGE

PRACTICE

Guided and Independent

Reviews You could use **Review B** as guided practice and have students complete **Review C** as independent practice.

HOMEWORK

Have students read the commentary in etiquette books on the importance of thank-you correspondence, and encourage them to study the models presented in the books.

Remind students to avoid mentioning amounts of money they might have received as gifts. Since people like to know the outcome of the acts of kindness they perform, remind students to say how they used the

3. I once read ~~where~~ the Roman general Julius Caesar was captured by pirates.   **3.** that

4. My history teacher ~~learned~~ my class about the pirates who disrupted shipping along the North African coast.   **4.** taught

5. As you may have seen in movies, these pirates preyed upon African, European, and American ships.   **5.** C

6. During the 1600s and 1700s, pirates lived off ~~of~~ the South American coast.

7. One of these pirates, Captain William Kidd, was a ~~real~~ dangerous cutthroat on the Caribbean Sea.   **7.** very

8. You may be surprised to learn that some fearsome pirates were women.   **8.** C

9. Anne Bonny and Mary Read attacked and robbed ~~alot~~ of ships on the Caribbean.   **9.** a lot

10. You may think that piracy is a thing of the past, but ~~its~~ still going on in some parts of the world.   **10.** it's

Review C Revising Sentences by Correcting Errors in Usage

ANSWERS

1. already—all ready
2. alot—a lot
3. among—between
4. this here—this
5. Like—As
6. how come—why
7. inside of—inside
8. than—then
9. their—there
10. couldn't of—couldn't have

Review C Revising Sentences by Correcting Errors in Usage

Revise the sentences in the following paragraph to correct each error in the use of formal, standard English.

EXAMPLE   **[1]** Our vacation along the Pan American Highway was real interesting.

   1. real—very (or *extremely*)

[1] My parents were already to leave as soon as school was out. [2] Mom and Dad had planned the trip themselves so that we'd see alot of country. [3] The Pan American Highway, as the map at left shows, runs among North America and South America. [4] Like a long bridge, this here highway connects the two continents. [5] Like you can see, Laredo, Texas, is one of the terminals for the highway. [6] That's how come we went to Laredo first. [7] I enjoyed visiting the towns and seeing the countryside deep inside of Mexico. [8] If you follow along on the map, you'll notice that we than drove through Central America. [9] We crossed the Panama Canal to get to Colombia; their we enjoyed touring the capital, Bogotá. [10] We couldn't of stayed in Venezuela and Chile any longer because both Mom and Dad had to get back to work.

280   **Chapter 12**   A Glossary of Usage

FAMILY/COMMUNITY ACTIVITY   *Continued from p. 279*

gift or how the favor affected them.

Allow students to work with others to evaluate and revise their thank-you letters. They should base their evaluations on cri-

teria spelled out or implied in the etiquette books they consult. They should also follow the proper format for personal letters and check for errors in usage.

Chapter Review

Terms in brackets refer to concepts tested by the items in the Chapter Review.

1. [*good, well*]
2. [*had ought, hadn't ought*]
3. [*doesn't, don't*]
4. [*way, ways*]
5. [*hisself*]
6. [*good, well*]
7. [*than, then*]
8. [*use to, used to, suppose to, supposed to*]
9. [*where*]
10. [*your, you're*]

Some answers may vary.

11. effects [*affect, effect*]
12. all right [*all right*]
13. badly [*bad, badly*]
14. why [*how come*]

A. Identifying Correct Usage

Identify the correct word or expression of the italicized pair in parentheses in each sentence.

1. Aunt Mary felt (*good, well*) about winning the contest.
2. Mr. Yglesias always believed that people (*had ought, ought*) to look after their families.
3. A parrot that (*don't, doesn't*) talk may be a bored parrot.
4. The cyclists have a long (*way, ways*) to go.
5. Trent bought (*hisself, himself*) a CD player.
6. An ability to speak (*well, good*) can help a person go far in life.
7. Mount Everest is higher (*then, than*) Mont Blanc.
8. She (*used to, use to*) be a track-and-field star.
9. I read in a magazine (*where, that*) a new treatment for acne is being developed.
10. (*Your, You're*) probably the calmest person I've ever met.

B. Identifying and Correcting Errors in Usage

One sentence in each of the following sets contains an error in usage. Choose the letter of the sentence that contains an error. Then, correctly write the sentence, using formal, standard English.

11. a. I rode a unicycle.
    b. Everyone came except Michael.
    c. What are the side affects of this medicine?
12. a. We had already been there.
    b. She feels alright now.
    c. We looked everywhere for him.
13. a. He behaved bad.
    b. She felt bad about being late.
    c. There is no talking between classes.
14. a. I know how come she left.
    b. It's windy.
    c. He likes this kind of movie.

15. [*of*]
16. [*this here, that there*]
17. very [*real*]
18. [*he, she, it, they*]
19. can [*hardly, scarcely*]
20. Its [*its, it's*]

15. **a.** She looks as though she is exhausted.
   (b.) Meet me outside ~~of~~ the building.
   c. He wrote the letter and mailed it.

16. **a.** I just bought those shoes.
   (b.) This ~~here~~ coffee mug is broken.
   c. Try to relax.

17. **(a.)** Tamir is ~~real~~ sad.
   b. Let's study now and go outside later.
   c. They're new in school.

18. **a.** Take the report when you go.
   b. She might have gone home.
   (c.) Mr. Bennigan ~~he~~ is my English teacher.

19. **a.** We worked for an hour.
   b. She accepted your invitation.
   (c.) They ~~can't~~ hardly see the sign.

20. **a.** You should have told me.
   b. Less sugar is needed.
   (c.) ~~It's~~ pedal is stuck.

C. Proofreading a Paragraph for Correct Usage

Each sentence in the following paragraph contains at least one ~~error in formal, standard usage~~. Rewrite each sentence to correct the error.

Some answers may vary.
21. Among [*between, among*]
22. who [*or that*] [*who, which, that*]
23. have [*could of*]
24. doesn't [*doesn't, don't*]
25. taught [*learn, teach*]
26. that [*reason . . . because*]
27. As [*like, as*]
28. [*he, she, it, they*]

[21] ~~Between~~ soccer fans worldwide, the name Zinedine Zidane became famous after the World Cup soccer match in July 1998. [22] Zidane is the player ~~which~~ led the French team to victory over Brazil by scoring two goals. [23] Not many people would ~~of~~ predicted such an impressive future for the son of a poor Algerian immigrant. [24] In some ways, this French success story ~~don't~~ seem different from many American success stories. [25] As a boy, Zidane ~~learned~~ himself to play soccer on the streets of his neighborhood in Marseille, France's second largest city. [26] One reason Zidane made his professional debut at sixteen was ~~because~~ he had an amazing ability to dribble. [27] ~~Like~~ others have done, he followed his dream out of poverty. [28] In 1994, Zidane ~~he~~ made his debut with the French national team by scoring two goals after only seventeen minutes

of play. **[29]** By 2001, Zidane's "magic feet" had taken him to a ~~real~~ promising deal with Real Madrid. **[30]** Four years later he decided to retire, but he came back in 2005 and played very ~~good~~.

29. very [*real*]
30. well [*good, well*]

Writing Application
Using Formal, Standard English in a Speech

Formal, Standard English   A local radio station is sponsoring a speech contest for Earth Day. To enter, contestants must write a speech about an environmental issue. Write a three-minute speech for the contest. Use only formal English in your speech.

Prewriting   You will need to choose a specific topic about the environment. You may wish to discuss one of the following subjects: local recycling efforts, pollution, endangered species, or rain forests. When you have selected a topic, jot down some notes about it. List not only facts and information you have read or heard about the topic but also your feelings about it. Then, make an informal outline of what you want to say.

Writing   Use your notes from the prewriting activities as you write the first draft of your speech. Make the main point of your speech very clear in a thesis statement early in your speech. Then, discuss each supporting point in a paragraph or two. Restate your main point in your conclusion. Time your speech to be sure it is no longer than three minutes.

Revising   Ask a friend to listen to your speech and to time it. Is the speech clear, informative, and persuasive? Did your listener hear any informal English? If your speech is too long, you will need to cut or revise some information.

Publishing   Review the rules and guidelines of standard English given in this chapter. Make any necessary corrections in usage. Publish your speech by presenting it to your class. If Earth Day is near, you could offer to read your speech at an Earth Day event.

APPLICATION

Writing Application
Prewriting Tip. Suggest that students structure their speeches by analyzing cause and effect. They can use the following format:

- Topic: Choose a topic.

- Effect: State one specific problem within the topic.

- Cause: List two or three specific factors or causes of the problem.

- Action: Identify one or two specific actions that will lessen the harmful effect—that is, things that can be done to help solve the problem.

Publishing Tip. When students are ready to give their speeches, spend some time discussing effective oral presentation. Play a brief tape of a professional newscast. Point out that professionals speak clearly, and they time their pauses to add emphasis.

Scoring Rubric. While you will want to pay particular attention to students' use of formal English, you will also want to evaluate their overall writing performance. You may want to give a split score to indicate development and clarity of the composition as well as usage skills.

13

13 Capital Letters
Rules for Capitalization

Diagnostic Preview

A. Proofreading Sentences for Correct Capitalization

Proofread the following sentences, correcting all errors in the use of capital and lowercase letters.

EXAMPLE
1. The shubert Theater is located at 222 West Forty-Fourth Street in New York City.

    1. *Shubert; Forty-fourth*

1. the planet mars was named for the roman God of war.
2. In History class we memorized the Capitals of all the states.
3. Uncle Dave owns one of the first honda Motorcycles that were sold in north America.
4. my cousin gave me a terrific book, *rules of the game.*
5. Rajiv Gandhi, who was then the prime minister of India, visited Washington, d.c., in June of 1985.
6. The Indus river flows from the Himalayas to the Arabian sea.
7. The writings and television appearances of dr. Carl Sagan increased public interest in Science.
8. In the afternoons i help Mrs. Parkhurst deliver the *Evening Independent*, a local Newspaper.
9. Many people I know have moved to the south and west recently.
10. The Writers Ernest Hemingway, an american, and Robert Service, a canadian, served in the red cross during World war I.
11. Could you please tell me how to get to ventura hall on highway 21 and riverside road?
12. For father's day, let's buy Dad a new power saw.

13. In 1978, the <u>president</u> of <u>egypt</u> and the <u>prime</u> <u>minister</u> of <u>israel</u> shared the <u>nobel</u> <u>peace</u> <u>prize</u>.

14. After we read "<u>fire and ice</u>" by Robert Frost, <u>i</u> wanted to read more of the <u>Poet's</u> work.

15. The knight knelt, saying "<u>o</u> noble sir, have mercy."

B. Proofreading Sentences for Correct Capitalization

Proofread the following sentences, correcting all errors in the use of capital and lowercase letters.

EXAMPLE   **1.** The national park service celebrated its seventy-fifth Anniversary in 1991.

       1. *National Park Service; anniversary*

16. The <u>national</u> <u>park</u> <u>service</u> was set up as a <u>Bureau</u> of the <u>department</u> of the <u>interior</u> on <u>august</u> 15, 1916.

17. However, the beginnings of today's park system go back to 1872, when <u>congress</u> established Yellowstone <u>national</u> <u>park</u> in <u>idaho</u>, <u>montana</u>, and <u>wyoming</u>.

18. In 1906, <u>president</u> Theodore Roosevelt signed the Antiquities <u>act</u>, which authorized the <u>president</u> to declare <u>spanish</u> missions and ancient <u>american</u> <u>indian</u> villages to be monuments.

19. Of the more than three hundred areas now under the <u>Agency's</u> protection, the one located farthest <u>North</u> is Noatak <u>national</u> <u>preserve</u> in northern Alaska.

20. Farthest east is the Buck Island National Monument on <u>st.</u> Croix, in the <u>u.s.</u> Virgin <u>islands</u>.

21. One park is both the farthest <u>South</u> and the farthest west: the <u>national</u> <u>park</u> of <u>american</u> Samoa, in the South <u>pacific</u>.

22. Continuing to expand its services to visitors, the <u>national</u> <u>park</u> <u>service</u> in 1991 began compiling a computerized directory of the 3,500,000 <u>civil</u> <u>war</u> <u>Soldiers</u>.

23. The <u>Directory</u>, installed at all twenty-eight <u>civil</u> <u>war</u> sites, is maintained by the <u>national</u> <u>park</u> <u>service</u>.

24. Almost 11,000,000 people visit those <u>Sites</u> each year.

25. Historians estimate that more than one third of all <u>americans</u> have <u>Relatives</u> who fought in the <u>civil</u> War, and the question visitors ask most often is, "<u>did</u> my <u>Great</u>-great-grandfather fight here?"

13. [13h(1), e(2, 9)]
14. [13h(3), b, e]
15. [13c]

Words that should be lowercased or capitalized are underscored. Double underscore indicates optional capitalization.

16. [13e(4), e, e(5)]
17. [13e(4, 2)]
18. [13h(1, 3), f]
19. [13e, e(2)]
20. [13e(2)]
21. [13e(2)]
22. [13e(4, 5), e]
23. [13e, e(5, 4)]
24. [13e]
25. [13e(6), e, e(5), a, h(2)]

■ The chapter closes with a **Chapter Review** including a **Writing Application** that asks students to write a biographical essay, using capital letters and lowercase letters correctly.

■ For help in integrating this chapter with writing assignments in *Holt Literature and Language Arts,* see the **Teaching Strands** chart on pp. T24–T25.

ASSESSING

Entry-Level Assessment

Diagnostic Preview. The **Diagnostic Preview** can help you identify particular rules of capitalization for which students need instruction and practice.

MECHANICS

Differentiating Instruction

■ *UA: Differentiating Instruction*

■ *UA: Supporting Instruction in Five Languages*

■ *Family Involvement Activities: In Five Languages*

Assessment

■ *Formal Assessment*

■ *Progress-Monitoring Tests,* pp. 25–26, 48

■ *Test Generator (Teacher One Stop DVD-ROM)* 🎧

Other Language Resources

■ *Spelling Lessons & Activities*

■ *WordSharp: An Interactive Vocabulary Tutor*

■ *Reading and Writing Transparencies*

MECHANICS

First Words, Pronoun *I*, Interjection *O*

Rules 13a–d *(pp. 286–288)*

OBJECTIVE

- To correct sentences by capitalizing words

PRETEACHING

Lesson Starter

Motivating. To illustrate that the correct usage of capital letters is vital to effective communication, write the following sentences on the chalkboard for students to discuss.

1. We need that lovely rose from Glenda's Garden to decorate the Library.

2. We need that lovely Rose from Glenda's garden to decorate the library.

[Sentence 1 indicates that a lovely flower from a store called Glenda's Garden is needed to decorate a place with the proper name, Library. Sentence 2 indicates that a person named Rose, who is in the garden belonging to Glenda, is needed to decorate a library that does not have a proper name, such as a private library in someone's home.]

Have pairs of students create similar sentences in which the incorrect usage of capital letters may cause ambiguity. Have pairs switch sentences and decipher the intended meanings.

Using Capital Letters Correctly

Capital letters are used to

- mark the beginnings of sentences
- distinguish proper nouns from common nouns
- indicate other words that deserve special attention

13a. Capitalize the first word in every sentence.

EXAMPLES   **M**ore and more people are discovering the benefits of exercise.

Daily workouts at the gymnasium or on the running track strengthen the heart.

Regular exercise has many other benefits. **F**or instance, it can help you sleep well at night.

Capitalize the first word of a directly quoted sentence.

EXAMPLES   "**O**ne of the hamsters looks sick," said Felipe.

Gwen asked, "**H**ow long did you study for the test?"

> **Reference Note**
>
> For more information about **using capital letters in quotations,** see page 344.

NOTE Capitalize the first word of a sentence fragment used in dialogue.

EXAMPLE   "**N**ot now," Vanessa replied. "**M**aybe later."

When quoting only part of a sentence, capitalize the first word of the quotation only if the person you are quoting capitalized it or if it is the first word in your sentence.

EXAMPLES   According to the speaker in the poem "My Last Duchess," the Duchess looks "**a**s if she were alive." [*As* is not capitalized in the original poem, nor does it begin this sentence.]

What does the speaker mean when he says his last Duchess was "**T**oo easily impressed"? [*Too* is capitalized in the original poem.]

"**T**he white mule / She rode with round the terrace" is another important image from the poem. [Although *the* is not capitalized in the poem, it is capitalized here because it begins this sentence.]

RESOURCES

First Words, Pronoun *I*, Interjection *O*
Practice

- *Language & Sentence Skills Practice,* p. 258
- *Developmental Language & Sentence Skills,* pp. 93–94

Traditionally, the first word in a line of poetry is capitalized.

EXAMPLES   **H**old fast to dreams
                For if dreams die
                Life is a broken-winged bird
                That cannot fly.

Langston Hughes, "Dreams"

NOTE   Some modern poets and writers do not follow this style. When you quote from a writer's work, use capital letters as the writer uses them.

13b. Capitalize the pronoun *I.*

EXAMPLES   They took my lover's tallness off to war,
                Left me lamenting. Now **I** cannot guess
                What **I** can use an empty heart-cup for.

Gwendolyn Brooks, "The Sonnet-Ballad"

Reference Note

For more about **pronouns,** see page 31.

13c. Capitalize the interjection *O.*

The interjection *O* is most often used on solemn or formal occasions. It is usually followed by a word in direct address.

EXAMPLES   **O** our Mother the Earth, **O** our Father the Sky,
                Your children are we, and with tired backs
                We bring you the gifts you love.

a traditional song of the Tewa people

                Protect us in the battle, **O** great Athena!

Reference Note

For more about **interjections,** see page 71.

The interjection *oh* requires a capital letter at the beginning of a sentence. Otherwise, *oh* usually is not capitalized.

EXAMPLES   **O**h, I wish I could tell you how lonely I felt.

Rudolfo A. Anaya, *Tortuga*

                We felt tired but, **o**h, so victorious.

13d. Capitalize the first word in both the salutation and the closing of a letter.

EXAMPLES   **D**ear Lauren,   **S**incerely yours,

                Dear Mr. Chuen: **Y**ours truly,

Notice that people's names and titles are also capitalized in salutations.

Reference Note

For information on **using colons and commas with salutations and letter closings,** see pages 335 and 328.

DIRECT TEACHING

Modeling and Demonstration

First Words, Pronoun *I*. Model how to proofread sentences for correct capitalization by using the incorrect example *last summer i went swimming for the first time.* First, ask students whether the first word in the sentence should be capitalized. [*yes*] Next, ask students to identify another capitalization error in the sentence. [*The pronoun* I *should be capitalized.*] Point out that the first word in a sentence and the pronoun *I* should be capitalized. Now, have a volunteer use another example from this chapter to demonstrate how to proofread sentences for correct capitalization.

DIFFERENTIATING INSTRUCTION

English-Language Learners

General Strategies. Because they see so much variation in handwriting in the United States, some English-language learners may feel uncertain when they try to form cursive capitals. Post a chart of properly formed capital cursive letters in the classroom to aid students.

Cantonese. Cantonese writers use ideographs, a graphic form of writing that does not use an alphabet. Consequently, there is no need for capitalization in Cantonese. Therefore, students who write Cantonese may need extra explanation and practice to learn the rules and conventions of English capitalization.

MECHANICS

Proper Nouns

Rule 13e *(pp. 288–298)*

OBJECTIVES

- To recognize the correct use of capital letters in sentences
- To identify and correct capitalization errors in sentences

MECHANICS

Reference Note

For more about **common and proper nouns,** see page 28.

COMPUTER TIP

If you use a computer, you may be able to use your spellchecker to help you capitalize people's names and other proper nouns correctly. Each time you use a new proper noun in your writing, make sure you have spelled and capitalized it correctly. Then, add the word to your computer's dictionary or spellchecker.

Exercise 1 Correcting Sentences by Capitalizing Words

Most of the following sentences contain errors in capitalization. If there are errors in the use of capitals, identify the <u>word or words that should be changed</u>. Then, write the word or words correctly. If a sentence is already correct, write *C*.

EXAMPLE 1. save us, o Poseidon, on this stormy sea.

  1. *save—Save; o—O*

1. If <u>i</u> need a ride, <u>i</u> will give you a call.
2. Loretta is spending her vacation in Maine, but <u>Oh</u>, how she would like to visit Paris.
3. Ana exclaimed, "<u>oh</u> no, I left my backpack on the bus!"
4. Please accept these gifts, <u>o</u> Lord.
5. Have I told you that Tara and Sandra teach aerobics at the community center? **5.** C
6. <u>this</u> is the hottest day yet this year.
7. My wish, <u>o</u> Great Spirit, is to be one with the universe.
8. Han said, "<u>no</u>, but thanks."
9. Ms. Garibay said, "<u>don't</u> forget to put away the art supplies and clean up your work area."
10. The letter begins with "<u>dear</u> Ms. Catalano."

13e. Capitalize proper nouns.

A *common noun* names one of a group of persons, places, things, or ideas. A *proper noun* names a particular person, place, thing, or idea.

A common noun is generally not capitalized unless it begins a sentence or is part of a title. Proper nouns are capitalized.

Common Nouns	Proper Nouns
athlete	**S**heryl **S**woopes
river	**N**ile
month	**F**ebruary

Some proper nouns consist of more than one word. In these names, short prepositions (those of fewer than five letters) and articles (*a, an, the*) are generally not capitalized.

EXAMPLES   Statue **o**f Liberty   Alexander **t**he Great

---

(1) Capitalize the names of persons and animals.

Given Names	Alice	Franklin	Christy
Surnames	Walker	Chang-Diaz	Sandoz
Animals	Trigger	Socks	Rover

NOTE For names containing more than one part, capitalization may vary.

EXAMPLES **De La Garza** **FitzGerald** **van Gogh**

de **H**oyos **Fitzgerald** **Van** der **Meer**

┌─HELP─
Always check the spelling of a name containing more than one part with the person whose name it is, or look up the name in a reference source.

Capitalize initials in names and abbreviations that come before or after names.

EXAMPLES **H. G.** Wells Isabel Robinson, **M.D.**

Ms. Levine Gary Stamos, **S**r.

Reference Note
For more information about **capitalizing titles used with names,** see page 301. For information on **punctuating abbreviations** that come before or after names, see page 313.

(2) Capitalize geographical names.

Type of Name	Examples	
Towns, Cities	Jamestown Manor	San Diego St. Paul
Counties, States	Cook County Bedford County	Tennessee New Hampshire
Countries	Germany	New Zealand
Islands	Wake Island	Isle of Wight
Bodies of Water	Lake Erie Kentucky River	Tampa Bay Indian Ocean
Forests, Parks	Tahoe National Forest	Chimney Rock Park
Streets, Highways	Madison Avenue West Fourth Street	Route 44 Interstate 75

Reference Note
Abbreviations of the names of states are capitalized. See page 313 for more about using and punctuating such abbreviations.

Reference Note
In addresses, abbreviations such as *St., Blvd., Ave., Dr.,* and *Ln.* are capitalized. For information about **punctuating abbreviations,** see page 313.

EXTENSION

Map Skills
Have students brainstorm names of cities, towns, or parks in the United States that they have visited or would like to visit. List some of these places on the chalkboard, and let pairs of students choose one destination and then create a travel route telling how to get to it. Provide maps of the United States, and ask students to spell and capitalize correctly the names of cities, towns, states, mountains, and rivers along the route. Students should define the route using complete sentences, but you might want to allow them to include a visual representation of the route as well.

DIFFERENTIATING INSTRUCTION

English-Language Learners
Spanish. Students may need practice capitalizing the words *Street, Avenue, Lane, Drive,* and so on, since these words are not capitalized in Spanish unless they begin a sentence.

MINI-LESSON **Mechanics**

Punctuation and Abbreviations.
Remind students that abbreviations usually end with periods. Ask students to volunteer abbreviations for each of the following categories.

Titles: [*Mr. Brown*]
Personal Names: [*A. J. Foyt*]
Times of Day: [*7:00 A.M.*]
Years: [*A.D. 1776*]
Addresses: [*500 Rabbit Tr.*]

DIRECT TEACHING

Correcting Misconceptions

Capitalizing Direction Words.
Students may mistakenly capitalize words indicating direction, such as *north* and *south*. You might help students understand the difference between words used to indicate direction and the same words used to indicate a section of the country by telling them that an article (*a, an,* or *the*) will be used before a section of the country, such as *the West*. If there is no article, there should be no capital letter.

Meeting the Challenge

ANSWERS
You may want to point out to students that many, but not all, of these new words have become common nouns even though they are taken from proper nouns.

1. the Fahrenheit and Celsius temperature scales
2. cologne, the frankfurter, and the hamburger
3. the graham cracker
4. sardines
5. the sandwich

| STYLE | | TIP |

Words such as *north, east,* and *southwest* are not capitalized when they indicate direction.

EXAMPLES
flying **s**outh for the winter

northeast of Atlanta

However, these words are capitalized when they name a particular place.

EXAMPLES
states in the **S**outhwest

driving in the **E**ast

MEETING THE CHALLENGE

Proper nouns are one source of new words in English. Many objects or concepts are named for the people who invented them or for the places in which they originated.

See if you can determine the English words or phrases that are derived from the following names.

1. the scientists Gabriel Daniel Fahrenheit and Anders Celsius
2. the German cities Cologne, Frankfurt, and Hamburg
3. the dietary reformer Sylvester Graham
4. Sardinia, a Mediterranean island known for fishing
5. the Earl of Sandwich

NOTE In a hyphenated street number, the second part of the number is not capitalized.

EXAMPLE   East Seventy-**e**ighth Street

Type of Name	Examples	
Mountains	**M**ount **W**ashington	**B**ig **H**orn **M**ountains
	Sawtooth **R**ange	**E**mory **P**eak
Continents	**A**ustralia	**A**sia
	North **A**merica	**A**frica
Regions	the **W**est **C**oast	the **B**alkans
	the **N**orth	the **M**idwest
Other Geographical Names	**M**alay **P**eninsula	**P**ainted **D**esert
	Seneca **R**ocks	**B**ering **S**trait
	Suez **C**anal	**D**ismal **S**wamp

Exercise 2   Proofreading for Correct Capitalization

Most of the following sentences contain an error in capitalization. Identify and correct each word or words that should be capitalized. If a sentence is already correct, write *C.*

EXAMPLE   1. If you like horses, you would enjoy reading mary O'Hara's books.

1. *Mary*

1. Ms. O'Hara was born in New jersey in 1885.
2. She began writing as a child with a short story she titled   **2. C**
"Lonely Laurie" and continued writing the rest of her life.
3. Her books about horses are loved even by people who live in the heart of a city, such as on Thirty-third street in New York City.
4. O'Hara's first book, *My Friend Flicka*, introduced a boy named kennie, who loves horses.
5. Kennie lives in wyoming, where Mary O'Hara also lived while she was writing the story.
6. The filly Flicka is given to Kennie, and he learns to take care of her.   **6. C**

7. Other characters in the story include Kennie's mother, Nell; father, Rob; and brother, <u>howard</u>.
8. O'Hara's second book, *Thunderhead,* continues the story of life on the <u>mcLaughlins</u>' ranch.
9. *Green Grass of Wyoming* is O'Hara's third and final book about Kennie and his life in the <u>west</u>.
10. O'Hara moved to <u>california</u>, where she wrote screenplays for movies and composed music.

(3) Capitalize the names of planets, stars, constellations, and other heavenly bodies.

EXAMPLES   **J**upiter   **S**irius   the **B**ig **D**ipper

NOTE   The word *earth* is not capitalized unless it is used along with the names of other heavenly bodies that are capitalized. The words *sun* and *moon* are generally not capitalized.

EXAMPLES   Is **E**arth located in the galaxy called the **M**ilky **W**ay?

The **e**arth is not the only planet that has a **m**oon.

(4) Capitalize the names of teams, organizations, institutions, and government bodies.

Type of Name	Examples
Teams	**D**etroit **P**istons **K**arr **C**ougars **S**eattle **S**eahawks
Organizations	**A**frican **S**tudies **A**ssociation **L**eague of **W**omen **V**oters **A**merican **G**eographical **S**ociety
Institutions	**S**t. **J**ude **C**hildren's **R**esearch **H**ospital **H**illcrest **J**unior **H**igh **S**chool **A**ntioch **C**ollege
Government Bodies	**A**ir **N**ational **G**uard **D**epartment of **A**griculture **L**ouisiana **S**tate **S**enate

STYLE   TIP

The names of organizations, businesses, and government bodies are often abbreviated to a series of capital letters.

EXAMPLES
American Telephone & Telegraph   **AT&T**

National Science Foundation   **NSF**

Reference Note

For more information about **abbreviations,** see page 313.

Using Capital Letters Correctly   **291**

**Learners Having
Difficulty/Advanced**

Resource Teams. Some students
may have difficulty with one or more
of the concepts in this chapter, while
others may have no difficulty with
the concepts at all. You can assist
both groups by allowing students
with a strong understanding of capitalization to serve as a resource team
for those who need assistance.
Encourage the members of the
resource team to explain the rules
about which students have questions, instead of merely telling them
the correct answers.

STYLE   TIP

The word *party* in the
name of a political party
may or may not be capitalized. Either way is correct.

EXAMPLE
  Democratic **p**arty or
  Democratic **P**arty

  However, within a par-
ticular piece of writing, be
consistent in your use of
capitals.

STYLE   TIP

The words *black* and *white*
may or may not be capitalized when they refer to
races. Either way is correct.
However, within a particular piece of writing, be
consistent in your use of
capitals.

Do not capitalize such words as *democratic, republican,* and
socialist when they refer to principles or forms of government.
Capitalize these words when they refer to a specific political party.

EXAMPLES   a **d**emocratic country

            the **R**epublican candidate

**(5) Capitalize the names of historical events and periods,
special events, holidays, and other calendar items.**

Type of Name	Examples
Historical Events	**B**attle of **B**unker **H**ill **W**orld **W**ar II **Y**alta **C**onference
Historical Periods	**G**reat **D**epression **A**ge of **R**eason **M**iddle **A**ges
Special Events	**W**orld **S**eries **O**lympic **G**ames **O**klahoma **S**tate **F**air
Holidays	**F**ather's **D**ay **K**wanzaa **V**eterans **D**ay
Other Calendar Items	**H**ispanic **H**eritage **M**onth **F**riday **O**ctober

NOTE The name of a season is usually not capitalized unless it is part
of a proper name.

EXAMPLES   the last day of **s**ummer

            the Oak Ridge **W**inter Carnival

(6) Capitalize the names of nationalities, races, and peoples.

EXAMPLES   **G**reek   **H**ispanic   **C**aucasian

           African **A**merican   **A**sian   **L**akota **S**ioux

(7) Capitalize the names of religions and their followers, holy days and celebrations, sacred writings, and specific deities.

Type of Name	Examples	
Religions and Followers	**C**hristianity **Z**en **B**uddhism	**M**uslim **A**mish
Holy Days and Celebrations	**A**sh **W**ednesday **E**aster	**R**amadan **Y**om **K**ippur
Sacred Writings	**K**oran the **T**orah	the **B**ible **N**ew **T**estament
Specific Deities	**G**od **B**rahma	**H**oly **S**pirit **J**ehovah

NOTE The words *god* and *goddess* are not capitalized when they refer to deities of ancient mythology. However, the names of specific mythological gods and goddesses are capitalized.

EXAMPLE **D**iana, the Greek **g**oddess of the hunt, is the subject of my report.

(8) Capitalize the names of buildings and other structures.

EXAMPLES **S**ydney **O**pera **H**ouse **G**olden **G**ate **B**ridge

Shubert **T**heater **F**airmont **H**otel

Hoover **D**am **T**ower of **L**ondon

Do not capitalize words such as *hotel, theater, church,* and *school* unless they are part of a proper name.

EXAMPLES a new **s**chool

Rocky Mount Junior High **S**chool

COMPUTER TIP

If you use a word processor when you write, the spell-checker might be able to help you find errors in capitalization. Spellcheckers are not perfect, though. When the spellchecker questions a certain word, you will need to decide whether it should be capitalized or not, depending on how you have used it in your sentence.

Oral Practice **Capitalizing Words in Sentences**

Read each of the following sentences aloud. Then, tell which words in each sentence should begin with a capital letter. Words that are already capitalized are correct.

CONTENT-AREA CONNECTIONS

Social Studies

Government. Have students work in groups of three or four to research the structure of the local government. Have groups create a graphic showing the local governmental bodies and the names and titles of local officials. (Students may use a computer graphics program if one is available.) Remind students to capitalize all proper nouns correctly.

MECHANICS

EXAMPLE   1. Towering over the surrounding countryside, the san esteban mission is visible for miles.

1. *san esteban mission—San Esteban Mission*

1. The mission sits atop a sandstone mesa in valencia county, new mexico.

2. Near San Esteban is the Pueblo village of acoma, which is fifty-four miles west-southwest of albuquerque.

3. Almost one thousand years old, acoma is believed to be the oldest continuously inhabited community in the united states.

4. In the seventeenth and eighteenth centuries, the spanish established dozens of missions in new mexico to promote catholicism.

5. The main purpose of the missions was to spread Christianity among the native peoples, but the outposts also served political and military purposes.   5. C

6. This photo of San esteban, which was built between 1629 and 1651, shows the type of mission architecture that developed in that region of the united states.

7. Adobe, a sandy clay commonly used in construction throughout the southwest, covers all the outside surfaces of the building.

8. The building's design is based on the designs of churches in central mexico.

9. Those churches, in turn, are regional variations of church buildings in spain.

10. Thus, san esteban, like other new mexican missions, combines various elements of three main cultures: american indian, mexican, and spanish.

(9) Capitalize the names of monuments, memorials, and awards.

Type of Name	Examples
Monuments and Memorials	the **G**reat **S**phinx **S**tatue of **L**iberty **C**ivil **R**ights **M**emorial **W**ashington **M**onument
Awards	**A**cademy **A**ward **N**obel **P**rize **N**ewbery **M**edal **P**urple **H**eart

(10) Capitalize the names of trains, ships, aircraft, and spacecraft.

Type of Name	Examples
Trains	*Silver Rocket* *Orient Express*
Ships	USS *Olympia* *Mayflower*
Aircraft	*Spruce Goose* *Silver Dart*
Spacecraft	*Mir* *Columbia*

(11) Capitalize the names of businesses and the brand names of business products.

BUSINESSES	**A**pple **C**omputer, **I**nc.®	**A**merican **A**irlines®
	International **B**usiness **M**achines®	**N**ational **B**roadcasting **C**ompany®
BRAND NAMES	**N**ike® shoes	**W**rangler® jeans

Reference Note

For information on using **italics for names,** see page 342.

HELP

Notice that the names of the types of products are not capitalized.

EXAMPLES
Nike **s**hoes
Wrangler **j**eans

Most word-processing programs have search features that are particularly useful for correcting a recurring word that has been incorrectly left lowercase or uppercase in a composition. Some programs allow the user to enter a word in the search mode and to specify either lowercase or uppercase for the first letter of the word. Other programs will find every version of the word, whether it begins with an uppercase or lowercase letter.

MECHANICS

PRACTICE

Guided and Independent

Review A You may wish to use items 1–10 in **Review A** as guided practice. Then, have students complete items 11–20 as independent practice. **HOMEWORK**

Review A Common Nouns and Proper Nouns

POSSIBLE ANSWERS

1. Rocky Mountains
2. talk show host
3. D-day
4. Mississippi River
5. *Enola Gay*
6. country
7. monument
8. *Enterprise*
9. Cheerios
10. government agency
11. Indian Ocean
12. playwright
13. Tahoe National Forest
14. literary prize
15. Sony
16. city
17. Ocean Spray
18. Dell
19. artist
20. *Titanic*

Review A Common Nouns and Proper Nouns

For each proper noun, give a corresponding common noun. For each common noun, give a proper noun.

EXAMPLES
1. Independence Hall
1. *building*

2. city
2. *San Francisco*

1. mountain range
2. Oprah Winfrey
3. historical event
4. river
5. aircraft
6. Ethiopia
7. Lincoln Memorial
8. spacecraft
9. cereal
10. Environmental Protection Agency
11. ocean
12. William Shakespeare
13. national forest
14. Newbery Medal
15. television set
16. Seattle
17. bottled fruit juice
18. computer
19. Leonardo da Vinci
20. ship

Review B Using Capital Letters Correctly

Correct each of the following expressions, using capital letters as needed.   Words that should be capitalized are underscored.

EXAMPLES
1. a member of the peace corps
1. *a member of the Peace Corps*

2. received an academy award
2. *received an Academy Award*

1. decisions of the <u>united</u> <u>states</u> <u>supreme</u> <u>court</u>
2. the <u>apaches</u> of the <u>southwest</u>
3. <u>hoover</u> <u>dam</u>
4. <u>tomb</u> of the <u>unknown</u> soldier
5. 512 <u>west</u> <u>twenty-fourth</u> <u>street</u>
6. pictures of <u>saturn</u> sent by *voyager 2*
7. in <u>hawaii</u> on <u>maui</u> <u>island</u>
8. the <u>great</u> <u>lakes</u>
9. <u>monday</u>, <u>april</u> 29
10. the <u>stone</u> <u>age</u>

Correcting Capitalization Errors

Each of the following sentences contains at least one error in capitalization. Identify the <u>word or words that should be capital-ized</u>. Then, write each word correctly.

EXAMPLE   1. Imagine how many flowers it must take to cover just one of the floats in the rose parade!

    1. *rose parade—Rose Parade*

1. I don't have plans for <u>new</u> <u>year's</u> <u>eve</u> yet, but <u>i</u> know where <u>i'll</u> be on <u>new</u> <u>year's</u> <u>day</u>.
2. <u>watching</u> the <u>rose</u> <u>parade</u> on TV is a <u>new</u> <u>year's</u> <u>day</u> tradition in my family.
3. The parade takes place each year in <u>pasadena</u>, <u>california</u>, which is northeast of <u>los</u> <u>angeles</u>.
4. The parade is sponsored by the <u>pasadena</u> <u>tournament</u> of <u>roses</u> <u>association</u>.
5. Did you know that the name *pasadena* comes from an <u>ojibwa</u> expression meaning "valley town"?
6. That's a fitting name for a town overlooking a valley at the base of the <u>san</u> <u>gabriel</u> <u>mountains</u>.
7. After the parade, we watch the <u>rose</u> <u>bowl</u> game, which is played in <u>pasadena's</u> <u>brookside</u> <u>park</u>.
8. The oldest postseason college football game in the <u>united</u> <u>states</u>, the <u>rose</u> <u>bowl</u> traditionally pits the winner of the <u>big</u> <u>ten</u> <u>con-ference</u> against the win-ner of the <u>pacific</u> <u>ten</u> <u>conference</u>.
9. <u>New</u> <u>year's</u> <u>day</u> is nearly always bitterly cold in <u>cleveland</u>, Ohio, where we live.
10. By the end of the game, we feel as though we've started the new year off with a minivacation in <u>california</u>.

PRACTICE

Guided and Independent

Reviews You may wish to use **Review C** as guided practice and have students complete **Review D** as independent practice.

HOMEWORK

MECHANICS

Reference Note

For more about **proper adjectives,** see page 42.

MECHANICS

Proper Adjectives

Rule 13f (pp. 298–299)

OBJECTIVE

■ **To correct sentences by capitalizing proper adjectives**

DIRECT TEACHING

Modeling and Demonstration

Proper Adjectives. Model how to correct sentences by capitalizing proper adjectives, using the incorrect example *Many american chefs study french cooking.* First, explain that a proper adjective is formed from a proper noun and is used to describe a noun. Then, ask students to identify any proper adjectives in the example. [*american, french*] Next, ask whether *american* and *french* should be capitalized. [*yes*] Point out that proper adjectives, like proper nouns, should be capitalized. Now, have a volunteer use another example from this chapter to demonstrate how to correct sentences by capitalizing proper adjectives.

Review D **Correcting Sentences by Capitalizing Words**

Each of the following sentences contains errors in capitalization. Identify the underlined word or words that should be capitalized. Then, write each word correctly.

EXAMPLE
    1. our class visited abraham lincoln's home in springfield, illinois.

    1. *our—Our; abraham lincoln's—Abraham Lincoln's; springfield—Springfield; illinois—Illinois*

1. the federal aviation administration regulates airlines only in the united states and not throughout the world.
2. when she was a child, ethel waters lived in chester, pennsylvania.
3. the sacred muslim city of mecca is located in saudi arabia.
4. in chicago, the sears tower and the museum of science and industry attract many tourists.
5. when did the florida marlins win the world series?
6. the valentine's day dance is always the highlight of the winter.
7. several of my friends bought new adidas® shoes at the big sporting goods sale in the mall.
8. the local food pantry is sponsored and operated by protestants, catholics, and jews.
9. the second-place winners will receive polaroid cameras.
10. jane bryant quinn writes a magazine column on money management.

13f. Capitalize proper adjectives.

A ***proper adjective*** is formed from a proper noun and is capitalized.

Proper Noun	Proper Adjective
China	**C**hinese doctor
Rome	**R**oman army
Islam	**I**slamic culture
King **A**rthur	**A**rthurian legend

RESOURCES

Proper Adjectives

Practice

■ *Language & Sentence Skills Practice,* p. 265
■ *Developmental Language & Sentence Skills,* pp. 103–104

Exercise 3 Correcting Sentences by Capitalizing Proper Adjectives

Capitalize the <u>proper adjectives</u> in each of the following sentences.

EXAMPLE **1.** A finnish architect, Eliel Saarinen, designed a number of buildings in the detroit area.

  1. Finnish, Detroit

1. The <u>alaskan</u> wilderness is noted for its majestic beauty.
2. The <u>syrian</u> and <u>israeli</u> leaders met in Geneva.
3. The <u>european</u> cities I plan to visit someday are Paris and Vienna.
4. Our <u>american</u> literature book includes <u>hopi</u> poems and <u>cheyenne</u> legends.
5. The <u>south</u> <u>american</u> rain forests contain many kinds of plants and animals.
6. Maria has watched two <u>shakespearean</u> plays on television.
7. Did you see the exhibit of <u>african</u> art at the library?
8. Our program will feature <u>irish</u> and <u>scottish</u> folk songs.
9. Where do the <u>amish</u> people live?
10. My family almost always sits down together for a <u>sunday</u> meal.

13g. Do not capitalize the names of school subjects, except course names followed by numerals and languages.

EXAMPLES You must pass **A**rt I before taking **A**rt II.

  I have tests in **E**nglish, **L**atin, and **m**ath.

Exercise 4 Using Capital Letters Correctly

Correct each of the following expressions, using capital letters and lowercase letters as needed.

EXAMPLE **1.** taking japanese and history 201

  1. taking Japanese and History 201

Words that should be lowercased or capitalized are underscored.

1. a lesson in <u>spanish</u>
2. report for <u>english</u> II
3. a syllabus for <u>Home</u> <u>Economics</u>
4. problems in <u>geometry</u> I
5. studying <u>german</u>, <u>Chemistry</u>, and <u>government</u> II
6. problems for <u>algebra</u> 101
7. ready for <u>computer</u> III

Proper Nouns and Proper Adjectives

Divide students into groups of three to create stories using proper nouns and proper adjectives. First, have each student write on four slips of paper a type of proper noun covered by one of the subrules of **Rule 13e** or directions for using a proper adjective. Example slips could be *a dog's name, a monument, create a proper adjective from* California, and *use* Valentine *as a proper adjective.* Each group should place their slips in a pile. Then, one student will select a slip and begin the story by writing an opening sentence containing the type of proper noun or adjective on the slip. *(When I was awakened by Butch barking ferociously, I knew something was wrong.)* Other members of the group will take turns adding to the story until all slips have been selected.

School Subjects, Titles
Rules 13g, h *(pp. 299–306)*

OBJECTIVE

■ To use capital letters correctly in school subjects and titles

School Subjects

Activity. If students are confused about when to capitalize a school subject, point out that subjects that aren't ordinarily capitalized might be capitalized in certain circumstances, such as on report cards or on library signs. Explain that these are special uses of the course names, to which the ordinary rule does not apply. Encourage students to follow the rules in their own writing.

DIRECT TEACHING

Modeling and Demonstration

School Subjects, Titles. Model how to use correct capitalization by using the incorrect example *We studied the emancipation proclamation in History.* First, ask students to identify a word that is incorrectly capitalized. [*History*] Remind students that school subjects are not capitalized, except language classes and course names followed by numbers. Next, ask students to identify other capitalization errors in the example. [*emancipation proclamation*] Explain that titles of historical documents, such as the *Emancipation Proclamation,* should be capitalized. Now, have a volunteer use another example from this chapter to demonstrate how to use correct capitalization.

EXTENSION

Critical Thinking

Metacognition. After students have completed **Review E,** ask them to write brief answers to the following questions.

1. How did you use the rules and examples in the chapter to help you complete the review?

2. Which rules gave you the most trouble? How will you remember these rules in the future?

---

8. choosing between <u>french</u> and <u>Civics</u>
9. taking <u>history</u> 4
10. in <u>english</u> and drama

Review E **Correcting Sentences by Capitalizing Proper Nouns and Proper Adjectives**

Capitalize the <u>proper nouns</u> and <u>proper adjectives</u> in each of the following sentences.

EXAMPLE **1.** The natchez trace developed from a series of trails made long before hernando de soto explored the area in 1540.

  1. *Natchez Trace; Hernando de Soto*

1. As this map shows, the <u>natchez</u> <u>trace</u> linked the present-day cities of <u>natchez</u>, <u>mississippi</u>, and <u>nashville</u>, <u>tennessee</u>.
2. From <u>natchez</u>, the 450-mile route ran northeast between the <u>big</u> <u>black</u> <u>river</u> and the <u>pearl</u> <u>river</u>.
3. Turning east a few miles north of <u>tupelo</u>, it crossed the <u>tennessee</u> <u>river</u> near <u>muscle</u> <u>shoals</u>, <u>alabama</u>, and then headed into <u>tennessee</u>.
4. Among the peoples living along the trail were the <u>natchez</u>, the <u>chickasaw</u>, the <u>choctaw</u>, and the <u>cherokee</u>.

5. Finding no gold or silver in the area, the <u>spanish</u> explorers turned their attention to what is now the <u>u.s.</u> <u>southwest</u>.
6. At the conclusion of the <u>french</u> and <u>indian</u> <u>war</u> (1754–1763), <u>france</u> was forced to give most of its territory east of the <u>mississippi</u> <u>river</u> to <u>great</u> <u>britain</u>.
7. Near the time of the <u>louisiana</u> <u>purchase</u> of 1803, the <u>natchez</u> <u>trace</u> was improved for use by mail and military wagons traveling to the <u>west</u>.

8. Traffic along the trail increased steadily until the 1830s, when regular steamboat service provided a less dangerous, more comfortable means of travel on the <u>mississippi</u> <u>river</u>.

9. Today a modern highway named the <u>natchez</u> <u>trace</u> <u>parkway</u> follows the general route of the ancient path.

10. In an effort to reclaim history, volunteers with the <u>natchez</u> <u>trace</u> <u>trail</u> <u>conference</u> are carving out a hiking trail the entire length of the parkway.

13h. Capitalize titles.

(1) Capitalize a person's title when the title comes before the person's name.

EXAMPLES   There will be a short address by **G**overnor Halsey.

Report to **L**ieutenant Engstrom, please.

Does **M**s. Tam know **D**r. Politi?

This is the church in which the **R**everend Henry Ward Beecher preached.

Generally, a title used alone or following a person's name is not capitalized, especially if the title is preceded by *a*, *an*, or *the*.

EXAMPLES   An **a**ttorney for the defense made a brief statement.

Is he the **r**abbi at the new synagogue?

Katie Dobbs, **c**hair of the entertainment committee, gave the status report.

However, a title used alone in direct address is usually capitalized.

EXAMPLES   Is the patient resting comfortably, **N**urse?

What is your name, **S**ir [*or* **s**ir]?

(2) Capitalize a word showing a family relationship when the word is used before or in place of a person's name, unless the word follows a possessive noun or pronoun.

EXAMPLES   I received a letter from **A**unt Christina and **U**ncle Garth.

When will **M**om and **D**ad be home?

Angela's **m**other and my **a**unt Daphne coach the girls' softball team.

Reference Note

For information about **abbreviating titles,** see page 313.

S T Y L E   T I P

Titles used alone or following a person's name may be capitalized for clarity or special emphasis.

EXAMPLES

The **A**ttorney **G**eneral has served our state with distinction.

Ben Cayetano, **G**overnor of **H**awaii, delivered the keynote speech.

MECHANICS

DIFFERENTIATING INSTRUCTION

Learners Having Difficulty

Making It Real. To make the capitalization rules about titles relevant to students, use examples drawn from students' lives. Titles of books, CDs, television shows, and magazines that are familiar to students might be useful. Have students brainstorm about titles they see in their everyday lives, and make a list on the chalkboard.

EXTENSION

Relating to Writing

Have students imagine that they have created works like the ones listed on this page and p. 303. Have students name their imagined work, correctly punctuate the title, and write a brief synopsis of the work. [*comic strip:* Dogwood—*A canine hero is noted for his eating habits and his adventures in space; computer game:* Space Race—*The object is to be the first pilot to travel the entire galaxy.*]

Reference Note

For a list of **prepositions,** see page 66. For information about **coordinating conjunctions** and **articles,** see pages 69 and 39.

(3) Capitalize the first and last words and all important words in titles and subtitles.

Unimportant words in titles include

- prepositions of fewer than five letters (such as *at, of, for, from,* and *with*)
- coordinating conjunctions (*and, but, for, nor, or, so, yet*)
- articles (*a, an, the*)

Type of Name	Examples
Books	*Dust Tracks on a Road* *River Notes: The Dance of the Herons*
Magazines	*Sports Illustrated* *Entertainment Weekly* *Woman's Day*
Newspapers	*The Boston Globe* *St. Petersburg Times*
Poems	"Refugee Ship" "With Eyes at the Back of Our Heads"
Short Stories	"The Tell-Tale Heart" "My Wonder Horse" "Gorilla, My Love"
Historical Documents	Mayflower Compact Emancipation Proclamation Monroe Doctrine
Movies	*The Wizard of Oz* *Casablanca*
Television Series	*Touched by an Angel* *FBI: The Untold Stories* *Family Matters*

 Learning for Life

Creating a Newspaper Ad. For practice in capitalizing words in real-life situations, ask students to prepare a newspaper ad for a book fair. The ad should include the name of the event; information about dates, times, places, and prices; and a list of featured books. If scanning equipment is available, students may include a scanned photograph of the cover of a featured book. Otherwise, they could use a drawing.

Ask students to work in groups of four. Have each group start by generating a list

Type of Name	Examples
Works of Art	*The Ballet Class* *Bird in Space*
Musical Works	*Moonlight Sonata* "Unforgettable" *The Magic Flute* "On Top of Old Smoky"
Plays	*I Never Sang for My Father* *Barefoot in the Park* *The Music Man*
Comic Strips	*Hagar the Horrible* *Garfield*
Videos	*Mariah Carey at Madison Square Garden* *It's a Wonderful Life*
Video Games	*Sonic the Hedgehog* *Star Wars: Shadow of the Empire*
Albums and CDs	*Sgt. Pepper's Lonely Hearts Club Band* *To the Faithful Departed*

Reference Note

For information on using **italics with titles**, see page 342. For information on using **quotation marks with titles**, see page 349.

Capitalize the titles of chapters and other parts of books.

EXAMPLES   José has already read **C**hapter 11, "**T**he **T**ropical **R**ain **F**orest."

The book's first section, titled "**L**egends of **B**aseball," includes a fun trivia quiz.

NOTE   Capitalize an article (*a, an,* or *the*) at the beginning of a title or subtitle only if it is the first word of the official title or subtitle.

EXAMPLES   Does your uncle subscribe to **t**he *Los Angeles Times*?

I read an interesting story in *The New Yorker.*

┌HELP┐

The official title of a book is found on the title page. The official title of a newspaper or other periodical is found on the masthead, which usually appears on the editorial page or the table of contents.

If you need help deciding which words should be capitalized—especially with the titles of newspapers and magazines—you can check the title page or masthead.

MECHANICS

of titles to be included in the ad. Then, have students create dummy layouts of the ads.

During the drafting phase, remind students to be careful about the use of capital letters.

Ask students to evaluate and revise their drafts, using the requirements of the assignment and the rules for capitalization as criteria. Have students proofread the final drafts for errors in spelling, usage, and punctuation. You can publish the ads by posting them in the classroom.

PRACTICE

Guided and Independent

You may wish to use **Exercise 5** as guided practice. Then, have students complete **Review F** as independent practice. **HOMEWORK**

DIFFERENTIATING INSTRUCTION

Special Education Students

Because it contains so many errors, **Review F** may be distracting to students. Set specific tasks such as "Find and correct errors with place names." Have students work on the review with a helper—one error at a time—until all the rules that apply have been covered.

Learners Having Difficulty

As an alternative to **Review F**, give students copies of different kinds of application forms—such as those for jobs, schools, and driver's licenses—to fill out using correct capitalization. Point out that correct mechanics will often be an important criterion to the people evaluating such applications.

Exercise 5 **Correcting Capitalization Errors**

Most of the following sentences contain at least one error in capitalization. If there are errors in the use of capitals, identify the word or words that should be capitalized. Then, write the word or words correctly. If a sentence is already correct, write *C*.

EXAMPLE　**1.** My uncle Kevin recommended "love must not be forgotten," a short story by Zhang Jie.

　　　　　1. "love must not be forgotten"—"Love Must Not Be Forgotten"

1. During <u>president</u> Woodrow Wilson's term, sheep grazed on the front lawn of the White House.
2. When my aunt Inez visited Mexico, she met <u>grandmother</u> Villa's brothers and sisters for the first time.
3. All of these pronunciations are correct according to *the <u>american heritage</u> dictionary*.
4. Well, <u>mom</u>, have you met <u>dr.</u> Brinson?
5. Did you hear <u>commissioner</u> of <u>education smathers's</u> speech recommending a longer school day?
6. Was Carrie Fisher in *return of the jedi*?
7. After the secretary read the minutes, the treasurer reported on the club's budget.　**7.** C
8. Elizabeth Speare wrote *calico captive*.
9. My older brother subscribes to *field and stream*.
10. The first politician to make a shuttle flight was <u>senator</u> Jake Garn of Utah.

Review F **Correcting Capitalization Errors**

Each of the following sentences contains errors in capitalization. Identify the word or words that should be capitalized. Then, write the word or words correctly.
Double underscore indicates optional capitalization.

EXAMPLE　**1.** My cousin's class went on a field trip to the science museum of virginia, which is in richmond.

　　　　　1. science museum of virginia—Science Museum of Virginia; richmond—Richmond

1. The <u>andersons</u> hosted an exchange student from <u>argentina</u> last year.
2. Did you know that the <u>king ranch</u> in <u>texas</u> is larger than <u>rhode island</u>?

3. At rand community college, ms. epstein is taking three courses: computer programming I, japanese, and english.
4. The sixth day of the week, friday, is named for the norse goddess of love, frigg.
5. The christian holiday of christmas and the jewish holiday of hanukkah are both celebrated in december.
6. My uncle ronald was stationed in the south pacific when he was an ensign.
7. The liberty bell, which is on display in independence hall in philadelphia, was rung to proclaim the boston tea party and to announce the first public reading of the declaration of independence.
8. Is your mother still teaching an art appreciation class at the swen parson gallery?
9. In the 1920s, zora neale hurston and countee cullen were both active in the literary movement known as the harlem renaissance.
10. I walk to the eagle supermarket each sunday to buy a copy of the *post* and a quart of zipee orange juice.

Review G — Proofreading Sentences for Correct Capitalization

Each of the following sentences contains at least one error in capitalization. Identify each word that should be changed. Then, write the word or words correctly.

EXAMPLE   1. Osaka, one of the largest Cities in japan, lies on the Southern coast of honshu island.

1. *Cities—cities; japan—Japan; Southern—southern; honshu island—Honshu Island*

1. president Roosevelt's saturday talks from the white house were broadcast on the radio.
2. In History class, we learned about these suffragists: elizabeth cady stanton, susan b. anthony, and lucretia c. mott.
3. In April the cherry blossom festival will be celebrated with a Parade through the heart of the City.
4. The 1996 olympics were held in atlanta.
5. The rio grande, a major river of north america, forms the Southwestern border of Texas.
6. jane addams, an American Social Reformer who cofounded hull house in chicago, was awarded the 1931 nobel peace prize.

MECHANICS

7. Many of the countries of <u>europe</u> are smaller than some states in our country.
8. In the <u>southeast</u>, William Least Heat-Moon began the journey that he tells about in his book *blue highways*.
9. Can we have a surprise <u>Birthday</u> party for <u>uncle</u> Victor, <u>mom</u>?
10. The <u>panama</u> <u>canal</u> connects the <u>atlantic</u> <u>ocean</u> and the <u>pacific</u> <u>ocean</u>.

Review H **Proofreading Sentences for Correct Capitalization**

Each of the following sentences contains at least one error in capitalization. Identify each <u>word that should be changed</u>. Then, write the word or words correctly. Double underscore indicates optional capitalization.

EXAMPLE   1. The south african vocal group Ladysmith Black Mambazo sings without instrumental accompaniment.

1. *south african—South African*

1. Ladysmith's music is based on the work songs of <u>black</u> <u>south</u> <u>african</u> miners.
2. In a sense, their music is the <u>south</u> African version of the <u>american</u> blues, which grew out of the work songs of enslaved Africans.
3. In 1985, <u>ladysmith</u> was featured on two songs on <u>paul</u> <u>simon</u>'s album *graceland*.
4. Those two songs, "<u>homeless</u>" and "<u>diamonds</u> on the <u>soles</u> of <u>her</u> <u>shoes</u>," helped to make the album an enormous hit; it even won a <u>grammy</u> <u>award</u>.
5. To promote the album, <u>Ladysmith</u> and <u>simon</u> toured the United <u>states</u>, <u>europe</u>, and <u>south</u> America.
6. Most of Ladysmith's songs are in the performers' native language, <u>zulu</u>.
7. Even people who don't understand the <u>Lyrics</u> enjoy the music's power and beauty.
8. Ladysmith has also appeared in a Hollywood movie, in the music <u>Video</u> *moonwalker,* and on the television shows *Sesame street* and the *Tonight show*.
9. The group's exposure to <u>american</u> music is reflected in two songs on its 1990 album, *two worlds, one heart*.
10. One song is a gospel number, and the other adds elements of <u>Rap</u> music to <u>ladysmith</u>'s distinctive sound.

DIFFERENTIATING INSTRUCTION

English-Language Learners

Spanish. Before students begin **Review H,** remind them to look specifically for proper adjectives, since these words are not capitalized in Spanish. Remind them also that in English, names of languages are capitalized, even though in Spanish, names of languages are capitalized only as part of a course title.

Chapter Review

A. Proofreading Sentences for Correct Capitalization

Numerals in brackets refer to rules tested by the items in the Chapter Review.

1. [13e(2), e(8)]
2. [13h(1), e(2)]
3. [13e(5)]
4. [13e(4)]
5. [13f, h(3), e(2)]
6. [13e(4, 2)]
7. [13e(2)]
8. [13e(11)]
9. [13e, e(7)]
10. [13g]
11. [13e(5), b]
12. [13e(2)]
13. [13e, h(1)]
14. [13c]
15. [13e(7)]
16. [13e(9)]
17. [13h(3)]
18. [13e(6, 4)]

Each of the following sentences contains at least one error in capitalization. Rewrite the sentences to correct the errors by changing capital letters to lowercase letters or lowercase letters to capital letters.

1. The Maxwells enjoyed visiting the southwest, particularly the alamo in San Antonio.

2. Is dr. Powell's office at Twenty-first street and Oak drive?

3. On labor day we went to Three Trees State Park.

4. Our junior high school had a much more successful carnival than Lakeside junior high school had.

5. Did you know that the german folk tale "cinderella," which is included in *grimm's fairy tales*, is similar to a tale from ninth-century china?

6. Arthur's cousin joined the Peace corps and lived in a small village on the west coast of africa.

7. No fish live in the Great salt lake in Utah.

8. Save money by shopping at Al's discount city.

9. We have studied Japanese Culture and the shinto religion.

10. This semester I have English, American History, and Spanish in the morning, and Industrial Arts I in the afternoon.

11. On saturday and sunday, my mother and i are going to a family reunion in the town where she grew up.

12. The Robinsons live near route 41, not far from Memorial parkway on the South side of town.

13. At our Wednesday Night meeting, the reverend Terry DeWitt gave a talk on the beliefs of Lutherans.

14. We salute you, o Caesar!

15. Was Thursday named after the Norse God Thor?

16. Awe-struck, the tourists paused to admire the sphinx.

17. Dale Evans and Roy Rogers sang the song "Happy trails to you" at the end of their television programs.

18. Thurgood Marshall was the first african american appointed to the Supreme court.

Chapter Review **307**

19. [13h(2), e(9, 5)]

19. My Grandfather won a purple heart during the Vietnam war.

20. [13e(5)]

20. The American revolution took place toward the end of the Age of Enlightenment, in the 1700s.

B. Proofreading a Paragraph for Correct Capitalization

Each sentence in the following word groups contains at least one error in capitalization. Write the correct form of each word that contains an error.

21. [13b, e(2), e]
22. [13e(2, 7)]
23. [13e, e(2)]
24. [13e(8)]
25. [13a, e(2), e]
26. [13e(6), f]
27. [13e(6)]
28. [13e(2), f]
29. [13e(2)]
30. [13b, e(2)]

[21] For a couple of years, i have had a pen pal named Habib who lives in tunisia, an Arabic Country in africa, on the Mediterranean sea. **[22]** Habib was born in the city of kairouan, a muslim holy city famous for its carpets. **[23]** He now lives in the Capital city, Tunis, on the Northeastern coast. **[24]** He is going to a Secondary School in the Capital. **[25]** not far from his home are the ruins of carthage, which in ancient times was a Great Power led by the famous general Hannibal. **[26]** After many centuries, Carthage was defeated by the romans and became a roman colony. **[27]** Greeks, Romans, Carthaginians, normans, turks—Tunisia has seen them all in its 3,000-year history. **[28]** Along with all that history, there are beautiful beaches near Habib's home, along the mediterranean coast, where he goes swimming and water-skiing during his free time. **[29]** In his last letter he told me about going camel-trekking in the sahara, in the South. **[30]** It's a long way to go, but someday i want to visit Habib in tunisia.

C. Using Capital Letters Correctly

Each of the following word groups contains at least one error in capitalization. Rewrite each expression to correct all the errors in capitalization.

31. [13e(11)]
32. [13e(2)]
33. [13e(2), f]
34. [13e(10)]
35. [13e(5)]
36. [13h(1), e(1)]
37. [13e(2)]

31. the bank of mexico
32. 211 fourteenth street
33. the himalayan peaks
34. the titanic
35. thursday, january 28
36. emperor marcus aurelius
37. lake powell

MECHANICS

38. the <u>united states</u> <u>department</u> of the <u>treasury</u>
39. <u>mount washington</u>
40. a <u>general</u> <u>motors</u> executive

Writing Application
Using Capital Letters in an Essay

Correct Capitalization   Your class is putting together a booklet of biographical sketches on the most-admired people in your community. Each student in your class will contribute one biography. Write a short essay about someone you admire. The person can be a friend, a family member, or someone you have never met. In your essay, use capital letters and lowercase letters correctly to help your readers understand precisely what you mean.

Prewriting   Write a list of people you admire. Then, read over your list, and choose the person you admire most. Jot down information about his or her background, personality traits, and major achievements. In the case of someone you know, you may wish to interview him or her to gather additional information. Finally, organize your information in an outline.

Writing   Begin your essay with a sentence or two that catches your audience's attention and identifies your subject. Using your notes and outline, write your first draft. In your conclusion, sum up the points you have made, or restate the main idea.

Revising   Re-read your paper to make sure you have clearly shown why you admire this person. Did you give enough information about him or her, and is the information correct? Add, delete, or rearrange information to make your essay clearer and more interesting.

Publishing   Read over your essay again, correcting any errors in grammar, punctuation, and spelling. Pay special attention to your use of capital letters and lowercase letters. Photocopy or print out your essay. With your classmates, create a booklet of your compositions. You may also wish to include photographs or sketches of the people about whom you have written. Invite other classes, friends, neighbors, and family members to read your booklet.

38. [13e(4)]
39. [13e(2)]
40. [13e(11)]

Chapter Review   **309**

MECHANICS

STANDARDS FOCUS

Grade-Level Standards
(Boldface indicates concepts that are taught and tested in this chapter.)

- Language Convention 1.0: **Students write and speak with a command of standard English conventions appropriate to this grade level.**

- Sentence Structure 1.3: **Use** subordination, coordination, **apposition**, and other devices to indicate clearly the relationship between ideas.

- Grammar 1.4: **Edit written manuscripts to ensure that correct grammar is used.**

- Punctuation and Capitalization 1.5: **Use correct punctuation and capitalization.**

Prerequisite/Review Standards

- Grammar 1.3: Identify all parts of speech and types and structure of sentences.

- Grammar 1.4: Demonstrate the mechanics of writing (e.g., quotation marks, commas at end of dependent clauses) and appropriate English usage (e.g., pronoun reference).

- Punctuation 1.5: Identify hyphens, dashes, brackets, and semicolons and use them correctly.

Standards Coming Up in the Next Grade Level

- Grammar and Mechanics of Writing 1.1: Identify and correctly use clauses (e.g., main and subordinate), phrases

(continued)

1.0 Written and Oral English Language Conventions
Students write and speak with a command of standard English conventions appropriate to this grade level.
1.3 Use apposition.
1.4 Edit written manuscripts to ensure that correct grammar is used.
1.5 Use correct punctuation.

Punctuation
End Marks, Commas, Semicolons, and Colons

Diagnostic Preview

Correcting Sentences by Adding End Marks, Commas, Semicolons, and Colons

Rewrite the following paragraphs, inserting periods, question marks, exclamation points, commas, semicolons, and colons where they are needed.   Optional commas are underscored.

EXAMPLE [1] Did I ever tell you how our washing machine which usually behaves itself once turned into a foaming monster

1. *Did I ever tell you how our washing machine, which usually behaves itself, once turned into a foaming monster?*

[1] "Oh no! The basement is full of soapsuds," my youngest sister Sheila yelled. [2] When I heard her, I could tell how upset she was. [3] Her voice had that tense, strained tone that I know so well. [4] To see what had alarmed her, I ran down to the basement. [5] Imagine the following scene: The washing machine, the floor, and much of my sister were completely hidden in a thick, foamy flow of bubbles. [6] I made my way gingerly across the slippery floor, fought through the foam, and turned off the washing machine .

[7] Doing so, of course, merely stopped the flow. [8] Sheila and I now had to clean up the mess, for we didn't want Mom and Dad to see it when they got home. [9] We mopped up soapsuds, we sponged water off the floor, and we dried the outside of the

Numerals in brackets refer to rules tested by the items in the Diagnostic Preview.

1. [14j(1), c, a]
2. [14j(2), a]
3. [14g, a]
4. [14j(2), a]
5. [14p, f, g, a]
6. [14f, a]
7. [14i(4), a]
8. [14h, a]
9. [14f, h, a]

CHAPTER RESOURCES

Internet
- go.hrw.com (keyword: HLLA)

go. hrw .com

Planning
- *Teacher One Stop DVD-ROM*
- *On Course: Mapping Instruction*
- *Family Involvement Activities: A Guide to Standards Mastery*

Practice & Review
- *Language & Sentence Skills Practice,* pp. 280–294; 295–298
- *Developmental Language & Sentence Skills,* pp. 107–112 ·

Application & Enrichment
- *Language & Sentence Skills Practice,* pp. 299, 302; 279, 300–301

0

washing machine.[10] After nearly an hour of steady effort at the task,we were satisfied with our work and decided to try the washer.

[11] Everything would have been fine if the machine had still worked,however,it would not even start.[12] Can you imagine how upset we both were then?[13] Thinking things over,we decided to call a repair shop.

[14] We frantically telephoned Mrs.Hodges,who runs the appliance repair business nearest to our town.[15] We told her the problem and asked her to come to 21 Crestview Drive,Ellenville,as soon as possible.

[16] When she arrived a few minutes after 4:00,Mrs.Hodges inspected the machine,asked us a few questions,and said that we had no real problem.[17] The wires had become damp;they would dry out if we waited a day or two before we tried to use the machine again.

[18] Surprised and relieved,we thanked Mrs.Hodges and started toward the stairs to show her the way out.[19] She stopped us,however,and asked if we knew what had caused the problem with the suds.[20] We didn't want to admit our ignorance,but our hesitation gave us away.[21] Well,Mrs.Hodges suggested that from then on we measure the soap instead of just pouring it into the machine.

[22] Looking at the empty box of laundry powder,I realized what had happened.[23] It was,I believe,the first time Sheila had used the washing machine by herself;she hadn't followed the instructions on the box.

[24] This incident occurred on November 10,2007,and we have never forgotten it.[25] Whenever we do the laundry now,we remember the lesson we learned the day the washer overflowed.

End Marks

An **end mark** is a mark of punctuation placed at the end of a sentence. The three kinds of end marks are the *period*, the *question mark*, and the *exclamation point*.

14a. Use a period at the end of a statement (or declarative sentence).

EXAMPLES   One of the figure skaters was Tara.

A small brown bird flitted from branch to branch.

---

10. [14j(2), a]
11. [14m, a, i(4)]
12. [14b]
13. [14j(2), a]
14. [14e, i(1), a]
15. [14k(1), a]
16. [14r(1), j(2), e, f, a]
17. [14l, a]
18. [14j(2), e, a]
19. [14i(4), a]
20. [14h, a]
21. [14j(1), e, a]
22. [14j(2), a]
23. [14i(4), l, a]
24. [14k(1), h, a]
25. [14j(2), a]

| STYLE   TIP |

As you speak, the tone and pitch of your voice, the pauses in your speech, and the gestures and expressions you use all help make your meaning clear. In writing, marks of punctuation, such as end marks and commas, show readers where these nonverbal cues occur.

Punctuation alone won't clarify the meaning of a confusing sentence, however. If you have trouble punctuating a sentence, check to see whether rewording it would help express your meaning more clearly.

Reference Note

For information about **how sentences are classified according to purpose,** see page 19.

End Marks   **311**

(e.g., gerund, infinitive, and participial), and mechanics of punctuation (e.g., semicolons, colons, ellipses, hyphens).

■ **Manuscript Form 1.4:** Produce legible work that shows accurate spelling and correct use of the conventions of punctuation and capitalization.

▼

INTRODUCING THE CHAPTER

■ This chapter allows students to review and build on past knowledge of punctuation. The first part of the chapter discusses end marks and abbreviations. Then, comma rules are presented, followed by rules for the use of semicolons and colons.

■ The chapter concludes with a **Chapter Review** including a **Writing Application** in which students write a business letter using correct punctuation.

■ For help in integrating this chapter with writing assignments in *Holt Literature and Language Arts,* see the **Teaching Strands** chart on pages T24–T25.

ASSESSING

Entry-Level Assessment

Diagnostic Preview. If students are having problems with punctuation in their writing, you can use the **Diagnostic Preview** to pinpoint error patterns and specific strengths and weaknesses. The preview asks students to correct sentences by adding end marks, commas, semicolons, and colons. Students' responses can help you determine which rules of punctuation students need to review.

MECHANICS

Differentiating Instruction
■ *UA: Differentiating Instruction*
■ *UA: Supporting Instruction in Five Languages*
■ *Family Involvement Activities: In Five Languages*

Assessment
■ *Formal Assessment*

■ *Progress-Monitoring Tests,* pp. 27–28, 48
■ *Test Generator (Teacher One Stop DVD-ROM)* 🎧

Other Language Resources
■ *Spelling Lessons & Activities*
■ *WordSharp: An Interactive Vocabulary Tutor*
■ *Reading and Writing Transparencies*

Lesson Starter

Background Information. Tell students that punctuation rules and marks vary in different languages. Ask volunteers who may speak other languages to share punctuation rules and marks that differ from those in English. Use the following examples to show how the question mark takes different forms in various languages.

1. Spanish—¿Where is Bill?
2. Farsi—Where is Bill؟ (Farsi is spoken in Iran, Afghanistan, Pakistan, Southern Russia, and India.)
3. Arabic—؟Where is Bill?
4. Greek—Where is Bill; (The question mark in Greek is the English semicolon.)

End Marks and Abbreviations

Rules 14a–e *(pp. 311–315)*

OBJECTIVES

- To correct paragraphs by adding end marks to sentences
- To correct sentences by adding end marks and by adding periods to abbreviations

---

Reference Note

For more information about **interjections,** see page 71.

⌐HELP⌐

The paragraphs in Exercise 1 contain a total of ten sentences.

14b. Use a question mark at the end of a question (an interrogative sentence).

EXAMPLE   Did Gordon Parks write *The Learning Tree*?

14c. Use an exclamation point at the end of an exclamation (an exclamatory sentence).

EXAMPLE   That's the biggest salad I've ever seen!

NOTE   Interjections that express a strong emotion may be set off from the rest of the sentence with an exclamation point.

EXAMPLE   Wow! What a view that is!

14d. Use a period or an exclamation point at the end of a request or a command (an imperative sentence).

EXAMPLES   Please give me the scissors. [a request]
Give me the scissors! [a command]

Exercise 1 **Using End Marks**

In the following paragraphs, sentences have been run together without end marks. Identify the last word of every sentence, and supply the proper end mark.

EXAMPLE   1. A visit to New Salem reveals that life in Lincoln's time was harder than it is today

1. *today.*

In New Salem Park, Illinois, you can find a reproduction of the little village of New Salem, just as it was when Abraham Lincoln lived there.Can you imagine what life was like in Abraham Lincoln's time?

The cabin of the Onstat family is not a reproduction but is the original cabin where Lincoln spent many hours.In that cabin, on that very floor, young Abe studied with Isaac Onstat.The cabin had only one room.

Across the way hangs a big kettle once used by Mr. Waddell for boiling wool.Mr. Waddell, the hatter of the village, made hats of wool and fur.

Do any of you think that you'd like to go back to those days? What endurance those people must have had!Could we manage to live as they did?

RESOURCES

End Marks and Abbreviations

Practice

- *Language & Sentence Skills Practice,* pp. 280–282, 295

Abbreviations

An *abbreviation* is a shortened form of a word or phrase.

14e. Many abbreviations are followed by a period.

Notice how periods are used with abbreviations in the following examples.

Types of Abbreviations	Examples		
Initials	Pearl S. Buck	I. M. Pei	
	W.E.B. DuBois	H. D. (Hilda	
	T. S. Eliot		Doolittle)
Titles Used with Names	Mr.	Mrs.	Ms.
	Jr.	Sr.	Dr.
States	N.Y.	La.	Mo.
	Mass.	N. Dak.	Wis.

NOTE A two-letter state abbreviation without periods is used only when it is followed by a ZIP Code. Both letters of the abbreviation are then capitalized.

EXAMPLE Austin, **TX** 78741-4144

Types of Abbreviations	Examples			
Times	A.M. (*ante meridiem,* used with times from midnight to noon)			
	P.M. (*post meridiem,* used with times from noon to midnight)			
	B.C. (before Christ)			
	A.D. (*anno Domini,* "in the year of the Lord")			
Addresses	St.	Ave.	Dr.	P.O. Box
Organizations and Companies	Co.	Inc.	Corp.	Ltd.

STYLE **TIP**

Leave a space between two initials in a person's name. Do not leave a space between three or more initials.

STYLE **TIP**

The abbreviations *A.D.* and *B.C.* need special attention. Place *A.D.* before a numeral and *B.C.* after a numeral.

EXAMPLES
124 **B.C.**   **A.D.** 720

For centuries expressed in words, place both *A.D.* and *B.C.* after the century.

EXAMPLES
seventh century **B.C.**

fourth century **A.D.**

MECHANICS

DIRECT TEACHING

Modeling and Demonstration

End Marks. Model how to add appropriate end marks by using the following examples: *One of the figure skaters was Tara; Did Gordon Parks write* The Learning Tree; *and That's the biggest salad I've ever seen.* First, ask students whether the first sentence is a statement, a question, or an exclamation. [*statement*] Explain that a period should be used at the end of a statement. Next, repeat the process for the second and third sentences. [*Sentence 2 is a question and takes a question mark. Sentence 3 is an exclamation and takes an exclamation point.*]

Now, use the examples *Please give me the scissors* and *Give me the scissors.* Ask students whether these two sentences are requests or commands. [*Sentence 1 is a request, and sentence 2 is a command.*] Ask which end marks identify requests and commands. [*period; exclamation point*] Explain that imperative sentences may take a period or an exclamation point.

Finally, have a volunteer use another example from this chapter to demonstrate how to add appropriate end marks.

DIFFERENTIATING INSTRUCTION

Learners Having Difficulty

It may be easier for some students to hear the differences in the sentence types than to recognize them visually. Give students oral examples of each type, and have students identify each sentence type and its proper end mark.

DIRECT TEACHING

Acronyms and Abbreviations

Activity. Science, technology, and politics use many abbreviations and acronyms, some of which eventually become part of our everyday vocabulary. Often when people use one of these terms, they may not know what words the individual letters represent. Ask students whether they know what the following acronyms and abbreviations represent.

FBI [*Federal Bureau of Investigation*]
RAM [*random-access memory*]
NASA [*National Aeronautics and Space Administration*]
SUV [*sport utility vehicle*]
DNA [*deoxyribonucleic acid*]

PRACTICE

End Marks and Abbreviations

Activity. To give students practice in using end marks and abbreviations, try a team game. Divide the class into five teams. Have each team create a sentence: Specify a type of sentence and a specific kind of abbreviation to be used in that sentence. You could combine the following items.

Type of Sentence	Abbreviation
statement	name (with title)
question	address
exclamation	organization
request	time
command	unit of measure

Team members may confer for thirty seconds, and then each team must send a member to the chalkboard to write the sentence. Continue the procedure by having teams rotate members sent to the chalkboard.

┌─HELP─
A few acronyms, such as *radar, laser,* and *sonar,* are now considered common nouns. They do not need to be spelled out on first use and are no longer capitalized. When you are not sure whether an acronym should be capitalized, look it up in a recent dictionary.

┌ STYLE   TIP ┐
Abbreviations are useful and appropriate in informal writing and in charts, tables, and footnotes. Only rarely should abbreviations be used in formal writing.

┌─HELP─
Use a period as a decimal point in numbers.

EXAMPLES
19.76 $7.25   .5 miles

An *acronym* is a word formed from the first (or first few) letters of a series of words. Acronyms are written without periods. If you are not sure that your readers will know what an acronym stands for, add the complete term in parentheses the first time you use the acronym.

EXAMPLES   Our school will have a fund-raising drive for **UNICEF.**

The **VISTA** (Volunteers in Service to America) program provides many services to our community.

NOTE   Abbreviations for government agencies and some widely used abbreviations are written as acronyms. Each letter of the abbreviation is capitalized.

EXAMPLES   FDA   CIA   NIMH
            PBS   YWCA   NBA
            URL   CD-ROM   VCR

Abbreviations for units of measure are usually written without periods. However, you should use a period with the abbreviation *in.* (for *inch* or *inches*) to prevent confusing it with the word *in.*

EXAMPLES   cm   kg   ml   oz
            lb   ft   yd   mi

NOTE   When an abbreviation with a period ends a sentence, another period is not needed. However, a question mark or an exclamation point is used if it is needed.

EXAMPLES   My dog's name is T. J.
            Why did you name your dog T. J.?

Review A   **Correcting Sentences by Adding Periods, Question Marks, and Exclamation Points**

Write the following sentences, adding periods, question marks, and exclamation points where they are needed.

EXAMPLE   **1.** Look at the beautiful costume the Japanese actor on the next page is wearing

           1. Look at the beautiful costume the Japanese actor on the next page is wearing!

1. The picture reminds me of our visit to Little Tokyo last year.
2. Have you ever heard of Little Tokyo?
3. It is a Japanese neighborhood in Los Angeles, Calif, bordered by First St, Third St, Alameda St, and Los Angeles St.
4. Some friends of ours who live in Los Angeles, Mr. and Mrs. Albert B. Cook, Sr, and their son, Al, Jr, introduced us to the area.
5. They met our 11:30 A.M. flight from Atlanta, Ga, and took us to a $9.95 lunch buffet at a restaurant in the Japanese Plaza Village.
6. Later we stopped at a bakery for *mochigashi*, which are Japanese pastries, and then we visited the Japanese American Cultural and Community Center on San Pedro St.
7. Outside the center is a striking abstract sculpture by Isamu Noguchi, who created the stone sculpture garden at the UNESCO headquarters in Paris, France.
8. Next door is the Japan America Theater, which stages a wide variety of works by both Eastern and Western artists.
9. Soon, it was time to head for the Cooks' home, at 6311 Oleander Blvd, where we spent the night.
10. What a great afternoon we had exploring Japanese culture!

Commas

A *comma* is generally used to separate words or groups of words so that the meaning of a sentence is clear.

Items in a Series

14f. Use commas to separate items in a series.

Words, phrases, and clauses in a series are usually separated by commas to show the reader where one item in the series ends and the next item begins.

Commas **315**

MECHANICS

Commas
Rules 14f–k *(pp. 315–331)*

OBJECTIVES

■ To correct sentences by adding commas to separate items in a series

■ To correct sentences by adding commas to separate two or more adjectives preceding a noun

■ To correct compound sentences by adding commas

■ To use commas in sentences containing nonessential phrases and clauses

■ To use commas in sentences to set off nonessential appositives and appositive phrases

■ To use commas in sentences to set off words of direct address

■ To use commas in sentences to set off parenthetical expressions

■ To use commas in sentences with introductory phrases and clauses

■ To correct dates, addresses, and parts of letters by adding commas

DIRECT TEACHING

Modeling and Demonstration

Commas. Model how to proofread sentences for correct use of commas by using the incomplete example *Always stop look and listen before crossing railroad tracks.* Ask students whether there is a series of three or more items in the sentence. [yes; *stop, look, listen*] Next, ask whether all the items in the series are joined by *and, or,* or *nor.* [no] Therefore, the items in the series *stop, look, and listen* need to be separated by commas. Now, have a volunteer use another example from this chapter to demonstrate how to proofread sentences for correct use of commas.

DIFFERENTIATING INSTRUCTION

Learners Having Difficulty

Because the section on commas contains many rules, you might want to create a chart listing the rules for using commas and including examples of each. Keep the chart posted in the classroom. As students work through each rule, you can add it to the chart, enlisting students' help to come up with examples.

Reference Note

For more about **phrases,** see Chapter 5. For more about **clauses,** see Chapter 6.

Reference Note

For more information about **semicolons,** see page 331.

S T Y L E   T I P

Including a comma before the conjunction in a series is not incorrect, so some writers prefer always to use a comma there. Follow your teacher's instructions on this point.

Words in a Series

Barbecue, hammock, canoe, and *moccasin* are four of the words that the English language owes to American Indians. [nouns]

Always stop, look, and listen before crossing railroad tracks. [verbs]

In the early morning, the lake looked cold, gray, and calm. [adjectives]

Phrases in a Series

Checking his shoelaces, fastening his helmet strap, and positioning his kneepads, Toshio prepared for the skateboarding competition. [participial phrases]

We found seaweed in the water, on the sand, under the rocks, and even in our shoes. [prepositional phrases]

Clearing the table, washing the dishes, and putting everything away took almost an hour. [gerund phrases]

Clauses in a Series

We didn't know where we were going, how we would get there, or when we would arrive. [subordinate clauses]

The lights dimmed, the curtain rose, and the orchestra began to play. [short independent clauses]

NOTE Independent clauses in a series can be separated by commas only if the clauses are short. Independent clauses that are long or that contain commas are usually separated by semicolons.

In your reading, you will find that some writers omit the comma before a conjunction such as *and, or,* or *nor* when it joins the last two items of a series. However, such a comma is sometimes necessary to make the meaning of a sentence clear. Notice how the comma affects the meaning in the following examples.

UNCLEAR Luanne, Zack and I are going riding. [Is Luanne being addressed, or is she going riding?]

CLEAR Luanne, Zack, and I are going riding. [Three people are going riding.]

If all the items in a series are joined by *and, or,* or *nor,* do not use commas to separate them.

EXAMPLES   I voted for Corey **and** Mona **and** Ethan in the student council officers election.

For your report you may want to read Jean Toomer's *Cane* **or** Ralph Ellison's *Invisible Man* **or** Richard Wright's *Native Son.*

Exercise 2   Correcting Sentences by Adding Commas

Rewrite each of the following sentences, inserting commas where they are needed.   Optional commas are underscored.

EXAMPLE   **1.** On their expedition, the explorers took with them 117 pounds of potatoes 116 pounds of beef and 100 pounds of fresh vegetables.

   1. On their expedition, the explorers took with them 117 pounds of potatoes, 116 pounds of beef, and 100 pounds of fresh vegetables.

1. Carlos and Anna and I made a piñata, filled it with small toys, and hung it from a large tree.
2. I sanded the boards, Ignacio primed them, and Paul painted them.
3. Last week I read the novel *The Lucky Stone,* the short story "Flowers for Algernon," and the poem "Legacy II."
4. Most flutes used by professional musicians are made of sterling silver, fourteen-carat gold, or platinum.
5. We know what we will write about, where we will find sources, and how we will organize our reports.
6. Squanto became an interpreter for the Pilgrims, showed them how to plant corn, and stayed with them throughout his life.
7. Sylvia Porter wrote several books about how to earn money and how to spend it, borrow it, and save it.
8. Joe looked for the cat under the bed, on the sofa, in the bathtub, and inside the empty cardboard box.
9. The San Joaquin kit fox, the ocelot, the Florida panther, and the red wolf are only some of the endangered mammals in North America.
10. I want to visit Thailand, Nepal, China, and Japan.

DIFFERENTIATING INSTRUCTION

Learners Having Difficulty

Students will probably be familiar with the use of commas to separate single-word items in a series, but they may not be familiar with using commas to separate phrases and clauses in a series. You may want to review **Chapter 5: The Phrase** and **Chapter 6: The Clause** and to give additional examples of phrases and clauses in a series.

APPLICATION

Using Commas in a Series

Activity. Give teams of four students five minutes to write as many sentences using commas in a series as they can. To help students get started, list the following examples on the chalkboard. Then, when the time is up, ask teams to share a few of their sentences with the rest of the class.

Words in a Series
Red, gold, and blue were her favorite colors.

Phrases in a Series
Counting the money, writing checks, and making deposits took four hours.

Clauses in a Series
The runners took their marks, the gun sounded, and the race began.

DIFFERENTIATING INSTRUCTION

Advanced Learners

The English language seems to require that some sets of two or more adjectives before a noun be placed in a particular order. For example, "big red apple" sounds ungrammatical and awkward when put in the order "red big apple." Ask students to find other examples of this phenomenon (for example, *little green car; big fat hen; lovely white flowers; huge, old brick building;* and so on). Ask students to try to write a rule that speakers of other languages could use to help them learn how to put in order adjectives of this type. Have them share their rules with the class.

TIPS & TRICKS

If you are not sure whether the final adjective and the noun make up a compound noun, use this test. Insert the word *and* between the adjectives. If *and* makes sense, use a comma. In the example on the right, *and* makes sense between *skillful* and *enthusiastic*. *And* does not make sense between *enthusiastic* and *dog*.

Another test you can use is to switch the order of the adjectives. If you can switch them and the sentence still makes sense, use a comma.

Reference Note

For more information about **compound nouns**, see page 26.

14g. Use commas to separate two or more adjectives preceding a noun.

EXAMPLES   Jack Russell terriers are small, energetic dogs.

These intelligent, loyal, playful pets always enjoy a challenge.

When the final adjective in a series is thought of as part of the noun, do not use a comma before that adjective.

EXAMPLE   A skillful, enthusiastic dog trainer can teach a Jack Russell to perform many exciting tricks. [No comma is used between *enthusiastic* and *dog* because the words *dog* and *trainer* make up a compound noun.]

A comma should never be used between an adjective and the noun immediately following it.

INCORRECT   The cute, clever, terrier who stars in TV's *Wishbone* is really named Soccer.

CORRECT   The cute, clever terrier who stars in TV's *Wishbone* is really named Soccer.

Exercise 3   Correcting Sentences by Adding Commas

Write the following sentences, adding commas where they are needed.

EXAMPLE   1. A squat dark wood-burning stove stood in one corner.

1. *A squat, dark wood-burning stove stood in one corner.*

1. They made a clubhouse in the empty, unused storage shed.
2. This book describes the harsh, isolated lives of pioneer women in Kansas.
3. What a lovely, haunting melody that song has!
4. Katie Couric's upbeat, intelligent approach to interviewing makes her an effective television anchor.
5. The delicate, colorful wings of the hummingbird vibrate as many as two hundred times each second.
6. The hot, unrelenting wind blew across the desert.
7. The movie is about a bright, active girl who is badly injured while riding a horse.

8. Jade Snow Wong's strong, focused determination led to her success as an author.

9. What is the quickest, easiest, most scenic way to get to Juneau?

10. Lupe likes to read true stories about daring, adventurous mountain climbers.

Compound Sentences

14h. Use a comma before a coordinating conjunction (*and, but, for, nor, or, so,* or *yet*) when it joins independent clauses in a compound sentence.

EXAMPLES   I enjoyed *The King and I*, **but** *Oklahoma!* is still my favorite musical.

Oscar Hammerstein wrote the words, **and** Richard Rodgers wrote the music.

The musical comedy began as an American musical form, **yet** its popularity has spread throughout the world.

When the independent clauses are very short, the comma before *and, but,* or *or* is sometimes omitted.

EXAMPLES   I'm tired but I can't sleep.

The cat can stay inside or it can go out.

A comma is almost always used before *nor, for, so,* or *yet* when it joins independent clauses.

EXAMPLES   We will not give up, **nor** will we fail.

Everyone seemed excited, **for** it was time to begin.

No one else was there, **so** we left.

The water was cold, **yet** it looked inviting.

NOTE   Do not confuse a compound sentence with a simple sentence that has a compound verb. A simple sentence has only one independent clause.

SIMPLE SENTENCE WITH COMPOUND VERB — Margo likes golf but doesn't enjoy archery.

COMPOUND SENTENCE — Margo likes golf, but she doesn't enjoy archery. [two independent clauses]

STYLE   TIP

The word *so* is often overused. If possible, try to reword a sentence to avoid using *so.*

EXAMPLE
It was late, so we went home.

REVISED
Because it was late, we went home.

STYLE   TIP

For clarity, some writers prefer always to use the comma before a conjunction joining independent clauses. Follow your teacher's instructions on this point.

Reference Note

For more information about **compound sentences,** see page 142. For more about **compound verbs,** see page 16.

Commas   **319**

DIFFERENTIATING INSTRUCTION

English-Language Learners

General Strategies. Not all languages have the same comma rules. Three languages that use a comma without a linking word to join independent clauses are Turkish, Dutch, and Arabic. Students who speak these languages may use comma splices, such as "My hometown is not large, it is very pretty." When you correct such punctuation, acknowledge that you are asking students to change rules they have already mastered in their native writing systems.

RETEACHING

Using Commas in Compound Sentences

Activity. Give students index cards that are lined on one side and blank on the other, and ask students to work in pairs to write sentences using each of the coordinating conjunctions given in **Rule 14h.** On the lined side of the card, they should write the sentence without the comma joining the independent clauses. On the unlined side, they should include the comma.

When students have finished writing their sentences, collect the cards, shuffle them, and distribute them to pairs of students. Students should decide where to place commas and then immediately check their work by looking on the unlined side of the card. If any pairs discover errors in the original sentences, ask them to write the sentences on the chalkboard and to explain the errors to the class.

Reference Note
For more information about **semicolons,** see page 331.

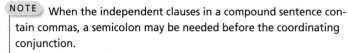

N O T E When the independent clauses in a compound sentence contain commas, a semicolon may be needed before the coordinating conjunction.

EXAMPLE   Our class will read Chapter 4, Chapter 7, and Chapter 9; and Larry, Dana, and Louis will present reports on them.

Oral Practice

DISTRIBUTED REVIEW
Ask students to find the following types of phrases in sentences 1, 3, and 6.

1. an infinitive phrase [*to become architects*]

3. a participial phrase containing a prepositional phrase [*covered with brilliant tropical flowers*]

6. two prepositional phrases [*in tropical trees, above the ground*]

DIFFERENTIATING INSTRUCTION

Learners Having Difficulty

To help students distinguish between a compound sentence and a simple sentence with a compound verb, write the following sentence pairs on the chalkboard.

1. Fred loves fruit yet hates pears.
Fred loves fruit, yet he hates pears.

2. Pam swims often and jogs daily.
Pam swims often, and she jogs daily.

Have volunteers underline the subjects with one color of chalk and the verbs with a different color. Also, ask volunteers to circle the comma in each compound sentence. Emphasize that compound sentences have two or more independent clauses, each of which has its own subject and verb.

Oral Practice   Correcting Compound Sentences by Adding Commas

Read each of the following sentences aloud, and identify the two words that should be separated by a comma. For sentences that do not need commas, say *correct*.

EXAMPLE   **1.** Have you read this article or do you want me to tell you about it?
   1. *article, or*

1. Human beings must study to become architects‸yet some animals build amazing structures by instinct.
2. The male gardener bower bird builds a complex structure and carefully decorates it to attract a mate.   **2.** C
3. This bird constructs a dome-shaped garden in a small tree‸ and underneath the tree he lays a carpet of moss covered with brilliant tropical flowers.
4. Then he gathers twigs and arranges them in a three-foot-wide circle around the display.   **4.** C
5. Tailor ants might be called the ant world's high-rise workers‸ for they gather leaves and sew them around tree twigs to make nests like the one shown on the left.

6. These nests are built in tropical trees‸and the nests may be one hundred feet or more above the ground.
7. Adult tailor ants don't secrete the silk used to weave the leaves together‸but they squeeze it from their larvae.
8. The female European water spider builds a water-proof nest under water‸and she stocks the nest with air bubbles.
9. This air supply is very important‸for it allows the spider to hunt underwater.
10. The water spider lays her eggs in the waterproof nest‸and they hatch there.

Interrupters

14i. Use commas to set off an expression that interrupts a sentence.

Two commas are used to set off an interrupting expression—one before and one after the expression.

EXAMPLES   Mr. Agoya, born and raised in Mexico, moved to California at the age of twenty-four.

          The applications, by the way, were mailed three days ago.

Some expressions that are used as interrupters can also come at the beginning or the end of a sentence. In such cases, only one comma is needed.

EXAMPLES   Born and raised in Mexico, Mr. Agoya moved to California at the age of twenty-four.

          The applications were mailed three days ago, by the way.

(1) Use commas to set off nonessential participial phrases and nonessential subordinate clauses.

A *nonessential* (or *nonrestrictive*) phrase or clause adds information that is not needed to understand the basic meaning of the sentence. Such a phrase or clause can be omitted without changing the main idea of the sentence.

NONESSENTIAL PHRASES   This small turtle, **crossing the street slowly,** was in danger. [The main idea of the sentence remains *This small turtle was in danger.*]

          Harvard College, **founded in 1636,** is the oldest college in the United States. [The main idea of the sentence remains *Harvard College is the oldest college in the United States.*]

NONESSENTIAL CLAUSES   Kareem Abdul-Jabbar, **who retired from professional basketball,** holds several NBA records. [The main idea of the sentence remains *Kareem Abdul-Jabbar holds several NBA records.*]

          Joshua eventually overcame his acrophobia, **which is the abnormal fear of being in high places.** [The main idea of the sentence remains *Joshua eventually overcame his acrophobia.*]

Reference Note

For more about **commas after introductory elements,** see page 326.

Reference Note

For more information on **participial phrases,** see page 102. For more about **subordinate clauses,** see page 121.

Commas   **321**

EXTENSION

Using Commas to Set Off Nonessential Phrases and Clauses

Research. Have each student use various library resources (for example, encyclopedias, biographies, the *Readers' Guide to Periodical Literature,* and *Who's Who*) to find three names with which other students might not be familiar. Have students exchange these names with partners, who will research each person named and write two descriptive sentences about him or her. One of the sentences should contain a nonessential participial phrase, and the other should contain a nonessential clause.

DIFFERENTIATING INSTRUCTION

Learners Having Difficulty

Write on the chalkboard several sentences such as the ones below, omitting the underlining and the commas.

1. Jolene's only piano teacher, <u>who has over fifty students</u>, is one of the best in town.

2. This bouquet of tulips and baby's breath, <u>given to me by my dad</u>, is beautiful.

3. We will be spending most of June, <u>which is my favorite month</u>, with my grandmother Rogers.

Have volunteers use colored chalk to underline each nonessential phrase or clause and to insert commas.

MINI-LESSON   **Grammar**

Who, Which, That. To teach students more about the words that introduce essential and nonessential clauses, remind students that adjective clauses usually begin with a relative pronoun such as *who, which,* or *that. Who* refers to persons, *which* refers to things, and *that* can refer to persons or things. For more information about *who, which,* and *that,* refer students to **Chapter 6: The Clause** and **Chapter 12: A Glossary of Usage.**

Relating to Writing

Activity. To give students extra practice punctuating phrases and clauses, separate the class into groups of four students. Give each group four note cards, and ask the group members to write a participial phrase or a subordinate clause on each card. You could write the following examples on the chalkboard.

1. who found a million dollars

2. that she discovered

3. tortured by indecision

4. looking around carefully

Have the groups exchange their sets of cards and write a correctly punctuated story using the phrases and clauses from their acquired sets. You may want to have one member from each group read the group's story to the rest of the class.

┌─────────────────────┐
│ TIPS & TRICKS │
└─────────────────────┘

A clause beginning with *that* is usually essential.

EXAMPLE
A prize will be awarded to the contestant **that** spills the least water. [Omitting the clause *that spills the least water* changes the basic meaning of the sentence.]

Do not use commas to set off an *essential* (or *restrictive*) phrase or clause. Since such a phrase or clause tells *which one(s)*, it cannot be omitted without changing the meaning of the sentence.

ESSENTIAL PHRASES
All farmers **growing the new hybrid corn** should have a good harvest. [Without the essential phrase, the sentence says *All farmers should have a good harvest.*]

The theories **developed by Einstein** have changed the way people think about the universe. [Without the essential phrase, the sentence says *The theories have changed the way people think about the universe.*]

ESSENTIAL CLAUSES
The map **that we were using** did not show your street. [Without the essential clause, the sentence says *The map did not show your street.*]

Often, someone **who does a good deed** gains more than the person **for whom the deed is done.** [Without the essential clauses, the sentence says *Often someone gains more than the person.*]

Exercise 4 · Using Commas in Sentences Containing Nonessential Phrases and Clauses

Write the following sentences, adding commas to set off the nonessential phrases and clauses. If a sentence is already correct, write *C*.

EXAMPLE   **1.** My music teacher recently told me about Joan Baez who was a popular folk singer in the 1960s.

1. *My music teacher recently told me about Joan Baez, who was a popular folk singer in the 1960s.*

1. Baez born in Staten Island, New York went to high school in California.

2. Her father who was a physicist moved the family to Massachusetts after Joan's graduation.

3. In Boston and nearby Cambridge, Baez performed at small clubs and coffeehouses singing traditional folk songs in a beautiful soprano voice.

4. People attending her early shows were impressed, and Baez attracted a devoted following.   **4.** C

5. In 1959, Baez appearing with Bob Gibson sang at the first annual Newport Folk Festival.

6. The following year she released her first album, titled *Joan Baez*, to great success.

7. Baez, who was involved with many social causes, often sang songs with political messages.

8. She performed at concerts that benefited civil rights organizations and sang "We Shall Overcome" at the 1963 March on Washington.   8. C

9. Baez's political activities, including protests against the Vietnam War, made her a controversial figure in an era of conflict and change.

10. Today she continues to lend her unique voice, which fans have loved for decades, to peace efforts throughout the world.

(2) Use commas to set off nonessential appositives and nonessential appositive phrases.

A *nonessential appositive* or *appositive phrase* provides information that is unnecessary to the meaning of the sentence.

EXAMPLES My best friend, **Nancy,** is studying ballet.

We're out of our most popular flavor, **vanilla.**

Sara, **my cousin,** has won a dance scholarship.

The Rio Grande, **one of the major rivers of North America,** forms the border between Texas and Mexico.

An *essential appositive* adds information that makes the noun or pronoun it identifies more specific. Do not set off an essential appositive.

EXAMPLES The blues singer **Bessie Smith** wrote the song **"Backwater Blues."** [The appositive *Bessie Smith* tells which blues singer. The appositive *"Backwater Blues"* tells which song.]

Exercise 5 **Using Commas in Sentences to Set Off Nonessential Appositives and Appositive Phrases**

Rewrite the sentences that require commas, inserting the commas. If a sentence is already correct, write *C*.

EXAMPLE   **1.** The dog a boxer is named Branford.

1. The dog, a boxer, is named Branford.

Reference Note

For more information about **appositives,** see page 112.

MECHANICS

Commas **323**

PRACTICE

Using Commas with Direct Address

Writing Dialogue. To give students practice in using commas with words used in direct address, have pairs of students write an imaginary dialogue between two famous people, living or dead. To provide ideas, suggest famous athletes, explorers, politicians, artists, singers, inventors, or writers. Allow pairs to present their dialogues to the class in the form of skits. Then, have pairs exchange papers to check each other's sentences for correct comma placement.

1. Katy Jurado, the actress, has appeared in many fine films.
2. The composer Mozart wrote five short piano pieces when he was only six years old.   **2. C**
3. Harper Lee, the author of *To Kill a Mockingbird*, is from Alabama.
4. The card game canasta is descended from mah-jongg, an ancient Chinese game.
5. Jupiter, the fifth planet from the sun, is so large that all the other planets in our solar system could fit inside it.
6. The main character in many of Agatha Christie's mystery novels is the detective Hercule Poirot.   **6. C**
7. The writing of Elizabeth Bowen, an Irish novelist, shows her keen, witty observations of life.
8. Charlemagne, the king of the Franks in the eighth and ninth centuries, became emperor of the Holy Roman Empire.
9. Chuck Yeager, an American pilot, broke the sound barrier in 1947.
10. Effie Tybrec, a Sioux artist from South Dakota, decorates plain sneakers with elaborate beadwork.

(3) Use commas to set off words of direct address.

EXAMPLES   **Mrs. Clarkson,** this package is addressed to you.

Do you know, **Odessa,** when the next bus is due?

I'd like to go now, **Jeff.**

Exercise 6 **Using Commas in Sentences to Set Off Words of Direct Address**

Write the following sentences, adding commas to set off words of direct address.

EXAMPLE   1. Are you hungry Jan or have you had lunch?
         1. Are you hungry, Jan, or have you had lunch?

1. Ms. Wu, will you schedule me for the computer lab tomorrow?
2. Have you signed up for a baseball team yet, Aaron?
3. Your time was good in the hurdles, Juanita, but I know you can do better.
4. Wear sturdy shoes, girls; those hills are hard on the feet!
5. Run, Susan; the bus is pulling out!
6. Felipe, you might like to enter your drawings in the contest.

7. It won't be long until your birthday, Angela, and then you will know what's in the package.

8. Coach Garcia, do we really have to do twenty laps?

9. Which do you like better, Sally, rhymed or unrhymed poetry?

10. All right, boys and girls, let's pick up the litter in the schoolyard.

(4) Use commas to set off parenthetical expressions.

A *parenthetical expression* is a remark that adds information or shows a relationship between ideas.

EXAMPLES   The president said, **of course,** that he was deeply disappointed.

In my opinion, the movie was too violent.

Commonly Used Parenthetical Expressions		
after all	generally speaking	of course
at any rate	I believe (hope,	on the contrary
by the way	suppose, think)	on the other hand
for example	in my opinion	however
for instance	nevertheless	therefore

Some of the above expressions are not always used as interrupters. Use commas only when the expressions are parenthetical.

EXAMPLES   Sidney, **I think,** volunteers at the senior center.
[parenthetical]

I think Sidney volunteers at the senior center.
[not parenthetical]

Traveling by boat may take longer, **however.**
[parenthetical]

However you go, it will be a delightful trip.
[not parenthetical]

> **Exercise 7**   **Using Commas in Sentences to Set Off Parenthetical Expressions**

Write each of the following sentences, using a comma or commas to set off the parenthetical expression.

EXAMPLE   **1.** Mathematics I'm afraid is my hardest subject.

 1. Mathematics, I'm afraid, is my hardest subject.

DIFFERENTIATING INSTRUCTION

Special Education Students

Some students might be able to hear parenthetical expressions more easily than they can spot them on a page. You may wish to read the examples on this page of the textbook aloud and then read them again without the parenthetical expressions. Students should recognize that the sentences do not need the parenthetical expressions to make sense. Stress that parenthetical expressions always interrupt the flow of the sentence and that this interruption is indicated by the use of commas.

MECHANICS

Exercise 7

> **MEETING THE CHALLENGE**
>
> Write a one-page short story about any subject you like. In your short story, include five sentences that use introductory prepositional phrases and five sentences that use introductory verbal phrases. Be sure to punctuate the sentences correctly.

1. The review, of course, covered material from the entire chapter.
2. Your subject should, I think, be limited further.
3. *Cilantro* is the Spanish name for the herb coriander, by the way.
4. Flying, however, will be more expensive than driving there in the car.
5. After all, their hard work paid off.
6. In my opinion, we need to put ice in the picnic cooler.
7. Rabat is the capital of Morocco, I believe.
8. Cooking the rice slowly, therefore, will make it taste better.
9. Motorcycles, generally speaking, are very noisy.
10. On the other hand, they get better gas mileage than cars.

Introductory Words, Phrases, and Clauses

14j. Use a comma after certain introductory elements.

(1) Use a comma to set off a mild exclamation such as *well, oh,* or *why* at the beginning of a sentence. Other introductory words, such as *yes* and *no,* are also set off with commas.

EXAMPLES   **Well,** I think we should ask for help.

Yes, I understand the problem.

(2) Use a comma after an introductory phrase or clause.

Prepositional Phrases

A comma is used after an introductory prepositional phrase if the phrase is long or if two or more phrases appear together.

EXAMPLES   **In the darkening attic room,** the girls searched for the box of old photos.

At night in the desert, the temperature falls rapidly.

If the introductory prepositional phrase is short, a comma may or may not be used.

EXAMPLE   **In the morning,** we'll tour the Caddo burial mounds.
In the morning we'll tour the Caddo burial mounds.

Verbal Phrases

A comma is used after a participial phrase or an infinitive phrase that introduces a sentence.

CONTENT-AREA CONNECTIONS

Mathematics
Word Problems. To emphasize the importance of punctuation in mathematics, ask pairs of students to select several word problems from their math books. Have them copy problems that include commas onto sheets of paper, leaving out the commas. Then, have pairs exchange problems and attempt to solve them. Discuss any confusion that results from not having commas in the proper places.

| PARTICIPIAL PHRASE | **Signaling the referee for a timeout,** the coach gathered her players for a pep talk. |
| INFINITIVE PHRASE | **To keep your bones strong,** be sure to get regular exercise and eat foods rich in calcium. |

> **NOTE** Sometimes an infinitive phrase at the beginning of a sentence is the subject of the sentence. In such a case, the infinitive should not be followed by a comma.
>
> EXAMPLE **To become a museum curator** is Shanda's dream.

Adverb Clauses

An adverb clause may be placed at various places in a sentence. When it begins a sentence, the adverb clause is followed by a comma.

| EXAMPLES | **When March came,** the huge ice floe began to melt and break up. |
| | **Because I had a sore throat,** I could not audition for the school play. |

Reference Note

For more information on **prepositional phrases,** see page 96. For more information about **verbal phrases,** see page 101. For more about **adverb clauses,** see page 127.

Exercise 8 Using Commas in Sentences with Introductory Phrases or Clauses

If a sentence needs a comma, write the word or numeral the comma should follow, and add the comma. If a sentence is already correct, write *C*.

EXAMPLE 1. Patented in 1883 Matzeliger's lasting machine, which attached the sole of a shoe to its upper part, revolutionized the shoe industry.

1. *1883,*

1. Issued in 1991 this stamp honoring inventor Jan Matzeliger is part of the U.S. Postal Service's Black Heritage Stamp series.
2. Since the Postal Service began issuing the series in 1978 the stamps have become popular collectors' items.
3. Originally picturing only government officials or national symbols U.S. stamps now feature a wide variety of people, items, and events.
4. As stamps become more varied stamp collecting becomes even more popular.

5. Because stamps portray our country's <u>culture</u>,they fascinate many people.

6. In the United States <u>alone</u>,more than twenty million people enjoy stamp collecting.

7. To attract <u>collectors</u>,the Postal Service produces limited numbers of special stamps.

8. To find a valuable, rare stamp is the dream of many a collector. **8.** C

9. To keep their collections from becoming too <u>bulky</u>,many collectors concentrate on a single topic.

10. With their treasures safely stored in <u>albums</u>,collectors enjoy examining their first stamps as well as their most recent ones.

Conventional Situations

14k. **Use commas in certain conventional situations.**

(1) **Use commas to separate items in dates and addresses.**

EXAMPLES The United States officially observed Martin Luther King, Jr., Day for the first time on January 20, 1986.

Each year the Kentucky Derby is held in Louisville, Kentucky, on the first Saturday in May.

I think Passover begins on Wednesday, April 14, this year.

The company's new mailing address is 522 Candler Lane, York, PA 17404-8202.

Notice that a comma separates the last item in a date or in an address from the words that follow it.

(2) **Use a comma after the salutation of a personal letter and after the closing of any letter.**

EXAMPLES Dear Aunt Margaret,   Yours truly,

┌HELP┐

A comma does not separate a month from a day (*April 14*), a house number from a street name (*522 Candler Lane*), or a state abbreviation from a ZIP Code (*PA 17404-8202*). A comma also does not separate a month from a year if no day is given (*June 2001*).

Exercise 9 **Correcting Dates, Addresses, and Parts of a Letter by Adding Commas**

Write the following items, inserting commas as needed.

EXAMPLE **1.** Friday October 2 1998

1. *Friday, October 2, 1998*

PRACTICE

Guided and Independent

You may wish to use **Exercise 9** as guided practice. Then, have students complete **Review B** as independent practice. **HOMEWORK**

1. 11687 Montana Avenue,Los Angeles,CA 90049-4673
2. Dresser Road at North First Street in Lynchburg,Virginia
3. from December 1,2001,to March 15,2002
4. Dear Joanne,
5. Sincerely yours,
6. at 4020 Keeley Drive,Antioch,Tennessee,until May 2009
7. Best regards,
8. Thursday,September 14,1967
9 North Tenth Street at Nolana Loop in McAllen,Texas
10. Yours truly,

Review B **Proofreading a Letter for Correct Use of End Marks and Commas**

Copy the following letter, adding any needed commas and end marks.

EXAMPLE　　[1] You're the greatest Aunt Lucy
　　　　　　1. You're the greatest, Aunt Lucy!

[1] 1113 Collins St.
[2] Fort Worth,TX 76106-9299
[3] September 16,2009

[4] Dear Aunt Lucy,

　　[5] What a great time I had at your house last week![6] Your two dogs,Buffy and Pepper,certainly kept me entertained.[7] I've really missed taking them for walks and playing fetch. [8] When summer vacation begins,I could come visit again.[9] Anyway,thank you very much for inviting me.

　　　　　[10] Sincerely,

　　　　　James

HELP

Use a comma in numerals of more than three digits. Place the comma between groups of three digits, counting from the right. If a number includes a decimal, count starting from the left of the decimal.

EXAMPLES
18,408

1,000,000 grains

$4,967.50

HELP

If a preposition is used between items of an address, a comma is not necessary.

EXAMPLE
He lives at 144 Smith Street **in** Moline, Illinois.

EXTENSION

Relating to Writing

Activity. As a culminating activity for this section, you may wish to have students write letters to students who will be eighth-graders next year. Have your students tell what they like best and least about being eighth-graders. Ask students to use commas at least once in each of the following ways: to separate phrases or clauses in a series, to separate adjectives before a noun, to separate independent clauses that are joined by a conjunction, to set off an expression that interrupts a sentence, to set off an introductory phrase or clause, and to set off words or numbers in a conventional situation.

MECHANICS

Commas　**329**

Review C Correcting Sentences by Adding Periods, Question Marks, Exclamation Points, and Commas

Write the following sentences, adding periods, question marks, exclamation points, and commas where they are needed. If a sentence is already correct, write *C.*

EXAMPLE   1. I moved from Canton Ohio to Waco Texas in 1999

      1. I moved from Canton, Ohio, to Waco, Texas, in 1999.
Optional commas are underscored.

1. At the corner of Twelfth St. and Park Ave. I ran into a friend.
2. Have you ever made the long, tiring climb to the head of the Statue of Liberty, Alan?
3. Oh, by the way, remind Geraldine to tell you what happened yesterday.
4. To prepare for her role in that movie, the star observed lawyers at work.
5. Must turtles, crocodiles, alligators, frogs, and dolphins breathe air in order to survive?
6. His new address is 141 Park Dr. Hartford, CT 06101-1347.
7. Junko Tabei, one of a team of Japanese women, reached the summit of Mount Everest in 1975.
8. Students who are late must bring a note from home.   8. C
9. Did the twenty-first century begin officially on January 1, 2000, or on January 1, 2001, Sarah?
10. What a great fireworks display that was!

Review D Correcting a Paragraph by Adding Periods, Question Marks, Exclamation Points, and Commas

Write the following paragraph, adding periods, question marks, exclamation points, and commas where they are needed.

EXAMPLE   [1] Have you ever played chess

      1. Have you ever played chess?
Optional commas are underscored.

[1] To beginners and experts alike, chess is a complex, demanding game. [2] It requires mental discipline, intense concentration, and dedication to long hours of practice. [3] Displaying those qualities, the Raging Rooks of Harlem tied for first place at the National

Junior High Chess Championship,which was held in Dearborn, Mich.[4] Sixty teams competing with the Rooks came from all across the U.S.[5] The thirteen- and fourteen-year-old Rooks attended New York City's Public School 43.[6] When they returned to New York after the tournament,they were greeted by Mayor David Dinkins.[7] Becoming media celebrities,they appeared on television and were interviewed by local newspapers and national news services.[8] Imagine how proud of them their friends and families must have been![9] The Rooks' coach, Maurice Ashley,wasn't surprised that the team did so well in the tournament.[10] After all,Ashley,the first African American grandmaster,has guided two Harlem schools,P.S. 43 and Mott Hall Intermediate School,to national championship tournaments.

Semicolons

A *semicolon* is used primarily to join independent clauses that are closely related in meaning.

14l. Use a semicolon between independent clauses in a sentence when they are not joined by *and, but, for, nor, or, so,* or *yet.*

EXAMPLES
On our first trip to Houston, I wanted to see the Astrodome; my little brother wanted to visit the Johnson Space Center.

Our parents settled the argument for us; they took us to both places.

Use a semicolon between independent clauses only when the ideas in the clauses are closely related.

INCORRECT I called Leon; did you notice how windy it is?

CORRECT I called Leon. **D**id you notice how windy it is?

I called Leon; he will be here in ten minutes.

NOTE Very short independent clauses in a series may be separated by commas instead of semicolons.

EXAMPLE
The leaves whispered, the brook gurgled, the sun beamed brightly.

Semicolons   **331**

HELP

Notice that a semicolon looks like a combination of a period and a comma. In fact, you can think of a semicolon as part period and part comma. A semicolon signals a pause in thought and is stronger than a comma but not as strong as a period.

MECHANICS

Semicolons
Rules 14l–n *(pp. 331–334)*

OBJECTIVE

■ **To correct sentences by adding semicolons and commas**

DIRECT TEACHING

Modeling and Demonstration

Semicolons. Model how to proofread sentences for correct use of semicolons by using the example *On our first trip to Houston, I wanted to see the Astrodome; my little brother wanted to visit the Johnson Space Center.* First, ask students whether there are two independent clauses in this sentence. [*yes*] Next, ask whether the two clauses are joined by *and, but, for, nor, or, so,* or *yet.* [*no*] Then, ask whether the ideas in the two clauses are closely related. [*yes*] Point out that the two independent clauses are correctly joined by a semicolon, placed after *Astrodome,* to form a compound sentence. Now, have a volunteer use another example from the chapter to demonstrate how to proofread sentences for correct use of semicolons.

RESOURCES

Semicolons
Practice
■ *Language & Sentence Skills Practice,* pp. 292–293
■ *Developmental Language & Sentence Skills,* pp. 111–112

COMPUTER TIP

A computer can help you check your writing for the correct punctuation of conjunctive adverbs and transitional expressions. Use a computer's search function to find semicolons. Then, look at each conjunctive adverb or transitional expression carefully to see how it is used. Does it join clauses? Does it interrupt a clause? Add or delete commas and semicolons as needed, using the rules in this chapter.

14m. Use a semicolon between independent clauses that are joined by a conjunctive adverb or a transitional expression.

A *conjunctive adverb* or a *transitional expression* shows how the independent clauses that it joins are related.

EXAMPLES   English was Lou's hardest subject**;** **accordingly,** he gave it more time than any other subject.

The popular names of certain animals are misleading**;** **for example,** the koala bear is not a bear.

Commonly Used Conjunctive Adverbs			
accordingly	furthermore	instead	nevertheless
besides	however	meanwhile	otherwise
consequently	indeed	moreover	therefore

Commonly Used Transitional Expressions			
as a result	for example	for instance	that is
in addition	in other words	in conclusion	in fact

NOTE   When a conjunctive adverb or a transitional expression joins clauses, it is preceded by a semicolon and followed by a comma. When it interrupts a clause, however, it is set off by commas.

EXAMPLES   Dad got the snacks ready**;** **meanwhile,** Theo and I decorated the living room.

Dad got the snacks ready; Theo and I**,** **meanwhile,** decorated the living room.

14n. A semicolon (rather than a comma) may be needed to separate independent clauses joined by a coordinating conjunction when the clauses contain commas.

Use a semicolon in such a situation only to prevent confusion or misreading.

CONFUSING   Our strongest defensive players are Carlos, Will, and Jared, and Kareem and Matt are excellent on offense.

CLEAR   Our strongest defensive players are Carlos, Will, and Jared**;** and Kareem and Matt are excellent on offense.

Learning for Life

Writing a Newsletter. Have students work in small groups to create newsletters for school organizations. Each group's newsletter should contain several carefully punctuated articles related to an organization's activities. Encourage students to include illustrations with captions.

Pass out newsletters from local groups as samples for style. Each group member should write one article. Encourage

As long as the sentence is not confusing or hard to read without a semicolon, a comma is enough.

EXAMPLE   Otto, you are the sweetest, most lovable dog in the world, and I'm glad I found you.

NOTE Semicolons are also used between items in a series when the items contain commas.

EXAMPLE   He was born on September 27, 1983; began school on September 4, 1988; and graduated from high school on May 17, 2001.

Exercise 10 Correcting Sentences by Adding Semicolons and Commas

Write the following sentences, adding semicolons and commas where they are needed.

HELP—

Not all of the sentences in Exercise 10 need both semicolons and commas.

EXAMPLE   1. The gym is on the ground floor the classrooms are above it.

          1. *The gym is on the ground floor; the classrooms are above it.*

Optional commas are underscored.

1. Scientists have explored almost all the lands on earth;they are now exploring the floors of the oceans.
2. Some of the birds at the feeder were picky eaters; the blue jay, for instance,would eat only sunflower seeds.
3. St. Augustine, Florida, was the first European settlement in the United States;the Spanish founded it in 1565.
4. Mike Powell set a world record for the long jump in 1991;his leap of 29 feet and 4½ inches beat Bob Beamon's 1968 record by 2 inches.
5. Some reptiles like a dry climate;others prefer a wet climate.
6. We visited New Orleans,Louisiana;Natchez,Mississippi;and St. Louis,Missouri.
7. In April 1912, a new, "unsinkable" ocean liner, the *Titanic,* struck an iceberg in the North Atlantic;as a result,roughly 1,500 persons lost their lives.
8. The members of the swim team who won first-place medals were Sam Foster, in the fifty-meter freestyle;Philip Tucker, in the individual medley;and Earl Sinclair, in the one-hundred-meter backstroke.

students to use the *5W-How?* questions approach to journalistic writing. After the articles are written, have group members offer suggestions relating to clarity of writing, completeness of information, and the correct use of end marks, commas, and semicolons.

Students could offer their newsletters to the appropriate organizations as advertising or public relations tools.

9. Joanna, your team will include Fred, Marty, and Manny, and Josie. Sam, and Phuong will be on my team.
10. The kind of tuba that wraps around the player's body is actually called a sousaphone; it was named for John Philip Sousa, a famous band leader who came up with the idea for the shape.

Colons

14o. Use a colon before a list of items, especially after expressions like *as follows* or *the following*.

EXAMPLES   Beyond talent lie all the usual words: discipline, love, luck, but, most of all, endurance.

James Baldwin, *The Writer's Chapbook*

Minimum equipment for camping is as follows: a bedroll, utensils for cooking and eating, warm clothing, sturdy shoes, a pocketknife, and a rope.

NOTE   Do not use a colon between a verb and its object or between a preposition and its object.

INCORRECT   Marcelo's hobbies include: fishing, hiking, and painting.

Last fall the Cohens traveled through: New York, Vermont, New Hampshire, and Maine.

CORRECT   Marcelo's hobbies include fishing, hiking, and painting.

Last fall the Cohens traveled through New York, Vermont, New Hampshire, and Maine.

14p. Use a colon before a statement that explains or clarifies a preceding statement.

EXAMPLES   Luis felt that he had accomplished something worthwhile: He had written and recorded his first song.

Mark Twain tried many jobs before becoming a successful writer: He was a printer's apprentice, a riverboat pilot, a soldier, and a silver miner.

Colons

Rules 14o–r *(pp. 334–336)*

OBJECTIVE

■ To correct sentences by adding colons

DIRECT TEACHING

Modeling and Demonstration

Colons. Model how to add colons to sentences where needed by using the incorrect example *Minimum equipment for camping is as follows, a bedroll, utensils for cooking and eating, warm clothing, sturdy shoes, a pocketknife, and a rope.* First, ask students whether the sentence contains a list of items. [*yes*] Next, ask whether the list is the object of a preposition, since a colon should not come between a preposition and its object. [*no*] Then, ask whether the list is the object of a verb, since a colon should not come between a verb and its object. [*no*] Therefore, a colon should replace the comma after *follows* to signal that more information follows. Now, have a volunteer use another example from this chapter to demonstrate how to use colons correctly.

STYLE TIP

Semicolons do a better job if you do not use too many. Sometimes it is better to make two sentences out of a compound sentence or a heavily punctuated sentence rather than to use a semicolon.

ACCEPTABLE
Doubles tennis, as you know, is partly based on strategy; the two players must know each other's games, communicate well, and work together on their tactical approach.

BETTER
Doubles tennis, as you know, is partly based on strategy. The two players must know each other's games, communicate well, and work together on their tactical approach.

MECHANICS

RESOURCES

Colons
Practice
■ *Language & Sentence Skills Practice,* pp. 294, 297–298
■ *Developmental Language & Sentence Skills,* pp. 111–112

14q. Use a colon before a long, formal statement or quotation.

EXAMPLE   Patrick Henry concluded his revolutionary speech before the Virginia House of Burgesses with these ringing words**:** "Is life so dear, or peace so sweet as to be purchased at the price of chains and slavery? Forbid it, Almighty God! I know not what course others may take, but as for me, give me liberty or give me death!"

14r. Use a colon in certain conventional situations.

(1) Use a colon between the hour and the minute.

EXAMPLES   12**:**57 P.M.   4**:**08 A.M.

(2) Use a colon after the salutation of a business letter.

EXAMPLES   Dear Ms. Gonzalez**:**

Dear Sir or Madam**:**

To Whom It May Concern**:**

(3) Use a colon between chapter and verse in Biblical references and between titles and subtitles.

EXAMPLES   Matthew 6**:**9–13   "Easter**:** Wahiawa, 1959"
I Corinthians 13**:**1–2   *Akavak***:** *An Eskimo Journey*

> **Exercise 11**   Correcting Sentences by Adding Colons

Write each of the following sentences, inserting a colon where it is needed.

EXAMPLE   **1.** In Ruth 1 16, Ruth pledges her loyalty to Naomi, her mother-in-law.

        1. In Ruth 1:16, Ruth pledges her loyalty to Naomi, her mother-in-law.

1. During the field trip, our teacher pointed out the following trees**:**sugarberry, papaw, silver bell, and mountain laurel.
2. The first lunch period begins at 11**:**00 A.M.
3. This is my motto**:**Laugh and the world laughs with you.
4. Using a recipe from *Miami Spice***:***The New Florida Cuisine*, we made barbecue sauce.
5. The artist showed me how to make lavender**:**Mix blue, white, and a little red.
6. The shortest verse in the Bible is John 11**:**35.

┌ **HELP** ─────

When a list of words, phrases, or subordinate clauses follows a colon, the first word of the list is lowercase. When an independent clause follows a colon, the first word of the clause begins with a capital letter.

EXAMPLES

All entries must include the following items**:** **a**n original photograph, a brief essay, and a self-addressed stamped envelope.

That reminds me of my favorite saying**:** **H**e who laughs last laughs best.

DIRECT TEACHING

Correcting Misconceptions

Colons and Semicolons. Some students may confuse the colon and the semicolon or think that the two are interchangeable. Explain that ordinarily a colon indicates what the writer wants to emphasize, whereas a semicolon helps the reader avoid confusion. Have students create posters illustrating the uses of the colon and the semicolon. Display the posters in the classroom so that students can refer to them throughout the year.

EXTENSION

Relating to Speaking

Quotations. To reinforce the use of colons, have students select quotations that they like. If students need help, refer them to a dictionary of quotations or the sayings Benjamin Franklin published in *Poor Richard's Almanac*. Next, have them write sentences containing the quotations set off by a colon, such as the following one:

> I'll never forget Patrick Henry's stirring words: "Give me liberty, or give me death."

Have students work in groups of three to check each other's punctuation. Then, have each student write his or her sentence on the chalkboard, read it, and tell why he or she chose that quotation.

7. Dear Senator Lupino:
8. The train will leave at exactly 3:15.
9. When I look at the night sky, I am reminded of lines from a poem called "Stars," by Sara Teasdale: "And I know that I / Am honored to be / Witness / Of so much majesty."
10. The menu for the 1:00 P.M. lunch includes empanadas, egg rolls, curry, and hummus.

Review E Correcting a Paragraph by Adding Punctuation

Write the following paragraph, adding periods, question marks, exclamation points, commas, semicolons, and colons where they are needed.   Optional commas are underscored.

EXAMPLE   [1] Acadiana La isn't a town it's a region

1. *Acadiana, La., isn't a town; it's a region.*

[1] Known as Cajun country, the region includes the twenty-two southernmost parishes of Louisiana. [2] Did you know that the word *Cajun* is a shortened form of *Acadian*? [3] Cajuns are descended from French colonists who settled along the Bay of Fundy in what is now eastern Canada; they named their colony *Acadie*. [4] After the British took over the area, they deported nearly two thirds of the Acadians; in 1755, many families were separated. [5] Some Acadians took refuge in southern Louisiana's isolated swamps and bayous. [6] They didn't remain isolated, however. They incorporated into their dialect elements of the following languages: French, English, Spanish, German, and a variety of African and American Indian languages. [7] In 1847, the American poet Henry Wadsworth Longfellow described the uprooting of the Acadians in *Evangeline*, a long narrative poem that inspired Joseph Rusling Meeker to paint *The Land of Evangeline*, which is shown to the left. [8] Today most people associate Cajun culture with hot, spicy foods and lively fiddle and accordion music. [9] Remembering their often tragic past, Cajuns sum up their outlook on life in the following saying: *Lâche pas la patate*, which means "Don't let go of the potato." [10] What a great way to tell people not to lose their grip!

The Saint Louis Art Museum. Gift of Mrs. W.P. Edgerton, by exchange.

Numerals in brackets
refer to rules tested
by the items in the
Chapter Review.

1. [14i(2), b]
2. [14o, f, a]
3. [14j(2), e, a]
4. [14i(1), a]
5. [14i(3), d]
6. [14g, a]
7. [14j(1), r(3), a]
8. [14b]
9. [14h, m, i(4), a]
10. [14j(1), a]
11. [14c, a]
12. [14j(2), a]
13. [14e, k(1), b]
14. [14i(1), a]
15. [14f, n, a]
16. [14j(2), a]
17. [14j(2), a]
18. [14r(1), b]
19. [14e, k(1), a]
20. [14j(2), a]

Chapter Review

A. Correcting Sentences by Adding Punctuation

Each of the following sentences contains at least one error
in the use of periods, question marks, exclamation points,
commas, semicolons, and colons. Write each sentence,
correcting the punctuation errors.

Optional commas are underscored.

1. Have you seen our principal,Ms. O'Donnell,today?

2. We made a salad with the following vegetables from our garden: lettuce,cucumbers,zucchini,squash,and cherry tomatoes.

3. Running after the bus,Dr.Tassano tripped and fell in a puddle.

4. My first pet,which I got when I was six,was a beagle.

5. Come in,Randy,and sit down.

6. The soft,subtle colors of this beautiful Tabriz carpet are arranged in an intricate medallion pattern.

7. Well,I do know John 3:16 by heart.

8. Does anyone know where the can opener is?

9. The chickens clucked,and the ducks squawked;however,the dogs didn't make a sound.

10. Yes,I recognize her.She's in my math class.

11. Wow!That's the longest home run I've ever hit! **11.** [or . . . hit.]

12. After the rain stopped,the blue jays hopped around the lawn.

13. Wasn't President John F.Kennedy assassinated in Dallas,Tex., on November 22,1963?

14. Soy sauce,which is made from soybeans,flavors many traditional Chinese and Japanese foods.

15. The first ones to arrive were Matt, Juan,and Linda;and Pat and Phil came later.

16. Preparing for takeoff,the huge jetliner rolled toward the runway.

17. In one of the barns,we found an old butter churn.

18. Did you see the highlights of the Cinco de Mayo Fiesta on the 6:00 news?

19. Her address is 142 Oak Hollow Blvd.,Mendota,CA 93640-2316.

20. To get a better view of the fireworks,Josh and I rode our bikes to Miller's Hill.

Chapter Review **337**

B. Correcting a Paragraph by Adding Periods, Question Marks, Exclamation Points, and Commas

Each sentence in the following paragraph contains at least one error in the use of periods, question marks, exclamation points, and commas. Write the paragraph, adding correct punctuation. Optional commas are underscored.

21. [14f, a]
22. [14j(2), a]
23. [14i(2), a]
24. [14h, f, a]
25. [14b]
26. [14h, i(2), a]
27. [14i(2), g, f, a]
28. [14j(2), f, b]
29. [14c]
30. [14j(1), h, i(4), b]

[21] Sixty miles south of Sicily is an ancient culturally diverse and quite fascinating island called Malta. [22] After being a British colony for over 150 years Malta became an independent nation in 1964. [23] The Maltese are a Mediterranean people whose language Maltese is a West Arabic dialect interspersed with Italian words. [24] Malta's history goes back to the Stone Age and the area has been colonized by Phoenician Greek Roman and Arab conquerors. [25] Have you ever heard of the Knights of Malta? [26] They successfully resisted a siege by the Ottoman Turks in the sixteenth century and Malta's capital Valletta is named after the Grand Master of the Knights at that time Jean de la Vallette. [27] Valletta Malta's capital since 1571 is a compact city with narrow winding streets an ancient cathedral and a harbor on the Mediterranean Sea. [28] With its sunny climate friendly people and multicultural heritage doesn't Malta sound like a great place for a vacation? [29] Let's go! [30] Well maybe we can't but we can dream can't we?

C. Correctly Using Semicolons and Colons

Each of the following items contains errors in the use of semicolons or colons. Write each item, correcting the punctuation.

31. [14m]
32. [14o]
33. [14n (Note)]
34. [14m]
35. [14o]

31. Emma felt shy; however, she soon made new friends.
32. Additional supplies are as follows: a ballpoint pen, some construction paper, scissors, and an eraser.
33. Dr. Termi has sent me letters from Dublin, Ireland; Geneva, Switzerland; Florence, Italy; and Athens, Greece.
34. Our music class is very busy; for example, Maria is giving a violin recital next week.
35. In the main hall we saw flags of five countries: the United Kingdom, Canada, India, Jamaica, and South Africa.

Writing Application
Using Correct Punctuation in a Business Letter

End Marks, Commas, Semicolons, and Colons   A local radio station is sponsoring a contest to select items to put in a time capsule. To enter the contest, write a business letter suggesting one item to include in the time capsule, which will be buried for one hundred years. In your letter, use punctuation marks correctly and follow the rules of business correspondence.

Prewriting   List tangible items (ones you can touch) that show what life is like now in the United States. Next, choose the item you think would give people one hundred years from now the clearest picture of life today. Finally, make up a name, address, and call letters for the radio station.

Writing   As you draft your letter, keep in mind that a business letter calls for a businesslike tone. Explain why the item you are suggesting should be included in the time capsule. Keep your letter brief, and stick to the point.

Revising   To evaluate your letter, ask yourself the following questions: Is the letter easy to follow? Have I used standard English to present my ideas clearly and reasonably? Based on your answers to these questions, revise your letter to make it clearer and easier to follow.

Publishing   Proofread your letter carefully, paying special attention to your use of end marks, commas, semicolons, and colons. Make sure that you have followed the proper form for a business letter. Type your letter on a computer, or handwrite a final copy and photocopy it. Compare it with those of your classmates. The class could vote on what ten items they would choose to put in a time capsule.

MECHANICS

15

Punctuation

Underlining (Italics), Quotation Marks, Apostrophes, Hyphens, Parentheses, Brackets, Dashes

Diagnostic Preview

A. Proofreading Sentences for the Correct Use of Quotation Marks and Underlining (Italics)

Each of the following sentences requires underlining (italics), quotation marks, or both. Write each sentence correctly, inserting the appropriate punctuation.

Numerals in brackets refer to rules tested by the items in the Diagnostic Preview.

1. [15l, c]
2. [15d, h, f]
3. [15a]
4. [15l]
5. [15b, l]
6. [15d, h]

EXAMPLE
1. Ted, can you answer the first question? Ms. Simmons asked.

1. *"Ted, can you answer the first question?"* *Ms. Simmons asked.*

1. The best chapter, "More Word Games," has a game involving the word enthusiasm.
2. "I answered all the questions," Todd said, "but I think that some of my answers were wrong."
3. The Wizard of Oz was more exciting on the big movie screen than it was on our small television set.
4. Every Christmas Eve my uncle recites "The Night Before Christmas" for the children in the hospital.
5. There is a legend that the band on the Titanic played the hymn "Nearer, My God, to Thee" as the ship sank.
6. "Play the Freddie Jackson CD again, Sam," Rebecca called.

7. Wendy wrote an article called "Students, Where Are You?" for our local newspaper, the <u>Morning Beacon</u>.

8. In the short story "Thank You, M'am" by Langston Hughes, a woman helps a troubled boy.

9. "Can I read <u>Treasure Island</u> for my report?" Carmine asked.

10. Mr. Washington asked Connie, "Which flag also included the slogan 'Don't Tread on Me'?"

7. [15l, a, i]
8. [15l]
9. [15a, d, g, i]
10. [15m, i]

B. Proofreading Sentences for the Correct Use of Apostrophes, Hyphens, Parentheses, Brackets, and Dashes

Each of the following sentences contains at least one error in the use of apostrophes, hyphens, parentheses, brackets, or dashes. Write each sentence correctly. Dashes are indicated by ‾λ.

EXAMPLE   1. Ive been thinking about rivers names that come from American Indian words.

1. *I've been thinking about rivers' names that come from American Indian words.*

Some answers may vary.

11. ~~Boater's~~ on the Missouri River may not know that *Missouri* means "people of the big canoes."

12. Have you ever heard the song about the South's famous Shenandoah River?

13. The committee has voted to help keep the walkway clean a‾long the Connecticut River.

14. I cant remember‾I wonder how many people have this sa‾me problem‾how many *i*s are in the word *Mississippi*.

15. Mount Vernon (the home of George Washington ‾(1732–1799)) overlooks the Potomac River.

16. Alicia said, "Don't you remember their story about catching twenty-two fish in the Arkansas River?"

17. Three fourths of the class couldnt pronounce the name *Monongahela* until we broke it into syllables‾Mo-non-ga-he-la.

18. Eliseo's oil painting of the Mohawk River was very good, but ‾her's was better.

19. Ricardos guidebook(the one he ordered last month)states that the Suwannee is one of Floridas major rivers.

20. Shes lived in Massachusetts for thirty-one years but has never before seen the Merrimack River.

11. Boaters [15o (Note)]
12. [15n]
13. along [15t(4)]
14. same [15r, z, t(2), s]
15. [1732–1799] [15y]
16. [15u]
17. [15r, z]
18. hers [15p]
19. [15n, x]
20. [15r, u]

INTRODUCING THE CHAPTER

- The first part of this chapter covers underlining (italics) for titles, names of trains, ships, aircraft, and space-craft, and for words, letters, and numbers referred to as such. The correct use of quotation marks and the punctuation rules for direct quotations are reviewed. Lessons on the use of apostrophes to form posses-sives, contractions, and some plurals are covered as well as the usage rules for hyphens, parentheses, brackets, and dashes.

- This chapter closes with a **Chapter Review** including a **Writing Application** that asks students to use underlining and quotation marks cor-rectly in writing a report based on actual interviews.

- This chapter could serve as a useful reference in the proofreading stage of writing assignments. For help in integrating this chapter with writing assignments in *Holt Literature and Language Arts,* see the **Teaching Strands** chart on pp. T24–T25.

ASSESSING

Entry-Level Assessment

Diagnostic Preview. The **Diagnostic Preview** contains two parts. You may wish to use **Part A,** which focuses on underlining (italics) and quotation marks, to determine whether students need a review of these punctuation marks before writ-ing literary analyses, research reports, or stories containing dialogue.

You may wish to use **Part B,** which focuses on the correct use of apostro-phes, hyphens, parentheses, brackets, and dashes, prior to giving writing assignments that may require these punctuation marks.

Differentiating Instruction

- *UA: Differentiating Instruction*
- *UA: Supporting Instruction in Five Languages*

Assessment

- *Formal Assessment*
- *Progress-Monitoring Tests,* pp. 29–30, 48

- *Test Generator (Teacher One Stop DVD-ROM)* 🎧

Other Language Resources

- *Spelling Lessons & Activities*
- *WordSharp: An Interactive Vocabulary Tutor*
- *Reading and Writing Transparencies*

MECHANICS

PRETEACHING

Lesson Starter

Prerequisite Skills. Point out to students that one way to tell whether a noun that ends in *s* forms a possessive and not a plural is to rewrite the sentence using *of.* For example, *the dog's collar* can be rewritten as *the collar of the dog,* but *the dogs barked* can't be rewritten in this way. Have students try this technique with the following examples.

Our neighbors' kitten followed us home. [*the kitten of our neighbors*]

Our neighbors have a kitten.

They will visit the Clarks' home. [*the home of the Clarks*]

The Clarks have a home near the lake.

Underlining (Italics)

Rules 15a–c *(pp. 342–344)*

OBJECTIVE

■ To identify words that should be underlined (italicized) in sentences

DIFFERENTIATING INSTRUCTION

Advanced Learners

Newspapers and magazines may have their own house styles regarding punctuation of titles. For example, some publications use quotation marks rather than italics for movie titles.

Have students research the use of italics in various newspapers and magazines from your school library. Suggest that students look at art, music, and film reviews to find examples of the use of italics. Ask volunteers to share their findings with the class.

COMPUTER TIP

If you use a computer, you may be able to set words in italics. Most fonts can be set in italics.

Reference Note

For examples of **titles** that are not italicized but are enclosed in **quotation marks,** see page 349.

TIPS & TRICKS

Generally, the title of an entire work (book, magazine, TV series) is italicized while the title of a part (chapter, article, episode) is enclosed in quotation marks.

HELP

To find the official title of a newspaper or magazine, look at the masthead. In a newspaper, the masthead usually appears on the editorial page. In a magazine, the masthead can be found on one of the first few pages, usually following the table of contents.

Underlining (Italics)

Italics are printed letters that lean to the right, such as *the letters in these words.* In your handwritten or typewritten work, indicate italics by underlining. If your work were printed for publication, the underlined words would appear in italics. For example, if you were to write

Born Free is the story of a lioness that became a pet.

the printed version would look like this:

Born Free is the story of a lioness that became a pet.

15a. Use underlining (italics) for titles and subtitles of books, plays, periodicals, works of art, films, television series, and long musical compositions and recordings.

Type of Title	Examples	
Books	*The Storyteller*	*Little Women*
	Lincoln: A Photo-biography	*The Adventures of Tom Sawyer*
Plays	*The Piano Lesson*	*A Doll's House*
	The Flying Tortilla Man	*Visit to a Small Planet*
Periodicals	*The New York Times*	*Hispanic*
	Scientific American	*Transitions Abroad*
	Sky and Telescope	*The Nation*

NOTE Underline (or italicize) an article (*a, an,* or *the*) at the beginning of a title or subtitle only if it is the first word of the official title or subtitle.

EXAMPLES   During vacation she read ***The*** *Woman Warrior,* by Maxine Hong Kingston. [The article *The* is part of the title.]

My parents subscribe to **the** *San Francisco Chronicle.* [The article *the* is not part of the official title.]

RESOURCES

Underlining (Italics)
Practice
■ *Language & Sentence Skills Practice,* pp. 304–306
■ *Developmental Language & Sentence Skills,* pp. 113–114

Type of Title	Examples	
Works of Art	*The Thinker*	*American Gothic*
Films	*The Wizard of Oz*	*Casablanca*
Television Series	*Dateline*	*Wall Street Week*
	Boy Meets World	*Animaniacs*
Long Musical Compositions and Recordings	*Don Giovanni*	*The Four Seasons*
	Fidelio	*Appalachian Spring*

15b. Use underlining (italics) for names of ships, trains, aircraft, and spacecraft.

Type of Title	Examples	
Ships	*Calypso*	*Titanic*
Trains	*Silver Meteor*	*Santa Fe Chief*
Aircraft	*Enola Gay*	*Air Force One*
Spacecraft	*Eagle*	*Columbia*

15c. Use underlining (italics) for words, letters, and numerals referred to as such.

EXAMPLES   Jean sometimes confuses the words **affect** and **effect.**

Don't forget to double the **p** when you add **–ed.**

Does your number begin with a **5** or an **8**?

Exercise 1 **Using Underlining (Italics) in Sentences**

Write and underline the words that should be italicized in each of the following sentences.

EXAMPLE   **1.** Have you read The Call of the Wild?

    1. The Call of the Wild

1. The magazine rack held current issues of National Wildlife, Time, Essence, Jewish Monthly, and Sports Illustrated.
2. Sometimes I forget to put the first o in the word thorough, and by mistake I write through.

Reference Note

For information on **capitalizing titles,** see page 302.

STYLE   TIP

Writers sometimes use italics for emphasis, especially in written dialogue. The italic type shows how the sentence is supposed to be spoken. Read the following sentences aloud. Notice that by italicizing different words, the writer can change the meaning of the sentence.

EXAMPLES
"Are you *sure* the quarterback hurt his ankle?" asked Michelle. [Are you sure, not just guessing?]

"Are you sure the *quarterback* hurt his ankle?" asked Michelle. [Was it the quarterback, not some other player, who hurt his ankle?]

"Are you sure the quarterback hurt his *ankle*?" asked Michelle. [Did the quarterback hurt his ankle, not his knee?]

Italicizing (underlining) words for emphasis is a handy technique that should not be overused. It can quickly lose its impact.

DIRECT TEACHING

Modeling and Demonstration

Underlining (Italics). Model how to identify words that should be underlined (italicized) by using the example *During vacation she read The Woman Warrior by Maxine Hong Kingston.* First, ask students to identify *The Woman Warrior.* [*title of a book*] Next, ask whether this title should be underlined (italicized). [*yes*] Then, ask whether the word *The* is part of the book's title. [*yes*] Point out that when *the* is part of a title, it should be underlined (italicized). Now, have a volunteer use another example from this chapter to demonstrate how to use underlining (italics) correctly.

Correcting Misconceptions

Titles. Many students have trouble distinguishing between titles that should be underlined (italicized) and those that should be placed in quotation marks. You could teach **Rules 15a** and **15l** (p. 349) together. Directly compare the two charts following the rules. Point out that titles that are underlined (italicized) name longer works or works that are whole. Titles in quotation marks usually name shorter works or portions of works.

Using an overhead projector, present a scrambled list of kinds of titles covered by these two rules. Show one item at a time. As each item is uncovered, have students call out either "italics" or "quotation marks."

MECHANICS

MINI-LESSON **Mechanics**

Using Italics. To help students remember to italicize words, letters, and numerals referred to as such, encourage them to look for phrases like *the word, the letter,* or *the numeral* before a word, letter, or numeral.

If one of these expressions is present, or could be added without changing the meaning of the sentence, then the word, letter, or numeral should be italicized or underlined.

Exercise 1

DISTRIBUTED REVIEW
Ask students to classify sentences 2, 4, 6, and 8 according to sentence structure. [2. *compound*, 4. *complex*, 6. *complex*, 8. *simple*]

Quotation Marks
Rules 15d–m *(pp. 344–351)*

OBJECTIVES

- To revise sentences containing direct quotations by adding capital letters, quotation marks, and other punctuation

- To use correct punctuation in paragraphs containing dialogue

- To correct sentences by adding double and single quotation marks

DIRECT TEACHING

Modeling and Demonstration

Quotation Marks. Model how to revise sentences for correct use of quotation marks by using the example *Has anyone here swum in the Great Salt Lake asked my cousin.* First, ask students whether the example contains the speaker's exact words. [*yes*] Explain that this is a direct quotation, and therefore the speaker's words should be enclosed in quotation marks. Then, ask where the quotation marks should be placed. [*before* Has *and after* Lake] Point out that since the quotation is a question, a question mark should be placed after *Lake* and inside the quotation marks. Now, have a volunteer use another example from this chapter to demonstrate how to use quotation marks correctly.

MEETING THE CHALLENGE

Write the following categories in a column: book, play, newspaper, magazine, movie, television series, painting, long musical work. Next to each category, write the title of your favorite work. Then, make up a sentence using each of these titles. After you have finished, check your work against the examples given in **Rule 15a**.

Answers will vary, but students should mark answers with underlining (italics) according to the guidelines in **Rule 15a**.

---

3. The final number will be a medley of tunes from George Gershwin's opera Porgy and Bess.
4. Jerry Spinelli won the Newbery Medal for his book Maniac Magee, which is about an unusual athlete.
5. Picasso's painting Guernica is named for a Spanish town that was destroyed during the Spanish Civil War.
6. My father reads the Chicago Sun-Times because he likes its columnists.
7. The first battle between ironclad ships took place between the Monitor and the Merrimack in 1862.
8. The Irish movie Into the West features the adventure of two brothers and their magical horse.
9. I had never traveled by train until we rode the Hill Country Flyer.
10. Melissa asked Christopher whether he and his family ever watch the show Nova.

Quotation Marks

15d. Use quotation marks to enclose a ***direct quotation***—a person's exact words.

Be sure to place quotation marks both before and after a person's exact words.

EXAMPLES   "Has anyone here swum in the Great Salt Lake?" asked my cousin.

Peggy Ann said, "I swam there last summer."

Do not use quotation marks for an ***indirect quotation***—a rewording of a direct quotation.

| DIRECT QUOTATION | Kaya asked Christopher, "What is your interpretation of the poem?" |
| INDIRECT QUOTATION | Kaya asked Christopher what his interpretation of the poem is. |

| DIRECT QUOTATION | As Barbara Jordan said in her keynote address to the Democratic National Convention in 1976, "We are willing to suffer the discomfort of change in order to achieve a better future." |
| INDIRECT QUOTATION | Barbara Jordan said that people will put up with the discomfort of change to have a better future. |

RESOURCES

Quotation Marks
Practice

- *Language & Sentence Skills Practice,* pp. 307–311, 320
- *Developmental Language & Sentence Skills,* pp. 115–118

15e. A direct quotation generally begins with a capital letter.

EXAMPLES Brandon shouted, "**L**aura! Over here!"

Abraham Lincoln said, "**T**hose who deny freedom to others deserve it not for themselves."

15f. When the expression identifying the speaker interrupts a quoted sentence, the second part of the quotation begins with a lowercase letter.

EXAMPLES "Do you know," asked Angelo, "**w**hat the astronauts learned when they landed on the moon?"

"One thing they found," answered Gwen, "**w**as that the moon is covered by a layer of dust."

Notice in the examples above that each part of a divided quotation is enclosed in a set of quotation marks. In addition, the interrupting expression is set off by commas.

When the second part of a divided quotation is a complete sentence, it begins with a capital letter.

EXAMPLE "Any new means of travel is exciting," remarked Mrs. Perkins. "**S**pace travel is no exception."

Notice that in such cases a period, not a comma, follows the interrupting expression.

15g. A direct quotation is set off from the rest of the sentence by a comma, a question mark, or an exclamation point, but not by a period.

EXAMPLES Alyssa said**,** "Mrs. Batista showed us a short film about Narcissa Whitman."

"Was she one of the early settlers in the Northwest**?**" asked Delia.

"What an adventure**!**" exclaimed Iola.

15h. A period or a comma is placed inside the closing quotation marks.

EXAMPLES Ramón said, "Hank Aaron was a better player than Babe Ruth because he hit more home runs in his career**.**"

"Hank Aaron never hit sixty homers in one year, though**.**" Paula responded.

┌HELP─┐

When you leave out part of a quotation, use three spaced periods, called *ellipses,* to show where the words have been omitted.

ORIGINAL
Stephanie said, "The stars shining above the prairie twinkle with an unusual glimmer tonight."

WITH ELLIPSES
Stephanie said, "The stars • • • twinkle with an unusual glimmer tonight."

You can also use ellipses to show a pause in dialogue or a stumble in speech.

EXAMPLE
Roger stammered, "You can't • • • I mean, that just isn't possible."

APPLICATION

Quotations
Activity. Explain to students that they may need to use direct and indirect quotations in a variety of real-life situations. Have students brainstorm examples of such situations. [*submitting a letter with a job application; writing a letter about a problem with a bill; filing a complaint with a business*] Then, ask volunteers to create sentences with direct or indirect quotations that might be used in some of the situations.

DIFFERENTIATING INSTRUCTION

English-Language Learners
General Strategies. Students sometimes make mistakes using the verbs *said* and *told,* resulting in sentences such as "He said me, 'Look out!'" Give the following examples of how these verbs differ. Draw students' attention to the fact that *told* usually takes an indirect object and is normally used in an indirect quotation rather than a direct quotation.

1. He said, "Look out!" (He told me to look out.)
2. Maria said, "This is a good book." (Maria told us that this is a good book.)

MECHANICS

DIFFERENTIATING INSTRUCTION

DIFFERENTIATING INSTRUCTION

Learners Having Difficulty

On separate strips of paper, print direct quotations, dialogue tags, opening and closing quotation marks, commas, and end marks. Distribute the strips to students. Have them stand with their strips and arrange themselves in an order that makes a complete sentence. A variation would be to have each student arrange sets of strips on a table or on the floor to form complete sentences.

Learners Having Difficulty

Have students cut comic strips from newspapers and write dialogues based on the strips. Students will need to add attributions, quotation marks, and other punctuation, and to correctly format the dialogues into paragraphs. Tell them to follow all of the rules of capitalization and punctuation. Have partners proofread each other's dialogues for correct capitalization and punctuation, and then discuss any revisions they have made. Ask volunteers to read their dialogues aloud to the class.

English-Language Learners

Vietnamese. Instead of using quotation marks in direct speech, as English does, Vietnamese generally uses a dash. *—I saw the game.* Quotation marks, when they are used, resemble marks used in French: << >>. Point out the use of quotation marks in books the students read in class, and provide students with exercises to reinforce the use of quotation marks.

15i. A question mark or an exclamation point is placed inside the closing quotation marks when the quotation itself is a question or an exclamation. Otherwise, it is placed outside.

EXAMPLES "Is the time difference between Los Angeles and Chicago two hours?" asked Ken. [The quotation is a question.]

Linda exclaimed, "I thought everyone knew that!" [The quotation is an exclamation.]

What did Jade Snow Wong mean in her story "A Time of Beginnings" when she wrote, "Like the waves of the sea, no two pieces of pottery art can be identical"? [The sentence, not the quotation, is a question.]

I'm so happy that Mom said, "You are allowed to stay out until 10:00 P.M. on Friday night"! [The sentence, not the quotation, is an exclamation.]

When both the sentence and a quotation at the end of that sentence are questions (or exclamations), only one question mark (or exclamation point) is used. It is placed inside the closing quotation marks.

EXAMPLE What is the title of the Gwendolyn Brooks poem that begins "Oh mother, mother, where is happiness?"

Exercise 2 Correcting Sentences by Adding Capital Letters and Punctuation

Revise the following sentences by supplying capital letters and marks of punctuation as needed. If a sentence is already correct, write *C*.

EXAMPLE 1. Of the early art of the Americas asked Julian which piece of art is your favorite?

1. "Of the early art of the Americas," asked Julian, "which piece of art is your favorite?"

1. Ms. Chung said that of the Incas is probably my favorite, because it was beautiful and varied.
2. There are wonderful pictures in this book said Pedro let's look at it.
3. The inlaid gold earrings are fantastic exclaimed Francine.

4. "The Incas' worship of the sun is expressed in many pieces of art," said Tonya, "such as in this tapestry."

5. "I found a picture of what the Inca capital of Cuzco looked like," Craig said. "It is easy to see that it was a large, technologically advanced city."

6. Matina said that it was wonderful to be left so much art, but that it was a shame the Incas didn't have a written language. **6. C**

7. "They did leave *quipus*," said Louella, "but no one completely understands their use; it's thought that the knotted strings assisted memory."

8. "A bit like tying a string around your finger," said Mahlon, "but more complicated."

9. Cohila said, "Let's make a *quipu* for the classroom."

10. "We each need one for the algebra test," laughed Marc.

Exercise 3 **Correcting Sentences by Adding Capital Letters and Punctuation**

Write the following sentences, supplying capital letters and marks of punctuation as needed.

EXAMPLE **1.** Why she asked can't we leave now

  1. "Why," she asked, "can't we leave now?"

1. "Mom, will you take us to the soccer field?" asked Libby.

2. "Please hold my backpack for a minute, Dave," Josh said. "I need to tie my shoelace."

3. Cary asked, "What is pita bread?"

4. Alison answered, "It's a round, flat Middle Eastern bread."

5. "Run! Run!" cried the boys, "a tornado is headed this way!"

6. Our cat caught a little rabbit and paid no attention when I yelled, "drop that!"

7. "Have you ever eaten enchiladas made with homemade tortillas?" asked Martin.

8. "The computers are all ready to be used," said Gary, "we'd better get to work."

9. "Oh no!" shouted Katrina, "not all of the chess pieces were put away with the board."

9. or "Oh, no!"

10. "If California is in the Pacific time zone," asked Ernesto, "in what time zone is Arizona?"

EXTENSION

Relating to Literature

If your literature textbook contains Toni Cade Bambara's "Raymond's Run," have students read and discuss the selection. Highlight lines of dialogue in which the characters are clearly differentiated. Point out that much of the story is told by narration, and ask why the author might have chosen to include direct quotations. [*The direct quotations give the reader a direct and immediate experience of the characters' personalities. The quotations add a dimension that cannot be achieved through description and narration alone.*]

Exercise 4   Correcting Dialogue by Adding Punctuation

POSSIBLE ANSWERS

[1] "Gordon, do you ever think about pencils?" Annie asked.

[2] "I'm always wondering where I lost mine," Gordon replied.

[3] "Well," said Annie, "let me tell you some of the things I learned about pencils."

[4] "Okay," Gordon said. "I love trivia!"

[5] "People have used some form of pencils for a long time," Annie began. [6] "The ancient Greeks and Romans used lead pencils. [7] However, pencils as we know them weren't developed until the sixteenth century, when people started using graphite."

(continued on p. 349)

15j. When you write dialogue (conversation), begin a new paragraph each time the speaker changes.

EXAMPLE   "Ay, no, señor!" Don Anselmo hastily blessed himself. "To bring a white horse into these mountains is not wise. *El Caballo Blanco* would not like it."

"*El Caballo Blanco* is dead. You yourself said this yesterday."

"Dead he may be in body, but the goatherds often see him on the trails in the moonlight, his hand on his gun, his hat on the back of his head, and his white horse between his knees."

"Have you ever seen him?"

Josephina Niggli, "The Quarry"

15k. When a quotation consists of several sentences, place quotation marks only at the beginning and at the end of the whole quotation.

EXAMPLES   "Memorize all your lines for Monday. Be sure to have someone at home give you your cues. Enjoy your weekend!" said Ms. Goodwin.

Monica said, "We spent all day Saturday at the beach. In the morning, we went swimming in the surf. After lunch, we hiked over the dunes in search of seashells."

Exercise 4   Correcting Dialogue by Adding Punctuation

Rewrite the following dialogue, adding commas, end marks, quotation marks, and paragraph indentions where necessary.

EXAMPLE   [1] Which would you rather use, a pencil or a pen asked Jody

1.   "*Which would you rather use, a pencil or a pen?*" *asked Jody.*

[1] Gordon, do you ever think about pencils Annie asked [2] I'm always wondering where I lost mine Gordon replied [3] Well said Annie let me tell you some of the things I learned about pencils [4] Okay Gordon said I love trivia [5] People have used some form of pencils for a long time Annie began [6] The ancient Greeks and Romans used lead pencils [7] However, pencils as

we know them weren't developed until the sixteenth century, when people started using graphite [8] What's graphite asked Gordon [9] Graphite is a soft form of carbon Annie explained that leaves a mark when it's drawn over most surfaces [10] Thanks for the information, Annie Gordon said Now, do you have a pencil I can borrow

15l. Use quotation marks to enclose titles and subtitles of short works such as short stories, poems, essays, articles, songs, episodes of television series, and chapters and other parts of books.

Reference Note

For examples of **titles that are italicized,** see page 342.

Type of Title	Examples
Short Stories	"A Worn Path" "The Rule of Names" "The Tell-Tale Heart" "A Rose for Emily"
Poems	"Mother to Son" "Birches" "Calling in the Cat" "Easter 1916"
Essays and Articles	"The Creative Process" "Free Speech and Free Air" "How to Make a Budget" "A Modest Proposal"
Songs	"Joy to the World" "Amazing Grace" "Duke of Earl" "Yesterday"
Episodes of Television Series	"Heart of a Champion" "The Trouble with Tribbles" "Journey's End"
Chapters and Other Parts of Books	"Learning About Reptiles" "English: Origins and Uses" "Creating a Federal Union"

Reference Note

Remember that the **titles of long musical works are italicized,** not enclosed in quotation marks. See the examples on page 343.

[8] "What's graphite?" asked Gordon.

[9] "Graphite is a soft form of carbon," Annie explained, "that leaves a mark when it's drawn over most surfaces."

[10] "Thanks for the information, Annie," Gordon said. "Now, do you have a pencil I can borrow?"

MECHANICS

15m. Use single quotation marks to enclose a quotation within a quotation or a title of a short work within a quotation.

EXAMPLES   "I said, 'The quiz will cover Unit 2 and your special reports,'" repeated Mr. Allyn.

"Which Shakespeare character speaks the line 'Good night, good night! Parting is such sweet sorrow'?" Carol asked.

Sharon said, "I just read 'Broken Chain.'"

Exercise 5   Correcting Sentences by Adding Quotation Marks

Write the following sentences, using quotation marks as needed.

EXAMPLE   1. We sang Greensleeves for the assembly, said Hiu.

      1. *"We sang 'Greensleeves' for the assembly," said Hiu.*

1. "Has anyone read the story To Build a Fire?" asked the teacher.
2. "I think Eileen said, Please go on without me," said Judy.
3. Do you know the poem To Make a Prairie?
4. Our chorus will sing When You Wish upon a Star today.
5. In the chapter Workers' Rights, the author discusses Cesar Chavez's efforts to help migrant workers.
6. "The first song I learned to accompany on guitar was Shenandoah," said Jack.
7. "When I was only seven I memorized Lewis Carroll's poem Jabberwocky," claimed Damita.
8. My favorite episode of *Nova* is the one titled The Doomsday Asteroid.
9. The magazine article How to Make the Most of Your Life contains very good advice.
10. "Danny, would you like to read Robert Frost's poem The Road Not Taken at graduation?" asked Dr. Washington.

Review A   Correcting Sentences by Adding Punctuation and Capital Letters

Write the following sentences, using marks of punctuation and capital letters as needed. If a sentence is already correct, write *C.*

EXTENSION

Critical Thinking

Metacognition. After students complete **Review A,** ask them to write brief answers to the following questions.

1. Which rule for using quotation marks gave you the greatest challenge?

2. How do you plan to deal with your most challenging rule in your future writing?

EXAMPLE
1. Did you read the article about NASA in USA Weekend Lynn asked.

1. "Did you read the article about NASA in <u>USA Weekend</u>?" Lynn asked.

1. Won't you stay?pleaded Wynnie﹘there will be music and refreshments later.
2. Hey, Jason,said Chen,you play the drums like an expert!
3. The girls asked whether we needed help finding our campsite.
4. Elise, do you know who said,The only thing we have to fear is fear itself asked the teacher.
5. What a wonderful day for a picnic on the levee exclaimed Susan to Rafiq.
6. I've read,Connie said,that Thomas Jefferson loved Italian food and ordered pasta from Italy.
7. When President Lincoln heard of the South's defeat, he requested that the band play Dixie.
8. The latest issue of <u>National Geographic</u> has a long article on rain forests.
9. Langston Hughes's Dream Deferred is a subtle, thought-provoking poem.
10. What can have happened to Francine this time, Tina? Didn't she say,I'll be home before you leave? Justin asked.

3. C

4. itself ?

Apostrophes

An *apostrophe* is used to form the possessive case of nouns and some pronouns, to indicate in a contraction where letters or numerals have been omitted, and to form some plurals.

Possessive Case

The *possessive case* of a noun or a pronoun shows ownership or possession.

Sandra's boat	an **hour's** time
Mother's job	**Julio's** sister
your book	**everyone's** choice

Apostrophes **351**

RESOURCES

Apostrophes

Practice
- *Language & Sentence Skills Practice,* pp. 312–317, 321
- *Developmental Language & Sentence Skills,* pp. 119–120

MECHANICS

Apostrophes
Rules 15n–s *(pp. 351–357)*

OBJECTIVES

- To supply apostrophes for singular possessive nouns in sentences

- To form plural possessives

- To form contractions from pairs of words

- To correct contractions in a letter by adding apostrophes

DIFFERENTIATING INSTRUCTION

English-Language Learners

Hmong. Because written Hmong relies upon a possessive noun classifier to indicate possession, the language does not include the use of the possessive apostrophe. Therefore, Hmong speakers may find the mark confusing in both translation and use. Be sure to offer Hmong-speaking students extra time for review and practice in using the apostrophe to signify possessives.

DIFFERENTIATING INSTRUCTION

English-Language Learners

General Strategies. Use a sample passage to review possessive forms with students. First, have students underline words ending in *'s,* and then have them read the sentences aloud. Some English-language learners may overlook *'s* endings as they concentrate on more important cues in sentences, but after this practice they will be better prepared to complete the exercises on possessives.

DIRECT TEACHING

Modeling and Demonstration

Apostrophes. Model how to use apostrophes correctly by using the examples *a dogs collar, womens suits,* and *customers complaints.* First, ask students what is being expressed in the phrase *a dogs collar.* [*possession*] Ask where the apostrophe should be placed to show possession. [*before the s—dog's*] Next, ask how to form the possessive of *women.* [*women's*] Then, ask how to form the possessive of *customers.* [*customers'*] Point out that plural nouns that do not end in *s* form the possessive by adding an apostrophe and an *s,* and that plural nouns that end in *s* form the possessive by adding an apostrophe after the *s.* Now, have a volunteer use another example from this chapter to demonstrate how to use apostrophes to show possession.

┌ H E L P ─

A proper noun ending in *s* may take only an apostrophe to form the possessive case if the addition of *'s* would make the name awkward to pronounce.

EXAMPLES
Marjorie Kinnan Rawlings' novels

Hercules' feats

Mr. Fuentes' plans

15n. To form the possessive case of a singular noun, add an apostrophe and an *s*.

EXAMPLES   a dog's collar   one dollar's worth

                 a moment's notice   Willis's typewriter

Exercise 6   Supplying Apostrophes for Possessive Nouns

Write each noun that should be in the possessive case in the following sentences. Then, add the apostrophe.

EXAMPLE   **1.** The dogs leash is made of nylon.

          1. dog's

1. That trucks taillights are broken.
2. By the end of the demonstration, the judges were impressed with Veronicas project.
3. Last weeks travel story was about Mindanao, the second largest island of the Philippines.
4. Matthews dream is to have a palomino.
5. Robin, please pack your mothers books.
6. Several cats and dogs were adopted during the animal shelters open house.
7. When the Martins came to visit, we played my fathers favorite game, Yahtzee.
8. The science museums schedule of summer events did not list an astronomy class.
9. A roosters crowing could wake up the soundest sleeper.
10. Much of E. E. Cummings poetry appeals to both adults and children.

15o. To form the possessive case of a plural noun ending in *s*, add only the apostrophe.

EXAMPLES   actors' scripts   doctors' opinions

              customers' complaints   the Haines' invitations

     To form the possessive case of a plural noun that does not end in *s*, add an apostrophe and an *s*.

EXAMPLES   women's suits   geese's noise

             sheep's pasture   children's books

NOTE In general, you should not use an apostrophe to form the plural of a noun.

INCORRECT   The passenger's showed their tickets to the flight attendant.

CORRECT   The **passengers** showed their tickets to the flight attendant. [plural]

Reference Note

For information on using an apostrophe and an *s* to form the **plurals of letters, numerals, symbols, and words used as words,** see page 357.

Exercise 7 Forming Plural Possessives

Correctly write each of the following plural possessives.

EXAMPLE   **1.** artists paintings
           1. *artists' paintings*

1. boys boots
2. ~~women~~ careers
3. friends comments
4. three days homework
5. girls parents
6. Joneses cabin
7. ~~men~~ shoes
8. ~~children~~ game
9. cities mayors
10. ~~oxen~~ yokes

11. sisters closet
12. schools playgrounds
13. teachers lounge
14. actors costumes
15. ~~deer~~ tracks
16. trees branches
17. birds nests
18. tadpoles ponds
19. Thomases house
20. classes schedules

2. women's

15. deer's

7. men's
8. children's
10. oxen's

15p. Do not use an apostrophe with possessive personal pronouns.

EXAMPLES   These keys are **yours,** not **mine.**

            Are these tapes **ours** or **theirs**?

            His pantomime was good, but **hers** was better.

NOTE The possessive case form of *it* is *its*. The expression *it's* is a contraction of the words *it is* or *it has*.

Reference Note

For more information about **possessive personal pronouns,** see page 225. For more about the **difference between** *its* **and** *it's,* see page 272.

15q. To form the possessive case of some indefinite pronouns, add an apostrophe and an *s*.

EXAMPLES   someone**'s** pencil

            no one**'s** fault

            anybody**'s** guess

PRACTICE

Guided and Independent

Exercise 7 You may want to have students complete the first ten items in **Exercise 7** as guided practice and the last ten items as independent practice. **HOMEWORK**

RETEACHING

Apostrophes

Possessive Case. An exercise that uses possessive-case nouns and pronouns to describe objects in students' lives might make the use of apostrophes more personally relevant. Have students write down three things that belong to them, three things that belong to someone they know, and three things that are shared by two people. Then, have students write the possessive-case form of the name of the owner or owners in front of each object listed. Have students exchange lists with partners and check each other's punctuation.

PRACTICE

Guided and Independent

Review B You may want to have students complete the first ten items in **Review B** as guided practice and the last ten items as independent practice. **HOMEWORK**

Review B Forming **Singular Possessives and Plural Possessives**

ANSWERS

1. book's; books'
2. puppy's; puppies'
3. donkey's; donkeys'
4. mouse's; mice's
5. calf's; calves'
6. hero's; heroes'
7. elephant's; elephants'
8. tooth's; teeth's
9. school's; schools'
10. family's; families'
11. hand's; hands'
12. roof's; roofs'
13. hour's; hours'
14. chalkboard's; chalkboards'
15. foot's; feet's
16. politician's; politicians'
17. moose's; moose's
18. canoe's; canoes'
19. zoo's; zoos'
20. country's; countries'

—HELP—
For information on forming the plurals of nouns, see page 376.

Review B **Forming Singular Possessives and Plural Possessives**

Form the singular possessive and the plural possessive of each of the following nouns.

EXAMPLES
1. citizen
1. citizen's; citizens'

2. city
2. city's; cities'

1. book	**6.** hero	**11.** hand	**16.** politician
2. puppy	**7.** elephant	**12.** roof	**17.** moose
3. donkey	**8.** tooth	**13.** hour	**18.** canoe
4. mouse	**9.** school	**14.** chalkboard	**19.** zoo
5. calf	**10.** family	**15.** foot	**20.** country

Contractions

15r. To form a contraction, use an apostrophe to show where letters or numerals have been omitted.

A **contraction** is a shortened form of a word, a numeral, or a group of words. The apostrophe in a contraction indicates where letters or numerals have been left out.

Common Contractions	
I am . . . . I'm	they had . . . . they'd
1993 . . . . '93	where is . . . . where's
let us . . . . let's	we are . . . . we're
of the clock . . . . . . o'clock	he is . . . . he's
she would . . . . she'd	you will . . . . you'll

The word *not* can be shortened to *n't* and added to a verb, usually without changing the spelling of the verb.

EXAMPLES
is not . . . . isn't	has not . . . . hasn't
are not . . . . aren't	have not . . . . haven't
does not . . . . . . doesn't	had not . . . . hadn't
do not . . . . don't	should not . . . . . shouldn't

| was not . . . . wasn't | would not . . . . . . wouldn't |
| were not . . . . . weren't | could not . . . . couldn't |

EXCEPTIONS will not . . . . **won't** cannot . . . . **can't**

Do not confuse contractions with possessive pronouns.

Contractions	Possessive Pronouns
He said **it's** snowing. [*it is*]	**Its** front tire is flat.
It's been a long time. [*It has*]	
Who's next in line? [*Who is*]	**Whose** idea was it?
Who's swept? [*Who has*]	
You're writing an essay. [*You are*]	**Your** writing has improved.
They're not here. [*They are*]	**Their** dog is barking.
There's a trophy for first place. [*There is*]	This trophy is **theirs**.

Oral Practice Forming Contractions

Read the following word pairs aloud, and say the contraction for each one.

EXAMPLE 1. he is
1. *he's*

1. will not	8. should not	15. we are
2. there is	9. let us	16. I am
3. who will	10. I have	17. had not
4. they are	11. you are	18. she is
5. who is	12. does not	19. you will
6. are not	13. he would	20. could not
7. it is	14. has not	

Exercise 8 Correcting Contractions by Adding Apostrophes

The letter on the following page contains ten punctuation errors. Write each incorrect contraction, and add an apostrophe.

EXAMPLE 1. When you visit Glacier National Park, youre in for a treat.
1. *you're*

English-Language Learners

Hmong. Since written Hmong does not use apostrophes, Hmong speakers may find English contractions confusing. Remind students that English uses apostrophes in contractions to indicate missing letters. Have students practice forming contractions.

EXTENSION

Relating to Literature

Have students find passages containing contractions in a story such as "The Treasure of Lemon Brown" by Walter Dean Myers. Have students rewrite the passages, spelling out the contracted forms. Then, ask volunteers to read each version of their passages aloud for the class. Next, lead the class in a discussion of how contractions help make the passage sound friendlier and more personal. You might also wish to discuss how the lack of contractions makes the passage sound more formal or otherwise different from the tone the writer intended to create.

Oral Practice Forming Contractions

ANSWERS

1. won't	11. you're
2. there's	12. doesn't
3. who'll	13. he'd
4. they're	14. hasn't
5. who's	15. we're
6. aren't	16. I'm
7. it's	17. hadn't
8. shouldn't	18. she's
9. let's	19. you'll
10. I've	20. couldn't

STYLE TIP

In formal writing, avoid using a contraction of a year. In informal writing, if the reader cannot determine the time period from the context of the sentence, it is best to write out the year.

EXAMPLE
The famous tenor toured Europe in '01. [Did the tenor tour in 1801, 1901 or 2001?]

REVISED
The famous tenor toured Europe in **1901**.

MECHANICS

August 7, 2009

Dear Granddad,

You'll love the pictures I'm sending you from here. Glacier National Park is awesome, and we're having a wonderful time. Thank you for telling us about it. We've been here two weeks now, but it doesn't seem like more than two days. We weren't planning to spend all day yesterday canoeing on Swiftcurrent Lake, but it's so beautiful we didn't want to go back to our hotel. Last night the rangers warned us to be careful on the trails because there are often bears. Just to be safe, we won't walk alone or after sundown, which is around seven o'clock.

Love,

Cal

Plurals

15s. Use an apostrophe and an *s* to form the plurals of letters, numerals, and symbols, and of words referred to as words.

EXAMPLES   There are two *d*'s in the word *hidden*.

Your *2*'s look like backward *5*'s.

Jazz became quite popular in the 1920's.

Don't use too many *so*'s and *and*'s.

He wrote *$*'s before all the amounts.

> **Review C**   **Correcting Sentences by Adding Apostrophes**

Write the correct form of each item that requires an apostrophe in the following sentences.

EXAMPLE   **1.** Dont you know what youre doing?

1. *Don't, you're*

1. The girls didnt say when theyd be back.
2. Lets find out when the next game is.
3. My cousin Blanca usually gets As and Bs on her report card.
4. It isnt correct to use &s in your compositions.
5. Many of the scores on the math test were in the 80s and 90s.
6. They cant come to the bar mitzvah with us; they've been delayed.
7. Theyll meet us, if its all right to tell them where were going.
8. Whos signed up for the talent show?
9. Dont those 9s look like gs to you?
10. Your capital Ls and Is are hard to tell apart.

Hyphens

15t. Use a hyphen to divide a word at the end of a line.

EXAMPLES   What percentage of U.S. households have sub-scribed to cable television?

You can probably find the answer in the alma-nac in the library.

MECHANICS

Hyphens, Parentheses, Brackets, and Dashes
Rules 15t–z *(pp. 357–364)*

OBJECTIVES

■ To hyphenate numbers and fractions

■ To correct sentences by inserting parentheses and brackets

■ To correct sentences by inserting dashes

DIRECT TEACHING

Modeling and Demonstration

Hyphens. Model how to use hyphens correctly by using the example *My great aunt read thirty six books last year.* First, ask students whether there are any written numbers in the sentence. [*yes; thirty-six*] Explain that compound numbers from *twenty-one* to *ninety-nine* should be punctuated with hyphens. Next, ask whether any other words in the example sentence need hyphens. [*yes; great-aunt*] Point out that hyphens should be used with the prefixes *ex–, self–, all–,* and *great–.* Now, have a volunteer use another example from this chapter to demonstrate how to use hyphens correctly.

DIFFERENTIATING INSTRUCTION

English-Language Learners

General Strategies. Some students may not know how to divide English words into syllables and so may hyphenate incorrectly at the end of a line. Let students know that there are rules for the division of most words (one vowel **sound** per syllable; divide between a double consonant) and that they can check in a dictionary for correct word divisions.

COMPUTER TIP

Some word-processing programs will automatically divide a word at the end of a line and insert a hyphen. Sometimes, such a division will break one of the rules of hyphenation.

Check a printout of your writing to see how the computer has hyphenated words at the ends of lines. If a hyphen is used incorrectly, revise the line by moving the word or by redividing the word and inserting a "hard" hyphen (one that the computer cannot move).

STYLE **TIP**

Hyphens are often used in compound names. In such cases, the hyphen is thought of as part of the spelling of the name.

EXAMPLES
Jean-Phillipe Rameau

Chiang Kai-shek

Henri Cartier-Bresson

Wilkes-Barre

If you are not sure whether a compound name is hyphenated, ask the person with that name or look in a reference source.

When dividing a word at the end of a line, remember the following rules:

(1) Divide a word only between syllables.

INCORRECT	Lisa wrote her science report on the tyra-nnosaurs, the largest meat-eating dinosaurs.
CORRECT	Lisa wrote her science report on the tyran-nosaurs, the largest meat-eating dinosaurs.

NOTE If you are not sure how to divide a word into syllables correctly, look up the word in a dictionary.

(2) Do not divide a one-syllable word.

INCORRECT	The fans stood and sang while the band play-ed the school song.
CORRECT	The fans stood and sang while the band played the school song.

(3) Divide an already hyphenated word at a hyphen.

INCORRECT	Keisha and I went to the fair with our great-un-cle James.
CORRECT	Keisha and I went to the fair with our great-uncle James.

(4) Do not divide a word so that one letter stands alone.

INCORRECT	While moving to Chicago last week, Anthony i-magined what the new house would be like.
CORRECT	While moving to Chicago last week, Anthony imag-ined what the new house would be like.

15u. Use a hyphen with compound numbers from *twenty-one* to *ninety-nine* and with fractions used as modifiers.

EXAMPLES	thirty-five students
	forty-eighth state
	one-third pint of milk

When a fraction is a noun, do not use a hyphen.

EXAMPLE	**one third** of a pint

Learning for Life

Writing a Letter. The punctuation discussed in this chapter is used in many kinds of writing, including personal letters. Ask each student to write a letter using as many different punctuation marks as possible.

Let students brainstorm ideas for their letters. Remind them that the tone of their letters should be light and personal.

As students draft their letters, remind them that they should get their ideas on paper first. They can correct any errors later. Encourage students to begin their let-

15v. Use a hyphen with the prefixes *all–*, *ex–*, *great–*, and *self–* and with the suffixes *–elect* and *–free* and with all prefixes before a proper noun or proper adjective.

EXAMPLES

all-star	president-elect
ex-principal	sugar-free
great-aunt	mid-September
self-confidence	pro-American

15w. Hyphenate a compound adjective when it precedes the noun it modifies.

EXAMPLES   a **well-worn** book [but *a book that is well worn*]

         a **small-town** girl [but *a girl from a small town*]

Do not use a hyphen if one of the modifiers is an adverb that ends in *ly*.

EXAMPLES   a **terribly bad** cold

         a **nicely turned** phrase

NOTE   Some compound adjectives are always hyphenated, whether they precede or follow the nouns they modify.

EXAMPLES   a **brand-new** stereo

         a stereo that is **brand-new**

Exercise 9   **Hyphenating Numbers and Fractions**

Write the following expressions, inserting hyphens as needed. If an expression is already correct, write *C*.

EXAMPLE   **1.** thirty one days

         1. thirty-one days

1. a two-thirds majority
2. one half of the coconut   **2.** C
3. one hundred thirty-five pages
4. Forty-second Street
5. twenty-two Amish quilts
6. one-third cup of water
7. ninety-nine years
8. fifty-five dollars and twenty cents
9. three eighths of the pizza   **9.** C
10. the twenty-first amendment

STYLE ✏ TIP

The prefix *half–* often requires a hyphen, as in *half-life, half-moon,* and *half-truth*. However, sometimes *half* is used without a hyphen, either as part of a single word (*halftone, halfway, halfback*) or as a separate word (*half shell, half pint, half note*). If you are not sure how to spell a word containing *half*, look up the word in a dictionary.

HELP

To find out whether a compound adjective is always hyphenated, look it up in a current dictionary.

TECHNOLOGY TIP

Because most computer programs simply move words that are too long to the next line or automatically insert hyphens to divide words, students may question the purpose of studying the rules for hyphens. Point out that in order to proofread word-processed text accurately and to be able to write by hand when computers are not available, students need to know the rules for dividing words.

MECHANICS

ters in a way that gets their reader's attention and that reflects their own voice.

Students should evaluate their letters for clarity and for appropriate tone and content. Also, ask them to take note of the punctuation they used. After students finish their revisions, have them proofread their letters for correct use of the punctuation marks discussed in this chapter as well as other punctuation, grammar, and spelling errors. You may wish to have students send their letters.

Review D Adding Apostrophes, Hyphens, and Underlining (Italics)

Write the following sentences, inserting apostrophes, hyphens, and underlining as needed.

EXAMPLE   1. Isnt the preface to that edition of Frankenstein twenty four pages long?

          1. *Isn't the preface to that edition of <u>Frankenstein</u> twenty-four pages long?*

1. There's where they live.
2. Who'll go to next week's showing of the film <u>Small Change</u>?
3. The Lockwood sisters' golden retriever is named Storm.
4. One third of Holly's allowance goes into the bank.
5. The park on Fifty-third Street has a well-lit jogging trail.
6. Twenty-six members of the student council (more than a three-fourths majority) voted to change the school song.
7. Shelly said that she's always wanted to read Amy Tan's book <u>The Joy Luck Club</u>.
8. If two thirds of the class have scores below seventy-five, we'll all have to retake the test.
9. Let's find out about Henry VIII's flagship, the <u>Mary Rose</u>.
10. Ninety-seven years ago my great-grandparents left Scotland for the United States.

STYLE TIP

Too many parenthetical expressions in a piece of writing can distract readers from the main idea. Keep your meaning clear by limiting the number of parenthetical expressions you use.

Parentheses

15x. Use parentheses to enclose material that is added to a sentence but is not considered of major importance.

EXAMPLES   Mohandas K. Gandhi **(**1869–1948**)** led India's struggle for independence from British rule.

             Mrs. Matsuo served us the sushi **(**so͞o' shē**)** that she had prepared.

Material enclosed in parentheses may range from a single word or number to a short sentence. A short sentence in parentheses may stand by itself or be contained within another sentence. Notice that a sentence within a sentence is not capitalized; such a sentence may be followed by a question mark or exclamation point, but not by a period.

CONTENT-AREA CONNECTIONS

Art

Collages. Ask students to search newspapers and magazines for headlines that use the marks of punctuation covered in this chapter. Have them cut out the headlines and create collages with them. Some students may wish to find a theme or unifying idea to serve as a focus for their collages. Others may wish to concentrate on one or two marks of punctuation and use their collages to illustrate the many ways the marks are used. You can display the finished collages in the classroom.

EXAMPLES   You should try the orange juice. **(It's freshly squeezed.)**

No, set that ladder **(watch out!)** over there.

My great-uncle Ed **(he's Grandma's brother)** is odd.

Brackets

15y. Use brackets to enclose an explanation or added information within quoted or parenthetical material.

EXAMPLES   At the press conference, Detective Stamos stated, "We are following up on several leads regarding the [Mills Sporting Goods] robbery."

During the Revolutionary War, Mohawk leader Joseph Brant (his Indian name was Thayendanegea [1742–1807]) became a colonel in the British Army.

Exercise 10 **Writing Sentences with Parentheses and Brackets**

For each of the following sentences, insert parentheses or brackets where they are needed. Be sure not to enclose any words or marks of punctuation that do not belong inside the parentheses or brackets.

EXAMPLE   **1.** One popular pet is the house cat *Felis cattus.*

    1. *One popular pet is the house cat* (Felis cattus).

1. The old fort(it was used during the Civil War)has been rebuilt and is open to the public.
2. The final speaker said, "If you don't allow them[the umpires] to do their jobs, we might as well not play the games."
3. The American writer Langston Hughes(1902–1967)is best known for his poetry.
4. Alligators use their feet and tails to dig water holes(also called "gator holes")in marshy fields.
5. On the Sabbath my family eats braided bread called challah(pronounced khä´lə).
6. Komodo dragons(the largest of all monitor lizards)can be found in Indonesia.
7. Antonin Dvořák(1841–1904)was a Czech composer who wrote beautiful symphonies.

┌─HELP─

The brackets in the first example for 15y tell the reader that *Mills Sporting Goods* is not part of Detective Stamos's sentence but was added to the quotation for clarity.

MECHANICS

8. The town's historic district(it dates from the nineteenth century)is a popular meeting place.
9. Block print all addresses(use blue or black ink).
10. The next president (he was Ulysses S. Grant[1822–1885]) continued the Reconstruction program while trying to protect the rights of former slaves.

Dashes

Many words and phrases are used *parenthetically;* that is, they break into the main thought of a sentence. Most parenthetical elements are set off by commas or parentheses.

EXAMPLES   The tomato**, however,** is actually a fruit, not a vegetable.

The outcome **(which candidate would be elected governor?)** was in the hands of the voters.

Sometimes, parenthetical elements demand stronger emphasis. In such instances, a dash is used.

15z. Use a dash to indicate an abrupt break in thought or speech.

EXAMPLES   Ms. Alonzo—she just left—will be one of the judges of the talent show.

"Right over here—oh, excuse me, Mr. Mills—you'll find the reference books," said the librarian.

Alisha began, "The burglar is—but I don't want to give away the ending."

Reference Note

For more information about **using commas with parenthetical expressions,** see page 325. For more about **using parentheses,** see page 360.

Exercise 11 Writing Sentences with Dashes

For each of the following sentences, insert dashes where they are needed.   Dashes are indicated by ⌃ .

EXAMPLE   1. Paul Revere he imported hardware made beautiful jewelry and utensils.

1. Paul Revere—he imported hardware—made beautiful jewelry and utensils.

1. A beautiful grand piano it was once played by Chopin was on display in the museum.

Exercise 11

DISTRIBUTED REVIEW
For a quick review of verbs and other parts of speech in **Exercise 11,** ask students to find the following forms in the designated sentences.

1. a pronoun [*it*]

2. a proper noun [*Josh*]

3. a linking verb [*is*]

4. a verb phrase [*was nominated*]

2. "I'd like the red—no, give me the blue—cycling shorts and white socks," said Josh.

3. Frederic Remington—artist, historian, and lover of the frontier—is famous for his paintings of the West.

4. On July 7, 1981, Sandra Day O'Connor—she was the first female associate justice—was nominated to the U.S. Supreme Court.

5. Cheryl wondered aloud, "Where in the world—oh, my poor Muffy—could that hamster be?"

6. Kohlrabi—an odd-looking vegetable—is part of the cabbage family.

7. You may cut some of the roses—oh, here, use the garden shears—to give to your mother.

8. We put up the banners—don't tell me they've fallen down—for the pep rally.

9. "The dog—stop jumping on the people, Punkin—doesn't bite," says our neighbor every time we visit her.

10. Most planets have Greek or Roman names—Mercury, Venus, Mars, Jupiter, and Saturn were all Roman gods—while the word *Earth* is Old English.

Review E Correcting Sentences by Adding Punctuation

Write the following sentences, supplying punctuation marks where needed. If a sentence is already correct, write *C*.

EXAMPLE 1. Stans going to the Washingtons Birthday cele bration in Laredo, Texas Teresa said.
Dashes are indicated by —.

1. "Stan's going to the Washington's Birthday celebration in Laredo, Texas," Teresa said.

1. "Some say that Laredo's festivities are the country's biggest celebration of Washington's birthday," Juan said. "Isn't that surprising?"

2. "No, not really," said Frank. "The city's large Hispanic population chose to honor George Washington, whom they consider a freedom fighter."

3. Teresa said, "The citizens there also have great respect for Washington's abilities as a leader."

4. Juan said that the annual event began back in the 1800's.   4. C

5. "Did you know that they've extended the birthday party to both sides of the Texas-Mexico border?" Teresa asked.

6. That's right, Juan said. The citizens of Nuevo Laredo in Mexico really enjoy the celebration, too.
7. Just look at the colorful costumes in the photograph! exclaimed Teresa. Can you tell what famous couple these people are portraying?
8. Teresa continued, Mrs. Serrano—she's Juan's aunt who lives in Houston—has gone to the festivities in Laredo for the past twenty-two years.

9. jalapeño-eating

9. Today the <u>Laredo Morning Times</u> reported that a jalapeño-eating contest was part of this year's celebration, Anna reported.
10. In honor of Washington's birthday [February 22], three fourths of our class read the book <u>Washington</u> by William Jay Jacobs, said Juan.

Numerals in brackets refer to rules tested by the items in the Chapter Review.

1. [15a]
2. [15d, h]
3. [15a]
4. [15l]
5. [15d, i]
6. [15l]
7. [15b]
8. [15m, h]
9. [15l]
10. [15d, h, f]

Chapter Review

A. Proofreading Sentences for the Correct Use of Quotation Marks and Underlining (Italics)

Each of the following sentences contains at least one error in the use of quotation marks or underlining (italics). Write each sentence correctly.

1. Uncle Ned reads The Wall Street Journal every day.
2. Fill in all the information on the form, the secretary said.
3. How many times have you seen the movie version of Margaret Mitchell's novel Gone with the Wind?
4. Many of the students enjoyed the humor and irony in O. Henry's short story The Ransom of Red Chief.
5. My little sister asked, Why can't I have a hamster?
6. Please don't sing I've Been Working on the Railroad.
7. Last summer my older sister played in a band on a Caribbean cruise ship named Bright Coastal Star.
8. "Read James Baldwin's essay Autobiographical Notes and answer both of the study questions," the teacher said.
9. Dudley Randall's poem Ancestors questions why people always seem to believe that their ancestors were aristocrats.
10. "That artist," Mr. Russell said, was influenced by the Cuban painter Amelia Pelaez del Casal.

B. Proofreading Sentences for the Correct Use of Apostrophes, Hyphens, Parentheses, and Dashes

Each of the following sentences contains at least one error in the use of apostrophes, hyphens, parentheses, or dashes. Write each sentence correctly. Dashes are indicated by $\bar{\wedge}$.

11. Marsha is this year's captain of the girls basketball team.
12. Susan B. Anthony(1820–1906)worked to give women the right to vote in the United States.
13. I'd never heard of a Greek bagpipe before, but Mr. Protopapas played one at his great-uncle's birthday party.

ASSESSING

Monitoring Progress
Chapter Review. To assess student progress, you may want to compare the types of items missed on the **Diagnostic Preview** with those missed on the **Chapter Review.** If students have not made significant progress, you may want to refer them to **Chapter 17: Correcting Common Errors, Exercises 30–32,** for additional practice.

MECHANICS

RESOURCES

Punctuation: Underlining (Italics), Quotation Marks, Apostrophes, Hyphens, Parentheses, Brackets, Dashes
Review
■ *Language & Sentence Skills Practice,* pp. 320–323

Assessment
■ *Formal Assessment*
■ *Progress-Monitoring Tests,* pp. 29–30, 48
■ *Test Generator (Teacher One Stop DVD-ROM)*

14. [15q]
15. [15r]
16. twenty-one [15n, t(3)]
17. [15r]
18. [15u]
19. [15n, u]
20. *or* ( ) [15z, w]

14. We couldn't have done the job without everyone's help.
15. He's strict about being on time.
16. On my older brother's next birthday, he will turn twen-ty one.
17. We'd have forgotten to eat if Maggie hadn't reminded us.
18. The recipe said to add two eggs and one-quarter cup of milk.
19. My mother's office is on the twenty-second floor.
20. Our dog—he's a giant schnauzer—is gentle and nicely behaved.

C. Proofreading a Paragraph for the Correct Use of Punctuation

Write the following sentences, supplying punctuation marks and starting new paragraphs where needed. If a sentence is already correct, write *C*.   New paragraphs indicated by ¶.

21. [15r]
22. ¶ [15j, d, i, r, k, h]
23. ¶ [15j, d, r, g, h]
24. ¶ [15j, d, g, f, r, i]
25. ¶ [15j, d, g, f, r, k, w]
26. [15d, g, f, r, h]
27. ¶ [15j, d, r, i]
28. ¶/ C [15j, d]
29. [15d, r, h]
30. ¶ [15j, d, g, r, i]

[**21**] "I'm on my way to curling practice," announced Andy. [**22**] Really? said Lori. What's curling, exactly? I've heard of it, but I get it confused with hockey. [**23**] Actually, there's one main similarity, said Andy. They're both played indoors, on ice. [**24**] I don't know much about them, said Lori, but I'm from South Texas, and we don't have too many ice sports down there! [**25**] Actually, said Andy, it's in my blood. I'm from Wisconsin, where curling is a well-established tradition, and I've played it since I was ten. [**26**] In fact, he continued, it's been around since the 1800's, thanks to Scottish immigrants who brought the sport over with them. [**27**] That's interesting, but how do you play it? asked Lori. [**28**] "It's not too complicated, as long as you don't let go of your stone," explained Andy. [**29**] That's a round stone with a handle that you slide as far as possible across the rink toward the center of a circle, called the bottom. [**30**] Oh, I see! exclaimed Lori. It's a bit like shuffleboard, isn't it?

D. Writing Sentences with Brackets and Parentheses

The following sentences contain errors in the use of brackets and parentheses. Write the sentences, correcting the errors.

31. [15x, y]

31. During the nineteenth century, novelist George Eliot (pen name of Mary Ann Evans [1819–1880]) wrote some of English literature's most important works.

32. John Singer Sargent(1856–1925)was a prominent American painter of portraits and landscapes.

33. Fill in the entire application form(type or print).

34. A common greeting among friends in France is "Salut!" (pronounced sä-lo͞o′).

35. One of the nineteenth century's most eloquent defenders of civil rights was Frederick Douglass(1817–1895).

32. [15x]
33. [15x]
34. [15x]
35. [15x]

Writing Application

Using Quotation Marks in a Report

Using Correct Punctuation Your class is taking a survey of people's reading habits. Interview at least five people, and based on the information you gather, write a brief report about people and their reading habits. In your report, use underlining and quotation marks correctly.

Prewriting   First, think of questions to ask. These questions could be about what, how often, when, and why people read. Next, select at least five people to interview. Record the name, age, and occupation of each person. As you conduct your interviews, write down or tape-record what people say. If you want to tape the interview, be sure to ask the interviewee for permission to do so. Jot down some notes to help you organize your information.

Writing   In the first paragraph of your rough draft, include a statement that summarizes the main idea of your project and findings. Then, use people's answers to your survey questions to support your main idea.

Revising   After you have finished your rough draft, take another look at your main idea. Add, cut, or rearrange details to present your findings clearly. State your conclusions in the last paragraph of your report.

Publishing   Proofread your report for any errors in grammar, usage, and mechanics. Be sure that you have correctly used quotation marks and underlining for titles. You and your classmates may want to collect your reports in a binder or create multimedia presentations based on your findings.

MECHANICS

16

Spelling
Improving Your Spelling

Diagnostic Preview

Proofreading for Misspelled Words and Words Often Confused

Identify and correct the errors in the following sentences.

EXAMPLE **1.** If you go too the store, pick up some of those lovly pears.

    1. too—to, lovly—lovely

1. "Does a mature elephant ~~wiegh~~ more ~~then~~ a ton?" Andy asked Roseanne at the zoo.   **1.** weigh/than

2. "~~Your~~ finally coming home!" my young sister ~~happyly~~ shouted over the phone.   **2.** You're/happily

3. ~~They're~~ plan to hold a fund-raiser met with the school board's ~~approval.~~   **3.** Their/approval

4. Our mother and father are very ~~industryous~~ people, and they are good parents, ~~to.~~   **4.** industrious/ too

5. Dr. Silvana ~~adviced~~ us boys to work harder ~~weather~~ we wanted to or not.   **5.** advised/whether

6. The ~~editor in chiefs~~ of the major newspapers met last Tuesday and agreed on a clear ~~coarse~~ of action to deal with the strike.   **6.** editors in chief/ course

7. The Gobi, a large ~~dessert~~ in Asia, stretches across vast ~~planes~~ in China and Mongolia.   **7.** desert/plains

8. Our ~~principle~~, Ms. Rios, who moved here last year, was ~~formally~~ the superintendent of schools in her hometown.   **8.** principal/formerly

9. As long as the meaning of this paragraph is clear, it will be ~~unnecessary~~ to change the paragraphs that ~~preceed~~ it.

10. The ~~whether~~ in the mountains can change several times ~~dayly~~, so be prepared.

9. unnecessary/precede [16d, c]

10. weather/daily [16i; *weather, whether*]

Good Spelling Habits

As your vocabulary grows, you may have difficulty spelling some new words. You can improve your spelling by using the following methods.

1. *Pronounce words correctly.* Pronouncing words carefully can often help you to spell them correctly.

EXAMPLES   athlete: ath•lete [not *ath•e•lete*]

probably: prob•a•bly [not *pro•bly*]

library: li•brar•y [not *li•bar•y*]

2. *Spell by syllables.* When you have trouble spelling long words, divide them into syllables. A *syllable* is a word part that is pronounced as one uninterrupted sound.

EXAMPLES   gymnasium: gym•na•si•um [four syllables]

representative: rep•re•sent•a•tive [five syllables]

Learning to spell the syllables of a word one at a time will help you master the spelling of the whole word.

3. *Use a dictionary.* When you are not sure about the spelling of a word, look it up in a dictionary. A dictionary will also tell you the correct pronunciations and syllable divisions of words.

4. *Keep a spelling notebook.* The best way to master words that give you difficulty is to list the words and review them frequently. Divide each page of a notebook into four columns.

COLUMN 1   Correctly write the words you frequently misspell.

COLUMN 2   Write the words again, dividing them into syllables and marking the accents. (If you are not sure how to do this, use a dictionary.)

> **STYLE** **TIP**
>
> In some names, marks that show how to say the word are as important as the letters are.
>
> **PEOPLE**
> Gréban   Jiménez
> Luís   Döbereiner
> Dvořák   Bjørn
>
> **PLACES**
> Alençon   Bâle
> Cáceres   Espíritu Santo
> El Faiyûm   João Pessoa
>
> If you are not sure about the spelling of a name, ask the person with that name or look it up in a dictionary.

students can use to improve their spelling. The chapter then presents a series of basic spelling rules and a list of words that are often confused. Further information on the usage of some of these words can be found in **Chapter 12: A Glossary of Usage.**

■ The chapter closes with a **Chapter Review** including a **Writing Application** that asks students to write a three-paragraph essay using at least five words from the **Words Often Confused** list.

■ For help in integrating this chapter with writing assignments in *Holt Literature and Language Arts,* see the **Teaching Strands** chart on pp. T24–T25.

ASSESSING

Entry-Level Assessment

Diagnostic Preview. You may wish to use the **Diagnostic Preview** to determine which spelling rules individual students should study. You might want to have students record on a chart the rules they have trouble with so that they can proofread their writing with these rules in mind.

MECHANICS

Differentiating Instruction

■ *UA: Differentiating Instruction*
■ *UA: Supporting Instruction in Five Languages*
■ *Family Involvement Activities: In Five Languages*

Assessment

■ *Formal Assessment*

■ *Progress-Monitoring Tests,* pp. 31–32, 48
■ *Test Generator (Teacher One Stop DVD-ROM)*

Other Language Resources

■ *Spelling Lessons & Activities*
■ *WordSharp: An Interactive Vocabulary Tutor*
■ *Reading and Writing Transparencies*

PRETEACHING

Lesson Starter

Motivating. To conduct a spelling bee with a twist, first divide the class into teams of five students each. Compile a list of commonly misspelled words, or use a list of problem words taken from students' writing. Choose one team to go first. Then, say a word, and have one student on the team give the first letter of the word. Another student on the same team names the second letter, and so on. If a student misses a letter, the word goes to the next team, and the process continues until the word is correctly spelled. The spelling bee continues until all the words on the list have been spelled correctly. For reinforcement, you may want to record the correctly spelled words on the chalkboard.

Spelling Rules

Rules 16a–y *(pp. 370–379)*

OBJECTIVES

- To spell words with *ie* and *ei*
- To proofread for misspelled words ending in *–cede, –ceed,* and *–sede*
- To spell words with prefixes and suffixes
- To spell the plural forms of nouns
- To spell numbers

| COLUMN 3 | Write the words again, circling the parts that give you trouble. |
| COLUMN 4 | Jot down any comments that may help you remember the correct spelling. |

EXAMPLE

Correct Spelling	Syllables and Accents	Trouble Spot	Comments
escape	es•cape′	e(sc)ape	Pronounce correctly.
calendar	cal′•en•dar	calend(a)r	Think of <u>days</u> marked on the calend<u>a</u>r.
casually	cas′•u•al•ly	casua(ll)y	Study rule 16e.

5. *Proofread for careless spelling errors.* Whenever you write, proofread your paper carefully for spelling errors and unclear letters. By slowly re-reading what you have written, you can correct careless errors such as uncrossed *t*'s, undotted *i*'s, and crossed *l*'s.

TIPS & TRICKS

To help you spell words containing *ei* and *ie*, remember this rhyme:
I before *e* except after *c* or when sounded like *a,* as in *neighbor* and *weigh.*

If you use this rhyme, remember that "*i* before *e*" refers only to words in which these two letters are in the same syllable and stand for the sound of long *e,* as in the examples under Rule 16a.

Spelling Rules

ie and *ei*

16a. Write *ie* when the sound is long *e,* except after *c.*

| EXAMPLES | ach**ie**ve | bel**ie**ve | ch**ie**f | f**ie**ld | p**ie**ce |
| | c**ei**ling | conc**ei**t | dec**ei**t | dec**ei**ve | rec**ei**ve |

| EXCEPTIONS | **ei**ther | l**ei**sure | n**ei**ther | |
| | prot**ei**n | s**ei**ze | sh**ei**k | |

16b. Write *ei* when the sound is not long *e,* especially when the sound is long *a.*

| EXAMPLES | for**ei**gn | forf**ei**t | h**ei**ght | sl**ei**gh | th**ei**r |
| | fr**ei**ght | n**ei**ghbor | r**ei**gn | v**ei**l | w**ei**gh |

| EXCEPTIONS | anc**ie**nt | consc**ie**nce | effic**ie**nt | sc**ie**nce |
| | fr**ie**nd | misch**ie**f | pat**ie**nce | anx**ie**ty |

RESOURCES

Spelling Rules
Practice
- *Language & Sentence Skills Practice,* pp. 329–344, 350
- *Developmental Language & Sentence Skills,* pp. 123–128

Exercise 1 Spelling Words with *ie* and *ei*

The following paragraph contains ten words with missing letters. Add the letters *ie* or *ei* to spell each numbered word correctly.

EXAMPLE   Many people know **[1]** th_____r signs in the Chinese zodiac.

        1. their

My **[1]** n_ei_ghbor, Mrs. Yee, told me about the Chinese zodiac signs. Not all Chinese people **[2]** bel_ie_ve in the zodiac. My parents don't, and **[3]** n_ei_ther do I, but I do think it is interesting. The Chinese zodiac is an **[4]** anc_ie_nt set of twelve-year cycles named after different animals. According to Mrs. Yee, the **[5]** ch_ie_f traits in your personality come from your animal sign. At first, I thought this notion was an odd **[6]** conc_ei_t, but it is not hard to understand. For example, a tiger is supposed to **[7]** s_ei_ze opportunities **[8]** f_ie_rcely. That description perfectly fits my brother's **[9]** fr_ie_nd Mike Chen, who was born in 1974. Mrs. Yee showed me a chart like the one on this page so that I could figure out the signs of all **[10]** _ei_ght members of my family.

| RAT
1972, 1984, 1996 | OX
1973, 1985, 1997 | TIGER
1974, 1986, 1998 | RABBIT
1975, 1987, 1999 | DRAGON
1976, 1988, 2000 | SNAKE
1965, 1977, 1989 |
| HORSE
1966, 1978, 1990 | SHEEP
1967, 1979, 1991 | MONKEY
1968, 1980, 1992 | ROOSTER
1969, 1981, 1993 | DOG
1970, 1982, 1994 | BOAR
1971, 1983, 1995 |

–cede, –ceed, and –sede

16c. In English, the only word ending in *–sede* is *supersede.* The only words ending in *–ceed* are *exceed, proceed,* and *succeed.* Most other words with this sound end in *–cede.*

EXAMPLES   con**cede**   inter**cede**   pre**cede**   re**cede**   se**cede**

DIRECT TEACHING

Modeling and Demonstration

Spelling Rules. Model how to spell correctly words that contain *ie* or *ei* by using the examples *believe, deceit, foreign, freight, protein,* and *friend.* First, ask students what sound *ie* makes in *believe.* [*long* e] Point out that a word is spelled with *ie* when the sound is long *e.* Next, ask what sound *ei* makes in *deceit.* [*long* e] Explain that after *c* the long *e* sound is spelled *ei.* Point out that *ei* is also the correct spelling when the sound is not long *e,* especially when the sound is long *a.* [*foreign, freight*] Show that *protein* and *friend* represent exceptions to these rules. Now, have a volunteer use another example from this chapter to demonstrate how to spell words with *ie* or *ei.*

DIFFERENTIATING INSTRUCTION

Learners Having Difficulty

Some students may benefit from seeing a visual diagram of **Rule 16c.** Arranging the three classifications of words as follows might help students recall the information.

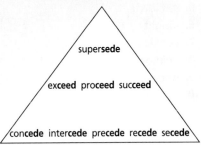

Encourage students to pronounce new or problem words and to spell the words aloud as they practice writing them.

EXTENSION

Proofreading

Strategy. To help students find misspelled words as they proofread their writing, suggest that they review their work backwards so that they read each word in isolation. Have them circle any spelling they question and check circled words in a dictionary.

DIFFERENTIATING INSTRUCTION

Learners Having Difficulty

Explain to students that one means of remembering the correct spelling of problem words is to use problem words in writing. Have each student use four problem words from **Exercises 3, 4,** and **5** in sentences and share their sentences with classmates.

Exercise 3 Spelling Words with Prefixes
ANSWERS

1. immigrate
2. resettle
3. uncertain
4. illegal
5. semicircle
6. insight
7. reaction
8. unknown
9. disbelief
10. semifinalist

Reference Note

Sometimes a prefix is used with a hyphen, as in *self-propelled*. For more about using **hyphens,** see page 357.

Exercise 2 Proofreading for Misspelled Words Ending in *–cede, –ceed,* and *–sede*

Each of the following sentences contains a misspelled word ending in *–cede, –ceed,* or *–sede*. Identify the errors, and spell the words correctly.

EXAMPLE   **1.** The guitarist could not procede until the electricity came back on.

    1. procede—proceed

1. Clarence Leo Fender succeeded in changing the music business in the 1950s.   **1.** succeeded
2. He improved the design of electric guitars, which quickly superceded acoustic guitars in popular music.   **2.** superseded
3. The great success of Fender's invention probably exceded his wildest dreams.   **3.** exceeded
4. Music critics consede that a new era began with the invention of the electric guitar.   **4.** concede
5. Concerts that preceeded Fender's invention were not nearly as loud as modern ones.   **5.** preceded

Adding Prefixes

A **prefix** is a letter or group of letters added to the beginning of a word to create a different meaning.

EXAMPLES   dis + honest = **dis**honest

    un + selfish = **un**selfish

16d. When adding a prefix to a word, do not change the spelling of the word itself.

EXAMPLES   mis + spell = mis**spell**   over + rate = over**rate**

Exercise 3 Spelling Words with Prefixes

Spell each of the following words, adding the prefix given.

EXAMPLE   **1.** un + wrap

    1. unwrap

1. im + migrate
2. re + settle
3. un + certain
4. il + legal
5. semi + circle
6. in + sight
7. re + action
8. un + known
9. dis + belief
10. semi + finalist

Adding Suffixes

A *suffix* is a letter or group of letters added to the end of a word to create a different meaning.

EXAMPLES stay + ing = stay**ing**

comfort + able = comfort**able**

walk + ed = walk**ed**

16e. When adding the suffix –*ly* or –*ness* to a word, do not change the spelling of the word itself.

EXAMPLES slow + ly = **slow**ly   dark + ness = **dark**ness

usual + ly = **usual**ly   late + ness = **late**ness

shy + ly = **shy**ly   shy + ness = **shy**ness

EXCEPTIONS For words that end in *y* and have more than one syllable, change the *y* to *i* before adding –*ly* or –*ness.*

happy + ly = happ**ily**   lazy + ness = laz**iness**

16f. Drop the final silent *e* before adding a suffix beginning with a vowel.

EXAMPLES line + ing = **lin**ing

approve + al = **approv**al

EXCEPTIONS Keep the final silent *e*

• in a word ending in *ce* or *ge* before adding a suffix beginning with *a* or *o*:

trace + able = tra**ceable**

courage + ous = coura**geous**

• in *dye* before –*ing*:   dy**eing**

• in *mile* before –*age*:   mil**eage**

16g. Keep the final silent *e* before adding a suffix beginning with a consonant.

EXAMPLES hope + less = hop**e**less   care + ful = car**e**ful

awe + some = aw**e**some   love + ly = lov**e**ly

nine + ty = nin**e**ty   amuse + ment = amus**e**ment

Spelling Rules   **373**

MEETING THE CHALLENGE

Base words (such as *hon-est* and *walk*) can stand alone or combine with other word parts (*dishon-est* or *walked*, for example). *Word roots* (such as –*crit*– and –*fer*–), like pre-fixes and suffixes, cannot stand alone and are com-bined with other word parts to form words (*critical* or *transfer*, for example).

Form new words by adding a prefix, a suffix, or both to the following base words and word roots.

BASE WORDS
cycle, element, quick, verse

WORD ROOTS
–*dict*–, –*gest*–, –*loc*–, –*vis*–

ANSWERS
Answers will vary. Here are some possibilities:

BASE WORDS
recycle, elementary, quickly, universe

WORD ROOTS
dictionary, digestible, relocate, visible

DIFFERENTIATING INSTRUCTION

Learners Having Difficulty

You can encourage students to think of **Rules 16e, f,** and **g** as a series of "if . . . then" statements. For example, **Rule 16e** could be rephrased "If you are adding –*ly* or –*ness,* then don't change the spelling of the base word." After giving students this example, ask them to write and share with the class "if . . . then" statements with examples for the other two rules.

Learners Having Difficulty

Ask students to go through some of their writing and list any misspelled words they find. Have students cor-rect the words in their writing, com-pile a personal list of words that are troublesome for them, and identify the applicable spelling rule (if any) for each word listed.

In addition, ask students to compare their list to other students' lists. If the same word appears on more than one list, then add that word to a master list for the class. The master list can be printed on poster board and dis-played in the classroom for reference during in-class writing assignments.

English-Language Learners

General Strategies. Since mispro-nunciation of words may hinder their spelling ability, have English-language learners repeat new words orally. Assign partners to check their pronunciations. Write new words or terms on the chalkboard, and have students pronounce them with you. Highlight unusual spellings, such as *Wednesday.*

MECHANICS

MINI-LESSON | **Grammar** | *Continued on p. 374*

Suffixes and Parts of Speech. Explain that adding a suffix to a root word sometimes changes the root word's part of speech. Review the suffixes in **Rules 16e–g,** and then write the following items on the chalkboard.

1. *nice* (adj.) + –*ly* = *nicely* (adv.)

2. *kind* (adj. *or* n.) + –*ness* = *kindness* (n.)

3. *sense* (n.) + –*ible* = *sensible* (adj.)

DIFFERENTIATING INSTRUCTION

Learners Having Difficulty

Word Games. Word games can help students learn to spell. Give students groups of two or three words, and have them make as many other words as they can using letters from the word groups. (For example, *three blind mice* could be used to produce words such as *he, dim, melt,* and *birth.*) Allow students to use dictionaries. Also, encourage students to play other word games, such as crossword puzzles and word searches.

TECHNOLOGY TIP

Some word-processing programs contain an auto-correct feature allowing users to input words they often misspell. The programs will automatically correct these errors when they are typed. If students have access to this feature, suggest that they add to the program any problem words with suffixes.

DIRECT TEACHING

Correcting Misconceptions

Spelling. Some students may have the misconception that correct spelling is unimportant in contemporary life. Ask students to jot down a list of reasons why correct spelling is important. Ask students whether correct spelling may be less important sometimes, such as when taking class notes or writing in personal diaries. Lead students to understand that always using correct spelling is good practice. Doing so helps break bad spelling habits and prevents such poor habits from developing.

EXCEPTIONS	nine + th = **nin**th	argue + ment = **argu**ment
	true + ly = **tru**ly	whole + ly = **whol**ly
	awe + ful = **aw**ful	

Answers
Exercise 4
1. naturally
2. adorable
3. surely
4. dryness
5. teasing
6. luckily
7. tuneful
8. noticeable
9. confinement
10. advantageous

Exercise 4 Spelling Words with Suffixes

Spell each of the following words, adding the suffix given.

EXAMPLE   1. hope + ful
          1. *hopeful*

1. natural + ly
2. adore + able
3. sure + ly
4. dry + ness
5. tease + ing
6. lucky + ly
7. tune + ful
8. notice + able
9. confine + ment
10. advantage + ous

16h. For words ending in *y* preceded by a consonant, change the *y* to *i* before any suffix that does not begin with *i.*

EXAMPLES	cry + ed = cr**ied**	duty + ful = dut**iful**
	easy + ly = eas**ily**	try + ing = tr**ying**

16i. For words ending in *y* preceded by a vowel, keep the *y* when adding a suffix.

EXAMPLES	pray + ing = pra**ying**	pay + ment = pa**yment**
	obey + ed = obe**yed**	boy + ish = bo**yish**

EXCEPTIONS	day + ly = da**ily**	lay + ed = la**id**
	pay + ed = pa**id**	say + ed = sa**id**

16j. Double the final consonant before adding a suffix beginning with a vowel if the word (1) has only one syllable or has the accent on the last syllable and (2) ends in a single consonant preceded by a single vowel.

EXAMPLES	sit + ing = si**tt**ing	refer + ed = refe**rr**ed
	swim + er = swi**mm**er	begin + er = begi**nn**er
	drop + ed = dro**pp**ed	forbid + en = forbi**dd**en

MINI-LESSON Grammar   *Continued from p. 373*

4. *use* (n. or v.) + *–ful* = *useful* (adj.)

5. *argue* (v.) + *–ment* = *argument* (n.)

Ask volunteers to use both words in each numbered item in separate sentences.

Finally, explain that knowing how suffixes can change a word's part of speech may help students to expand their vocabularies. Refer students to **Chapters 2** and **3** for a review of the parts of speech.

Otherwise, the final consonant is usually not doubled before a suffix beginning with a vowel.

EXAMPLES   sing + er = singer   final + ist = finalist

               speak + ing = speaking   center + ed = centered

NOTE In some cases, the final consonant may or may not be doubled.

EXAMPLES   cancel + ed = canceled *or* cancelled

               travel + er = traveler *or* traveller

Most dictionaries list all the spellings above as correct.

Exercise 5 **Spelling Words with Suffixes**

Spell each of the following words, adding the suffix given.

EXAMPLE   **1.** study + ed

           1. *studied*

1. tiny + est   **5.** display + ed   **9.** submit + ing
2. trim + ing   **6.** enjoy + ment   **10.** win + er
3. dry + ing   **7.** refer + al
4. pity + ful   **8.** jog + er

Review A **Proofreading for Misspelled Words**

Most of the following sentences contain a spelling error. Identify and correct each error. If a sentence is already correct, write *C*.

EXAMPLE   **1.** The man shown on the next page is not Sam Houston or Jim Bowie, but he is a certifyed Texas hero.

           1. *certifyed—certified*

1. This ~~industryous~~ blacksmith is William Goyens.   **1.** industrious
2. In 1820, he moved from North Carolina to Texas, where he ~~succeded~~ in several businesses.   **2.** succeeded
3. Goyens ~~acheived~~ his greatest fame as a negotiator with the Comanche and the Cherokee peoples.   **3.** achieved
4. He easily made ~~freinds~~ with the American Indians who traded in the small town of Nacogdoches.   **4.** friends

---

┌**HELP**

When you are not sure about the spelling of a word, it is best to look it up in a dictionary.

Answers
Exercise 5
  1. tiniest
  2. trimming
  3. drying
  4. pitiful
  5. displayed
  6. enjoyment
  7. referral
  8. jogger
  9. submitting
10. winner

┌**HELP**

None of the proper nouns in Review A are misspelled.

English-Language Learners
Hmong. The Hmong language's Romanized Popular Alphabet uses unvoiced final consonants as tonal markers whose only purpose is to indicate a word's stress and pitch. Therefore, when reading, some Hmong students may leave English end consonants unvoiced. Because pronunciation is so crucial to spelling, this omission may result in dropped final consonants by Hmong spellers. Have students practice reading aloud, emphasizing final consonants as they read, until they begin to voice end consonants consistently.

EXTENSION

Relating to Dictionary Skills

Some dictionaries contain reference material on learning to spell correctly. Ask students to study this material in a dictionary from home, school, or a public library and to share with the class any rules or tips they discover that are not included in the textbook.

Because dictionaries sometimes give more than one spelling for a word, you may want to have students study the introductory material that explains the dictionary's policy regarding multiple spellings. For example, the first spelling given is usually the one most commonly used. If two spellings are joined by the word *or*, both may be equally acceptable.

DIFFERENTIATING INSTRUCTION

English-Language Learners

General Strategies. Students may not notice *s* endings on plurals when reading or listening and, in turn, might fail to pronounce these endings in speaking or to use them in writing. To heighten awareness of *s* endings, have students read aloud a portion of text containing many plurals; whenever they miss an *s*, say the word aloud yourself and have students pronounce it after you, emphasizing the *s*.

Hmong. Hmong places the word *cov* before nouns to make them plural. Explain to Hmong-speaking students that many English nouns are made plural by adding *s* or *es* to the end of the word. This addition, except for its attachment to the noun itself, is much like the Hmong use of *cov*. Review and practice creating English plurals with students.

William Goyens, tinted print (1820s). Courtesy of Hendrick-Long Publishing Co.

┌─HELP─
Make sure that you do not confuse the plural form of a noun with its possessive form. Generally, you should not use an apostrophe to form the plural of a word.

Reference Note
For a discussion of **possessive forms of nouns,** see page 351.

5. Later, he assisted the Mexican government and then the Texas army in ~~makking~~ peace with their American Indian neighbors.
6. General Sam Houston asked Goyens to ~~interceed~~ on behalf of the settlers.   **5.** making **6.** intercede
7. Because of Goyens's efforts, the Comanches and Cherokees agreed to remain on ~~peacful~~ terms with the settlers.   **7.** peaceful
8. In addition to negotiating peace treaties, Goyens ~~studyed~~ law to protect his own and others' freedoms.   **8.** studied
9. People started coming to him with their legal problems, and he unselfishly tried to help them.   **9.** C
10. William Goyens was ~~truely~~ an important force in shaping Texas history.   **10.** truly

Forming the Plurals of Nouns

16k. To form the plurals of most nouns in English, add *s*.

SINGULAR	pest	isle	blue	opera	Taylor
PLURAL	pest**s**	isle**s**	blue**s**	opera**s**	Taylor**s**

16l. For nouns ending in *s, x, z, ch,* or *sh,* add *es*.

SINGULAR	gas	box	waltz	wrench	wish	Paz
PLURAL	gas**es**	box**es**	waltz**es**	wrench**es**	wish**es**	Paz**es**

NOTE Some one-syllable words ending in *z* double the final consonant when forming plurals.

EXAMPLES   quiz   fez
            quiz**zes**   fez**zes**

Oral Practice   Spelling the Plural Forms of Nouns

For each of the following words, say the plural form aloud. Then, say whether the plural form takes an –*s* or an –*es*.

EXAMPLE   **1.** right
           1. rights

1. dish **1.** es   5. address **5.** es 9. Gómez **9.** es
2. plumber **2.** s 6. march **6.** es 10. tax **10.** es
3. candle **3.** s   7. parade **7.** s
4. watch **4.** es   8. republic **8.** s

16m. For nouns ending in *y* preceded by a vowel, add *s*.

SINGULAR	valley	weekday	boy	journey	Murray
PLURAL	valley**s**	weekday**s**	boy**s**	journey**s**	Murray**s**

16n. For nouns ending in *y* preceded by a consonant, change the *y* to *i* and add *es*.

SINGULAR	puppy	library	lily	navy	story
PLURAL	pupp**ies**	librar**ies**	lil**ies**	nav**ies**	stor**ies**

EXCEPTIONS   For proper nouns, add *s*.

Kennedy—Kennedy**s**   Curry—Curry**s**

16o. For some nouns ending in *f* or *fe*, add *s*. For others, change the *f* or *fe* to *v* and add *es*.

SINGULAR	roof	sheriff	giraffe	knife	thief
PLURAL	roof**s**	sheriff**s**	giraffe**s**	kni**ves**	thie**ves**

┌HELP──
When you are not sure about how to spell the plural of a noun ending in *f* or *fe*, look it up in a dictionary.

16p. For nouns ending in *o* preceded by a vowel, add *s*.

SINGULAR	radio	ratio	video	igloo	Romeo
PLURAL	radio**s**	ratio**s**	video**s**	igloo**s**	Romeo**s**

16q. For nouns ending in *o* preceded by a consonant, add *es*.

SINGULAR	tomato	potato	echo	hero
PLURAL	tomato**es**	potato**es**	echo**es**	hero**es**

EXCEPTIONS   For musical terms and proper nouns, add *s*.

piano—piano**s**   soprano—soprano**s**

solo—solo**s**   Nakamoto—Nakamoto**s**

NOTE   To form the plural of some nouns ending in *o* preceded by a consonant, you may add either *s* or *es*.

SINGULAR	domino	mosquito	banjo	flamingo
PLURAL	domino**s**	mosquito**s**	banjo**s**	flamingo**s**
or	*or*	*or*	*or*	*or*
	domino**es**	mosquito**es**	banjo**es**	flamingo**es**

┌HELP──
When you are in doubt about the way to form the plural of a noun ending in *o* preceded by a consonant, check the spelling in a dictionary.

16r. Some nouns have irregular plural forms.

SINGULAR	ox	goose	foot	tooth	child	mouse
PLURAL	ox**en**	g**ee**se	f**ee**t	t**ee**th	child**ren**	m**i**ce

---

MECHANICS

Exercise 6 Spelling the Plurals of Nouns

ANSWERS

1. monkeys
2. trophies
3. Masseys
4. diaries
5. hoofs *or* hooves
6. proofs
7. palominos
8. children
9. cargoes *or* cargos
10. women
11. mothers-in-law
12. sit-ups
13. *8*'s
14. trout *or* trouts
15. drive-ins
16. *t*'s
17. salmon *or* salmons
18. spoonfuls
19. @'s
20. *him*'s

Reference Note

For more information on **compound nouns,** see page 26.

STYLE TIP

In your reading, you may notice that some writers do not use apostrophes to form the plurals of numerals, capital letters, symbols, and words used as words.

EXAMPLES

Their music is as popular today as it was in the **1970s.**

When dividing, remember to write **Rs** before the remainders in the quotients.

However, using an apostrophe is not wrong and may be necessary for clarity. Therefore, it is better to use the apostrophe.

HELP

Some words in Exercise 6 have more than one correct plural form. You need to give only one form for each word. You may want to use a dictionary to check your work.

16s. For most compound nouns, form the plural of the last word in the compound.

SINGULAR	bookshelf	pull-up	blue jay	four-year-old
PLURAL	bookshel**ves**	pull-up**s**	blue jay**s**	four-year-old**s**

16t. For compound nouns in which one of the words is modified by the other word or words, form the plural of the word modified.

SINGULAR	sister-in-law	guest of honor	ninth-grader
PLURAL	sister**s**-in-law	guest**s** of honor	ninth-grader**s**

16u. For some nouns, the singular and the plural forms are the same.

SINGULAR AND PLURAL	aircraft	sheep
	deer	Sioux
	moose	Vietnamese

16v. For numerals, letters, symbols, and words used as words, add an apostrophe and *s*.

EXAMPLES   The product of two **4**'s is twice the sum of four **2**'s.

Notice that the word *Mississippi* has four *i*'s, four *s*'s, and two *p*'s.

Write **$**'s before, not after, amounts of money.

This composition contains many *us*'s and *them*'s.

Exercise 6 Spelling the Plurals of Nouns

Spell the plural form of each of the following nouns.

EXAMPLE   **1.** volcano
    1. volcanoes or volcanos

1. monkey	**8.** child	**15.** drive-in
2. trophy	**9.** cargo	**16.** *t*
3. Massey	**10.** woman	**17.** salmon
4. diary	**11.** mother-in-law	**18.** spoonful
5. hoof	**12.** sit-up	**19.** @
6. proof	**13.** *8*	**20.** *him*
7. palomino	**14.** trout	

Spelling Numbers

16w. Spell out a number that begins a sentence.

EXAMPLE   **Fifteen thousand** tickets to the concert went on sale.

16x. In a sentence, spell out numbers that can be written in one or two words. Use numerals for other numbers.

EXAMPLES   Do you have **two** nickels for **one** dime?

Our school's concert band has **twenty-six** members.

The movie theater has **270** seats.

NOTE   If you use several numbers, some short and some long, write them all the same way. Usually, it is better to write them all as numerals.

INCORRECT   We sold eighty-six tickets to the fall dance and 121 tickets to the spring dance.

CORRECT   We sold **86** tickets to the fall dance and **121** tickets to the spring dance.

16y. Spell out numbers used to indicate order.

EXAMPLE   Our team placed **third** [not *3rd*] in the regional track meet this season.

Exercise 7   Spelling Numbers

Write each of the following sentences correctly. If a sentence is already correct, write *C*.

EXAMPLE   **1.** 3 quarters were sitting on the table.

1.   Three quarters were sitting on the table.

1. David was scheduled to be the 4th speaker at the banquet.
2. Kerry counted 349 pennies in her penny jar.
3. The new cafeteria had a capacity of over 300 people.
4. Shannon correctly answered 96 of the 125 items on the test.
5. 1286 tickets were sold for the weekend performances of the senior play.

1. fourth
2. C
3. three hundred
4. C
5. One thousand two hundred eighty-six

Words Often Confused

(pp. 380–392)

OBJECTIVE

- To complete sentences by choosing between pairs of words often confused

DIRECT TEACHING

Modeling and Demonstration

Words Often Confused. Model the correct usage of often confused words with the examples *The eruption of Krakatau affected the sunsets all over the world* and *The phases of the moon have an effect on the tides of the earth's oceans.* First, point out that correct usage can often be determined by asking what the confusing word means in a sentence. Ask students what *affected* means in the first example. [*to influence*] Since *affected* describes an action, it is a verb. Next, ask what *effect* means in the second example. [*the consequence or result of an action*] Explain that *effect* is a noun. Now, have a volunteer use other examples from this chapter to demonstrate the correct usage of words often confused.

EXTENSION

Oral Presentation

Divide the class into groups of three, and assign each group one set of words often confused. Ask each group to create a plan for teaching the set of words to other students. Encourage groups to use visuals in their lessons. Then, have each group teach its words to the rest of the class.

Reference Note

If there is a word you cannot find in the following list, refer to the Glossary of Usage, Chapter 12, or look up the word in a dictionary.

┌HELP─

All right should be written as two words. The spelling *alright* is not standard English.

Words Often Confused

People frequently confuse the words in each of the following groups. Some of these words are **homonyms.** The pronunciations of homonyms are the same, but their meanings and spellings are different. Others have the same or similar spellings but have different meanings.

accept	[verb] *to receive with consent; to give approval to* In 1964, Dr. Martin Luther King, Jr., *accepted* the Nobel Prize for peace.
except	[verb] *to leave out from a group;* [preposition] *other than; but* We were *excepted* from the requirement. Everyone *except* Ruben will be there.
advice	[noun] *a recommendation about a course of action* *Advice* may be easy to give but hard to follow.
advise	[verb] *to recommend a course of action; to give advice* I *advise* you to continue your music lessons.
affect	[verb] *to influence; to produce an effect upon* The eruption of Krakatau *affected* the sunsets all over the world.
effect	[noun] *the result of an action; consequence* The phases of the moon have an *effect* on the tides of the earth's oceans.
all ready	[adjective] *all prepared* The players are *all ready* for the big game in San Diego next week.
already	[adverb] *previously* Our class has *already* taken two field trips.
all right	[adjective] *satisfactory;* [adverb] *satisfactorily* Was my answer *all right*? Maria did *all right* in the track meet.

RESOURCES

Words Often Confused

Practice

- *Language & Sentence Skills Practice*, pp. 345–349, 351–353
- *Developmental Language & Sentence Skills*, pp. 129–134

Exercise 8 Using Words Often Confused

From the choices in parentheses, select the <u>correct word or words</u> for each of the following sentences.

EXAMPLE 1. Anh and her family are (*all ready, already*) to celebrate Tet, the Vietnamese New Year.

1. *all ready*

1. Do you think my work is (*all right, alright*)?
2. The (*affect, effect*) of the victory was startling.
3. The scientists were (*all ready, already*) to watch the launching of the rocket.
4. Whose (*advice, advise*) are you going to take?
5. The coach (*advices, advises*) us to stick to the training rules.
6. Why did you (*accept, except*) Carla from the rule?
7. Her weeks of practice have finally (*affected, effected*) her game.
8. Juan has (*all ready, already*) learned how to water-ski.
9. The president offered most of the rebels a full pardon, which they (*accepted, excepted*), but the leaders were (*accepted, excepted*) from the offer.
10. Gabriel took my (*advice, advise*) and visited the home of Frederick Douglass in Washington, D.C.

altar	[noun] *a table for a religious ceremony* The *altar* was covered with lilies.
alter	[verb] *to change* The outcome of the election may *alter* the mayor's plan.
all together	[adjective] *in the same place;* [adverb] *at the same time* The family was *all together* then. Please sing *all together,* everybody.
altogether	[adverb] *entirely* Nishi seemed *altogether* thrilled to see us.
brake	[noun] *a device to stop a machine* Can you fix the *brake* on my bicycle?
break	[verb] *to fracture; to shatter* A high-pitched noise can *break* glass.

(continued)

COMPUTER TIP

Most word-processing programs have a spellchecker that can help you catch spelling mistakes. Remember, though, that a computer's spellchecker cannot point out homonyms that are used incorrectly. For example, if you use *affect* where you should use *effect,* the computer probably will not catch the mistake. Learn how to proofread your own writing, and never rely entirely on a spellchecker.

MECHANICS

Words Often Confused **381**

DIFFERENTIATING INSTRUCTION

Advanced Learners

Changes in English. Just as the meanings of words can change over time, so can their spellings. To illustrate this point, share with students these Old English spellings and their modern English equivalents.

Old English	Modern English
cild	child
muth	mouth
regn	rain
blæc	black
hwit	white

Even within what is considered modern English, spelling continues to evolve. Some dictionaries have introductory sections that recount the history of spelling. If such dictionaries are available, you may want to ask students to read this material and then have each student report to the class three things he or she learned from it.

Exercise 9

DISTRIBUTED REVIEW

For a quick review of complements, ask students to find the complements in sentences 5, 8, and 9. Then, have students identify each complement as a direct object, indirect object, predicate nominative, or predicate adjective. [5. *complicated—predicate adjective;* 8. *menace—predicate nominative;* 9. *plans—direct object*]

┌ TIPS & TRICKS ┐

To remember how to spell *capitol*, use this memory aid: There's a d**o**me on the capit**o**l.

(continued)

capital	[noun] *a city; the seat of a government* Olympia is the *capital* of Washington.
capitol	[noun] *building; statehouse* Where is the *capitol* in Albany?
choose	[verb; rhymes with *whose*] *to select* Did you *choose* speech or art as your elective?
chose	[verb; past tense of *choose*, rhymes with *grows*] *selected* Sara *chose* a red pen, not a blue one.

FRANK & ERNEST reprinted by permission of Newspaper Enterprise Association, Inc.

Exercise 9 Using Words Often Confused

From the choices in parentheses, select the correct word or words for each of the following sentences.

EXAMPLE **1.** Mr. Conway said he (*choose, chose*) teaching as a career because he wants to help young people.

   1. chose

1. The building with the dome is the (*capital, capitol*).
2. By working (*all together, altogether*), we can succeed.
3. Alma (*choose, chose*) a difficult part in the school play.
4. Be careful not to (*brake, break*) those dishes.
5. That book is (*all together, altogether*) too complicated.
6. The candles on the (*altar, alter*) glowed beautifully.
7. Why did you (*choose, chose*) that one?
8. A car without a good emergency (*brake, break*) is a menace to pedestrians and other vehicles.
9. Will Carrie's accident (*altar, alter*) her plans?
10. Tallahassee is the (*capital, capitol*) of Florida.

clothes	[noun] *wearing apparel* One can learn much about a historical period by studying its styles of *clothes*.
cloths	[noun] *pieces of fabric* Some cleaning *cloths* are in the drawer.
coarse	[adjective] *rough; crude* The beach is covered with *coarse* brown sand.
course	[noun] *path of action; unit of study; route;* [also used in the expression *of course*] If you follow that *course*, you'll succeed. My mother is taking a *course* in accounting. The wind blew the ship slightly off its *course*. You know, of *course*, that I'm right.
complement	[noun] *something that completes or makes perfect;* [verb] *to complete or make perfect* The chef's kitchen features a full *complement* of appliances. The white tulips *complemented* the crystal vase.
compliment	[noun] *a remark that expresses approval, praise, or admiration;* [verb] *to praise someone* Mrs. Chung paid Miranda a *compliment* on her model of Notre Dame. The ambassador *complimented* Agent Makowski on her quick thinking.
consul	[noun] *a representative of a government in a foreign country* Who is the Guatemalan *consul* in Miami?
council	[noun] *a group of people who meet together* The mayor called a meeting of the city *council*.
counsel	[noun] *advice;* [verb] *to give advice* When choosing a career, seek *counsel* from your teachers. Ms. Jiménez *counseled* me to pursue a career in teaching.

(continued)

┌─────────────────┐
│ TIPS & TRICKS │
└─────────────────┘

You can remember the difference in spelling between *complement* and *compliment* by remembering that a compl**e**ment compl**e**tes a sentence.

DIFFERENTIATING INSTRUCTION

Special Education Students

Spelling presents problems for students with visual-processing deficiencies. To help such students, offer a multisensory approach. Have the students or a helper print in large letters on flashcards the correct spellings of words they are studying. Students can then study the words by simultaneously tracing the letters with their fingers and pronouncing the word on the card. For an added sensory dimension, letters can be written in puff paint so that students can actually feel the letters once the paint has dried.

Advanced Learners

Some students will not have problems spelling the words in the **Words Often Confused** list. Allow such students to work as a group to compile a list of words that they have encountered in their reading and have had difficulty spelling. Students can then study the words from the list they have compiled instead of spending time studying words they already know how to spell.

MECHANICS

councilor	[noun] *member of a council* The *councilors* discussed several issues.
counselor	[noun] *one who advises* Who is your guidance *counselor*?
desert	[noun, pronounced des'•ert] *a dry, sandy region* The Sahara is the largest *desert* in Africa.
desert	[verb, pronounced de•sert'] *to abandon;* *to leave* Most dogs will not *desert* a friend in trouble.
dessert	[noun, pronounced des•sert'] *the sweet, final* *course of a meal* Fruit salad is my favorite *dessert*.

Exercise 10 Using Words Often Confused

From the choices in parentheses, select the correct word for each of the following sentences.

EXAMPLE   1. Egypt, of (*course, coarse*), is an ancient country in northeastern Africa.

   1. *course*

1. The student (*council, counsel*) voted to have "A Night on the Nile" as its dance theme.
2. In this photograph, many shoppers at an Egyptian market wear Western (*clothes, cloths*).

3. Others wear traditional garments, including (*clothes, cloths*) called *kaffiyehs* wrapped loosely around their heads.
4. In ancient Egypt, pharaohs did not always follow the advice of their friends and other wise (*councilors, counselors*).
5. The surfaces of some famous Egyptian monuments look (*coarse, course*) from years of exposure to wind and sand.

DIFFERENTIATING INSTRUCTION

Learners Having Difficulty

Memory tricks such as the following ones can be helpful for some students.

1. all right—If it's not *all right,* it's all wrong.
2. de**ss**ert—When dessert is served, we often want two (two *s*'s).
3. h**ear**—We hear with our <u>ears</u>.

RETEACHING

Words Often Confused

Activity. You may want to introduce students to several pairs of words that are spelled in exactly the same way but are different parts of speech, are pronounced differently, and have different meanings (such as *des*ert and de*sert*). When used as a noun or adjective, the stress is on the first syllable. When used as a verb, the stress falls on the second syllable. Other examples include *con*flict—con*flict, per*mit—per*mit, pres*ent—pre*sent,* and *pro*duce—pro*duce.* Have students repeat these words as you model the correct pronunciations. Then, have students work with partners to create sentences using the word pairs, for example, "My father won't per*mit* me to get a driv-ing *per*mit until next year."

MECHANICS

6. In my geography (*coarse, course*), I learned that Nubians make up the largest minority group in Egypt's population.
7. The U.S. (*consul, council*) in Cairo welcomed the vice-president to Egypt.
8. Camels did not (*desert, dessert*) their owners when they crossed the Egyptian (*desert, dessert*).
9. Figs, grapes, and dates have been popular (*deserts, desserts*) in Egypt for a long time.
10. In Cairo, the confused tourists looked to their tour director for (*council, counsel*).

formally	[adverb] *with dignity; according to strict rules or procedures* The mayor delivered the speech *formally.*
formerly	[adverb] *previously; in the past* Adele Zubalsky was *formerly* the principal of the school.
hear	[verb] *to receive sounds through the ears* Dogs can *hear* sounds that people can't *hear.*
here	[adverb] *in this place* The treasure is buried *here.*
its	[possessive form of *it*] *belonging to it* Mount Fuji is noted for *its* beauty.
it's	[contraction of *it is* or *it has*] *It's* [It is] a good idea to relax. *It's* [It has] been a long time.
lead	[verb, rhymes with *feed*] *to go first; to be a leader* A small town in New Hampshire often *leads* the nation in filing its election returns.
led	[verb, past tense of *lead*] *went first* Mr. Tanaka *led* the scout troop back to camp.
lead	[noun, rhymes with *red*] *a heavy metal; graphite in a pencil* Many fishing nets are weighted with *lead* to hold them to the sea bottom. Is your mechanical pencil out of *lead*?

(continued)

CONTENT-AREA CONNECTIONS

Art

Spelling Quilt. Have each student design a nine-inch quilt square illustrating a pair of words often confused. (For example, a student might illustrate *peace* and *piece* by drawing a large *peace* sign and a *piece* of pie.) Encourage students to use various methods to create the squares (collages, computer graphics, needlework, batik, and so forth). Then, have students stitch or tape their squares together to make a spelling quilt to display in the classroom.

(continued)

| **loose** | [adjective, rhymes with *moose*] *not securely attached; not fitting tightly*
If the knot is too *loose,* the piñata will fall out of the tree. |
| **lose** | [verb, rhymes with *whose*] *to suffer loss*
Vegetables *lose* some of their vitamins when they are cooked. |

Exercise 11 Using Words Often Confused

From the choices in parentheses, select the correct word for each of the following sentences.

EXAMPLE 1. Mary Beth did not (*loose, lose*) her Southern accent even after she moved to Boston.

       1. *lose*

1. According to Ethan's map, (*its, it's*) a very long way from (*hear, here*) to the park.
2. The ancient Chinese, Greeks, and Romans used (*lead, led*) in their coins.
3. If you don't wait (*hear, here*), we may (*loose, lose*) you in the crowd.
4. "Before the club takes up any new business," said Mr. Burr, "the secretary (*formally, formerly*) reads the minutes of the previous meeting."
5. (*Its, It's*) too bad that the oak tree has lost (*its, it's*) leaves so early in the season.
6. Didn't you (*hear, here*) me, Charlotte? Come over (*hear, here*) right now!
7. The Chipmunks were ten runs behind, and it seemed certain that they were going to (*loose, lose*).
8. Venus Williams (*lead, led*) after the first set of the tennis match at the U.S. Open.
9. Our new mayor, Mr. Brown, was (*formally, formerly*) an actor but has been in politics for ten years now.
10. That (*loose, lose*) bolt could cause trouble if we have to fly during a storm.

EXTENSION

Relating to Vocabulary Skills

Vocabulary and spelling problems are closely linked in the words covered in this segment. Ask students to choose from the **Words Often Confused** list five words that are not part of their usual vocabularies and to record the definitions of these words in their spelling notebooks. Then, have students write several original sentences using each word on their list correctly. Finally, have students revise the sentences to create a fill-in-the-blank or a multiple-choice exercise. Assign the exercises that students have written to those students who need extra practice.

MECHANICS

passed	[verb, past tense of *pass*] *went by* The people in the car waved as they *passed* us.
past	[noun] *that which has gone by;* [preposition] *beyond;* [adjective] *ended* Some people long to live in the *past.* They walked *past* the dozing guard. He forgot his *past* concerns.
peace	[noun] *security and quiet order* We are striving for *peace* and prosperity.
piece	[noun] *a part of something* Some people can catch fish with a pole, a *piece* of string, and a bent pin.
plain	[adjective] *simple, common, unadorned;* [noun] *a flat area of land* The actors wore *plain* costumes. What is the difference between a prairie and a *plain*?
plane	[noun] *a tool; an airplane; a flat surface* The *plane* is useful in the carpenter's trade. Four single-engine *planes* are in the hangar. In geometry class, we learned how to measure the angles of *planes* such as squares and triangles.
principal	[noun] *the head of a school;* [adjective] *main or most important* The *principal* of the school is Mr. Arimoto. What are the *principal* exports of Brazil?
principle	[noun] *a rule of conduct; a main fact or law* Judge Rios is a woman of high *principle.* We discussed some of the basic *principles* of democracy.
quiet	[adjective] *still and peaceful; without noise* Let's find a *quiet* room so that we can study.
quite	[adverb] *wholly or entirely; to a great extent* Winters in New England can be *quite* severe.

TIPS & TRICKS

Here's a way to remember the difference between *peace* and *piece*: You eat a p**ie**ce of p**ie.**

TIPS & TRICKS

Here is an easy way to remember the difference between *principal* and *principle:* The princi**pal** is your **pal.**

RETEACHING

Memory Aids

Words Often Confused. Students may find it helpful to compose a single sentence containing both words in a pair of frequently confused words. Here are two examples.

   I will not *desert* my *dessert.* desert/dessert

   In the *past* I *passed* all my exams. past/passed

Each longer line contains a sentence using both of the words being studied, while the shorter lines list the words. Suggest that each student use this technique for any words he or she frequently confuses and keep the sentence in his or her notebook. Ask volunteers to share a few sentences they have written.

MECHANICS

Explain to students that a computer program will query any spellings that are not in its dictionary, and it will suggest alternative spellings. Remind students, though, of the danger of depending entirely on computers for spelling. Most spellcheckers will not question sentences such as "Their having a good time at there family reunion." Discuss the importance of careful proofreading in addition to the use of spellcheckers.

TIPS & TRICKS

Here is an easy way to remember the difference between *stationary* and *stationery*: You write a lett**er** on station**er**y.

Exercise 12 **Using Words Often Confused**

From the choices in parentheses, select the correct word for each of the following sentences.

EXAMPLE 1. Summer (*passed, past*) by too quickly!

1. *passed*

1. In some Filipino villages, you can still find (*plain, plane*), practical houses built on bamboo stilts.
2. The summer was not (*quiet, quite*) over before the beginning of school brought a (*quiet, quite*) household once more.
3. This is a main (*principal, principle*) in mathematics.
4. On July 11, 1991, the moon (*passed, past*) between the earth and the sun, causing a total solar eclipse.
5. A (*plain, plane*) is a useful tool.
6. Save me a (*peace, piece*) of that blueberry pie.
7. The new (*principal, principle*) used to be a student here.
8. You can learn much from the (*passed, past*), Eduardo.
9. After the long war came a long period of (*peace, piece*).
10. Cattle were grazing on the (*plains, planes*).

shone	[verb, past tense of *shine*] *gleamed; glowed* The Navajo jeweler polished the silver-and-turquoise ring until it *shone*.
shown	[verb, past participle of *show*] *revealed* A model of the new school will be *shown* to the public next week.
stationary	[adjective] *in a fixed position* Most of the furnishings of a space station must be *stationary*.
stationery	[noun] *writing paper* I need a new box of *stationery*.
than	[conjunction used for comparisons] The Amazon River is longer *than* the Mississippi River.
then	[adverb] *at that time* If the baby is awake by four o'clock, we will leave *then*.

their	[possessive form of *they*] *belonging to them* *Their* team seems very skillful.
there	[adverb] *at or in that place;* [also used to begin a sentence] Go *there* in the fall when the leaves are turning. *There* were no objections.
they're	[contraction of *they are*] *They're* rehearsing for a summer production of *A Soldier's Story.*
threw	[verb, past tense of *throw*] *tossed, pitched* Our relief pitcher *threw* nine strikes in succession.
through	[preposition] *in one side and out the other side, across* The ship went *through* the series of locks in the Panama Canal.

Exercise 13 **Using Words Often Confused**

From the choices in parentheses, select the correct word for each of the following sentences.

EXAMPLE **1.** (*There, Their*) are some truly amazing tunnels used for transportation throughout the world.

    1. There

1. Take a good look at the workers in the photograph on the next page because (*there, they're*) part of history.
2. (*Their, They're*) labor helped link England with France by creating a tunnel under the English Channel.
3. A documentary about the tunnels through the Alps will be (*shone, shown*) at the library.
4. Huge exhaust fans had to be constructed to move the (*stationary, stationery*) air in the Holland Tunnel in New York.
5. To run railroad lines all across the United States, workers had to dig many tunnels (*threw, through*) mountains.
6. Used for blasting tunnels in mountainsides, explosives (*threw, through*) enormous boulders into the air.
7. The warm sun (*shone, shown*) brightly on the snowy top of Mont Blanc, but in the mountain's tunnel it was dark and chilly.

Learning for Life

Continued on p. 390

Writing Technical Instructions. As technology assumes a larger role in society, so does technical writing. Ask students to write a set of instructions for using a specific technological device.

    Have students brainstorm devices they might use. Encourage them to choose a fairly simple device so their instructions will not be too complicated.

    Have each student select a specific audience and keep its needs in mind as he or she drafts the instructions. As part of

8. We rode the underground, or subway, into London, where I bought some (*stationary, stationery*).
9. Boston's subway is older (*than, then*) New York City's subway.
10. In Paris, we took the subway, called the *métro*, to the Eiffel Tower and (*than, then*) to the Louvre museum.

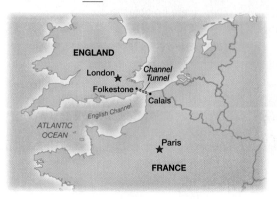

to	[preposition] *in the direction of; toward* [also part of the infinitive form of a verb] Marco Polo began his trip *to* China in 1271. Do you know how *to* make tortillas?
too	[adverb] *also; more than enough* We have lived in Iowa and in Alaska, *too.* It is *too* cold for rain today.
two	[noun] *cardinal number between one and three;* [adjective] *one more than one* I've got *two* of their CDs. She borrowed *two* dollars from me.
waist	[noun] *the middle part of the body* These pants are too big in the *waist.*
waste	[noun] *unused material;* [verb] *to squander* Most of the *waste* can be recycled. Don't *waste* your money on popcorn and soda.
weak	[adjective] *not strong; feeble* The patient is too *weak* to have visitors.
week	[noun] *seven days* Josh's bar mitzvah is planned for next *week.*

Learning for Life

Continued from p. 389

prewriting, have students make an ordered list of the steps involved.

As students write, encourage them to imagine someone actually trying to use the instructions. Tell students to include enough details to communicate effectively.

Have partners evaluate one another's papers, focusing on clarity and accuracy. As students proofread, encourage them to refer to the spelling rules in this chapter whenever they are unsure of the spelling of a word.

MECHANICS

weather	[noun] *condition of the air or atmosphere* The *weather* is hot and humid.
whether	[conjunction] *if* Jessica wondered *whether* she should go.
who's	[contraction of *who is* or *who has*] *Who's* [Who is] representing the yearbook staff? *Who's* [Who has] read today's newspaper?
whose	[possessive form of *who*] *belonging to whom* *Whose* report are we hearing today?
your	[possessive form of *you*] *belonging to you* *Your* work in math is improving.
you're	[contraction of *you are*] *You're* right on time!

Exercise 14   Using Words Often Confused

From the choices in parentheses, select the correct word for each of the following sentences.

EXAMPLE   **1.** (*Your, You're*) class gets to visit Minnehaha
              Park in Minneapolis.

          1. Your

1. Jason felt (*weak, week*) after skiing all day in the Sangre de Cristo Mountains of New Mexico.
2. (*Weather, Whether*) we'll go to the park or not depends on the (*weather, whether*).
3. (*Whose, Who's*) books are you carrying?
4. Find out (*whose, who's*) going to the annual football banquet if you can.
5. Learning (*to, too, two*) roll carved sticks for the Korean game of *yut* wasn't (*to, too, two*) difficult.
6. (*Your, You're*) off your course, captain.
7. We took (*to, too, two*) (*weaks, weeks*) for our trip to France and Switzerland last summer.
8. Twirl the hoop around your (*waste, waist*).
9. Would you enjoy a trip (*to, too, two*) Mars, Flo?
10. Aren't you using (*your, you're*) compass?

EXTENSION

Relating to Writing

Rhyme. Students who are interested in writing rhyming poetry or song lyrics might find rhyming dictionaries useful for finding words that rhyme and for learning how to spell the words. Ask interested students to write four-line rhyming poems and to use a rhyming dictionary from the classroom, library, or a computer program. You may want to suggest several rhyming words that would lend themselves to humorous lines, such as *hippopotamus* or *metropolis*. Students might use poems by Ogden Nash as models.

TECHNOLOGY TIP

You may want to point out that some word-processing programs have rhyming dictionaries. Students can indicate the words for which they need rhymes, determine how many syllables they wish to rhyme, and let the computer suggest possible words.

MECHANICS

EXTENSION

Critical Thinking

Metacognition. After students have completed **Review B,** ask them to write brief answers to the following questions.

1. How did completing **Review B** compare with completing the other exercises on using words that are often confused?

2. How did you make use of the rules and examples in the textbook to complete **Review B**?

3. What advice would you give others regarding correcting spelling errors while proofreading?

Review B **Proofreading for Words Often Confused**

Identify and correct each error in words often confused in the following sentences.

EXAMPLE   **1.** Anne Shirley, here portrayed by actress Megan Follows, found a pieceful life and a loving family on Prince Edward Island.

      1. pieceful—peaceful

1. Does the scenery shone in the picture on this page appeal to you? **1.** shown

2. My family enjoyed the green hillsides and rugged seashore during our two-weak vacation there last summer. **2.** week

3. Prince Edward Island is quite a beautiful spot, and its Canada's smallest province. **3.** it's

4. Everyone who lives there calls the island PEI, and now I do, to. **4.** too

5. During our visit, the weather was quite pleasant, so I lead my parents all over PEI on foot. **5.** led

6. We walked to several places of interest in Charlottetown, the capitol. **6.** capital

7. I got to chose our first stop, and I selected the farmhouse that's the setting for the novel *Anne of Green Gables.* **7.** choose

8. That novel's main character, Anne Shirley, is someone who's ideas I admire. **8.** whose

9. Walking around "The Garden Province," we passed many farms; the principle crop is potatoes. **9.** principal

10. Take my advise and visit Prince Edward Island if you get the chance. **10.** advice

16

┌HELP┐

None of the proper nouns in the Chapter Review are misspelled.

Terms and numerals in brackets refer to concepts and rules tested by the items in the Chapter Review.

1. Fifteen thousand [16w]
2. 135 [16x]
3. quite [*quiet, quite*]
4. puppies, fifth [16y]
5. succeeded [16c]
6. week [*weak, week*]
7. adorable [16f]
8. C [16a; *passed, past*]
9. achievement, peace [16a; *peace, piece*]
10. swimmer, intercede [16j, c]
11. waltzes [16l]
12. igloos [16p]
13. heroes, bookshelves [16q, o]
14. brothers-in-law [16t]
15. altar [*altar, alter*]
16. advantageous [16f]
17. easily [16h]
18. oxen [16r]

Chapter Review

A. Proofreading for Misspelled and Misused Words

Most of the following sentences contain at least one error in spelling or in words often confused. Write the sentences, correcting each error. If a sentence is already correct, write *C*.

1. 15,000 young salmon were released into the river last week by the fishing club.
2. Phil and his family drove one hundred thirty-five miles to visit his cousins.
3. "It is quiet foolish," said Mr. Vohra, "to hope for success but to do nothing."
4. The puppys didn't get tired until the 5th time they had run around the house.
5. Finally, we succeded in getting the pig out of the backyard.
6. Last weak I felt ill, but now I'm fine.
7. How adoreable that puppy is!
8. We were relieved to discover that the storm had passed and that everyone was all right.
9. "Woodrow Wilson's most remarkable acheivement," said Mrs. Levine, "was to make a broken promise look like leadership by declaring war after promising piece."
10. Our neighbor, who is also a swimer, agreed to interceed on our behalf.
11. How many waltzs did they dance back in old Vienna?
12. Fewer and fewer Inuit live in iglooes nowadays.
13. They told us the books on heros were on one of the bookshelfs at the back.
14. Teddy has two brother-in-laws, and they're both nice.
15. The alter of a church is a table or stand used for religious services.
16. "Closing the deal now would be personally advantagous to you," the sales representative assured us.
17. After the mechanic put in a new alternator, the engine started very easyly.
18. Weren't oxes used in the old days to pull plows?

ASSESSING

Monitoring Progress
Chapter Review. To assess student progress, you may want to compare the types of items missed on the **Diagnostic Preview** with those missed on the **Chapter Review.** If students have not made significant progress, you may want to refer them to **Chapter 17: Correcting Common Errors, Exercises 33–35,** for additional practice.

RESOURCES

Spelling: Improving Your Spelling

Review

■ *Language & Sentence Skills Practice,* pp. 350–353

Assessment

■ *Formal Assessment*

■ *Progress-Monitoring Tests,* pp. 31–32, 48

■ *Test Generator (Teacher One Stop DVD-ROM)*

19. Romeos [16p]
20. *n's* [*or* C] [16v]

19. My little brother calls my sisters' boyfriends ~~Romeoes~~.
20. "How many ~~n's~~ are there in *Tennessee*?" asked Kim.

B. Using Words Often Confused

From the choices in parentheses, choose the <u>correct word</u> or words for each of the following sentences.

21. [*brake, break*]
22. [*capitol, capital*]
23. [*hear, here*]
24. [*past, passed*]
25. [*desert, dessert*]
26. [*counsel, council*]
27. [*plain, plane*]
28. [*to, too, two*]
29. [*whose, who's*]
30. [*waist, waste*]

21. A carelessly thrown baseball can (*brake*, <u>*break*</u>) a window.
22. New Delhi is the (*capitol*, <u>*capital*</u>) of India.
23. Turn up the sound so you can (<u>*hear*</u>, *here*) the program.
24. The car (*past*, <u>*passed*</u>) us at high speed.
25. We must not (<u>*desert*</u>, *dessert*) a friend in need.
26. All of the members of the United Nations Security (*Counsel*, <u>*Council*</u>) voted against intervention.
27. Our (*plain*, <u>*plane*</u>) finally took off after a two-hour delay.
28. I know that aardvarks eat ants, and I think they eat termites, (*to*, *two*, <u>*too*</u>).
29. (<u>*Whose*</u>, *Who's*) raincoat is on the coat rack?
30. At those prices, buying those new CDs would be a serious (*waist*, <u>*waste*</u>) of money.

C. Proofreading a Paragraph for Misspelled and Misused Words

Each sentence in the following paragraph contains at least one misspelled or misused word. Correctly write each incorrect word.

31. whose [*whose, who's*]
32. to [*to, too, two*]
33. passed [*past, passed*]
34. There [*their, there, they're*]
35. 1770's [*or* C]/ clothes [16v; *clothes, cloths*]
36. led [*lead, led, lead*]
37. quite/principal [*quiet, quite; principal, principle*]

[31] My mother, ~~who's~~ birthplace is Alexandria, Virginia, has always wanted to go back there. **[32]** Last year, we finally traveled from our home in the Midwest ~~too~~ see where she was born. **[33]** Strolling around the Old Town section of Alexandria, a beautiful old city just outside Washington, D.C., we ~~past~~ many historic buildings. **[34]** ~~Their~~ were churches, homes, old taverns, and several shops on our tour. **[35]** At a building called Gadsby's Tavern, built in the ~~1770s~~, a man dressed in Colonial-era ~~cloths~~ greeted us. **[36]** He was a guide, and he ~~lead~~ us on a tour of the building, which is now a museum. **[37]** As one of the very few eighteenth-century taverns remaining in the United States, Gadsby's, he explained, is ~~quiet~~ a special place: George Washington, the Marquis de Lafayette, and Thomas Jefferson were some of the ~~principle~~ visitors. [38] When our guide told us that, it didn't take much for us to imagine those famous people climbing up the front steps to the ~~lovly~~ old tavern. [39] By the end of the day, Mother had ~~shone~~ us where she was born and had taken us to see the Potomac riverfront. [40] She said she would ~~readyly~~ move back to Alexandria, and we completely understood how she felt.

38. lovely [16g]
39. shown [*shone, shown*]
40. readily [16h]

Writing Application
Using Words Correctly in an Essay

Correctly Using Words Often Confused   Write a three-paragraph essay on the favorite hobbies of your family or your friends. Use at least five words from the Words Often Confused list in this chapter.

Prewriting   First, make a list of family members or friends, and beside each name, write what you know about that person's favorite hobby or pastime. If you're not sure about someone's hobbies, ask him or her. Then, choose at least five words from the Words Often Confused list, and use them in your essay.

Writing   As you jot down notes for your first draft, think about ways to organize your information. You could list the information by age of friend or family member, hobbies in common, variety of interests and pastimes, and so on.

Revising   Ask a friend or classmate to read your essay. Is each person's hobby or pastime clearly described? Add, cut, or rearrange information to make your essay as clear and descriptive as possible.

Publishing   Read through your essay to check for errors in grammar, usage, punctuation, and spelling. Have you correctly used words often confused? You and your classmates may want to share your essays with your class, either by reading them aloud or posting them on a class bulletin board or Web page.

Writing Application
Scoring Rubric.   While you will want to pay particular attention to students' spelling, you will also want to evaluate overall writing performance. You may want to give a split score to indicate development and clarity of the composition as well as skill in spelling.

MECHANICS

TEACHING TIP

The number of each word group in the **Spelling Words** list corresponds to a lesson number in the *Spelling Lessons and Activities* workbook.

Lesson 1: OBJECTIVE
■ To spell words that are formed by joining two different words

Lesson 2: OBJECTIVE
■ To recognize and spell homonyms (homophones)

Lesson 3: OBJECTIVE
■ To spell inflected forms of words

Lesson 4: OBJECTIVE
■ To spell words that are formed from the same base word

Lesson 5: OBJECTIVE
■ To spell words that have similar pronunciations

Lesson 6: OBJECTIVE
■ To spell words that contain a form of the prefixes *in–* and *ad–*

Lesson 8: OBJECTIVE
■ To spell words that have French origins

Lesson 9: OBJECTIVE
■ To spell words that have adjective endings

Lesson 10: OBJECTIVE
■ To spell words that have Greek word parts

Lesson 11: OBJECTIVE
■ To spell words that have Greek origins

Lesson 12: OBJECTIVE
■ To spell words that come from science and technology

Lesson 14: OBJECTIVE
■ To spell words that contain the Latin roots *–serv–*, *–dict–*, *–migr–*, and *–port–*

Spelling Words

1.
- homemade
- long-term
- underground
- handkerchief
- large-scale
- gingerbread
- furthermore
- heart attack
- stagecoach
- good-natured
- headquarters
- loudspeaker

2.
- boarder
- bard
- stationary
- principle
- palette
- stationery
- burro
- pallet
- Capitol
- burrow
- foul
- barred

3.
- programming
- refused
- omitted
- produced
- acquired
- abilities
- submitted
- justified
- forbidding
- petrified
- nutrients
- resources

4.
- continue
- profession
- dramatic
- despair
- awe
- professionally
- continuous
- strenuous
- continuously

- dramatically
- desperately
- strenuously

5.
- conscious
- excess
- bizarre
- finely
- breadth
- persecuted
- conscience
- prosecuted
- futile
- access
- anecdote
- feudal

6.
- inspection
- insisted
- illustrated
- advice
- approved
- agreeable
- investigated
- announcement
- impressed
- accomplished
- affectionate
- irresponsible

8.
- suite
- matinee
- blouse
- debris
- surgeon
- embarrassed
- chauffeur
- croquet
- amateur
- crochet
- plateau
- coup

9.
- historic
- ragged
- magnetic
- barefooted
- democratic
- passionate

- rigid
- contented
- poetic
- undersized
- metallic
- confederate

10.
- symbolic
- microphone
- generation
- cyclone
- symptoms
- genius
- synonyms
- generator
- synthetic
- genes
- sympathetic
- symphony

11.
- physical
- aroma
- episode
- marathon
- chorus
- pneumonia
- rhythm
- labyrinth
- melancholy
- philosophy
- phenomenon
- architecture

12.
- chemical
- scientists
- sonar
- instruments
- atmosphere
- experiments
- hemisphere
- environment
- laser
- probability
- technological
- molecules

14.
- predicting
- dictator
- supported

- verdict
- dictionaries
- reservation
- preservation
- conservation
- observatory
- indictment
- emigrate
- immigration

15.
- combine
- combination
- patriots
- patriotic
- distribute
- distribution
- repeated
- repetition
- oblige
- obligation
- medicine
- medicinal

16.
- provisions
- international
- interview
- telescopes
- underlying
- underneath
- profitable
- proceeds
- intermediate
- prosperity
- interrupted
- intercept

17.
- abstract
- transaction
- absolute
- extravagant
- subdued
- abolished
- translation
- submerged
- transferred
- transient
- extraordinary
- extraterrestrial

Lesson 15: OBJECTIVE
■ To spell related forms of words

Lesson 16: OBJECTIVE
■ To spell words with the prefixes *pro–*, *under–*, *inter–*, and *tele–*

Lesson 17: OBJECTIVE
■ To spell words with the prefixes *ab–*, *sub–*, *trans–*, and *extra–*

18. • hesitate
demonstrate
investigate
delegate
concentrate
mandate
eliminate
advocate
simulate
participate
negotiate
phosphate

20. • multicolored
magnitude
equality
multitude
microscope
equation
multimedia
equator
microorganism
multicultural
magnificently
equivalent

21. • scattering
polluted
summoned
satellite
vaccination
intellectual
narrative
penniless
parallel
embassy
exaggerated
torrential

22. • tourism
loyalty
robbery
uncertainty
patriotism
cruelty
specialty
realism
novelty
optimism

mechanism
criticism

23. • occupation
obtained
offering
obviously
offensive
opportunity
obscure
occupant
obstacle
opposition
obsessions
occasionally

25. • perimeter
circumstances
permanently
circumference
perception
intrastate
introvert
perspective
periodic
peripheral
persuaded
circuit

26. • politics
sophisticated
metropolitan
optic
scholarship
philosopher
optical
optometrist
archaic
automatically
sophomore
archaeologist

27. • carnival
chipmunk
parakeet
monsoon
hickory
heroic
skeleton

spaghetti
walrus
yacht
macaroni
barbecue

28. • geographic
astronauts
geology
geometry
supervision
nautical
navigation
odometer
asterisk
altimeter
cosmonauts
seismometer

30. • spoonerism
malapropism
sequoia
boycott
mackintosh
frankfurter
pasteurize
Braille
Celsius
Fahrenheit
odyssey
zeppelin

31. • detained
sentimental
productive
deceived
attended
adjustments
justice
acceptable
acceptance
sensation
sensory
perceived

32. • yearling
diskette
luncheonette
particle

icicle
sapling
banquet
cabinet
bracelet
cassette
pamphlet
statuette

33. • duplicate
financial
complicated
vocal
conjunction
infinite
vocabulary
vocational
definitely
territorial
juncture
applicable

34. • igloo
karate
harpoon
kimono
kindergarten
caucus
toboggan
kayak
tundra
persimmon
hibachi
haiku

35. • historically
favorably
eventually
governmental
fortunately
economically
architectural
sensationally
naturalization
significantly
mysteriously
rhythmically

Spelling Words   397

Lesson 18: **OBJECTIVE**
■ To spell words with the suffix –ate

Lesson 20: **OBJECTIVE**
■ To spell words with prefixes that tell size and amount

Lesson 21: **OBJECTIVE**
■ To spell words that have doubled consonants

Lesson 22: **OBJECTIVE**
■ To spell words that have noun-forming suffixes

Lesson 23: **OBJECTIVE**
■ To spell words with the prefix *ob–* and its variations

Lesson 25: **OBJECTIVE**
■ To spell words with the prefixes *peri–, per–, intra–, intro–,* and *circu(m)–*

Lesson 26: **OBJECTIVE**
■ To spell words formed from Greek word parts

Lesson 27: **OBJECTIVE**
■ To spell common words that come from other languages

Lesson 28: **OBJECTIVE**
■ To spell and understand relationships among word parts

Lesson 30: **OBJECTIVE**
■ To spell words that come from names

Lesson 31: **OBJECTIVE**
■ To spell words that have Latin roots

Lesson 32: **OBJECTIVE**
■ To spell words that have diminutive suffixes

Lesson 33: **OBJECTIVE**
■ To spell words that have Latin roots

Lesson 34: **OBJECTIVE**
■ To spell words from other languages

Lesson 35: **OBJECTIVE**
■ To spell words that have suffixes in combination

Spelling Words   **397**

CHAPTER
17

Correcting Common Errors

─HELP─

Remember that all of the exercises in Chapter 17 test your knowledge of the rules of **standard, formal English.** These are the rules you should follow in your schoolwork.

Reference Note

For more about **standard** and **nonstandard English** and **formal** and **informal English,** see page 265.

Key Language Skills Review

This chapter reviews key skills and concepts that pose special problems for writers.

- **Sentence Fragments and Run-on Sentences**
- **Subject-Verb and Pronoun-Antecedent Agreement**
- **Verb Forms**
- **Pronoun Forms**
- **Comparison of Modifiers**
- **Misplaced and Dangling Modifiers**
- **Standard Usage**
- **Capitalization**
- **Punctuation—Commas, End Marks, Colons, Semicolons, Quotation Marks, and Apostrophes**
- **Spelling**

Most of the exercises in this chapter follow the same format as the exercises found throughout the grammar, usage, and mechanics sections of this book. You will notice, however, that two sets of review exercises are presented in standardized test formats. These exercises are designed to provide you with practice not only in solving usage and mechanics problems, but also in dealing with these kinds of problems on standardized tests.

Exercise 1 — Identifying Word Groups as Sentence Fragments or Sentences

Identify each of the following word groups as either a *sentence fragment* or a *sentence*. If the word group is a fragment, correct it by adding or deleting words to make a complete sentence. You may need to change punctuation and capitalization, too.

EXAMPLE   **1.** Those basketballs over there.

           1. *Those basketballs over there are for tomorrow's game.*

                    or

           Please gather up those basketballs over there.

1. Fourteen years ago today.   **1.** frag.
2. In 1810, when Miguel Hidalgo started the independence movement in Mexico.   **2.** frag.
3. Drought and dust plagued Oklahoma and adjoining states in the 1930s.   **3.** sent.
4. If she decides to become a doctor.   **4.** frag.
5. Let us see what will happen next.   **5.** sent.
6. He thinks the 1997 movie about the *Titanic* is the best movie ever made.   **6.** sent.
7. Running in from the pouring rain.   **7.** frag.
8. When he wrote the letter to the editor.   **8.** frag.
9. To keep from using foam cups, my uncle Louis carries a reusable plastic cup.   **9.** sent.
10. Another example of being environmentally conscious. **10.** frag.

Exercise 2 — Correcting Sentence Fragments

Most of the groups of words on the following page are sentence fragments. If a word group is a fragment, correct it either by adding or deleting words to make a complete sentence or by attaching it to a complete sentence. You may need to change the punctuation and capitalization, too. If a word group is already a complete sentence, write *S*.

EXAMPLE   **1.** The movie about Cleopatra.

           1. *The movie about Cleopatra is playing downtown.*

                    or

           Have you seen the movie about Cleopatra?

HELP

Most of the word groups in Exercise 1 can be correctly revised in more than one way. You need to give only one revision for each word group.

Reference Note

For information on **sentence fragments,** see page 4.

HELP

Most of the word groups in Exercise 2 can be correctly revised in more than one way. You need to give only one revision for each word group.

Reference Note

For information on **sentence fragments,** see page 4.

OBJECTIVE

- To distinguish between sentences and sentence fragments and to revise fragments to make them complete sentences

Exercise 1 — Identifying Word Groups as Sentence Fragments or Sentences

POSSIBLE ANSWERS

1. Fourteen years ago today, my older sister was born.

2. In 1810, when Miguel Hidalgo started the independence movement in Mexico, Napoleon Bonaparte was still alive.

4. If she decides to become a doctor, she will probably want to specialize in homeopathic medicine.

7. I saw our cat running in from the pouring rain.

8. When he wrote the letter to the editor, Dad was very concerned about the number of traffic accidents near the middle school.

10. Another example of being environmentally conscious is the city council's stand against development in ecologically sensitive areas.

COMMON ERRORS

Assessment

- *Formal Assessment*
- *Progress-Monitoring Tests,* pp. 33–34, 48
- *Test Generator* (Teacher One Stop DVD-ROM)

Other Language Resources

- *Spelling Lessons & Activities*
- *WordSharp: An Interactive Vocabulary Tutor*
- *Reading and Writing Transparencies*

Exercise 2 Correcting Sentence Fragments

POSSIBLE ANSWERS

1. My little sister answered the telephone politely.

2. An armadillo's covering of bony plates is like armor.

3. Because Alan prefers volleyball to any other team sport, he is trying to organize an intramural team.

4. After the first winter snow melted, we thought spring had arrived.

5. S

6. When she returns to the house this afternoon, Mom will be surprised that the chores have all been done.

7. The post office will not be delivering the package with postage due.

8. The recycling center is not accepting magazines and catalogs.

9. S

10. Gretchen's family moved here from Germany so that she could study at the institute.

Exercise 3

OBJECTIVE

■ To correct run-on sentences

---

1. Answered the telephone politely.
2. An armadillo's covering of bony plates like armor.
3. Because Alan prefers volleyball to any other team sport.
4. After the first winter snow.
5. Someone gave the museum those photographs of settlers in the Ozarks.
6. When she returns to the house this afternoon.
7. Delivering the package with postage due.
8. The recycling center accepting magazines and catalogs.
9. The kitten walked across the computer keyboard.
10. Moved here from Germany so that she could study at the institute.

┌HELP┐

Most of the sentences in Exercise 3 can be correctly revised in more than one way. You need to give only one revision for each sentence.

Reference Note

For information about **run-on sentences,** see page 441.

Exercise 3 Correcting Run-on Sentences

Correct each of the following run-on sentences by making two separate sentences or by combining the two parts of the run-on sentence to make one complete sentence. Be sure to use capitalization and punctuation correctly.   Answers may vary.

EXAMPLE   1. Sign language, or manual speech, is not new, in fact, it has a long history.

1. *Sign language, or manual speech, is not new; in fact, it has a long history.*

or

Sign language, or manual speech, is not new. In fact, it has a long history.

1. , but

3. , and

5. , and

1. Some people may think that manual speech dates from this century the beginnings of manual speech go much further back.

2. An Italian physician played a very important role in the development of manual speech. I had never heard of him.

3. His name was Girolamo Cardano he lived during the sixteenth century.

4. Cardano proposed the theory that people unable to hear could learn to associate written symbols with objects or actions he thought that people who could not hear or speak could then use such symbols to communicate.

5. In the 1700s, Abbé Charles Michel de L'Epée opened the first free school for people with impaired hearing he devised a manual sign version of spoken French.

6. In 1778, Samuel Heinicke began a school in Germany for people unable to hear, it was the first such school to receive government recognition.

7. The first school in the United States for those unable to hear was founded in 1817 ~~its founder was~~ Thomas Hopkins Gallaudet, a minister from Philadelphia.   7. by

8. Laurent Clerc was the first deaf person to teach other deaf people in a school in the United States in 1816 he came to the United States to help Gallaudet found the Hartford School for the Deaf.

9. Gallaudet College is in Washington, D.C. it is still the world's only liberal arts college specifically for people who are deaf or hard of hearing.

10. Today, American Sign Language is used by at least 500,000 people in the United States and Canada, it is the fourth most common language in the United States.

Exercise 4 Correcting Sentence Fragments and Run-on Sentences

The following word groups contain sentence fragments, run-on sentences, and complete sentences. Identify each word group by writing *F* for a fragment, *R* for a run-on, or *S* for a complete sentence. If a word group is a fragment, correct it by adding or deleting words to make a complete sentence. Correct each run-on by making it into two separate sentences or by combining the two parts of the run-on to make one complete sentence. You may also need to change the punctuation and capitalization.

EXAMPLE   1. The old truck drove very slowly up the hill, a long line of cars followed it.

1. *R—The old truck drove very slowly up the hill. A long line of cars followed it.*

or

R—The old truck drove very slowly up the hill, and a long line of cars followed it.

1. One of the most famous photographs taken during World War II shows soldiers raising the U.S. flag at Iwo Jima.

2. I hope to travel to Asia someday, I want to climb the Himalayas.

┌─HELP─
Most of the sentences in Exercise 4 can be correctly revised in more than one way. You need to give only one revision for each sentence.

Reference Note
For information on **sentence fragments,** see page 4. For information on **run-on sentences,** see page 441.

COMMON ERRORS

Grammar and Usage   **401**

Exercise 5

OBJECTIVE

- To identify word groups as sentence fragments, run-on sentences, or complete sentences; and to correct the sentence fragments and run-on sentences

Exercise 5 Correcting **Sentence Fragments and Run-on Sentences**

POSSIBLE ANSWERS

1. R—There have been many milestones in the history of food production. The development of canned food is one of the most important.

2. F—Because canned goods fill our stores today, most people generally take these foods for granted.

3. S

4. R—The story of canned goods begins in the 1700s with Lazzaro Spallanzani; his experiments in preserving food were some of the earliest to succeed.

5. S

6. F—They used processes in which the bottles of food were heated to very high temperatures.

7. F—Bottles were later replaced with containers made of tin-plated iron.

8. S

9. F—Heat kills the bacteria that cause food to spoil, as Louis Pasteur discovered in the mid-1800s.

10. R—The development of this process, now called pasteurization, made eating canned food safer, and the eventual invention of the can opener made it easier!

┌HELP┐

Most of the word groups in Exercise 5 can be correctly revised in more than one way. You need to give only one revision for each word group.

Reference Note

For information on **sentence fragments,** see page 4. For information on **run-on sentences,** see page 441.

---

3. To uproot the stumps of the trees we cut down in the front yard.

4. Some kinds of spiders, such as the bolas spider, that do not make webs.

5. We played a variety of music from different countries for the dancers.

6. Robin, my best friend since fourth grade.

7. Into the forest and across the valley they rode it took until sundown to reach the camp.

8. When a cicada comes out of the ground.

9. My mother's favorite movie is about the composer Mozart, I can't remember its title.

10. Sirius, which is the brightest star that can be seen from Earth at night.

Exercise 5 Correcting Sentence Fragments and Run-on Sentences

The following paragraph contains sentence fragments, run-on sentences, and complete sentences. First, identify each numbered word group by writing *F* for a fragment, *R* for a run-on, or *S* for a complete sentence. Then, revise the paragraph to correct the fragments and run-ons.

EXAMPLE **[1]** The history of food a delicious subject.

    1. *F—The history of food is a delicious subject.*

                   or

    F—I just saw a documentary on the history of food, a delicious subject.

[1] There have been many milestones in the history of food production, the development of canned food is one of the most important. [2] Because canned goods fill our stores today. [3] Most people generally take these goods for granted. [4] The story of canned goods begins in the 1700s with Lazzaro Spallanzani his experiments in preserving food were some of the earliest to succeed. [5] Other early experimenters preserved vegetables, fruit, and meat in glass bottles. [6] Using processes in which the bottles of food were heated to very high temperatures. [7] Bottles later replaced with containers made of tin-plated iron. [8] Heat kills the bacteria that cause food to spoil. [9] As Louis Pasteur

discovered in the mid-1800s. [10] The development of this process, now called pasteurization, made eating canned food safer the eventual invention of the can opener made it easier!

Exercise 6 Identifying Verbs That Agree in Number with Their Subjects

For each of the following sentences, choose the form of the verb in parentheses that agrees with the subject.

EXAMPLE   **1.** (*Do, Does*) you know much about clouds?

      1. *Do*

1. Learning about clouds (*help*, *helps*) you predict the weather.
2. Some of the books that I used in my report about weather (*give*, *gives*) detailed information about clouds.
3. Water droplets and ice crystals (*form*, *forms*) clouds.
4. Many of us (*like*, *likes*) to look for faces and familiar shapes in clouds overhead.
5. One of the most common types of clouds (*is*, *are*) the cumulonimbus rain cloud.
6. People often (*call*, *calls*) these clouds thunderstorm clouds.
7. Clouds of this kind (*produce*, *produces*) tornadoes and hail at times.
8. My friends Jeffrey and Kate (*don't*, *doesn't*) remember the name of cloud formations that look like wisps of cotton.
9. Several of these cirrus clouds (*was*, *were*) in the sky yesterday.
10. Stratus clouds, which often produce drizzle, (*look*, *looks*) like smooth sheets.
11. The basic types of clouds (*include*, *includes*) cumulus, nimbus, stratus, and cirrus.
12. Many cloud names (*combine*, *combines*) these basic names.
13. A cumulonimbus cloud (*have*, *has*) combined characteristics of cumulus and nimbus.
14. Another type of cloud, which combines features of nimbus and stratus clouds, (*are*, *is*) called a nimbostratus.
15. Other combinations (*take*, *takes*) the names stratocumulus and cirrostratus.
16. This information (*sounds*, *sound*) complicated but is easy to learn and fun to use.

Reference Note

For information on **subject-verb agreement,** see page 156.

COMMON ERRORS

17. Think how impressed your friends will be when you say, "Those (*appear, appears*) to be nimbostratus clouds over there; we may get rain later."
18. Cloud names (*come, comes*) from Latin words such as *cumulus,* meaning "heap."
19. *Nimbus,* in Latin, (*mean, means*) "rainstorm"; nimbus clouds are dark and full of rain.
20. *Cirrus* and *stratus* (*derive, derives*) from Latin words meaning "to curl" and "to spread out."

Reference Note

For information on **subject-verb agreement,** see page 156.

Exercise 7

OBJECTIVE

- To correct sentences with errors in subject-verb agreement

Exercise 7 Proofreading Sentences for Correct Subject-Verb Agreement

Most of the following sentences contain ~~errors in subject-verb agreement.~~ If a verb does not agree with its subject, give the ⌃correct form of the verb. If a sentence is already correct, write *C.*

EXAMPLE 1. Spanish explorers and missionaries is important in New Mexico's history.

1. *are*

1. Spanish missions throughout New Mexico ~~attracts~~ many tourists nowadays. **1.** attract
2. Some of these missions ~~has~~ been in continuous use for centuries. **2.** have
3. Two missions especially ~~interests~~ me. **3.** interest
4. I can't decide whether the Mission of San Agustin de Isleta or Santa Fe's Mission of San Miguel ~~are~~ my favorite. **4.** is
5. Both of these beautiful missions date from the early seventeenth century. **5.** C
6. Each of them ~~have~~ survived damage caused by fires and centuries of wear. **6.** has
7. Antique objects and priceless art ~~lends~~ their beauty to these old missions. **7.** lend
8. One of the most noteworthy features of the Santa Fe mission is a bell. **8.** C
9. The bell, which was brought to Santa Fe in the 1800s, ~~were~~ cast in 1356 in Spain. **9.** was
10. Churches in Spain and Mexico ~~was~~ home to the bell before it was brought to New Mexico. **10.** were

Identifying Pronouns That Agree with Their Antecedents

For each of the following sentences, choose the <u>pronoun or pair</u> <u>of pronouns in parentheses</u> that agrees with its antecedent or antecedents.

EXAMPLE   **1.** The horse and mule walked toward (*its, their*) owner.

         1. their

1. Did your uncle or your father take (*<u>his</u>, their*) fishing license to the pier?
2. Does one of the coats have Kim's initials on (*their, <u>its</u>*) label?
3. Everyone has had (*<u>his or her</u>, their*) turn to play in the game.
4. Ms. Torres and Ms. Lawrence gladly accepted (*her, <u>their</u>*) Community Appreciation Certificates.
5. Anyone may recite (*<u>his or her</u>, their*) poem during the program tonight.
6. Did Alejandro or Tim put on (*<u>his</u>, their*) jacket?
7. Neither of my twin stepbrothers has had (*<u>his</u>, their*) first haircut.
8. Each of the twenty women cast (*their, <u>her</u>*) vote.
9. Neither Ramona nor Isabel recalled (*<u>her</u>, their*) dream from the night before.
10. The first grade and the second grade will be taking (*its, <u>their</u>*) field trip tomorrow.
11. Either Eileen or Alicia has forgotten (*their, <u>her</u>*) raincoat.
12. Did your brother and your cousin Brad intend to exchange (*his, <u>their</u>*) tickets?
13. The cat has eaten all of (*<u>its</u>, their*) food.
14. Carlton joined the band but then forgot to bring (*<u>his</u>, their*) guitar to practice.
15. Each of the women will need (*their, <u>her</u>*) copy of the newsletter.
16. Many U.S. presidents were reelected and therefore served (*his, <u>their</u>*) second terms.
17. The track team and the cross-country team have (*its, <u>their</u>*) competitions tomorrow.
18. Neither Chris nor Luke has had (*their, <u>his</u>*) bicycle repaired yet.
19. Has either Cristina or Rachael lost all of (*their, <u>her</u>*) baby teeth yet?
20. The cast and director hope (*his, <u>their</u>*) production succeeds.

Reference Note

For information on **pronoun-antecedent agreement,** see page 173.

COMMON ERRORS

Exercise 9

OBJECTIVE

■ To correct errors in pronoun-antecedent agreement

Exercise 10

OBJECTIVE

■ To give the past or past participle form of verbs

Reference Note

For information on **pronoun-antecedent agreement,** see page 173.

Snowy! It's up to you to save us now, Snowy ...You must carry this message and get help from the monastery ...

HERGE/MOULINSART 1999

Reference Note

For information on **verb forms,** see page 186.

1. hiked

2. known

Exercise 9 Proofreading Sentences for Correct Pronoun-Antecedent Agreement

Most of the following sentences contain errors in pronoun-antecedent agreement. Identify each incorrect pronoun, and supply the correct form or forms. If the sentence is already correct, write *C*.

EXAMPLE   1. Tintin, whose adventures spanned the globe, traveled with their dog, Snowy.

   1. *their—his*

1. The Belgian cartoonist Georges Remi created the comic strip character Tintin in the 1920s and set their first adventures in the Soviet Union. **1.** his
2. Everybody in class who had read Tintin stories had their favorite tales of the adventurous reporter. **2.** his or her
3. Both of this character's closest companions, Captain Haddock and Professor Cuthbert Calculus, help his friend Tintin. **3.** their
4. Each of these men has their own unusual characteristics. **4.** his
5. Thomson and Thompson, detectives who look alike, add his own silliness to Tintin's travels.   **5.** their
6. Several of the students said that he or she had read the comic strip. **6.** they
7. Which one of the seven girls remembered to bring their own copy of *Tintin in Tibet*? **7.** her
8. Julia showed us her drawing of Tintin's dog, Snowy. **8.** C
9. My grandparents still have some of his or her old Tintin books. **9.** their
10. Did *Tintin's Travel Diaries* inspire James or Reginald to keep their own travel diary during the summer? **10.** his

Exercise 10 Writing Correct Verb Forms

For each of the following sentences, fill in the blank with the correct past or past participle form of the verb given before the sentence.

EXAMPLE   1. *draw*   Kevin has _____ a Japanese pagoda.
   1. *drawn*

1. *hike*   Most of the club members have _____ on the Appalachian Trail.
2. *know*   I have _____ the Katsanos family for years.

3. *steal*	Can you believe that Jean Valjean was put in prison because he had ____ a loaf of bread?	3. stolen
4. *try*	The baby giraffe ____ to stand immediately after its birth.	4. tried
5. *spin*	The car ____ around twice on the wet road.	5. spun
6. *build*	My dad and my sister have ____ a workbench.	6. built
7. *make*	Who ____ this delicious Irish soda bread?	7. made
8. *swim*	Our team has ____ in pools this size, but we prefer Olympic-size pools.	8. swum
9. *suppose*	Gary was ____ to rent a funny movie for us to watch tonight.	9. supposed
10. *shake*	The wet puppy ____ itself and got water all over Phuong's dress.	10. shook
11. *take*	She ____ the opportunity to work in Nigeria.	11. took
12. *climb*	They had ____ Mount McKinley before trying Mount Everest.	12. climbed
13. *join*	To meet others with similar interests, many people have ____ clubs.	13. joined
14. *think*	They ____ Elena would like the new computer.	14. thought
15. *write*	Everything he ____ entertained his readers.	15. wrote
16. *play*	The dogs have ____ with the toy so long that it is in shreds.	16. played
17. *show*	The teacher has ____ the film to both classes.	17. shown
18. *bring*	We had ____ fry bread to go with the stew.	18. brought
19. *stand*	They have ____ by the window all morning, waiting for the rain to stop.	19. stood
20. *go*	The train to Seattle ____ by two hours ago.	20. went

Exercise 11 **Proofreading for Correct Past and Past Participle Verb Forms**

If a sentence contains an ~~incorrect verb~~ form, write the correct form. If a sentence is already correct, write *C*.

EXAMPLE **1.** Have you ever saw a sundial?
　　　 1. seen

1. I have read Anne Frank's *The Diary of a Young Girl*.
2. The song that Ann and Brian sang ~~use~~ to be popular in the 1950s.
3. Caitlin ~~begun~~ swimming lessons around the age of six.
4. Ben ~~perform~~ that routine for the judges last year.

Reference Note
For information on **verb forms,** see page 186.

1. C
2. used
3. began
4. performed

COMMON ERRORS

5. did [or had done]
6. written
7. told
8. gave
9. ran
10. C
11. rung
12. bought
13. blew
14. stole
15. taught
16. C
17. worn
18. left
19. frozen
20. bit

5. The lizard ~~done~~ its best to catch the fly, but the fly flew away unharmed.
6. Have you ~~wrote~~ a letter recently?
7. The performer ~~telled~~ jokes and stories while he danced.
8. Excited about her new idea, Marie ~~gived~~ up on her first plan.
9. Is it true that the winner actually ~~run~~ backward in the race?
10. Did Sara say that Bill "Bojangles" Robinson made up the word *copacetic,* which means "fine" or "excellent"?
11. The bells for class have ~~rang~~ already.
12. I ~~buyed~~ three CDs on sale yesterday.
13. During the storm, the billboards ~~blowed~~ down.
14. Hoping to get to home plate, Sammi ~~stealed~~ third.
15. My second-grade teacher ~~teached~~ me how to tell time.
16. I'll never forget the times I have spent with my cousin.
17. The clothes that I haven't ~~weared~~ in a long time, I'll give to the thrift store.
18. Thank goodness they have ~~leaved~~ the lights on.
19. We have ~~freezed~~ the leftover tortillas to use next week.
20. The dog chased and ~~bited~~ its own tail.

Exercise 12

OBJECTIVE

■ To proofread sentences for correct past and past participle verb forms

Reference Note

For information on **verb forms,** see page 186.

Exercise 12 Proofreading for Correct Past and Past Participle Verb Forms

If a sentence contains an ~~incorrect verb form~~, write the correct form. If a sentence is already correct, write *C.*

EXAMPLE 1. I have took several lessons in aikido.
    1. *taken*

1. Aikido, a Japanese system of self-defense, has ~~interest~~ me for some time. **1.** interested
2. A month ago, I ~~begun~~ lessons at a local martial arts studio. **2.** began
3. Every time I have ~~went~~ to class, I have been nervous, but I am finally becoming more confident. **3.** gone
4. Our instructor has ~~teached~~ us that the Japanese word *aikido* means "the way of blending energy." **4.** taught
5. He ~~sayed~~ that I can "accept" an attacker's energy and redirect the attack away from myself. **5.** said
6. Today in class, I saw how redirecting an opponent's energy really works. **6.** C
7. The aikido holds and movements I ~~choosed~~ played off my opponent's strength. **7.** chose

COMMON ERRORS

8. I ~~maked~~ these movements without using any unnecessary
   force. **8.** made
9. My opponent lunged at me, but he ~~losed~~ his footing. **9.** lost
10. My instructor said that attackers are usually ~~throwed~~ off
    balance by such movements because a person under attack
    usually uses force to fight back. **10.** thrown

Exercise 13 Identifying Correct Pronoun Forms

Choose the correct form of each pronoun in parentheses in the
following sentences.

EXAMPLE 1. The new rules do not apply to any of (*us, we*) eighth-
graders.

1. *us*

1. Please give (*her, she*) the sequins for the costume.
2. The new paramedics at the stadium are (*they, them*).
3. Sasha and (*him, he*) are good at trivia games.
4. Coach Mendoza adjusted the parallel bars for Paul and (*me, I*).
5. The usher showed (*us, we*) to our seats.
6. My sister and (*me, I*) will help Dad paint our house this
   summer.
7. A friend of ours sent (*us, we*) a new book of short stories
   by a popular Venezuelan author.
8. The retirement home where Brad's grandmother lives
   impressed (*him, he*).
9. Did you give the oranges and apples to (*they, them*) for
   the picnic?
10. The first ones to arrive there in the morning are always
    (*she and I, her and me*).

Exercise 14 Identifying Correct Pronoun Forms

Choose the correct form of the pronoun in parentheses in each
of the following sentences.

EXAMPLE 1. Facts about first ladies interest (*me, I*).

1. *me*

1. Hillary Rodham Clinton wrote a book titled *It Takes a
   Village;* last week she autographed copies for (*us, we*).
2. James and (*I, me*) were surprised to learn that Lucy Hayes
   was the first president's wife to earn a college degree.

Reference Note

For information on
pronoun forms, see
page 216.

Reference Note

For information on
pronoun forms, see
page 216.

Exercise 13

OBJECTIVE

■ To identify correct pronoun forms

Exercise 14

OBJECTIVE

■ To identify correct pronoun forms

COMMON ERRORS

3. It was (*her, she*) who was nicknamed Lemonade Lucy.
4. The school librarian gave (*him, he*) an article about Grace Coolidge, who taught children with hearing impairments.
5. Jack showed Caroline, Heather, and (*me, I*) a picture of Mrs. Coolidge with Helen Keller.
6. Tell (*them, they*) about Martha Washington's role as hostess of the new nation.
7. The artist who painted the portrait of the elegant Elizabeth Monroe could have been (*him, he*).
8. In a report on Edith Wilson, Nathaniel said that (*she, her*) sewed clothes to send to soldiers during World War I.
9. When she was a delegate to the United Nations, Eleanor Roosevelt, shown here, championed human rights and worked to secure (*it, them*) for all people.
10. With (*she, her*) as chairperson, the United Nations' Human Rights Commission drafted the Universal Declaration of Human Rights.

Reference Note

For information on **pronoun forms,** see page 216.

Exercise 15 Identifying Correct Pronoun Forms

Choose the correct form of the pronoun in parentheses in each of the following sentences.

EXAMPLE
1. Anika has a book that she asked David and (*I, me*) to read.

1. *me*

1. The book is *In a Sacred Manner I Live,* and David and (*I, me*) are eager to read it.
2. Several of (*we, us*) who are interested in American Indian writings are getting together to read the book aloud.
3. The writings are beautiful, and the wisdom contained in (*they, them*) should be shared.
4. For Anika and (*I, me*) the writings have special meaning because of our American Indian ancestry.
5. David says the stories are interesting for (*he, him*) because his great-grandmother was a Cherokee Indian.
6. The one who researched their family history was (*she, her*).
7. Asa, whose grandfather is Navajo, hopes (*he, him*) will speak to our group.
8. (*We, Us*) students all like the beautiful Navajo chant, "In Beauty May I Walk," which is in the book.

Exercise 15

OBJECTIVE

■ To identify correct pronoun forms

9. The editor of the book, Neil Philip, has published a collection of American Indian poems that (*he, him*) titled *Earth Always Endures.*

10. Our group discussions are such fun that (*we, us*) will get that book, too.

Exercise 16 Choosing Correct Regular and Irregular Modifiers

Choose the correct form of the modifier in parentheses in each of the following sentences.

EXAMPLE **1.** *The Fantasticks* is Jorge's (*favorite, favoritest*) musical.

      1. favorite

1. The original off-Broadway production of *The Fantasticks* had the (*longer, longest*) run of any musical in New York City.

2. It ran for nearly 42 years and was the (*oldest, older*) continuously running musical in the United States.

3. My aunt says that the performance she saw at New York's Sullivan Street Playhouse in 1996 was the (*better, best*) show of any she'd ever seen.

4. She told me that *The Fantasticks* was created by one of the (*most talented, talentedest*) teams of writers for the stage— Tom Jones and Harvey Schmidt.

5. Jones and Schmidt have also written other musicals, but *The Fantasticks,* which opened in New York City in 1960, is generally considered to be the (*popularest, most popular*) of their works.

6. Have you ever seen a musical with a character called something (*more strange, stranger*) than The Man Who Dies?

7. The play has both serious and funny songs; many people like the funny songs (*best, better*).

8. The Handyman, who appears only during the play's intermission, and The Mute, who has no lines to speak, are among the (*most odd, oddest*) roles in modern theater.

9. The students who put on our school's recent production of *The Fantasticks* performed (*good, well*).

10. If the play ever comes to your town, you might find it (*more, most*) enjoyable to see than a movie.

Reference Note

For information on **using modifiers correctly,** see page 236.

COMMON ERRORS

Exercise 17

OBJECTIVE

- To identify and correct double comparisons and double negatives

Exercise 18

OBJECTIVE

- To revise sentences to correct misplaced modifiers

Reference Note

For information on **double comparisons,** see page 248. For information on **double negatives,** see page 249.

1. one

3. anywhere
4. safe
5. anybody

6. common

8. ever

9. could

11. any

13. fierce
14. can

18. ever

20. clean

Reference Note

For information on **misplaced modifiers,** see page 251.

Exercise 17 **Correcting Double Comparisons and Double Negatives**

Identify the incorrect modifier in each of the following sentences. Then, rewrite the sentence to correct the error. Revisions may vary.

EXAMPLE 1. Some of the most prettiest candles are made of beeswax.

1. Some of the prettiest candles are made of beeswax.

1. We wanted to rent a movie but couldn't find none that we all wanted to see.
2. Both Ted and I are learning Spanish, but I am more shyer about speaking it than he is.
3. Kim never wanted to go nowhere near the icy rapids.
4. People in cars are less safer when they do not wear seat belts.
5. We volunteered to help with the preschool art classes because there wasn't nobody else who had the time.
6. Of all the kinds of trees in our neighborhood, which do you think is the least commonest?
7. Moose are the most largest members of the deer family.
8. Don't never use the elevator to escape if the building you are in is on fire.
9. Carrie couldn't scarcely walk after she broke her toe.
10. Kudzu is a Japanese vine that grows more faster than many other plants.
11. We never get no interesting mail.
12. It was the most tiniest mouse that ever lived.
13. The storm couldn't have been more fiercer.
14. When Jake and Fido jog together, Jake can't hardly keep up.
15. Filing all the papers was the most best I could do.
16. You can't never be too careful about avoiding double negatives.
17. The Pacific Ocean is the most biggest ocean in the world.
18. None of us would never throw litter out of a car window.
19. Ostriches lay more bigger eggs than any other birds do.
20. The movie theater is less cleaner on Saturday afternoons.

Exercise 18 **Revising Sentences to Correct Misplaced Modifiers**

Each of the following sentences contains a misplaced modifier. Revise each sentence to correct the error. Revisions may vary.

EXAMPLE   1. Bathing in the mud, the photographer snapped several photographs of the elephants.

               1. *The photographer snapped several photographs of the elephants bathing in the mud.*

1. My dad said ~~today~~ we are going to the beach.
2. The children could see the bacteria ~~using their microscope.~~
3. Richard saw the announcement for the book sale ~~on the bulletin board.~~
4. Yesterday evening, I saw a raccoon ~~going to check the mail.~~
5. I gave flowers ~~to my friends~~ that I had picked along the roadside.
6. ~~Looming in the road ahead~~ I saw a large moose.
7. I could see the constellations clearly ~~sitting on the roof.~~
8. I was startled by the large grasshopper ~~leaning down to smell the flowers.~~
9. Luís went to a baseball game ~~using his season pass.~~
10. We watched a film about how volcanoes form ~~in science class.~~

Exercise 19 Revising Sentences to Correct Misplaced and Dangling Modifiers

Each of the following sentences contains a misplaced or dangling modifier. Revise each sentence to correct the error.

EXAMPLE   1. Growing in the root cellar, my aunt found a red mushroom.

               1. *My aunt found a red mushroom growing in the root cellar.*

1. I read a book about how the Egyptian pyramids were built yesterday.
2. While making lunch for the visitors, the stove caught on fire.
3. The children played in the puddle with no boots on.
4. Don announced at the meeting he will be asking for volunteers.
5. Running to catch the bus, several books fell out of his backpack.
6. Wobbling, the crowd anxiously watched the tightrope walker.
7. My sister described the giraffe she had seen during our flight back to the United States.
8. Tired of the drought, the rain was greeted with loud cheers.

1. today
2. Using their microscope,
3. on the bulletin board
4. Going to check the mail
5. to my friends
6. looming in the road ahead
7. Sitting on the roof,
8. Leaning down to smell the flowers,
9. Using his season pass,
10. In science class

Reference Note

For information on **misplaced and dangling modifiers,** see page 251.

OBJECTIVE

■ To correct misplaced and dangling modifiers

Exercise 19 Revising Sentences to Correct Misplaced and Dangling Modifiers

POSSIBLE ANSWERS

1. Yesterday I read a book about how the Egyptian pyramids were built.
2. The stove caught on fire while I was making lunch for the visitors.
3. The children played with no boots on in the puddle.
4. At the meeting, Don announced he will be asking for volunteers.
5. Several books fell out of his backpack as he ran to catch the bus.
6. The crowd anxiously watched the tightrope walker wobbling.
7. During our flight back to the United States, my sister described the giraffe she had seen.
8. Tired of the drought, we greeted the rain with loud cheers.
9. Although the sapphire ring sparkled in the sunlight, the mockingbird showed no interest in it.
10. While I was walking along the shoreline, a large, black fossilized shark's tooth caught my eye.

COMMON ERRORS

Grammar and Usage   **413**

Grammar and Usage   **413**

Exercises 20–21

OBJECTIVE

■ To revise sentences to correct misplaced and dangling modifiers

Exercise 20 Revising
Sentences to Correct Misplaced
and Dangling Modifiers

POSSIBLE ANSWERS

1. The recent polls did not please
   the politician who was facing
   an election.

2. On a car trip to Texas, my uncle
   told me about armadillos.

3. Neighboring land has been
   donated to expand the park.

4. Looking at the x-rays, the doctor
   discovered that my leg was
   bruised and not broken.

5. Wearing our swimsuits, we were
   let into the pool area by the security guard.

6. When I was a little girl, my mother
   showed me where she had gone
   to kindergarten.

7. With sunglasses on, the mountain
   climbers looked at the glittering
   glacier.

8. While checking the grocery list, I
   bumped the cart into a stack of
   cans.

9. While I was watching the sunset, a
   barking dog chased a cat through
   the yard.

10. From a local store we bought a
    bicycle that had ten speeds.

Exercise 21 Revising
Sentences to Correct Misplaced
and Dangling Modifiers

POSSIBLE ANSWERS

1. The musicians returned to the
   stage in response to the cheering
   audience yelling "More! More!"

2. Because I was wearing a hard hat,
   the falling icicle didn't hurt me.

---

9. Sparkling in the sunlight, the mockingbird showed no interest
   in the sapphire ring.
10. While walking along the shoreline, a large, black fossilized
    shark's tooth caught my eye.

Exercise 20 Revising Sentences to Correct Misplaced
and Dangling Modifiers

Each of the following sentences contains a misplaced or dangling
modifier. Revise each sentence to correct the error.

EXAMPLE   **1.** Swimming in the pond, the cat watched the goldfish.

         1. The cat watched the goldfish swimming in the pond.

1. Facing an election, the recent polls did not please the politician.
2. My uncle told me about armadillos on a car trip to Texas.
3. To expand the park, neighboring land has been donated.
4. Looking at the x-rays, my leg was bruised and not broken.
5. Wearing our swimsuits, the security guard let us into the
   pool area.
6. My mother showed me where she had gone to kindergarten
   when I was a little girl.
7. The mountain climbers looked at the glittering glacier with
   sunglasses on.
8. Checking the grocery list, the cart bumped a stack of cans.
9. Watching the sunset, a barking dog chased a cat through
   the yard.
10. We bought a bicycle from a local store that had ten speeds.

Exercise 21 Revising Sentences to Correct Misplaced
and Dangling Modifiers

Each of the following sentences contains a misplaced or dangling
modifier. Revise each sentence to correct the error.

EXAMPLE   **1.** Grabbing for the rope, the boat was swept away.

         1. While we were grabbing for the rope, the boat
          was swept away.

1. Yelling "More! More!" the musicians returned to the stage
   in response to the cheering audience.
2. Wearing a hard hat, the falling icicle didn't hurt me.

Reference Note
For information
on **misplaced and
dangling modifiers,**
see page 251.

Reference Note
For information
on **misplaced and
dangling modifiers,**
see page 251.

3. Listening to the concert, her purse fell to the floor.
4. To enter the contest, many questions must be answered.
5. Lifted by the wind, capture was impossible.
6. After picking up the litter, the trash can was full.
7. Shining in the night sky, I tried to remember the names of some constellations.
8. The waves washed under the net while playing volleyball.
9. Using the can opener, the cat always knows it's time to be fed.
10. Driving carefully, the mountain road didn't seem as winding.

Exercise 22 Identifying Correct Usage

For each of the following sentences, choose the word or word group in parentheses that is correct according to the rules of formal, standard English.

EXAMPLE   1. About (*a, an*) hour before sunrise, the dam almost (*burst, busted*).

　　　　　　1. *an, burst*

1. (*Doesn't, Don't*) the long-term (*affects, effects*) of global warming concern you?
2. There (*use to, used to*) be (*fewer, less*) people jogging in my neighborhood.
3. (*Without, Unless*) we have permission, I don't think we ought to (*bring, take*) Dad's new CD player to the beach tomorrow.
4. Marshall (*would of, would have*) gone to the picnic in the park, but (*then, than*) he changed his mind.
5. We had a difficult time choosing (*between, among*) the two puppies playing together (*inside, inside of*) the large basket.
6. My clarinet playing has improved (*some, somewhat*), but I really (*had ought, ought*) to practice more.
7. Everyone (*accept, except*) John thinks the weather will be (*allright, all right*) for the powwow.
8. I (*try and, try to*) go to all of my aunt's softball games because her team plays so (*good, well*).
9. (*Who's, Whose*) going to sleep outside with so many of (*them, those*) mosquitoes around?
10. Randy talks (*like, as if*) he has to ride his bike a very long (*way, ways*) on his paper route.

Reference Note

For information on **common usage errors**, see page 262.

Exercise 21 Revising Sentences to Correct Misplaced and Dangling Modifiers

ANSWERS continued

3. While she was listening to the concert, her purse fell to the floor.
4. To enter the contest, one must answer many questions.
5. Because the papers were lifted by the wind, capture was impossible.
6. After I picked up the litter, the trash can was full.
7. I tried to remember the names of some constellations shining in the night sky.
8. While we were playing volleyball, the waves washed under the net.
9. When I use the can opener, the cat always knows it's time to be fed.
10. Because Mom was driving carefully, the mountain road didn't seem as winding.

Exercise 22

OBJECTIVE

■ To identify correct usage

Reference Note

For information on **common usage errors,** see page 262.

Exercise 23 Correcting Errors in Usage

Each of the following sentences contains ~~an error in the use of formal, standard English.~~ Identify and correct each error.

EXAMPLE   **1.** Patrick did so good at the spelling bee that he qualified for the national contest.

   1. good—well

1. If the shrimp enchiladas taste ~~badly,~~ don't eat any more of them. **1.** bad

2. My stepsister said she would ~~learn~~ me how to play the piano.   **2.** teach

3. Please ~~bring~~ these vegetables to your grandmother when you visit her this Friday. **3.** take

4. I read ~~where~~ a waterspout is the name for a tornado that occurs over a lake or an ocean. **4.** that

5. The cartoonist ~~which~~ works for our local newspaper has a wonderful sense of humor. **5.** who [*or* that]

6. The *ruble* is ~~an~~ unit of currency used in both Russia and Tajikistan. **6.** a

7. A friendly rivalry arose ~~between~~ all of the members of the soccer team. **7.** among

8. Late last night, Jack saw a light shining ~~somewheres~~ across the river. **8.** somewhere

9. Mr. Catalano said that the smallest dinosaurs ~~weren't~~ scarcely larger than chickens. **9.** were

10. I knew that we should ~~of~~ brought the umbrella with us when we left the house today. **10.** have

11. Mr. Stevens would not ~~except~~ any final history papers turned in after Friday. **11.** accept

12. ~~Alot~~ of students wanted to work on the play.   **12.** A lot

13. Although he had ~~less~~ hits than Corey, Jorge scored more runs.   **13.** fewer

14. Maryanne wanted to know ~~how come~~ the bus was late. **14.** why

15. Jan used smooth brush strokes on the painting, ~~like~~ the teacher had shown him. **15.** as

16. Is a cheetah faster ~~then~~ a cougar? **16.** than

17. Mrs. Koontz asked us to try ~~and~~ memorize our music for the concert by Monday. **17.** to

18. The bus driver said we still had quite a ~~ways~~ to go before we arrived in St. Louis. **18.** way

19. ~~Whose~~ going to the dance this weekend? **19.** Who's

20. Don't forget to bring ~~you're~~ favorite book to class. **20.** your

Exercise 24 Correcting Errors in Usage

Each of the following sentences contains an ~~error in the use of formal, standard English~~. Identify and correct each error.

EXAMPLE 1. Our class has all ready read about the life of José Luis Muñoz Marín (1898–1980).

  1. all ready—already

1. Where was Muñoz Marín born ~~at~~?
2. I read in this ~~here~~ biography that he was born in San Juan, the capital of Puerto Rico.
3. For more ~~then~~ a quarter of a century, Muñoz Marín was Puerto Rico's chief political leader. 3. than
4. He worked to help the people of Puerto Rico build better lives for ~~theirselves~~. 4. themselves
5. ~~Like~~ Muñoz Marín himself discovered, he had been born at a major turning point in the history of his country. 5. As
6. He must ~~of~~ been very popular, for he was elected governor four times. 6. have
7. When I read his biography, I learned ~~how come~~ he founded the Popular Democratic Party. 7. why
8. John F. Kennedy was the president ~~which~~ awarded Muñoz Marín the Presidential Medal of Freedom. 8. who [or that]
9. ~~Its~~ fascinating to think of Muñoz Marín's being both a poet and a politician. 9. It's
10. Did you know that ~~their~~ is a U.S. postage stamp featuring Muñoz Marín? 10. there

Reference Note

For information on **common usage errors,** see page 262.

OBJECTIVE

■ To correct errors in usage

Using the Grammar and Usage Tests. A Correcting Common Errors Test Answer Sheet that students may use for these **Grammar and Usage Tests** is provided on p. 49 of the *Progress Assessment for the Holt Handbook* ancillary.

Students may benefit from reading "Test Smarts" (pp. 498–503 of their textbook) before they take the **Grammar and Usage Tests.**

Grammar and Usage Test: Section 1

DIRECTIONS Read the paragraph below. For each numbered blank, select the word or word group that best completes the sentence. Indicate your response by shading in the appropriate oval on your answer sheet.

EXAMPLE The word *organic* __(1)__ "of or related to living things."

1. **(A)** it means
   (B) meant
   (C) is meaning
   (D) means

ANSWER 1. (A) (B) (C) (**D**)

Scientists __(1)__ study the prehistoric world __(2)__ carbon dating to determine the age of organic materials such as wood and bone. All living things absorb carbon-14 from the environment into __(3)__ tissues. An organism that has died __(4)__ carbon-14 because __(5)__ no longer takes in air and food. Carbon-14 that was previously absorbed into the organism's tissues __(6)__ at a specific rate. Knowing the rate of breakdown, scientists measure the amount of carbon-14 in an organism's remains to determine how much time __(7)__ since the organism died. Scientists cannot use carbon dating to determine the age of organic material __(8)__ is __(9)__ about 120,000 years, because carbon-14 __(10)__ down and becomes untraceable after that length of time.

---

1. **(A)** which
   (B) who
   (C) whom
   (D) what

2. **(A)** they use
   (B) use
   (C) uses
   (D) used

3. **(A)** its
   (B) his or her
   (C) they're
   (D) their

4. **(A)** doesn't absorb no more
   (B) don't absorb more
   (C) doesn't absorb any more
   (D) don't absorb any more

5. **(A)** he
   (B) she
   (C) it
   (D) they

6. **(A)** it decays
   (B) decays
   (C) decay
   (D) were decaying

7. **(A)** passes
   (B) is passing
   (C) have passed
   (D) has passed

8. **(A)** that
   (B) what
   (C) who
   (D) whom

9. **(A)** more old then
   (B) older than
   (C) older then
   (D) more older than

10. **(A)** busts
    (B) busted
    (C) break
    (D) breaks

Grammar and Usage Test: Section 2

DIRECTIONS   Either part or all of each of the following sentences is under-lined. Using the rules of formal, standard English, choose the answer that correctly expresses the meaning of the underlined word or word group. If there is no error, choose A. Indicate your response by shading in the appropriate oval on your answer sheet.

EXAMPLE   1. The first Cuban-born woman to become a U.S. Army officer was Mercedes O. Cubria, <u>whom</u> served in the Women's Army Corps.

   (A) whom
   (B) who
   (C) that
   (D) which

ANSWER   1.

1. In basketball, one kind of illegal dribbling <u>is when</u> a player stops dribbling and then begins dribbling again.
   (A) is when
   (B) is that
   (C) is because
   (D) occurs when

2. Karen's sandwich is <u>more tastier than</u> the one I brought.
   (A) more tastier than
   (B) more tastier then
   (C) tastier than
   (D) tastier then

3. Tonya said she had seen a hummingbird at her feeder in the mall today.
   (A) Tonya said she had seen a hummingbird at her feeder in the mall today.
   (B) In the mall today, Tonya said she had seen a hummingbird at her feeder.
   (C) Tonya said in the mall today she had seen a hummingbird at her feeder.
   (D) Tonya said in the mall today at her feeder she had seen a hummingbird.

4. Have the Glee Club and they set down to discuss the program?
   (A) Have the Glee Club and they set
   (B) Have the Glee Club and them sat
   (C) Have the Glee Club and they sat
   (D) Has the Glee Club and they sat

5. For many years, Matthew Henson accompanied Robert Peary on expeditions, together, in 1908, they set out for the North Pole.
   (A) expeditions, together, in 1908, they set
   (B) expeditions, together, in 1908, they setted
   (C) expeditions; together, in 1908, they setted
   (D) expeditions. Together, in 1908, they set

6. The reason you should wear a helmet is because it can prevent head injuries.
   (A) is because it
   (B) is that it
   (C) is that they
   (D) is when it

7. A dedicated and creative teacher, Anne Sullivan learned Helen Keller how to communicate effectively.
   (A) learned
   (B) taught
   (C) was learning
   (D) teached

8. Between Josh and <u>him lay</u> the exhausted puppy.
   (A) him lay
   (B) he lay
   (C) him laid
   (D) him has laid

9. <u>The treasure that was buried in the abandoned mine.</u>
   (A) The treasure that was buried in the abandoned mine.
   (B) The treasure found buried in the abandoned mine.
   (C) The treasure buried in the abandoned mine.
   (D) The treasure was buried in the abandoned mine.

10. <u>Peering behind the bookcase, a secret passage was
    discovered by the detective.</u>
    (A) Peering behind the bookcase, a secret passage was
        discovered by the detective.
    (B) Peering behind the bookcase, the detective discovered a
        secret passage.
    (C) The detective discovered a secret passage peering behind
        the bookcase.
    (D) While peering behind the bookcase, a secret passage was
        discovered by the detective.

Exercise 25

OBJECTIVE

■ To correct errors in capitalization

Exercise 26

OBJECTIVE

■ To correct sentences with errors in capitalization

COMMON ERRORS

Reference Note

For information on **capitalization rules,** see page 284.

Reference Note

For information on **capitalization rules,** see page 284.

Exercise 25 Correcting Errors in Capitalization

Each of the following word groups contains at least one error in capitalization. Correct the errors either by changing capital letters to lowercase letters or by changing lowercase letters to capital letters.

EXAMPLE   1. central avenue in albuquerque, New mexico
          1. *Central Avenue in Albuquerque, New Mexico*

1. venus and jupiter
2. my Aunt Jessica
3. wednesday morning
4. the Jewish holiday hanukkah
5. Thirty-Fifth street
6. the stone age
7. nobel peace prize
8. Minute maid® orange juice
9. spanish, earth science, and algebra I
10. secretary of state madeleine albright
11. the washington Monument
12. Portland, oregon
13. my Mother
14. the japanese fan
15. social studies and french
16. where fifty-first street crosses Collins avenue
17. Lake erie
18. president of the pta
19. the mexican flag
20. the thirteenth of october

Exercise 26 Correcting Errors in Capitalization

Each of the following sentences contains errors in capitalization. Correct the errors either by changing capital letters to lowercase letters or by changing lowercase letters to capital letters.

EXAMPLE   1. many african americans lived and worked in the western United states after the civil war.
          1. *Many African Americans lived and worked in the western United States after the Civil War.*

1. one of the most interesting people from that era is bill pickett, who was born on December 5, 1870.

2. His father worked on ranches near austin, texas, and pickett grew up watching cowhands work.
3. Bill began performing rodeo tricks at county fairs, and in 1905 he joined the 101 wild west show in the region then called the oklahoma territory.
4. With this show, Pickett toured the united states, south america, canada, and great britain.
5. i wish i could have seen all the cowboys, cowgirls, horses, buffalo, and longhorn cattle that were part of the show!
6. My uncle Larry told me that Pickett portrayed himself in a 1923 silent movie.
7. Pickett, who died in 1932, was later inducted into the national rodeo cowboy hall of fame.
8. in 1977, the university of oklahoma press published a biography, *bill pickett, bulldogger*, written by colonel bailey c. hanes.
9. a bronze statue of Bill Pickett was dedicated at the fort worth cowtown coliseum in 1987.
10. The Bill Pickett invitational rodeo, which tours all over the united states, draws rodeo talent from around the nation.

Exercise 27 Correcting Sentences by Adding Commas

Each of the following sentences lacks at least one comma. Write the word that comes before each missing comma, and add the comma. Optional commas are underscored.

EXAMPLE   **1.** When the Spanish brought the first horses to North America the lives of many American Indians changed dramatically.

     1. America,

1. Native peoples bred the Spanish horses and developed ponies that could survive on the stubby, coarse grasses of the Great Plains.
2. These hardy ponies may not have been considered as beautiful as the Spanish horses, but they were faster, stronger, and smarter.
3. Because horses were so highly valued, they came to signify status and wealth.
4. These ponies, which were useful in the daily activities of American Indians, were also ridden into battle.
5. Before riding into a battle, Crow warriors painted symbolic designs on themselves and on their ponies.

Reference Note
For information on **using commas,** see page 315.

Exercise 27

OBJECTIVE

■ **To correct sentences by adding commas**

COMMON ERRORS

6. These designs might show that the rider possessed "medicine power," had been on successful horse raids,or had lost someone special to him.

7. Just as designs did,color had special meanings.

8. The color blue,for example,represented wounds; red,which symbolized courage and bravery,represented bloodshed.

9. Often painted on the pony's flanks or under its eyes,white clay stripes indicated the number of horses a warrior had captured.

10. Among the Plains Indians,warriors who disgraced their enemies by tapping them at close range earned horizontal stripes called "coup" marks.

O B J E C T I V E

- To correct sentences by providing end marks, commas, and periods for abbreviations

Reference Note

For information on **using end marks and commas,** see page 310.

Exercise 28 **Using Periods, Question Marks, Exclamation Points, and Commas Correctly**

The following sentences need periods, question marks, exclamation points, and commas. Write the word or numeral that comes before each missing punctuation mark, and add the proper punctuation. Optional commas are underscored.

EXAMPLE   1. Did you sign up for the class trip to Washington Baltimore and Roanoke

   1. *Washington, Baltimore, Roanoke?*

1. What,for instance,would you suggest doing to improve wheelchair access to the theater?

2. Well,I was standing on the ladder,but I still couldn't reach the apples.

3. Marta,a friend of mine,always recycles her aluminum cans and newspapers.

4. When I draw with pastels,charcoal,or chalk,I'm careful to wash my hands before touching anything else.

5. Amy,watch out for the wasp! 5. [*or* wasp.]

6. Is the Spanish Club meeting scheduled for today or tomorrow,Lee?

7. Adela wrote one letter on May 19,2001,and another on October 5,2001.

8. Mr.N.Q.Galvez,Ms.Alma Lee,and Dr.Paul M.Metz spoke at the nutrition seminar last week.

9. What a great idea that is,Edward!

10. My friends and I like to hike in the mountains,water-ski on the lake,and jog along the park trails.

Exercise 29 — Using Semicolons and Colons Correctly

The following sentences lack necessary colons and semicolons. Write the <u>word or numeral that comes before and after each missing punctuation mark</u>, and add the proper punctuation.

EXAMPLE   **1.** Friday is the day for the band concert all of my family is attending.

        1. *concert; all*

1. I put bread in the oven at 4<u>15</u>it should be done soon.
2. We have been keeping the highway clean for three <u>years</u> naturally, no one in the club litters.
3. My brother's favorite movie is *Homeward Bound<u>The Incredible Journey.</u>*
4. We gathered driftwood, shells, and <u>rocks</u>and we bought sand, glass, and paint for the sculpture.
5. My stepsister Sarah, who is deaf, uses the following electronic <u>devices</u>a doorbell that makes the lights flicker, a telephone that converts speech to written words, and a television with closed captioning.
6. The counselor used Proverbs 15<u>1</u> as the basis for her talk.
7. To paint the clubhouse we needed the <u>following</u>brushes, paint, masking tape, and water.
8. We are going to Dallas for the <u>rally</u>however, first we need to raise the money.
9. The swimmers will compete in three <u>divisions</u>backstroke, breaststroke, sidestroke.
10. Her business letter began with "To Whom It May <u>Concern</u>I am a student at Lincoln Middle School."

Exercise 30 — Correcting Sentences by Adding Quotation Marks, Other Marks of Punctuation, and Capital Letters

Revise the following sentences by supplying capital letters and marks of punctuation as needed.

EXAMPLE   **1.** Diane asked where is Denali National Park?

        1. *Diane asked, "Where is Denali National Park?"*

1. Gloria Estefan is my favorite singer said Stephen but I haven't heard her newest song yet.
2. Aunt Caroline exclaimed what a beautiful origami swan that is!

Reference Note

For information on using **semicolons,** see page 331. For information on using **colons,** see page 334.

Reference Note

For information on **using quotation marks,** see page 344. For information on **using other punctuation marks,** see page 345. For information on **using capital letters,** see page 345.

Exercise 29

OBJECTIVE

- To correct sentences by adding colons and semicolons

Exercise 30

OBJECTIVE

- To correct sentences by adding capital letters and marks of punctuation

Exercise 30 Correcting Sentences by Adding Quotation Marks, Other Marks of Punctuation, and Capital Letters

ANSWERS

1. "Gloria Estefan is my favorite singer," said Stephen, "but I haven't heard her newest song yet."
2. Aunt Caroline exclaimed, "What a beautiful origami swan that is!"
3. "To block some of the traffic noise," Russell commented, "the city should plant some trees along this street."
4. The first episode of that new television series is called "Once upon a Twice-Baked Potato."
5. "Did you see that?" Francis asked. "That player bumped the soccer ball into the goal with his heel!"
6. Beverly asked, "Why doesn't Janet want to be president of the club?"

COMMON ERRORS

Exercise 30 Correcting Sentences by Adding Quotation Marks, Other Marks of Punctuation, and Capital Letters

ANSWERS continued

7. "I'll go with you," Dee said. "That sack of birdseed will be too heavy for you to carry back by yourself."

8. "I just finished reading the chapter titled 'Noah Swims Alone,' and I really enjoyed it," Shawn said.

9. "Did Stephanie actually yell, 'I'm out of here!' before she left the room?" asked Joel.

10. Jonathan said, "'You've Got a Friend in Me' is one of the songs in the movie *Toy Story*."

Exercise 31

OBJECTIVE

■ To punctuate written dialogue correctly

Exercise 31 Proofreading a Dialogue for Correct Punctuation

ANSWERS

1. ¶"It's an organization that renovates and builds houses for people who are poor and do not own homes," Henry replied.

2. ¶"Oh, now I remember," Lynn said. "Many volunteers help with the work, right?"

3. ¶"Yes, that's true," Henry answered, "and the people who will live in the houses also help with the renovating or building of these houses."

4. ¶"Are they required to help paint, hammer, and do whatever else needs to be done?" Lynn asked.

5. ¶"Yes, and over an extended period of time, they also pay back the building costs," Henry explained.

3. To block some of the traffic noise Russell commented the city should plant some trees along this street.

4. The first episode of that new television series is called Once upon a Twice-Baked Potato.

5. Did you see that Francis asked. That player bumped the soccer ball into the goal with his heel

6. Beverly asked why doesn't Janet want to be president of the club?

7. I'll go with you Dee said that sack of birdseed will be too heavy for you to carry back by yourself.

8. I just finished reading the chapter titled Noah Swims Alone, and I really enjoyed it Shawn said.

9. Did Stephanie actually yell I'm out of here before she left the room asked Joel.

10. Jonathan said You've Got a Friend in Me is one of the songs in the movie *Toy Story*.

Exercise 31 Proofreading a Dialogue for Correct Punctuation

Correct any errors in the use of quotation marks and other marks of punctuation in the following dialogue. Also, correct any capitalization errors, and begin a new paragraph each time the speaker changes.

EXAMPLES **[1]** Guess what! Henry exclaimed This Saturday I'm going with my youth group to work on a Habitat for Humanity project **[2]** What is Habitat for Humanity Lynn asked

    1.   *"Guess what!" Henry exclaimed. "This Saturday I'm going with my youth group to work on a Habitat for Humanity project."*

    2.   *"What is Habitat for Humanity?" Lynn asked.*

[1] It's an organization that renovates and builds houses for people who are poor and do not own homes Henry replied. [2] Oh, now I remember Lynn said. Many volunteers help with the work, right [3] Yes that's true Henry answered and the people who will live in the houses also help with the renovating or building of these houses

[4] Are they required to help paint, hammer, and do whatever else needs to be done? Lynn asked. [5] Yes, and over an extended period of time, they also pay back the building costs Henry explained

Reference Note

For information on **punctuating dialogue,** see page 348.

[6] Lynn asked Isn't it expensive to build a house [7] Well Henry responded it does take a lot of money, but volunteer labor, donated construction materials, and skillful management keep the cost of building affordable.

[8] How long has Habitat for Humanity existed, and who started it Lynn asked [9] Our youth group leader told us that Millard and Linda Fuller started Habitat for Humanity in Georgia in 1976 Henry replied.

[10] Hey, I think I'll go with you to work on the building project Lynn said.

Exercise 32 Correcting Sentences by Adding Apostrophes

Write the correct form of each word that requires an apostrophe in the following sentences. If a sentence is already correct, write *C*.

EXAMPLE   1. Didnt the womens team win the tournament last year, too?
           1. *Didn't, women's*

1. They're looking for Rodney's bucket of seashells that he gathered at the beach.
2. It's anybody's guess who will win!
3. I'm glad you enjoyed staying at the Caldwells' cabin last weekend.
4. If you help me wash my car this afternoon, I will help you wash yours tomorrow. 4. C
5. Isn't ten dollars' worth going to be enough?
6. I haven't a clue about that.
7. Charles Dickens's "A Christmas Carol" is a story that you'll really enjoy.
8. The men's clothing shop is closed today.
9. Let's go swimming next Wednesday.
10. Tonya's Mexican casserole is always a hit at the church's annual cook-off.

Exercise 33 Correcting Spelling Errors

If a word in the list on the following page is spelled incorrectly, write the correct spelling. If a word is already correctly spelled, write *C*.

EXAMPLE   1. superceed
           1. *supersede*

Habitat for Humanity

This Is The New Home Of:
Michelle Burrough

Reference Note
For information on **using apostrophes,** see page 351.

Reference Note
For information on **spelling rules,** see page 370.

Exercise 31 Proofreading a Dialogue for Correct Punctuation

ANSWERS continued

6. ¶Lynn asked, "Isn't it expensive to build a house?"

7. ¶"Well," Henry responded, "it does take a lot of money, but volunteer labor, donated construction materials, and skillful management keep the cost of building affordable."

8. ¶"How long has Habitat for Humanity existed, and who started it?" Lynn asked.

9. ¶"Our youth group leader told us that Millard and Linda Fuller started Habitat for Humanity in Georgia in 1976," Henry replied.

10. ¶"Hey, I think I'll go with you to work on the building project," Lynn said.

Exercise 32

OBJECTIVE

- To correct sentences by adding apostrophes

Exercise 33

OBJECTIVE

- To correct spelling errors

COMMON ERRORS

Mechanics   **427**

Exercise 33 Correcting Spelling Errors

ANSWERS

1. fried
2. recede
3. C
4. wives
5. tempos
6. Lopezes
7. freeways
8. casually
9. disfiguring
10. mothers-in-law
11. C
12. sleigh
13. C
14. misshapen
15. managing
16. measurement
17. denies
18. ratios
19. sheep
20. tablecloths
21. thieves
22. C
23. intercede
24. immature
25. C
26. monkeys
27. aircraft
28. C *or* deers
29. commanders in chief
30. switches

Exercise 34

OBJECTIVE

■ To choose correctly between words often confused

---

1. fryed
2. receed
3. brief
4. wifes
5. tempoes
6. Lopezs
7. freewayes
8. casualy
9. disfigureing
10. mother-in-laws
11. dimmer
12. sliegh
13. receipt
14. mishapen
15. manageing
16. measurment
17. denys
18. ratioes
19. sheeps
20. tablescloth
21. thiefs
22. freight
23. intersede
24. imature
25. courageous
26. monkies
27. aircrafts
28. deer
29. commander in chiefs
30. switchs

Reference Note

For information on **words often confused,** see page 380.

Exercise 34 Using Words Often Confused

Choose the correct word or words from the choices in parentheses in each of the following sentences.

EXAMPLE   1. My brother's (*advise, advice*) is usually good.
    1. *advice*

1. When will you hear (*whether, weather*) your poem has been (*accepted, excepted*) for publication?
2. We have (*all ready, already*) planned the field trip.
3. Do you think we will need to (*alter, altar*) our plans?
4. If you could (*choose, chose*) any place in the world to visit, where would you go?
5. Did the town (*counsel, council, consul*) meet today?
6. I'd rather experience the (*piece, peace*) and quiet of the beach (*then, than*) the noise and crowds of the city.
7. (*Its, It's*) good manners to hold the door open for anyone (*whose, who's*) hands are full.
8. The floats (*shown, shone*) brightly in the sunlight as the parade (*passed, past*) our house.
9. If the (*whether, weather*) is bad, will that (*effect, affect*) our party, or are we having the party indoors?
10. Before turning in plastic bags for recycling, we reuse them (*to, too, two*) or three times.
11. (*You're, Your*) collection of glass animals is fascinating.
12. The (*course, coarse*) texture of this cloth bothers me.
13. Some people prefer to live in the (*dessert, desert*).
14. Ms. Chen will be (*formally, formerly*) installed as president.
15. Mr. Martinez (*led, lead*) us through the museum.

16. Logan has been (*excepted*, _accepted_) by the architecture program at Rice University.
17. Jamie (*through*, _threw_) the stick for Chauncey to fetch.
18. Isaiah prefers (*plane*, _plain_) cloth for his shirts.
19. No matter how much she practiced, Kate couldn't get the music (*quiet*, _quite_) right.
20. The wind and lightning have (*past*, _passed_), but it is still raining.

Exercise 35 Proofreading for Errors in Spelling and Words Often Confused

For each of the following sentences, correct any error in spelling or words often confused.

EXAMPLE 1. Have you noticeed the advertisments for the exhibit of rare manuscripts?

 1. *noticed, advertisements*

1. The manuscript known as the *Book of Kells* was produced in Ireland around the 8th century.
2. At that time, printing presss had not yet been invented, and manuscripts had too be written by hand.
3. Christian scribes, who created books of great beauty for monasterys and churchs, copied and illustrated the Gospels in the *Book of Kells*.
4. The beauty of it's illustrations distinguishes the *Book of Kells* from other copys of the Gospels.
5. The book's drawings, made with great care and artistry, display vibrant and harmonyous colors.
6. The rich, interlaceing patterns of decoration, which are sometimes wraped around still other patterns, often contain figures of animals and people.
7. These ornate drawings do not yeild there secrets to casual readers.
8. Many of the anceint illustrations express they're meanings threw symbols.
9. Those symbols include butterflys, oxes, eagles, mouses, lions, and fish.
10. Unfortunatly, many pages of the manuscript are missing, perhaps lost or destroied by Viking warriors during raids.

┌HELP┐
No proper nouns in Exercise 35 are misspelled.

Reference Note
For information on **spelling rules,** see page 370. For information on **words often confused,** see page 380.

COMMON ERRORS

TEACHING **TIP**

Using the Mechanics Tests. A
**Correcting Common Errors Test
Answer Sheet** that students may use
for these **Mechanics Tests** is provided
on p. 49 of the *Progress Assessment
for the Holt Handbook* ancillary.

Students may benefit from reading
"Test Smarts" (pp. 498–503 of
their textbook) before they take the
Mechanics Tests.

Mechanics Test: Section 1

DIRECTIONS   Each numbered item below contains an underlined group of
words. Choose the answer that shows the correct capitalization, punctuation,
and spelling of the underlined part. If there is no error, choose answer D
(Correct as is). Indicate your response by shading in the appropriate oval on
your answer sheet.

EXAMPLE   Thank you very **[1]** much Mr. and Mrs. Fernandez for a great visit.

(A) much Mr. and Mrs. Fernandez,

(B) much, Mr. and Mrs. Fernandez,

(C) much Mr. and Mrs. Fernandez;

(D) Correct as is

ANSWER   1.

1201 Palm Circle
[1] Jacksonville Fla. 32201

[2] April 11 2009

[3] Dear Mr. and Mrs. Fernandez,

  I am so glad that you and Pedro invited me to stay at your home this
[4] past weekend, I had a great time. The **[5]** whether I think was perfect for
the activities you planned. The **[6]** picnic lunches volleyball games, and boat
rides were so much fun! I especially enjoyed going fishing in your boat
[7] the ugly duckling.

  Next weekend my parents are going to have a barbecue party to
celebrate **[8]** my aunt Jessicas birthday. If you would like to join us this
coming **[9]** Saturday at 5:30 P.M. please give us a call sometime this week.

[10] Sincerely yours,

Todd Grinstead

Todd Grinstead

1. **(A)** Jacksonville, FL 32201
   (B) Jacksonville Fla 32201
   (C) Jacksonville FL 32201
   (D) Correct as is

2. **(A)** April, 11 2009
   (B) April Eleventh 2009
   (C) April 11, 2009
   (D) Correct as is

3. **(A)** Dear Mr. and Mrs. Fernandez:
   (B) Dear Mr and Mrs Fernandez:
   (C) Dear Mr. and Mrs Fernandez,
   (D) Correct as is

4. **(A)** passed weekend; I had
   (B) past weekend; I had
   (C) passed weekend, I had
   (D) Correct as is

5. **(A)** weather, I think, was
   (B) weather, I think was
   (C) whether, I think was
   (D) Correct as is

6. **(A)** picnic lunchs,
   (B) picnic lunchs
   (C) picnic lunches,
   (D) Correct as is

7. **(A)** *the Ugly Duckling.*
   (B) *The Ugly Duckling.*
   (C) "The Ugly Duckling."
   (D) Correct as is

8. **(A)** my Aunt Jessica's
   (B) my Aunt Jessicas'
   (C) my aunt Jessica's
   (D) Correct as is

9. **(A)** Saturday, at 5:30 P.M.
   (B) Saturday at 5:30 P.M.,
   (C) Saturday, at 530 P.M.,
   (D) Correct as is

10. **(A)** Sincerely yours',
    (B) Sincerly yours,
    (C) Sincerely yours:
    (D) Correct as is

Mechanics Test: Section 2

DIRECTIONS   Each of the sentences on the following page contains an underlined word or group of words. Choose the answer that shows the correct capitalization, punctuation, and spelling of the underlined part. If there is no error, choose answer D (Correct as is). Indicate your response by shading in the appropriate oval on your answer sheet.

EXAMPLE   1. King Louis Philippe of France created the <u>foreign legion</u> in 1831.

   (A) Foreign Legion
   (B) Foriegn Legion
   (C) foriegn legion
   (D) Correct as is

ANSWER   1.

1. My music teacher, Mrs. O'Henry will sing two solos at our school's talent show.
   (A) Mrs. O'Henry, will sing two soloes
   (B) Mrs. O'Henry will sing two solos
   (C) Mrs. O'Henry, will sing two solos
   (D) Correct as is

2. "Do we have enough pickets to build the fence," asked Michelle.
   (A) fence"
   (B) fence?"
   (C) fence"?
   (D) Correct as is

3. Last Friday my sister-in-laws nephew stopped by.
   (A) my sister-in-law's
   (B) my sister's-in-law
   (C) my sister-in-law
   (D) Correct as is

4. The short story Over the Fence is about three oxen and a frog.
   (A) 'Over the Fence' is about three oxes
   (B) 'Over The Fence' is about three oxen
   (C) "Over the Fence" is about three oxen
   (D) Correct as is

5. Turn left on Ninety-eighth Street.
   (A) Ninty-eighth Street
   (B) Ninety-Eighth Street
   (C) Ninety-eighth street
   (D) Correct as is

6. Roberto Clemente twice lead the Pittsburgh Pirates to victory in the World Series.
   (A) lead The Pittsburgh Pirates
   (B) led the Pittsburgh Pirates
   (C) led the Pittsburgh pirates
   (D) Correct as is

7. "How many of you," asked Mr. Reynolds "have seen a painting by the young Chinese artist Wang Yani?"
   (A) Mr. Reynolds, "have
   (B) Mr. Reynolds," have
   (C) Mr. Reynolds, "Have
   (D) Correct as is

8. Those who studied for the test of course, did better than those who did not.

   (A) Those, who studied for the test,
   (B) Those, who studied for the test
   (C) Those who studied for the test,
   (D) Correct as is

9. "Did you say that "it's time to go?" asked Raul.

   (A) say, that 'it's time to go'?"
   (B) say that it's time to go?"
   (C) say that 'It's time to go'?"
   (D) Correct as is

10. My younger sister excels in the following classes Art II, social studies, and English.

    (A) classes: Art II, social studies,
    (B) classes, Art II, Social Studies,
    (C) classes art II, social studies,
    (D) Correct as is

RESOURCES

Review
■ *Language & Sentence Skills Practice*, pp. 389–391

Assessment
■ *Formal Assessment*
■ *Progress-Monitoring Tests*, pp. 33–34, 48
■ *Test Generator (Teacher One Stop DVD-ROM)* 💿

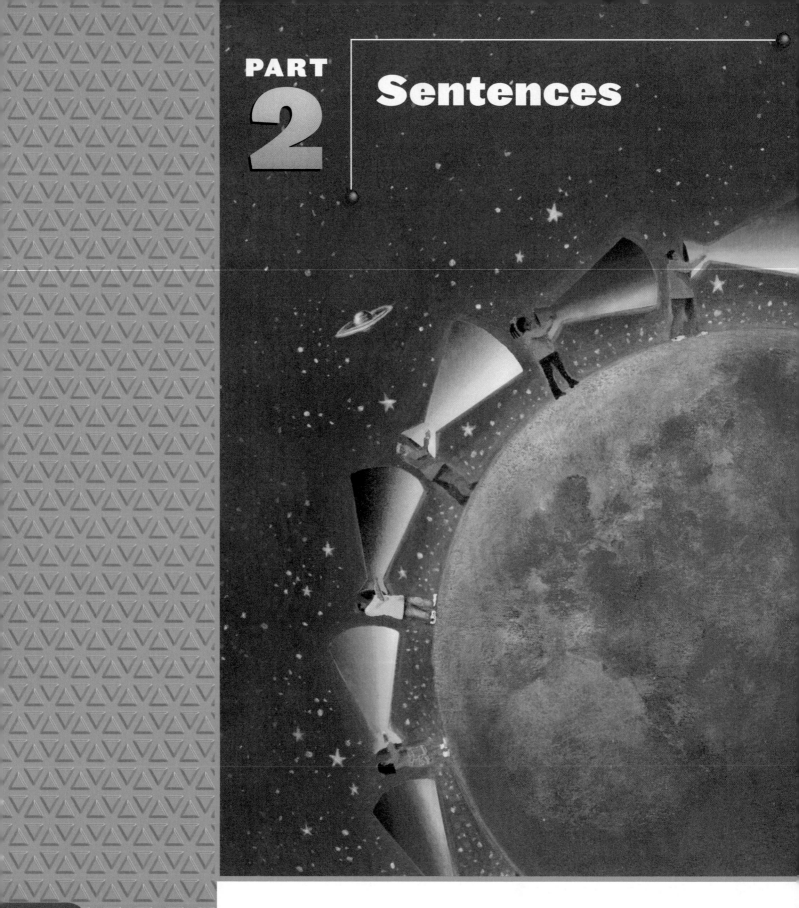

18 Writing Effective Sentences

19 Sentence Diagramming

go.hrw.com

GO TO: go.hrw.com
KEYWORD: HLLA

Sentences   435

Writing Effective Sentences

STANDARDS FOCUS

Grade-Level Standards

(Boldface indicates concepts that are taught and tested in this chapter.)

- Language Convention 1.0: **Students write and speak with a command of standard English conventions appropriate to this grade level.**

- Sentence Structure 1.1: **Use correct and varied sentence types and sentence openings to present a lively and effective personal style.**

- Sentence Structure 1.2: **Identify and use parallelism, including similar grammatical forms, in all written discourse to present items in a series and items juxtaposed for emphasis.**

- Sentence Structure 1.3: **Use subordination, coordination, apposition, and other devices to indicate clearly the relationship between ideas.**

Prerequisite/Review Standard

- Sentence Structure 1.1: Place modifiers properly and use the active voice.

Standards Coming Up in the Next Grade Level

- Grammar and Mechanics of Writing 1.2: Understand sentence construction (e.g., parallel structure, subordination, proper placement of modifiers) and proper English usage (e.g., consistency of verb tenses).

- Grammar and Mechanics of Writing 1.3: Demonstrate an understanding of proper English

(continued)

1.0 Written and Oral English Language Conventions

Students write and speak with a command of standard English conventions appropriate to this grade level.

1.1 Use correct and varied sentence types and sentence openings to present a lively and effective personal style.

1.2 Identify and use parallelism, including similar grammatical forms, in all written discourse to present items in a series and items juxtaposed for emphasis.

1.3 Use subordination, coordination, apposition, and other devices to indicate clearly the relationship between ideas.

Terms in brackets refer to concepts tested by the items in the Diagnostic Preview.
1. frag—We stopped [frag]
2. sentence [sent]
3. frag—, we could meet our goal. [frag]
4. run-on [run-on]
5. run-on [run-on]
6. and Eric [combining sentences]
7. talented [combining sentences]

Diagnostic Preview

A. Identifying Sentences, Sentence Fragments, and Run-ons

Identify each of the following word groups as a *sentence*, a *sentence fragment*, or a *run-on sentence*. Rewrite each sentence fragment to make it a complete sentence. Rewrite each run-on sentence to make it one or more complete sentences.

Possible revisions appear below.

EXAMPLE   **1.** Because you have to leave early.

    1. sentence fragment—I packed a lunch for you because you have to leave early.

1. In front of a very large sailboat with yellow and white sails.
2. When you say your lines, look at the audience.
3. If more people donate food to the food bank this month‸
4. I enjoyed lunch‸Joey made my favorite dish.
5. At night, we watched a meteor shower‸I saw several meteors.

B. Combining Sentences

Combine the sentences in the following items.

Possible revisions appear below.

EXAMPLE   **1.** The pancreas is a gland. It produces insulin.

    1. The pancreas is a gland that produces insulin.

6. Randy‸will go to Chicago this summer. ~~Eric will, too.~~
7. The concert showcased several‸performers. ~~They were talented.~~

CHAPTER RESOURCES

Internet
- go.hrw.com (keyword: HLLA)

Planning
- *Teacher One Stop DVD-ROM*
- *On Course: Mapping Instruction*
- *Family Involvement Activities: A Guide to Standards Mastery*

Practice & Review
- *Language & Sentence Skills Practice,* pp. 397–402; 405–414, 417–420, 423–426; 403–404, 415–416, 421–422, 427–428

- *Developmental Language & Sentence Skills,* pp. 137–154

Differentiating Instruction
- *UA: Differentiating Instruction*

8. Gary Soto is a well-known author~~, He~~ grew up in California.
9. My family has a reunion every year~~. It is held~~ in the spring.
10. We looked up Dalmatians in the encyclopedia, ~~We~~ learned that they originated in Europe.

C. Revising Stringy and Wordy Sentences

Some of the following sentences are stringy or wordy. Revise each sentence so that the writing is simple, clear, and effective.

Possible revisions appear below.

EXAMPLE   **1.** The bird was building a nest, and it used twigs and string, and it built the nest on our chinaberry tree.

   1. *The bird was using twigs and string to build a nest in our chinaberry tree.*

11. ~~Due to the fact that~~ we were late, we missed the previews.
12. The painters spread dropcloths, ~~and they~~ mixed the paint, and ~~then they~~ began to paint the living room.
13. ~~With great happiness,~~ the toddler unwrapped the present.
14. Soon after ~~the time that~~ the drought ~~was happening~~, the farmers began preparing the soil for the fall crop.
15. Tim wanted to play soccer Monday, but he forgot his cleats ~~so~~ he hurried home, and ~~then he~~ returned for practice.

D. Revising a Paragraph to Improve Sentence Style

Rewrite the following paragraph, varying sentence openings, varying sentence structures, and adding transitions to make the meaning clearer and make the paragraph easier to read.

Possible revisions appear below.

EXAMPLE   Sharon wanted to make a birthday present for her older brother. She didn't have much time.

   Sharon wanted to make a birthday present for her older brother. However, she didn't have much time.

Sharon tried to think of a good present for her brother. She thought about buying him a CD that he wanted, She couldn't find it anywhere, Sharon tried to find a shirt he would like, He is very picky, She wasn't sure which one to choose. ~~Sharon is~~ good at sketching, She decided to make a wall calendar for him. She drew a different sketch for each month, ~~The calendar~~ included sketches of their house and school, ~~It also included pictures of~~ his dog, his favorite basketball player, and the nearby lake.

8. who [combining sentences]
9. [combining sentences]
10. and [combining sentences]

11. Because [wordy]
12. [stringy]
13. happily [wordy]
14. [wordy]
15. [stringy]

, but
Next,/However,
, so
Sharon finally
and

usage and control of grammar, paragraph and sentence structure, diction, and syntax.

INTRODUCING THE CHAPTER

■ Students should recognize that complete and concise sentences are essential to clear writing. In this chapter, they will learn how to identify and correct sentence fragments and run-on sentences. In addition, students will learn strategies for combining sentences, revising stringy and wordy sentences, and varying sentence openings and patterns in their writing. Students will also practice using transitions and parallel structure. You may use this chapter to teach the concepts of combining sentences and improving sentence style or as a reference tool for students as they complete writing assignments throughout the year.

ASSESSING

Entry-Level Assessment

Diagnostic Preview. Use the **Diagnostic Preview** to identify areas in which students need instruction and practice in writing effective sentences. You could use the results of the preview to decide which lessons to teach to the entire class and which ones to assign to small groups.

■ *UA: Supporting Instruction in Five Languages*
■ *Family Involvement Activities: In Five Languages*

Assessment
■ *Formal Assessment*
■ *Progress-Monitoring Tests,* pp. 35–39, 48

■ *Test Generator (Teacher One Stop DVD-ROM)*

Other Language Resources
■ *Spelling Lessons & Activities*
■ *WordSharp: An Interactive Vocabulary Tutor*
■ *Reading and Writing Transparencies*

Lesson Starter

Motivating. Write the following quotation on the chalkboard. "Style is the dress of thoughts." (Philip Dormer Stanhope, fourth earl of Chesterfield, 1694–1773, English statesman) Ask students to think about what this sentence means and to record their ideas on paper. Then, lead a discussion in which students share their interpretations. [*Clothing choices may help people express themselves; writing style adds expression and character to thoughts.*]

Writing Clear Sentences

(pp. 438–443)

OBJECTIVES

- To identify and revise sentence fragments
- To identify and revise run-on sentences

Writing Clear Sentences

No matter who your audience is, you want your writing to be clear and understandable. One of the easiest ways to make your writing clear is to use complete sentences. A **complete sentence** is a word group that

- has a subject
- has a verb
- expresses a complete thought

EXAMPLES   The Great Wall of China was begun in 214 B.C.

It spans 1,450 miles and is twenty-five feet high.

Is the wall the longest structure ever built?

Be careful not to fall!

Each of the previous examples meets all the requirements of a sentence. At first glance, the fourth example may not appear to have a subject. The subject, *you*, is understood in the sentence even though it is not stated: "(You) be careful not to fall!"

Two stumbling blocks to the development of clear sentences are *sentence fragments* and *run-on sentences*. Once you learn how to recognize fragments and run-ons, you can revise them to create clear, complete sentences.

Sentence Fragments

A **sentence fragment** is a group of words that has been capitalized and punctuated as if it were a complete sentence. Like a fragment of a painting or photograph, a sentence fragment is confusing because it fails to give the whole picture.

FRAGMENT   Commanded the American Continental army during the Revolutionary War. [The subject is missing. *Who* commanded the American Continental army during the Revolutionary War?]

SENTENCE   George Washington commanded the American Continental army during the Revolutionary War.

FRAGMENT	On December 25, 1776, Washington his troops across the icy Delaware River into Trenton, New Jersey. [The verb is missing. *What did Washington do* on December 25, 1776?]
SENTENCE	On December 25, 1776, Washington led his troops across the icy Delaware River into Trenton, New Jersey.

FRAGMENT	Even though the American Continental army captured a British outpost at Trenton in 1776. [This group of words has a subject and a verb, but it does not express a complete thought.]
SENTENCE	Even though the American Continental army captured a British outpost at Trenton in 1776, it would still face many challenges.

NOTE Often, sentence fragments are the result of writing in a hurry or being a little careless. For example, you might accidentally chop off part of a sentence by putting in a period and a capital letter too soon.

EXAMPLE	Raphael had finished his homework. Before his mother came home from the grocery store. [The second word group is a fragment.]

You can correct the sentence fragment by combining it with or attaching it to the sentence with which it belongs.

EXAMPLE	Raphael had finished his homework **before his mother came home from the grocery store.**

Oral Practice Identifying Sentence Fragments

Read each of the following groups of words aloud, and say whether each group is a sentence or a fragment.

EXAMPLE 1. One of the most notable First Ladies in the history of this nation.
1. *fragment*

1. Eleanor Roosevelt was First Lady of the United States from 1933 to 1945. **1.** S
2. Raised by her grandmother because both of her parents had died by the time she was ten. **2.** F

┌HELP─
Use this simple three-part test to find out which word groups are sentence fragments and which are complete sentences.
1. Does the group of words have a subject?
2. Does it have a verb?
3. Does it express a complete thought?

DIRECT TEACHING

Modeling and Demonstration

Sentence Fragments. Model how to identify and correct sentence fragments by using the incorrect example *Commanded the American Continental army during the Revolutionary War.* First, ask students whether the group of words is punctuated like a sentence. [*yes*] Then, ask students whether the group of words has a subject. [*no*] Tell students that the word group is a fragment because it lacks a subject. Next, ask whether the group of words has a verb. [*yes—Commanded*] Ask students how to turn the fragment into a sentence. [*add a subject*] Ask what subject can logically complete the fragment. [*George Washington*] Finally, ask whether the word group expresses a complete thought now that a subject has been added. [*yes*] Now, have a volunteer use another example from this chapter to demonstrate how to identify and correct sentence fragments.

Oral Practice

DISTRIBUTED REVIEW
After students have completed the **Oral Practice,** have them rewrite the items as sentences in a coherent paragraph, complete with transitions.

Learning for Life   **Continued on p. 440**

Communicating with Fragments.
Explain to students that while complete sentences are desirable and make sense, time or space constraints may force people to communicate by means of sentence fragments. Writers frequently use fragments in classified advertisements and in street signs. Offer your students the following two examples and ask them to explain what each means.

EXTENSION

Critical Thinking

Consider using a selection such as Robert Cormier's "The Moustache," in which the author intentionally uses sentence fragments. First, discuss what effect the author creates by using fragments. [*The fragments convey emotion and help the dialogue sound more realistic.*] Then, ask students to suggest how the fragments might be made into complete sentences. Discuss the effects of these changes. [*Complete sentences make the characters and dialogue seem artificial.*]

3. Wrote a popular newspaper column titled "My Day" as well as many magazine articles and several books. **3.** F
4. As First Lady, worked for the rights of the poor and underprivileged. **4.** F
5. Because she felt strongly about the struggle of children and minorities. **5.** F
6. Eleanor Roosevelt traveled all over the world. **6.** S
7. Hundreds of press conferences at which she discussed important issues. **7.** F
8. Important role in forming the United Nations and a delegate to the General Assembly. **8.** F
9. Chairperson of the United Nations Commission on Human Rights. **9.** F
10. After a long life of public service, died in 1962. **10.** F

Exercise 1 Finding and Revising Sentence Fragments

Some of the following groups of words are sentence fragments. Revise each fragment by (1) adding a subject, (2) adding a verb, or (3) attaching the fragment to a complete sentence. You may need to change the punctuation and capitalization, too. If the word group is already a complete sentence, write *S*.

EXAMPLE **1.** Before the sun rose.
   1. *We awoke before the sun rose.*

Possible revisions appear below.

1. We
2. We heard
3. The bear came
4. It
5. S
6. , I jumped.
7. I
8. the bear
9. S
10. the bear

1. Felt very tired because we had not gotten much sleep the night before.
2. A bear growling in the bushes outside the tent sometime after midnight.
3. Because we had left food in the fire ring.
4. Came from the bushes and circled the area where our campfire had been.
5. Our eyes grew large as the bear stood up and revealed its teeth.
6. When my friend let out a screeching yell and began to back away
7. Put my hand over his mouth.
8. Then growled at us menacingly.
9. We stood still.
10. Dropping to all fours, ran back into the forest.

Learning for Life

Continued from p. 439

Classified Ad: For Sale: Solid wood table with four chairs, never used, $100 for all. Call evenings. [*The price for a wood table and four chairs is $100.*]
Street Sign: This area for buses only. [*Only buses may park here.*]

Provide students with magazines, newspapers, or fliers with advertising. Have students in groups of four examine the ads and note the use of fragments. Then, ask the groups to analyze why each fragment was used.

Run-on Sentences

If you run together two complete sentences as if they were one sentence, you create a ***run-on sentence.*** Run-ons are often confusing because the reader cannot tell where one idea ends and another one begins.

RUN-ON	Margaret Bourke-White was a famous photographer she worked for *Life* magazine during World War II.
CORRECT	Margaret Bourke-White was a famous photographer**.** **S**he worked for *Life* magazine during World War II.

RUN-ON	Bourke-White traveled all over the world taking photographs in Africa and other parts of the world won her fame and respect.
CORRECT	Bourke-White traveled all over the world**.** **T**aking photographs in Africa and other parts of the world won her fame and respect.

To spot run-ons, try reading your writing aloud. A natural, distinct pause in your voice usually marks the end of one thought and the beginning of another. If you pause at a place where you have no end punctuation, you may have found a run-on sentence. Take care not to use just a comma between two sentences. If you do, you will create a run-on sentence.

RUN-ON	Our dog finally came home late last night, she was dirty and hungry.
CORRECT	Our dog finally came home late last night**.** **S**he was dirty and hungry.

Revising Run-on Sentences

Here are three ways you can revise run-on sentences.

1. You can make two sentences.

RUN-ON	Kite building is an ancient art the Chinese made the first kites around three thousand years ago.
CORRECT	Kite building is an ancient art**.** **T**he Chinese made the first kites around three thousand years ago.

Reference Note

For more information and practice on **commas,** see page 315.

DIRECT TEACHING

Correcting Comma Splices

Tell students that the term *comma splice* refers to two complete sentences incorrectly joined by a comma. A comma splice may be corrected in one of three ways.

- Replace the comma with a period, as shown at left in the correct example sentence about the dog.

- Keep the comma and add a conjunction. Example: Our dog finally came home late last night, and she was dirty and hungry.

- Replace the comma with a semicolon. Example: Our dog finally came home late last night; she was dirty and hungry.

Writing Clear Sentences   **441**

Reference Note

For more information about **coordinating conjunctions,** see page 69.

Reference Note

For more information about **semicolons,** see page 331.

2. You can use a comma and a coordinating conjunction such as *and, but,* or *or.*

RUN-ON   The Chinese sometimes used kites in religious ceremonies, they usually used them for sport.

CORRECT   The Chinese sometimes used kites in religious ceremonies**, but** they usually used them for sport.

3. You can use a semicolon.

RUN-ON   Classical music varies greatly in length, individual pieces range from a few minutes to many hours.

CORRECT   Classical music varies greatly in length**;** individual pieces range from a few minutes to many hours.

Exercise 2   Identifying and Revising Run-on Sentences

Decide which of the following groups of words are run-ons. Then, revise each run-on by (1) making it into two separate sentences, (2) using a comma and a coordinating conjunction, or (3) inserting a semicolon. If the group of words is already correct, write *C*.   Possible revisions follow.

EXAMPLE   1. Museums can be entertaining as well as educational, I go as often as I can.

1. *Museums can be entertaining as well as educational; I go as often as I can.*

1. The Louvre is the largest museum in the world, it is also one of the oldest.   **1.** , and
2. The first works of art in the Louvre were bought by the kings of France, each ruler added more treasures.
3. King Francis I was a great supporter of the arts, he bought the *Mona Lisa.*
4. As other French rulers made additions, the collections of fine works of art grew.   **4.** C
5. The Louvre is now a state-owned museum, its new pieces are either bought by the museum or received as gifts.   **5.** ;
6. Each year, about one and a half million people from all over the world come to see the artwork at the Louvre.   **6.** C
7. The buildings of the Louvre form a rectangle, there are courtyards and gardens inside the rectangle.   **7.** , and

8. The Louvre covers about forty acres‸it has about eight miles of gallery space. **8.** and

9. Over one million works of art are exhibited in the Louvre. **9.** C

10. Many of the buildings of the Louvre have been expanded and modernized‸this photograph shows how the Louvre looks today. **10.** ⊙

Review A Revising Sentence Fragments and Run-on Sentences

The following paragraph is confusing because it contains some sentence fragments and run-on sentences. First, identify the fragments and run-ons. Then, revise each fragment and run-on to make the paragraph clearer.   Possible revisions follow.

EXAMPLE   **1.** All too often, the remake not as good as the original movie.

1. *All too often, the remake is not as good as the original movie.*

The 1956 movie <u>Godzilla</u>‸about a huge is reptile. Godzilla looks like a dinosaur‸ , but he breathes fire like a dragon. He comes up out of the ocean. After an atomic bomb wakes him up. Godzilla can melt steel with his atomic breath‸he is big enough , and to knock down huge buildings. In the original film he destroys the city of Tokyo‸he gets killed at the end. , but

COMPUTER TIP

Use a word-processing program when you revise your draft for sentence fragments, run-on sentences, or style. The cut and paste commands make it easy for you to move words or phrases within a sentence and to move sentences within your draft.

Review A Revising Sentence Fragments and Run-on Sentences

ANSWERS

Sentences 1 and 4 are fragments; 2, 5, and 6 are run-ons; 3 is a complete sentence.

Combining Sentences

(pp. 444–454)

OBJECTIVES

- To combine sentences by inserting words and phrases

- To combine sentences by creating compound subjects and verbs, by creating compound sentences, and by using subordinate clauses

DIRECT TEACHING

Modeling and Demonstration

Combining Sentences. Model how to combine sentences by using the examples *The Persians landed at Marathon in 490 B.C.* and *The Persians invaded Greece.* Write the two sentences on the chalkboard so that the first one appears directly above the other. Ask students to identify similarities between the two sentences. [The Persians *is the subject of both sentences.*] Next, ask how the two sentences can be combined. [*add the conjunction* and—The Persians landed at Marathon in 490 B.C. and invaded Greece. *Answers may vary.*] Now, have a volunteer use other examples from this chapter to demonstrate how to combine sentences.

Combining Sentences

Would you enjoy reading a book that contains only one simple character facing ordinary, uncomplicated situations? Of course not. To hold your attention, a writer must include a *variety* of characters who encounter many different and interesting situations. A writer must also *vary sentence length and structure* to keep the reader's interest. Consider the following example in which the author mainly uses short, choppy sentences:

> The Persians landed at Marathon in 490 B.C. The Persians invaded Greece. The mighty Persians outnumbered the small Greek army. The Greeks defeated the Persians. The Greek commander sent Phidippides (fī•dip'i•dēz') to Athens to spread the good news. Phidippides was his fastest runner. Phidippides ran the entire way. Phidippides proudly announced the Greek victory. Then he died. We get the term "marathon" from Phidippides's run. Phidippides's run was historic.

Now, read the revised version. To make the paragraph more interesting, the writer combined some of the short, choppy sentences into longer, smoother ones. Notice how the ***sentence combining strategies*** listed to the right of the paragraph have helped to eliminate some repeated words and ideas. Explanations of these strategies appear on the following pages.

The Persians landed at Marathon in 490 B.C. and invaded Greece. Although the mighty Persians outnumbered the small Greek army, the Greeks defeated the Persians. The Greek commander sent Phidippides, his fastest runner, to Athens to spread the good news. After running the entire way, Phidippides proudly announced the Greek victory. Then he died. We get the term "marathon" from Phidippides's historic run.	Using conjunction Inserting clause Inserting phrase Inserting phrase Inserting word

RESOURCES

Combining Sentences

Practice

- *Language & Sentence Skills Practice,* pp. 405–416
- *Developmental Language & Sentence Skills,* pp. 141–146

Combining by Inserting Words

One way to combine short sentences is to take an important word from one sentence and insert it into another sentence. Sometimes you will need to change the form of the word before you can insert it.

Inserting Without a Change

ORIGINAL   Louis Armstrong was a famous musician. He was a jazz musician.

COMBINED   Louis Armstrong was a famous **jazz** musician.

Inserting with a Change

ORIGINAL   Armstrong was an easygoing person. He was a friend to many people.

COMBINED   Armstrong was an easygoing, **friendly** person.

Exercise 3 Combining Sentences by Inserting Words

Combine each of the following sentence pairs by taking the italicized word from the second sentence and inserting it into the first sentence. Some sentences have hints in parentheses for changing the forms of words.

EXAMPLE   1. Young Louis Armstrong first showed his talent on the streets of New Orleans. His talent was for *music*. (Add *–al*.)

     1. *Young Louis Armstrong first showed his musical talent on the streets of New Orleans.*

1. Louis Armstrong became a jazz musician. He received *acclaim* for his music. (Add *–ed* and change *a* to *an*.)
2. Louis started playing at a New Orleans nightspot. He played *cornet*.
3. He recorded a solo in 1923. It was *his first* recorded solo. (Delete *a*.)
4. He was coached by Lil Hardin, a pianist who later became his wife. Lil Hardin was a *classically trained* pianist.
5. He became famous as a solo trumpet player. He was famous on an *international* level. (Add *–ly*.)
6. Louis Armstrong also sang jazz. His jazz singing was *brilliant*. (Add *–ly*.)

| TIPS & TRICKS |

You can often move a key word from one sentence to another by adding certain endings. The endings *–ed* and *–ing* can turn some verbs into words that act like adjectives or nouns. Adding *–ly* can turn some adjectives into adverbs and some nouns into adjectives.

EXAMPLES
  relieve: The reliev**ed** student sighed.

  sing: A sing**ing** canary flew overhead.

  fortunate: Fortunate**ly**, we were finished.

  cost: The cost**ly** necklace gleamed.

Reference Note

For more information on **adjectives,** see pages 38 and 238. For more information on **adverbs,** see pages 61 and 238.

DIFFERENTIATING INSTRUCTION

Advanced Learners

Have students brainstorm words that can be changed by adding certain endings as shown in the **Tips & Tricks**. Then, ask each student to choose three words from the list and write two sentences for each word. The first sentence should use the word in its original form, such as *In five minutes I will* relieve *the goalie*. The second sentence should use the word in its form as an adjective or adverb, such as *The relieved* goalie limped to the bench.

Learners Having Difficulty

Students may be unsure about where to place the key words when they combine sentences in **Exercise 3**. Ask leading questions to help them position the words they are inserting. For example, in the example sentence, you could ask what kind of talent Armstrong first showed in New Orleans. [*musical*]

Exercise 3 Combining Sentences by Inserting Words

ANSWERS

1. Louis Armstrong became an acclaimed jazz musician.

2. Louis started playing cornet at a New Orleans nightspot.

3. He recorded his first solo in 1923.

4. He was coached by Lil Hardin, a classically trained pianist who later became his wife.

5. He became internationally famous as a solo trumpet player.

6. Louis Armstrong also sang jazz brilliantly.

MINI-LESSON **Mechanics**   *Continued on pp. 446–447*

Using Commas with Adjectives. Explain that a comma usually separates two or more adjectives that come before a noun. To decide whether a comma is needed, students should try inserting *and* between the adjectives. If *and* sounds natural, as in *rainy (and) humid afternoon,* a comma is needed [*rainy, humid afternoon*]. If *and* does not sound natural between the adjectives, a comma should not be used. [In the sentence *It is a rainy*

Exercise 3 Combining
Sentences by Inserting Words

ANSWERS continued

7. Louis Armstrong had a deep, rough voice.

8. In the 1926 song "Heebie Jeebies," Armstrong first employed scat singing, a form of rhythmic, wordless singing.

9. A new generation of fans in the 1950's and 1960's knew him primarily as a singer.

10. The song "Hello, Dolly!" is one of Armstrong's best-known vocal recordings.

---

7. Louis Armstrong had a deep voice. His voice was *rough*.

8. In the 1926 song "Heebie Jeebies," Armstrong employed scat singing, a form of rhythmic, wordless singing. This was his *first* use of scat singing.

9. A generation of fans in the 1950's and 1960's knew him primarily as a singer. This generation of fans was *new*.

10. The song "Hello, Dolly!" is one of Armstrong's vocal recordings. The song is one of Armstrong's *best-known* works.

Combining by Inserting Phrases

A *phrase* is a group of words that acts as a single part of speech and that does not have both a subject and a verb. You can combine sentences by taking a phrase from one sentence and inserting it into the other sentence.

ORIGINAL	Brown bears gather in groups. They gather around the banks of rivers.
COMBINED	Brown bears gather in groups **around the banks of rivers.**

Reference Note

For more about **using commas with introductory phrases,** see page 326. For more information and practice on **using commas with appositive phrases,** see page 323.

Sometimes you will need to put commas after or around the phrase you are inserting. For example, if the prepositional phrase above appeared at the beginning of the sentence, it would be followed by a comma because the phrase consists of two smaller phrases. However, a single short prepositional phrase usually does not require a comma. Also, ask yourself whether the phrase renames or describes a noun or pronoun in the sentence. If it does, it is an *appositive phrase,* and you may need to use a comma or commas to set off the phrase from the rest of the sentence.

ORIGINAL	Alaska is home to the big brown bears. The big brown bears are the largest kind of bear.
COMBINED	Alaska is home to the big brown bears, **the largest kind of bear.** [The phrase in boldface type describes the noun *bears.*]

ORIGINAL	The brown bear eats fish caught from the stream. The brown bear is a skilled and patient hunter.
COMBINED	The brown bear, **a skilled and patient hunter,** eats fish caught from the stream. [The phrase in boldface type renames the noun *bear.*]

MINI-LESSON **Mechanics**   *Continued from p. 445*

(and) spring afternoon, and does not sound natural; delete *and* and do not insert a comma.] Finally, remind students that a comma should not be used between a single adjective and the noun immediately following it. [*My friend and I had a long chat.*]

Write the following sentences on the chalkboard and ask students to read them. If a comma is needed, have them write the word that the comma should follow. If a sentence is correct, have them write *C.*

Another way to combine sentences is to change the verb in a sentence to make a new phrase. You change the verb by adding *–ing* or *–ed* or by putting the word *to* in front of it. You can then use the new phrase to modify a noun, verb, or pronoun in another sentence.

Reference Note

For more information and practice on **verb forms using *–ing, –ed,* or *to,*** see pages 101 and 108.

ORIGINAL   The bear prepares his winter retreat. He digs a burrow in a bank.

COMBINED   **Digging a burrow in a bank,** the bear prepares his winter retreat. [The phrase in boldface type modifies the noun *bear.*]

ORIGINAL   Bears dig in the ground. This is how they find roots and sweet bulbs.

COMBINED   Bears dig in the ground **to find roots and sweet bulbs.** [The phrase in boldface type modifies the verb *dig.*]

NOTE   When you combine sentences, be sure to keep the compound elements ***parallel,*** or matching in form. In other words, use the same kind of word or phrase in each of the compound elements.

ORIGINAL   Julie likes **fishing** in a mountain stream. Julie also likes **to swim** in a cool mountain stream.

NOT PARALLEL   Julie likes **fishing** and **to swim** in a mountain stream. [*Fishing* is a gerund; *to swim* is an infinitive.]

PARALLEL   Julie likes **fishing** and **swimming** in a cool mountain stream. [*Fishing* and *swimming* are both gerunds.]

Exercise 4 **Combining Sentences by Inserting Phrases**

Combine each pair of sentences by taking the italicized words from the second sentence and inserting them into the first sentence. The hints in parentheses tell you how to change the forms of words. Add commas where needed.

EXAMPLE   **1.** The Empire State Building was completed in 1931. It *towers above New York City at a height of 1,454 feet.* (Change *towers* to *towering.*)

    1. *Towering above New York City at a height of 1,454 feet,* the Empire State Building was completed in 1931.

1. My friend is a caring trustworthy person with a mischievous streak. [*caring*]

2. Our conversations are usually about our many funny adventures. [*C*]

3. She decided to help me prepare for a long difficult history exam. [*long*]

4. My friend role-played famous historical characters I had to identify. [*C*]

5. I will not forget the witty meaningful quotations she used to coach me. [*witty*]

Exercise 4 · Combining Sentences by Inserting Phrases

POSSIBLE ANSWERS

1. Once the tallest building in the world, the Empire State Building was constructed in one year and forty-five days.

2. A gigantic structure, the building cost over twenty-four million dollars to complete.

3. It is a fine example of art deco, a sleek, geometric style popular in the 1920's and 1930's.

4. The building rises in a series of steplike shapes called setbacks.

5. Weighing 365 million tons and containing 102 floors, the building is a popular tourist attraction.

6. The building has 1,860 stairs from street level to the 102nd floor.

7. The building was the site of a tragic event in 1945.

8. An Army B-25 cargo plane flying through heavy fog crashed into the seventy-ninth floor, killing fourteen people.

9. A commemorative cornerstone celebrating the fiftieth anniversary of the building was added in 1981.

10. The Empire State Building has an official Web site providing verified information about the building.

---

1. The Empire State Building was constructed in one year and forty-five days. The Empire State Building was *once the tallest building in the world.*

2. The building cost over twenty-four million dollars to complete. The building was *a gigantic structure.*

3. It is a fine example of art deco. Art deco was *a sleek, geometric style popular in the 1920's and 1930's.*

4. The building rises in a series of steplike shapes. The steplike shapes are *called setbacks.*

5. The building is a popular tourist attraction. It *weighs 365 million tons and contains 102 floors.* (Change *weighs* to *weighing* and *contains* to *containing.*)

6. The building has 1,860 stairs. This number includes the stairs *from street level to the 102nd floor.*

7. The building was the site of a tragic event. The event occurred *in 1945.*

8. An Army B-25 cargo plane crashed into the seventy-ninth floor, killing fourteen people. The plane *flew through heavy fog.* (Change *flew* to *flying.*)

9. A commemorative cornerstone was added in 1981. The new cornerstone *celebrated the fiftieth anniversary of the building.* (Change *celebrated* to *celebrating.*)

10. The Empire State Building has an official Web site. The Web site *provides verified information about the building.* (Change *provides* to *providing.*)

Combining by Using Connecting Words

You can also combine sentences by using the coordinating conjunctions *and, but,* or *or.* Doing so is called **coordination.** With one of these connecting words, you can form a *compound subject,* a *compound verb,* or a *compound sentence.*

Compound Subjects and Verbs

Sometimes two sentences with different subjects have the same verb. You can combine the sentences by linking the two subjects with *and* or *or.* When you do this, you create a **compound subject.**

ORIGINAL   Kangaroos carry their young in pouches. Koalas carry their young in pouches.

COMBINED   **Kangaroos and koalas** carry their young in pouches.

TIPS & TRICKS

When you form a compound subject, make sure that it agrees with the verb in number.

ORIGINAL
Tasmania is in Australia. Queensland is in Australia.

REVISED
Tasmania and Queensland are in Australia. [The plural subject takes the verb *are*.]

If two sentences with different verbs have the same subject, you can link the verbs with *and, but,* or *or* to form a *compound verb.*

ORIGINAL   Kangaroos can hop on their hind legs. They can walk on all four legs.

COMBINED   Kangaroos can **hop** on their hind legs **or walk** on all four legs.

Reference Note

For more information and practice on **subject and verb agreement,** see page 156.

Exercise 5 Combining by Forming Compound Subjects and Compound Verbs

Combine each of the following sentence groups by forming a compound subject or a compound verb. Make sure your new subjects and verbs agree in number.

EXAMPLE   **1.** Alligators are among the largest living reptiles. Crocodiles are among the largest living reptiles.

1. *Alligators and crocodiles are among the largest living reptiles.*

1. Crocodiles have strong tails. They are excellent swimmers.   **1.** and
2. To hunt, the crocodile submerges itself in water. It waits for prey to swim near.   **2.** and
3. Crocodiles have sharp, piercing teeth. Alligators have sharp, piercing teeth.   **3.** and alligators
4. Crocodiles feed mostly on small animals such as turtles and fish. Crocodiles can live up to one hundred years.   **4.** and   **5.** and
5. Alligators are classified as a threatened species. They enjoy the protection of state and federal law.
6. The Indian gharial is related to alligators and crocodiles. It has a narrower snout.   **6.** but
7. A caiman is a type of alligator. It lives in Central and South America.   **7.** and
8. A crocodile usually stays underwater for between 10 to 15 minutes. It may stay submerged for 30 minutes or more if hiding from a threat.   **8.** but
9. Alligators in colder climates are inactive during the winter months. In warmer climates they remain active year-round.
10. Florida provides a habitat for the American alligator. Louisiana provides a habitat for the American alligator. Other states provide a habitat for the American alligator.

9. but in warmer climates
10. , Louisiana, and other states provide habitats

Combining Sentences   **449**

English-Language Learners

General Strategies. Some students may have trouble choosing among the conjunctions *and, but,* and *or.* As you show students how to create compound sentence structures, point out that *and* is used to connect similar ideas, *but* is used for contrasting ideas, and *or* is used when a choice is offered between ideas. Ask students to think of symbols or illustrations to show the differences among the three conjunctions. For example, a plus sign (+) could represent *and.*

SENTENCES

MINI-LESSON **Usage**

Compound Subjects. Remind students that a compound subject does not always take a plural verb. For example, when using the conjunctions *either . . . or* and *neither . . . nor,* one part of the compound subject can be singular and one part can be plural. Explain that in this situation the verb agrees with the subject that is closer to the verb. Here are two examples.

- Neither yeast nor <u>raisins were</u> used in the bread.
- Neither raisins nor <u>yeast was</u> used in the bread.

DIRECT TEACHING

Correcting Misconceptions

Compound Verbs or Compound Sentences? Some students may incorrectly think they need to use commas before conjunctions that link compound verbs. Remind students that a comma is used before a conjunction when two sentences are combined to create a compound sentence. Write the following sentences on the chalkboard and discuss them with students.

1. Julian went to the store but forgot the grocery list. [*Sentence 1 is a simple sentence with a compound verb. Julian went but forgot.*]

2. Julian went to the store, but he forgot the grocery list. [*Sentence 2 is a compound sentence containing two independent clauses joined by a comma and the conjunction* but. *Julian went to the store. He forgot the grocery list.*]

Use colored chalk to highlight the subject and the compound verb in sentence 1 (*Julian, went, forgot*) and the two subjects and two verbs in sentence 2 (*Julian went; he forgot*). Now, ask students to write compound sentences and simple sentences with compound verbs. Then, have partners identify one another's sentences.

┌ TIPS & TRICKS ┐

Before you create a compound sentence out of two simple sentences, make sure the thoughts in the sentences are closely related to each other. If you combine two sentences that are not closely related, you will confuse your reader.

UNRELATED
  Kim chopped the vegetables, and I like soup.

RELATED
  Kim chopped the vegetables, and I stirred the soup.

Compound Sentences

Sometimes you may want to combine two sentences that express equally important ideas. You can connect the two sentences by using a comma and the coordinating conjunction *and, but,* or *or.* When you link sentences in this way, you create a ***compound sentence.***

| ORIGINAL | Many nations throughout the world use the metric system. The United States still uses the old system of measurement. |
| COMBINED | Many nations throughout the world use the metric system**, but** the United States still uses the old system of measurement. |

Exercise 6 **Combining Sentences by Forming a Compound Sentence**

The sentences in each of the following pairs are closely related. Make each pair into a compound sentence by adding a comma and the coordinating conjunction *and, but,* or *or.*

EXAMPLE   1. The kilogram is the basic unit of weight in the metric system. The meter is the basic unit of length.

        1. *The kilogram is the basic unit of weight in the metric system, and the meter is the basic unit of length.*

1. The metric system was developed in France‿It became popular in many countries.   **1.** , but (*or* and)
2. Scientists make measurements in metric units‿Other people worldwide rely on metric units, too.   **2.** , and
3. Most people in the United States still use the English system‿In 1988, Congress declared the metric system better for trade and commerce.   **3.** , but
4. We can keep the old system of measurement‿We can switch to the metric system.   **4.** , or
5. Using both systems usually does not cause problems‿It did cause the loss of a Mars lander in 1999.   **5.** , but
6. One group of NASA scientists was using the English system‿Another group was using the metric system.   **6.** , and (*or* but)
7. The old system of measurement has more than twenty basic units of measurement‿The metric system has only seven.
8. A meter equals ten decimeters‿A decimeter equals ten centimeters.   **8.** , and   **7.** , but

9. Counting by tens is second nature to most people_∧ Many people still find the metric system difficult to learn.   **9. , but**

10. Most temperature readings need to be converted from Fahrenheit to Celsius_∧ Forty degrees below zero is the same on both scales.   **10. , but**

Combining by Using a Subordinate Clause

A *clause* is a group of words that contains a verb and its subject. An *independent clause* can stand alone as a sentence. A *subordinate* (or *dependent*) *clause* cannot stand alone as a sentence because it fails to express a complete thought.

INDEPENDENT CLAUSE	In the 1850's, Elizabeth Cady Stanton was a civil rights activist. [This clause can stand alone as a sentence.]
SUBORDINATE CLAUSE	who fought to win women of all states the right to vote in federal elections [This clause cannot stand alone as a sentence.]

If two simple sentences are closely related but unequal in importance, you can combine them by using a subordinate clause. Doing so is called *subordination.* Just turn the less important idea into a subordinate clause and attach it to the other sentence. The result is a *complex sentence.* The subordinate clause will give additional information about an idea expressed in the rest of the sentence.

ORIGINAL	Many women could not cast a vote in a federal election. The Nineteenth Amendment was ratified in 1920.
COMBINED	Many women could not cast a vote in a federal election **until the Nineteenth Amendment was ratified in 1920.**

Clauses Beginning with *Who, Which,* or *That*

You can make a short sentence into a subordinate clause by inserting *who, which,* or *that* in place of the subject.

ORIGINAL	The Aztecs were an American Indian people. They once ruled a mighty empire in Mexico.
COMBINED	The Aztecs were an American Indian people **who once ruled a mighty empire in Mexico.**

Reference Note

For more information and practice on **complex sentences,** see page 145.

Reference Note

A clause that begins with *who, which,* or *that* and that modifies a noun or pronoun is an **adjective clause.** For more information on **adjective clauses,** see page 124.

Combining Sentences   **451**

DIRECT TEACHING

Subordinate Clauses

When combining sentences using subordinate clauses, some students may have difficulty deciding which sentence should be turned into a subordinate clause. Ask students to follow the steps below when they combine sentences like these:

Henry David Thoreau lived in a simple hut. He built the hut at Walden Pond.

1. What are the ideas in the simple sentences? [*Thoreau lived in a simple hut. He built the hut at Walden Pond.*]

2. Which idea seems more important? [*Living in a hut seems more important than where the hut was built, but I can't tell for sure.*]

3. If you can't decide which idea seems more important, turn each sentence into a subordinate clause and attach it to the other sentence. Then, see which sentence makes more sense.

Henry David Thoreau, *who lived in a simple hut,* built the hut at Walden Pond. [*This sentence is awkward.*]

Henry David Thoreau lived in a simple hut *that he built at Walden Pond.* [*This sentence makes more sense.*]

DIFFERENTIATING INSTRUCTION

English-Language Learners

Cantonese. Cantonese sentences sometimes contain adverb clauses as coordinating rather than subordinating elements: *Although I worked on homework, but I did not finish.* Show students that complex sentences beginning with a subordinating conjunction, or connecting word, should not have *and* or *but* between clauses.

English-Language Learners

Vietnamese. In Vietnamese, an introductory clause may be followed by a "balancing" word in the main clause. English: *Because* he runs fast, he is on the track team. Vietnamese: *Because* he runs fast, *therefore,* he is on the track team.

Some Vietnamese speakers may omit the subordinating word, using only the balancing word: This usage may create a run-on sentence. *He runs fast, therefore, he is on the track team.* Others may use *also* as a balancing word. *Even if I had a bike, I would also not ride to school.* Show students that when sentences combine with a subordinating conjunction, or connecting word, to form complex sentences, they do not need any other connecting words between the clauses. Have them locate connecting words in sample sentences, and check their writing for correct usage.

Reference Note

A clause that is used to give information about time and place and that modifies a verb, adjective, or adverb is an **adverb clause.** For more information on **adverb clauses,** see page 127.

Reference Note

For more about **commas after subordinate clauses,** see page 321.

STYLE   TIP

Varying sentence beginnings by moving a phrase or clause to the beginning of a sentence can make your writing more interesting. If you put a time or place clause at the beginning of a sentence, you will need to put a comma after the clause.

ORIGINAL
The Aztec empire grew. Aztec warriors conquered nearby territories.

COMBINED
When Aztec warriors conquered nearby territories, the Aztec empire grew.

Clauses Beginning with Words of Time or Place

You can also make a subordinate clause by adding a word that indicates time or place, such as *after, before, since, where, wherever, when, whenever,* or *while.* You may need to add, delete, or change some words to insert the clause into another sentence.

| ORIGINAL | The Aztecs built the capital city of Tenochtitlán. They moved into Mexico in the twelfth century. |
| COMBINED | The Aztecs built the capital city of Tenochtitlán **after they moved into Mexico in the twelfth century.** |

| ORIGINAL | The capital city of the Aztec empire was in central Mexico. Mexico City stands in that spot today. |
| COMBINED | The capital city of the Aztec empire was in central Mexico, **where Mexico City stands today.** |

Exercise 7 **Combining Sentences by Using a Subordinate Clause**

Combine each of the following sentence pairs by making the second sentence into a subordinate clause and attaching it to the first sentence. The hint in parentheses will tell you what word to use at the beginning of the clause. To make a smooth combination, you may need to delete one or more words in the second sentence of each pair.

EXAMPLE   1. The Aztecs practiced a religion. It affected every part of their lives. (Use *that.*)

1. *The Aztecs practiced a religion that affected every part of their lives.*

1. Aztec craft workers made drums and rattles. ~~Drums and rattles~~ were their main musical instruments. (Use a comma and *which.*) **1. , which**
2. Aztec cities had huge temples. The people held religious ceremonies ~~there.~~ (Use *where.*) **2. where**
3. Their empire was destroyed by the Spanish. ~~The Spanish~~ conquered it in 1521. (Use a comma and *who.*) **3. , who**
4. The Spanish invaders were joined by many Indians. ~~The Indians~~ had been conquered by the Aztecs and resented their heavy taxes. (Use a comma and *who.*) **4. , who**

CONTENT-AREA CONNECTIONS

Science

Writing Directions. Have students select directions for an experiment in their science books. Working in pairs, students should combine the sentences from these directions into longer sentences. Then, pairs can exchange papers and compare the new directions with the original ones. [*The revised directions may be more difficult to follow.*] Discuss with students why, in some writing, using many short sentences may be necessary. [*to provide directions that might otherwise be confusing*]

5. At first, the Aztec leader Montezuma II did not oppose the Spaniards, He thought the Spanish leader Hernando Cortés represented the Aztec god Quetzalcoatl. (Use *because*.) **5.** because

6. The Aztecs rebelled against the Spaniards, The Spaniards made Montezuma II a prisoner. (Use *because*.) **6.** because

7. The Aztecs surrendered, Cortés launched a fierce counter-attack. (Use *after*.) **7.** after

8. There was very little left of the Aztec civilization, The Spanish invaders tore down most of the Aztec buildings. (Use *after*.) **8.** after

9. However, the site of the Great Temple in Mexico City has been excavated by archaeologists, ~~The archaeologists~~ have recovered thousands of artifacts. (Use a comma and *who*.) **9.** , who

10. Today, people around the world enjoy chili, chocolate, and tacos, ~~These foods~~ are Aztec in origin. (Use a comma and *which*.) **10.** , which

Review B Revising a Paragraph by Combining Sentences

The paragraph on the next page sounds choppy because it has too many short sentences. Use the methods you have learned in this section to combine some of the sentences. You will notice the improvement when you finish.

ANSWERS

Here is a possible revision.

In 1886, the area became an exclusive neighborhood for the wealthy. Eventually, the word *tuxedo* was given to a style of clothing worn by many fashionable men of Tuxedo Park. However, most of these men probably did not know that the word *tuxedo* actually came from the American Indian word *p'tuksit,* which means "he has a rounded foot." American Indians used this word to describe the wolves which were plentiful around the lake. See how funny the English language can be? Just picture the men of Tuxedo Park dining and dancing at a formal party and not knowing that their tuxedo jackets were really "wolf" jackets.

Improving Sentence Style

(pp. 454–460)

OBJECTIVES

- To identify and revise stringy sentences

- To identify and revise wordy sentences

- To revise sentences to create parallel structure

┌HELP─

The word
syntax denotes the way words, phrases, and clauses are arranged to make meaning. Being mindful of your syntax, especially taking care to avoid stringy and wordy sentences, can help make your speaking and writing effective.

EXAMPLE   In 1814, a man acquired some land. This land was located around Tuxedo Lake in the state of New York.

In 1814, a man acquired some land around Tuxedo Lake in the state of New York.

In 1886, the area became an exclusive neighborhood for the wealthy. Eventually, the word *tuxedo* was given to a style of clothing. This style of clothing was worn by many of the men of Tuxedo Park. These men were fashionable. However, most of these men probably did not know something. They probably did not know that the word *tuxedo* actually came from the American Indian word *p'tuksit*. This word means "he has a rounded foot." American Indians used this word to describe wolves. Wolves were plentiful around the lake. Of course, now you can see how funny the English language can be. Just picture the men of Tuxedo Park at a formal party. Picture them dining and dancing. Most of these men probably did not know that their tuxedo jackets were really "wolf" jackets.

Improving Sentence Style

You have learned how to improve choppy sentences by combining them into longer, smoother sentences. Now, you will learn how to improve *stringy* and *wordy sentences* by making them shorter and more precise.

Revising Stringy Sentences

Stringy sentences just ramble on and on. They have too many independent clauses, or complete thoughts, strung together with coordinating conjunctions such as *and* or *but*. If you read a stringy sentence out loud, you may run out of breath.

Mary McLeod Bethune dreamed of
being a teacher, and she attended
a college in Chicago, and she won
a scholarship for her hard work, and
Bethune eventually became a teacher,
and she earned the respect of educators and presidents.

As you can see, stringy sentences are confusing
because they do not show how the ideas fit together.
To fix a stringy sentence, you can

- break the sentence into two or more sentences
- turn some of the independent clauses into
  phrases or subordinate clauses

Now, read the revised version of the stringy
sentence. Notice how the writer turned two of the
independent clauses into subordinate clauses.

Mary McLeod Bethune dreamed of being
a teacher. She attended a college in
Chicago after she won a scholarship
for her hard work. Bethune eventually
became a teacher who earned the respect
of educators and presidents.

NOTE When you revise a stringy sentence, you may decide to keep
and or *but* between two closely related independent clauses. If you
do leave the sentence in compound form, be sure to use a comma
before the *and* or *but* to show a pause between the two complete
thoughts.

ORIGINAL   Mary McLeod Bethune went on to found Bethune
           Cookman College and she also directed the Division
           of Negro Affairs under President Franklin Delano
           Roosevelt.

REVISED   Mary McLeod Bethune went on to found Bethune
           Cookman College**, and** she also directed the Division
           of Negro Affairs under President Franklin Delano
           Roosevelt.

Improving Sentence Style   **455**

Exercise 8 Revising Stringy Sentences

ANSWERS

Possible revisions follow.

1. Harriet Ross grew up as a slave on a plantation in Maryland. In 1844, she married John Tubman, a freed slave.

2. Believing that people should not be slaves, Harriet Tubman decided to escape. Late one night she began her dangerous trip to the North.

3. C

4. New friends told her about the Underground Railroad, a secret group of people who helped runaway slaves get to the North.

5. Tubman decided she would rescue more slaves from the South. Using the North Star as her guide, she led groups of slaves along the road to freedom. She made nineteen trips in twelve years.

6. C

7. Although Tubman never learned to read or write, she was a powerful speaker at many antislavery meetings.

8. When the Civil War broke out, Tubman volunteered to help the Union army. She served as a cook and a nurse and later became a spy.

9. When the war ended, Tubman settled in Auburn, New York, where she started a home for elderly black men and women.

10. C

Exercise 8 Revising Stringy Sentences

Some of the following sentences are stringy and need revision. First, identify the stringy sentences. Then, revise them by using the methods you have learned. If a numbered item needs no revision, write *C* for correct.

EXAMPLE
1. This country has a history of slavery, and that history is sad, but that history includes examples of brave resistance, and the story of Harriet Tubman is one good example.

1. *This country has a sad history of slavery, but that history includes examples of brave resistance. The story of Harriet Tubman is one good example.*

1. Harriet Ross grew up as a slave in Maryland, and she worked on a plantation there, but in 1844 she married John Tubman, and he was a freed slave.

2. Harriet Tubman did not believe that people should be slaves, and she decided to escape, and late one night she began her dangerous trip to the North.

3. She made the long journey to Philadelphia, Pennsylvania, by traveling at night.

4. New friends told her about the Underground Railroad, and it was a secret group of people, and they helped runaway slaves get to the North.

5. Tubman decided she would rescue more slaves from the South, and she used the North Star as her guide, and she led groups of slaves along the road to freedom, and she made nineteen trips in twelve years.

6. The slaves hid during the day and continued their journey at night.

7. Tubman never learned to read or write, but she was a powerful speaker, and she spoke at many antislavery meetings.

8. The Civil War broke out, and Tubman volunteered to help the Union army, and she served as a cook and a nurse and later she became a spy.

9. The war ended, and Tubman settled in Auburn, New York, and she started a home for elderly black men and women.

10. The people of Auburn built Freedom Park in memory of Tubman.

Revising Wordy Sentences

Sometimes you may use more words than you really need. Extra words do not make writing sound better. They just get in the reader's way. You can revise *wordy sentences* in several different ways.

1. Replace a group of words with one word.

WORDY	I did not get to school on time yesterday due to the fact that I missed the bus.
REVISED	I did not get to school on time yesterday **because** I missed the bus.

WORDY	Christopher opened his birthday gift with a great eagerness.
REVISED	Christopher **eagerly** opened his birthday gift.

2. Replace a clause with a phrase.

WORDY	When the play had come to an end, we walked to a restaurant and treated ourselves to pizza.
REVISED	**After the play,** we walked to a restaurant and treated ourselves to pizza.

WORDY	I ordered a slice with mushrooms and onions, which are my favorite toppings.
REVISED	I ordered a slice with mushrooms and onions, **my favorite toppings.**

3. Take out a whole group of unnecessary words.

WORDY	What I mean to say is that Carlos did not go to the movie with us.
REVISED	Carlos did not go to the movie with us.

WORDY	We all liked the movie because it had some very funny scenes that were the kinds of scenes that make you laugh.
REVISED	We all liked the movie because it had some very funny scenes.

STYLE TIP

Extra words and phrases tend to make writing sound awkward and un-natural. As you revise your writing, try reading your sentences aloud to check for wordiness or a stringy style. If a sentence sounds like a mouthful to you, chances are it is stringy, wordy, or both.

EXTENSION

Critical Thinking

To show students that there is more than one correct way to revise a sentence, have groups of three revise the same set of stringy and wordy sentences. Each student should first revise the set individually, share his or her results with the group, and discuss the strategies used in the revisions. The group should then decide which revision of each sentence is preferable. After groups have completed and chosen their revisions, have a representative from each group write the group's work on the chalkboard. As a class, discuss and compare the revisions, noting any differences. Ask students to decide which sentences are most effective and why.

Exercise 9 **Exercise 9** **Revising Wordy Sentences**

Decide which of the following sentences are wordy and need revision. Then, revise each of the wordy sentences. You can (1) replace a group of words with one word, (2) replace a clause with a phrase, or (3) take out unnecessary words. If the sentence is effective as it is, write *C*.   Possible revisions appear below.

EXAMPLE   1. Many people are full of a great deal of fear of wasps.

1. *Many people are afraid of wasps.*

1. Most wasps are helpful to humanity because ~~of the fact that~~ they eat harmful insects.
2. ~~What I want to say is that~~ wasps do far more good than harm.
3. Social wasps ~~are the type that~~ live together as groups and work as a team to build their nests.
4. Social wasps make their nests from old wood and tough plant fibers.   **4.** C
5. They chew ~~and chew~~ the wood and fiber until the mixture becomes pasty and mushy.
6. The mixture becomes a material ~~that is~~ called wasp paper.
7. According to some historians, the Chinese invented paper after watching wasps make it.   **7.** C
8. A wasp colony lasts only through the summer.   **8.** C
9. The queen wasp, ~~being the only member of the colony to survive~~ the winter, comes out of hibernation in the spring.
10. The queens start new colonies by ~~means of~~ building nests and laying eggs.   **9.** Only/survives/and

Review C **Revising Stringy and Wordy Sentences**

The following paragraph is hard to read because it contains stringy and wordy sentences. First, identify the stringy and wordy sentences. Then, revise them to improve the style of the paragraph.   Here is a possible revision.

EXAMPLE   Sometimes an audience thinks that fictional stories, which are made up, are actually true.

Sometimes an audience thinks that fictional stories are true.

On October 31, 1938, an amazing event took place̥that was very surprising. Many families were gathered around their radios⌐ and they were listening to music⌐ ∧and then when they heard that Martians had invaded Earth. Actually, the fact is that the news report was a radio version of H. G. Wells's novel <u>The War of the Worlds</u>. Orson Welles, who was the producer of this famous hoax, made the show very realistic. Thousands of Americans were frightened and upset∧ and ⊙ <u>m</u>any people jumped in their cars to escape from the aliens∧ and <u>s</u>ome people even ⊙ reported seeing the Martians and their spaceships.

THE FAR SIDE®   **By GARY LARSON**

"YEEEEEHAAAAAAAAA!"

Using Parallel Structure

When you combine several related ideas in one sentence, it is important to make sure that your combinations are balanced. You create balance in a sentence by using the same grammatical form or part of speech to express each idea. For example, you balance a noun with a noun, a phrase with a phrase, and a clause with a clause. This balance is called *parallelism,* or *parallel structure.*

Review C **Revising Stringy and Wordy Sentences**

ANSWERS
Stringy: 2, 5; Wordy: 1, 3, 4

Improving Sentence Style   **459**

NOT PARALLEL	I enjoy baseball, soccer, and playing lacrosse. [two nouns and a phrase]
PARALLEL	I enjoy, **baseball, soccer,** and **lacrosse.** [three nouns]
NOT PARALLEL	I plan to play basketball, finish my homework, and my chores.
PARALLEL	I plan to **play basketball, finish my homework,** and **do my chores.**
NOT PARALLEL	Jordan said to be there early and that you shouldn't eat supper beforehand.
PARALLEL	Jordan said **that you should be there early** and **that you shouldn't eat supper beforehand.**

Exercise 10 **Revising Sentences to Create Parallel Structure**

Bring balance to the following sentences by putting the ideas in parallel form. You may need to add or delete some words. If a sentence is already correct, write *C*. Possible revisions follow.

EXAMPLE **1.** We visited London in 1996, 1998, and went again in 2002.

1. *We visited London in 1996, 1998, and 2002.*

1. London, the capital of England, is famous for its history, culture, and ~~having a~~ lively theater district.
2. The River Thames runs through the city and empties into the North Sea. **2.** C
3. Walking through Trafalgar Square, visiting the British Museum, and ∧Buckingham Palace are all favorite pastimes of tourists. **3.** seeing
4. Did you know ∧~~about London's history as~~ a Roman city or that London has existed for nearly two thousand years? **4.** that London was
5. London is known for being home to many of the world's greatest scientists, artists, politicians, and ~~having great~~ poets.
6. Weather in London is often rainy, cool ~~temperatures~~, and unpredictable.
7. London has a busy business district, noisy traffic, and ~~spreads across~~ miles of suburbia.
8. We want to see a play at the new Globe Theatre, to eat at a Chinatown restaurant, and ∧enough time to see every room in the National Gallery. **8.** to have
9. London athletes enjoy cricket and ~~playing~~ rugby.
10. London is my favorite city and ∧very rainy. **10.** a/place

Beyond Sentence Style

You've learned how to improve individual sentences, but to make your writing the best it can be, you'll need to take a step back and look at how your sentences go together. Good writers use a variety of sentence beginnings and a variety of sentence structures to keep readers interested. Good writers also use transitions to show the connections between ideas in a paragraph or other composition.

Varying Sentence Beginnings

Basic English sentences begin with a subject followed by a verb, perhaps with a few adjectives and adverbs included. If you use too many basic sentences in a row, your sentences will sound too much the same, and you very likely will bore your reader—even if each separate sentence is itself interesting. Notice how dull the following paragraph sounds.

> Roberto plays soccer. He has played on
> the team called the Northridge Tornadoes
> for four years. He played fullback at
> first and helped defend the goal. He
> moved up to halfback after a season or
> two and usually plays forward now. The
> Northridge Tornadoes have played four
> games this season, and Roberto has
> already made several important goals.
> He scored three goals in their last game,
> including the final, winning goal.

One good way to make sure you don't bore your reader is to vary sentence beginnings. Instead of starting most or all of the sentences with the subject of the basic sentence, you can begin some of them with one-word modifiers, with introductory phrases, or with subordinate clauses.

> Roberto plays soccer. For four years,
> he has played on the team called the
> Northridge Tornadoes. Playing fullback at
> first, he helped defend the goal. He
> moved up to halfback after a season or two
> and usually plays forward now. In the four
> games that the Northridge Tornadoes have

Beyond Sentence Style   **461**

played so far this season, Roberto has already made several important goals. In fact, he scored three goals in their last game, including the final, winning goal.

Varying Sentence Beginnings	
One-Word Modifiers	**Fortunately,** I have a plan. [adverb]
	Shivering, Tony wished he had worn a jacket. [adjective]
Phrases	**Before supper,** Gina usually goes for a run or walk. [prepositional phrase]
	Galloping madly, the horse disappeared over the hill. [participial phrase]
	To save money, we should pack lunches, not buy them there. [infinitive phrase]
Subordinate Clauses	**Because the streets were icy,** we stayed home. [adverb clause]
	If you will help me study, I'll help you. [adverb clause]

Exercise 11 **Revising a Paragraph to Vary Sentence Beginnings**

Rewrite the following paragraph to vary sentence beginnings so that the paragraph is more interesting. You can add one-word modifiers, introductory phrases, or subordinate clauses to the sentences, and you can rearrange other words as necessary.

Possible revisions follow.

A Labrador retriever,
Adopted by my family when he was a puppy,

he barks,

ʌMy dog is named Sandy, and he is a Labrador retriever. ʌSandy is about five years old now, and my family adopted him when he was a puppy. He is well-trained,ʌ ⱨe knows how to sit, heel, and shake hands. He also barks when he thinks anyone in my family is in danger, ʌbut he stops barking when we say, "Hush, Sandy." I walk him every morning, and my sister takes him to the park several times a week.

Varying Sentence Structure

You have learned that if you start all of your sentences the same way, you will very likely bore your reader. Likewise, if all of your sentences are about the same length or if they are all constructed much the same, your reader may get bored and tune out what you are saying. An important way to keep your reader's attention is to mix sentences of different lengths and structures.

Read the following passage, which contains mostly short simple sentences.

```
    Frederick walked to the foot of the
great staircase. He thought he had heard
footsteps. He waited uncertainly for
a few seconds. Then he walked up the
stairs. He looked in the three rooms
on the second floor. No one was there.
Frederick then noticed the door to the
attic. It was partly open. That door
opened downward into the dark end of the
hallway. The attic door had a set of
folding stairs. He pulled the door open
completely. Then he unfolded the stairs
and stood still, unsure of the situation.
Then he began to climb the stairs to the
attic.
```

Now, read the revised paragraph. Notice how the writer has varied sentence length and has used a mix of simple, compound, complex, and compound-complex sentences.

```
    Frederick walked to the foot of the
great staircase, for he thought he had
heard footsteps. He waited uncertainly
for a few seconds; then he walked up the
stairs. He looked in the three rooms on
the second floor, but he found no one
there. Frederick then noticed that the
door to the attic was partly open. That
door, which opened downward into the dark
end of the hallway, had a set of folding
stairs. He pulled the door open completely
```

and then unfolded the stairs and stood
still, unsure of the situation. Then he
began to climb the stairs to the attic.

Below is a chart that shows you the four sentence structures. Using a balance of these four structures will help you keep your reader interested in what you have to say.

Reference Note
For more information about **identifying sentence structures,** see Chapter 7.

Sentence Structures	Example
simple sentence contains one independent clause	A sparrow flew quickly past.
compound sentence contains two or more independent clauses	A sparrow flew quickly past, and a blue jay followed.
complex sentence contains one independent clause and at least one subordinate clause	After a sparrow flew quickly past, a blue jay followed.
compound-complex sentence contains two or more independent clauses and at least one subordinate clause	A sparrow that had been at our bird feeder flew quickly past, and a blue jay followed.

Exercise 12 Revising a Paragraph to Vary Sentence Length and Structure

Rewrite the following paragraph to vary sentence length and structure so that the paragraph is more interesting.

EXAMPLE   We don't have anything else to do. We
           could go to the park.

           Since we don't have anything else to do, we could go to the park.
                                    Possible revisions appear below.

           The park is full of life this time of
           year. White ducks and mallards swim on the
and   pond's surface⹁ They eat the stale bread
           we bring for them. Minnows and perch dart

```
underwater‸ Red-eared turtles sun them-
selves on logs‸ They quickly plop into the
water as we walk by. Large rodents called
nutria‸make homes along the shore. They
look a little like otters. Songbirds sing
in the trees‸ Clover flowers bloom and
attract bees and butterflies. In the
picnic shelter we notice tiny‸ frogs⊙
The frogs are bright green.
```

, and
, quickly plopping

, which look a little
like otters,
, and

, bright green

Using Transitions

Imagine that you are reading a passage that is full of clear, complete
sentences. Each sentence is itself interesting, and the writer has used
a variety of sentence beginnings and a variety of kinds of sentences.
However, you can't tell how the sentences are related to each other.
You find yourself re-reading the passage and trying to puzzle out
the connections between thoughts. What could be wrong? Chances
are, the writer failed to include transitions. *Transitional words and
phrases* help connect ideas. Acting as signposts, they lead readers
along, pointing out the relationships between thoughts.

Transitional Words and Phrases		
also	finally	meanwhile
another	first	moreover
as a result	for example	on the other hand
at last	for instance	soon
besides	furthermore	then
but	however	therefore
consequently	in fact	though
eventually	last	thus

Read the following passage, which includes underlined
transitional words and phrases. As you read, stop when you
get to each underlined transition. Before you read the rest of
the sentence, predict what kind of information will be in that
sentence. For instance, will the sentence support the one before
it? Will it present a contrast? Watch for transitional "signposts"
that tell you that the passage is going to keep going straight or
that tell you the writer is changing direction.

Taylor and Kate arrived at the trail-head and eagerly began their hike. <u>Soon, though</u>, they stopped to look at the map, which showed that the peak was several miles further than their guidebook said. <u>Also</u>, dark thunderheads had appeared on the horizon, and the wind had picked up. <u>However</u>, they both had rain gear and wanted to get in a good hike. <u>In fact</u>, the girls were determined to make the climb. <u>Nevertheless</u>, they knew that they didn't have enough water for such a long hike and that hiking uphill in stormy weather could be difficult and dangerous. They decided, <u>therefore</u>, to take a shorter and easier loop of the trail that day and to tackle the peak later in the week.

Notice how the transitional words and phrases tell the reader what kind of ideas to expect. When you write, you can include words and phrases like these to guide your reader. Doing so will help you express your ideas more clearly and help you keep the interest of your reader.

Exercise 13 **Identifying Transitional Words and Phrases**

The transitional words and phrases in the following paragraph show how the ideas are related to one another. Make a list of the transitions in the paragraph. Use the chart of transitional words and phrases to help you.

Richard had trouble keeping track of money. <u>In fact</u>, he almost always ran out of money well before he received his allowance. <u>Moreover</u>, he often borrowed money from his friends and his sister, and he did not always keep track of how much he owed. <u>As a result</u>, his sister and friends were all getting tired of lending him cash. He had <u>even</u> quarreled with two of them about how much he had borrowed and when he was supposed to repay it. <u>However</u>, he realized that constantly borrowing and owing money was a problem. <u>At last</u>, tired of having money troubles, he decided to get organized. He listed his debts and made a plan for earning enough extra money to pay them within the month. <u>Then</u> he looked over his expenses, decided where he could cut back, and created a budget. <u>Finally</u>, he promised himself that he would stick to his budget.

Exercise 14 **Revising a Paragraph to Show Transitions**

The sentences in the following paragraph do not clearly show how one idea is related to another. Rewrite the paragraph, adding appropriate transitions to show how the ideas are related.

EXAMPLE   The cook was going outside to gather parsley. He noticed a strange young man near the gate.

The cook was going outside to gather parsley. Suddenly, he noticed a strange young man near the gate.
                                        Possible revisions follow.

The mysterious stranger had lingered outside the palace all afternoon. The servants said he might have been there since before breakfast. Some guessed that he must want to see the queen. He did not knock or come to the palace doors. The queen left in the carriage. The stranger did not look up or approach the carriage. Some said that he was up to no good and was waiting for a chance to sneak in. The cook suggested that perhaps the stranger was the long lost prince. It began to storm. The stranger disappeared from view. The servants agreed that he had been a harmless idler. There came a great clatter outside and someone pounding at the door.

In fact,

also

, but
Eventually,
However,

therefore
Then

Meanwhile,
Suddenly,
Consequently,
Soon, though,

Review D Applying Sentence Revision Strategies

ANSWERS

A possible revision appears below.

Stone buildings were common here, but the largest and most impressive was the "Great Zimbabwe," the home of the king. The massive circular walls built around the king's home were thirty-two feet high. When visitors came to the city, they had to walk through a passage between the two circular walls to reach the chief's home. In the center of the circle, they saw a magnificent cone-shaped building, the "Great Zimbabwe." The present-day country of Zimbabwe gets its name from this building, which means "dwelling of the chief."

Review D Applying Sentence Revision Strategies

Using the skills you have learned throughout this chapter, revise fragments, run-ons, and stringy and wordy sentences in the following paragraph. Try to combine at least five sentences so that the revised paragraph includes compound and complex sentences.

EXAMPLE   A wealthy and rich kingdom emerged in southeast Africa this was in the twelfth century.

A wealthy kingdom emerged in southeast Africa in the twelfth century.

Stone buildings were common structures here, and the largest and biggest of the stone buildings was called the "Great Zimbabwe," and this was the most impressive building. The word *Zimbabwe* means "dwelling of the chief." This was the home of the king. Massive walls were built around the king's home. These walls were in the shape of a circle that was round. They were thirty-two feet high. Visitors came to the city. Visitors had to walk through a passage. They did this to reach the chief's home. The passage was situated in a location between the two circular walls. Passed through the circular walls. They saw a magnificent building. It was in the center of the circle's circumference. This building was the "Great Zimbabwe." This building was cone-shaped. The present-day country of Zimbabwe. Gets its name from this building.

Chapter Review

Monitoring Progress

Chapter Review. To assess student progress, you may want to compare the types of items missed on the **Diagnostic Preview** with those missed on the **Chapter Review.** You may want to set specific goals with individual students who are still having difficulty mastering essential information.

Terms in brackets refer to concepts tested by the items in the Chapter Review.

A. Identifying Sentences, Sentence Fragments, and Run-ons

Identify each of the following word groups as a *sentence*, a *sentence fragment*, or a *run-on sentence*. If a word group is a sentence fragment, rewrite it to make a complete sentence. If a word group is a run-on sentence, rewrite it to make it one or more complete sentences.   Possible revisions follow.

1. fragment—is at 1:00. [frag]

1. The earliest appointment at the orthodontist⌃

2. fragment—is very smart. [frag]

2. The person who wrote that letter to the editor⌃

3. sentence [sent]

3. Tonight, I should study for tomorrow's social studies test.

4. run-on [run-on]

4. Go to the end of the hall⌃the room you are looking for will be to your left.

5. fragment—I [frag]

5. ⌃Asked whether I could have another helping of the rice and beans.

6. fragment—seems sad. [frag]

6. The man wearing the blue jacket and standing on the front steps of the building⌃

7. fragment—, they deserved that grade. [frag]

7. Because Kevin, Heather, and Jimmy worked hard on that presentation⌃

8. run-on—; [run-on]

8. The ferry is usually on time⌃however, it was about ten minutes late this morning.

9. sentence [sent]

9. The printer was out of paper, so I loaded about three hundred sheets.

10. fragment—, we went home. [frag]

10. After the hot-air balloon rose up into the morning sky and sailed across the prairie⌃

B. Combining Sentences

Each of the following items contains two complete sentences. Combine these sentences to make a single sentence that is clear and interesting. To combine the sentences, you can add connecting words, insert words or phrases, or use compound or complex sentences.   Possible revisions follow.

11. and [sent. combining]

11. Justin makes money mowing lawns⌃ ~~He~~ usually saves the money in his bank account.

12. handmade [sent. combining]

12. Aunt Shirley gave me a⌃sweater for my birthday. ~~It is hand-made.~~

RESOURCES

Writing Effective Sentences

Review

■ *Language & Sentence Skills Practice,* pp. 403–404, 415–416, 421–422, 427–428

Assessment

■ *Formal Assessment*

■ *Progress-Monitoring Tests,* pp. 35–39, 48

■ *Test Generator* (Teacher One Stop DVD-ROM)

13. The puffin, a shore-bird with a large, brightly colored beak, dives for fish. [sent. combining]
14. because [sent. combining]
15. , spewing [sent. combining]
16. [sent. combining]
17. [sent. combining]
18. four [sent. combining]
19. , working [sent. combining]
20. , so [sent. combining]

Review C [sent. style]

13. ~~The puffin dives for fish. It is~~ a shorebird with a large, ~~brightly colored beak.~~
14. I will send a thank-you note to Sandra₍ₐ₎ ~~S~~he helped me study for final exams.
15. The volcano erupted suddenly₍ₐ₎ ~~It spewed~~ ashes and lava all across the region.
16. When you leave town, please stop at Dave's house~~. Stop there~~ to say goodbye.
17. I'm expecting an important letter~~. It should arrive~~ in the mail today.
18. The₍ₐ₎deer were grazing alongside the dusty road. ~~There were four deer.~~
19. The salmon traveled steadily for days₍ₐ₎ ~~They worked~~ their way inland.
20. Mr. Barrera's car is making a strange noise₍ₐ₎ ~~H~~e has taken it to a mechanic for repair.

C. Revising a Passage to Improve Sentence Style

The passage below contains stringy sentences, wordy sentences, and nonparallel structures. It also lacks variety in sentence openings and sentence structure. Also, the passage needs transitions to show the relationships between ideas. Rewrite the passage to make it clearer and to improve the sentences.

A possible revision follows.

```
     The students considered having a car
wash. They could donate the money they
made to a charity. They talked about
having a walkathon and how they could
raise money for a charity. The students
discussed helping Habitat for Humanity
build a house for a family that needed
one, and they decided that helping to
build a house for Habitat for Humanity
would be the most fun of the three
projects, and they asked one student to
contact Habitat for Humanity about help-
ing on a house-building project. That
student's name was Reginald.
     Due to the fact that Habitat for
Humanity was working on a house that was
nearby, the organization told Reginald
they could use the class's help. The
organization sent a person to the class
```

```
to tell them about Habitat for Humanity.
The person was Mr. Ramirez. He told the
students what the students would need to
do and about the organization's goals.
Mr. Ramirez invited the students to come
as a group the next weekend. They did.
The class had a number of members total-
ing about eighteen. They could get a
great deal of work done together. Some
of them helped paint the inside walls,
and some of them helped install cabinets,
and some of them cleared the backyard of
trash and weeds. The students were very
pleased. The reason was that they had
accomplished so much. It was also fun to
do the work themselves.
```

First, the students considered having a car wash or a walkathon to raise money for a charity. Then the students discussed helping Habitat for Humanity build a house for a family that needed one. They decided that helping to build a house for Habitat for Humanity would be the most fun of the three projects, so they asked one student, Reginald, to contact Habitat for Humanity about helping on a house-building project.

Since Habitat for Humanity was working on a nearby house, the organization told Reginald they could use the class's help. Mr. Ramirez, the person Habitat for Humanity sent to tell the class about the organization, told the students what they would need to do and what the organization's goals are. Mr. Ramirez invited the students to come as a group the next weekend, and they did. The class totaled about eighteen and therefore could get a great deal of work done together. Some of them helped paint the inside walls, some helped install cabinets, and some helped clear the backyard of trash and weeds. The students were very pleased because they had accomplished so much, and it was also fun to do the work themselves.

Sentence Diagramming

1.0 Written and Oral English Language Conventions

Students write and speak with a command of standard English conventions appropriate to this grade level.

Reference Note

For information on **subjects and verbs,** see Chapter 1.

The Sentence Diagram

A *sentence diagram* is a picture of how the parts of a sentence fit together. It shows how the words in the sentence are related.

Subjects and Verbs

To diagram a sentence, first find the simple subject and the verb (simple predicate), and write them on a horizontal line. Then, separate them with a vertical line.

EXAMPLES   The reporter dashed to the fire.

reporter	dashed

Have you been studying?

you	Have been studying

Notice that a diagram shows the capitalization but not the punctuation of a sentence.

Understood Subjects

To diagram an imperative sentence, place the understood subject *you* in parentheses on the horizontal line.

EXAMPLE   Listen to the beautiful music.

$$\text{(you)} \mid \text{Listen}$$

Reference Note
For information on **understood subjects,** see page 19.

Exercise 1 Diagramming Simple Subjects and Verbs

Diagram only the simple subjects and the verbs in the following sentences.

EXAMPLE   **1.** Midas is a character in Greek mythology.

$$\text{Midas} \mid \text{is}$$

1. Midas ruled the kingdom of Phrygia.
2. One of the gods gave Midas the power to turn anything into gold.
3. Soon this gift became a curse.
4. Do you know why?
5. Read the story of King Midas in a mythology book.

Compound Subjects

EXAMPLES   **Vines** and **weeds** grew over the old well.

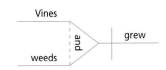

Reference Note
For information on **compound subjects,** see page 15.

Either **Daphne** or **Teresa** plans to report on Thailand.

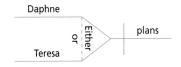

Exercise 1 **Diagramming Simple Subjects and Verbs**

ANSWERS

1. $\text{Midas} \mid \text{ruled}$

2. $\text{One} \mid \text{gave}$

3. $\text{gift} \mid \text{became}$

4. $\text{you} \mid \text{Do know}$

5. $\text{(you)} \mid \text{Read}$

Compound Verbs

EXAMPLE   We **ran** to the corner and barely **caught** the bus.

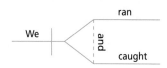

Compound Subjects and Compound Verbs

EXAMPLE   **Ken** and **LaDonna dived** into the water and **swam** across the pool.

Reference Note
For information on **compound verbs,** see page 16.

Exercise 2 **Diagramming Compound Subjects and Compound Verbs**

Diagram the subjects and the verbs in the following sentences.

EXAMPLE   1. Nikki and Chris chopped the cilantro and added it to the salsa.

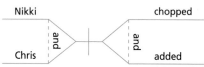

1. Mr. Carrington collects aluminum cans and returns them for recycling.
2. The students and the faculty combined their efforts and defeated the proposal.
3. The plane circled above the landing field but did not descend.
4. Pencil and paper are needed for tomorrow's math assignment.
5. Angela and her costar prepared for the scene.

Exercise 2 **Diagramming Compound Subjects and Verbs**

ANSWERS

1.
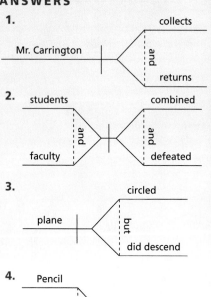

2.

3.

4.

5.
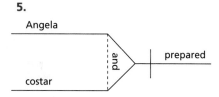

Adjectives and Adverbs

Both adjectives and adverbs are written on slanted lines below the words they modify.

Reference Note

For information on **adjectives** and **adverbs**, see page 38 and page 61.

Adjectives

EXAMPLES **bright** star   **a special** person   **her favorite** class

┌─**HELP**──

Possessive nouns and pronouns are diagrammed in the same way adjectives are.

Two or more adjectives joined by a connecting word are diagrammed this way:

EXAMPLE a **lovely** and **quiet** place

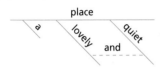

Exercise 3 Diagramming Adjectives

Diagram the following word groups.

EXAMPLE **1.** that old clock

1. mighty warrior
2. long, exciting movie
3. my final offer
4. short and funny story
5. the slow but persistent turtle

Exercise 3 Diagramming Adjectives

ANSWERS

1.   warrior
          mighty

2.   movie
          long   exciting

3.   offer
          my   final

4.   story
          short   funny
             and

5.   turtle
          the   slow   persistent
                   but

Reference Note

For information on **adverbs,** see page 61.

Adverbs

EXAMPLES   studies **hard**   does **not** exercise **daily**

When an adverb modifies an adjective or another adverb, it is placed on a line connected to the word it modifies.

EXAMPLES   **extremely** strong wind   tried **rather** hard

Exercise 4 Diagramming Adverbs

Diagram the following word groups.

EXAMPLE   **1.** very seldom breaks

1. answered quickly
2. listened quite intently
3. dangerously sharp curve
4. may possibly happen
5. never plans very carefully

Review A Diagramming Sentences That Contain Adjectives and Adverbs

Diagram the following sentences.

EXAMPLE   **1.** The blue car quickly swerved left.

```
    car  |  swerved
   The  blue  quickly  left
```

476   **Chapter 19**   Sentence Diagramming

Exercise 4 Diagramming Adverbs

ANSWERS

1.
```
answered
   quickly
```

2.
```
listened
   intently
     quite
```

3.
```
curve
   sharp
     dangerously
```

4.
```
may happen
   possibly
```

5.
```
plans
  never    carefully
              very
```

476   Sentence Diagramming

1. Our turn finally came.
2. We are definitely leaving tomorrow.
3. The anxious motorist drove too fast.
4. The shutters rattled quite noisily.
5. The new car had not been damaged badly.

Objects

Direct Objects

A direct object is diagrammed on the horizontal line with the subject and verb. A vertical line separates the direct object from the verb. Notice that this vertical line does not cross the horizontal line.

EXAMPLE   The rain cleaned the **street.**

Compound Direct Objects

EXAMPLE   We sold **lemonade** and **oranges.**

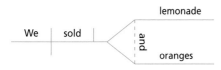

Indirect Objects

To diagram an indirect object, write it on a short horizontal line below the verb. Connect the indirect object to the verb by a slanted line.

EXAMPLE   The artist showed **me** his painting.

Reference Note

For information on **objects,** see page 81.

Reference Note

For information on **direct objects,** see page 81.

Reference Note

For information on **compound direct objects,** see page 82.

Reference Note

For information on **indirect objects,** see page 83.

SENTENCES

Review A   Diagramming Sentences That Contain Adjectives and Adverbs

ANSWERS

1.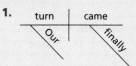

2.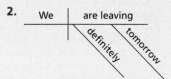

3.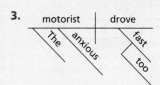

4.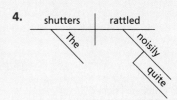

5.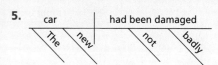

Exercise 5 Diagramming Sentences That Contain Direct Objects and Indirect Objects

ANSWERS

1.

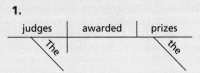

2.

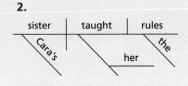

3.

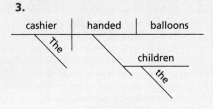

4.

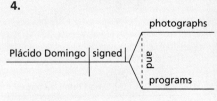

5.

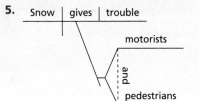

Reference Note

For information on **compound indirect objects,** see page 83.

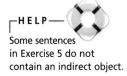

HELP

Some sentences in Exercise 5 do not contain an indirect object.

Reference Note

For information on **subject complements,** see page 85.

Reference Note

For information on **predicate nominatives,** see page 85.

Compound Indirect Objects

EXAMPLE   The company gave **Jean** and **Corey** summer jobs.

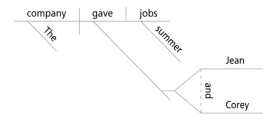

Exercise 5 Diagramming Sentences That Contain Direct Objects and Indirect Objects

Diagram the following sentences.

EXAMPLE   **1.** They gave her a present.

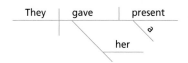

1. The judges awarded the prizes.
2. Cara's sister taught her the rules.
3. The cashier handed the children balloons.
4. Plácido Domingo signed photographs and programs.
5. Snow gives motorists and pedestrians trouble.

Subject Complements

A subject complement is placed on the horizontal line with the simple subject and the verb. The subject complement comes after the verb and is separated from it by a line slanting toward the subject. This slanted line shows that the complement refers to the subject.

Predicate Nominatives

EXAMPLE   William Least Heat-Moon is an **author.**

Compound Predicate Nominatives

EXAMPLE   The contestants are **Joan** and **Dean.**

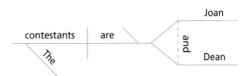

Predicate Adjectives

EXAMPLE   The river looked **deep.**

Compound Predicate Adjectives

EXAMPLE   This Chinese soup tastes **hot** and **spicy.**

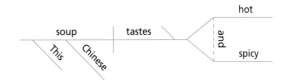

Exercise 6 **Diagramming Sentences That Contain Subject Complements**

Diagram the following sentences.

EXAMPLE   **1.** Some dogs are good companions.

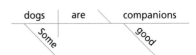

1. My shoes looked dusty.
2. Sir Francis Drake was a brave explorer.
3. The air grew cold and damp.
4. The chimpanzees seemed tired but happy.
5. My favorite months are September and May.

Reference Note

For information on **compound predicate nominatives,** see page 86.

Reference Note

For information on **predicate adjectives,** see page 87.

Reference Note

For information on **compound predicate adjectives,** see page 87.

SENTENCES

Exercise 6 **Diagramming Sentences That Contain Subject Complements**

ANSWERS

1.

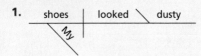

2.

Sir Francis Drake | was | explorer — a, brave

3.

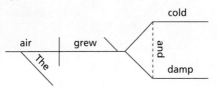

4.

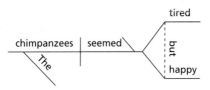

5.

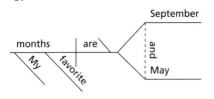

The Sentence Diagram   **479**

Review B Diagramming Sentences That Contain Complements

ANSWERS

1.

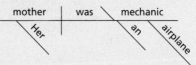

2.

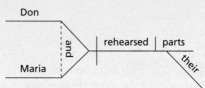

3.

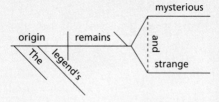

4.

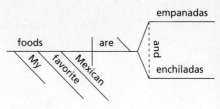

5.

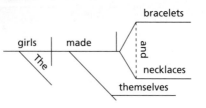

Reference Note

For information on **phrases,** see Chapter 5. For information on **prepositional phrases,** see page 96.

Reference Note

For information on **adjective phrases,** see page 97.

Review B Diagramming Sentences That Contain Complements

Diagram the following sentences.

EXAMPLE   **1.** That cockatiel is friendly.

1. Her mother was an airplane mechanic.
2. Don and Maria rehearsed their parts.
3. The legend's origin remains mysterious and strange.
4. My favorite Mexican foods are empanadas and enchiladas.
5. The girls made themselves bracelets and necklaces.

Phrases

Prepositional Phrases

Prepositional phrases are diagrammed below the word or word group they modify. Write the preposition that introduces the phrase on a line slanting down from the modified word. Then, write the object of the preposition on a horizontal line extending from the slanting line.

Adjective Phrases

EXAMPLES   paintings **by famous artists**

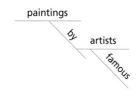

cloth **from Costa Rica and Guatemala**

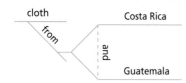

Adverb Phrases

EXAMPLES walked **along the road**

went **with Hollis and Dave**

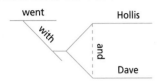

When a prepositional phrase modifies the object of another prepositional phrase, the diagram looks like this:

EXAMPLE camped on the side **of a mountain**

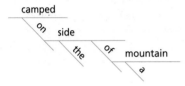

Exercise 7 **Diagramming Prepositional Phrases**

Diagram the following word groups.

EXAMPLE **1.** drove through the Maine woods

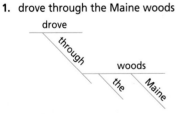

1. invited to the celebrations
2. a glimpse of the famous ruler

For information on **adverb phrases,** see page 99.

Reference Note

Exercise 7 **Diagramming Prepositional Phrases**

ANSWERS

1. invited

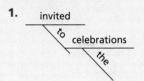

2. glimpse

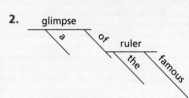

3. one

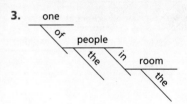

4. drove

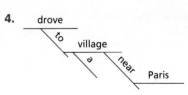

5. wrote

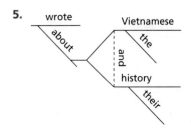

Review C Diagramming Sentences That Contain Prepositional Phrases

ANSWERS

1.
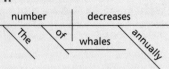

2.
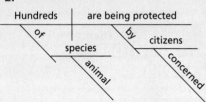

3.
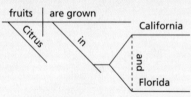

4.
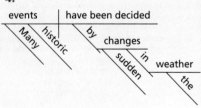

5.
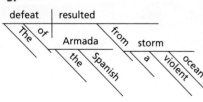

3. one of the people in the room
4. drove to a village near Paris
5. wrote about the Vietnamese and their history

Review C Diagramming Sentences That Contain Prepositional Phrases

Diagram the following sentences.

EXAMPLE　**1.** The steep slopes of the mountains are covered with forests.

1. The number of whales decreases annually.
2. Hundreds of animal species are being protected by concerned citizens.
3. Citrus fruits are grown in California and Florida.
4. Many historic events have been decided by sudden changes in the weather.
5. The defeat of the Spanish Armada resulted from a violent ocean storm.

Reference Note

For information on **verbals** and **verbal phrases,** see page 101.

Verbals and Verbal Phrases

Participles and Participial Phrases

Participles are diagrammed differently from other adjectives.

EXAMPLE　José comforted the **crying** baby.

Participial phrases are diagrammed as follows:

EXAMPLE   **Shaking the manager's hand,** Teresa accepted her
new job.

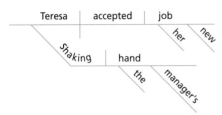

Reference Note

For information on
participles and **participial phrases,** see
pages 101 and 102.

Notice that the participle has a direct object (*hand*), which is
diagrammed in the same way that the direct object of a main
verb is.

Gerunds and Gerund Phrases

EXAMPLES   I enjoy **swimming.** [gerund used as direct object]

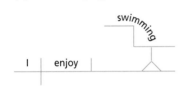

Reference Note

For information on
gerunds and **gerund
phrases,** see pages 105
and 106.

Being slightly ill is no excuse for **missing two days
of piano practice.** [Gerund phrases used as subject and
as object of preposition. The first gerund has a subject
complement (*ill*); the second gerund has a direct object
(*days*).]

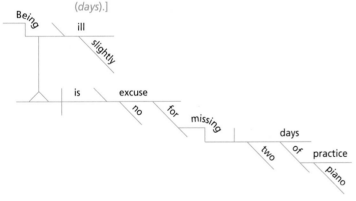

Infinitives and Infinitive Phrases

EXAMPLES **To write** is her ambition. [infinitive used as subject]

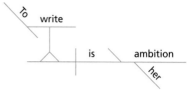

Reference Note

For information on **infinitives** and **infinitive phrases,** see pages 108 and 109.

He was the first one **to solve that tricky problem.**
[infinitive phrase used as adjective]

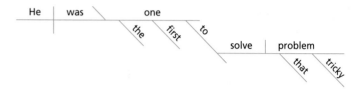

Marge was hoping **to go with us.** [infinitive phrase used as direct object]

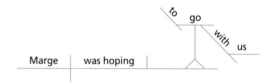

She called **to invite us over.** [infinitive phrase used as adverb]

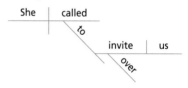

Exercise 8 Diagramming Sentences That Contain Verbals and Verbal Phrases

Diagram the following sentences.

EXAMPLE   **1.** I heard them **laughing.**

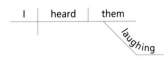

1. Taking that shortcut will cut several minutes off the trip.
2. I want to watch television tonight.
3. That is my cat licking its paws.
4. Checking the time, Wynetta rushed to the gym.
5. Did he go to the store to buy oranges?

Appositives and Appositive Phrases

To diagram an appositive or an appositive phrase, write the appositive in parentheses after the word it identifies.

EXAMPLES   Our cousin **Iola** is a chemical engineer.

Jerry Seinfeld, **the popular comedian,** is also the author of a bestselling book.

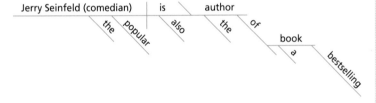

Reference Note

For information on **appositives** and **appositive phrases,** see page 112.

The Sentence Diagram   **485**

Exercise 8 Diagramming Sentences That Contain Verbals and Verbal Phrases

ANSWERS

1.

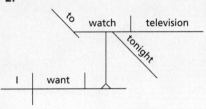

2.

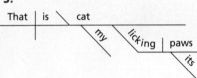

3.

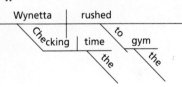

4.

5.

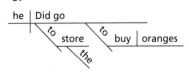

SENTENCES

The Sentence Diagram   **485**

Subordinate Clauses

Adjective Clauses

Diagram an adjective clause by connecting it with a broken line to the word it modifies. Draw the broken line between the relative pronoun and the word to which it relates.

EXAMPLE   The grade **that I got yesterday** pleased my parents.

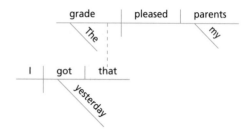

NOTE A relative pronoun relates an adjective clause to the word the clause modifies. The relative pronouns are *that, which, who, whom,* and *whose.*

Adverb Clauses

Diagram an adverb clause by using a broken line to connect the adverb clause to the word it modifies. Place the subordinating conjunction that introduces the adverb clause on the broken line.

EXAMPLE   **When I got home from school,** I ate an apple.

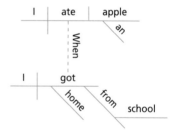

NOTE An adverb clause is introduced by a subordinating conjunction. Some common subordinating conjunctions include *because, before, since, though,* and *whether.*

Reference Note
For information on
adjective clauses, see
page 124.

—HELP—
The relative
pronouns are *who, whom, whose, which,* and *that.*

Reference Note
For information on
relative pronouns,
see page 124.

Reference Note
For information on
adverb clauses,
see page 127.

Noun Clauses

Diagram a noun clause by connecting it to the independent clause with a solid line.

EXAMPLE   Olivia knew **what she wanted.** [The noun clause is the direct object of the independent clause. The word *what* is the direct object in the noun clause.]

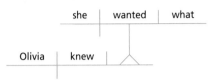

When the introductory word of the noun clause does not have a specific function in the noun clause, the sentence is diagrammed in this way:

EXAMPLE   The problem is **that they lost the map.** [The noun clause is the predicate nominative of the independent clause. The word *that* has no function in the noun clause.]

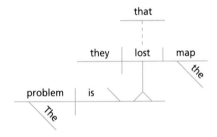

Reference Note

For information on **noun clauses,** see page 130.

Exercise 9   **Diagramming Sentences That Contain Subordinate Clauses**

Diagram the sentences on the following page.

EXAMPLE   **1.** The box that contained the treasure was wooden.

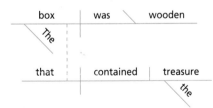

Exercise 9 Diagramming Sentences That Contain Subordinate Clauses

ANSWERS

1.
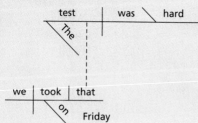

2.
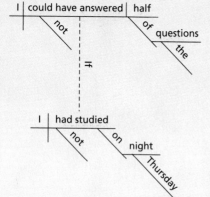

3.
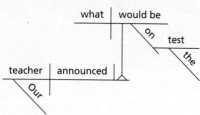

4.
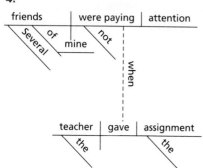

1. The test that we took on Friday was hard.
2. If I had not studied on Thursday night, I could not have answered half of the questions.
3. Our teacher announced what would be on the test.
4. Several friends of mine were not paying attention when the teacher gave the assignment.
5. Some of them did not know what they should study and are worried now about their grades.

Sentences Classified According to Structure

Reference Note

For information on **simple sentences,** see page 140.

Simple Sentences

EXAMPLE   Tracy is building a birdhouse in industrial arts class. [one independent clause]

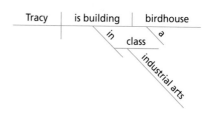

Reference Note

For information on **compound sentences,** see page 142.

Compound Sentences

The second independent clause in a compound sentence is diagrammed below the first and is joined to it by a coordinating conjunction.

EXAMPLE   Darnell threw a good pass, but Clay did not catch it. [two independent clauses]

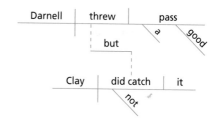

488   Chapter 19   Sentence Diagramming

5.
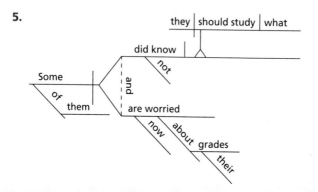

Exercise 10) Diagramming Compound Sentences

Diagram the following compound sentences.

EXAMPLE 1. A strange dog chased us, but the owner came to our rescue.

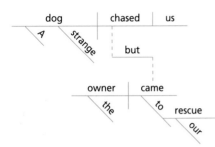

Reference Note

For information about **coordinating conjunctions,** see page 69.

1. I want a motorboat, but Jan prefers a sailboat.
2. The bus stopped at the restaurant, and all of the passengers went inside.
3. Our club is very small, but it is growing.
4. Shall we meet you at the station, or will you take a taxi?
5. In Arizona the temperature is often high, but the humidity always remains low.

Complex Sentences

EXAMPLE Before they left the museum, Lester and Jessica visited the exhibit of masks from Nigeria and the Ivory Coast.
[one subordinate clause and one independent clause]

Reference Note

For information on **complex sentences,** see page 145.

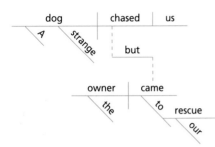

Exercise 10) Diagramming Compound Sentences

ANSWERS

1.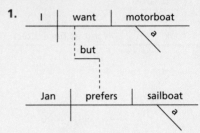

2.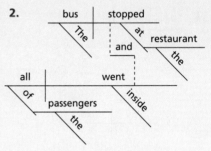

3.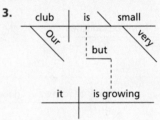

4.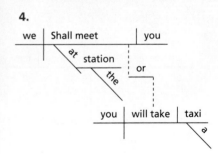

5.

Exercise 11 Diagramming Complex Sentences

ANSWERS

1.

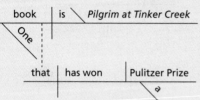

2.

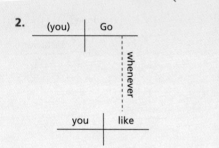

3.

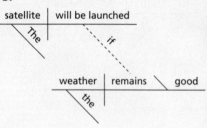

4.

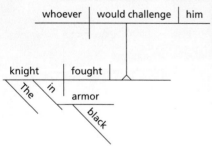

5.

Exercise 11 **Diagramming Complex Sentences**

Diagram the following complex sentences.

EXAMPLE   1. As night fell, the storm grew worse.

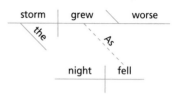

1. One book that has won a Pulitzer Prize is *Pilgrim at Tinker Creek*.
2. Go whenever you like.
3. The satellite will be launched if the weather remains good.
4. The knight in black armor fought whoever would challenge him.
5. Alexander the Great, who conquered most of the known world, died at the age of thirty-three.

Compound-Complex Sentences

EXAMPLE   Hamako, whose father is a musician, studies piano, but her cousin Akio prefers to play tennis. [two independent clauses and one subordinate clause]

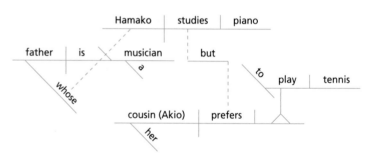

Reference Note

For information on **compound-complex sentences,** see page 147.

Review D **Diagramming Sentences**

Diagram the following sentences.

EXAMPLE   **1.** The room that Carrie painted had been white, but she changed the color.

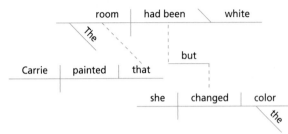

1. Diego Rivera and Frida Kahlo were two important Mexican artists of the twentieth century.
2. Mom wanted to fly to Utah, but Dad and I wanted to drive there.
3. Our new neighbors, the Chens, come from Taiwan, which is an island off the coast of China.
4. For my report, I wrote about Katherine Anne Porter and Eudora Welty, two Southern authors.
5. When I returned to the store, the purple shirt had been sold, so I bought the blue one.

The answers for **Review D** appear on pp. T491A–T491B.

Review D Diagramming Sentences

ANSWERS *(for items appearing on p. 491)*

1.

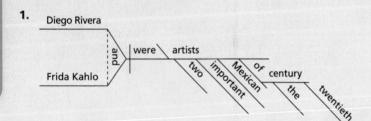

2.

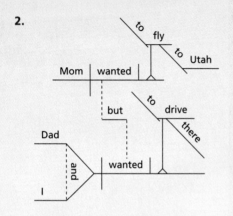

3.

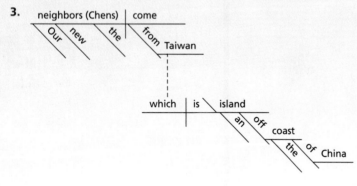

ANSWERS continued

4.

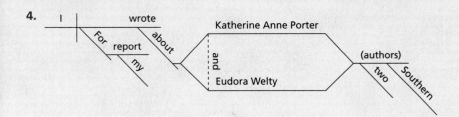

5.

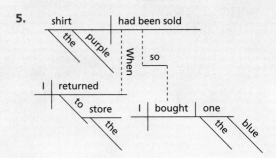

PART 3 Resources

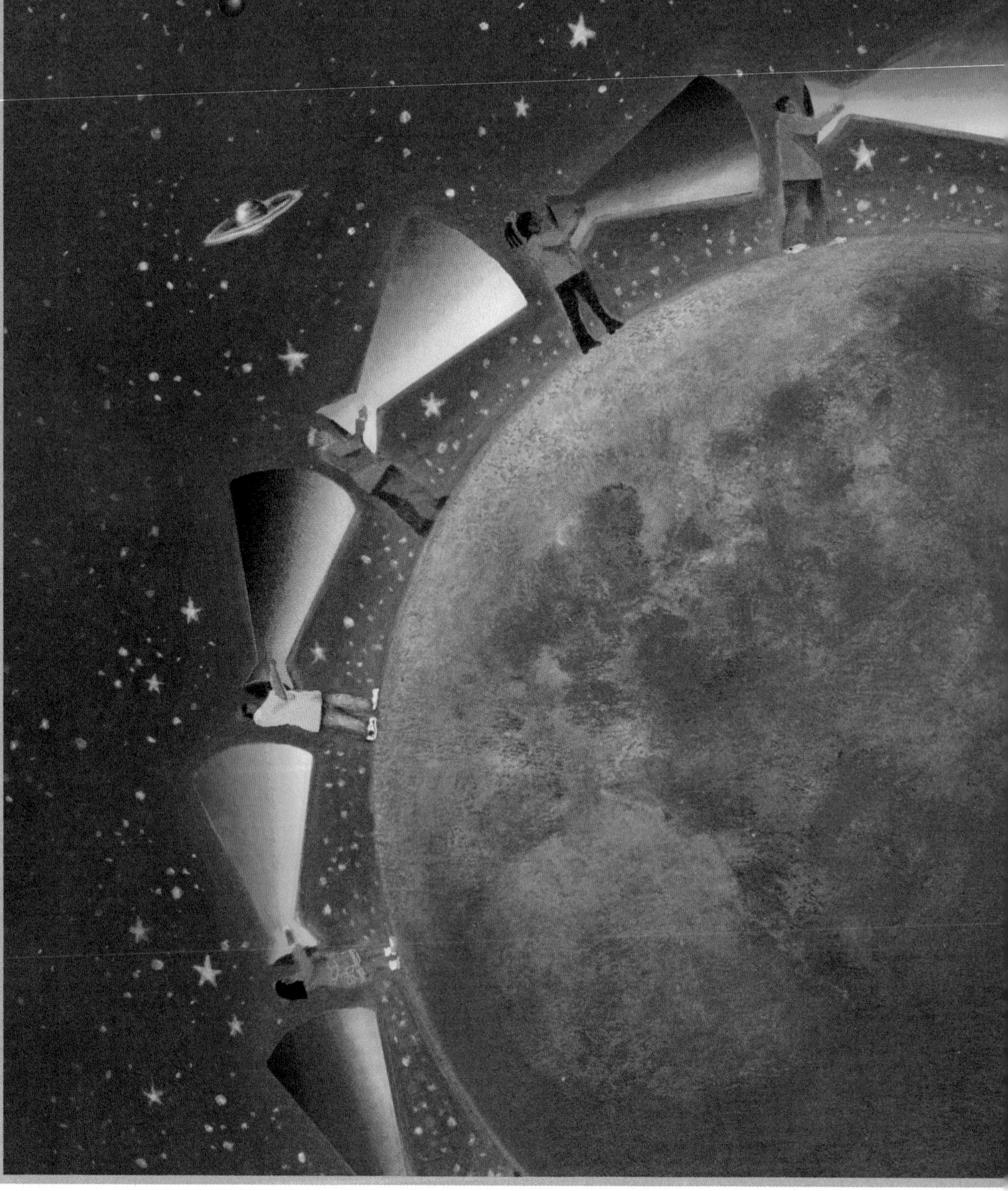

The History of English

Test Smarts

Grammar at a Glance

The History of English

Origins and Uses

No one knows exactly when or how English got started. We do know that English and many other modern-day languages come from an early language that was spoken thousands of years ago. The related languages still resemble that parent language, just as you resemble your parents. For example, notice how similar the words for *mother* are in the following modern-day languages.

ENGLISH mother	FRENCH mère
SPANISH madre	ITALIAN madre
SWEDISH moder	

Over 1,500 years ago, a few small tribes of people invaded the island that is now Britain. These tribes, called the Angles and Saxons, spoke the earliest known form of English, called **Old English.** Old English was very different from the English we speak.

English continued to evolve through a form known as **Middle English.** While our language has always changed and grown, some of our most basic words have been around since the very beginning.

EARLY WORD
hand   dohtor   andswaru   hleapan

PRESENT-DAY WORD
hand   daughter   answer   leap

Changes in Meaning   It may be hard to believe that the word *bead* once meant "prayer." Many English words have changed meaning over time. Some of these changes have been slight. Others have been more obvious. Below are a few examples of words that have changed their meanings:

naughty—In the 1300s, *naughty* meant "poor or needy." In the 1600s, the meaning changed to "poorly behaved."

lunch—In the 1500s, a *lunch* was a large chunk of something, such as bread or meat.

caboose—*Caboose* entered the English language in the 1700s when the word meant "the kitchen of a ship."

Even today the meanings of words may vary depending on where they are used. For example, in the United States a *boot* is a type of shoe, but in Great Britain, a *boot* may refer to the trunk of a car.

Changes in Pronunciation and Spelling

If you traveled back in time a few hundred years, you would probably have a hard time understanding spoken and written English.

■ **Changes in Pronunciation** English words used to be pronounced differently from the way they are pronounced today. For example, in the 1200s, people pronounced *bite* like *beet* and *feet* like *fate.* They also pronounced the vowel sound in the word *load* like the vowel sound in our word *awe.*

You may have wondered why English words are not always spelled as they sound. Changes in pronunciation help account for many strange spellings in English. For example, the *w* that starts the word *write* was not always silent. Even after the *w* sound was dropped, the spelling stayed the same. The *g* in *gnat* and the *k* in *knee* were once part of the pronunciations of those words, too.

■ **Changes in Spelling** The spellings of many words have changed over time. Some changes in spelling have been accidental. For example, *apron* used to be spelled *napron.* People mistakenly attached the *n* to the article *a,* and *a napron* became *an apron.* Here are some more examples of present-day English words and their early spellings.

EARLY SPELLING

| jaile | locian | slæp | tima |

PRESENT-DAY SPELLING

| jail | look | sleep | time |

■ **British vs. American Spelling and Pronunciation** Pronunciations and spellings still vary today. For instance, the English used in Great Britain differs from the English used in the United States. In Great Britain, people pronounce *bath* with the vowel sound of *father* instead of the vowel sound of *cat.* The British also tend to drop the *r* sound at the end of words like *copper.* In addition, the British spell some words differently from the way people in the United States do.

AMERICAN

| theater | pajamas | labor |

BRITISH

| theatre | pyjamas | labour |

Word Origins

English grows and changes along with the people who use it. New words must be created for new inventions, places, or ideas. Sometimes, people borrow words from other languages to create a new English word. Other times, people use the names of people or places as new words.

■ **Borrowed words** As English-speaking people came into contact with people from other cultures and lands, they began to borrow words. English has borrowed hundreds of thousands of words from French, Hindi, Spanish, and African languages, and from many other languages spoken around the world. In many cases, the borrowed words have taken new forms.

FRENCH	ange	HINDI	champo
ENGLISH	angel	ENGLISH	shampoo
KIMBUNDU	mbanza	SPANISH	patata
ENGLISH	banjo	ENGLISH	potato

■ **Words from Names**   Many things get their names from the names of people or places. For example, in the 1920s, someone in Bridgeport, Connecticut, discovered a new use for the pie plates from the Frisbie Bakery. He turned one upside down and sent it floating through the air. The new game sparked the idea for the plastic flying disk of today.

Dialects of American English

You probably know some people who speak English differently from the way you do. Different groups of people use different varieties of English. The kind of English we speak sounds most normal to us even though it may sound unusual to someone else. The form of English a particular group of people speaks is called a *dialect.* Everyone uses a dialect, and no dialect is better or worse than another.

Ethnic Dialects   Your cultural background can make a difference in the way you speak. A dialect shared by people from the same cultural group is called an *ethnic dialect.* Because Americans come from many cultures, American English includes many ethnic dialects. One of the largest ethnic dialects is the Black English spoken by many African Americans. Another is the Hispanic English of many people whose families come from Mexico, Central America, or Cuba.

Regional Dialects   Do you *make* the bed or *make up* the bed? Would you order a *sub* with the *woiks* or a *hero* with the *werks*? In the evening, do you eat *supper* or *dinner*? How you answer these questions is probably influenced by where you live. A dialect shared by people from the same area is called a *regional dialect.* Your regional dialect helps determine what words you use, how you pronounce words, and how you put words together.

Not everyone from a particular group speaks that group's dialect. Also, an ethnic or regional dialect may vary depending on the speaker's individual background and place of origin.

Standard American English

Every dialect is useful and helps keep the English language colorful and interesting. However, sometimes it is confusing to try to communicate using two different dialects. Therefore, it is important to be familiar with *standard American English.* Standard English is the most commonly understood variety of English. You can find some of the rules for using standard English in this textbook. Language that does not follow these rules and guidelines is called **nonstandard English.** Nonstandard English is considered inappropriate in many formal environments, such as school or business.

> NONSTANDARD   I don't want no more spinach.
>
> STANDARD   I don't want **any** more spinach.
>
> NONSTANDARD   Jimmy would of gone hiking with us.
>
> STANDARD   Jimmy would **have** gone hiking with us.

Formal and Informal   Read the following sentences.

> Many of my friends are excited about the game.
>
> A bunch of my friends are psyched about the game.

Both sentences mean the same thing, but they have different effects. The first sentence is an example of **formal English,** and the second sentence is an example of **informal English.**

Formal and informal English are each appropriate for different situations. For instance, you would probably use the formal example if you were talking to a teacher about the game. If you were talking to a friend, however, the second sentence might sound natural. Formal English is frequently used in news reports and in schools and businesses.

■ **Colloquialisms**   Informal English includes many words and expressions that are not appropriate in more formal situations. The most widely used informal expressions are *colloquialisms.* **Colloquialisms** are colorful words and phrases of everyday conversation. Many colloquialisms have meanings that are different from the basic meanings of words.

EXAMPLES
I wish Gerald would *get off my case.*
Don't get *all bent out of shape* about it.
We were about to *bust* with laughter.

■ **Slang**   *Slang* words are made-up words or old words used in new ways. Slang is highly informal language. It is usually created by a particular group of people, such as students, or people who hold a particular job, like computer technicians or artists. Often, slang is familiar only to the groups that invent it.

Sometimes slang words become a lasting part of the English language. Usually, though, slang falls out of style quickly. The slang words in the following sentences will probably seem out of date to you.

That was a really *far-out flick.*
Those are some *groovy duds* you're wearing.
I don't have enough *dough* to buy a movie ticket.

TEACHING TIP

You can reinforce the material in this section with practice tests found on pages 418, 419, 430, and 431 of the pupil's textbook and with chapter tests found in the ancillary *Progress Assessment for the Holt Handbook*.

RESOURCES

Test Smarts
Taking Standardized Tests in Grammar, Usage, and Mechanics

Becoming "Test-Smart"

Standardized achievement tests, like other tests, measure your skills in specific areas. Standardized achievement tests also compare your performance to the performance of other students at your age or grade level. Some language arts standardized tests measure your skill in using correct capitalization, punctuation, sentence structure, and spelling. Such tests may also measure your ability to evaluate sentence style.

The most important part of preparing for any test, including standardized tests, is learning the content on which you will be tested. To do this, you must

- listen in class
- complete homework assignments
- study to master the concepts and skills presented by your teacher

In addition, you also need to use effective strategies for taking a standardized test. The following pages will teach you how to become test-smart.

General Strategies for Taking Tests

1. **Understand how the test is scored.** If no points will be taken off for wrong answers, plan to answer every question. If wrong answers count against you, plan to answer only questions you know the answer to or questions you can answer with an educated guess.

2. **Stay focused.** Expect to be a little nervous, but focus your attention on doing the best job possible. Try not to be distracted with thoughts that aren't about the test questions.

3. **Get an overview.** Quickly skim the entire test to get an idea of how long the test is and what is on it.

4. **Pace yourself.** Based on your overview, figure out how much time to allow for each section of the test. If time limits are stated for each section, decide how much time to allow for each item. Pace yourself, and check every five to ten minutes to see if you need to work faster. Try to leave a few minutes at the end of the testing period to check your work.

5. **Read all instructions.** Read the instructions for each part of the test carefully. Also, answer the sample questions to be sure you understand how to answer the test questions.

6. **Read all answer choices.** Carefully read *all* of the possible answers before you choose an answer. Note how each possible answer differs from the others. You may want to make an *x* next to each answer choice that you rule out.

7. **Make educated guesses.** If you do not know the answer to a question, see if you can rule out one or more answers and make an educated guess. Don't spend too much time on any one item, though. If you want to think longer about a difficult item, make a light pencil mark next to the item number. You can go back to that question later.

8. **Mark your answers.** Mark the answer sheet carefully and completely. If you plan to go back to an item later, be sure to skip that number on the answer sheet.

9. **Check your work.** If you have time at the end of the test, go back to check your answers. This is also the time to try to answer any questions you skipped. Make sure your marks are complete, and erase any stray marks on the answer sheet.

Strategies for Answering Grammar, Usage, and Mechanics Questions

The questions in standardized tests can take different forms, but the most common form is the multiple-choice question. Here are some strategies for answering that kind of test question.

Correcting parts of sentences

One kind of question contains a sentence with an underlined part. The answer choices show several revised versions of that part. Your job is to decide which revised version makes the sentence correct or whether the underlined part is already correct. First, look at each answer carefully. Immediately rule out any answer in which you notice a grammatical error. If you are still unsure of the correct answer, try approaching the question in one of these two ways.

- **Think how you would rewrite the underlined part.** Look at the answer choices for one that matches your revision. Carefully read each possible answer before you make your final choice. Often, only tiny differences exist between the answers, and you want to choose the *best* answer.

■ **Look carefully at the underlined part and at each answer choice, looking for one particular type of error, such as an error in capitalization or spelling.** The best way to look for a particular error is to compare the answer choices to see how they differ both from each other and from the underlined part of the question. For example, if there are differences in capitalization, look at each choice for capitalization errors.

After ruling out incorrect answers, choose the answer with no errors. If there are errors in each of the choices but no errors in the underlined part, your answer will be the "no error" or "correct as is" choice.

EXAMPLE

Directions: Choose the answer that is the **best** revision of the underlined words.

1. My neighbor is painting his <u>house and my brother helped him.</u>

   A. house; and my brother is helping him.
   B. house, and my brother had helped him.
   C. house, and my brother is helping him.
   D. Correct as is

Explanation: In the example above, the possible answers contain differences in punctuation and in verb tense. Therefore, you should check each possible answer for errors in punctuation and verb tense.

   A. You can rule out this choice because it has incorrect punctuation.
   B. This choice creates inconsistent verb tenses, so you can rule out this answer.
   C. This choice has correct punctuation and creates consistent verb tenses.
   D. You can rule out this choice because the original sentence lacks correct

punctuation between the clauses.

Answer: Choice C is the only one that contains no errors, so the oval for that answer choice is darkened.

Correcting whole sentences

This type of question is similar to the kind of question previously described. However, here you are looking for mistakes in the entire sentence instead of just an underlined part. The strategies for approaching this type of question are the same as for the other kind of sentence-correction questions. If you don't see the correct answer right away, compare the answer choices to see how they differ. When you find differences, check each choice for errors relating to that difference. Rule out choices with errors. Repeat the process until you find the correct answer.

EXAMPLE

Directions: Choose the answer that is the **best** revision of the following sentences.

1. After Brad mowed the lawn, he swept the sidewalk and driveway, then he took a shower. And washed his hair.

   A. After Brad mowed the lawn, he swept the sidewalk and driveway. Then he took a shower and washed his hair.
   B. After Brad mowed the lawn, he swept the sidewalk and driveway. Then he took a shower, and washed his hair.
   C. After Brad mowed the lawn. He swept the sidewalk and driveway; then he took a shower and washed his hair.
   D. Correct as is

Explanation: The original word groups and answer choices have differences in sentence structure and punctuation, so you should check each answer choice for errors in sentence structure and punctuation.

- **A.** This choice contains two complete sentences and correct punctuation.
- **B.** This choice contains two complete sentences and incorrect punctuation.
- **C.** This choice begins with a sentence fragment, so you can rule it out.
- **D.** You can rule out this choice because the original version contains a sentence fragment.

Answer: Choice A is the only one that contains no errors, so the oval for that answer choice is darkened.

Identifying kinds of errors

This type of question has at least one underlined part. Your job is to determine which part, if any, contains an error. Sometimes, you may also have to decide what type of error (capitalization, punctuation, or spelling) exists. The strategy is the same whether the question has one or several underlined parts. Try to identify an error, and check the answer choices for that type of error. If the original version is correct as written, choose "no error" or "correct as is."

EXAMPLE

Directions: Read the following sentences and decide which type of error, if any, is in the underlined part.

1. Marcia, Jim, and Leroy are participating in <u>Saturday's charity marathon. they</u> are hoping to raise one hundred dollars for the new children's museum.

- **A.** Spelling error
- **B.** Capitalization error
- **C.** Punctuation error
- **D.** Correct as is

Explanation: If you cannot tell right away what kind of error (if any) is in the original version, go through each answer choice in turn.

- **A.** All the words are spelled correctly.
- **B.** The sentences contain a capitalization error. The second sentence incorrectly begins with a lowercase letter.
- **C.** The sentences are punctuated correctly.
- **D.** The sentences contain a capitalization error, so you can rule out this choice.

Answer: Because the passage contains a capitalization error, the oval for answer choice B is darkened.

Revising sentence structure

Errors covered by this kind of question include sentence fragments, run-on sentences, repetitive wording, misplaced modifiers, and awkward construction. If you don't immediately spot the error, examine the question and each answer choice for specific types of errors, one type at a time. If you cannot find an error in the original version and if all of the other answer choices have errors, then choose "no error" or "correct as is."

EXAMPLE

Directions: Read the following word groups. If there is an error in sentence structure, choose the answer that best revises the word groups.

1. Mary Lou arranged the mozzarella cheese and fresh tomatoes. On a platter covered with lettuce leaves.

   A. Mary Lou arranged the mozzarella cheese and fresh tomatoes on a platter covered with lettuce leaves.

   B. Mary Lou arranged the mozzarella cheese and fresh tomatoes, on a platter covered with lettuce leaves.

   C. Mary Lou arranged the mozzarella cheese and fresh tomatoes; on a platter covered with lettuce leaves.

   D. Correct as is

Explanation: The original sentences and answer choices have differences in sentence structure and punctuation.

   A. This choice is correctly punctuated and contains a correct, complete sentence.

   B. This choice contains an incorrect comma, so you can rule it out.

   C. This choice contains an incorrect semicolon, so you can rule it out.

   D. The original word groups contain a sentence fragment, so D cannot be correct.

Answer: Choice A is the only one that contains no errors, so the oval for that answer choice is darkened.

Questions about sentence style

These questions are often not about grammar, usage, or mechanics but about content and organization. They may ask about tone, purpose, topic sentences, supporting sentences, audience, sentence combining, appropriateness of content, or transitions. The questions may ask you which is the *best* way to revise the passage, or they may ask you to identify the *main* purpose of the passage. When you see words such as *best*, *main*, and *most likely* or *least likely*, you are not being asked to correct errors; you are being asked to make a judgment about style or meaning.

If the question asks for a particular kind of revision (for example, "What *transition* is needed between sentence 4 and sentence 5?"), analyze each answer choice to see how well it makes that particular revision. Many questions ask for a general revision (for example, "Which is the *best* way to revise the last sentence?"). In such situations, check each answer choice and rule out any choices that have mistakes in grammar, usage, or mechanics. Then, read each choice and use what you have learned in class to judge whether the revision improves the original sentence. If you are combining sentences, be sure to choose the answer that includes all important information, that demonstrates good style, *and* that is grammatically correct.

EXAMPLE

Directions: Choose the answer that shows the **best** way to combine the following sentences.

1. Jacques Cousteau was a filmmaker and author. Jacques Cousteau explored the ocean as a diver and marine scientist.

   A. Jacques Cousteau was a filmmaker and author; Jacques Cousteau explored the ocean as a marine scientist.

   B. Jacques Cousteau was a filmmaker and author, he explored the ocean as a diver and marine scientist.

   C. Jacques Cousteau was a filmmaker

and author who explored the ocean as a diver and marine scientist.
  D. Jacques Cousteau was a filmmaker, author, diver, and scientist.

Explanation:
  A. Answer choice A is grammatically correct but unnecessarily repeats the subject *Jacques Cousteau* and leaves out some information.
  B. Choice B is a run-on sentence, so it cannot be the correct answer.
  C. Choice C is grammatically correct, and it demonstrates effective sentence combining.
  D. Choice D is grammatically correct but leaves out some information.

Answer: Because answer choice C shows the best way to combine the sentences, the oval for choice C is darkened.

Fill-in-the-blanks
This type of question tests your ability to fill in blanks in sentences, giving answers that are logical and grammatically correct. A question of this kind might ask you to choose a verb in the appropriate tense. A different question might require a combination of adverbs (*first, next*) to show how parts of the sentence relate. Another question might require a vocabulary word to complete the sentence.

To approach a sentence-completion question, first look for clue words in the sentence. *But, however,* and *though* indicate a contrast; *therefore* and *as a result* indicate cause and effect. Using sentence clues, rule out obviously incorrect answer choices. Then, try filling in the blanks with the remaining choices to determine which answer choice makes the most sense. Finally, check to be sure your choice is grammatically correct.

EXAMPLE

Directions: Choose the words that **best** complete the sentence.
1. When Jack _____ the dog, the dog _____ water everywhere.
  A. washes, splashed
  B. washed, will be splashing
  C. will have washed, has splashed
  D. washed, splashed

Explanation:
  A. The verb tenses (present and past) are inconsistent.
  B. The verb tenses (past and future) are inconsistent.
  C. The verb tenses (future perfect and present perfect) are inconsistent.
  D. The verb tenses (past and past) are consistent.

Answer: The oval for choice D is darkened.

Using Your Test Smarts
Remember: Success on standardized tests comes partly from knowing strategies for taking such tests—from being test-smart. Knowing these strategies can help you approach standardized achievement tests more confidently. Do your best to learn your classroom subjects, take practice tests if they are available, and use the strategies outlined in this section. Good luck!

Test Smarts   **503**

Grammar at a Glance

A

┌HELP┐

Grammar at a Glance is an alphabetical list of special terms and expressions with examples and references to further information. When you encounter a grammar or usage problem in the revising or proofreading stage of your writing, look for help in this section first. You may find all you need to know right here. If you need more information, **Grammar at a Glance** will show you where in the book to turn for a more complete explanation. If you do not find what you are looking for in **Grammar at a Glance,** turn to the index.

abbreviation An abbreviation is a shortened form of a word or a phrase.

■ **capitalization of** (See pages 301 and 289.)

TITLES USED WITH NAMES	**M**rs.	**G**ov.	**J**r.	**M.D.**
KINDS OF ORGANIZATIONS	**C**o.	**I**nc.	**A**ssn.	**C**orp.
PARTS OF ADDRESSES	**B**lvd.	**S**t.	**A**ve.	**P.O. B**ox
NAMES OF STATES	[without ZIP Codes]		**A**riz.	**M**d.
			Conn.	**N. M**ex.
	[with ZIP Codes]		**AZ**	**MD**
			CT	**NM**
TIMES	**A.M.**	**P.M.**	**B.C.**	**A.D.**

■ **punctuation of** (See page 313.)

WITH PERIODS	(See preceding examples.)			
WITHOUT PERIODS	MVP	PBS	USAF	NASA
	kg	mi	qt	C	cm

[Exception: inch = in.]

action verb An action verb expresses physical or mental activity. (See page 53.)

EXAMPLE   She **hoped** Myron **would leave** on time.

active voice Active voice is the voice a verb is in when it expresses an action done by its subject. (See page 200. See also **voice.**)

EXAMPLE   Peggy **climbed** the old oak tree.

adjective An adjective modifies a noun or a pronoun. (See page 38.)

EXAMPLE   Arthur likes **action-packed crime** thrillers.

adjective clause An adjective clause is a subordinate clause that modifies a noun or a pronoun. (See page 124.)

EXAMPLE   The actor **who starred in that TV film** is Robert Duvall.

adjective phrase A prepositional phrase that modifies a noun or a pronoun is called an adjective phrase. (See page 97.)

EXAMPLE   The clothes **from Italy** are the best **in the store.**

adverb An adverb modifies a verb, an adjective, or another adverb. (See page 61.)

EXAMPLE   **Usually,** the linguini is **very** good **here.**

adverb clause An adverb clause is a subordinate clause that modifies a verb, an adjective, or an adverb. (See page 127.)

EXAMPLE   They stayed **until darkness fell.**

adverb phrase A prepositional phrase that modifies a verb, an adjective, or an adverb is called an adverb phrase. (See page 99.)

EXAMPLE   **In the afternoon,** we will go **to the park.**

affix An affix is a word part that is added before or after a base word or root. (See **prefix** and **suffix.**)

EXAMPLES   sub + total = **sub**total

                 re + route = **re**route

                 optimist + ic = optimist**ic**

                 fame + ous = fam**ous**

agreement Agreement is the correspondence, or match, between grammatical forms. Grammatical forms agree when they have the same number and gender.

■ **of pronouns and antecedents** (See page 173.)

SINGULAR	**Ernesto** is saving **his** money to buy a new pair of in-line skates.
PLURAL	Having tuned **their** instruments, the mariachi band **members** were ready to rehearse.

SINGULAR	**Everyone** in the science class is hard at work on **his or her** ecology project.
PLURAL	**All** of the science students are hard at work on **their** ecology projects.

SINGULAR	**Neither Julie nor Erin** was pleased with **her** performance in the piano recital.
PLURAL	**Julie and Erin** were not pleased with **their** performances in the piano recital.

■ **of subjects and verbs** (See page 156.)

SINGULAR	The space shuttle **commander is** optimistic that the rescue mission will be successful.
SINGULAR	The space shuttle **commander,** as well as her crew members, **is** optimistic that the rescue mission will be successful.
PLURAL	The space shuttle crew **members are** optimistic that the rescue mission will be successful.
PLURAL	The space shuttle crew **members,** as well as their commander, **are** optimistic that the rescue mission will be successful.

SINGULAR	Does Charlene know that **each** of these library books **is** overdue?
PLURAL	Does Charlene know that **all** of these library books **are** overdue?

SINGULAR	**Either Ben or Cameron is** in charge of ticket sales.
PLURAL	**Both Ben and Cameron are** in charge of ticket sales.

SINGULAR	Here **is** a **recipe** for making the famous Korean dish kimchi.
PLURAL	Here **are** the **ingredients** you will need for making the famous Korean dish kimchi.

SINGULAR	*Little Heroes* **is** a heartwarming movie.
PLURAL	The young **heroes** in the movie **are** an eleven-year-old girl named Charley and her dog, Fuzz.

SINGULAR	**Gymnastics is** not yet a part of our school's athletics program.
PLURAL	The **Summer Olympics are** not **held** in the same year as the Winter Olympics.

SINGULAR	A common **problem** at picnics **is** ants.
PLURAL	**Ants are** a common problem at picnics.

antecedent An antecedent is the word or words that a pronoun stands for. (See page 31.)

EXAMPLE **Tamara** told **Ben** and **Tracy she** was thinking of **them.**
[*Tamara* is the antecedent of *she. Ben* and *Tracy* are the antecedents of *them.*]

apostrophe

■ **to form contractions** (See page 354. See also **contractions.**)
EXAMPLES   can°t   they°ll   o°clock   °99

■ **to form plurals of letters, numerals, symbols, and words used as words** (See page 357.)
EXAMPLES   dotting *i*°s and crossing *t*°s   writing *R*°s and *B*°s

in the 1900°s   learning the ABC°s

using *and*°s instead of &°s or +°s

■ **to show possession** (See page 351.)
EXAMPLES   the student°s schedule

the students° schedules

children°s toys

someone°s backpack

Tommy and Eric°s pet-sitting service

Katrina°s and Simon°s paper routes

one year°s [or twelve months°] salary

appositive An appositive is a noun or a pronoun placed beside another noun or pronoun to identify or describe it. (See page 112.)

EXAMPLE   The great soccer player **Pelé** is also a composer and businessman.

appositive phrase An appositive phrase consists of an appositive and its modifiers. (See page 112.)

EXAMPLE   Mrs. Grabovski, **our upstairs neighbor,** has become a good friend to our family.

article The articles, *a, an,* and *the,* are the most frequently used adjectives. (See page 39.)

EXAMPLE   **A** favorite cartoon character around **the** world, and **an** ageless hero, is **the** Belgian reporter Tintin.

B

bad, badly (See page 267.)

NONSTANDARD   This sour milk smells badly.
STANDARD   This sour milk smells **bad.**

base Base words (such as *prove* or *will*) can stand alone or combine with other word parts (as in *disprove* or *willing*). (See page 373. See also **root.**)

base form The base form, or infinitive, is one of the four principal parts of a verb. (See page 186.)

EXAMPLE   We saw him **leave** the building.

brackets (See page 361.)

EXAMPLES   According to an African proverb, "It is not only giants [extraordinary people] that do great things [heroic deeds]."

The United States Congress comprises the House of Representatives (435 members [each up for reelection every two years]) and the Senate (100 members [each up for reelection every six years]).

C

capitalization

■ **of abbreviations** (See page 289. See also **end marks.**)
■ **of first words** (See page 286.)

EXAMPLES **M**any students are in favor of attending school year-round.

Mr. Inouye told us, "**T**he Hawaiian alphabet consists of five vowels and seven consonants."

Dear Ms. Evans:

Sincerely yours,

■ **of proper nouns and proper adjectives** (See pages 288 and 298.)

EXAMPLES Have you ever visited **Canada**? [proper noun]

I can sing the **Canadian** national anthem. [proper adjective]

Proper Noun	Common Noun
Alfred the **G**reat	leader
South **A**merica	continent
Saudi **A**rabia	country
San **M**iguel **C**ounty	county
Saskatchewan **P**rovince	province
Galápagos **I**slands	islands
Gulf of **T**onkin	body of water
Mount **P**inatubo	mountain
Chaco **C**ulture **N**ational **H**istorical **P**ark	park
Sherwood **F**orest	forest
Mammoth **C**ave	cave
Zion **C**anyon	canyon
the **S**outheast	region
Forty-second **S**treet	street
Democratic **P**arty (or **p**arty)	political party
Battle of **S**an **J**uan **H**ill	historical event
Super **B**owl	special event
Presidents' **D**ay	holiday
January, **T**hursday	calendar items
Quapaw **S**ioux	people
Taoism	religion

(continued)

(continued)

Proper Noun	Common Noun
Buddhist	religious follower
God (*but* the **g**od **A**pollo)	deity
Hanukkah	holy day
Koran	sacred writing
Statue of **L**iberty	monument
Texas **C**ommerce **T**ower	building
Spingarn **M**edal	award
Neptune	planet
Beta **C**rucis	star
Ursa **M**inor	constellation
*S*candinavian *S*tar	ship
*E*nterprise	spacecraft

■ **of titles** (See page 301.)

EXAMPLES   **S**enator Ben Nighthorse Campbell [preceding a name]

Ben Nighthorse Campbell, a **s**enator from Colorado [following a name]

Thank you, **S**enator. [direct address]

Uncle Omar [*but* my uncle Omar]

*T*he *W*orld's *G*ame: *A* *H*istory of *S*occer [book]

*M*ythic *W*arriors: *G*uardian of the *L*egend [TV series]

*D*og *B*arking at the *M*oon [work of art]

*T*he *T*hree-*C*ornered *H*at [musical composition]

"**M**y **O**ld **K**entucky **H**ome" [song]

"**T**he **L**egend of **S**leepy **H**ollow" [short story]

"**E**legy for the **G**iant **T**ortoises" [poem]

*T*een *P*eople [magazine]

the *S*t. *L*ouis *P*ost-*D*ispatch [newspaper]

*D*ennis the *M*enace [comic strip]

case of pronouns Case is the form a pronoun takes to show how it is used in a sentence. (See page 216.)

NOMINATIVE   For social studies, **she** and **I** built a model of the White House.

      The chairperson of the dance committee is **he.**

      Either basketball player, Carmen or **she,** is an excellent point guard.

      We eighth-graders are learning how beneficial the rain forests are.

      Is I. M. Pei the architect **who** designed the Mile High Center in Denver, Colorado?

      Do you know **who** the new exchange student is?

      We have known Ramon longer than **she.** [subject of an elliptical clause meaning *longer than she has known Ramon*]

OBJECTIVE   My parents took **me** to Memphis, Tennessee, to visit the museum honoring the legacy of Dr. Martin Luther King, Jr., and his civil rights efforts.

      Ms. Wu read **us** the Cambodian folk tale "Judge Rabbit and the Tree Spirit."

      The final footrace was between Lupe and **him.**

      The reward money was divided equally among the three rescuers, Leo, Chen, and **her.**

      In the locker room, Coach Alvarez showed **us** players the videotape of last night's game.

      One leader about **whom** I would like to know more is Kofi Annan, who was elected secretary-general of the United Nations in 1997.

      We have known Ramon longer than **her.** [direct object of an elliptical clause meaning *longer than we have known her*]

POSSESSIVE   **Your** camera takes better pictures than **mine** does.

clause A clause is a group of words that contains a subject and a verb and is used as part of a sentence. (See page 119.)

EXAMPLES   While Molly sang a song [subordinate clause]

      Brendan played the pipes [independent clause]

colon (See page 334.)

■ **before lists**

EXAMPLES   The Nobel prizes are awarded each year to those who have made the greatest contributions in the following fields: chemistry, physics, medicine or physiology, economics, literature, and world peace.

Only four women have been featured on United States currency: Martha Washington, the first first lady; Matoaka, better known as Pocahontas; Susan B. Anthony, a pioneer in the women's rights movement; and Sacajawea, the American Indian guide of Lewis and Clark.

▪ before statements that explain or clarify

EXAMPLE   This is one of the most popular computers: It is inexpensive, easy to use, and comes in designer colors.

▪ before a long, formal statement or quotation

EXAMPLE   Mark Twain's philosophy was simple and straight-forward: "Let us so live that when we come to die even the undertaker will be sorry."

▪ in conventional situations

EXAMPLES   10:15 P.M.

Exodus 20:3–17

Heart of Lions: The History of American Bicycle Racing

Dear Ms. Zahn:

comma (See page 315.)

▪ in a series

EXAMPLES   In 1999, the lira, the franc, the deutsche mark, and eight other currencies were all replaced by a currency called the euro.

A good night's sleep in the cool, crisp, clean mountain air had invigorated the weary rock climbers.

▪ in compound sentences

EXAMPLES   The highest point in the United States is Mount McKinley in Alaska, and the lowest is Death Valley in California.

I have read *The Education of Little Tree,* but I have not seen the film version of the book.

- **with nonessential phrases and clauses**

EXAMPLES   Eileen Collins, a lieutenant colonel in the United States Air Force, was the first woman to command a space shuttle mission.

Halley's comet, named for the scientist Edmund Halley, orbits the sun about every seventy-six years.

The name *Minnesota* comes from the Dakota Sioux word *mnisota,* which means "cloudy or milky water."

- **with introductory elements**

EXAMPLES   On her way to her karate lesson, Courtney stopped by the library to return a book for her grandfather.

After he had graduated from college, my brother Giovanni joined the Peace Corps.

- **with interrupters**

EXAMPLES   The most impressive exhibit at the art gallery, in my opinion, is the one called "Ancient Art of Olmec Mexico."

"May 5, of course, is the day on which the Cinco de Mayo Fiesta will be held," the mayor reminded her staff.

- **in conventional situations**

EXAMPLES   On Saturday, August 16, 2008, Mr. Diaz and his daughter began their hot-air balloon trip from Savannah, Georgia, to Cheyenne, Wyoming.

Please ship this package to 701 Loyola Ave., Portsmouth, New Hampshire, on 12 January 2009.

comma splice A comma splice is a run-on sentence in which only a comma separates two complete sentences. (See **fused sentence, run-on sentence.**)

COMMA SPLICE   This baseball card is valued at two hundred dollars, to some collectors it may be worth more than that.

REVISED   This baseball card is valued at two hundred dollars, **and** to some collectors it may be worth more than that.

REVISED   This baseball card is valued at two hundred dollars; **t**o some collectors it may be worth more than that.

REVISED   This baseball card is valued at two hundred dollars. **T**o some collectors it may be worth more than that.

comparison of modifiers (See page 241.)

- ### comparison of adjectives and adverbs

Positive	Comparative	Superlative
short	short**er**	short**est**
lucky	luck**ier**	luck**iest**
valuable	**more (less)** valuable	**most (least)** valuable
swiftly	**more (less)** swiftly	**most (least)** swiftly
bad/badly	**worse**	**worst**

- ### comparing two

EXAMPLES   Of Venus and Mars, which planet is **farther** from Earth?

My sister keyboards **faster** and **more accurately** than I.

Don't you think that Kaya and Russell perform this routine **more gracefully** than **any other** couple in the dance company?

- ### comparing more than two

EXAMPLES   Weighing approximately ninety tons, the seismosaurus was the **largest** dinosaur.

Of the four golfers, Chen plays **most skillfully.**

complement A complement is a word or word group that completes the meaning of a verb. (See page 79. See also **direct object, indirect object, subject complement, predicate nominative,** and **predicate adjective**)

EXAMPLES   The teacher asked **everyone** in the room three **questions.**

It's an old **car,** but it is **fast.**

complex sentence A complex sentence has one independent clause and at least one subordinate clause. (See page 145.)

EXAMPLES   Aboriginal art, which is the artwork of the Australian Aborigines, includes cave paintings, rock engravings, and tree carvings.

If we are going to make gazpacho for dinner tonight, I want you to promise that you'll help in the kitchen.

compound-complex sentence A compound-complex sentence has two or more independent clauses and at least one subordinate clause. (See page 147.)

EXAMPLE My pen pal e-mails me a poem every week; sometimes it is one that he has composed, but most of the time it is one that a famous poet, such as Langston Hughes or Robert Frost, has written.

Our aunt Junko came to visit us last week, and with her she brought a new computer game, which she had helped to design.

compound sentence A compound sentence has two or more independent clauses but no subordinate clauses. (See page 142.)

EXAMPLES The first person to reach the North Pole was the American explorer Robert Peary, and the first to reach the South Pole was Roald Amundsen, an explorer from Norway.

The Big Dipper consists of seven stars; it is part of the constellation Ursa Major.

compound subject A compound subject is made up of two or more subjects that are connected by a conjunction and that have the same verb. (See page 15.)

EXAMPLES A technical **school** in Oklahoma and a two-year **college** in Texas offered my sister scholarships.

Mindy, Kristen, Rudolf, and **Thad** won trophies in the chess tournament.

compound verb A compound verb consists of two or more verbs that are joined by a conjunction and that have the same subject. (See page 16.)

EXAMPLES A deer **ran** across the road and **jumped** the fence.

Moshe **trimmed** the hedges, **mowed** the yard, and **cleaned** the kitchen before the party.

conjunction A conjunction is a word or words that join together two or more words or word groups. (See pages 69 and 128.)

COORDINATING CONJUNCTIONS	Ken **or** Tia can help you with your math homework, **but** I have to finish my science report.
CORRELATIVE CONJUNCTIONS	Mikhail **not only** plays basketball and runs track, **but** he **also** sings in the choir.
SUBORDINATING CONJUNCTION	Venice called her grandfather **before** she left for school.

contraction A contraction is a shortened form of a word, a numeral, or a group of words. Apostrophes in contractions indicate where letters or numerals have been omitted. (See page 354. See also **apostrophe.**)

EXAMPLES			
	you've [you have]	**where's** [where is]
	who's [who is *or* who has]	**they're** [they are]
	wouldn't [would not]	**it's** [it is *or* it has]
	can't [cannot]	**won't** [will not]
	'39–'45 war [1939–1945 war]	**o'clock** [of the clock]

coordinating conjunction (See **conjunction.**)

coordination Coordination is the use of a conjunction to link ideas of approximately equal importance. (See page 448. See also **conjunction.**)

EXAMPLE   Sierra looked through the box of clothes, **but** she did not find her favorite wool sweater.

correlative conjunction (See **conjunction.**)

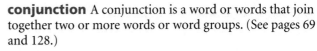

dangling modifier A dangling modifier is a modifying word, phrase, or clause that does not clearly and sensibly modify a word or a word group in a sentence. (See page 251.)

DANGLING   Searching the Internet for information about American Indian customs, an article about the Shawnee leader Tenskwatawa, Chief Tecumseh's brother, captured my interest. [Is the article searching the Internet?]

REVISED	**Searching the Internet for information about American Indian customs, I** found an interesting article about the Shawnee leader Tenskwatawa, Chief Tecumseh's brother.
REVISED	**While I was searching the Internet for information about American Indian customs,** an article about the Shawnee leader Tenskwatawa, Chief Tecumseh's brother, captured my interest.

dash (See page 362.)

EXAMPLE	Kerri—she's the top algebra student—is the only one who finished the extra-credit homework assignment.

declarative sentence A declarative sentence makes a statement and is followed by a period. (See page 19.)

EXAMPLE	Whales and dolphins are marine mammals**.**

dependent clause (See **subordinate clause.**)

diction *Diction* refers to word choice, especially as it affects clarity and tone. *Diction* can also refer to the clarity of pronunciation. (See page 265.)

direct object A direct object is a word or word group that receives the action of the verb or shows the result of the action. A direct object answers the question *Whom?* or *What?* after a transitive verb. (See page 81.)

EXAMPLE	Did you read the **newspaper** today?

double comparison A double comparison is the nonstandard use of two comparative forms (usually *more* and *–er*) or two superlative forms (usually *most* and *–est*) to express comparison. In standard usage, the single comparative form is correct. (See page 248.)

NONSTANDARD	Devon would have had a more better time on the camping trip if he had not forgotten his allergy medication.
STANDARD	Devon would have had a **better** time on the camping trip if he had not forgotten his allergy medication.

double negative A double negative is the nonstandard use of two negative words to express a single negative idea. (See page 249.)

NONSTANDARD	This morning, my throat was so sore that I couldn't hardly swallow.
STANDARD	This morning, my throat was so sore that I **could hardly** swallow.

NONSTANDARD	The tickets to the local science center to see the documentary *Africa's Elephant Kingdom* won't cost the students nothing.
STANDARD	The tickets to the local science center to see the documentary *Africa's Elephant Kingdom* **won't cost** the students **anything.**
STANDARD	The tickets to the local science center to see the documentary *Africa's Elephant Kingdom* **will cost** the students **nothing.**

double subject A double subject occurs when an unnecessary pronoun is used after the subject of a sentence. (See page 271.)

NONSTANDARD	Dr. Yaeger, who lives next door to me, she is one of the veterinarians at the animal clinic.
STANDARD	**Dr. Yaeger,** who lives next door to me, **is** one of the veterinarians at the animal clinic.

E

ellipses An ellipsis (three equally spaced periods) is used to mark an omission from a quoted passage or to reflect a pause or hesitation in speech. (See page 345.)

EXAMPLES	The mayor said, "I would like to dedicate this monument to **. . .** all those who fought in the Persian Gulf War."
	"Well, **. . .** maybe you shouldn't go," Amalia replied thoughtfully.

end marks (See page 311.)

■ **with sentences**

EXAMPLES	Jambalaya, a spicy Creole dish, is made of rice, vegetables, and various kinds of meat**.** [declarative sentence]

Have you ever eaten jambalaya? [interrogative sentence]

Wow! [interjection] What a hot, spicy dish this is! [exclamatory sentence]

Pass the jambalaya, please. [imperative sentence]

Sit down! [strong imperative sentence]

■ **with abbreviations** (See page 313. See also **abbreviations.**)

EXAMPLES   One of the guest speakers was Jesse Jackson, Jr.

Wasn't one of the guest speakers Jesse Jackson, Jr.?

essential clause/essential phrase An essential, or restrictive, clause or phrase is necessary to the meaning of a sentence and is not set off by commas. (See page 322.)

EXAMPLES   Participants **who have not received an I.D. card** must come to the front desk. [essential clause]

Students **entered in the relay race** should meet with Coach Peterson. [essential phrase]

exclamation point (See **end marks.**)

exclamatory sentence An exclamatory sentence expresses strong feeling and is followed by an exclamation point. (See page 19.)

EXAMPLE   I've never been so surprised!

fragment (See **sentence fragment.**)

fused sentence A fused sentence is a run-on sentence in which no punctuation separates complete sentences. (See **comma splice, run-on sentence.**)

FUSED   The Underground Railroad was not an actual railroad it was a network of people who helped fugitive slaves secure their freedom.

REVISED   The Underground Railroad was not an actual railroad. It was a network of people who helped fugitive slaves secure their freedom.

REVISED   The Underground Railroad was not an actual railroad; it was a network of people who helped fugitive slaves secure their freedom.

future perfect tense (See **tense of verbs.**)

future tense (See **tense of verbs.**)

gerund A gerund is a verb form ending in *–ing* that is used as a noun. (See page 105.)

EXAMPLE   **Singing** is her main interest.

gerund phrase A gerund phrase consists of a gerund and its modifiers and complements. (See page 106.)

EXAMPLE   They improved the insulation of the apartment by **adding solar screens to the windows.**

good, well (See page 269.)

EXAMPLE   The gymnast's performance on the uneven parallel bars was especially **good.** [*not* well]

hyphen (See page 357.)

■ **for division of words**

EXAMPLE   The labor leader Cesar Chavez worked hard to organize the migrant farm workers in the United States.

■ **in compound numbers**

EXAMPLE   Wasn't the price of a postage stamp twenty-three cents?

■ **with prefixes and suffixes**

EXAMPLES   The construction of the new high school should be completed by mid-June.

The speech will be given by the club's president-elect, Catherine French.

imperative sentence An imperative sentence gives a command or makes a request and is followed by either a period or an exclamation point. (See page 19.)

EXAMPLES   All those in favor, say "Aye**.**"

Sit down**!**

indefinite pronoun An indefinite pronoun does not refer to a definite person, place, thing, or idea. (See page 36.)

EXAMPLE   **Most** of the books Carlos reads are autobiographies.

I would like to try a **few** of the bread recipes in this cookbook.

independent clause An independent clause (also called a *main clause*) expresses a complete thought and can stand by itself as a sentence. (See page 120.)

EXAMPLE   Because she wanted to celebrate spring, **Josie bought a bouquet of daffodils and placed them in a vase on the hallway table.**

indirect object An indirect object is a word or word group that often comes between a transitive verb and its direct object and tells to whom or to what or for whom or for what the action of the verb is done. (See page 83.)

EXAMPLE   Roman told **Natalya** and **Stefan** a fascinating tale of old Warsaw. [The direct object is *tale*.]

infinitive An infinitive is a verb form, usually preceded by *to*, that is used as a noun, an adjective, or an adverb. (See page 108.)

EXAMPLE   These apples are the kind **to bake.**

infinitive phrase An infinitive phrase consists of an infinitive and its modifiers and complements. (See page 109.)

EXAMPLE   Dr. Matissot is the one **to ask about matters of French grammar.**

interjection An interjection expresses emotion and has no grammatical relation to the rest of the sentence. (See page 71.)

EXAMPLE   **Wow!** That's some fish!

Grammar at a Glance   **521**

interrogative sentence An interrogative sentence asks a question and is followed by a question mark. (See page 19.)

EXAMPLE   Is *Petrushka* a ballet by Igor Stravinsky**?**

intransitive verb An intransitive verb is a verb that does not take an object. (See page 59.)

EXAMPLE   The crowd **cheered** for a full five minutes.

irregular verb An irregular verb is a verb that forms its past and past participle in some way other than by adding *d* or *ed* to the base form. (See page 188. See also **regular verb.**)

Base Form	Present Participle	Past	Past Participle
be	[is] being	was, were	[have] been
bring	[is] bringing	brought	[have] brought
build	[is] building	built	[have] built
burst	[is] bursting	burst	[have] burst
choose	[is] choosing	chose	[have] chosen
cost	[is] costing	cost	[have] cost
drive	[is] driving	drove	[have] driven
grow	[is] growing	grew	[have] grown
speak	[is] speaking	spoke	[have] spoken
swim	[is] swimming	swam	[have] swum

italics (See **underlining.**)

its, it's (See page 272.)

EXAMPLES   One of **its** [Hawaii's] nicknames is the Aloha State.

It's [It is] located in the North Pacific.

It's [It has] been a U.S. state since 1959.

lie, lay (See page 203.)

EXAMPLES   For nearly one hundred years, the wrecked ship **lay** on the ocean floor.

Before we set out the food, we **laid** a clean tablecloth on the picnic table.

linking verb A linking verb connects the subject with a word that identifies or describes the subject. (See page 54.)

EXAMPLE   Before long, the sea **became** rough and choppy.

misplaced modifier A misplaced modifier is a word, phrase, or clause that seems to modify the wrong word or words in a sentence. (See page 251.)

MISPLACED   The explorers discovered a sack of old Spanish gold coins winding their way through a maze of stalagmites and stalactites. [Are the coins winding their way through a maze?]

REVISED   **Winding their way through a maze of stalagmites and stalactites,** the explorers discovered a sack of old Spanish gold coins.

REVISED   The explorers, **winding their way through a maze of stalagmites and stalactites,** discovered a sack of old Spanish gold coins.

modifier A modifier is a word or group of words that makes the meaning of another word more specific. (See page 238.)

EXAMPLE   **Suddenly,** a **tiny** rabbit appeared **on the lawn.**

The book **that I just finished reading** is about Tiger Woods.

nonessential clause/nonessential phrase A nonessential, or nonrestrictive, clause or phrase adds information not necessary to the main idea in the sentence and is set off by commas. (See page 321.)

EXAMPLES   That man, **who lives across the street from us,** has some strong opinions. [nonessential clause]

The scouts, **exhausted by the hike,** dozed by the campfire. [nonessential phrase]

noun A noun names a person, place, thing, or idea. (See page 25.)

RESOURCES

EXAMPLE   On **Friday,** the lead **car** in the **expedition** blew a **gasket,** and the **team** wasted no **time** in contacting **Colonel MacPherson** at **headquarters** over the **radio.**

noun clause A noun clause is a subordinate clause used as a noun. (See page 130.)

EXAMPLE   **How she won the race** is an amazing story.

number Number is the form a word takes to indicate whether the word is singular or plural. (See page 155.)

SINGULAR	foot	I	essay	solo
PLURAL	feet	we	essays	solos

object of a preposition An object of a preposition is the noun or pronoun that ends a prepositional phrase. (See page 96.)

EXAMPLE   The timid deer ran from **us.** [*From us* is a prepositional phrase.]

parallelism Parallelism is the repetition of sentence patterns or of other grammatical structures. (See page 459.)

NOT PARALLEL   For our New Year's resolutions, Sonia and I decided to exercise more often, eat healthier food, and on a budget for next semester.

PARALLEL   For our New Year's resolutions, Sonia and I decided to exercise more often, eat healthier food, and plan a budget for next semester.

parentheses (See page 360.)

EXAMPLES   The Heimlich maneuver **(**see the diagram below**)** is an emergency technique that can be used to help a person who is choking.

The Heimlich maneuver is an emergency technique that can be used to help a person who is choking. **(S**ee the diagram below**.)**

participial phrase A participial phrase consists of a participle and any complements and modifiers it has. (See page 102.)

EXAMPLE   They were surprised to find their goat Daisy **grazing in the neighbors' yard.**

participle A participle is a verb form that can be used as an adjective. (See page 101.)

EXAMPLE   Colin calmed the **snarling** dog.

passive voice The passive voice is the voice a verb is in when it expresses an action done to its subject. (See page 200. See also **voice.**)

EXAMPLE   We **were told** to meet him here.

past perfect tense (See **tense of verbs.**)

past tense (See **tense of verbs.**)

period (See **end marks.**)

phrase A phrase is a group of related words that does not contain both a verb and its subject and that is used as a single part of speech. (See page 95.)

EXAMPLES   The court chamberlain **had been thinking** recently **about his position.** [*Had been thinking* is a verb phrase. *About his position* is a prepositional phrase.]

Running swiftly, the gazelle escaped **from the cheetah.** [*Running swiftly* is a participial phrase. *From the cheetah* is a prepositional phrase.]

To know me is **to love me.** [*To know me* and *to love me* are infinitive phrases.]

Painting the bedroom is our next project. [*Painting the bedroom* is a gerund phrase.]

predicate The predicate is the part of a sentence that says something about the subject. (See page 9.)

EXAMPLE   They **spent all their leisure time painting the apartment.**

predicate adjective A predicate adjective is an adjective that completes the meaning of a linking verb and that modifies the subject of the verb. (See page 87.)

EXAMPLE   Of all the cities the Podestas visited in the United States, Santa Fe seemed **friendliest** and most **hospitable.**

predicate nominative A predicate nominative is a noun or pronoun that completes the meaning of a linking verb and identifies or explains the subject of the verb. (See page 85.)

EXAMPLE   The highest jumper in that heat was **Oscar.**

prefix A prefix is a word part that is added before a base word or root. (See page 372.)

EXAMPLES   un + important = **un**important

il + legal = **il**legal

re + construct = **re**construct

pre + recorded = **pre**recorded

self + conscious = **self**-conscious

ex + governor = **ex**-governor

mid + Atlantic = **mid**-Atlantic

pre + Revolution = **pre**-Revolution

preposition A preposition shows the relationship of a noun or a pronoun to some other word in a sentence. (See page 66.)

EXAMPLE   **From** July 6 **until** July 14 each year, the running **of** the bulls takes place **in** Pamplona, the capital **of** Navarre province **in** northeastern Spain.

prepositional phrase A prepositional phrase includes a preposition, a noun or pronoun called the object of the preposition, and any modifiers of that object. (See page 96. See also **object of a preposition.**)

EXAMPLE   Riding **on a fast horse,** the pony express carrier never lingered.

present perfect tense (See **tense of verbs.**)

present tense (See **tense of verbs.**)

pronoun A pronoun is used in place of one or more nouns or pronouns. (See page 31.)

EXAMPLES   Zita told Patrick **her** frank opinion of **his** plan.

            Someone helped **himself** or **herself** to my yogurt.

            That is a good idea, Jeremy.

question mark (See **end marks.**)

quotation marks (See page 344.)

- **for direct quotations**
  EXAMPLE   **"**Take nothing but pictures,**"** our nature guide reminded us, **"**and leave nothing but footprints.**"**

- **with other marks of punctuation** (See also preceding example.)
  EXAMPLES   **"**What is the capital of Uruguay**?"** asked Albert.

              Doesn't the word *fortuitous* mean **"**occurring by chance**"?**

              The teacher asked**,** **"**What are the names of the speaker's children in Li Po's poem **'**Letter to His Two Small Children**'?"**

- **for titles**
  EXAMPLES   **"**Raymond's Run**"** [short story]

              "Quiet Night Thoughts**"** [short poem]

              "When You Wish upon a Star**"** [song]

regular verb A regular verb is a verb that forms its past and past participle by adding *d* or *ed* to the base form. (See page 187. See also **irregular verb.**)

Base Form	Present Participle	Past	Past Participle
ask	[is] asking	asked	[have] asked
believe	[is] believing	believed	[have] believed

RESOURCES

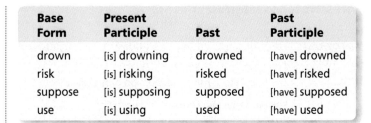

Base Form	Present Participle	Past	Past Participle
drown	[is] drowning	drowned	[have] drowned
risk	[is] risking	risked	[have] risked
suppose	[is] supposing	supposed	[have] supposed
use	[is] using	used	[have] used

rise, raise (See page 205.)

EXAMPLES For nine days in a row, the temperature **rose** higher than 100°F.

Adjusting the thermostat, Mother **raised** the temperature in the room to 78°F.

root Word roots (for example, *–dict–* or *–vis–*), like prefixes and suffixes, cannot stand alone and are combined with other word parts to form words (for example, *dictionary* or *visible*). (See page 373. See also **base.**)

run-on sentence A run-on sentence is two or more complete sentences run together as one. (See page 441. See also **comma splice** and **fused sentence.**)

RUN-ON Ms. Micklewhite, Tom's supervisor, told Tom he was at the top of the list for a promotion however, she said that the promotion might mean Tom would have to relocate to Chicago.

REVISED Ms. Micklewhite, Tom's supervisor, told Tom he was at the top of the list for a promotion. **H**owever, she said that the promotion might mean Tom would have to relocate to Chicago.

REVISED Ms. Micklewhite, Tom's supervisor, told Tom he was at the top of the list for a promotion; however, she said that the promotion might mean Tom would have to relocate to Chicago.

semicolon (See page 331.)

■ **in compound sentences with no conjunction**

EXAMPLE In 1993, Vicki Van Meter became the youngest girl to pilot an airplane across the United States; she was eleven years old.

- **in compound sentences with conjunctive adverbs or transitional expressions**

  EXAMPLE The Hubble Space Telescope, which entered Earth's orbit in 1990, has proved to be a valuable resource for astronomers; for example, in 1996, the telescope provided them views of the surface of the planet Pluto.

- **between items in a series when the items contain commas**

  EXAMPLE Joshua made a chart that classifies the different species of dinosaurs as carnivorous, or meat eating; herbivorous, or plant eating; or omnivorous, or meat eating and plant eating.

sentence A sentence is a group of words that contains a subject and a verb and expresses a complete thought. (See page 4.)

                  S   V
EXAMPLE Many children are curious about animals of all species.

sentence fragment A sentence fragment is a group of words that is punctuated as if it were a complete sentence but that does not contain both a subject and a verb or that does not express a complete thought. (See pages 4 and 438.)

FRAGMENT Sweeping across the Sahara, a hot, violent wind called a simoom.

SENTENCE Sweeping across the Sahara, a hot, violent wind called a simoom causes the formation of huge sand dunes.

FRAGMENTS The reason for building the Great Wall of China. To protect the country from invaders.

SENTENCE The reason for building the Great Wall of China was to protect the country from invaders.

simple sentence A simple sentence has one independent clause and no subordinate clauses. (See page 140.)

EXAMPLES The French expression *joie de vivre* means "joy of living."

Emilia and Jeffrey are running for class president.

sit, set (See page 201.)

EXAMPLES The students **sat** quietly, listening to the Japanese folk tale "Green Willow."

Did you see who **set** this package on my desk?

stringy sentence A stringy sentence is a sentence that has too many independent clauses. Usually, the clauses are strung together with coordinating conjunctions like *and* or *but*. (See page 454.)

STRINGY In Roman mythology, Arachne was a peasant girl, and she was a skillful weaver, too, and she claimed that her skill was superior to that of the goddess Minerva.

REVISED In Roman mythology, Arachne, a peasant girl who was a skillful weaver, claimed that her skill was superior to that of the goddess Minerva.

subject The subject tells whom or what a sentence is about. (See page 7.)

EXAMPLE ***The Jungle*** by Upton Sinclair is a strong criticism of the meat-packing industry in the early years of the twentieth century.

subject complement A subject complement is a word or word group that completes the meaning of a linking verb and identifies or modifies the subject. (See page 85.)

EXAMPLES Before he emigrated, my great-grandfather was a **farmer.**

He was always very **resourceful.**

subordinate clause A subordinate clause (also called a *dependent clause*) contains a subject and verb but does not express a complete thought and cannot stand alone as a sentence. (See page 121. See also **adjective clause, adverb clause, noun clause.**)

EXAMPLES The student **who studies hardest** will get the highest score. [adjective clause]

That they came back to win in the final two minutes didn't surprise the team. [noun clause]

While you write your names, I will hand out the papers. [adverb clause]

subordinating conjunction (See **conjunction.**)

subordination Subordination is the use of a subordinate clause to show that an idea is not as important as the idea in the independent, or main, clause. (See page 451.)

EXAMPLE   The basketball slipped through the hoop **before the buzzer sounded.** [*Before the buzzer sounded,* the subordinate clause, is not as important to the sentence as the independent clause *The basketball slipped through the hoop.*]

suffix A suffix is a word part that is added after a base word or root. (See page 373.)

EXAMPLES

safe + ly = safe**ly**	lucky + ly = lucki**ly**
open + ness = open**ness**	portray + ing = portray**ing**
move + able = mov**able**	peace + able = peace**able**
begin + er = beginn**er**	dream + er = dream**er**

syllable A syllable is a word part that can be pronounced as one uninterrupted sound. (See page 369.)

EXAMPLES   bought [one syllable]

prob • lem [two syllables]

sen • si • tive [three syllables]

syntax Syntax is the structure of a sentence (the grammatical arrangement of words, phrases, and clauses). (See page 454.)

tense of verbs The tense of verbs indicates the time of the action or state of being expressed by the verb. (See page 196.)

Present Tense	
I take	we take
you take	you take
he, she, it takes	they take

Past Tense	
I took	we took
you took	you took
he, she, it took	they took

(continued)

(continued)

Future Tense

I will (shall) take	we will (shall) take
you will (shall) take	you will (shall) take
he, she, it will (shall) take	they will (shall) take

Present Perfect Tense

I have taken	we have taken
you have taken	you have taken
he, she, it has taken	they have taken

Past Perfect Tense

I had taken	we had taken
you had taken	you had taken
he, she, it had taken	they had taken

Future Perfect Tense

I will (shall) have taken	we will (shall) have taken
you will (shall) have taken	you will (shall) have taken
he, she, it will (shall) have taken	they will (shall) have taken

their, there, they're (See page 389.)

EXAMPLES   **Their** mother owns and operates a home-repair store. [*Their* tells whose mother.]

The information booth is over **there** under the blue tent. [*There* tells where the information booth is.]

There are four concert tickets for sale in the newspaper. [*There* begins the sentence but does not add to the sentence's meaning.]

Do you know if **they're** still on vacation? [*They're* is a contraction of *they are.*]

transitions Transitions are words or word groups that link words, phrases, sentences, or paragraphs together. (See page 465.)

EXAMPLES   I was worried about Leah, but **the next day,** she assured me that she was fine.

Our house survived the storm without damage; **however,** other houses will need to be repaired.

transitive verb A transitive verb is an action verb that takes an object. (See page 59.)

EXAMPLE   Jill **passed** the exam.

underlining (italics) (See page 342.)

U

- **for titles**

EXAMPLES   *The Deep End of the Ocean* [book]

USA Today [periodical]

The Potato Eaters [work of art]

Rhapsody in Blue [long musical composition]

- **for words, letters, and symbols used as such and for foreign words**

EXAMPLES   Notice that the *f* sounds in the word *photography* are spelled *ph.*

The friendly, gracious server at the French restaurant wished us *bon appétit.*

verb A verb expresses an action or a state of being. (See page 51.)

V

EXAMPLES   Tamara **walks** to school every day.

Tamara **is** in school today.

verbal A verbal is a form of a verb used as a noun, an adjective, or an adverb. (See page 101. See also **participle, gerund,** and **infinitive.**)

EXAMPLES   **Smiling,** Mr. Patel invited us in.

I liked his **yodeling.**

It's not easy **to yodel** well.

verbal phrase A verbal phrase consists of a verbal and any modifiers and complements it has. (See page 101. See also **participial phrase, gerund phrase,** and **infinitive phrase.**)

EXAMPLES   **Experienced in foreign-car repair,** Darryl was soon hired by a big local dealership and began **to specialize in transmissions.**

He liked **working there.**

verb phrase A verb phrase consists of a main verb and at least one helping verb. (See page 52.)

EXAMPLE   **"Should** I **speak** to her?" wondered Mrs. Callaghan.

voice Voice is the form a transitive verb takes to indicate whether the subject of the verb performs or receives the action. (See page 200.)

ACTIVE VOICE   Vincent van Gogh **painted** *The Night Café* in 1888.
PASSIVE VOICE   *The Night Café* **was painted** by Vincent van Gogh in 1888.

well (See *good, well.*)

who, whom (See page 226.)

EXAMPLES   Everyone **who** has applied for the job is well qualified.
Everyone **whom** I have interviewed for the job is well qualified.

wordiness Wordiness is the use of more words than necessary or the use of fancy words where simple ones will do. (See page 457.)

WORDY   Theo Marshall, who is the athlete who regularly plays the position of quarterback for their football team, will not play in the game that is scheduled for tonight due to the fact that he sprained his ankle during the practice that was held yesterday.

REVISED   Theo Marshall, their regular quarterback, will not play in tonight's game because he sprained his ankle during yesterday's practice.

INDEX

C

End marks (sentence punctuation), 518–19
    abbreviations and, 313–14, 519
    definition of, 311
    exclamation points, 312, 314, 345, 346
    periods, 311–12, 314, 345–46
    question marks, 312, 314, 345, 346
    quotation marks and, 345–46
English language
    British vs. American spelling, 495
    colloquialisms, 497
    ethnic dialects, 496
    formal English, 265, 497
    history of, 494–97
    informal English, 265, 497
    Middle English, 494
    nonstandard English, 265, 497
    Old English, 494
    regional dialects, 496
    slang, 497
    standard English, 190, 265, 496–97
Essays and articles, quotation marks for, 349
Essential appositives and appositive phrases, 323
Essential clauses/essential phrases, 322, 519
Ethnic dialects, 496
Everywheres, 266
Except, accept, 265, 380
Exclamation points, 19, 314, 345
    with direct quotations, 346
    with interjections, 312
Exclamations, commas with, 326
Exclamatory sentences, 19, 519

Fall, **principal parts of,** 190
Feel, **principal parts of,** 190
Feminine pronouns, agreement and, 173–74
Fewer, less, 269
Fight, **principal parts of,** 190
Films, underlining (italics) of title, 343
Find, **principal parts of,** 190
First-person pronouns, 32, 33
Fly, **principal parts of,** 190
For, 69, 70
Forgive, **principal parts of,** 190
Formal English. *See also* English language.
    definition of, 265
Formally, formerly, 385
Fractions
    hyphens with, 358
    subject-verb agreement with expressions of, 171
Fragments. *See* Clauses; Phrases; Sentence fragments.
Freeze, **principal parts of,** 190
Fused sentences, 519–20
Future perfect progressive tense, 198

Future perfect tense, 196, 532
Future progressive tense, 198
Future tense, 196, 532

Gender
    pronoun agreement in, 173–74
    of singular antecedents, 174
Geographical names, capitalization of, 289–90
Gerund phrases, 106–107, 520
    definition of, 106
    diagram of, 483
Gerunds, 105–106, 520
    definition of, 105
    diagram of, 483
Get, **principal parts of,** 190
Give, **principal parts of,** 190
Glossary, definition of, 264–65
Go, **principal parts of,** 190
Gods and goddesses, capitalization of names of, 293
Good, well, 240, 269, 520
Government bodies
    abbreviations (acronyms) of, 314
    capitalization of names of, 291
Grow, **principal parts of,** 190, 522

Had of, 268
Had ought, hadn't ought, 269–70
Half–, **as prefix,** 359
Hardly, scarcely, 270
Have
    forms of, 52
    as helping verb, 52, 186
Have, **principal parts of,** 191
Hear, here, 385
Hear, **principal parts of,** 191
Heavenly bodies, capitalization of names of, 291
Helping verbs, 52–53, 186
    and compound verbs, 16
Her, **pronoun-antecedent agreement and,** 174
He, she, it, they, 271
Hide, **principal parts of,** 191
Himself, themselves, 227–28
His, **pronoun-antecedent agreement and,** 174
Hisself, 227, 271
Historical documents, capitalization of, 302
Historical events and periods, capitalization of names of, 292
Hit, **principal parts of,** 191
Hold, **principal parts of,** 191

semicolons, 142, 320, 331–33, 528–29
underlining (italics), 342–43, 533
Put, **principal parts of,** 191

"Quarry, The" (Niggli), 348
Question marks, 312, 345
    with direct quotation, 346
Quiet, quite, 387
Quotation(s)
    capitalization in, 286
    direct quotations, 344–46
    divided quotations, 345
    indirect quotations, 344
    within quotations, 350
Quotation marks
    dialogue and, 348
    for direct quotations, 344–46, 527
    with long quotations, 348
    with other punctuation, 345–46, 527
    single quotation marks, 350
    for titles and subtitles of short works, 349, 527

Races, capitalization of names of, 292
Raise, **principal parts of,** 205
Raise, rise, 205, 528
Read, **principal parts of,** 191
Real, 275
Reason . . . because, 275
Reflexive pronouns, 33, 227–28
Regional dialects, 496
Regions, capitalization of names of, 290
Regular comparison of modifiers, 242–43
Regular verbs, 187, 527–28
Relative adverbs, 125
Relative pronouns, 35, 484
    adjective clauses and, 124–25
    definition of, 124
Religions, capitalization of names of, 293
Ride, **principal parts of,** 191
Ring, **principal parts of,** 189, 191
Rise, **principal parts of,** 191, 205
Rise, raise, 205, 528
Risk, **principal parts of,** 528
Root words, 373, 528
Run, **principal parts of,** 191
Run-on sentences, 438, 441–42
    comma splice and, 513

    definition of, 441, 528
    fused sentences and, 519–20

–s, **nouns endings in,** 155–57
Sacred writings, capitalization of titles of, 293
Salutation of letter
    capitalization in, 287
    colons with, 335
    commas with, 328
Say, **principal parts of,** 191
Scarcely, hardly, 270
School subjects, capitalization of names of, 299
Seasons, capitalization of names of, 292
Second-person pronouns, 32, 33
–sede, –cede, –ceed, **spelling rule for,** 371
See, **principal parts of,** 191
Seek, **principal parts of,** 191
Sell, **principal parts of,** 191
Semicolons, 331–33, 442, 528–29
    compound sentences and, 142, 528, 529
    independent clauses and, 320, 331–33
    with items in a series, 333, 529
Send, **principal parts of,** 192
Sentence(s). *See also* Combining sentences; headings
    beginning with Sentence.
    adjectives in, 40
    awkward sentences, 457
    capitalization in, 14, 286
    choppy sentences, 96, 103, 113
    classification of, 19, 139–47
    combining sentences, 444–52
    complete sentences, 438
    complex sentences, 145, 451, 464, 489, 514–15
    compound-complex sentences, 147, 464, 490, 515
    compound sentences, 142–43, 319–20, 448, 450,
        464, 486, 512, 515
    declarative sentences, 19, 311, 517
    definition of, 4, 529
    diagrams of, 488–90
    exclamatory sentences, 19, 519
    fused sentences, 519–20
    imperative sentences, 19, 312, 520–21
    interrogative sentences, 19, 312, 522
    inverted order of, 167
    parallel structure and, 459–60
    run-on sentences, 438, 441–42, 513, 519–20, 528
    sentence structure variety and, 147, 463–64
    sentence style improvement, 454–60
    simple sentences, 140, 319, 464, 488, 529
    stringy sentences, 454–55, 530
    structure of, 139–47
    varying sentence beginnings, 452, 461–62
    wordy sentences, 457

ACKNOWLEDGMENTS

For permission to reprint copyrighted material, grateful acknowledgment is made to the following sources:

From "the sonnet-ballad" from *Blacks* by Gwendolyn Brooks. Copyright © 1987, 1991 by Gwendolyn Brooks. Published by The David Company. Reissued by Third World Press, 1991. Reproduced by permission of **Brooks Permissions**.

From "Dreams" from *The Collected Poems of Langston Hughes*. Copyright © 1994 by The Estate of Langston Hughes. Reproduced by permission of **Alfred A. Knopf, Inc., a division of Random House, Inc.,** and electronic format by permission of **Harold Ober Associates Incorporated**.

From *Mexican Village* by Josefina Niggli. Copyright © 1945 by **The University of North Carolina Press**; copyright renewed © 1972 by Josefina Niggli. Reproduced by permission of the publisher.

PHOTO CREDITS

ABBREVIATIONS USED: (tl)top left, (tc)top center, (tr)top right, (l)left, (lc)left center, (c)center, (rc)right center, (r)right, (b)bottom, (bl)bottom left, (bc)bottom center, (br)bottom right.

TABLE OF CONTENTS: Page v, SuperStock; vii, Image Copyright ©2001 PhotoDisc, Inc.; viii, Stephen Simpson/FPG International; ix, Alan Schein/The Stock Market; xi, Image Copyright ©2001 Photodisc, Inc.; xiv, U.S. Postal Service; xvi, Michelle Bridwell/Frontera Fotos; xvii, Copyright 1996 David Eisenberg/Development Center for Appropriate Technology; xix, Image Copyright ©2001 Photodisc, Inc.

CHAPTER 1: Page 5, The Granger Collection, New York; 9, Image Copyright ©2001 Photodisc, Inc.; 12, Red-figure amphora, showing the slaying of Medusa by Perseus/British Museum, London/Bridgeman Art Library, London/New York; 15, Image Copyright ©2001 Photodisc, Inc.; 17, AP/Wide World Photos.

CHAPTER 2: Page 26, William S. Soule/National Anthropological Archives/National Museum of Natural History/Smithsonian Institute, neg. #1380A; 30, Alan Schein/The Stock Market; 36, Lindsay Hebberd/CORBIS; 38, Bryan Bedder/Getty Images; 43 (rc), Ken Dequaine/The Picture Cube; 43 (bc), George Cassidy/The Picture Cube.

CHAPTER 3: Page 56, Phototone/Letraset; 58, Image Copyright ©2001 Photodisc, Inc.; 62 (cl), Image Copyright ©2001 Photodisc, Inc.; 62 (b), Shutterstock; 65 (c), The Stock Market; 65 (tr), Frank Schreider/Photo Researchers, Inc.; 68, Corbis Images; 71, Stephen Simpson/FPG International; 74, Bonnie Timmons/Image Bank.

CHAPTER 4: Page 80, The Granger Collection, New York; 84, Professional Rodeo Cowboy Assoc.; 86 (lc), Barry L. Runk/Grant Heilman Photography; 86 (bl), Barry L. Runk/Grant Heilman Photography; 86 (bc), Barry L. Runk/Grant Heilman Photography; 86 (br), SuperStock; 89, Earl Kogler/HRW Photo.

CHAPTER 5: Page 97, Nati Harnik/AP/Wide World Photos; 100, Autry Museum of Western Heritage, Los Angeles; 105 (tr), SuperStock; 105 (c), Bob Daemmrich Photography; 105 (lc), Bob Daemmrich Photography; 111, Cahokia Mounds State Historical Site.

CHAPTER 6: Page 133 (rc), The Museum of Appalachia; 133 (b), The Museum of Appalachia.

CHAPTER 7: Page 141, Musee de'l Armee, Paris/Art Resource, NY; 143, HRW Photo; 144, Everett Collection; 149, Michelle Bridwell/Frontera Fotos.

CHAPTER 8: Page 158, Gregory Shamus/NBAE via Getty Images; 162, A. Scibilia/Art Resource, NY; 166, Eric Beggs/HRW Photo; 170, Rob Atkins/Image Bank; 180, Rayli McLinde/Shooting Star International.

CHAPTER 9: Page 195, HRW Photo Research Library; 199, ©1997 Radlund & Associates for Artville; 204, Image Copyright ©2001 Photodisc, Inc.; 206, Image Copyright ©2001 Photodisc, Inc.; 208 (br), Steve Allen/Peter Arnold, Inc.; 208 (bc), Jerry Jacka Photography; 210, Image Copyright ©2001 Photodisc, Inc.

CHAPTER 10: Page 217 (bc), Michael Ochs Archives/Venice, CA; 217 (rc), Michael Ochs Archives/Venice, CA; 217 (br), Michael Ochs Archives/Venice, CA; 220 (bl), IBM Corporation; 220 (bc), Fielder Kownslar/IBM Corporation; 229, Everett Collection, Inc.

CHAPTER 11: Page 246, Bob Daemmrich/Stock Boston; 247, Image Copyright ©2001 PhotoDisc, Inc.; 250, SuperStock; 258, EyeWire, Inc. Image Club Graphics ©1998 Adobe Systems, Inc.

CHAPTER 12: Page 267, SuperStock; 273, Corbis Images; 277, Chris Falkenstein.

CHAPTER 13: Page 291, Corbis Images; 294, Wolfgang Kaehler Photography; 297, Ric Francis/AP/Wide World Photos; 300, Courtesy of McGraw-Hill.

CHAPTER 14: Page 315, Mike Powers; 320, Kjell B. Sandved/Photo Researchers, Inc.; 323, Tim Mosenfelder/Getty Images; 327, U.S. Postal Service; 331, Image Copyright ©2001 Photodisc, Inc.

CHAPTER 15: Page 347, Werner Forman Archive/Museum fur Volkerkunde, Berlin/Art Resource, NY; 348, Image Copyright ©2001 Photodisc, Inc.; 356, VEER/Christopher Talbot Frank/Photonica/Getty Images; 364, Bob Dammrich/The Image Works.

CHAPTER 16: Page 376, Courtesy of Hendrick-Long Publishing Co.; 384, SuperStock; 390, Reuters/Pascal Rossignol/Archive Photos; 392 (bl), Richard Sullivan/Shooting Star; 392 (bc), SuperStock.

CHAPTER 17: Page 401, Image Copyright ©2001 PhotoDisc, Inc.; 402, Image Copyright ©2001 PhotoDisc, Inc.; 410, Courtesy of Franklin Delano Roosevelt Library Historical Pictures Service; 423 (tr), Image Copyright ©2001 PhotoDisc, Inc.; 423 (br), Theodor Gentilz; 427, Copyright 1996 David Eisenberg/Development Center for Appropriate Technology; 429, Trinity College Dublin Library.

CHAPTER 18: Page 438, Chromo Sohm/Sohm/Stock Boston; 441, Helen Brush/Everett Collection; 443, SuperStock; 445, Archive Photos/Express Newspapers; 447, SuperStock; 449, Image Copyright ©2001 Photodisc, Inc.; 453, Owen Franken/Stock Boston; 455, Archive Photos; 458, Image Copyright ©2001 Photodisc, Inc.; 468, SuperStock.